Modern European History

A Garland Series of Outstanding Dissertations

MODERN EUROPEAN HISTORY

Nineteenth-Century Churches

The History of a New Catholicism
in Württemberg, England, and France

R.W. Franklin

Garland Publishing, Inc.
New York and London 1987

Library of Congress Cataloging-in-Publication Data

Franklin, R.W., 1947–
    Nineteenth-century churches.

    (Modern European history)
    Revision of the author's thesis (Ph.D.—Harvard
University, 1975)
    Bibliography: p.
    1. Europe—Church history—19th century.
2. Tübingen School (Catholic theology) 3. Möhler,
Johann Adam, 1796–1838. 4. Oxford movement—
England—History. 5. Anglo-Catholicism. 6. Liturgical movement—Catholic Church—History—19th
century. 7. Benedictines—France—History—19th
century. 8. Gueranger, Prosper, 1806–1875. 9. Abbaye Sainte-Pierre de Solesmes—History—19th century. 10. Catholic Church—Europe—History—19th
century. 11. Church of England—History 19th century. 12. Anglican Communion—England—History—19th century. I. Title. II. Series.
BR477.F69 1987   282'.4   87-25853
ISBN 0-8240-8067-X

Printed in the United States of America

Nineteenth Century Churches:

The History of a New Catholicism

in

Württemberg, England, and France

R. W. Franklin

Saint John's University

Collegeville, Minnesota

Dedication

To the Memory of

Bessie Thompson and Eddie Cain

Table of Contents

Abbreviations

B.C.   The British Critic, Quarterly Theological Review, and
         Ecclesiastical Record

OLP   Questions liturgiques et paroissiales

ThQ   Theologische Quartalschrift

Preface

The following pages are a shortened version of the Ph.D. thesis I presented to the Department of History of Harvard University in April, 1975. As a Southerner who came North to school, I grew curious about two features which dominated the landscape but had been almost absent in our culture: Industry and Catholicism. I set out to find how the recasting of the shape of the church is caused by and mirrors the ideological, economic, and political shifts of Western history.

A traveling fellowship from Harvard University in 1972-1973 allowed me a year in Oxford, Tübingen, and Solesmes collecting most of the material on which the thesis is based. Additional archival research was made possible from 1977 through 1985 by grants particularly from the German Federal Republic through <u>Deutscher Akademischer Austauschdienst</u>.

The revisions reflect other experiences of the decade since 1975. I gained a theological education from my work with Harris Kaasa of Luther College and Joseph Shaw of St. Olaf College in the Christian Humanism Project. I have been taught to appreciate the ecumenical significance of the new Catholicism by William Norgren, Ecumenical Officer of The Episcopal Church, and Robert Wright of the General Theological Seminary, as we have sought to represent Anglicans in official dialogue with the Roman Catholic Church. As a professor at St. John's University in Minnesota, an American outpost of the new Catholicism, I have been the grateful recipient of the support of Hilary Thimmesh, Eva Hooker, Sylvester Theisen, and Robert Spaeth, the example of the Benedictine monastic community, and the instruction of Michael Blecker, Michael Marx, and Abbot Jerome Theisen.

Collegeville, Minnesota
1986

i

Acknowledgments

A long thesis can only have been done with the generous assistance of many individuals. The searching and counting which were necessary for these pages were made possible by the kindness of each bishop, priest and abbot whose diocese, parish, or monastery are named here. Of these Dom Philippe Jobert, Librarian of the Abbey of Solesmes in France, Dr. K. W. Noakes, Librarian of Pusey House, at Oxford, and Herr Helmut Baur, Archivist of the Diocese of Rottenburg in West Germany, provided months of counsel and hospitality as well as manuscripts, letters, and registers. I have been fortunate to have had the suggestions of Prof. H. Stuart Hughes on this topic, both in seminar and as a reader of this thesis.

At every stage of the project I have had the support of Dr. H. J. Hanham and Carmela Vircillo Franklin. This could never have been done without them. More than the details of the history of three countries, more than years of advice, he has provided a model of zeal which has inspired me to go on at occasions of tangle and disappointment. She has delayed her own research to crawl through ecclesiastical attics, penetrate monasteries, proofread through blizzards, suffer theological texts, to count and advise and improve.

Cambridge, Massachusetts
1975

CHAPTER I

1833: Three Catholic Revivals

On July 11, 1833, Prosper Guéranger assembled followers for prayer in a damp priory church on the banks of the Sarthe River at Solesmes in western France and began the Benedictine-liturgical revival, the first stage of the world-wide liturgical movement that has reshaped the worship of many branches of Christendom.[1] Three days later, July 14, 1833, John Keble preached his "Assize Sermon" in the University Church at Oxford, a protest leading on to the Oxford Movement that under the leadership of E. B. Pusey transformed the established Church of England and eventually the member churches of the Anglican Communion.[2] In September 1833 the German Roman Catholic theologian Johann Adam Möhler was attacked by Protestant opponents from throughout Germany for the polemical tone of his Symbolik. This was the beginning of a period of bitter Catholic-Protestant confessional conflict in Württemberg, the Rhineland, Prussia, and other German states which involved members of the Roman Catholic Tübingen School.[3]

----

[1]Prosper Louis Pascal Guéranger (1805-1875) refounded the Benedictine priory of Solesmes on July 11, 1833, the feast day that marks the translation of the relics of St. Benedict into France.

[2]John Keble (1792-1866) preached the Sermon "National Apostasy" July 14, 1833, before the Court of Assizes which sat at Oxford. J. H. Newman (1801-1890) was the first person to keep Keble's Assize Sermon as the beginning of the Oxford Movement (1833-1845). Keble, Newman, and Edward Bouverie Pusey (1800-1882) guided the movement until 1845, when Newman was received into the Roman Catholic Church. After 1845 the Anglican Catholic revival was known as "Anglo-Catholicism" or "Tractarianism" and Pusey was clearly the leader until his death.

[3]Johann Adam Möhler published Symbolik oder Darstellung der

Catholic Revivals

The coincidence of the appearance, of the survival, and of the eventual triumph of these three movements, quite similar in their expressions of Christianity, demands a proper explanation today. The French Benedictines and Guéranger, the Oxford Tractarians and Pusey, Möhler and the Tübingen School were each movements launched to restore the Catholic conception of Christianity for the first generation of Europeans forced to confront a democratic, industrial and predominantly secular civilization. The Benedictines, the Tractarians, and the Tübingen theologians all proclaimed that religion unnourished by the visible Catholic Church with liturgical worship, the eucharist or the mass, at its heart could not long maintain vital spiritual life in an age of secularism and revolution. Through the efforts, in part, of Guéranger, Pusey, and Möhler Catholicism was successfully restored in France, England, and Germany before the disdainful frowns and sneers of liberal, secularist skeptics who looked upon churches and religion as more or less archaic hangovers from the past, destined, like warfare, to fade away in the light of reason and self-interest.

Time has brought its surprises. In the nineteenth century Catholicism was on the defensive as a moral and political force, threatened not only by secularism and science but also by Marxism and other challenges to its authority. Today, however, Catholicism is still with us, not just in the service of those intractable mysteries and worship which eluded Marx and the secularists but also in some

----

dogmatischen Gegensatze der Katholiken und Protestanten nach ihren offentlichen Bekenntnisschriften in 1832. In October 1833, Möhler was attacked by the notable Protestant spokesman D. Marheineke in Jahrbücher für Wissenschaftliche Kritik No. 76, pp. 601–606, No. 77, pp. 609–613, No. 78, pp. 616–622, No. 79, pp. 626–631, and in November 1833 in No. 83, pp. 622–633, No. 84, pp. 665–670, No. 85, pp. 673–678, No. 86, p. 681. The leading Tübingen liberal Protestant theologian F. C. Baur attacked Möhler in the fall of 1833 in "Gegensatz des Katholicismus und Protestantismus, nach den Principien und Hauptdogmen der beiden Lehrbegriffe, mit besondere Rucksicht auf Hrn. D. Möhlers Symbolik," Tübingen Zeitschrift für Theologie, Third Quarter, 1833, pp. 1–43.

parts of the world itself now a powerful, revolutionary force over-shadowing even contemporary Marxism, which is on the wane as a living ideology.

Dom Guéranger, who felt called to a liturgical vocation in 1829 and who refounded the Benedictine priory of Solesmes in 1833 as a center of Christian revitalization, believed that in the advanced secularism of France a revival of Christianity could only be achieved through the restoration of the church as an institution with a marked emphasis on the liturgy, the official cycle of Catholic worship. Guéranger was concerned that the commitment of modern revolutions to the individual and to a predominantly materialistic civilization would have to lead to the subversion of all social order in Europe. As the claims of revolutionary secular humanism seemed to prove empty, Guéranger lifted before France the church and its liturgy as a source and model of human endeavor.

In 1887 at the fiftieth anniversary celebration of the refounding of Solesmes, Dom Guéranger was spoken of as the instigator of a Catholic renaissance that had reawakened an interest in worship both among French intellectuals and the faithful, after generations of neglect. In providing materials for the French public on the meaning of Catholic ritual, devotées of 1887 perceived that Guéranger had contributed to diminishing the separation of worship from daily affairs, of the faithful from the liturgy, of the priests from their congregations.[4]

By 1900 Guéranger's revival of the liturgy had come to be accepted by the French Catholic literary establishment. In J. K. Huysman's L'Oblat the Catholic liturgy is found to be a thing of "extraordinary beauty," the supreme medium for the translation of art into life. Charles Péguy was attracted to the "mystery of holiness" and Paul

---

[4]The sentiments expressed at the fiftieth anniversary were collected in Les Fêtes Jubilaires de l'Abbaye de Saint-Pierre de Solesmes, 9, 10, et 11 Juillet, 1887 (Solesmes, 1887).

Claudel to the "mystical realism" of Catholic ceremonies; and the singular appeal of the beauty of liturgical ritual is found in the novels of Francis Jammes, Camille Mayran, Joseph Malègue, François Mauriac, and André Billy.[5]

When abbots and bishops from several countries gathered in the summer of 1933 to celebrate the centenary of the refounding of Solesmes, Guéranger was perceived as a figure whose influence had extended far beyond the borders of France. It was now acknowledged that "Solesmes meant the awakening of the liturgical sense for half the world...Abbot Guéranger must above all be spoken of as the father of the contemporary liturgical movement."[6] Guéranger had first used the phrase "liturgical movement" in 1851 to define the recovery of the eucharist or mass in the life and teaching of the churches.[7] The

----

[5]Charles Desportes, MS La Vocation monastique: Dom Delatte et Huysmans, MS Mélanges Dom Germain Cozien, pp. 53–70, H Ma/5–6/22, Library, Abbey of Solesmes; A. L. Mayer, "Die Geistesgeschichtliche Situation der liturgischen Erneuerung in der Gegenwart," Archiv für Liturgiewissenschaft, IV (1955), 1–51; Robert d'Harcourt, "Romano Guardini et l'éducation liturgique," Ecclesia, CXXXII (1960), 107–11.

[6]P. Beda Danzer, "Solesmes in Jubelkranz," Benediktinische Monatschrift 15 (1933) 253–260; Placidus Glogger, "Monastischer Lenz, Monastischer Sommer," Benediktinische Monatschrift 16 (1934) 53–59 (published by Beuron); the Archabbot of Beuron telegraphed Solesmes 8 July 1933, "Soror Junior Congaudet Seniori in Cordis Laetitia et Gratitudine"; "Monk of Clervaux," "Solesmes," Metzer Katholisches Volksblatt (30 July, 1933); D. B. Capelle, Coadjutor abbot of Mont-César in Belgium, "Le mouvement liturgique," Les questions liturgiques et paroissiales (1934) 222–224; D. B. Capelle, "Dom Guéranger et l'esprit liturgique," Les questions liturgiques et paroissiales (1937) 131–146; F. A. Genestout, "Dom Guéranger et la restauration de Solesmes," Le correspondant 105, no. 1701 (10 August, 1933) 391–405; Victor Giraud, "La résurrection de Solesmes," Revue des deux mondes (15 July, 1933); 448–454; French articles which stressed Guéranger's significance as the founder of the liturgical revival of the church appeared in Les cahiers du cercle de la femme française, no. 7 (October 1933); l'Express du Midi (13–15 July, 1933); Journal de Sablé (15 July, 1933); La Sarthe (12 July, 1933); L'Ouest-Eclair (12 July, 1933); Semaine religieuse d'Autun, Chalon et Maçon (9 September, 1933); Bulletin religieux de Rouen (22 July, 1933); Semaine religieuse de Cambrai (15 July, 1933).

[7]"Our intention is to produce a movement," Guéranger announced in 1840 in the first volume of Institutions liturgiques, lxxi. He first

liturgical movement came to be marked by its effort to teach women and men to find in prayer a meaningful activity with social implications in the midst of economic hardship. In a nineteenth century society in which worship had been cut off from daily affairs and relegated to the strictly spiritual plane, the liturgical movement dramatized the bond between the eucharist and social justice and found in Catholic worship an act that held up a pattern of more dignified human relationships which actually could be realized in the temporal order.

The Oxford Movement (1833-1845) was the beginning of a Catholic revival within the Church of England.[8] Its leaders, primarily John Keble, John Henry Newman, and Edward Bouverie Pusey, argued that the established church was not the Protestant Church of England, but the Catholic Church in England, and they fashioned the Oxford Movement's Tracts for the Times into instruments for a second, and Catholic, reformation in England. In his incisive Tracts, which came out until 1841 and earned the appellation Tractarian for the movement, Newman revived the notion of a Catholic understanding of Christianity as the firmest bulwark against "all-corroding, all-dissolving scepticism."[9] Newman feared that the scientific world he saw growing up around him conveyed the popular impression that religion had been discredited and that it was no longer necessary to trouble with the institutional

----

used the phrase "liturgical movement" in 1851 in the third volume of the Institutions (Paris, 1851) p. 167. Three other places where the term can be found in this period are Abbé Jouve, Du Mouvement liturgique en France durant le XIXe siècle (Paris, 1860); M.-D.-A. Sibour, Mandement de Mgr. l'Archêveque de Paris sur le retour à la liturgie romaine (Paris, 1856); De la situation de la question liturgique en France en 1851 (Paris, 1851).

[8]1833-1845 were firmly established as the dates of the Oxford Movement in 1891 by R. W. Church in the The Oxford Movement: Twelve Years, 1833-1845 (most recent edition with a modern introduction, Chicago, 1970). However, these dates are arbitrary and perhaps focus too much on J. H. Newman.

[9]Newman quoted in Piers Brendon, "A High Road to Anglican UDI," The London Times (9 July, 1983).

church. The Tracts for the Times asserted that in modern times Jesus continued to be encountered in the historic church. Against Evangelical views of faith that had often dwindled into self-regard, the Tractarians argued that the church is a spiritual organism deriving its life and its authority from Jesus Christ and his apostles and their successors, rather than from the British Crown, the laws of Parliament, or the actions of the sixteenth century English reformers. The Oxford Movement with its emphasis on tradition, ritual, and dogma, was thus another attempt, a parallel to the French Benedictines, to return the church to a character consistent with its authentic Catholic past.

Of the key figures of the Oxford movement E. B. Pusey is ignored today. To Victorians generally, Pusey and "Puseyism" were terms of disapprobation and mockery, suggesting troglodytic crankiness and unpatriotic oddity, as in Thomas Carlyle's phrase, "to procreate a spectral Puseyism."[10] The sound of his name itself, his paunchy, bookish looks, his opaque literary style overshadowed by the genius of John Henry Newman who possessed the imagination and the literary talents of a great artist, his mysterious penitential life in Cardinal Wolsey's rooms behind the walls of Christ Church in Oxford—where he was said by some to wear hair cloth, to eat unpleasant food, and to sacrifice a lamb every Good Friday—his tubercular hunchback children, all of these things did nothing to dispel shadows Pusey cast in his life and after.

It is conventionally said that Pusey became the central figure in the Anglican Catholic revival only after 1845, when Newman was received into the Roman Catholic Church and the Tractarians became more commonly known as Puseyites. But Pusey's significance extends far beyond that. It is E. B. Pusey who most closely parallels within England and Anglicanism the thought and influence of Guéranger within the Roman Catholic Church. It was Pusey, not Newman, who turned the Oxford Movement away from the better funded parishes controlled by some of the most reactionary elements in British society and urged that the English

----

[10]Thomas Carlyle, Life of Sterling (New York, 1897), pp. 61-62.

Catholic revival should of necessity focus on the modern cities, rather than on areas of former population concentration where the comfortable parishes were located. E. B. Pusey had the courage to challenge the Tractarians to "grapple with our manufacturing system as the apostles did with the slave system of the ancient world...if by God's grace we would wrest from the principalities and powers of evil those portions of his kingdom, of which, while unregarded by the church, they have been taking full possession."[11]

In addition Pusey, like Guéranger, related liturgical worship to human beings as they existed in the industrial order. Reviving the eucharist in the parishes was the way in which Pusey opposed those loud voices, claiming to represent biblical faith, which were making broad-side attacks on liturgical worship and propagating the notion in Britain that Evangelical preaching should be at the heart of Christian worship. Against a one-sided Puritan spirituality which had deprecated the body and its senses and portrayed material externals as signs of hypocrisy in religion, Pusey held up liturgical worship as the noble heritage of the Church of Christ.

For the Puseyites, the eucharist gave new significance to earth as well as to eternity, to matter as well as to spirit. In their parishes justice began to flow from the eucharist: funds for workers' compensation, funds for worthy burial, and distribution centers for clothing, food and other necessities. From 1840 to 1900 the bond between Catholic worship and social justice was also vividly dramatized in Puseyite parishes in English commercial districts; and in one sense the future lay with the Puseyites in the entire Anglican Communion, for throughout the world the more Catholic emphasis on the eucharist led to the more Protestant morning prayer and evensong being supplanted by the mass as the chief form of Anglican worship. As the centenary of the Oxford Movement approached in 1933, an Anglican monk could write that the Catholic conception of the church and of worship had "come at last

---

[11]E. B. Pusey, The Councils of the Church from the Council of Jerusalem to the Council of Constantinople (Oxford, 1857), pp. 4-5.

into its own."[12]

Pusey's stature and his contribution to the wide-spread transition of Anglicanism from Protestantism to Catholicism has only occasionally been recognized, but it was noted by The London Times on his death in 1882:

> If Cranmer was the most conspicuous ecclesiastical personage in the sixteenth century, Laud in the seventeenth, then no one could dispute with Dr. Pusey the honour of giving his name to the great Anglican reaction of the nineteenth. Half the English theological world has reverenced him as a saint, risen whenever he has shown himself. Half have found no charge or insinuation too bad for him. It is Dr. Pusey who has been the Reformer, or the Heresiarch of this century.[13]

German Catholic ecclesiology, or the theology of the churches, was dominated in the nineteenth century by the work of Johann Adam Möhler. Möhler grew up amid the ruins of the Catholic Church in southwestern Germany which were the result of the secularization of Catholic lands and institutions in Germany by Napoleon Bonaparte in 1803, acting in the name of revolutionary France. In 1822 the young Catholic seminarian made the unprecedented gesture of traveling north to Berlin to study with the leading Continental Protestant theologian, Friedrich Schleiermacher. Möhler returned to the Protestant University of Tübingen in the small German state of Württemberg and proceeded to publish two of the most important books of nineteenth century Catholic theology: The Unity in the Church (1825) and Symbolism (1832).

Möhler's theology was shaped by his growing fears of the might of the state. In 1835 the young teacher was forced out of Tübingen by the Protestant government of Württemberg. The King of Württemberg was attempting to eliminate the possibility that the Catholic Church or Catholic professors might emerge as an independent political influence. From exile in Munich, Möhler closely followed religious developments to the north in Prussia: the imprisonment of a Rhineland archbishop and then a Polish archbishop because both refused to sanction

---

[12]A. G. Hebert, Intercommunion (London, 1932), p. vii.

[13]The London Times, September 18, 1882.

9

government orders directed at their clergy. Behind these events Möhler saw already dawning upon humankind the monstrous figure of the totalitarian state.

"If there will be no higher power than the state in Europe, then human freedom has come to an end," Möhler wrote in 1837.[14] To offset the divisive tendencies of nineteenth century nationalism, he spread abroad the Christian vision of the unity of all in the church. Only in a free, international religious community, the Catholic Church, could the liberties of the individual be guaranteed.

Möhler knew of the young Hegelians in Germany who described religion as the destroyer of the community. But the Catholic theologian defended religious institutions. Möhler argued that a restored church could once again be the source of social stability in Europe. Like many of his German contemporaries, Möhler found freedom only in the imposition of external social bonds. He wrote that the individual controlled by the will of the community was freed from personal aberration and made healthy and normal. A social body is thus necessary for the survival of civilization, and the Catholic Church alone can be that body. To Möhler the church was the architect of social cohesion in a revolutionary age of atomization, individualism, and fragmentation.

The rediscovery of the social dimension of the Catholic Church, the renewal of its social mission, was also brought together with a revival of liturgical worship in German Catholicism by Johann Adam Möhler. Möhler's restoration of social mission and liturgy were carried into the parishes of Germany by a Möhlerian Party made up of Möhler's Tübingen seminarians and continued at Tübingen after his death by his successor and former pupil Karl Josef Hefele, who was later appointed a bishop in the Roman Catholic Church in Germany.[15] Hefele

----

[14]J. A. Möhler, "Uber die neueste Bekämpfung der Katholischen Kirche," Gesammelte Schriften, 2 (Regensburg, 1839-1840) p. 229.

[15]Some influential members of the Möhlerian Party and parishes reformed according to its principles are J. M. Mack (Ziegelbach), Thomas Moser (Dürnau, Friedberg, Sauggart), J. B. Hafen (Gattnau), F. A. Scharpff (Mengen, Rottenburg). See also Karl Josef Hefele, Beitrage

and the Möhlerian Party fostered in the laity a love of the church and its services and reasserted the strongly humanistic potential of worship as a basis for Catholics to deal with a hostile secular order in Germany.

The force of Möhler's combination of Catholic social mission with liturgical reform was so great that in 1866 a biographer remarked that the history of the spiritual awakening and renewal of Catholic Germany must be connected with his name and bound to his memory.[16] One of the seminarians who carried the Tübingen professor's ideas of renewal out into German parishes summed up the testimony of many German Catholics to Möhler's influence:

> An ardent love for the Church distinguished Möhler from all others of his day. The unity and freedom of the Church came before everything for him. His fervor contributed a certain element of charm to his new standpoint. His ardor worked on his students. He called forth in Tübingen, he called forth in Württemberg, and he called forth in Germany, as teacher and author, a new, or rather an old--actually, more precisely, a renewed theological spirit. He departed from Tübingen, he departed from life on the earth. But his spirit has remained behind.[17]

Möhler's theology, born in the fire of controversy with the German state of Württemberg, made the closest identification of Christ with the Catholic Church as an institution. Only in an international religious community, with a marked transcendent dimension could a full humanism be guaranteed for nineteenth century Europeans. Like Guéranger, Möhler came to appreciate celibacy and the papacy as nurturing the transcendent aspect of the church.

This transposition allowed Möhler to fuse his theology of worship and his theology of the church into one whole based upon the incarnation, the doctrine of God becoming human in the life of Jesus

---

zur Kirchengeschichte, Archäologie und Liturgik (Tübingen 1864).

[16]Balthasar Wörner, Johann Adam Möhler. Ein Lebensbild (Regensburg, 1866), p. 388.

[17]J. B. Hafen, Möhler und Wessenberg (Ulm, 1842), p. 11.

Christ. His teaching that the mystery of the incarnation is reflected in both eucharistic worship, or the mass, and the institutional church became one of the fundamental theological contributions of the nineteenth century to modern Catholic thought. The church is a visible, divinely constituted, society which is the sacramental manifestation of God's saving mercy. The celebration of the eucharist is the supreme action by which each Christian comes into her or his own as a member of Christ's body and experiences union with the community. This linking of corporate worship to the concrete institutions of the church and Möhler's phrase "the church as the mystical body of Christ" came to stand behind the thinking of almost all modern German and French Catholic theologians.

At the centenary of Möhler's death, in 1938, a collection of essays by scholars from all over Europe was published simultaneously in France and Germany. Die Eine Kirche Zum Gedenken J. A. Möhlers 1838–1938 was a recognition of the theologian's importance for Europe as a whole, not only for Germany. The liturgical scholar J. A. Jungmann was the Austrian representative. To him the picture of the church in Möhler's The Unity in the Church of 1825 filled up the gap left by the collapse of the ecclesiastical structures of the Hapsburg empire after World War I with its decadent hierarchies and individualistic piety. Another essayist was Gustave Bardy who attested to a spiritual awakening among young French priests through a reading of Möhler's works. Pierre Chaillet and Pierre Chenu were two such French clerics who led Yves Congar to an understanding of Möhler.[18] Congar wrote:

> Thanks to Pierre Chenu, I was given the first idea, global in its implication, of Möhler and the Tübingen School—that was in 1928. I felt that I had not only found a breach in the bastion of the post-Tridentine church, but an inspiration, a source, a new synthesis.[19]

----

[18]J. A. Jungmann, "Die Kirche im religiösen Leben der Gegenwart," in Heman Tüchle, Die Eine Kirche zum Gedenken J. A. Möhlers. 1838–1938 (Paderborn, 1939), pp. 373–390; Gustave Bardy, "Die Stimme der Väter," ibid., pp. 63–86.

[19]Yves Congar, "Johann Adam Möhler," ThQ (1970), 47; Yves Congar, "Sur l'évolution et l'interpretation de la pensée de Moehler," Revue des Sciences Philosophiques et Théologiques, 27, II (1938), 204–212.

Through the thirties and forties Congar's work popularized Möhler's phrase "the church as the mystical body of Christ" and expanded on the implications that were contained within it. Möhler's understanding of the doctrine of the church became so prevalent by the 1940's, it was said to be in the very atmosphere of Catholicism, that Pope Pius XII issued the 1943 encyclical Mystici Corporis, in which the Pope adopted elements of Möhler's theory of the church and voiced a willingness to further its acceptance through the world-wide church.

Reading the history of these three movements together results in an altered comprehension of the traditional interpretation of each. Common time suggests common origin, and the parallel development of churches in England, France, and Germany can be explained if these new theological ideas of restoring church and worship derived from one source or were the product of a common set of social forces. Guéranger, Pusey, and Möhler are no longer understood as the product of a single national tradition, and their contribution to European religion, taken as a whole, is made clear. The justification of a comparative presentation is that only in this manner will the revivals of the 1830's be seen as part of a general transformation of European culture and together contributing to a new period of church history.

The New Catholicism: The Theme of Community

The "new Catholicism" means the Catholicism of our own time which, while never rejecting the hierarchical dimension of the church, has restored the communal dimension of Christianity. From the sixteenth century to the nineteenth century the church was conceived both by Roman Catholics and by Anglicans primarily either in terms of its hierarchical or its political structures. In both churches a majority of theologians pictured worship as a way of piety for the individual soul, rather than as an action celebrated by a community. "Watching" and "hearing" had become the dominant role of Roman Catholic and Anglican laity at worship, and the church and its worship were fragmented and divided by symbols of status, party, and class, both ecclesiastical and social.

Today an entirely new note is being sounded among Anglicans and Roman Catholics. "The people" has become the primary association of the church. Theology has moved from juridical concepts such as "perfect society" to defining the church, clergy and laity alike, as "one people." Anglicans and Roman Catholics are making the bold proclamation that Jesus continues to make his dwelling on earth in all his faithful people. There has been a renewed sense that God calls the whole of humanity to become God's daughters and sons: God's purpose is that all should share in the fellowship and worship of the church; mission and worship are carried out in the context of a "fellowship of believers"; the corporate character of Catholic worship and witness today springs from a wider grasping of the church as one community, the body of Christ.[20]

A popular appreciation of the new sense of community in eucharistic worship among Anglicans and Roman Catholics appears in a recent hymn:

As Christ breaks bread for all to share
each proud division ends.
That love that made us makes us one,
and strangers now are friends.
Together met, together bound,
We'll go our different ways,
and as his people in the world,
We'll live and speak his praise.[21]

Recent Catholic thought, Anglican and Roman, has been driven by the insight that God's creative and redemptive work in the world is intended to bring all of humankind into one community. How to realize this wider unity of the human family has become one of the immediate tasks of the two churches.

----

[20]Anglican/Roman Catholic Commission in the U.S.A., "Agreed Statement on the Purpose of the Church," Ecumerical Bulletin, 38 (November/December, 1979) 24-32.

[21]Brian A. Wren, "I Come with Joy," The Hymnal 1982 (New York, 1985), p. 304.

For Roman Catholics, the restoration of the communal dimension of
Catholicism was the most significant achievement of the Second Vatican
Council (1962-1965). The documents of Vatican II point out how pro-
foundly Christianity is a communion of people together with God. To
the Vatican Council, social conscience reflects the communal dimension
of human beings that is brought to fulfillment in the church understood
as the body of Christ. To insist upon an individual experience of God
and a secular commitment to man makes Christianity the enemy of
integral human life, and to the Council such a dichotomy contradicts
the New Testament description of the church as a koinonia, a
community.22

Another preeminent idea of the Council is that the primary means
of living the Christian life is active participation in eucharistic
worship, not by the clergy alone but also by laymen and women as well.
The fostering of a renewed corporate Catholicism in the mass has been
confined to the laity and ordained persons. This new understanding of
the church at Vatican II, expressed in the 1960's and 1970's in a
global emphasis upon communal forms of worship: the liturgy, eucharistic communion, and the liturgical year, rather than on individual acts
of piety: the rosary, private prayer or sermons, has transformed the
face of Christendom, in the shift of altars from dark sanctuaries into
the middle of congregations, and in the style of the great new public
edifices, like Liverpool Catholic Cathedral, which was the first round
cathedral to be built since the ninth century. The sound of Catholicism
has changed, too, for within all these structures mass has been said in
the language of the people for the first time in a thousand years.

In the 1970's, following the directives of the Vatican Council,
the Roman Catholic Church gave resonance to a new ecumenical
theological concept, "regional and international bilateral consulta-
tions and commissions." This new network of relationships among world
families of churches has led to significant advancement in the "new

---

22Walter M. Abbot, The Documents of Vatican II (New York, 1966);
Louis Bouyer, The Liturgy Revived (Notre Dame, 1964).

Catholicism." The first major example of international ecumenical theology has been the document released in 1982 by the Anglican-Roman Catholic International Commission known as The Final Report. The Final Report is a treatise of one hundred pages in which eighteen scholars drawn from the Anglican Communion and the Roman Catholic Church express their unanimous agreement on such formerly divisive issues as the eucharist, the nature of the ordained ministry, and authority in the church. The Final Report, a result of twelve years of study, research, and dialogue, has now been officially accepted by the Church of England and the Episcopal Church in the United States as consistent with and expressive of the faith of Anglicans.

The Final Report is a significant landmark for the triumph of the "new Catholicism," for within it a second world family of churches, the Anglican Communion, documents the restoration of the communal dimension of Catholicism, as the Catholic Church is defined in this way: "The Church is the community of those reconciled with God and with each other because it is the community of those who believe in Jesus Christ. It is also the reconciling community, because it has been called to bring to all mankind, through the preaching of the Gospel, God's gracious offer of redemption."[23] "Community for Service" is the key phrase of The Final Report; and the eucharist is understood as an action celebrated by the whole body of believers: "When we gather around the same table in this communal meal at the invitation of the same Lord and when we 'partake of the one loaf,' we are one in commitment not only to Christ and to one another, but also to the mission of the Church in the world."[24]

One source of this distinctively communal modern Catholicism lies in the three coincident Catholic restorations of the 1830's, most of all in their similar attempts to overcome the subjective and individualistic tendencies of Christian and secular thought since the

---

[23]Anglican/Roman Catholic International Commission, The Final Report (London, 1982), p. 8.

[24]Ibid., pp. 6-7, 13.

late middle ages by substituting an objective conception of Christianity based on the life of a community. Solesmes, Oxford, and Tübingen may be seen as one beginning of a reaction against those who had considered religion to be individualistic, moralistic, rationalistic, or nationalistic, most recently Wesleyans, Evangelicals, and Noetics in England; Gallicans in France; and Wessenbergians, Febronians, and Josephists in Germany.

The religious agitation of the 1830's was a revolt against the anticommunal spirit in two guises: in the Reformation churches with their pew boxes, prominent pulpits, and scriptural exercises and the Counter-Reformation churches, with their confessional boxes, baroque pulpits, and extraliturgical cults. Solesmes, Oxford, and Tübingen constituted a break not only with the eighteenth century but with a form of the church which had become dominant long before, and they shared a kinship with groups which revolted for the sake of community in the secular sphere, the Marxists, the Owenite socialists, the Comteans, the Saint-Simonians, the English who followed Ruskin, Carlyle, and Morris, the Germans Paul de Lagarde, Julius Langbehn, and Moellar van den Bruck. It is the coincidence of this transformation in theology with secular economic and intellectual developments in the nineteenth century, particularly the weakening of pre-industrial communities by the industrial revolution and consequent alienation, which accounts for the strength of the contribution of the Catholic revivals of 1833 to the general evolution of the theme of community within Anglican and Roman Catholic churches.

Guéranger's chief contribution to this transformation was the rediscovery of the liturgy as an instrument of the destruction of individualism. Guéranger taught very clearly that the eucharist was both the praise of God and the means for being incorporated into a human community, the church. Both of these aspects of worship were of fundamental importance to him. His most intriguing sentences in the introduction to The Liturgical Year (1841) emphasize above all that the eucharist is not just prayer, but prayer conceived of as social action. The introduction goes so far as to assert that the social dimension of prayer is the basis for all true worship and that the eucharist is a common offering, the work of all the people, in which the assembly of the laity must unite in the closest possible manner with everything that is said and done by the priest at the altar.[25]

To find nostalgic pleasure in decaying ecclesiastical structures was not a rare experience among nineteenth century men and women. But Dom Guéranger differed from a host of contemporaries in relating buildings and rites to what he perceived to be a social need, the necessity of community. His zeal for ritual led to a new evaluation of its importance: ritual could overcome alienation if people understood what it meant. In the midst of an actively participating congregation a community is born, Guéranger said. The church grows from communal worship. Its art, in fact all of Christian civilization, flows from the liturgy. In time Guéranger's notions of the 1830's became the basis of a new ecclesiology and his liturgical revival became one source that led on to a general revival of the Roman Catholic Church.

Johann Adam Möhler was the first Roman Catholic theologian for a thousand years to argue that the ground of the church was not the clergy or the state, but the communal life of all believers. The fundamental shift in his ecclesiology matched the radical change in the social context of Europe. For example, in the seventeenth century the Jesuit theologian Robert Bellarmine had nurtured the ideal of unity in the absolute monarchy of the papacy. To be a member of the church was to be a subject of the sovereignty of the pope. Bellarmine perceived the church as a militant "perfect society" of ordered ranks "like the Kingdom of France or the Republic of Venice."[26]

By contrast in the nineteenth century, Möhler beheld Christianity not as rules and dogma but as a life lived in common. Möhler's

----

[25]Prosper Guéranger, L'Année liturgique: L'Avent (Paris, 1874), pp. VIII-XIII.

[26]Bellarmine in Peter Nichols, The Pope's Divisions (London, 1981), p. 294.

definition of the church as a corporate unity, rather than as a legal entity, is based on his concept of the incarnation: Jesus continues to dwell on earth in his church. The goal of the incarnation, the joining of matter and spirit and divinity and humanity in Christ, continues to be carried out in the assembly of Christians.   Christ touches the world through the members of the church; they are his agents for forging bonds of human unity. Christ the cornerstone in this way "unites with the strongest bonds of love and holds [humanity] together in the covenant of eternal unity."[27]

After 1825, Möhler published on the humanistic dimensions of the church. He found that humans are, in a deeply mysterious way, instruments of the salvation of which they are also the beneficiaries. Liturgical acts are the chief signs of human participation in the redemptive process, and it is for this reason that all members of the community are actively to perform their proper role in a church service.   Möhler campaigned against private masses, for such noncommunal worship by priests alone introduced a magical element into Christianity. He called for a return of the communion cup to lay people at mass, after a millenium of denial. In the Theologische Quartalschrift he mocked the current arguments that the language of the liturgy should be Latin because of its antiquity and its ability to transmit unity to the church: "Such a unity! A unity based on ignorance and as for antiquity, why not use Hebrew in the liturgy? It is even older. Let the people understand their prayers."[28]

By relating the liturgy and the sacraments to the essential corporate nature of the church, Möhler found a way to overcome the extremely individualized sacramental theology of early nineteenth century Europe in such a way that his thinking stands behind the work

----

[27]J. A. Möhler, Symbolism, quoted in J. M. Shaw, R. W. Franklin, H. Kaasa, Readings in Christian Humanism (Minneapolis, 1982), p. 453.

[28]J. A. Möhler, "Rezension: F. Walter, Lehrbuch des Kirchenrechts mit Berücksichtigung der neuesten Verhältnisse", ThQ (1823) 294-98; "Rezension: L. Schaaf, Die Kirchenagenden-Sache in dem preussischen Staate, ThQ (1825) 286.

of those theologians who fashioned a revised understanding of the relationship of the laity to the church at the Second Vatican Council. All the great theologians who prepared the way for the restoration of the lay, communal dimension of the church at the Second Vatican Council, from Cardinal Ratzinger to Hans Küng, have admitted some debt to Johann Adam Möhler. Rarely in history has an Ecumenical Council owed so much to one man. In the documents of Vatican II, such as Lumen gentium and Gaudium et spes, the great mystery of the church as a royal priestly people pilgrimaging in time can be expressed in no more fitting terminology than Möhler's "the church as the body of Christ."[29]

In 1842, Möhler's Munich colleague, the great church historian J. J. Döllinger recognized the same spirit of a "new Catholicism" in E. B. Pusey that he perceived in J. A. Möhler. Döllinger wrote to Pusey in 1842 that "everything, with us in Germany also, points more and more distinctly towards a drawing together of kindred elements... Inwardly we are united in our religious conviction, although externally we belong to two separated churches."[30]

It is significant that from 1833 Pusey regarded the Oxford Movement as "new Catholicism" rather than as a return to seventeenth century high church doctrines now to be dipped in the fog of English romanticism. To Pusey the old Anglican establishment--the episcopal palace, the country parsonage, the Thirty-Nine Articles, the bare worship--would never make a breach in factory walls, could never lay hold of an industrial population. The times required communities of faith showing how to keep the fast as well as the festival. Pusey's

---

[29]Ecclesiam Suam of Vatican II, in Peter Foote, Vatican II's Dogmatic Constitution on the Church (New York, 1969). pp. 16, 18; Alberic Stacpoole, Vatican II Revisited By Those Who Were There (Minneapolis, 1986).

[30]MS letters to E. B. Pusey, 7 February 1842, and 30 May 1866, Pusey House, Oxford. On relations between Möhler, the Catholic Tübingen School, and the Oxford Movement see J. S. von Drey, "Die rücklaufige Bewegung im Protestantismus und ihre Bedeutung," ThQ 26 (1844) 4-56; "Das Wesen der Puseyitschen Doctrin," ThQ 26 (1844) 417-457.

growing insight that the city required community was nurtured from 1825 to 1840 by lectures and monographs of the Berlin Protestant church historian Augustus Neander. Neander set before Pusey the forgotten world of the patristic church: the intense consciousness of human solidarity expressed in the writings of the Fathers; the fellowship, sharing, and corporate celebration the early church experienced in its liturgical worship; the essential vision of the patristic church as that of a community propagating itself in opposition to the dominant pagan power.

By 1843 Pusey's study of the Fathers had issued in this interpretation of the gospel for Victorian society: the good news about Jesus is that faith in him establishes a living, organic relationship with others. He reminded his English contemporaries, who for the most part were concerned primarily with personal salvation, that from ancient to modern times Christianity has been concerned with the relationship between the believer and a community, and that therefore celebration of the eucharist is an essential part of any renewal of Christian fellowship. The eucharist can become this bond of fellowship, but only if the English recover a Catholic belief in the "true and objective" presence of Jesus Christ in the holy eucharist.

In the atmosphere of the mechanized world Pusey reversed the work of the sixteenth century reformer-liturgist Thomas Cranmer who had sought to turn the English mass into communion by eliminating any explicit mention of the real presence from the Book of Common Prayer. Pusey found that in order to make worship the act of all present who are members of Christ's body, the people's work, the eucharist had to be celebrated so as to express Christ as a living presence in the midst of his church on earth. This joining of the real presence to a communal understanding of the church and of its worship is captured in a hymn of W. E. Gladstone, the great liberal and Tractarian-influenced British prime minister of the nineteenth century. Gladstone wrote in "O Lead My Blindness by the Hand": "We who with one blest Food are fed, Into one body may we grow."[31]

Pusey advocated a Catholic liturgy which involved the people. He defended the new Puseyite ritualism "as a lay rather than a clerical movement."[32] He wrote in 1848, while himself bringing out books of popular instruction aimed at "building up our own people" in liturgical piety, that "the difference between Roman Catholic public devotion and ours eminently is that theirs being in a foreign language is so much addressed to the eye, ours to the understanding."[33] Ritual at first was not introduced into a parish until it could be explained to the people. For the early Puseyites active participation in worship—through bodily gestures, singing hymns, joining in responses and processions, and frequent communion—was the primary way a parish and its people witnessed for Jesus Christ in the industrial city, and Pusey wished no ceremonial or architectural practice to undermine the sense of community in the celebration of the eucharist. And yet some later generations of Anglo-Catholics have been slow to see that the world-wide push for liturgical renewal in many Christian churches, the restoration of full lay participation in the eucharist, is part of the "consummatio" of which Döllinger saw Pusey to be one of the pioneers.

The Cultural Dynamic

The new communal Catholicism of Guéranger, Möhler and Pusey survived and became useful in the twentieth century because, however

----

[31]W. E. Gladstone, "O Lead My Blindness By the Hand," The English Hymnal (London, 1933), p. 454.

[32]MS letter to William B. Pusey, 11 February 1866, Pusey House, Oxford. Pusey restated the lay character of the ritual movement in letters to Liddon (11/21/1880) and the Bishop of Oxford (6/21/1881). Leonard Prestige, Pusey (Oxford, 1982), calls his chapter on ritualism "The Revolt of the Catholic Laity," pp. 142-159.

[33]MS Letter to A. J. P. Beresford-Hope, 18 March 1848, Pusey House, Oxford. Pusey's "adapted books" are A Guide for Passing Advent Holily (1844); The Year of Affections (1845); The Spiritual Combat (1846); The Foundations of the Spiritual Life (1847).

new twentieth century problems appeared to be, they arose from those essential societal conditions already evident in the first half of the nineteenth century which the Catholic revivals had addressed: weak human beings isolated before monoliths of state, business, and industry which were withdrawn from the kingdom of the spirit, and the situation of the masses in the great cities, innumerable people threatened in their freedom as the state powers sought to force them into chains. Solesmes, Oxford, and Tübingen must be seen as part of a larger cultural dynamic, a cluster of parallel movements in politics, the arts, and labor relations opposing the individualizing tendencies of the agricultural, industrial, and democratic revolutions. The coincident Catholic revivals came at a moment in the nineteenth century when the transformation of human life following these political and economic revolutions was being worked out in many European countries. It was then, with the spread of mechanical power and the displacement of monarchy, that the social order that had been in existence for over a thousand years in western civilization came to an end.

Solesmes, Oxford, and Tübingen were thus, in part, a reaction against a great transformation in the patterns of life in villages, towns, and cities, which had begun in the eighteenth century under the impact of the agricultural and industrial revolutions, and resulted in social dislocation and the alienation of the individual from organic integration into society. The sense of rural community which had bound men in secure traditional relationships was disrupted by the commercialization of agriculture and the depopulation of country districts after industry created a demand for urban workers. The changes in farming and land ownership which reached a climax around 1760 were a product of economics and ideas. The great population growth in Europe in the first decades of the eighteenth century created a greater demand for agricultural products, and higher prices stimulated the interest of new investors in land.

Enlightened agricultural theorists like Arthur Young and the Physiocrats urged that traditional group farming techniques be abandoned and that rational business skill be applied to raising crops. A greater efficiency was introduced which led to the spread of enclosure, a prerequisite for capitalist agriculture, the decline of the open field, and the end of collective systems of farming. These forces liquidated communal rights and common ownership. Furthermore, the Revolution of 1789 in France and the Napoleonic régime in Württemberg ended the church's corporate land systems and resulted in an increase in the number of bourgeois investors with little regard for traditional rural relationships. In England, the competition of commercial agriculture drove small, independent traditional farmers from their property. In each country these displaced farmers were forced to find employment in small local manufacturing works which were springing up at the turn of the century.

Many observers had a negative reaction to this change. De Tocqueville saw that with the introduction of individualistic agricultural methods a sense of family and community was ending in rural France. Goldsmith in England, Adam Müller and Baader in Germany and Sismondi, the Swiss, argued that capitalistic agriculture was leading to the disintegration of social unity. William Cobbett saw commercial agriculture to be an oppressive system, destructive of the old rural relationships.

The reaction of the rural population was to try to protect their traditional system in face of the intrusion of the market economy. Their discontent was often expressed in isolated country rebellions or larger movements like the Vendée in France or Captain Swing in England.

There was a similar realization of the loss of community in cities. Old towns began to grow in the late eighteenth century because the demographic revolution allowed a surplus population to migrate from the land. The expansion of factories and the opportunity for higher industrial wages were added inducements which account for the transfer of population from the country to the city. The crowded, unplanned new living conditions created anomie, loneliness and rootlessness in the urban masses. Capitalism, which had produced the industrial city, enhanced the separation of individuals. It was in essence a competitive system which set businessman against businessman, worker against worker.

The history of urban protest in the nineteenth century is evidence of dissatisfaction with a new state of affairs, although some theorists were pleased with the individualism of the age. Bentham regarded the ideal world as a collection of persons each pursuing separate interests and pleasures. Nineteenth century idealism from Kant to the neo-Kantians led to a cultivation and worship of the Self, a philosophy of the world as essentially a private affair. In Appearance and Reality J. H. Bradley, the English idealist, describes the delights of individuality: "My external sensations are no less private to my thoughts or my feelings. In either case my experience falls within my own circle, a circle closed on the outside; and, with all its elements alike, every sphere is opaque to the others which surround it....In brief, regarded as an existence which appears in a soul, the whole world for each is peculiar and private to that soul."[34]

There were, however, many criticisms of industrialization as de-humanizing precisely because of its atomization of society, its destruction of relationships among individuals. Many nineteenth century writers argued that social well-being would return only if there were common values, if men fit into a community. Marx made the most famous German protest against the situation. Bourgeois industry is destructive because "it has left no other bond between man and man than naked self-interest, than callous 'cash-payment.' It has drowned the most heavenly ecstacies of religious fervour, of chivalrous enthusiasm...in the icy water of egotistical calculation."[35] The emancipation from capitalist alienation would come by the uniting of men into an organic whole and the end of individual ownership of property. F. E. D. Schleiermacher commented on the end of common values in industrial society: The "whole sense of a common material progress is without value...the work of humanity is carried out by an

---

[34]J. H. Bradley quoted in A. G. Hebert, The Form of the Church (London, 1948), p. 68.

[35]Karl Marx, The Communist Manifesto (New York, 1955), p. 12.

'ingenious system' in which each man is forced to restrict his powers."[36]

The late nineteenth century German apostles of cultural despair Paul de Lagarde, Julius Langbehn, and Arthur Moeller van den Bruck longed for a new Germanic political community which would overcome the industrial civilization which had destroyed social unity and all social values. In the early twentieth century the Blaue Reiter movement argued that collective art makes social integration possible and in 1923 Walter Gropius, speaking for the Bauhaus group, expressed the same ideas in terms of architecture: "The idea of a contemporary world is already recognized....The old dualistic world-picture which showed the individual in opposition to society is losing ground. In its place is rising the idea of a universal unity in which all opposing forces exist in a state of community."[37]

In France, Fourier realized that capitalism was reducing men and women by separating them from spiritual values and transforming them into material things. To Saint-Simon a state which functioned to unite men and women into a community would make values possible. His student Auguste Comte thought that empirical science would check the egotistical tendencies of France and make social order possible.

English writers maintained a sustained protest in the name of community. Robert Southey contrasted the human deformity of the mechanized world in his Colloquies. Robert Owen built the community of New Lanark to overcome the isolating effect of factories. Coleridge would have restored a nation alienated by individualism from its cultural heritage by means of a National Church. Carlyle sought de-mechanization through an organic literary class, Ruskin through a paternal state, the Fabians by means of collectivism, D. H. Lawrence

---

[36]H. G. Schenk, The Mind of the European Romantics (Garden City, 1969), p. 25.

[37]Walter Gropius in Idee und Aufbau des Staatliches Bauhauses Weimar quoted in Reyner Banham, Die Revolution der Architektur (Munich, 1964), pp. 241-244.

through literature: "We have frustrated that instinct of community which could make us unite in pride and dignity....Our civilization... has almost destroyed the natural flow of common sympathy between men and men, and men and women....It is this that I want to restore into life."[38]

The parish church, which in its primitive state had been in essence a communal organization was now unable to minister to the needs of parishioners suffering from the effects of this age of individualism, because it also was under the influence of post-Reformation religious theories. In the villages of Württemberg, in parts of France, and in Anglican churches, worship and the corporate aspects of Christianity were relegated to the background. Spiritual life assumed very largely a subjective and private character dominated by rational sermons, religious readings, extraliturgical pilgrimages, and special devotions.

The parish church was an outpost of the secular government as much as a link in the ecclesiastical hierarchy. It was understood to be a center of secular education, public charity, and local administration even more than a place for religious services. In England, France, and Germany there was little liturgical participation by the people; eucharistic communion was de-emphasized and was given little meaning. The few church organizations which existed for laypersons did not meet social needs. Almost no care was shown for ritual and music and their meaning within the cycle of the liturgical year was ignored. The physical condition of the church fabric was often poor. Sections of the church building were rented to individual families for their use at religious functions. The structure was cluttered and divided by galleries, pew-boxes, shrines and statues, and the main altar was often hidden from the worshippers' view. The bishop rarely visited. This resulted in few confirmations and a diminished sense of belonging to a larger ecclesiastical community.

---

[38]D. H. Lawrence in Raymond Williams, Culture and Society (New York, 1958), pp. 205, 215.

City churches were as unable to provide a sense of community to
the displaced masses of the urban workers. They suffered essentially
from the same institutional debility and had the added problem of a
vast increase in the number of their parishioners living in radically
altered circumstances. St. George-in-the-East in London, for example,
with one rector and 30,000 parishioners in 1838 had four services a
week, communion four times a year and an average attendance of a few
hundred. Some Berlin churches like Zum Heilige Kreuz had 100,000
parishioners, four ministers and one service a week.

There was no conception of a structural change in the administration of such parishes which could meet the needs of the new city
dwellers. Neither the number of services, the way of dispensing the
sacraments, the character of worship, nor pastoral methods could deal
with new social problems. The round of learned sermons continued
without any attempt to add beauty or a sense of fellowship through
Christian worship to the needs of people caught in the dismal
industrial situation.

A common solution to the question of church and society was
realized by the French Benedictines, the Tübingen School, and the
Oxford Movement. Guéranger, Pusey, and Möhler are part of the many
attempts in the nineteenth century to reintegrate a Western culture
fragmented by the new set of economic and social circumstances
associated with modernization. They found that the communal conception
of early Christianity could offer an ideal of community to contemporary
society. This resolution was the product of witnessing the effects of
social change in the light of a new paradigm of Christianity. The
exact manner by which the paradigm came to be adopted by these
movements has escaped scholars for a hundred years.

The Question of the Correct Intellectual Link

The hunt for a connection between Möhler and J. H. Newman, Pusey's
great friend and Oxford colleague who abandoned the innovative ideas of
the Oxford Movement when he went over to the Roman Church in 1845 and

began to combat the work of his former comrades, has engaged the most research.

Even contemporaries were aware that there were striking similarities in the theories of Newman and Möhler about the manner in which the tradition of the Christian church developed. Indeed, in The Development of Christian Doctrine Newman himself cites Möhler as one who had already said much the same thing.[39] Lord Acton was convinced that Möhler had directly influenced Newman's view of the church and the way it developed either because Newman had read a comparison of himself to the German in a Roman theological work, Perrone's Praelectiones Theologicae, or through the influence of a Pembroke College undergraduate.[40] Edmond Vermeil, a French scholar, concludes that the Oxford don's idea of the church as the continung earthly form of Christ, which contains within it a living and therefore developing tradition, was a reproduction of the Tübingen School in England. Although the common influence of biological theory and romantic organicism as well as the similar conflicts with Protestant governments could have produced the same ideas in Möhler and Newman, Vermeil argues that there must have been a direct link between the two movements.[41]

Henry Tristram's opinion was that the most plausible mediating influence between J. A. Möhler and J. H. Newman was Cardinal Wiseman, the head of the English College at Rome, later the first Archbishop of Westminster, who knew Newman and had been a great advocate of Möhler's theories. Tristram finds in both the idea that the living tradition of the church is embodied in the liturgy and the episcopate.[42] Wilfrid

----

[39]J. H. Newman, An Essay on the Development of Christian Doctrine (2nd ed. London, 1878), p. 27. Möhler discusses development in the preface to Einheit and in Symbolik, part 1, ch. 5, sect. 40.

[40]Owen Chadwick, From Bossuet to Newman (Cambride, 1957), p. 112.

[41]Edmond Vermeil, Jean-Adam Möhler et l'Ecole Catholique de Tübingen (Paris, 1913), p. 454ff.

[42]Henry Tristram, "J. A. Moehler et J. H. Newman, la pensée allemande et la renaissance catholique," Revue des Sciences Philosophiques et Théologiques, No. 2 (April, 1938), 184-204.

Ward, the Newman biographer, more cautiously admits only that Newman and Möhler had similar ideas of development, but he does not offer any explanation for the coincidence.[43] To J. R. Geiselmann, a leading Möhler scholar, the striking similarity of the German with Newman is not the common views of tradition but skepticism regarding the religious knowledge of the individual and a high regard for the sensus fidelium, the entire body of the faithful as the organ which transmits religious knowledge and the true tradition of the church.[44]

Another group of observers has resolved the question of similarity of ideas by stressing that both Newman and Möhler had read and were strongly influenced by the Fathers of the first five centuries of the Christian church. Both wrote on Athanasius.[45] T. D. Acland writing to Newman from Bologna on May 11, 1834 said: "Wiseman has desired me to draw your attention to a German work by Möhler, on Athanasius and his times. Very Roman Catholic, I believe."[46] Two German studies of Newman in the 1950's emphasize the parallel picture which Newman and Möhler formed of Athanasius, and state further that their identification of the church with the body of Christ is a very important revival of a viewpoint which Newman and Möhler both found in many theologians of the

----

[43]Wilfrid Ward, The Life of John Henry Cardinal Newman I (London, 1927), 308, 315.

[44]Joseph Rupert Geiselmann, The Meaning of Tradition (Freiburg, 1966), pp. 19, 20, 53-72 on Möhler and p. 152 on Newman; J. R. Geiselmann, unpublished lectures Grundlegung der Dogmatik in MS Gf 2480 HS, Tübingen Wilhelmstift, pp. 8, 9, 46, 47. This is a position which is very close to the communal theory of knowledge, epistemological traditionalism. A more recent view is found in John Coulson, Newman and the Common Tradition (London, 1970), which stresses the relation of Newman's epistemology to a common tradition also preserved in Möhler and that "this common tradition is confirmed and supported by the documents of Vatican II."

[45]Möhler's Athanasius der Grosse und die Kirche seiner Zeit appeared in 1827 and Newman's The Arians of the Fourth Century in 1833; also Newman's Athanasius Alexandrinus (London, 1844).

[46]Anne Mozley, Letters and Correspondence of John Henry Newman (London, 1891), pp. 39-40.

patristic period.[47]   And yet other scholars, particulary Roger Aubert
and Alexander Dru, argue that, rather than rediscoverers, Möhler and
Newman are pioneers in stressing a communal and spiritual conception of
the church and not the hierarchical one emphasized in post-Tridentine
ecclesiology.[48]

By a close reading of Newman's notebooks Owen Chadwick provided
evidence which disproved all theories of any direct or indirect Newman-
Möhler link that had appeared before 1957.[49] Yet some scholars have
noticed that Möhler was read by other Tractarians and their sympathizers such as W. E. Gladstone who reviewed Möhler's Symbolism in 1845,
by William Palmer of Worcester, and most importantly by Frederick
Oakeley and W. G. Ward who cited Möhler frequently in their articles
in the British Critic, one of the main organs of the Oxford Movement.[50]

----

[47]Norbert Schiffers, Die Einheit der Kirche nach John Henry Newman,
(Düsseldorf, 1956), pp. 31-32, note 42 discusses Fathers, p. 115, note
58 discusses development, p. 137, ideas about lay theology, see also
pp. 195, 197; Alfred Läpple, Der Einzelne in der Kirche (Munich, 1952),
pp. 140-141, note 48, p. 221, note 107.

[48]Alexander Dru, The Church in the Nineteenth Century: Germany
1800-1918 (London, 1963), pp. 15, 64, 108, 121; Roger Aubert, "Die
Ekklesiologische Geographie im 19 Jahrhundert," in Jean Daniélou and
Herbert Vorgrimler, ed., Sentire Ecclesiam (Freiburg, 1961),
pp. 430-473.

[49]Chadwick, op. cit., p. 118.   Those who have discussed the
Döllinger-Newman relationship reveal nothing that is evidence that the
German church historian passed on any of the ideas of his friend
Möhler. See Heinrich Fries, "Newman und Döllinger," pp. 29-76, in
Newman-Studien, I (Nürnberg, 1948); Tristram, loc. cit., p. 194;
Schiffers, op. cit., p. 137; H. A. MacDougall, The Acton-Newman
Relations (New York, 1962). From the point of view of this thesis the
over-studied Newman is neither the most revolutionary nor the most
important figure in the Oxford Movement and he demonstrates his
rejection of the new conception of the church by joining the English
Roman Catholics in 1845 and arguing against Pusey's treatise on
communal Catholicism, the Eirenicon.

[50]Chadwick, op. cit., pp. 114-118; W. G. Roe, Lamennais and England
(London, 1966), p. 107; Roger Greenfield, The Attitude of the
Tractarians to the Roman Catholic Church. 1833-1850, MS D.PHIL. thesis
d. 1726, Bodleian, Oxford, pp. 368-373. Frederick Oakeley, 1802-1880,
Fellow of Balliol College, Oxford, minister of Margaret Chapel, London,
one of the young extremists of the second group of Tractarians, joined

Palmer went as far as to say that Möhler and de Maistre were the two favorite authors of the British Critic.[51] Ward, it is argued, was pushed toward a new conception of Catholicism becaue of Möhler.[52] However, the influence of these articles and books by Ward, Oakeley, Gladstone and Palmer is not evident until the 1840's, much too late to have been responsible for the coincident ideas of 1833.

A third set of commentaries on nineteenth-century theology does not single out any direct links between Möhler and Newman or the minor Tractarians but concentrates rather on the broad similarity of Möhler's ecclesiology and that of all the major Tractarians taken together. Waldemar Trapp discovers a Catholic restoration at Tübingen and Oxford which leads to a deepened understanding of the church as a divine institution and a new conception of the importance of the liturgy. He adds E. B. Pusey to the discussion because of Pusey's emphasis on the objectivity of Catholic belief.[53] A. Härdelin demonstrates that Tübingen and Oxford share a definition of the church and the sacraments as an extension of the incarnation and therefore both the body of Christ.[54] Olivier Rousseau finds in Möhler, Newman, Keble, and Pusey a new emphasis on the contemporary significance of the patristic

---

the Roman Church in November, 1845, a month after Newman. William George Ward, 1812-1882, Fellow of Balliol, famous for his The Ideal of a Christian Church Considered in Comparison with Existing Practice, censured at Oxford in 1845, and as editor 1863-1878 of the Dublin Review, an Ultramontane journal, after he became a Roman Catholic.

[51]William Palmer, A Narrative of Events Connected with the Publication of the Tracts for the Times (Oxford, 1843), p. 45. The British Critic, and Quarterly Theological Review, hereafter B.C., appeared from 1793 to 1843. It became the organ of the Tractarians.

[52]Greenfield, op. cit., p. 368. The important Ward articles in the B.C. which discuss Möhler are "Arnold's Sermons," "Whately's Essays," and "The Synagogue and the Church."

[53]Waldemar Trapp, Vorgeschichte und Ursprung der liturgischen Bewegung (Regensburg, 1940), on the Oxford Movement and Pusey and Newman, pp. 256-259, on similarities, p. 256, on Möhler, pp. 230-233.

[54]Alf Härdelin, The Tractarian Understanding of the Eucharist (Uppsala, 1965), pp. 10, 80-87.

theologians of the early centuries, whose mystical understanding of the sacraments and allegorical interpretation of scripture account for the new ecclesiology and the revival of the liturgy and the liturgical year. There is more than an affinity between Möhler and the Tractarians, he argues, and Dr. Pusey's trip to Germany in the 1820's may account of that fact.[55]

Yngve Brilioth narrows the study of similarities to Pusey and Möhler, concentrating on the sacramental/incarnational definition of the church in both, and the understanding of justification as an evolutionary process of sanctification. He also notes that Pusey had Möhler's Symbolism in his library but that "it seems doubtful whether this work exercised any direct influence on the Oxford Movement proper. On the other hand the palpable convergence of the views is probably to be explained as the independent results of the same fundamental elements."[56]

Stephan Lösch, the Tübingen historian, comes closest to a proper explanation of the meeting of ideas in one of the first articles of his career "J. A. Möhler und die Theologie Englands im 19 Jahrhundert." Lösch posits the theory that Pusey influenced the other Tractarians in the Möhlerian direction because of a knowledge of Möhler gained through friendship with August Tholuck, the Berlin Evangelical theologian who was also acquainted with the southern German. The crucial role of Tholuck in the transmission of ideas was thus established.[57]

----

[55]Olivier Rousseau, Histoire du Mouvement Liturgique (Paris, 1945), pp. 10, 73, 77, 81-89, 112-127.

[56]Yngve Brilioth, The Anglican Revival (London, 1925), pp., 329, 336. In Dr. Pusey's Eirenicon Considered in Relation to Catholic Unity (London, 1866), p. 55, H. N. Oxenham, who knew the works of Pusey and Möhler, compared their notions of church union, but had no theory to explain any similarities which existed.

[57]Rottenburger Monatschrift für praktische Theologie, 6 (1922/ 1923), 198-202, 221-227. Friedrich August Gottreu Tholuck, 1799-1877, student of Neander in Berlin, 1821, lecturer at University of Berlin to 1826, after 1826 professor at Halle, Evangelical New Testament critic whose works concentrate on the Epistles.

Contrary to the opinion of many, it is quite clear that Pusey did read his copy of Möhler's Symbolism. He knew that book well, but that knowledge does not account for the similarity of so many of the ideas of Pusey and Möhler.[58] A crucial factor which explains the development of the Oxford Movement was Dr. Pusey's period of study in northern German universities in the 1820's which resulted in a deep interest in German theology and long friendships with German scholars.[59] On the whole, commentators on the life and work of Pusey have noted but discounted the effects of two trips to Germany and Pusey's German correspondence. H. P. Liddon, Pusey's student and primary biographer, set the pattern of de-emphasis by portraying the main result of contact with leading German Protestant theologians Schleiermacher, Neander, and Tholuck to be the re-inforcement of a great fear of rationalism in the Tractarian rather than the acceptance of German patristic scholarship with its newly-discovered communal views of the church.[60] To the later Pusey biographer Maria Trench, a new line of professional study was opened to Pusey when he learned Hebrew, Arabic, and Syriac in the German schools.[61]

To others the importance of the German experience was not so much

----

[58]See E. B. Pusey, Eirenicon I (London, 1865), 259-260, Eirenicon II (London, 1869), 54-55, and copy of MS letter to Keble, Dec. 17, 1860, Pusey House, Oxford.

[59]The extent of contact may be judged by the fact that there are three volumes of collected German correspondence in Pusey House.

[60]Henry Parry Liddon, The Life of Edward Bouverie Pusey (2nd ed., London, 1893), I, 71ff.; Friedrich Ernst Daniel Schleiermacher, 1768-1834, professor of theology at Bonn and Berlin, founder of a new school of romantic Protestant theology; Johann August Wilhelm Neander, 1789-1850, born into Jewish family, converted to Protestantism in 1806, student of Schleiermacher, from 1813 professor of church history at University of Berlin.

[61]Maria Trench, The Story of Dr. Pusey's Life (London, 1900), p. 27f. Tristram, pp. 185, 186, concludes that he adopted the new critical positions of Heinrich Ewald, 1803-1875, the Göttingen orientalist, Hebraist, and theologian who was one of Pusey's teachers, while learning languages for Biblical research.

that if fitted E. B. Pusey for his role as Regius Professor of Hebrew
in the University of Oxford, but that it permanently altered the
theological position of his youth. In the opinion of G. W. E. Russel
it turned Pusey against the "dead orthodoxism" of the English High
Church, and according to Roger Greenfield it opened him to Evangelical
and Roman Catholic influences, broader interpretations of scripture and
forms of piety to satisfy the yearnings of the heart.[62] A. B. Donaldson
provides a hint that perhaps the combined result of the impact of the
Germans was Pusey's new treatment of the sacraments: "A visit from
Tholuck, for whom he had a warm regard, strengthened Pusey in his
anxiety to spend his life in defence of the Christian faith, and he
devoted himself in the next few months to the special study of the
Sacraments: the result of this was his celebrated Tract on Baptism."[63]

More specialized studies have suggested that the affinities of the
Oxford Movement and the German romantics and idealists might be
explained by Pusey's role in carrying German ideas to England and
producing there the new sacramentalism and ecclesiology associated with
the Oxford Movement. C. C. J. Webb sees that both the Tractarians and
the Hegelians stressed that the Christian life is a mysterious
incorporation of the individual personality into the humanity of God
incarnate by being drawn into the corporate life of the church through
the action of the sacraments. However, the German pietists are understood to be the only direct link joining Hegel and Pusey.[64] I. A.
Willoughby and E. A. Knox conclude that Schleiermacher's arguments
against rationalistic defenses of Christianity converted Dr. Pusey to
the opinion that "the original seat of religion is in the feeling, not
in the understanding."[65] A. M. Fairbairn views the English Catholic

---

[62]G. W. E. Russel, Dr. Pusey (London, 1907), p. 17ff.; Greenfield,
op. cit., pp. 51-55.

[63]A. B Donaldson, Five Great Oxford Leaders (London, 1902), p. 165.

[64]C. C. J. Webb, Religious Thought in the Oxford Movement (London,
1928), pp. 81, 84, 86, 90-91, 101.

[65]I. A. Willoughby, "On Some German Affinities with the Oxford
Movement," The Modern Language Review, XXIX, No. 1 (January, 1934),

revival not as an insular movement, but as part of a flood of Continental religious romanticism which swept across the English Channel. Pusey's earliest book, shown to be based on Tholuck who was a member of the romantic school of Schleiermacher, was a harbinger of that flood.[66]

Previous studies, then, have come close to answering the question of the coincident theologies at Oxford and Tübingen by demonstrating that Pusey brought German ideas home to England at the end of the 1820's. It has been rightly emphasized that Pusey's pioneering communal concepts were drawn from the group of German Evangelical romantics surrounding Schleiermacher at the University of Berlin, but the important role of another member of that group, August Neander, the great Protestant church historian, has been overlooked.

As early as 1826 and 1827, Pusey was directed by Neander to regard the church of the patristic age as a model. It is in his research into the theology of the Fathers that Pusey discovered the new view which he passed on to the Tractarians, that the church is a visible, objective community which is the body of Christ. Because of Neander and his student A. Tholuck, Pusey readjusted his thinking about the sacraments, and justification came to be seen as a process of development, of sanctification, and incorporation into Christ's body, the church. He arrived at his new theology by reading the New Testament in the light of the "sacramental" system of the Old Testament: that God conveys grace and religious knowledge not to individuals through their intellects but to the community by means of material objects. The allegorical interpretation of the Old Testament by the Fathers, to which Pusey was introduced by the Schleiermacher school, revealed this new concept to him. Thus it is made clear why the Anglican Catholic revival was highly influenced by the Regius Professor of Hebrew of the

---

52-66; E. A. Knox, The Tractarian Movement 1833-1845 (London, 1933), pp. 351-356.

[66]A. M. Fairbairn, Catholicism: Roman and Anglican (New York, 1899), pp. 88, 94, 97, 295, 305.

University of Oxford. Pusey's sacramentalism and ecclesiology are the foundations of Anglo-Catholicism. Therefore, the influence of German ideas upon Pusey and their transmission by Pusey must be seen as equally important in English intellectual history as the German intellectual relations of Coleridge, Wordsworth, and Carlyle, and infinitely more so than those of Newman.[67]

Yet if Möhler can not be shown to have been an influence on Pusey, the similarity and coincidence of their new understanding of Christianity remains to be explained. Furthermore, the possibility that it was Möhler who was first influenced by the Oxford Movement must be raised. The Tübingen theologian had a great interest in the Anglican Church, but his only direct contact was the English congregation at Baden-Baden where he would go for leisurely summer cures.[68] He wrote three articles in the Theologische Quartalschrift, the Tübingen theological journal, on English religion.[69] But there is never much discussion of the English in his letters, and he is mistaken in much of what he says about the Church of England in his Symbolism, hereafter referred to by its German title Symbolik. There were several other important articles by Johann Adam Möhler on British subjects in the organ of the Tübingen School. One is a review of Marsh's comparisons of English Protestantism and Roman Catholicism before the Emancipation, but it was printed in 1822 and although it may have influenced Möhler it was probably too early to have been written by

----

[67]René Wellek, Confrontations (Princeton, 1965), discusses Wordsworth and Coleridge in Germany, pp. 4, 9, 11, and Carlyle and Germany, p. 31. See also A. O. Lovejoy, "On the Discrimination of Romanticisms," Essays in the History of Ideas (Baltimore, 1948), pp. 228-253, and Mill on Coleridge in John Stuart Mill on Bentham and Coleridge (New York, 1950), pp. 99-168.

[68]Stefan Lösch, Prof. Dr. Adam Gengler 1799-1866. Die Beziehungen des Bamberger Theologen zu J. J. J. Döllinger und J. A. Möhler (Würzburg, 1963), p. 102 discusses Möhler with the English at Baden in July, 1833, and relations with Anglicans generally.

[69]ThQ (1827), 587; (1828), 337; (1830), 126. One is on Anselm and the church of his time, the second and third on Bishop Milner.

him.[70] There were two important discussions of Puseyism in numbers for 1844, but they appeared after Möhler's death and almost certainly were written by J. S. Drey, his teacher.[71]

There were no direct Tübingen-Oxford contacts, but there is one reason which explains the convergence: Möhler traveled to northern Germany in 1822-23 and attended the same lectures Pusey would later audit. He heard Schleiermacher, was deeply impressed by Neander, met and was written to by Tholuck.[72] One group of commentators pictures this northern trip as the crucial factor in the development of Möhler's ecclesiology, citing it as accounting for the new Catholic spirit of southwest Germany.[73]

The Frenchmen Georges Goyau and Edmond Vermeil argue pointedly that J. A. Möhler was influenced by both Neander and Schleiermacher. Goyau demonstrates that Neander and Schleiermacher were the first to posit the renewed ideal of the communal church and that the Catholic Möhler derived the concept from them, while Vermeil stresses that Möhler's Unity in the Church, hereafter referred to by its German title Einheit in der Kirche, where the church as community is first discussed, is a Catholic replica of Schleiermacher's Dogmatic, where the non-individualistic aspects of Christianity are revived. Both agree that it was from Neander that the Tübingen theologian learned of

----

[70]ThQ began in 1819 at Tübingen and is the oldest continuing theological quarterly in the world. Möhler's first articles began to appear in 1823, although since the pieces are unsigned there is often conjecture concerning authorship.

[71]"Die rucklaufige Bewegung im Protestantismus und ihre Bedeutung," ThQ (1844), 4-56, and "Das Wesen der Puseyitischen Doctrin," ThQ (1844), 415-457; Johann Sebastian Drey, 1777-1853, Prof. of Dogmatics at Ellwangen, 1812, and prof. at Tübingen from 1817. He began ThQ and was the father of the Tübingen School.

[72]This letter is included in Stephan Lösch, Johann Adam Möhler. Gesammelte Aktenstucke und Briefe (Munich, 1928), pp. 259-260.

[73]D. F. Strauss, Kleine Schriften (Berlin, 1866), p. 353. Karl Eschweiler, Johann Adam Möhlers Kirchenbegriff (Braunsberg Pr., 1930), p. 35.

a new kind of Catholicism which had existed in the first three centuries of the church and could now meet the needs of Catholics in the altered circumstances of the nineteenth century.[74]

Karl Eschweiler, Joseph Ranft, and Geiselmann differ in that to them only Schleiermacher is the important Prussian for Möhler. Schleiermacher's theology of experience, according to Eschweiler, is reflected in his description of a church grounded in the feelings of the community, and his definition of the bishop as merely the focal point of the love of that group. The Protestant's "outer-inner" distinctions, that outer religious symbols are the expression of the emotions of the group, are maintained in the Catholic's Einheit, where it is suggested that all outer forms in the church be related to the reality of an inner religious experience and that the inner spiritual unity of the church is as important as its hierarchical invisibility.[75] For Geiselmann, it is apparent that Möhler adopts Schleiermacher's language concerning the work of the Holy Ghost in the perfection and unification of mankind.[76] Ranft understands Möhler to have translated Schleiermacher's discussion of the importance of the religious self-consciousness of the individual into the symbols of the objective community of the Catholic Church.[77]

To Karl Bihlmeyer and Karl Adam, only Neander is the important outside influence. After hearing Neander's lectures and reading his studies of early Christians the young Möhler broke with the static, mechanical conceptions of the church of the Catholic Aufklärung and

----

[74]Georges Goyau, Moehler (Paris, 1905), pp. 14-18, and Goyau, "Frohes Streben zur Einheit," Herman Tüchle, Die Eine Kirche. Zum Gedenken J. A. Möhlers. 1838-1939, pp. 57-62, particularly p. 59; Vermeil, op.cit., pp. 13, 104, 153.

[75]Eschweiler, op. cit., pp. 29, 35, 46, 148.

[76]J. R. Geiselmann, "Einheit und Liebe. Ihr Gestaltwandel in Möhlers Theologie der Kirche" in Tüchle, op. cit., pp. 135-291, particularly p. 182.

[77]Joseph Ranft, "Lebendige Uberlieferung. Ihre Einheit und ihre Entwicklung," Tüchle, op. cit., pp. 109-134, particulary pp. 124-125.

began to describe the tradition of the church as a living, organic growth which responds to the development of the life of the Christian people.[78]

Of course there are arguments which denigrate the decisive influence of a Protestant school on Catholic theology. Some are that Möhler found his new ideas in other German romantics, particularly Novalis and Schelling, or from the completely Catholic tradition of the Bavarian Bishop Sailer.[79] Yet there is the internal evidence which Möhler himself provides to demonstrate the critical importance of his student journey in the Protestant German north. There are his reports to the Tübingen faculty and to his uncle at the episcopal office in Rottenburg which recount the strong impressions of the Schleiermacher group in Berlin and the unforgettable lectures of Neander in which he was introduced to the world of Origen, Tertullian, Augustine, and Chrysostom.[80] Möhler would later write that this contact with the Fathers transformed his conception of Christianity.[81] There is the letter of Tholuck, a witness to Möhler's personal relationship with the same Berlin Protestant circle with which Pusey was involved. Further evidence is provided by Möhler's articles in the Theologische Quartalschrift which praise Neander for his historical methodology and for providing the contemporary church with a picture of the devoted priesthood and inspired community life of the early Christian

----

[78]Karl Bihlmeyer, "J. A. Möhler als Kirchenhistoriker, seine Leistungen und Methode," ThQ (1919), 134-198, particulary 146; Karl Adam, "Die Katholische Tübinger Schule zur 450-Jahrfeier der Universitat Tübingen," Hochland 24, II (1927), 581-601.

[79]Many of these arguments are summarized in Stephan Lösch, "Der Geist der Ecclesia und das Werden ihrer sichtbaren Form: Der Weg von 'Einheit' zur 'Athanasius,'" Tüchle, op cit., pp. 241-257.

[80]These letters and reports of 30 January and 20 February 1823 are in Lösch-Möhler I, 83-84, 89.

[81]Heinrich Kihn, Professor Dr. J. A. Möhler ernannter Domdekan von Würzburg. Ein Lebensbild als Beitrag zur Geschichte der Theologie der Neuzeit (Würzburg, 1885), p. 9.

centuries.[82] His Tübingen lecture notes and the testimony of his
students tell of Möhler's regard for Neander as the greatest church
historian of the era.[83] We are left, then, with the novel conclusion
that the roots of important aspects of two Catholic revivals in England
and Württemberg lie in the influence of Protestant theology and church
history at Berlin on Pusey and Möhler.

The literature which has dwelt on the parallels and connections of
religious movements in France and England follows the pattern of the
discussions of German-English relations. There are notations of a
broad spirit of religious romanticism afoot at the beginning of the
nineteenth century.[84] There is a narrowing to several similar groups
and figures, and then a closing in on the greatest similarity of
Guéranger and the Anglo-Catholics.[85] A. M. Allchin in his study of the
early years of Anglo-Catholic monasticism notices that the ancien
régime religious orders were being refounded in France in the nineteenth century at the same moment that the first monastic institutions
were being re-opened in the Church of England since the Reformation.[86]
The largest number of books to investigate parallel religious
developments in France and England between 1820 and 1850 has
concentrated on the striking fact that at the same time that the Abbé
Lamennais published the French newspaper L'Avenir, the Oxford dons put

---

[82]ThQ (1824), 195-219, (1825), 646-664, (1833), 49-60.

[83]Johann Adam Möhler, Unpublished lecture notes on church history,
winter semester 1827-28, summer semester 1828, MS HS Gh 3280,
Wilhelmstift, Tübingen, pp. 52-53; C. F. Kling, "Aus dem Leben
Möhlers," in Lösch-Möhler I, 498; J. M. Mack, "Zum Gedachtnis an
Möhler," in Lösch-Möhler I, 538.

[84]J. H. Newman, Apologia pro Vita Sua (2nd ed., London, 1913),
p. 196; G. H. Harper, Cardinal Newman and William Froude (Baltimore,
1933), p. 30; Brilioth, op. cit., p. 57; Willoughby, loc. cit., p. 52.

[85]Ollard, op. cit., preface, p.11.

[86]A. M. Allchin, The Silent Rebellion (London, 1958), p. 50;
Fairbairn, op. cit., p. 294, compares the Oxford Movement to
Chateaubriand and de Maistre.

out their Tracts for the Times.[87] Both L'Avenir and the Tracts argued for a religious revival based on the independence of the church from control by the state. At first there were comparisons of Newman and Lamennais, sparkling writers, tragic figures, religious geniuses with an unexplained power over a group of devoted followers. Ward finds that Lamennais also has a developmental theory of tradition which is close to Newman's, and Acton and Geiselmann regard them both as traditionalists in their need for a religious authority which goes beyond reliance on the individual reason.[88]

Although there is not an overt comparison of the two in Alec Vidler's Birbeck Lectures on Lamennais, Newman and Oxford are unspoken presences. Vidler is moved to say openly of La Chesnaie, the Lamennais headquarters: "It stands in the history of the Church of France for at least as much as, say Oriel and Littlemore do in the history of the Church of England."[89] And then again Vidler says speaking of the school of La Chesnaie from 1828 to 1833: "...during those years it was as much a burning and a shining light in the Church of France as the tractarian school was in the Church of England when Newman was at the height of his power and influence."[90]

It has been suggested that R. H. Froude, Newman's closest associate, understood that Lamennais was carrying on a struggle for the separation of church and state very much like that of a segment of the

---

[87]Félicité Robert de Lamennais, 1782-1854, French priest; in 1817 the first volume of Essai sur l'indifférence en matière de religion appeared, and in 1825 and 1829 parts of De la religion considérée dans ses rapports avec l'ordre politique et civil; these are masterworks of traditionalist apologetic. His ideas were published by his school in the Parisian Catholic daily L'Avenir in 1830 and 1831. He left the Roman Catholic Church in 1834.

[88]Ward, op. cit., pp. 308, 315; Geiselmann, The Meaning of Tradition, introduciton, p. 152ff.

[89]Alec R. Vidler, Prophecy and Papacy (London, 1954), p. 31.

[90]Ibid., p. 143. He also remarks on the great similarity of the ecclesio-political theory of De la religion and Mr. Gladstone's 1838 book on relations between church and state.

English High Church when he visited France during a European tour in the winter of 1832 and the spring of 1833.[91] Froude was so impressed by what he saw in France that he imported the French priest's ideas and methods and inspired the English Catholic revival to assume the form which it took. Froude's biographer notes that he injected a new element of radical anti-Erastianism into the old High Church Party. A Froude letter of May 23, 1833, is recorded: "There is now in France a High Church party who are Republican, and wish for universal suffrage, on the ground that in proportion as the franchise falls lower the influence of the Church makes itself more felt;...Don't be surprised if one of these days you find us turning Radicals on similar grounds."[92] Before 1833 Froude had said that nothing could save the church, but a contemporary noted: "...now Froude's song is: 'If the State would but kick us off!' caught from Lamennais and the great democrat-Ultramontane agitation in France."[93]

E. A. Knox thinks that Lamennais' denunciation of the Erastian settlement of the Church of England drove Froude to be the first Tractarian to turn openly against the Reformation.[94] To Christopher Dawson, Froude was bolstered in his propaganda calling for the spiritual sovereignty of the church and the ousting of those who regarded the Church of England as the bulwark of the established political order by Lamennais' arguments. Like L'Avenir writers whom he quoted in the Tracts, Froude called for a return to the apostolic principles of independent spiritual authority in the church. Of the influence of France and the L'Avenir on Froude, Dawson is led to

----

[91]Richard Hurrell Froude, 1803-1836, was the bold, imaginative, and bigoted Fellow of Oriel who was Newman's great friend. He began to waste away with consumption in 1831 and after he died his literary Remains were published in 1838, scandalizing English Protestant opinion.

[92]L. I. Guiney, Hurrell Froude (London, 1904), p. 105.

[93]Ibid., p. 114.

[94]Knox, op. cit., p. 51.

speculate: "All his activity during the summer of 1833 was coloured by it, and it is even possible that the idea of the Tracts themselves... was first suggested by Froude at Oxford before Newman's return, [and] owed something to the influence of L'Avenir."[95]

There are books which suggest that Lamennais held sway over other Oxford men and that he influenced the Romeward trend among the younger Tractarians. R. W. Church produces a list of Frenchmen who correct the "insularity" of Pusey, Keble, and Newman. They are de Maistre, Lacordaire, Montalembert, and Lamennais, all more or less part of the same Ultramontane movement for the independence of the Church of France.[96] Wilfrid Ward says that it is de Maistre and Lamennais who pushed the second school of Tract writers into the Roman Church.[97]

W. G. Roe in Lamennais and England most comprehensively discusses the impact of the Frenchman on the Oxford Movement. Roe demonstrates that by the 1830's Lamennais was fairly well known in England. The Times carried extracts from the columns of L'Avenir and stories about its brushes with authority.[98] There was awareness of the Abbé's system, and the basis of his struggle was known in Roman Catholic and Anglican circles. But nothing decisive is concluded about any influence he might have had over Froude and Newman.[99] He sees in Newman's early

----

[95]Christopher Dawson, The Spirit of the Oxford Movement (New York, 1933), p. 68, other discussions of Froude, p. 50ff.

[96]R. W. Church, The Oxford Movement: Twelve Years (London, 1891), p. 295. It could be argued that all of them were members of the same Ultramontane school. Joseph, comte de Maistre, 1753-1821, issued Du Pape in 1819. Jean Baptiste Henri Lacordaire, 1802-61, and Charles Forbes René, comte de Montalembert, 1810-70, were followers of Lamennais and friends of Guéranger. The former refounded the Dominicans in France and the latter became a leading French liberal Catholic.

[97]Wilfrid Ward, W. G. Ward and the Catholic Revival (London, 1893), p. 82.

[98]20, 29, 30 November, 1830; 4, 14 February, 10, 16 May, 14 October, 1831.

[99]Roe, op. cit., p. 106.

Tracts the apocalyptic sense of L'Avenir and the similar philosophical
basis of belief founded upon the sensus fidelium. However, these
coincident views could be simply the result of the changing ecclesio-
political constructs of the era of the 1830 Revolution in France and of
the Reform Bill in England.[100] By 1837 Newman was criticizing the by
then apostate French priest in "The Fall of De La Mennais" for his sins
of rebellion.[101]

Other writers tend to minimize the connection of the Oxford
Movement and Lamennais' school, but in doing so they overlook the
important role played by Dom Guéranger in the transmission of some
Mennaisian concepts, particularly the importance of the liturgy and
ritual to the English church.[102] For a number of years Guéranger was
under the influence of Abbé Lamennais, and he wrote several articles
for L'Avenir. The fact that Lamennais' movement ended in 1832 with his
troubles and papal condemnation accounts in part, for the reason that
Guéranger began anew with the foundation of a Benedictine Abbey,
Solesmes, in 1833. It is Guéranger's Benedictine liturgical and
monastic revival which is the French counterpart of the Oxford
Movement.

There have been discussions before about Oxford and Solesmes, and
Newman and Guéranger. Daniel-Rops wrote that by studying the Fathers

---

[100]Ibid., p. 139. Acton was interested in why the idea of sens
commun appeared in both Lamennais and Newman.

[101]J. H. Newman, Essays Critical and Historical (2nd ed., London,
1872), I, 102-104. Roe, op. cit., pp. 97, 98, 103, 109. By 1836 the
sympathy for Lamennais was gone. Roe concludes that Dawson "may be
right" when he suggests that the idea of the Tracts came from L'Avenir.
He feels, however, that the English paper does not resemble the French
one at all, that the British Magazine seems a closer parallel, and that
if Froude changed the political consciousness of John Henry Newman
because of his contacts with France, there is no real evidence to prove
the point.

[102]Henry Tristram, "In the Lists with the Abbé Jager," John Henry
Newman: Centenary Essays (London, 1945), p. 201; F. L. Cross, John
Henry Newman (London, 1933), p. 49; B. Newman, Cardinal Newman (London,
1925), p. 53.

and early church history Newman and Guéranger both came to the conclusion that a new "sense of the Church" was necessary before there could be any revival of Christianity.[103] Roger Aubert defines this sentire ecclesiam to be the revolutionary idea that the church is in essence the mystical body of Christ composed equally of lay persons and clergy, not a hierarchy alone, of which the inner spirituality of its members must correspond to its visible power.[104] However, one must be careful in making too much of an affinity between Guéranger and Newman. In 1860 the Benedictine abbot visited Newman at the Birmingham Oratory and afterwards recorded all that need be said concerning expressions of mutual regard: "I made a visit to Dr. Newman. He didn't speak French and hardly any Italian: a true Saxon, cold as ice and refusing to open himself up....I tried to make him talk about Father Faber but I could not pull anything out of him. It appears that the two oratories of London and Birmingham do not get along."[105]

Another view is that the ideas of Guéranger and the Tractarians resulted in a liturgical revival which radically altered worship and art in the churches of England and France. To Trapp in Vorgeschichte und Ursprung der liturgischen Bewegung there is the rediscovery and purification of old ritual forms and combination of enlightenment and romantic improvements at Solesmes and Oxford which is a foundation of the modern liturgical movement.[106] The Tracts are liturgical documents and Pusey is the leader of an Anglican awakening which spreads beyond the universities and comes long before any similar renewal of English Roman Catholic worship.[107] It is the Abbot of Solesmes not Chateaubriand

----

[103]Daniel-Rops, "Dom Guéranger restaure la liturgie," Ecclesia, No. 132 (March 1960), 93-97, particularly 93.

[104]Aubert in Daniélou, op. cit., p. 430.

[105]Extract from Guéranger's journal from MS Listes de Rechanges, Archives of the Abbey of Solesmes, p. 1.

[106]Trapp, op. cit., p. 256.

[107]Trapp, op. cit., pp. 256, 258, 259.

who is the leader of the nineteenth century French return to the Roman liturgy, Gregorian chant, and Gothic services.[108] The important result of both the Oxford Movement and the Benedictine revival, according to D. A. Robeyna, is that they spur on scholarly research which leads to the simple, communal rites of Anglicans and Roman Catholics in the twentieth century.[109]

Olivier Rousseau's survey of the modern renewal of worship is at one with this sample of liturgical histories in its argument that the Benedictines and Anglicans parallel rather than directly influence one another. Yet Rousseau differs in suggesting that the early Fathers rather than the ideals of the Catholicism of the Middle Ages inspired the radical implications of the new ritualism. Rousseau also is the first to point to the parish church which Dr. Pusey founded at Leeds as a center of innovations which in time became characteristic of the liturgical movement.[110]

The Scandinavian scholar Härdelin, however, has discovered the effect of Dom Guéranger on Frederick Oakeley, the first Puseyite ritualist.[111] "Ritualists" here means Anglo-Catholics who practiced the externals of Catholic worship and emphasized the importance of renewal of the liturgy in the parishes of the Church of England. Oakeley discussed Guéranger's restoration of liturgical worship in an article "Rites and Ceremonies" which appeared in the British Critic in 1841. It is in effect a review of the first volume of the Institutions liturgiques, Guéranger's call for a reform of the books, music, and architecture used in nineteenth century worship. Oakeley introduces the French abbot as a great defender of forms in Christianity, a champion to counter the Puritan view that the religion of Jesus is anti-formalistic. It is clear that by summarizing in English

----

[108]Ibid., p. 252.

[109]D. A. Robeyna, "Les débuts du mouvement liturgique," QLP, 19 (1934), 276–298, particularly 278–279, and 282.

[110]Rousseau, op. cit., pp. 10, 112, 113, 114, 115, 120, 127.

[111]Härdelin, op. cit., p. 120.

Guéranger's arguments about mystery in church and the development of ritual and symbolism, Oakeley is telling Anglicans that the eye as well as the ear must be moved by worship and that a new understanding of the liturgy would end the customary question habitually asked of parties coming from church: "Whom did you hear?"[112]

A Catholic service, argues Oakeley after reading Guéranger, must now be introduced to correspond to the Catholic principles of the Church of England, and it is the non-national Catholicity of the Institutions which is most appealing to the Fellow of Balliol: "We cordially go along with the author whose work we have been reviewing, in what we may call his unnational spirit. We can have no sympathy with the Gallican party so far as it is at issue with the Ultramontane. National theories, even the Gallican (which is more or less the theory of every state in the Roman Communion), appear to us to involve a subtle Erastianism, besides betokening an inadequate estimate of the fullness of freedom of Gospel privileges."[113] In other articles Oakeley suggests that one of the best means for the Anglican churches to overcome their nationality and re-assert the unity of the undivided church is by the adoption of Gregorian chant, which, as Guéranger also argues, more than any other music exhibits the proper Catholic aesthetic, simplicity and purity.[114]

One old interpretation held that the Tractarians were introduced to ritual by the Leicestershire squire Ambrose Phillipps de Lisle.[115] Knox places de Lisle in Oxford during the year 1842 talking to Pusey and Newman about the corporate reunion of the Church of England with

----

[112]B.C., Vol. XXX (July 1841), No. LX, 422-465.

[113]Ibid., 465.

[114]B.C., No. LVI, 371-390, No. LXVIII, 278-320.

[115]Bishop Forbes, the ardent follower of Pusey, saw de Lisle as the real author and Grace-Dieu the home of modern ritualism. De Lisle, 1809-1878, converted to Roman Catholicsim in October, 1825, after attending solemn vespers at Notre Dame in Paris. In 1835 he opened a Trappist house on his estate.

the Roman Catholic Church.[116] E. S. Purcell, the biographer of de Lisle, provides a more useful date. Purcell says that in 1841 Newman's assistant Bloxam, Oakeley, F. W. Faber, and W. G. Ward visited de Lisle's house and monastery, Grace-Dieu, and there beheld the splendors of Roman ritual and Gregorian chant.[117] But Purcell describes his subject as "no ordinary insular, upper class" English Roman Catholic. De Lisle maintained close ties with the Catholic movement in France and provided the French with accurate reports on the progress of the Oxford Movement. Montalembert, an ally of Guéranger, wrote De Lisle on December 7, 1842: "Thanks to the Tablet and the Catholic I can follow with an anxious eye and heart every step your Puseyite friends are taking; and I do so with the most heartfelt sympathy....it is a thousand times more important not to put the slightest impediment in the way which these Puseyites are so marvelously treading in...."[118]

The archives at Solesmes reveal that a "Mr. Philips" was one of Guéranger's strongest contacts in England.[119] A biography of the Benedictine Cardinal Pitra, Guéranger's most important disciple, makes clear that "Mr. Philips" was Ambrose Phillipps de Lisle, for when Pitra went to England in 1844 he stopped for several days at Grace-Dieu. There he was shown the curious liturgical books of the new Anglican school and the works of Pusey. J. D. Dalgairns, a Tractarian who had previously visited Solesmes, took Pitra to a "Puseyite dinner" at Oakeley's house, and Pitra visited Charles Wordsworth at Harrow and Beresford-Hope in London.[120] This evidence suggest that since Oakeley

---

[116]Knox, op. cit., p. 100ff.

[117]E. S. Purcell, The Life and Letters of Ambrose Phillipps de Lisle (London, 1900), p. 277.

[118]Ibid., p. 236.

[119]MS L.R., p. 1.

[120]Albert Battandier, Le Cardinal Jean-Baptiste Pitra (Paris, 1893), pp. 152, 153, 156. J. D. Dalgairns, 1818-1876, who was one of those Tractarians who stayed with Newman at Littlemore, wrote a controversial letter "Anglican Church Parties" to the Univers, the newspaper edited by Guéranger's supporter Louis Veuillot, just before he joined the Roman Church in 1845.

first wrote about Guéranger in the summer of 1841 after visiting Grace-Dieu, it was probably de Lisle who introduced him to the liturgical ideas of the Abbot of Solesmes. De Lisle should not be seen as the father of ritualism but as rather the connection between the Tractarians and the French Catholic revival. The visits and contacts between Solesmes and Oxford before the many Anglican conversions to Roman Catholicism in 1845 molded English ritualism in a model set by the Benedictines. That explains the parallel development of French parishes influenced by Guéranger and the Puseyite congregations in England. The nurturing influence of relations between the English and French churches continued to be important to Pusey throughout his career.

Other links with France prepared Pusey for his conversion to ritualism and had an impact on the elucidation of his spirituality and ecclesiology. Pusey's chief biographer Liddon suggests that in the twenties Dr. Pusey was directed by the Bishop of Oxford, Dr. Lloyd, to break out of the traditions of the English Church.[121] Oakeley reveals in Personal Reminiscences of the "Oxford Movement" and "The Church Service" that to many Tractarians, Bishop Lloyd's lecture on the liturgy in the late 1820's were the first impulse toward a Catholic revival. Lloyd introduced many for the first time to the breviary, the ancient service books, and other forms of Catholic spirituality.[122] Willoughby and Roe demonstrate that Bishop Lloyd himself had been influenced by a group of French Catholic émigré clergy and that he had read Du Pape and the articles of the restoration periodical Ami de la religion et du roi. When his protégé Pusey began to adapt Roman Catholic spiritual guides for Anglicans, he turned almost entirely to French Catholic literature.[123] The manual for confessors which Pusey

----

[121]Liddon, op. cit., I, 23, 62-64, 97, 98, 100, 112, 113, 114, 117, 123, 178. 183, 184, 186, 187, 193, 199, 201, 202.

[122]Frederick Oakeley, Remeniscences (London, 1855), p. 4; "The Church Service," B.C., No. LIV, 251.

[123]Willoughby, loc. cit., p. 52-53; Roe, op. cit., p. 94.

50

translated for Anglican clergy was written by an abbé of the party of
Guéranger.[124] Both Liddon and Trench are aware that Pusey's treatise on
Catholicism, the Eirenicon, was based on conversations between the
English and French churches in the eighteenth century and Pusey's own
conversations with Gallican ecclesiastics in the nineteenth century.[125]
They do not divulge that Guéranger's name appears on one list of those
who where willing to hear Pusey's appeals.

The Abbot of Solesmes himself turned to the Oxford Movement for
financial help, manuscripts, and moral support. Guéranger's biographer, Dom Delatte, notes that the abbot reacted with pleasure to the news
that Anglicans across the channel were following sympathetically the
move for the purification of the liturgical practices of France. When
Solesmes was faced with bankruptcy because of the financial disaster of
a daughter priory in Paris, Dom Guéranger sent Dom Pitra to England to
collect funds from the Puseyites. Pitra attempted to enlist the
English Roman Catholic Benedictines in aiding the Solesmes Paris
foundation, but they refused. A plea for help was rebuffed by Newman.
The Puseyites Charles Wordsworth, Oakeley, and Dalgairns were friendly
and helpful. After Wordsworth became a canon at Westminster Abbey, he
allowed Pitra to use the Lambeth library and archives, and Wordsworth
and A. J. P. Beresford-Hope went on missions in search of manuscripts
to be used in the Gallia Christiana series edited and put out by
Solesmes.[126] In the Institutions liturgiques, Guéranger recognizes that

---

[124]Some of the French authors were Avrillon, Surin, and Noeut. He
was Jean Joseph Gaume; an edition of his Manuel des Confesseurs came
out in 1845. See Antoine Ricard, Etude sur Monseigneur Gaume. Ses
oeuvres, son influence, sa polémique.

[125]Liddon, op. cit., (London, 1897), IV, 154ff.

[126]Fernand Cabrol, Histoire du Cardinal Pitra (Paris, 1893),
pp. 94, 95; Battandier, pp. 146, 155, 156. Christopher Wordsworth,
1807-1885, Headmaster of Harrow, 1836, Canon of Westminster, 1844,
published a Diary of France, 1845, Bishop of Lincoln, 1868, strong
supporter of Anglo-Continental Society, after 1870 in close relations
with Döllinger. Alexander James Beresford-Hope, 1820-1887, M. P. for
Maidstone, 1841, M. P. for Cambridge, 1868, bought St. Augustine's
monastery at Canterbury for missionaires and raised the new All Saint's
Church, Margaret Street.

the work of liturgical reform and unification is going on in the Oxford
Movement as well as in the Benedictine revival:

> But, we affirm it first of all that the principal cause of
> their return to the antique faith [in Britain], of this
> dissolution of Anglican Protestantism...is nothing less than
> the development of the liturgical element...conserved in the
> midst of the established church....But it is principally in
> the things of the liturgy that the disciples of Doctor Pusey
> argue that it is useful to stress the meaning of Catholic
> usages....They have seen in the tradition of the Fathers of
> the Church, whose authority is already genuine for them, they
> have seen there that several papist ceremonies go back in
> origin to the cradle of Christianity. They dream to re-
> establish them. A vague desire for the Real Presence [of
> Christ in the eucharist] is at work in them....They speak of
> re-establishing the divine office....If the progress of
> liturgical tendencies accelerates the advance of England
> toward Catholic truth and unity, it is in other countries
> where the repression of the same tendencies leads to contrary
> results.[127]

Books and articles which treat Möhler and Guéranger fall into the
clearly established pattern which has appeared here before. To some
they are alike in rejecting the religious theories of the
Enlightenment. To others they both appear to have been subjected to
the ideas of religious community of the Lamennais circle. In
commenting on the work of Guéranger and Möhler in re-associating the
life of the individual soul to the life of the church, Daniel-Rops
says:

> There was to say truly, in this domain, a convergence of
> thoughts and intentions. In the first third of the century
> there were the theologians of Tübingen, and J. A. Möhler
> above all went deeply into the same notion of the Church [as
> Dom Guéranger], that it is a human society without a doubt
> but united and made a living reality by the Holy Ghost.[128]

----

[127]Prosper Guéranger, Institutions liturgiques (2nd ed., Paris,
1880), II, 652-657. Newman's large impact on France, though more as a
Roman Catholic than as a member of the Oxford Movement, is discussed
with extensive bibliography and attention to modernism in B. D. Dupuy,
"Newman's Influence in France," John Coulson and A. M. Allchin, The
Rediscovery of Newman: an Oxford Symposium (London, 1967).

[128]Daniel-Rops, loc. cit., p. 93.

Aubert, the Belgian historian, concludes that Guéranger's Ultramontane liturgical campaign had the indirect result of bringing the inner, supernatural aspect of the church to light again. He also maintains that the Tübingen theologians were part of an Ultramontane renaissance which rediscovered that the church was a mystical community:

> This leading idea which came from the founder of the school, J. S. Drey, was taken up and deepened by Möhler, so that it played a fundamental role in the shape of the ecclesiology of the nineteenth and twentieth centuries.[129]

The historians of the liturgical movement see Möhler and Guéranger either as the joint founders of aspects of its second stage or as independently, but simultaneously, reawakening interest in the services of the church. Trapp understands no direct connection between the two but rather a common synthesis of Aufklärung liturgical thinking, the necessity for purified forms, comprehension of rites, and the participation of all the lay people in the worship of the church. Trapp portrays Möhler as a pioneer in calling for the unity of laity and clergy, which is the ecclesiological basis of the liturgical revival. This is even more important to Trapp than Möhler's advocacy of vernacular masses and communion in both kinds. Secondly, Trapp maintains that Möhler is memorable for training and educating F. A. Staudenmaier whose Der Geist der Christentums, published in 1835, shares with Guéranger's Liturgical Year, the Frenchman's nine-volume meditation on the rites and ceremonies of the Christian liturgical cycle, the responsibility for popularizing in Europe the idea that the Catholic cult is a master-work of art, in fact the greatest work of collective art, comparable to medieval cathedrals.

Robeyna is certain that although Möhler and Guéranger are both responsible for the ecclesiological revolution of 1830-1840, it is primarily Möhler's students who fomented German liturgical change.[130] Rousseau, however, has proposed an entirely new model for the explanation of the origin of the modern liturgical movement. The

---

[129]Aubert in Daniélou, loc. cit., pp. 443, 445.

[130]Robeyna, loc. cit., pp. 277, 281.

liturgical movement arose when Dom Guéranger's ideal of the monastic liturgical apostolate was combined with Möhler's ecclesiology at the Abbey of Beuron in southwest Germany.[131] In a more recent work on the second stage of the liturgical movement, André Haquin expands Rousseau's idea and explains how the work of the two men could have been united in the founding of Beuron. The Wolter brothers of Cologne established the monastery of Beuron on the model of Solesmes in the 1860's following a period of study in France. After the Wolters had been influenced by the Rhineland theologian M. J. Scheeben, who maintained a corporate theology in "the wake" of J. A. Möhler, they felt a need for the institutional realization of Möhler's communal ideals in a Benedictine monastic community.[132]

There have been several attempts to place Tübingen within the context of the French traditionalism from which Solesmes also emerged. Lord Acton came to the conclusion that Möhler shared the Ultramontane and traditionalist ideas of de Maistre, Ventura, and Lacordaire.[133] Others compare Möhler's and de Maistre's attempts to resolve the question of the proper means for constructing the unity of the church in the post-revolutionary political situation of Europe, a period of weakened Gallican-Febronian, or Erastian, centers. Whereas the French traditionalists concluded that unity could only be established in the papacy, Möhler argued that there first must be a community of the faithful united in the local bishop and then a binding of the collective episcopate with the papacy into the true unity of the church. This group concludes that although there is a growth of papalism in Möhler, neither de Maistre nor the French are responsible for it.[134] In 1931 an opposite point of view was expressed when

----

[131]Rousseau, op. cit., pp. 10, 67-91, 93-97.

[132]André Haquin, Dom Lambert Beauduin et le Renouveau Liturgique (Gembloux, 1970), pp. 1-6, particularly p. 4.

[133]Cf. letter in Victor Conzemius, ed., Ignaz von Döllinger-Lord Acton Briefwechsel, Volume I (Munich, 1963), 295, to letters in Volume III (Munich, 1971), 260 and 282.

[134]Hermann König, "Die Einheit der Kirche nach Joseph de Maistre und

54

Geiselmann suggested that the French traditionalists surrounding
Lamennais are the cause of the new understanding of the church as
community which emerges in Möhler between the Einheit and the
Symbolik.[135] Möhler is shown to have held, in the French sense, that the
entire body of believers including the laity, guides the church into
all truth, although in an 1835 controversy with Abbé Bautain Möhler
modified his position by admitting that the individual's reason as well
as the tradition of the community as a whole can be a witness to the
existence of God.[136]

Although there have been no detailed investigations of the
channels through which Lamennais and other L'Avenir correspondents
exerted an influence over Johann Adam Möhler,[137] there are clear
indications of how that happened. The Möhler biographer Friedrich
reveals that in 1830 Möhler was reading the Mennaisian Mémorial and the
Revue catholique edited by the Abbé Gerbet and complaining of the fact

---

Johann Adam Möhler," ThQ, 115 (1934), pp. 83-140, particularly p. 97.
Fritz Vigener, "Gallikanismus und episkopalistische Strömungen im
deutschen Katholizismus zwischen Tridentinum und Vaticanum,"
Historische Zeitschrift, Vol. 111 (1913), 495-581, particularly 560,
561, 563, 564.

[135]Geiselmann, "Johann Adam Möhler und die Entwicklung seines
Kirchenbegriffs," ThQ (1931), pp. 1-91, particulary pp. 90-91.
Geiselmann's varying theories of the manner in which French
traditionalism shaped Möhler are set forth in the following books and
articles: Lebendiger Glaube aus Geheiligter Uberlieferung (Mainz,
1942), pp. 35, 300, 497; the lectures Grundlegung, pp. 9, 10; The
Meaning of Tradition, pp. 47-48.

[136]Geiselmann, The Meaning, pp. 19, 54, 57, 58, 62.

[137]Relations between France and Tübingen are discussed in the ThQ
(1830), 570-597; (1831), 328-329; (1832), 765-806. Stefan Lösch,
Döllinger und Frankreich. Eine Geistige Allianz. 1823-1871 (Munich,
1955), discusses in valuable detail the connections of Döllinger to
Lamennais, but nothing is said of any ideas being passed on to Möhler.
A book which argues the influence of Lemannais and traditionalism on
the Rhineland theologian J. W. J. Braun is Heinrich Schrörs, Ein
Vergessener Führer aus der Rheinischen Geistesgeschichte des
Neunzehnten Jahrhunderts (Bonn, 1925), pp. 105, 114f., 149f., 165f.,
286ff., 289ff.

that the editors were not better known in his part of Germany.[138] Lösch prints a letter in his Möhler-correspondence from the same year in which the German theologian praises the "very good" writers of France who are beginning a genuine revival of the church, and Möhler names in particular Lamennais and de Bonald.[139]

Of great importance is the fact that in another collection of Möhler correspondence Lösch includes a letter of 7 June 1832, in which Möhler records that a friend, Dr. Augustin Theiner, is sending back to him from France information on Lamennais, Gerbet, and Lacordaire.[140] This is a significant piece of information, for in 1831 J. A. Möhler reviewed Abbé Philippe Gerbet's Considérations sur Le Dogme Générateur de la Piété Catholique in the Theologische Quartalschrift .[141] Gerbet became the primary means of transmitting Lamennais' communal conceptions of a people's church, of a church grounded in the Christian people as a whole, into Möhler's theology.

Gerbet's Considérations is one of the first books written in the nineteenth century which sets forth a communal and mystical understanding of the structure of the church. Gerbet's Considérations argues that Protestantism is destructive of Christianity precisely because it declares the sovereignty of individual reason. Gerbet states that Catholicism alone can meet the needs of modern society because it combines the individual life of private devotion with the collective eucharistic worship of the public domain. The eucharist joins the individual with the community and therefore it should be at the center of the Christian life. A vital equality is established by Gerbet

---

[138]J. Friedrich, Johann Adam Möhler der Symboliker (Munich, 1894), p. 22. Philippe Gerbet, 1798–1864, later Bishop of Perpignan, and Salinis, both ardent disciples of Lamennais, were the editors of the Revue catholique, which lasted from 1824–1830 and was replaced by L'Avenir.

[139]Lösch, Möhler, I, 263, 264. Louis Gabriel Ambroise, vicomte de Bonald, 1754–1840, was another traditionalist.

[140]Lösch, Gengler, p. 88.

[141]in ThQ (1831), pp. 328–357.

between the incarnation and the church, which is defined as Christ continually present on earth, as well as between the eucharist and the incarnation, the body of Christ momentarily present. Eucharistic communion is emphasized in Considérations because it is the means by which the incarnation is individualized. Therefore, the eucharistic liturgy is the heart of the Christian system.[142]

Gerbet's Considérations was written in 1829 and in it are to be found many of the radical concepts of Möhler's most important treatise, the Symbolik of 1832. A number of those ideas are mentioned for the first time in Möhler's 1831 review of Gerbet: the realization that religion is primarily an affair of the community with God, the need for a rediscovery of the communal dimension of Catholic faith for modern times, the church and the eucharist understood as Christ continuing to dwell on earth, both church and eucharist defined as an extension of the incarnation, and the importance of the eucharist in the Catholic system of justification as the means by which the individual is engrafted into the communal body of Christ.[143] Möhler ends one of the most important reviews of his career by declaring: "...we observe here no criticism, but on the other hand only a conversion to the spirit of Abbé Gerbet."[144]

It is most significant that Dom Antoine de Mazis has concluded that Gerbet's Considérations was also the decisive influence which led to Guéranger's liturgical vocation and to the re-founding of Solesmes in 1833.[145] D. B. Capelle and Liselotte Ahrens had suggested that Abbé Gerbet was an influential figure for Guéranger, but de Mazis carefully dates Dom Guéranger's turning to a liturgical apostolate as a legitimate channel for the communal perceptions of the Lamennais school

---

[142]Philippe Gerbet, Considérations (Paris, 1829), pp. x-xi, 57, 59, 62, 81, 83, 116, 125, 230.

[143]ThQ, (1831), pp. 341f., 343, 353.

[144]Ibid., p. 357.

[145]Antoine de Mazis, La Vocation de Dom Guéranger, MS Archive of Abbey of Solesmes, dated 7 October 1972.

from his reading of Gerbet's <u>Considérations</u>.[146] Thus, the influence
exerted by the Abbé Gerbet's work is responsible for the similarity of
Möhler's and Guéranger's thought in 1833.

P. Charles Brandes provides another direct link between Möhler and
Guéranger, which has so far escaped attention. Brandes was a German
Protestant and friend of Montalembert who appeared at the Abbey of
Solesmes in 1835. He had the role of interpreting German works for the
monks at Solesmes because in the 1830's no one else in the community
could read the language, and Brandes maintained a passionate interest
in German Catholic theology. On 16 July 1836, Dom Guéranger added at
the end of a letter to Montalembert: "Father Brandes asks of you, if
it is possible, that you send him, for several weeks, the <u>Symbolik</u> of
Möhler."[147] Brandes stayed in Munich from September to November, 1840,
and again from the autumn of 1844 to September 1845. In Munich he was
in contact with Görres, Philips, and Döllinger, and there he read
extensively in the works of Möhler.[148] While he was in Germany, Brandes
wrote long reports for Dom Guéranger on German liturgical conditions,
Catholic literature, and the reception of Guéranger's books. On 19
July 1843, Brandes noted that "the four great men who are guiding me in
my work are Georres, Moehler, Klee, Doellinger." In the same letter he
reveals that his ambition is to educate the French public in the
splendors of Görres and Möhler.[149]

Until about 1840 Brandes was very close to Dom Guéranger and
accompanied him on trips to Rome. It is impossible to determine

----

[146]D. B. Capelle, "Dom Guéranger et l'esprit liturgique," QLP (1937),
pp. 131-146; Liselotte Ahrens, <u>Lamennais und Deutschland</u> (Münster,
1930), pp. 277-288.

[147]Germany, MS L.R., Solesmes, p. 1.

[148]Idem.

[149]Letters of Brandes to Guéranger, beginning 31 December 1840, MS
Archives, Abbey of Solesmes. In another of his reports, Feast of Peter
and Paul, 1841, Brandes describes in great detail the third volume of
the <u>Tracts for the Times</u>: "They are importing fruits of paradise into
their dry and arid climate with these fresh, beautiful plants of the
Church."

exactly what sort of influence he had over Guéranger in introducing him
to Möhler's thought, but long extracts from early volumes of
Guéranger's Liturgical Year appear as though they could have been taken
directly from Möhler's Einheit or Symbolik.[150] Guéranger's understanding
of the situation of Catholics in Germany is demonstrated in the second
volume of his Institutions liturgiques where he records that "no other
Catholic region today is able to show men at the same time so erudite
and so intelligent as Germany, viz. Möhler."[151]

So, despite their many differences, Christians in France, Germany,
and England, Anglicans as well as Roman Catholics, participated in an
overarching attempt to reestablish Catholicism with a marked communal
dimension for modern times, a development transcending national and
even confessional boundaries. None of the movements of 1833 can be
thought of solely as the product of a single national tradition; each
must be understood as part of some larger bedrock structure of
historical change, a reflection in the sphere of religion of a general
transformation of European culture.[152] The search for community within

----

[150]Prosper Guéranger, Liturgical Year, Pascal Time (Stanbrook, 1910),
II, 260: "[The Church] is the continuation of the mystery of the
Incarnation, the object of things invisible." Pascal Time (3rd ed.,
Stanbrook, 1909), III, 382:
"The Church is the body of Christ, and the Holy Ghost is the
principle which gives her life. He is her soul – not only in that
limited sense in which we have already spoken of the soul of the
Church, that is, of her inward existence, and which after all, is
the result of the Holy Spirit's action within her – but He is also
her soul, in that her whole interior and exterior life, and her
workings, proceed from Him. The Church is undying because the
love which has led the Holy Ghost to dwell within her, will last
forever: and here we have the reason of that perpetuity of the
Church, which is the most wonderful spectacle witnessed by the
world. Let us now pass on, and consider that other marvel, which
consists in the preservation of unity in the Church. Jesus would
have but one and not many to be His Church, His bride: the Holy
Ghost will, therefore, see to the accomplishment of His wish."

[151]I.L.., p. 649.

[152]Another book which uses a comparative approach to study a general
European phenomenon, in this case stabilization as it occurred in
France, Germany, and Italy after World War I, is Charles S. Maier,
Recasting Bourgeois Europe (Princeton, 1975). Maier examines how

many Christian churches in the last one hundred and fifty years was but one part of the general attempt to achieve a communal revival in a rapidly modernizing society.[153]

The emergence of similar themes in the churches of England, France, and Germany can be explained for two reasons. First, Guéranger, Möhler, and Pusey were influenced by a common set of social, political, and economic forces associated with the democratic and industrial revolutions of the late eighteenth and the early nineteenth centuries. Changes in politics and economics associated with the spread of mechanical power, the growth of nationalism, and the challenge to monarchy imposed a parallel set of strains upon the states of Europe and so dictated religious reactions in at least three countries resembling one another.

Secondly, the origin of the theme of community in the three Catholic revivals cannot be understood without taking seriously the role of multinational intellectual cross-fertilization in determining the theological and liturgical shape of the movements. Above all, Oxford, Solesmes, and Tübingen were under the influence of two circles which had begun to revive the ideal of community in their own ways prior to 1830. These were the north German Protestants of Berlin surrounding Schleiermacher and Neander and the Frenchmen of the school of Lamennais and Gerbet.

----

political and economic elites retained their power following World War I, anticipating political solutions achieved after 1945.

[153]On the "leftist" revival of the ideal of community in the nineteenth century see Robert Tucker, Philosophy and Myth in Karl Marx (Cambridge, 1967); Nikolaus Pevsner, Pioneers of Modern Design (London, 1966); David Watkin, Morality and Architecture (Oxford, 1977); Paul Meier, William Morris (Harvester Press, 1978); and Robert Macleod, Style and Society, 1835-1914 (London, 1971). On the "rightist" revival of the ideal of community see George L. Mosse, The Nationalization of the Masses (New York, 1975); Fritz Stern, The Politics of Cultural Despair (Garden City, 1965); and Barbara Miller Lane, Architecture and Politics in Germany (Cambridge, 1968). William J. McGrath, Dionysian Art and Populist Politics in Austria (New Haven, 1974) has linked some Wagnerians to the Benedictine monastic revival of the nineteenth century.

Evolution of the New Catholicism from 1833 to 1982:

The State of the Question

This comparative history might be superficial if it merely confined itself to an intensive examination of religion in three European countries during the one critical decade of the 1830's. A bouquet of three historical parallels provides little knowledge about European society or an institution such as the church if it goes nowhere. The three Catholic revivals must not be scrutinized just for the roles they played in the mid-nineteenth century, but also for the fundamental effect they had in ultimately contributing to a reshaping of the form of modern Catholicism, both Anglican and Roman Catholic. The goal of this comparative analysis is to reveal a common thread in the evolution of the European churches, a tidal flow of church history which stretches from the 1830's to the documents of Vatican II in the 1960's, to the promulgation and introduction of new liturgies into many churches of the Anglican Communion in the 1970's, and finally to the ecumenical convergence statements of the 1980's such as The Final Report and Baptism, Eucharist, and Ministry.[154]

If we view 1833-1982 as one distinct era of church history, then it should be divided into three subperiods: [1] 1833-1845: intellectual reaction in Oxford, Solesmes, and Tübingen to revolutionary (democratic and industrial) threats to community and Catholicism; [2] 1845-World War I: growing appeal of Catholic communalism, primarily in the parishes; [3] World War I-1982: widespread appearance of "liturgical movements" among Anglicans and Roman Catholics, growing acceptance of Catholic communalism by Roman Catholic and Anglican bishops.

----

[154]Baptism, Eucharist, and Ministry (Geneva, 1982), published by the Faith and Order Commission of the Word Council of Churches is the work of one hundred theologians representing the WCC churches, including Anglicans, and Roman Catholic theologians. BEM is another recent comprehensive theological defense for understanding the church as a sharing and healing community whose ministry is an extension of the actual power of Christ himself.

To make the case for this evolution from Pusey into Anglicanism, a connection must first be established between the role of the Oxford Hebrew professor in the first half of the nineteenth century and the so-called "ritualist parishes" of the second half of the century where frequent celebrations of the eucharist with lights, incense, vestments, and processions were first seen in the Church of England, combined in some parishes with growth in the corporate participation of the laity and increasing social protest against the status quo of the English political and economic order.   Next, a link has to be made between Pusey and the ritualist parishes and post-World War I liturgical reform activities, such as the Parish Communion Movement in the Church of England, that encouraged the active participation of the lay community in a single Sunday celebration of the eucharist around a simple, freestanding altar table, and that spoke of the relationship between the eucharist and the industrial social order.

In this country J. F. White's classic monograph on the Cambridge Movement has left a dominant impression that the Anglo-Catholic liturgical revival was a sudden recrudescence of medievalism in worship.   White describes the general English romantic retreat to the Middle Ages in the nineteenth century as an escape from the hideous processes of industrialization, an escape realized in the Gothic Revival and Pre-Raphaelitism.   White chose to stress the manner in which the Tractarians and the Cambridge Camden Society influenced liturgy and church architecture in anachronistic ways, leading to newfound clericalism.[155] Other surveys of the Oxford Movement argue that there was little connection between Tractarians and liturgical life, and that Pusey was ignorant of such matters.   For example, Yngve Brilioth finds it inappropriate to discuss ritual or the liturgy in The

----
[155]James F. White, The Cambridge Movement: The Ecclesiologists and the Gothic Revival (Cambridge, 1962, 1979).   White is concerned with and portrays accurately the Cambridge Movement.   He has written the standard history of the Cambridge Camden Society, which from 1839 to 1845 provided practical knowledge about Catholic liturgy and building to approximately six hundred English clergy.   But there were other, more progressive, influences from Oxford.

Anglican Revival (1933), one of the best books on the movement.[156]

But the oldest and correct understanding of the relationship between the Hebrew professor and ritual was maintained in the anti-Puseyite polemics. B. W. Saville, Rector of Shillingford, for example, wrote at Pusey's death in 1882 that his "new teaching" on the real objective presence of Christ in the eucharist was the foundation of the "frenzied Ritualists."[157] J. H. Rigg, a Methodist writing at the same time said, "Dr. Pusey's teaching, indeed, leads directly and necessarily to such Romish ritualizing as that of the late Father Lowder or Mr. Mackonochie."[158] The major Anglican biographers of Pusey have tended to avoid the conclusion that Pusey was either the father of the ritualists or that he had nothing to do with liturgical development in the parishes. They agree that Pusey's doctrinal teaching on the objectivity and centrality of the eucharist underlay the use of new liturgical externals, but that only gradually and at the end of his life did he identify himself with the advanced ritualist party and their parish churches.[159]

----

[156]Yngve Brilioth, The Anglican Revival (London, 1933) p. 325. Surveys which deemphasize the Tractarian-liturgical connection are Horton Davies, Worship and Theology in England (Princeton, 1962) pp. 244, 271; Geoffrey Faber, Oxford Apostles (London, 1933) pp. 378-379; C. P. S. Clark, The Oxford Movement and After (London, 1932) pp. 154, 159.

[157]Bourchier Wrey Savile, Dr. Pusey: An Historic Sketch (London, 1883), pp. 17, 23.

[158]J. H. Rigg, Dr. Pusey: His Character and Life Work (London, 1883), p. 67.

[159]To Miss Trench, Pusey does not show his unity with the ritualists until a University Sermon in May 1867. Russell, p. 132, says that after 1870 and the First Vatican Council, Pusey's "duty now was to defend what had come to be called 'Ritualism,' as expressing what he held to be revealed truth about the Sacrament of the altar." Donaldson argues that Pusey first appeared publicly to be a ritualist at an ECU meeting in 1866 when he said, p. 211:
"Now in these days, many of the difficulties which we had in the first instance to contend with have been removed. In the first place, I suppose that this [ritualism] is from its very centre a lay movement. The clergy have taught it to the people, and the people have asked it of the clergy. We taught it them, they felt

Another set of commentators, such as Ollard in his Short History, finds ritualism and Tractarianism to be in effect the same movement.[160] This is also the conclusion of one of the most complete surveys of the subject, Alf Härdelin's The Tractarian Understanding of the Eucharist which discusses "not so much the Tractarian contribution to the eucharistic liturgical revival, viewed from its merely external side, but rather the principles of worship, as they are discernible in the Tractarian sources."[161] The discussion in the present book differs from Härdelin in that it concentrates on an examination of the relationship between Dr. Pusey and leading Puseyite churches and seeks to gauge the effect of his ideas by charting changes in church participation and activity after their introduction into the parishes. By tracing the history of selected Puseyite parishes it illustrates the evolution of ritualist churches into centers of the liturgical movement, institutions which could deal with the social fragmentation wrought by the industrial revolution.

Until recently there was little bibliographical precedent for the contention that Pusey's churches were liturgically or socially radical. Knox and Vidler, in The Development of Modern Catholicism, recognize that important changes took place in some of the parishes which led to future forms of Anglican Catholicism: one was the Catholic socialism

----

it to be true, and they said, set it before our eyes."
This is Liddon's description of Pusey's mind in 1867:
"He wished it to be understood that he held and taught the doctrine which they [the ritualists] expressed by means of ceremonial, and desired to shield them if necessary by diverting prosecution to himself."

[160]Ollard, op. cit., p. 113; W. J. Sparrow Simpson, The History of the Anglo-Catholic Revival from 1845 (London, 1932), pp. 75, 76; Paul Thureau-Dangin, The English Catholic Revival in the Nineteenth Century (New York, 1919), II, 427, 428, 453, 467, 479, 509, 519, 539, 540, 553, 554; E. A. Down, "Pastoral Ideals and Methods of the Movement," in N. P. Williams and C. Harris, Northern Catholicism. Centenary Studies in the Oxford and Parallel Movements (London, 1933), pp. 263-289.

[161]Alf Härdelin, The Tractarian Understanding of the Eucharist (Uppsala, 1969), p. 225.

of Stuart Headlam and the Guild of St. Matthew, another was one of the "first attempts to reconcile Catholic theology with modern thought."[162] A. G. Hebert in The Parish Communion and Liturgy and Society takes the view that the best known Puseyite parish churches in London such as St. Alban's, Holborn, and St. Peter's, London Docks, did indeed make important liturgical advances which foreshadowed developments of the twentieth century.[163]

The designation of Pusey as an innovator who plays an important role in modern Catholic theology is even rarer. The group most often cited as the link between the Tractarians and modern Anglo-Catholicism are the Oxford priests of the late nineteenth century who wrote the essays in Lux Mundi, Charles Gore, Aubrey Moore, H. S. Holland, and Charles Illingworth. H. P. Liddon, Pusey's principal and conservative biographer, attempted to hide the influence of the Hebrew professor on that later group, and Lux Mundi is said by Liddon to be "a proclamation of revolt against the spirit and principles of Dr. Pusey and Mr. Keble."[164]

Ramsey, in discussing Anglican theology from Lux Mundi to Archbishop Temple notes the importance of the new definition of the church as the extension of the incarnation, so fundamental to twentieth century Anglican theologians, but there is not the slightest mention that the first English theologian to espouse that view in the nineteenth century was E. B. Pusey.[165] Other surveys credit Pusey with contributing a certain "spiritual tone" which lingers on in Anglo-Catholicism.[166] Yet most are silent about the Puseyite concepts in the

----

[162]Wilfred L. Knox and Alec R. Vidler, The Development of Modern Catholicism (London, 1933), p. 65.

[163]The Parish Communion (London, 1937), pp. 6-7; Liturgy and Society (London, 1935), pp. 209-229.

[164]Liddon quoted in Ragnar Ekstrom, The Theology of Charles Gore (Lund, 1944), p. 5.

[165]A. M. Ramsey, From Gore to Temple (London, 1960).

[166]Bernard M. G. Reardon, From Coleridge to Gore (London, 1971) and Thureau-Dangin, op. cit., passim.

background of leading figures of the Church of England at the end of the nineteenth century and at the beginning of the twentieth: Gore, Halifax, Hebert, Kelly, Benson.[167] Even those who properly credit Pusey as the restorer of Anglican monasticism, fail to demonstrate the realization of his communal theological concepts in the pioneer religious orders.[168]

C. C. J. Webb and Brilioth were the exceptions in the past generation to this refusal to accord the Oxford professor his proper place in nineteenth century church history. Webb cites the Pusey-Newman doctrine of justification as incorporation into God as the chief contribution of the Oxford Movement to systematic theology.[169] To Brilioth it is the definition of the church as the continuation of the incarnation which has a lasting effect on the churches.[170] A few monographs have dealt with the continuity of Pusey's ideas in later church history, such as those of William Perry on their primal role in Scottish Anglo-Catholicism and that of Ragnar Ekstrom on the importance of the incarnational ecclesiology of Pusey's Tract 67, with its ideal of communal Christian life, in the theology of Charles Gore.[171]

----

[167]A. S. Duncan Jones, "The Oecumenical Ideals of the Oxford Movement," Williams and Harris, loc. cit., pp. 446-477, never mentions Pusey's attempts at reunion or the Eirenicon. Davies, p. 282:
"...The Tractarians, in their fear of Liberalism, left to their successors the task of correlating the life of worship with the redemption of human society, and in this endeavour the Anglo-Catholics owed more to Maurice than to Pusey."
Others who minimize the role of Pusey are: Clarke, op. cit.; Roger Lloyd, The Church of England. 1900-1965 (London, 1966); Sparrow Simpson, op. cit.; Sheila Kaye-Smith, Anglo-Catholicism (London, 1925); H. L. Stewart, A History of Anglo-Catholicism (London, 1929).

[168]A. M. Allchin, op. cit., passim; Peter F. Anson, The Call of the Cloister (London, 1955); Thomas Jay Williams, The Park Village Sisterhood (London, 1965), and Priscilla Lydia Sellon (London, 1965).

[169]Webb, op. cit., p. 75.

[170]Brilioth, op. cit., pp. 329, 348.

[171]William Perry, Alexander Penrose Forbes. Bishop of Brechin. The Scottish Pusey (London, 1939), and William Perry, The Oxford Movement in Scotland (Cambridge, 1933); Ekstrom, op. cit., p. 15- on Tract 67 and Gore, p. 120 - Pusey's Parochial and Cathedral Sermons, No. XV, as

This one hundred and fifty year period of church history closed with a "renewed understanding of the importance of Pusey for today" and a recognition that any fresh appraisal of the significance of the Oxford Movement for Catholic renewal "will have to take greater cognizance of the contribution of Edward Bouverie Pusey." For David Jasper, Pusey's study of the Hebrew Bible, of the Fathers, and of the theology of Germany pointed toward "an approach to a sacramental theology which was of profound importance" for Catholic-minded Anglicans. To A. M. Allchin, the communal tradition of the early church "lives and grows and becomes more accessible to us here in Western Europe, now in the late twentieth century," because of Pusey.[172]

Louis Weil has shown that the affirmations of the first Anglo-Catholics about the church, the sacraments and worship raised some of the primary questions upon which the modern liturgical movement is now based, and Geoffrey Rowell has recently written that the soul of the rediscovered Catholicism of the Tractarians is "corporate experience." "If we look at the notable parishes of the Catholic revival," states Rowell, "we find that in a surprisingly large number of instances this community dimension was present as supplying an important element of the new patterns of ministry."[173]

---

important for the development of the common life, p. 232- "...the idea of the Church as the body of Christ plainly goes back to the Pusey tradition."

[172]Perry Butler, ed., Pusey Rediscovered (London, 1983), pp. 386, X, 68, 386. More traditional recent treatments of Pusey appear in John R. Griffin, The Oxford Movement: 1833-1983 (Edinburgh, 1984); Elisabeth Jay, The Evangelical and Oxford Movements (Cambridge, 1983); and A. G. Lough, Dr. Pusey: Restorer of the Church (Devon, 1981). A full and up-to-date bibliography of the Oxford Movement can be found in G. Rowell and P. Cobb, Revolution by Tradition (Oxford, 1983).

[173]Louis Weil, Sacraments and Liturgy: The Outward Signs (Oxford, 1983); Geoffrey Rowell, The Vision Glorious (Oxford, 1983), pp. 249, 123; See also J. Robert Wright, ed., Lift High the Cross (Cincinnati, 1983), p. 99. More traditional recent treatments of ritualism appear in James Bentley, Ritualism and Politics in Victorian Britain (Oxford, 1978); Colin Buchanan, Anglo-Catholic Worship (Bramcote, 1983); Charles Angell, A Ritual Controversy in the Victorian Church of England (Rome, 1983); and Nigel Yates, The Oxford Movement and Anglican Ritualism (London, 1983).

There are thus signs that the appreciation may be growing of the significant role of the Puseyite parishes in transmitting values of the Oxford Movement down to the churches of today. The evolution of the new Catholicism may be traced in parishes in which liturgical change was joined to a recovery of the communal dimension and social mission of the church. There the new Catholicism was kept alive as a continuing tradition after the nineteenth century, the parishes acting as a seedbed for twentieth century advance.[174]

There is a similar division in the evaluation of the role of Dom Guéranger in the evolution of the form of the church. A popular image is Guéranger the Ultramontane reactionary, obstructing progress at every turn. This is the picture in Louis Bouyer's history of liturgical piety since the Enlightenment which portrays the Abbot of Solesmes as one who hindered the spread of emerging changes in the celebration of the mass by diverting the reformed liturgical life into monastic channels. There it became the plaything of aristocrats and aesthetes rather than an inspiration for ordinary lay folk.[175] Aubert's position in La Théologie Catholique au milieu du XXe siècle is that the socially radical implications of the liturgical movement came not from Solesmes but from the Centre de Pastorale Liturgique, founded by Dominicans. Solesmes was too upper class, to esoteric to have had any impact on the church in the twentieth century.[176]

Notwithstanding the hostility traditionally shown to Guéranger by scholars, there is the witness of some liturgical historians that he was the first successful liberator of the church from the sentimentalities of individualistic piety,[177] that his Liturgical Year "caused the

---

[174]On the parishes see Kenneth Leech and Rowan Williams, Essays Catholic and Radical (London, 1983); Nigel Yates, The Anglican Revival in Victorian Portsmouth (Portsmouth, 1983); Ritual Conflict at Farlington and Wymering (Portsmouth, 1978).

[175]Bouyer, op. cit., pp. 23-29.

[176]Roger Aubert, La Théologie Catholique au milieu du XXe siècle (Paris, 1954).

[177]Robeyna, loc. cit., p. 277.

first boom of liturgical thinking in France,"[178] and that the radicalism of later Catholic liturgical reform was implied in that book.[179] Jungmann in his history of the evolution of the Roman mass points to Guéranger's decisive role in destroying the customs which had separated the mass from the people.[180] Yet only Rousseau suggests a method by which Guéranger's ideas eventually led to change in the church, by the route of parish churches and of Benedictine abbeys at Beuron and Maria Laach in Germany and Maredsous and Mont César in Belgium.[181] Two articles suggest that a very important stage of liturgical development between the first volume of the Liturgical Year and the transmission of Guéranger's principles to Central Europe by the Wolter brothers in 1863 was the liturgical war between Solesmes and the French bishops, corresponding in time and viciousness to the Anglo-Catholic ritualists' battles with the authority of the English bishops and state.[182]

Since the centenary of Dom Guéranger's death in 1975 debate over the origins in the nineteenth century of the new communal Catholicism associated with the liturgical movement has continued. The two most recent surveys of the history of worship are in general agreement, except about the nineteenth century. Writing in Geschiedenis van de Christelijke Eredienst, Herman Wegman states, "Guéranger's passion was to glorify the old (that is, medieval) Roman liturgy and to suppress whatever was in conflict with it. In a short while through his efforts

----

[178]Trapp, op. cit., p. 252.

[179]Capelle, loc. cit., pp. 145, 139.

[180]J. A. Jungmann, The Mass of the Roman Rite (New York, 1951), pp. 158-159.

[181]Rousseau, op. cit., pp. 93-97.

[182]Jacques d'Anglejan, "Un Défenseur de la Tradition Religieuse en France au XIXe Siècle," La Revue critique des Idées et des Livres, XIII, No. 75 (25 May 1911), 456-480 argues that in fighting against the diocesan liturgies Guéranger was ending individualism in religion. Daniel-Rops, loc. cit., maintains that in unifying the liturgy he was restoring it and creating a new sense of the church.

the neo-Gallican renewal was radically uprooted....Guéranger was a papal Zouave for the defense of the Roman liturgy! His restoration of the Roman liturgy did indeed do harm and for a long time blocked its development." On the other hand, in Il Culto Cristiano in Occidente Enrico Cattaneo arrived at a balanced appraisal of his career, in which Dom Guéranger sounds the trumpet opening the way to the modern pioneers of the liturgy.[183]

Louis Soltner is persuaded that Guéranger originally envisioned purified Benedictine monasticism to be an appropriate instrument for the rebuilding of the church at large in an age in which France witnessed three revolutions and six regimes. He, for whom monastic community is constituted on the model of the church—the church in microcosm—could perpetuate no more artificial barriers between an abbey and the laity of these circumstances. The monastery was to be created anew out of the dust of secularization as a hearth radiating and propagating a liturgical sense among the faithful. However the most recent book on Guéranger, though it demonstrates clearly his recovery of the ecclesial dimension of the liturgy and the communal structure of the church at prayer, still fails to make a definitive judgment on the abbot's place in history. Cuthbert Johnson's examination of Prosper Guéranger is neither an attempt to vindicate his work and resurrect a prophet nor a project to substantiate the claims of those who portray the Abbot of Solesmes as one who diverted reformed liturgical life into monasteries alone.[184]

New evidence is presented below that proves that Guéranger did influence parishes in which revolutionary elements of the liturgical

----

[183]Herman Wegman, Geschiedenis van de Christelijke Eredienst in het Westen en het Oosten (Hilversum, 1976), p. 259; Enrico Cattaneo, Il Culto Cristiano in Occidente (Rome, 1978), pp. 546-580; Guy Oury, "Aux origines du mouvement liturgique. Les Institutions liturgiques de Dom Guéranger," Esprit et Vie 86 (1976), 120-126, 139-143, 157-160; Tomás Moral, "Cien anos después de la muerte de dom Guéranger," Yermo 14 (1976), 103-132.

[184]Louis Soltner, Solesmes et Dom Guéranger: 1805-1875 (Solesmes, 1974); Cuthbert Johnson, Prosper Guéranger (1805-1875): A Liturgical Theologian (Rome, 1984).

movement can be seen to be evolving in a nineteenth century context. Guéranger linked the monastic liturgical revival to parishes at the outset of the 150-year development of the liturgical movement. The new Catholicism could not have advanced unless it had proffered to parishioners in the nineteenth century an attractive commodity, an objective religious organicism in the liturgical parishes of France that replaced the destruction of secular communities. For it was the success in the parishes—in villages like Mesnil-St. Loup, at Notre-Dame du Pré in Le Mans, and in Paris at St. Jacques du Haut-Pas and St. François Xavier, all influenced directly by Guéranger—which helped to overcome the opposition of the French hierarchy to the reform of worship.

The question of Guéranger's influence on change in worship is solved below by the demonstration of the evolution of elements of the liturgical movement in parishes which followed his thinking during the period of Solesmes' fight for the adoption of the Roman mass, the Gregorian chant, and patristic ritual practices. The histories of the parishes related below are evidence that in France as well as in Germany and Belgium the Ultramontane innovations of the Benedictine gradually led to the form of a new Catholicism.

In the case of Möhler, as in that of Pusey, the new ideas have been seen as creating a shift in theology as well as in ritual. In the German literature, however, there is a division between those who see the Tübingen professor as the father of a southwest German Ultramontane reaction which stifled the first evidence of creative theology in the area and others who picture him as the forerunner of the Catholic modernists, or of the neo-romantic German Catholic reform agitation of the 1920's, or even of all of modern Roman Catholic theology. The argument of the liturgical historians has already been stated. They held that an origin of twentieth-century eucharistic renovation lies in Möhler's communal ecclesiology and his influence on Staudenmaier and the founders of Beuron.[185] Rousseau sees the profound change wrought by

----

[185]Trapp, op. cit., pp. 230-233, 245, 246, 269, 359, 361; Rousseau, op. cit., pp. 67-91, 106.

Möhler to be so great that "he was incontestably the greatest ecclesiologist of the nineteenth century."[186] A recent essay on the German liturgical apostolate comments on the delayed value of his theology of community, the general priesthood, and the active participation of all believers in the building up of the church: "This ...meant that the liturgical movement became not simply a program for the outer form of the cult. But it took almost a hundred years for all these suppositions to come out."[187]

In Geiselemann's paradigm Möhler is not so much the instigator of the German ecclesiological revolution as was Bishop Michael Sailer of Ratisbon, but Möhler is such a strong advocate for the objectivity and communality of the church that his view remains to reemerge in the twentieth-century theology of Romano Guardini and Karl Adam.[188] To Alexander Dru the importance of Tübingen exceeds the sum of its achievements and lies in the creation of a school which kept the Catholic romantic theological tradition alive, so that when theology began to revive in the twentieth century it returned to the Tübingen tradition, not only in Germany but in France as well. Between 1848 and 1914 there is a period of stagnation in German Catholicism, a time when "poetry was a Protestant dialect." There is not then a constant evolution from Möhler to the new Catholics but a leap backward to him for inspiration in the twentieth century.[189]

---

[186]Oliver Rousseau in L'ecclésiologie au XIX siècle (Paris, 1960), p. 373.

[187]Ferdinand Kolbe, Die Liturgische Bewegung (Aschaffenburg, 1964), p. 19.

[188]J. R. Geiselmann, Die Lehre von der Kirche, unpublished lectures, MS HS Gf 1930 a, Wilhelmstift, Tübingen, lists various schools of ecclesiology, and under what may be called the new school he lists: J. M. Sailer, Grundlehren der katholischen Religion; A. Gugler, Einige Worte Uber den Geist des Christentums; J. A. Möhler, Einheit, J. S. Drey, Vom Geist und Wesen des Kath.; F. A. Staudenmaier, Das Wesen der Kath. Kirche; R. Guardini, Vom Sinn der Kirche; Karl Adam, Das Wesen des Kath.

[189]Dru, op. cit., pp. 64, 121.

A collection of essays published at the centenary of Möhler's death also suggests that he is a primary force in the background of the break with scholasticism in Catholic Germany of the twenties of this century.[190] J. A. Jungmann in his essay "Die Kirche im religiosen Leben der Gegenwart" maintains that the individualistic piety which had dominated the church since the period of Thomas à Kempis broke down in the face of the shattering disillusionments of the 1914-18 war. A communistic piety and a yearning for an organic whole to be found in the church were the result. Germans looked for an expression of those views and found Mohler's Die Einheit in der Kirche.[191] "Die Religiöse Aktualitat Möhlers" of J. E. Vierneisel explains the appeal of a theologian of the spiritual and lay aspect of the church in a period when post-war settlements and political fortunes had stripped the institution of any authority which it had once manifested in the public domain. Möhler's church of the Fathers matched the conditions of inter-war Catholicism, when the social essence of the church was called upon to respond to the needs of groups rather than individuals.[192]

At the death of Karl Adam, one of the leading Weimar Catholics, it was first suggested that Adam was the link between Möhler's early nineteenth century theology and the evolution of the German new Catholicism in the twentieth century. Because of Adam's grounding in the spirit of the Tübingen school, acquired while he was lecturing at that university, he was held responsible for transmitting the idea of

---

[190]Tüchle, op. cit.; on p. 13 of the introduction Pierre Chaillet emphasizes the importance for contemporary spirituality of Möhler's concept of finding Christ in the community of believers.

[191]J. A. Jungmann, "Die Kirche im religiosen Leben der Gegenwart," Tüchle, op. cit., 373-390.

[192]J. E. Vierneisel, "Die Religiose Aktualitat Möhlers," pp. 332-343, Tüchle, op. cit., particularly pp. 332, 334, 342. Another book which does not discuss Möhler specifically but does argue that the German Catholics of 1918-1933 returned to the romantics of 1800-1830 because of the delusion and destruction of the war is Klaus Breuning, Die Vision des Reiches. Deutscher Katholizismus zwischen Demokratie und Diktatur (1929-1934) (Munich, 1969), pp. 56 and 158.

the church as a community which is the body of Christ into the era of the Second Vatican Council:

> The Church is the body drenched with and intermingled with the saving power of the body of Jesus. From this conviction, which places Adam in the great line of Paul - Augustine - Thomas - Möhler - Newman, originates a completely new conception of the Dogma, morality, cult, and law of the Church....The realization of the Church as the new community of mankind stands, we say here, at the heart of the theology of Karl Adam....One must return to the theology of Augustine and Möhler if one wants to find such an intensive consciousness of the solidity of the bond which binds men together in sin and grace. Mankind is to him no variegated conglomerate of single individuals, but on the other hand an organic unity and whole, a single "we."[193]

Some German ecclesiastical historians, however, take exception to the portrayal of their countryman as a liberalizer of Catholic theology. Eschweiler considers Möhler to be responsible for pushing the German church in a conservative and idealistic direction.[194] Vigener and Bihlmeyer argue that Möhler ushered in a period of political Catholicism, the aim of which was the establishment and maintenance of the collective freedom of the church.[195] He increased the frequency of Catholic conflicts with Protestant governments. He was an apologist for the interference of the Vatican in German affairs.[196] Herman Tüchle and Rudolph Reinhardt show that in his own time and immediately after his death Möhler was regarded as the pioneer of the "papalistic, curialistic, Ultramontane system" in southwest Germany.[197] His protégé Hefele, as professor at Tübingen and Bishop of the Diocese of

----

[193]Fritz Hofmann, "Theologie aus dem Geist der Tübingen Schule," ThQ, 146 (1966), 277, 281, 282.

[194]Eschweiler, op. cit., pp. 167, 168, 169. It is suggested that Möhler was the Aquinas of Hegelianism.

[195]Bihlmeyer, loc. cit., pp. 163-167.

[196]Vigener, loc. cit., pp. 563, 564.

[197]Rudolph Reinhardt, "Unbekannte Quellen zur Hefeles Leben und Werk," ThQ, CLII (1972), 54-77. Also see Reinhardt's "Im Zeichen der Tübinger Schule," Attempto, 25, 25 (1968), 40-58.

Rottenburg, advanced the new Möhlerian "Kirchlichkeit," a basic institutional and dogmatic conservatism, against Protestant governments and Wessenbergian Catholic liberals. Möhler is seen by these historians as the beginning of the end of a period of daring theological experimentation in the area of Germany covered by the diocese of Rottenburg, as creating a new coterie of young Ultramontane priests who favored celibacy, Rome, and the Latin mass, and eventually stifled the creative spirit of the early Tübingen school.

This division in the interpretation and evaluation of Möhler has continued for the past decade, even in this country. On the one hand, Leonard Swidler places Möhler among the liturgical reformers of "Aufklärung Catholicism" because he lifted his voice in favor of liturgy in the language of the people, of a return of the chalice to the people at mass, and of the priority of communal celebrations of the liturgy over private prayer and popular devotions. Yet Swidler identifies no channel through which there is an evolution from the "Aufklärung Catholicism" of the early nineteenth century to the "substantially similar" reforms of Vatican II. To Swidler, the nineteenth century renewal had only ephemeral value and finally failed. Möhler's more radical influence ultimately evaporated and even vanished from the pages of most of our history books.[198]

On the other hand, Thomas F. O'Meara identifies Möhler with the German Catholic romantics, and O'Meara has found that some characteristics of German Catholic romantic idealism have exercised a lasting impact on the evolution of modern Catholicism, including the ideal of community.[199] To O'Meara, though the liturgical movement does not rise

----

[198]Leonard Swiderl, Aufklärung Catholicism: 1780-1850 (Missoula, 1978).

[199]Thomas F. O'Meara, Romantic Idealism and Roman Catholicism (Notre Dame, 1982); for other recent studies see also Heinz Brunner, Der organologische Kirchenbegriff in seiner Bedeutung für das ekklesiologische Denken des 19. Jahrhunderts (Frankfurt, 1979); Wayne L. Fehr, The Birth of the Catholic Tübingen School (Chico, 1981); Joseph Fitzer, Moehler and Baur in Controversy, 1832-38 (Tallahassee, 1974).

immediately out of the creative time of German romantic idealism, 1795 to 1845, it is within the religious renewal sparked by German romanticism that the origins and seeds of the liturgical movement lie.[200]

O'Meara has proposed that new research must look into people and institutions that link the cultural world of J. A. Möhler to Guéranger and the Abbeys of Beuron and Maria Laach. One way to solve the problem of evolution from Möhler to the modern church, and contradictions in the evaluation of Möhler, is to present here new evidence on the development of worship and parish life in Johann Adam Möhler's own diocese of Rottenburg, a diocese coextensive with the kingdom of Württemberg, and particularly the histories of parishes served by Möhler students. There the experience of England and France is repeated. What at first appeared to be reactionary tendencies evolved into aspects of the new Catholicism which gave fresh relevance to the parish as an institution with a communal dimension in the midst of a rapidly modernizing society.[201]

One stream of church history links Möhler and Guéranger directly to the twentieth century through the Benedictine congregation of Beuron, founded by Dom Maurus Wolter in Germany in 1863. Beuron and three of its daughter houses, Maredsous (1872) and Mont-César (1899) in Belgium and Maria Laach (1892) in the German Rhineland, bore the revival of communal worship into the twentieth century and stand behind the explicit recognition of liturgical renewal by the Vatican in the reign of Pius XI, the first pope to use the term "liturgical movement."[202] From Beuron the liturgical apostolate spread to Benedictine monasteries around the globe, houses that in turn began to touch

----

[200]Thomas F. O'Meara, "The Origins of the Liturgical Movement and German Romanticism," Worship, Volume 59, No. 4 (1985), 326–342.

[201]For more on Möhler and liturgical reform see the unpublished dissertation of Michael Grütering, Johann Adam Möhler und die Liturgie seiner zeit (Bonn, 1972).

[202]D. B. Capelle, "Le Saint Siège et le mouvement liturgique," Q L P 21 (1936), 125–147.

Lutherans, Methodists, the Reformed, and Anglicans in such a way that clear lines of convergence in the eucharistic renewal of the churches could begin to be seen.

The Möhlerian impact on southwestern Germany plays a part in this development. Beuron itself is fifty miles from the University of Tübingen. Many of the first and second generation of Beuronese monks had been students at Tübingen, studied Möhler with other German theologians or had been raised in the southern kingdom of Württemberg. Tübingen and the parishes of the diocese of Rottenburg are in the background of Anselm Schott, who directed the Beuron mass translations from 1868, and Suitbert Bäumer who after coming to Beuron from Tübingen in 1865 published on the history of the breviary and the role of the laity in the divine office. At Maredsous the Möhlerian tradition was passed on to Ildefons Herwegen, who as Abbot of Maria Laach until 1946 refashioned nineteenth century teaching for Germans who experienced the collapse of their empire and economy following World War I, by the master of novices Boniface Wolff and by Germain Morin, the first editor of the Revue Bénédictine.

Thus nineteenth century churches are crucial to the evolution of the new Catholicism. If aspects of modern Catholicism appeared at Oxford, Solesmes, and Tübingen before they did elsewhere, they also gradually emerged in parish churches and monastic communities under the influence of these centers of renewal. Parishes and monasteries are the neglected but important link between the revivals of 1833 and their twentieth century successors, Adam, Guardini, Herwegen, Casel, Congar, Chenu, Gore, Hebert, Dix, Ramsey, and others who continued to transform the churches during the first half of this century and laid the ground-work for what came to be the communal reforms of Vatican II and of modern Anglican Catholicism.

The extent of the impact of the Oxford Movement, the French Benedictines, and the Tübingen School on the church makes the choice of a descriptive term for them difficult. They have been called "restorations," "revivals," "renewals," but those words miss the

connotation of movements evolving along a creative "middle way" which
was at once conservative, in that it looked to the past for models, and
progressive, in that it sought to create a revived community life
appropriate for modern conditions.[203]

Perhaps "reformation" is the right word.   Perhaps a second
reformation did begin in the 1830's.   That word does convey the idea
that this was a religious change that was not confined to one country
or one religious communion, that it was a reaction occurring
simultaneously in many ecclesiastical centers. However, the change was
slower, less dramatic, more diffuse, subtler than the sixteenth century
events that go by the name reformation.

---

[203]A similar point about "confessional" neo-Lutherans and conservative Protestants in nineteenth century Germany, England, and America is
made by Walter H. Conser in his Church and Confession: Conservative
Theologians in Germany, England, and America 1815-1866 (Mercer, 1984),
"If their vision was anachronistic, they nevertheless understood a
message that the twentieth century has been at pains to recover—that
human development consists of a balance of intellect and emotions, and
that such a balance can only be found in community." (p. 329).

CHAPTER II

Württemberg and Berlin

"'And - and - what comes next?'

'Oh, yes, yes, what the dickens does come next? C'est la question, ma très chère demoiselle!'" The speaker is old Johann Buddenbrook. In Thomas Mann's Buddenbrooks, in the portrayal of a transition from the sceptical Enlightenment to the new religiosity of the 1830's in Lübeck, he represents Francophile and elegant local Senators of the Hanseatic town, the poet Jean Jacques Hoffstede, the eighteenth-century pastor Wunderlick remembered by old residents for his "tact and moderation," and also a host of northern and southern Germans, Protestant as well as Catholics, who were suspicious enough of orthodoxy to jest at a child's recitation of the Shorter Catechism. While his granddaughter enumerated the acts of the creator in providing "meat and drink, hearth and home, wife and child, acre and cow, old Johann Buddenbrook could not hold in longer. He burst out laughing, in a high, half smothered titter, in his glee at being able to make fun of the Catechism."[1]

"'There you go again, Father, making fun of sacred things.'" This is the voice of a new generation, the men of the thirties, and it is the voice of Thomas Buddenbrook, son of the Old Consul, who on the birth of his daughter in 1838 wrote in this manner in his journal:

> "'I have taken out...an insurance policy for my youngest daughter, of one hundred and fifty thaler current. Lead her, O Lord, in Thy ways....For inasmuch as our weak human hearts are prone to forget Thy priceless gift of the sweet blessed Jesus....' And so on for three pages....He cited whole pages

----

[1]Thomas Mann, Buddenbrooks (New York, 1955), pp. 3, 59.

of Scripture, he prayed for his parents, his wife, his children, and himself... and then, with a last quotation and three final 'Amens,' he strewed sand on the paper and leaned back with a sigh of relief."[2]

It was from this clash of generations, which occurred as much in his native Württemberg as in Lübeck, that Johann Adam Möhler emerged. The sharp contrast of two schools of religion, the enlightened and the romantic, impelled him to seek a synthesis. In the end he manufactured an ecclesiology which was an alloy of rationalism and romanticism, idealism and materialism. Such a theology of combination was born in and necessary for an era of institutional destruction. But the central thesis which emerged in Möhler, that the church is in essence a community of the faithful who themselves form the mystical body of Christ, lasted to do duty as one of the foundations of the liturgical movement and of modern Catholicism.

The idea of the communal church was the base of the Möhlerian synthesis. It reached beyond the dichotomies of Aufklärer and Die Romantik to the fresh and inductive thinking of the Fathers of the early church. Möhler discovered his solution when he broke out of the ghetto of Catholic thought in Württemberg, symbolically in a trip to the north German Protestants, and came upon patristic scholarship which had been rediscovered in Berlin. His exploit was a significant stage in bringing to an end the cultural isolation of the Roman Catholic Church in Germany.

The situation of Catholics in Germany had been unique since the Reformation when the Catholic churches withdrew into the world of their own diaspora. After the French Revolution the history of Catholicism in Germany is contained between two moments: the romantic renewal at the beginning of the nineteenth century and a second spring of revived worship and theology between World War I and World War II. In the middle lies an era of hesitation, tension, and conflict as German Catholics increasingly abandoned their ghetto and encountered the secular modern world.

----

[2]Ibid., pp. 5, 42.

Möhler's synthetic theological discourse joins the two moments. His theology was first compiled amid the sweep of German philosophy from Kant to Hegel, amid changes in the spiritual life of the parishes, revolution in the relation of church and state, and disruptions in the patterns of social life. Buffeted by new economies and by new directions of the state, the traditional communal spirituality of the parishes had almost disappeared during Möhler's life-time.

Möhler's works became popular again throughout Germany during the inter-war years of this century as large numbers of Catholics came to appreciate the altar as a center of community that transcends the totalitarian secular world. "The study of the intellectual history of Germany at the beginning of the nineteenth century is more than an academic exercise for us," Philip Funk wrote in 1929, "it touches on the living questions of the present."[3]

Johann Adam Möhler was born at the very end of the eighteenth century into a part of Germany which was a patchwork of tiny states, stitched together between Bavaria in the east and France in the west, Lake Constance in the south and the Rhineland and Pfalz in the north. The majority of the 483,000 people who lived in this complex of territories, at the end of the eighteenth century inhabited the lands of the Duke of Württemberg. They were all Protestant. The 200,000 Catholics of the region dwelt in the Breisgau and Oberschwaben districts, ruled by the Hapsburgs, or in the temporal realms of local prince-bishops, or on the ancient, independent estates which belonged to the great abbeys of the southwest, Zwiefalten, Rottenmünster, Schontäl, Heiligkreutztal, Stift-Comburg, Oberstenfeld, and Margerethenhausen, or in the Catholic free imperial cities of Rottweil, Weil der Stadt, Gmünd, Neresheim, and Ellwangen, or in the towns owned by the Teutonic Knights, Mergentheim and Neckarsulm.

Möhler's primary field of study was ecclesiology, and the history of Christian ecclesiology presents, even from the first centuries, the story of two warring factions. Both were represented among the

---

[3]Alexander Dru, The Church in the Nineteenth Century (London, 1963), p. 15.

Catholics of southwestern Germany. One had held that the church is a society of sinful men, founded for the appropriation of divine grace to the individual soul. The priesthood and hierarchy being the mediators of that grace, they are the essential element of the Christian body. The other contended that the church is a community of divine life, which life is communicated to all equally in a church whose essence is the faithful people. The Germans labelled this as part of the Gemeinschaft/Gesellschaft distinction which was very old in European civilization, appearing in pre-Christian authors. The early Fathers were representative of the Gemeinschaft type in Christianity. Tertullian, Irenaeus, Clement of Alexandria, and Cyprian maintained in opposition to the Gnostics and other schismatics that the Holy Spirit was grounded in the faithful, and therefore popular traditions were a guide to revelation. In Augustine the theory of the church and the city of God as the Corpus mysticum of Gemeinschaft pattern is contrasted to the "society of man." To answer the elitist Donatists Augustine preached that the entire church is the extension of Christ's body.

The tradition of independent communal organizations inspired originally by the Gemeinschaft theory had once been so strong in Möhler's part of Germany that in the Middle Ages the countryside which comprises Württemberg was known as "the cloister street of the Holy Roman Empire."[4] In the eleventh century thirteen Benedictine communities were established in the region. In the twelfth century four Cistercian and five Premonstratensian houses were opened and six foundations of secular canons established. In the thirteenth century these cloisters were built: eight for Cistercian women, nine for Franciscans and Dominicans, five for Augustinian hermits, two for Carmelites, six for Johannites, and five for the Teutonic Knights. Between the eleventh and the sixteenth century twenty other monasteries flourished.[5]

---

[4]August Willburger and Herman Tüchle, Geschichte der Katholischen Kirche in Württemberg (Rottenburg, 1954), p. 28.

[5]Ibid., pp. 28-31.

The Reformation, which in this district was quickly adopted in urban areas with a more educated population than in the surrounding countryside, was the first sustained attack on communal religious associations in Württemberg, and it almost completely destroyed the remnants of the Gemeinschaft theology. By 1550, twenty-eight monasteries had been dissolved. Luther, Zwingli, and Calvin, whose thought penetrated the area, retained the concept of divine revelation but made it co-extensive with the Bible. The concept of a divine Spirit evolving among the people or transmitted to the Pope and bishops was dropped. Among the Protestants the dogma of the invisible community of the predestined was all that remained of communal ecclesiology. To counter this, Roman Catholic theologians placed all emphasis upon the visible authority of pope and episcopate. The Catholic ideal of the visible community of Christians was forgotten. Canisius and Bellarmine allowed the essence of the church to be the Petrine primate with the body of bishops, and their concepts dominated German ecclesiology during the wasted years of the Thirty Years' War and after when Recktskirche was all and the Gnadenskirche of the Fathers and the medieval mystics had been lost. This tradition of thin scholastic polemic in defense of the hierarchy continued down through the eighteenth century and appeared in a last important fossil form in Benedikt Stattler's Allgemein Katholisch-Christlich-theoretische Religionslehre, published at Munich in two volumes in 1792-1793, picturing the church as a perfect society of unequal hierarchy joined to ecclesiastical monarchy.

Stattler was a fossil because the Enlightenment was a much more fundamental challenge to Catholicism than Protestantism had been. These later reformers argued elegantly, but none the less forcefully, against the whole notion of a divine revelation communicated to men either through a corporate institution or the Bible. As early as the mid-eighteenth century at Halle Jacob Baumgarten was saying, "My words are intended for those who are at once Christians and men of reason," but he was spreading a religion based only upon the reason of the single individual through the journals Nachrichten von einer Hallischen

<u>Bibliothek</u> and <u>Nachrichten von merkwürdigen Bücher</u>.[6] The next
generation at Halle was even more radical. Johann Semler taught that
the true spirit of religion, which he defined to be synonymous with the
inner moral life of the human, was being smothered under heaps of human
rules, ordinances, and rites.

Kant continued the subjective moralistic, anti-liturgical, and
critical disposition of German <u>Aufklärung</u> theology among the
Protestants. The only possible road to the knowledge of God for him
led through the conscience of the individual. In his <u>Religion within
the Limits of Reason</u>, which came out in 1793, religion is little more
than an appendix to an ethical code which is judged by personal acts
and practical results. Kant's dread of the traditional, the
authoritative, and the mysterious as arbitrary and destructive of the
ethical character of faith drew him to a depreciation of the devotional
and liturgical content of Christianity. He wrote, "I distinguish the
<u>teaching</u> of Christ from the report which we have of the teaching of
Christ, and in order to get at the former I try above all to extract
the <u>moral</u> teaching separated from all precepts of the New Testament."[7]
He held all external worship done in common to be idle. "Everything
that man, apart from a moral way of life, believes himself to be
capable of doing to please God is mere religious delusion and spurious
worship."[8] He himself abstained from all external religious custom and
in later years did not go to church.

The Enlightenment began to filter into the councils of the Roman
Catholics of the southern states of Germany at first through the
evidential theology of the Catholic philosopher and commentator
Reinhold. The theological faculty at Freiburg became an outpost for
the dissemination of the <u>Aufklärung</u> with the publication of the monthly

----

[6]Paul Hazard, <u>European Thought in the Eighteenth Century</u>
(Cleveland, 1967), p. 67.

[7]Letter of Immanuel Kant of 1775, quoted in S. Körner, <u>Kant</u>
(London, 1955), p. 170.

[8]<u>Idem</u>.

Der Freymütige from 1782 until 1787. The Archbishop of Salzburg sent his students to study directly with Kant. The notions of enlightened ecclesiastical reform were so pervasive in the second half of the eighteenth century that they began to determine the forms of religious life of the Catholic people who made up one-third of the population of southwest Germany.

Here, in fact, there were two varieties of Catholicism. The churches of the northern, non-Schwabian districts were dominated by the prince-bishops, and those of the southern Schwabian region felt the directing influence of the Hapsburg emperor at Vienna. Both northern and southern leaders attempted to overturn the liturgical and devotional habits of centuries. They did not, however, challenge the traditional German imperial ecclesiological principle that the church is a hierarchy which draws its power either from political or local ecclesiastical sovereignty. Möhler's hometown in the Frankish north was surrounded by the traditions of the prince-bishops' self-contained, separatist vision of the church which was shaped by the ambitions of the three episcopal electors of Cologne, Mainz, and Trier and the metropolitan of Salzburg to be politically independent of the emperor and free of the meddling power of the pope.

The theologians, who served these prince-bishops and were assigned the endless task of shoring up the crumbling power of the princelings, developed a custom of arguing that the church should be culturally and politically a free corporation. In reality, however, they were describing it as essentially an administrative body. The most famous of these German divines was John Nicholas von Hontheim, suffragan bishop to the elector of Trier, who issued in 1763 a defense of the independence of the northern episcopate, The Book of Justinus Febronius. This was an attack on all forms of corporate ecclesiastical authority other than the episcopate. Hontheim assaulted the religious orders and other bodies of men and women who sought to live the religious life in common. He called for the end of confraternities, the confiscation of the property of the contemplative orders, and the abandonment of celibacy, as well as the obstruction of communication between monasteries and Rome.

Liturgical legislation was passed by the German prince-bishops at Ems in 1785 which called for the service of God to be rational, educational, moral, and individualistic. Pictures depicting miracles, statues on the altar, and outdoor processions were banned from the churches. In Cologne in 1780 a new breviary was enforced which reduced the number of lessons on the miraculous legends of the saints. Franz Ludwig von Erthal, the prince-bishop of Würzburg, whose territory included Möhler's native village, ordered in 1784 that a service of preaching was to be held in the parishes on Sunday night. He introduced German hymns in 1787, and the Gregorian chant was suppressed. The number of pilgrimages, processions, and other communal exercises allowed in the parish churches was severely limited in 1789. A bulletin of May 1803 requested that useful subjects, philosophy, politics, and economics, be discussed in the pulpit. The bishop of Seggau curtailed the number of processions his priests could lead in 1783, and in 1787 the ordinary of Regensburg forbade his people and clergy to attend worship in any monasteries.

In the Schwabian parishes a program, which in many respects recapitulated that of the northern German bishops, was established by the Emperor Joseph II of Austria. All contemplative orders were dissolved. Monasteries were suppressed and their lands confiscated. In 1773 the Jesuits were exiled and in 1775 the Franciscans and their third orders in the parishes were disbanded. The liturgical polity of the Empire was equally anti-communal and anti-ritualistic. In 1786 the Austrian government decreed the abolition of traditional forms of piety. Processions were allowed but their frequency reduced. The Austrian Chancellor, the Febronian Prince Kaunitz, limited feasts to seventeen days in 1782 and disallowed Gregorian chant.

The Catholic people of the Austrian lands did not readily accept the destruction of their old forms of worship. In 1789 there was enough peasant unrest around Freiburg, in the Oppenau Valley, and near Achern and Bühl to evoke fears of another Bundschuh, the conservative peasants' revolt which took place after the Reformation. Two thousand country people marched for a restitution of unspecified "old rights" and for a return to common grazing privileges. The Prussian Ambassador at Stuttgart, von Madeweiss, noted that the peasant unrest occurred only in the Austrian–Catholic villages, and he reported to Berlin that the revolt was essentially a religious protest.[9]

The destruction of secular corporate institutions and communal work traditions had even preceded the ecclesiastical reform. First on Protestant lands and then on Catholic estates a gradual elimination of traditional farming techniques related to concepts of common use of land and social bonds, joining owner and worker in more than a cash relationship, had begun. The initial impulse for this transformation of agricultural labor came from a large population increase which began about 1745, after 100 years of demographic stagnation whose origin lay in the decimation of the region during the Thirty Years' War. There was a great demand for food, the price of agricultural products increased, and so a demand for a change in old farming techniques was heard throughout the southwest. Grazing rights were interrupted with the introduction of clover and new crops. Common land holdings were rapidly altered. In 1780 all servile labor in the Austrian territory was abolished and converted to a cash obligation. The church even changed its Gült, or tithe on grain production, into a money payment.

The pressure of increasing population disrupted other social patterns. In the shifting financial situation which accompanied the rise of food prices, the power and solvency of the free cities and their ancient guilds eroded. The surplus population forced off the land sought employment in trade without joining one of the old corporations. Cotton spinning and linen weaving were introduced through the area at the end of the eighteenth century, but in a putting out rather than a formal factory system. By 1819 there were 32,407 commercial workers in Württemberg, but only five hundred of these were employed in factories per se.[10] The reorganization of work which goes

---

[9]Jonathan B. Rubenstein, Society and Politics in Southwest German, MS Ph.D. thesis, Harvard Archives, HU 90.9650, Widener Library, p. 103.

[10]Ibid., pp. 43, 44, 49.

by the name Industrial Revolution in Württemberg followed the Continental pattern of being dispersed through the countryside rather than being concentrated in a few burgeoning towns as in England, so that social transformation in the southwest was focused in villages and small towns as much as in the cities.[11]

The destruction of the old way of life continued through the era of the French Revolution and Napoleonic wars. While Möhler was a little boy, the miniature political and ecclesiastical organisms of his region became battlefields. The French troops of Jourdan, Moreau, and Marceau engaged the imperial Hapsburg troops at Cannstadt, Neresheim, Amberg, and Würzburg, wreaking physical havoc upon the churches, monasteries, castles, and villages of the countryside. Spiritual and political dismemberment followed at the Imperial Diet in Regensburg on February 25, 1803, with the promulgation of the Reichsdeputation-shauptschluss which decreed the end of cuius regio eius religio, the ecclesio-political dictum of 1648 which had settled the Thirty Years' War. The way was open for the Paritätsstaat, pluralistic societies, and the hand of the prince was theoretically weakened in religious matters.

The Reichsdeputationshauptschluss was an utter disaster for the Catholics. It enacted a thorough secularization of all Catholic lands, territories, and institutions in Germany. The political and economic, the spiritual and outer ecclesiastical existence of the Roman Church as it had developed in its own form in Germany was destroyed. Foundations of secular and regular canons, monasteries, schools, universities,the estates of the Catholic knights, societies of Catholic nobles, cathedral chapters, all disappeared with one Napoleonic stroke. The twenty-two states ruled by bishops were abolished. Priceless books and manuscripts were thrown from the windows of Catholic libraries and left to rot in the streets. Chalices, chasubles, processional crosses, and reliquaries were melted down and the metal distributed to the French intruders and Protestant princes. The spiritual states with

---

[11]D. S. Landes, The Unbound Prometheus (Cambridge, 1969), p. 188.

their ecclesiastical culture and confessional self-confidence which had
so recently produced Mozart at Salzburg and an architectural flowering
at Würzburg were wiped from the map. "The historic German Church in
all its rich spiritual and worldly form had vanished from the earth,"
said the historian Vigener, and Schnabel observed, "Seldom in the past
was the situation of the Catholic Church (in Germany) so precarious as
it was at the turn of the nineteenth century."[12]

After 1803 there was a reallocation of Protestant and Catholic
populations. Catholic Bavaria received Lutheran Ansbach and Bayreuth.
The Rhineland, which was three-fourths Catholic, went to Reformed
Prussia. The Protestant Margrave of Baden took over sections of the
Breisgau and lands around Lake Constance which had long looked to
Vienna for spiritual direction. Napoleon's policy was to satisfy the
land hunger of the German princes with the dissolved free cities and
the bishops' temporal holdings. In the Peace of Pressburg of 1805 he
ejected the Austrians from the southwest and turned Württemberg into a
kingdom, which immediately engulfed half a dozen abbeys, principalities, most of the cities of the region which were Catholic, and the
district where Möhler grew up. The new king Friedrich now ruled
230,000 Catholics, whereas in the old Duchy of Württemberg there were
only 5,000. In Stuttgart they had been mostly transient ballet
dancers, artists, barbers, and opera singers who worshipped in
temporary prayer houses, for the public cult had been forbidden.[13]

By 1810, when he was fourteen years old, Möhler lived in a state
which was one-third Catholic and two-thirds Protestant, roughly
corresponding to the make-up of English society in the second half of
the nineteenth century when Roman and Anglo-Catholics made up one-third
of the population. The position of the Romanists was improved, for in

----

[12]Fritz Vigener, "Gallikanismus und episkopalistische Strömungen im
deutschen Katholizismus zwischen Tridentinum und Vaticanum,"
Historische Zeitschrift, 111 (1913), 530; A. Schnabel quoted in
Paul-Werner Scheele, Einheit und Glaube (Munich, 1964), p. 5.

[13]A. Hagen, Geschichte der Diözese Württemberg (Stuttgart, 1956), I,
140.

the eighteenth century Württemberg Catholics might not become <u>Bürgers</u> or enjoy the rights of citizenship. In fact, the destruction of the traditional patterns of religious life continued with the intrusion of the new state power. Friedrich sought to eliminate the privileges and authority of all the ancient institutions in his newly acquired kingdom so that all sovereignty in the realm might flow from his palace at Stuttgart. He therefore carried forward the rational ecclesiastical reform of the eighteenth century in order to serve his own purposes.

An "Organisationsedikt für NeuWürttemberg" was issued on January 1, 1803, to regulate the confessional affairs of the newly mixed population. Here the king awarded the Catholics the full rights of citizenship, but he assumed the right to make the parochial assignments of the clergy, except in a few cases. An annual report to the king was required of all parish priests which included a statement of the physical and financial condition of the church, as well as the state of organs and clocks, and the number of hosts, the amount of wine, and the quantity of incense consumed in a year. All government orders were required to be announced from the chancel. Parish business and any request for appointment to higher positions was required to be discussed with Stuttgart. The king controlled the Catholic educational apparatus.

From 1806 until 1816 all ecclesiastical affairs in Württemberg were conducted by the Royal Catholic Church Office in Stuttgart whose directors were the Protestant aristocrats Joseph von Camerer and Rudolf von Soden. The Ministry of the Interior and of School and Church Affairs was in charge of the parishes from 1817 to 1848. The chiefs of that department were also Protestants, C. F. von Schmidlin, S. E. von Kapff, Johannes von Schlayer, and Eduard von Schmidlin. These officers enacted many liturgical regulations. There could be no more than one celebration of the eucharist on work days. Each parish was allowed a single spiritual confraternity which could celebrate one feast day annually. The keeping of the feast of St. Joseph and the Assumption was prohibited. Pilgrimages were placed under police surveillance. Curates were required to report the names of all penitents to the central ministry.

Secular unsettlement continued when King Friedrich suppressed all guilds and other traditional forms of association in the name of bureaucratic uniformity. After 1803 villages were allowed only limited authority in the administration of communal property and in 1808 the country nobility were stripped of their historic prerogatives when the remaining vestiges of the feudal system were abolished. Public meadows were fenced off to prevent grazing. The right of the citizen to take wood from the public forests was suspended. In 1811 Stuttgart began to appoint its own rulers of cities and towns and discontinued the Bürgerausschüsse, citizens' assemblies. The Oberamtmann, a royal agent, began to sell all the common lands. Trusts and funds established before the Reformation for the general needs of the citizens of the free cities were taken over by the king.

In 1817, while Möhler was a student at Tübingen, a movement began for the re-establishment of old secular communal rights. The Bürgerfreunde, who lived mostly in the towns, appealed to the peasants to work with them for a new constitution which would grant more freedom and rights to the citizens. Der Volksfreund aus Schwaben was circulated to counteract the influence of the Stuttgart government in local elections. At Tübingen the Bürgerfreunder published this petition calling for a return to the rights of the communes:

> There exists in our time a spirit which parades under the appearance of wanting to preserve order, but actually destroys order.
> This spirit recognizes no more pressing concern than the exclusion of citizens from all public affairs and the retention of authority by a few privileged people. There are tyrannical aristocrats who decry the freedom of all citizens as an expression of the Jacobin spirit....Only the true friend...of the people of Württemberg knows that a free citizenry is the most solid support of the monarchy because they have the same interest: the prevention of devastating chaos. He knows that a free citizenry destroys the pressing and enervating chains of a bureaucratic aristocracy and raises the strength of the country to unimagined levels.[14]

---

[14]Rubenstein, op. cit., pp. 332-333.

By 1819 the king granted a constitution which provided for Estates to meet annually and to control finances. The legislature, however, had no voice in ecclesiastical spending. Church affairs were directed entirely from the Palace. The monarch attempted to eliminate any possibility that the Catholic Church might emerge as an independent political force. Protestant delegates dominated the legislative assemblies, although a majority of the nobility of the new Württemberg were Catholic.

-2-

Württemberg was beset by disunity and disarray in religious, political, and economic life. In the churches, disintegration was advanced by the destruction of the ecclesiastical configuration of the Holy Roman Empire, the hierarchy's inability to adjust to different economic and political circumstances, and the inroads of secular polities. Disharmony was not confined to Württemberg. Many Germans observed a connection between the unaccustomed multiplicity which had unmasked alienation and the post-Napoleonic predicament. There was a new sense that an absence of common feeling and excessive subjectivity were the seeds of social dissolution. Paradoxically, in the city, a place of collectivity, the absence of community was most apparent. Engels wrote in the 1840's:

> The very turmoil of the streets has something repulsive, something against which human nature rebels. The hundreds of thousands of all classes and all ranks crowding past each other, are they not all human beings...they crowd by one another as though they had nothing in common, nothing to do with one another....The brutal indifference, the unfeeling isolation of each in his private interest becomes the more repellent and offensive, the more these individuals are crowded together within a limited space....this isolation of the individual, this narrow self-seeking is the fundamental principle of our society everywhere....The dissolution of mankind into monads, of which each one has a separate principle, the world of atoms, is here carried out to its utmost extreme.[15]

----
[15]Raymond Williams, Country and the City (New York, 1973), pp. 214-215.

Until the 1840's in Germany such cultural criticism was usually united with a denigration of rationalism, for the Aufklärung was understood to have originated pernicious individualism. The Germans took up the theme of Gemeinschaft and Gesellschaft once again, organic community and individualistic society. Gesellschaft, with its weaker social bond, was linked to alienation. That notion is in Savigny and Puchta, and in the 1840's Lorenz von Stein at Kiel wrote in Der Socialismus und Communismus des heutigen Frankreichs that unless unity were restored to society by the channeling of communalism through appropriate social reforms, there would be a complete destruction of the civil order. Ferdinand Tonnies discovered an evolution of mankind from primitive communism to individualism and predicted a re-emergent unity if organic communities of blood, place, and kinship were taken seriously once again. Hegel found a restoration of unity in the state, for to him it was the supreme form of human association. It was God on earth, the divine substance, the highest form of objectification of Geist.

Ludwig Feuerbach progressed from Hegel to a conception of unity established in the emancipation of the human from religion. Alienation arises, according to Feuerbach, because religious man and his spokesman the theologian are self-centered. They are concerned only with the self in the form of a divine alter ego. Not an illusory God but other human beings are the basis of unity: "The being of man is given only in communion, in the unity of man with man, a unity resting on the reality of the distinction between I and thou...."[16]

This is the opposite of Johann Adam Möhler's answer to social disunity. Feuerbach and the young Hegelians described religion as the destroyer of community. Möhler said that the church produced it. He apologized for institutions, for to him they were the only architects of social cohesion. Above all, contemporary multiplicity could be cured by the church, but only if the church itself possessed true

---

[16]Robert Tucker, Philosophy and Myth in Karl Marx (Cambridge, 1967), p. 91.

unity. The hierarchical/territorial ecclesiological principle of the Holy Roman Empire had failed to account for unity. The religious theories of the Enlightenment did not unite men. Möhler looked to the past and found the Christian age of the Fathers. Then there was unity. Around him there was atomization. Then spiritual authority dispensed solicitous paternalism. Now it fostered compulsory exploitation. Then there were sympathetic relationships among kinsfolk and old acquaintances. Now there were strangers and aliens everywhere. Now the attitude of the businessman prevailed. Then men's simple needs were met by home production and barter. Now cold calculation was applied which deprived work of the personality of one's fellow man.

To Möhler, the unity in the church which was the source of its stability transcended the hierarchy. Its ground was not the clergy or the state but the communal life of believers. The essence of the church then and now, therefore, should be the people. The alienation of material existence could be once more overcome within the communal life of the Christian totality. Alienation, Möhler found, was born in a civilization of matter without spirit. Collective life was the only medium through which spirit could break into the world. Even classes are dissolved in the church, if it is truly an absorbing collectivity.

Like many other German contemporaries Möhler found freedom and spirituality only in the imposition of external bonds. He wrote that the individual controlled by the will of the community was freed from personal aberration and made healthy and normal. A social body is thus necessary for the survival of civilization and the Catholic Church alone can be that body. This is because the church is the single institution which possesses spirit, and spirit is the necessary requirement for community, for it is the agency of the transcendence of the ego.

Spirit is present in the church because it is the continuation of the incarnation, and the incarnation is the sole means for the intrusion of the spiritual into the material world. Möhler's definition of the church as a corporate unity with a mystical spirit, rather than as a legal entity, is based on the incarnation. The people themselves are the body of Christ, participators in divinity. That is why their collective life is the point of the obtrusion of spirit. The goal of the incarnation, uniting matter and spirit, is carried out in the assembly of Christians.

This abstract view of the church was grounded in the social reality of the Württemberg parishes by Möhler's theory of the sacraments. The eucharist is also an extension of the incarnation which transmits the unifying agency of the church into society. Physical aspects of religion and worship are essential, for they are the media which engraft men into the ecclesiastical community. A defense of forms and rites emerges in Möhler's works, but of those forms which are the exteriorization of the religious experience of the community, not of individual devotion. Social unity, he counseled, can only be built around such communal symbolic forms.

But Möhler's contemporary co-religionists in Württemberg first tried to repair the disaster of secularization by continuing the destruction of just those communal symbols. The spiritual as opposed to the temporal direction of the churches of Württemberg was once again divided between the north and the south, for there was no real diocese per se in the new country after secularization. The non-Schwabian districts fell under the ministrations of the newly created General Vicariate of Ellwangen and were supervised by the figurehead bishop Johann Baptist von Keller. He was consecrated titular bishop of Evara by Pius VII so that episcopal functions could be duly performed, but the actual leadership came from the spiritual advisors to the Catholic Church Office at Stuttgart, a corps of enlightened former monks, the Premonstratensian Mercy, the Cistercian Mayr, Frey, who had been at the Capuchin cloister at Biberach, the Dominican Neeb, and Jakob Danzer, once a Benedictine of Isny.

At the head stood Maria von Werkmeister who left the Benedictines at Neresheim to become court preacher at Stuttgart in 1784. While a member of the Catholic Church Office from 1807 to 1823, he adapted the liturgy to the needs of the new churches of Württemberg. Kantian notions are present in his directives and pamphlets, which contained sentiments such as "morality is the main subject of the Bible. Dogma makes up a trifling part of its contents."[17] He ordered that worship in the parishes be altered so as to make it more an occasion for ethical instruction that would "commend practical Christianity."[18] To accomplish this, pilgrimages, processions, folk devotions, the cult of the saints and the rosary ("an absurd, frivolous, and mechanical prayer") were denounced by Werkmeister and suspended along with brotherhoods and novenas.[19]

Werkmeister was assisted by the second Catholic figure of Stuttgart, Beda Pracher. He also had left the Benedictine Abbey of Neresheim. His Der Katholische Gottesdienst oder vollstandiges Gebetbuch was prefaced with the suggestion that the churches would have to be purified of mechanical and non-rational ceremonies if Christians were to adapt to modern times. "I and you and a thousand others with us no longer believe in the activities of witches and devils which our liturgy presumes to present to us. How can we thus give up our Hokus Pokus?"[20] Pracher's Neue Liturgie des Pfarrers provided a liturgical solution to the dilemma for the curates of the neighborhood. This guide directed that there be only one parish church service each week with no vestments, altar candles, Latin, or Gregorian chant. Neue Liturgie advocated the abandonment of the complications of the liturgical year. In 1806 Pracher published Entwurf eines neuen Rituale at Tübingen. In it the blessing of baptismal water and benediction were eliminated. The sacramental importance of confirmation was lessened by the suggestion that it not be performed by the bishop but by the local priest. To Pracher confirmation symbolized the completion of the religious education of young people.

----

[17]Waldemar Trapp, Vorgeschichte und Ursprung der liturgischen Bewegung (Regensburg, 1940), p. 44.

[18]Ibid., p. 47.

[19]Ibid., p. 48.

[20]Ibid., p. 60.

The former imperial lands of South Schwabia were shepherded by a Vicar General who was suffragan to the bishop of Constance, Freiherr Ignaz Heinrich von Wessenberg. He carried out reforms similar to those of Stuttgart. They were, if anything, more all-encompassing and part of a general plan of a second Reformation which was to attune the church to modern civilization. Wessenberg came down to Württemberg from Dresden, where he had been born in 1774, after being educated under the influence of Kant and the theologians who had surrounded the court of Joseph II.[21] From 1802 until 1819 he attempted to overcome the low state of religion in his parishes which had suffered a variety of devastation. He relied on the enlightened theories of his education and a strong party of parish priests to accomplish this task. Wessenberg created a corps to teach rationalized Catholicism to students in a Seminar for Pastoral Theology at the diocesan seminary of Meersburg and by holding conferences for older pastors for the discussion of parochial problems and remedies, beginning in 1803. The results of these meetings and Wessenberg's theories, practical suggestions, and pastoral directives were published in the quarterly Archiv für die Pastoralkonferenzen in den Landkapiteln des Bistums Konstanz, which appeared after 1804, and the monthly Geistlichen Monatsschrift.

In these fora Wessenberg professed a Christianity which was the organized form of the most moral way of life possible, whose mission was the propagation of brotherly love for the improvement of daily life. He wrote, "Religion is for man, not man for religion....(and) ....the whole goal of Christianity is love."[22] Wessenberg's version of renewal was to be the work of pastoral priests, not dogmatic theologians. Its goal was to have the parish church become the center of the educational and moral betterment of Christian people. The emphasis of the reform was placed upon preaching and moral instruction

---

[21]J. B. Hafen, Möhler und Wessenberg (Ulm, 1842), pp. 5, 23.

[22]Hagen, op. cit., I, 31; Hafen, op. cit., p. 21.

on Sunday afternoon and in the school. "Spiritually mechanical" liturgical forms of piety, the breviary for example, were shown to be devoid of moral value and priests were urged to give them up. To Wessenberg the function of liturgy was quite secondary.

He said that an emphasis upon liturgical ceremonies distorted the moral import of Christianity for "the sensual man is perpetually inclined to over-value the worth of forms, which are prone to get mixed up, unobserved, with the true Spirit....The more outer, blindly performed liturgical work, the less inner Christianity."[23] Towns in Württemberg like Haigerloch where remnants of the communal forms of piety were still practiced were made fun of: "So many confessions, communions, pilgrimages, and devotional exercises which bear no fruit at all in the heart, in religious education,or in morals."[24] He advised that all customs be dropped which prevented worship "in spirit and in truth."[25]

The Vicar General taught in the Archiv and in his Die grossen Kirchenversammlungen des XV und XVI Jahrhunderten in Beziehung auf Kirchenverbesserung, in four volumes, that the parochial clergy should look to the most primitive practices of the Christian church for a model of improvement. The first century A.D. was the golden age and all that had happened since, particularly the "darkness and slavery" of the Middle Ages, should be forgotten. Wessenberg turned to the individual bishops and the state, not to the Papacy, for the sanctioning of his new Reformation. He hated Roman institutions. "Rome," he wrote, "has through tricks and artifices, through unChristian methods of all kinds subjected the church to a domination, the like of which should not be found in this world....Here is Germany—there is Rome, here is freedom—there is servitude, here is truth—there is falsehood, here is law—there is lawlessness, here is Christian love—there is the

---

[23]Trapp, op cit., p. 140.

[24]Erwin Keller, "Die Konstanzer Liturgiereform unter Ignaz Heinrich von Wessenberg," Freiburger Diözesan-Archiv, 85 (1965), p. 40.

[25]Ibid., p. 48.

love of hunting heretics."[26] No rituals, liturgies, catechisms, or forms of music which had their origin in the curia at Rome should be admitted into the dioceses: "The determination of the liturgy belongs by right to the bishop as chief shepherd of the diocese."[27]

Yet Wessenberg made so many concessions to the control of the church by the state that he spoke of the parish priest as if he were an officer of the secular power. He defined the Christian community as "the reverend Catholic parish office...the royal parish office."[28] He advised that his priests obey every new law which came out of Stuttgart, even those which required that Catholic priests bless the mixed marriages of Romanists with Protestants. This presented no obstacle to Wessenberg and his party who regarded the Lutherans and Calvinists as adherents to another, equally valid, variety of the Christian faith. The Vicar General advocated frequent contacts between the two communions.[29] There was no such friendly regard for Catholic monks, however, for Wessenberg worked for the complete abolition of monasticism and against any restoration of the Jesuits. Such communities made no practical contribution to the world. "Monasticism," he wrote, "has lost the power to make an impact on society in our time, a society which has been affected by the light of knowledge, the extension of freedom, and the expansion of industry...."[30]

Since Wessenberg regarded the local hierarchy as the authority for renewal, he soon began to order his own theories into practice. In 1803 the gospel was required to be read in German, for Latin, it was felt, hindered the educational benefit of worship. He announced the following rule in that year: "In the future all processions which take

---

[26]Hafen, op cit., p. 32; Hagen, op. cit., I, 99.

[27]Keller, loc. cit., p. 73.

[28]Hafen, op. cit., p. 45.

[29]Ibid., pp. 69, 75.

[30]Ibid., p. 55.

place on the high feast days of the year, on Corpus Christi and its octave, on the feast day of Saint Mark, and during the Rogation days shall take place inside the Church."[31] He refused to allow banners and statues to be carried in those processions. In 1804 the Catholic people of southern Württemberg were forbidden to frequent any monastic chapels. All processions of brotherhoods and confraternities were banned in 1807, and after 1808 no child was admitted to communion until his education had been completed. Wessenberg's Hymnen für den Katholischen Gottesdienst eliminated Gregorian chants. On March 16, 1809, a "General Order for Church Services" encouraged more preaching, banned all brotherhoods except "the brotherhood of the love of God," and forbade pilgrimages to shrines. In 1810 Wessenberg discouraged confirmation by a bishop, and he reformed baptism by eliminating exorcisms and requiring that, in order to safeguard the health of the baby, the baptismal waters be warmed.

Württemberg priests began to utter similar sentiments. Ludwig Busch averred that "Religion here is really for men....Should not the outer garment of religion be adjusted to the advancement of mankind and its form made to fit the contemporary age?"[32] August Rugel in preaching against the "nuisance of mechanical prayer" said, "What is a better cure for mankind than moral improvement?"[33] Karl Wachter of Sulmingen asked, "How shall the liturgy of the Christian-Catholic Church be conditioned so that it can be grounded in reason and the scriptures?"[34] Others repeated, "We preach without discrepancy against the mechanical prayers which are no more than the movements of the lips, against... church ceremonies, the way of the cross, pilgrimages,...and brotherhoods."[35]

----

[31]Keller, loc. cit., p. 291.

[32]Ibid., p. 29.

[33]Ibid., pp. 192, 197.

[34]Ibid., p. 67.

[35]Ibid., p. 90.

The common people as well as the clerical leaders were faced with new conditions. In the southwest the churches had been centers of the traditional, communal elements of their life. In the early eighteenth century, after a period of war and plague, powerful spiritual confraternities grew up which enrolled many parishioners and controlled large sums of money. Many elements of Catholicism which Kant argued most forcefully against were strong in these societies. There was an elaborate and colorful liturgical cycle associated with the confraternities which maintained intimate connection with agriculture, daily life, and death through extended processions, pilgrimages, and recitation of the divine office.

Whether it was because of the directives of secular and ecclesiastical leaders or because of economic forces beyond the control of the parishioners, the communal spirituality began to disappear slowly as the eighteenth century advanced. An all-pervasive cult of death, which led to the foundation of numerous private masses said alone by the priest and the retention of messners who performed religious ceremonial only for the benefit of the dead, tended to break down the old forms. Religious orders became increasingly enclosed. Baroque architecture, widely adopted in the middle of the eighteenth century, separated worshippers by class with galleries and high box-pews and a concentration of architectural splendor upon the clerical office. New churches and monastic walls came after the population increased and agricultural prices went up. The priest's income rose too, and he soon was more of a middle class man, the product of the university who took his duty as official of the state and educator more seriously than his role as a man of the people. A gulf of class and religious conception began to separate priest and people, symbolized often by the erection of a new priest's house fitted out as a bureaucratic compound.

The stories of a handful of churches from representative regions of Württemberg show that change was accompanied by a decline in religious life, and the reforms of the Wessenbergians and Werkmeister did nothing to check this growing weakness. In many places ordinary people resisted the elimination of their communal religious rights as they had protested the destruction of common ownership in the secular sector. They kept on making pilgrimages, processing, reciting the offices, and attending mass, and when their church was transformed, they turned away. For a moment the parishioners of the small churches made a stand against the Enlightenment, even while there was no organized resistance to change.

In city churches like Saint Martin's in Rottenburg, with 2,500 people in the parish, under the influence of state legislation and Aufklärung liturgical directives vespers had become the only remnant of the divine office ever prayed publicly by the laity in church, and the population had acquiesced in the elimination of most corporate procession and other communal religious exercises. At Saint Martin's "All Latin choral singing ceased," and "the fulfilling of professional duties counts as going to church on work days."[36]

In contrast there were villages like Saulgau in 1804 and Mülheim in 1803, where there were momentary revolts against the discontinuation of the Rogation processions. The village of Moosheim just north of Lake Constance continued these practices in the 1820's though they had been forbidden by the government of Württemberg in 1817: Confraternities processed as a body on the first Sundays of the month, on feasts of Peter, Paul, and the Virgin Mary, on the Ascension, and the last Sunday of the liturgical year.[37] In the neighboring parish at Friedberg the community refused to discontinue its corporate processions which went out into the fields on ten days of the year. The community processions on Saint Mark's day and the Feast of the Holy Cross lasted six hours because the assembly passed through the fields of each

---

[36]MSS B74, 75 Verkündbuch, 1820-1840; MS directives from Catholic Church Office to parishes, 7/14/1807, 28/6/1808, 2/8/1808, Domarchiv, Rottenburg; MS B74 Verkündbuch, 1819, Domarchiv, Rottenburg; MS B98 Predigtbuch, 1820, 1823, Domarchiv, Rottenburg.

[37]MS Pfarrchronik Moosheim, MS Geschichte der Pfarrei Moosheim, Parish Archive, Moosheim; MS Z 7a Dekanat: Saulgau – Pfarr – Visitation – Moosheim – 1818, MS Z 7a Dekanat: Saulgau – Pfarr – Visitation – Moosheim – 1824, 1825, Diocesan Archive, Rottenburg.

parishioner. The Saint Vitus procession for protection against disease included a public parade of sacred pictures and relics. After each procession the community prayed vespers. To this office on the Epiphany the villagers brought the salt used during the year to be blessed. At the Purification and on Saint Blasius' day candles were consecrated. Seeds for summer planting were hallowed on the Annunciation, and the bullets of hunters were blessed on the feasts of Saint John and Saint Paul. Matins, in addition to vespers, was prayed by the community during Holy Week and during the octaves of Christmas, Pentecost, and All Saints. In October the entire parish went together on a pilgrimage to a miraculous chapel at Saulgau.[38]

Gattnau is a tiny village which contains a richly decorated Baroque church. In the nineteenth century it served a large number of rural folk who farmed the countryside on the shores of Lake Constance at the southernmost tip of Württemberg. For many generations there had been two confraternities in the parish. One, "For the Attainment of a Good Death," existed to insure that members of the community were at an individual's side when death came. Cornell Münch was pastor at Gattnau for the first decades of the nineteenth century. Münch was a typical Wessenbergian of the diocese of Constance who was more interested in his pfarramt, that is, the state, educational, and financial duties that went with his appointment, than in the traditional liturgical life of his people. In 1815 he abolished "For the Attainment of a Good Death," and soon after he began a campaign to halt the Rogation processions. But the people of Gattnau refused, and in 1824 Cornell Münch had to report to his bishop that "the Rogation processions are still being participated in because of outside influences."[39]

---

[38]MS Aus der Pfarr - Registratur in Friedberg, Kirchen-Kalendar, MS Verzeichnis der wichtigstem...Verkündigungen die Pfarrei Friedberg, Parish Archive, Friedberg; MS Z 7a Dekanat: Saulgau - Pfarr - Visitationen - Friedberg - 1818, Diocesan Archive, Rottenburg.

[39]MS Z 7a Dekanat: Tettnang - Pfarrvisitationen - Gattnau - 1823, 1824, Diocesan Archive, Rottenberg; J. B. Hafen, Gattnauer Chronik oder der Pfarrbezirk Gattnau (Lindau, 1854).

People of Saulgau, Mülheim, Friedberg, Moosheim, and Gattnau were raw material for a party. It was for these men and women that Möhler provided a theology which integrated their longing for the retention of corporate liturgical forms with elements of reform and renewal. For such parishes Möhler became a party symbol as well as a theologian.

Möhler himself was first formed in the highly conservative liturgical tradition of two parishes which were noted for their spiritual attainments and in which the church was the dominant institution, the real center of everyday life. When Möhler was born at Igersheim in 1796 that town of one thousand residents was still under the influence of what had once been the elaborate worship of the episcopal city of Würzburg, twenty miles away. His family was pious and large. They all lived in the inn which his father owned and where he did the baking for Igersheim. Like Beethoven, Johann Adam was forced to spend his childhood working in an inn. Antonin Möhler, unlike Beethoven's father, was so fanatically Catholic that he avoided sending his son to school until he was eleven.

The young Johann must have been struck by the contrast between life in the inn and the rich services in Igersheim Church, for he remembered as late as 1832 the great attraction the edifices of the Würzburg district held for him.[40] There, where the secular power had been so weak, the church was the greatest institution which one could behold. The most impressive architectural monuments were all ecclesiastical. The old Gothic church of Igersheim was still the scene of processions every feast day and during the period of Rogation and Corpus Christi. The office of vespers was said daily in the evening, matins in the morning on some feast days, and there were two masses on Sunday and one daily. A holy aura hung about the place. In 1825 an episcopal visitor noted the marked spirituality of Igersheim when

---

[40]Stefan Lösch, Prof. Dr. Adam Gengler 1799-1866. Die Beziehungen des Bamberger Theologen zu J. J. I. Döllinger und J. A. Möhler (Würzburg, 1963), p. 290.

compared to neighboring parishes. An 1828 report referred to it as "a religious town—a godly spirit dwells there." "The religiosity of the public church services" was observed in 1837, and an opinion of 1842 was that "Igersheim is made up of a completely moral, hardworking religious population."[41]

The impression of Igersheim was reinforced by Mergentheim, one of the chief ecclesiastical centers of the German southwest with a population of 2,300 and a parish church important enough to baptize an average of 69 children each year.[42] Mergentheim had been a strong center of communal institutions. The Teutonic Knights made the ninth-century Romanesque church their seat at the Reformation. Capuchins founded a large monastery and church in 1641. Lay brotherhoods continued to be numerous and active. "The Rosary" had 1,291 members in 1795.[43] "Corpus Christi" and "Christian Death" recited offices on Sunday afternoons.[44] Möhler came to Mergentheim for school because his uncle Philipp Messner was attached to the Teutonic Knights there. Johann Adam walked to Mergentheim every day for four years. There he witnessed what had once been the common liturgical cycle of the Catholic southwest containing remnants of a communal element. Before every feast solemn vespers were sung with lights and incense. Even minor holidays like the Circumcision were celebrated with festival services, and there were daily high masses with music. Severe fasts were enjoined upon all in Lent. There were two special services on Ash

---

[41]MS Bo - KapA Dekanat: Mergentheim - Pfarrvisitationen - Igersheim, 1825, 1828, p. 7, 1837, p. 176, 1842, pp. 60-62; Diocesan Archive, Rottenburg; "Igersheim ad S. Michael Archangel," "Rottweil," "Reidlingen," "Tettnang," "Waldsee," "Rottenburg," "Saulgau," "Mertgentheim," in S. J. Neher, Statistischer Personal - Katalog des Bistums Rottenburg (Schw. Gmünd, 1878).

[42]MS Pfarrchronik, p. 116; MS Taufregister, 1808-1830, Parish Archive, Mergentheim.

[43]"Rosenkranz Bruderschaft, 1795" (printed broadside with list of 1,291 names from four Mergentheim quarters), Parish Archive, Mergentheim.

[44]MS Verkündigungbuch, 1825-1836, Parish Archive, Mergentheim.

Wednesday and offices and processions on Maundy Thursday and Good Friday. The Miserere was sung every day in Lent. Corporate processions went down the road to Igersheim on All Saints' Day, St. Mark's Day, the Rogation days, and at Corpus Christi.[45] The general opinion was that the state of religion was "generally good."[46]

Möhler went from Mergentheim to the Lyzeum in Ellwangen which was penetrated by the Enlightenment. He set out, at the age of seventeen, to become a priest and took up the two-year philosophy course there. He was shocked, for, as one contemporary remembered, "the spirit which dominated there was not very theological and even less religious."[47] The professors taught out of manuals which were "completely rationalistic."[48] The inns were filled with drunken theological students. At the carnival they held a masked ball. A professor who spoke out against this laxity was boycotted. The majority of pupils went to communion once every other three months. Möhler was so unhappy at Ellwangen that he wanted to become a lawyer, but his father would not allow it. "If you do not like to be a priest," he wrote his son, "you may return to my inn and work there. So many good young men have lost their ancestral faith studying secular subjects that I will not take the responsibility for losing my son's soul."[49]

The son stayed on in Ellwangen and continued in philosophy and theology. A new Catholic faculty of higher learning had just opened in the city. It was at once more reverent toward past Roman thought and practice, yet open to anti-Aufklärung winds sweeping down from the

----

[45]Idem.

[46]MS BO KaPA – Visitationen – Mergentheim – 1830-31 (Abschnitt IV), 1828 (Abschnitt IV), Diocesan Archive, Rottenburg.

[47]Balthaser Wörner, Johann Adam Möhler. Ein Lebensbild (Regensburg, 1966), p. 5.

[48]Alois Knöpfler, Johann Adam Möhler. Ein Gedenkblatt zu dessen hundertstem Geburtstag (Munich, 1896), p. 13.

[49]Serge Bolschakoff, The Doctrine of the Unity of the Church in the Works of Khomyakov and Möhler (London, 1946), p. 218.

north. Of the five new university professors in town Möhler chose the most Romantic and traditional as his own, Johann Sebastian Drey.

This Ellwangen faculty was not connected to any former centers of Catholic thought, for it was founded to continue the Stuttgart policy that "the church should be a tool of the state."[50] In negotiating a concordat between the Holy See and the new Württemberg the nuncio Mgr. Della Genga urged the government to provide two dioceses for its Catholics. Recalling the Febronian bishops and seeking to continue the weakened state of the Roman Church in Württemberg, King Friedrich compromised in 1807 by establishing one bishop and five chairs in theology for the region. Following the ancient Württemberg policy of filling up old possessions before building anew, the king suggested that his decrepit castle at Tübingen be used by the theologians. The nuncio objected. A shadow would fall on "faith and morals" if the Catholic faculty were located in a Protestant city.[51] The Catholic Church Office, knowing the rationalistic character of Ellwangen, wanted to found the new Catholic university there. There being an empty set of five-hundred-year-old seminary buildings in Ellwangen, the king agreed to that site for a Katholische Landes-Universität in 1813.

It was actually nothing more than an academy, but King Friedrich was given to the typical Schwabian characteristic of exaggeration. To him these five professors were the Catholic University of Württemberg, just as he had appointed an admiral for his Lake Constance navy. However, to the Roman Catholic Church this was no complete university. So in 1817, when it became clear that the king's financial difficulties at the end of the Napoleonic wars would prevent any proper expansion, the decision was made to create a Catholic theological faculty in the University of Tübingen, by simply moving the five Ellwangen professors down to that ancient university town on the Neckar thirty miles from Stuttgart. The shift of location from enlightened Ellwangen was

---

[50]Rudolf Reinhardt, "Im Zeichen der Tübingen Schüle," Attempto, 25-26 (1968), 41.

[51]Idem.

The move to Tübingen was also significant because important Roman Catholic thinking would occur in a Protestant center. The famous Evangelical Stift of Tübingen had been in the vanguard of the revolt against Kant. Hegel and Schelling had been students there, and the town itself was becoming a center of Romantic poetry, with Hölderlin and Uhland as moderators. The merger of Ellwangen and Tübingen occurred in an atmosphere of revived and self-confident Protestantism arising from the festivities surrounding the Tercentenary of the Reformation and a new purposeful apologetic which applied recent developments in philosophy to a defense of Evangelical theology. The Protestant Tübingen School also created a synthesis of history and speculative theology, the technical tools of criticism of Aufklärung, with the epistemology of Die Romantik, and the leader of that effort, F. C. Baur, was an exact contemporary of Möhler.

There was intimate contact at first between the Protestant and Catholic Tübingen faculties. The Organic Statute of the Catholic faculty drawn up in 1818 insured the same rights and duties for Catholic teachers as for their Protestant colleagues and a voice in the senate in the election of the university rector. Catholic students could attend courses in the law and philosophy faculties. In Ellwangen the students had lived in inns and houses, but this could not be allowed in Protestant Tübingen, so the king bought a former Collegium illustre, which had been an academy for noblemen, and gave it to the Romanists. This became the Wilhelmstift.

Möhler said that in Tübingen the usual Catholic mediocrity was avoided because "the small isolated school [was set] in a new intellectual milieu [with] exterior stimulants."[52] The chief stimulant can be labelled accurately in the German context as Romanticism. In the religious field Romantics sought to escape the various dualisms of the Enlightenment, to unite mind and heart. Herder, who died in 1803 and was therefore too old to have been a member of the generation of

---

[52]Edmond Vermeil, Jean-Adam Möhler et l'École Catholique de Tubinque (1815-1840) (Paris, 1913), p. 6. This is a quote from Möhler's article in ThQ (1826), 82.

the high Romantics, tried to refute Kant by demonstrating that God is known through feelings rather than through reason alone. Far from having to do only with morality, he said that religion is the symbolic representation of emotional life. F. H. Jacobi, a student of Kant who died in 1819, ventured to redefine what Kant had meant by knowledge and knowing. He thereby opened the way for a philosophically justified faith. Jacobi outlined his Glaubensphilosophie most completely in an 1811 work, Von den göttlichen Dingen. Here, as in Fichte and Schelling, there is a blurring of the distinctions which had been made between the phenomenal and noumenal world. The faculty of imagination is shown to be a guide to eternal, noumenal realities. Experience is portrayed as leading to a realm inaccessible to reason, and faith is argued to be founded on religious experience. Religion has become in Jacobi a matter of feeling.

In Fichte and Schelling there was admission that in the immediacy of experience and intuition the way was open to absolute knowledge. Yet, as the Englishman Pusey observed, the transition from Kant to Jacobi, Fichte, and Schelling was an evolution without a complete break:

> ...It [Kant's moral foundation of religion] led many, who were not bound by the fetters of the new philosophy, to listen to the voice of nature, the revelation of God within them, and to seek as the direct result of consciousness the truths which speculation was unable scientifically to justify.[53]

Some of these men turned to mankind as a whole rather than to individuals for an accounting of knowledge, morality, and art. There was a rediscovery of the social basis of existence. The idea was developed in Schelling's philosophy that the individual ego does not exist in isolation, but that it is a particular in a larger world soul

---

[53]E. B. Pusey, An Historical Enquiry into the Probable Causes of the Rationalist Character Lately Predominant in the Theology of Germany (London, 1828), p. 164. For a recent review of the religious dimension of this period of German intellectual history with bibliography see J. Heywood Thomas, "Fichte and Schelling," in Ninian Smart et al., Nineteenth Century Religious Thought in the West, Volume I (Cambridge, 1985), pp. 41-79.

which unites all being into one unity, which is a part of the larger divine Oneness. Religion, in this system, is the product of the human organism as a whole, an organism which is not static but evolving. God is revealed in this evolution produced by historical experience transforming the form of human life. In Über des Wesen der menschlichen Freiheit of 1809, Schelling presents a cosmology in which God, rather than being disassociated from the human as in the Aufklärung view, is intimately associated with the evolution of humankind. Men and women are united with one another in the organic association of nature which is one with God.

Various concrete representations of the objective whole of humanity were sought after to overcome the subjectivism which some Romantics linked to alienation. In his Makroanthropos, Novalis wrote that "all men form in reality only one man," and that is the message of the greatest musical embodiment of German Romanticism, the fourth movement of Beethoven's Ninth Symphony.[54] The foundation of such a unity was the common people. The forms of art and life of ordinary folk were given new value, because they were said to reflect Gemeingeist, the spirit of a united humanity. The concept of life itself was approved, particularly as it was embodied in certain universal institutions which bound men together into the great unities.

There was soon a rediscovery of Kirche by secular Germans. Novalis' essay "Die Christenheit oder Europa" was an influential example of new secular praise for the church because it had provided a unified cultural basis for European culture in the Middle Ages. Similar sympathy for the cosmopolitan, universal, and authoritative character of the Christian body began to appear in the works of Zacharias Werner, Clemens Brentano, Count Friedrich Leopold von Stolberg, and the Schlegel brothers. Schelling became interested in the church because it appeared to be a historic unity always expressing itself in new forms, yet forever maintaining its essential intellectual content unchanged. His statements in Vorlesungen über die Methode des

----

[54]Josef Rupert Geiselmann, Lebendiger Glaube aus geheiligter Überlieferung (Mainz, 1942), p. 367.

akademischen Studiums that "Christianity is in its inner spirit and its highest sense historic," that is, that as an institution it is continually evolving, had a great influence on the new Tübingen Catholic faculty.[55]

These Romantic sentiments entered the Catholic world first at Münster, a suffragan see of Cologne, in the circle of Princess Gallitzin who was a close friend of Jacobi. A series of conversions to both Catholicism and Romanticism took place in her salon. One convert was Stolberg. Another was Friedrich Schlegel who turned to the Roman Church because only there could he realize the bond of religion and culture which was necessary for the restoration of unity. At the same time, the language of the Münster Romantics remained liturgically individualistic. Dorothea Schlegel is remembered for writing about religious experiences in her own room in this way: "I am alone in my chamber feeling in the same devotional spirit as in the church."[56]

The corporate nature of Catholicism came more into the open in Bavaria. Franz Baader, who had connections at Münster, brought Romanticism down to Munich. He portrayed the church as an ideal, living organism which could overcome the problems of the age if "the belief of the Church is not dead, rigid letters, but living real spirit."[57] Yet the Bavarian Romantic who made the strongest impression on Möhler's teacher Drey was Johann Michael Sailer. Sailer brought a new emotional piety to the Catholic southwest by emphasizing the forms of religious life of ordinary people and re-interpreting the church as a center of a way of life, not as a legal institution.

Sailer was born in Upper Bavaria in the middle of the eighteenth century and joined the Jesuits in 1770. He became a secular priest in 1799 and taught pastoral theology at the University of Landshut, which

---

[55]Ibid., p. 120, Thomas F. O'Meara, Romantic Idealism and Roman Catholicism (Notre Dame,1982).

[56]Trapp, op. cit., p. 100.

[57]Karl Adam, "Die Katholische Tübinger Schüle zur 450 - Jahrfeier der Universität Tübingen," Hochland 24, II (1927), 591.

was moved to Munich by Ludwig I. As a theologian Sailer turned against the scholastic method of his teacher Benedikt Stattler. He read Lessing, Jacobi, Mendelssohn, Kant, and Herder. The first indication of the new direction of his thinking appeared in his Vollständiges Lese- und Betbuch zum Gebrauch der Katholiken. Catholicizing Jacobi, he enunciated there a Verkündigungs Theologie (theology of experience) which maintained that in the post-revolutionary secular world of German Catholicism the only foundation of the church could be the religious experience of the individual. Faith here is the experience of noumenal reality in which imagination, a faculty of the mind higher than reason, leads the individual to knowledge of ultimate truth. God breaks in upon the imagination in the midst of religious experience, a process which Sailer described in biblical terms:

> How should I discover a living faith in the living Christ (in the Scriptures) if the Spirit of God did not send me a Philip to sit with me in the carriage and interpret Isaiah and show me the lamb that was offered for me?[58]

By Philip, the missionary who would guide the mind to truth, Sailer meant the heart. Like eighteenth-century pietists in England and Germany, Sailer was arguing for a renewal of Christianity in which inner life would correspond to dogma once again.

It was at this point that Sailer suggested vistas of the church as an organism. He fell more and more under the influence of non-Catholic German Romantics. "The influence of the romantic world showed him a deeper understanding of what a body is....The idea of community came in opposition to his concentration on the single individual," wrote Geiselmann.[59] First Sailer uncovered the old doctrine of the church as the invisible community of all Christians who have experienced holiness. "The Church," he said in his first definition, "is the

---

[58]Alexander Dru, The Church in the Nineteenth Century: Germany 1800-1918 (London, 1963), p. 44.

[59]Josef Rupert Geiselmann, Die theologische Anthropologie Johann Adam Möhlers: Ihr geschichtlicher Wandell (Freiburg, 1955), p. 95.

community of the holy ones."[60] When he published his prayerbook, Gebetbuch, he approached a new understanding of the church as a unity of all Christians:

> Those who are struggling and have already finished their struggle, those who are pure and are becoming pure, those who abide in Jesus and yearn after Jesus, those who are struggling and those who have triumphed—all, all are one Body under one Head.[61]

By the time his Pastoraltheologie was published in 1812, he defined the church as a form of life binding men and women on earth. Here it is "the life, the life streaming from Christ, the life penetrating all members, the life uniting them all with the head, uniting them with God."[62] And then in the Moraltheologie of 1818 there is a later definition full of Romanticism and only a few steps from Möhler's ecclesiology:

> The Church of Christ is understood as a spiritual society in connection with Christ. It is the unity, the community of all its living members with God the father through the one Christ in the one spirit of love.[63]

Sailer's communal church does not overcome contemporary alienation, nor is it related to the forms of life of the people. But Sailer opened the way for these developments, for he was the first German Catholic theologian to view the church as a dynamic organism rather than a static hierarchy. He defended the exterior aspects of the church as manifestations of the evolution of the Christian body, in fact as guides to the continuation of God's revelation.[64] Grundlehren

----

[60]Idem.

[61]Idem.

[62]Ibid., p. 96.

[63]Sebastian Merkle, "Möhler," Historischer Jahrbuch der Görres-Gesellschaft 58 (1938), 64.

[64]Josef Rupert Geiselmann, Geist des Christentums und des Katholizismus. Ausgewählte Schriften Katholischen Theologie im Zeitalter des Deutschen Idealismus und der Romantik (Mainz, 1940), p. xl.

der Religion of 1805 said that, "The church is the living tradition,"[65] and solemn public worship is, "in accordance with its original dignity, as it were, a living propagation of religion in the world around and a living transmission of religion to posterity."[66] Sailer argued for the retention of the traditional liturgical practices of the parishes because they provided for more than the intellectual needs of the people. These old traditions of the Christian folk should be retained because "Christianity is a completely irreplaceable religion. By no other means except Christian practices are all the needs of the human family so completely answered."[67]

Drey overcame the lingering subjectivism in Sailer, but at the same time he insured that science and research would continue to have a place in Catholic theology, that it would not dissolve into mere feeling, a direction in which the Bavarian theological movement tended. Drey connected anti-individualism with contemporary social conditions. Perhaps this was because of the variety of experiences which formed him. He was born in 1777, the son of a shepherd who tended sheep near the Württemberg town of Rölingen. Drey was educated like Sailer by the Jesuits and in the same rationalistic schools of Ellwangen which repelled Möhler. While studying theology at Augsburg he discovered Sailer, and this opened the way for Protestant influences. During his spare time while priest at Rölingen after 1801, he read most of the German philosophy which was coming out, from Kant to Schelling. This study resulted in a mastery of contemporary philosophical terminology. Drey favored Schelling over Jacobi, the organic developmentalism of the first idealists rather than the individualistic experientialism of the immediate post-Kantians. Schelling convinced Drey that God's objective revelation was being carried forth in the history of the church. Then

---

[65]MS Joseph Rupert Geiselmann, Die Lehre von der Kirche, unpublished lecture notes, MS GSGf 1930a, Wilhelmstift, Tübingen, p. XVI.

[66]Josef Rupert Geiselmann, The Meaning of Tradition (Freiburg, 1966), p. 18.

[67]Trapp, op. cit., p. 210.

came his new valuing of the role of the people in the church and the addition of scientific historical method to theology which became the hallmark of Tübingen Catholicism.[68]

Drey publicly broke with the non-dynamic mechanical definitions of the Enlightenment in 1812 in "Revision des gegenwartigen Zustandes der Theologie" which appeared in the Wessenbergian Archiv für die Pastoralconferenzen in den Landkapiteln des Bisthums Konstanz. He now defined Christianity as "...a living unbroken whole through the whole of time...the Church is its outer visible organism."[69] Drey separated himself from the Wessenbergians in their own journal, for instead of the customary call for rejection of the status quo in favor of primitive Christian practice, he issued a defense of old habits in the parishes, arguing that they had been the legitimate development of the teaching of Jesus. He said that the reform of Wessenberg was no true renewal but an artificial revival of antiquity which could not assist nineteenth century church people. Wessenberg was revolted when Drey maintained that popular liturgical patterns were related to continuing divine revelation. As a true disciple of Schelling, Drey wrote that the inner core of God's communication to humans was molded into ever changing outer phenomena by the forces of secular history. Therefore he urged that theology and history be studied together:

> So it would be possible and also perhaps interesting to consider the history of theology in our nation in parallel with the rest of its history....Consider science as a whole [and] its condition among a people will be parallel to their progress and in fact their whole history. Even more so can these same historical conditions explain literary history. In the same way should theology be considered, which, more than any other science, works on the entire body of the nation.[70]

----

[68]Adam, loc cit., pp. 581-601. A good review of the secondary literature on Drey appears in Wayne L. Fehr, The Birth of the Catholic Tübingen School: The Dogmatics of Johann Sebastian Drey (Chico, 1981), pp. 16-20.

[69]Geiselmann, Geist des Christentums, p. 126, quotes Drey from Archiv (1812), 1 Heft, 3-26.

[70]Particularly in this 1812 article, Drey's defense of present and past practices of the church would have been unthinkable without the Romantic concept of the organic development of history and

The shift of the Catholic faculty from Ellwangen to Tübingen forced Drey to address another audience. Now he had to defend Catholicism in a language which Protestants could understand, and he felt the need to restore the Catholic tradition in an increasingly profane civilization, which he regarded to be in essence Godless. In Kurze Einleitung in das Studium der Theologie mit Rücksicht auf den wissenschaftlichen Standpunkt, Drey related the decay of Catholicism to its subjection to the rational analysis of the Enlightenment and its separation from the mystical devotional life. In ignoring the organic development of Christianity by turning to a mythical ideal based on the first century alone, Catholic reformers had fallen into a dry moralism: "It [religion] is incomplete [if it only deals with morality]. The moral attributes of God are only a part of his attributes, not their fullness."[71] In opposition to ethical, intellectual religion, Drey recalled the theme of Sailer, that religion is feeling evoked by consciousness of God. But Drey here goes on to suggest that it is the life of the church as a whole which provides the experience which is the subject of theology, not the inner life of the individual. Practices, worship, and devotion are for the Catholic writer what an animal organism is for a biologist: "In the nature of things the teacher or writer in the church must emphasize the element of theoretical knowledge, but the living element in the church is not knowledge, but practical religiosity."[72]

By the time another pioneering article of 1819 "Vom Geist and Wesen des Katholizismus" had appeared, Drey was discussing the church

---

institutions. Geiselmann said, "This work of Drey's would have been impossible without the world of ideas of the romantics." Drey used Schelling's concept of the world system as dynamic organism, to defend the current practices of the contemporary church, the patristic church, and the medieval church, except that he replaced Schelling's cosmological organism with an ecclesiastical one. Geiselmann, Geist des Christentums, p. 86.

[71]Ibid., p. 120.

[72]Ibid., p. 253.

not as a corpus juris, but as a corporate unity with a mystical esprit
de corps. He began to inquire into the nature of "the inner binding of
the single members [of the Church] into the one community" that
transcended the institutional hierarchy.[73] Knowledge of the eternal is
only mediated through this community: "Reason by itself cannot
apprehend anything of the nature of positive truth. It is only a
receptive organ."[74]

The sacraments were important once again to Drey for they made
possible the uniting of men and women for this transmission of
revelation. The sacraments are the means of the intrusion of the
divine into the world: "The eucharist was considered at once by
Christ himself as a feast of union....That union [founded in the
eucharist] itself is a mysterious uniting of men with God and with the
supernatural in and through Christ."[75] Drey's colleague Johann Baptist
Hirscher was even more explicit about the social nature of Christian
worship. In his 1821 Missae genuinae notionem ejusque celebrandae
rectam methodus demonstrare tentavit, Hirscher portrayed the
eucharistic assembly as the highest realization of faith and love in
which doctrine is translated into social form. The essence of the mass
to Hirscher is the organic union which is achieved between the
Christians present and Christ. Hirscher proposed a liturgy which was
old and new. On the one hand he called for the retention of the old
parish customs of the Catholic southwest so that the eucharist would
be properly meaningful to congregants, but on the other hand, he called
for a return to practices which had not been seen for centuries, such
as the communion of the people in both kinds, in order to restore the
communal character of worship.[76]

----

[73]Ibid., p. 104; for additional discussion of Drey on the church see
Fehr, op. cit., pp. 241-242.

[74]MS Josef Rupert Geiselmann, Grundlegung der Dogmatik, unpulished
lectures, MS bf 2480HS, Wilhelmstift, Tübingen, p. 46.

[75]MS J. S. Drey, Mein Tagebuch, MS HS Gf 2836, Wilhelmstift,
Tübingen, p. 6.

[76]Vermeil, op. cit., p. 332.

The Tübingen professors founded a quarterly review, Theologische
Quartalschrift, to combat seriously the Wessenbergians. Theological
quarrels here as in France were not wars of faculties, monasteries, and
chapters but struggles between journals. In the twenties, a number of
anti-Aufklärung periodicals, corresponding in spirit and tone with
L'Avenir, began to appear: Der Katholik in Mainz, the Katholische
Kirchenzeitung of Aschaffenburg, and the Marburg Kirchenzeitung für das
katholische Deutschland. The Theologische Quartalschrift was more
conservative than these others in its attitude toward the Enlightenment. It espoused scientific research for the purification of the
church but also "churchly orthodoxy" and the "centrality of the
church."[77] It was the only one of all these contemporary journals to
survive, and the Theologische Quartalschrift is today the oldest Roman
Catholic theological quarterly in the world.

Its composition suggests that Tübingen had arrived at one level of
synthesis. But the weakness of the early Tübingen School was that it
was vague. It suggested that the church was a social body without
applying that notion to the solution of social problems, to the
relation of church and state, or to the disruption of the old secular
and parish communal organizations in Württemberg.

Möhler made the crucial connection between the abstractions of his
teachers and a model of the church which had actually existed in the
past, in the patristic period. The addition of historical models
allowed Möhler to speak of the communal church in appealing terms which
corresponded to human needs, whereas, in contrast, Drey and Hirscher
appeared to spin theoretical webs. Karl Adam spoke of this when he
accounted for Möhler's popularity in the twentieth century:

> If one goes with Möhler...one doesn't go through a
> stubblefield of abstract concepts, but, on the contrary, as
> to the Sea Genesareth, where Jesus preaches....that is why
> still today Möhler lives.[78]

---

[77]Fritz Vigener, loc. cit., p. 555.

[78]Adam, loc. cit., p. 588.

118

It was just at this moment, when Möhler had finished his studies
under Drey at Tübingen and a year at the seminary for priests at
Rottenburg, that he had a short experience in a parish at Riedlingen
which convinced him of the serious inadequacies of the local church as
it then existed in Württemberg. These months in Riedlingen parallel
Guéranger's service in Paris during the 1830 Revolution which were the
prelude to the founding of Solesmes.

Riedlingen was a large town (seventy-seven baptisms and fourteen
marriages during Möhler's years) with elaborate Baroque churches built
on the banks of the Danube.[79] The people and priests had practiced
religion in a more carefree manner than in the parishes in which Möhler
grew up. The feasts of the church year were kept with real feasting.
Once in the 1790's on the feast of Saint Anthony there was a sumptuous
meal after church "with music" not for the whole parish but only for "a
few notables, the clergy, and the guest preacher." This was not an
exception.[80] The architecture of church and chapel reflected a concept
of church as civic monument in Riedlingen. In 1724 these buildings had
been richly redecorated in the rococo style. Greater prominence was
given to statues of saints with local associations than to Christ.[81]

Möhler did not fit in here. The priest Urban Strobele noted in a
report to the Catholic Church Office that Möhler was different from
anyone who had been a priest in the town for many years. It was
strange to the old priest Strobele that Möhler had so much energy and
was filled with projects for the parish. The people thought him odd.
Those characteristics of the nineteenth century priest, which marked
him off from his predecessors, were already appearing. His preaching
consisted of "heartfelt expositions." His strangest characteristic was

---

[79]MSS Taufregister 1820, Eheregister 1820, Parish Archive,
Riedlingen. Möhler baptized twenty-one babies between June 9, 1820 and
October 30, 1820.

[80]MS Protocolbuch, 1788-1798, Parish Archive, Riedlingen.

[81]Weilerkapelle und Stadtpfarrkirche St. Georg, Riedlingen,
Württemberg (Munich, 1960).

"holy earnestness." He even "expressed love for and devotion to the entire community." Strobele reported to the government that Möhler's "strong church direction found expression in outer forms so that the old people of the neighborhood said, 'Such a learned young man appears to have another belief different from that of us old people,'" and he advised that Möhler be sent away from parish work and back to "scientific study" at the Wilhelmstift.[82]

Möhler returned to be a tutor in the Wilhelmstift in a mood of despair. He did not study theology but took up classical languages. In 1822 he applied to the king for an appointment in philology at Tübingen. But an accident occurred. A position in church history fell vacant at the end of the spring term in 1822, and the government suggested that Möhler be appointed. For preparation the Tübingen faculty sent him north to the centers of Protestant learning from the fall of 1822 to spring 1823.

Möhler embarked on his trip to Berlin filled with enthusiasm after the fit of parochial despair. His brother remembered that when Möhler came home to Igersheim for a vaction before his departure he was so full of ideas that he would jump up from the dinner table and run upstairs to write down some observation which had suddenly occurred to him.[83] This keen sense of observation produced theological results, for on his northern trip he combined new intellectual discoveries with investigations of social and intellectual conditions, and this led to his altered ecclesiology. He visited schools and seminaries at Würzburg, Bamberg, Breslau, and Munich. The famous center of enlightened Catholicism, the Collegium Carolinum, impressed upon him again how inadequate Aufklärung theology was.

At Jena he visited the dogmatician F. O. Baumgarten-Crusius, the

---

[82]Letter of Urban Strobele to Catholic Church Office, Stuttgart, 25 October, 1820, quoted in Stephan Lösch, Johann Adam Möhler. Gesammelte Aktenstücke und Briefe, I (Munich, 1928), pp. 24-25.

[83]Heinrich Kihn, Professor Dr. J. A. Möhler ernannter Domdekan von Würzburg. Ein Lebensbild (Würzburg, 1885), p. 18.

historian Heinrich Luden, and the exegete J. P. Gablen, and at Halle professors Niemeier, Knapp, Gesenius, and Wegscheider. He did not find these rationalistic gentlemen compelling, and so he went on to orthodox Leipzig and listened to H. G. Tschirner, W. T. Krug, E. F. K. Rosenmüller, G. Hermann, and G. Jacob Planck. Planck had found the roots of classical Protestantism in the age of the Fathers in his Geschichte des Entstehung, der Veränderungen und der Bildung unsers protestantischen Lehrbegriffs and Geschichte des Entstehung und Ausbildung des christlich-kirchlichen Gesellschaftsverassung, and he urged Möhler that if he would be an orthodox Christian in the contemporary situation he must study the resources of an earlier age.[84]

This was said amid the commercial boom and new weaving mills of Saxony and Thuringia which followed the founding of the German Zollverein in 1815. Of all the cities of central Germany, Planck's Leipzig was experiencing the most advanced rate of growth, and Möhler wrote back to the members of his faculty on 30 October, 1822, that he was troubled by the future pattern of life in such a great city of business.[85] He was investigating the new forms of Catholic education which had been created for these conditions, the adaptation of Andrew Bell's system to Catholic doctrine at Braunschweig, and he visited a Father Deleker near Magdeburg to witness how his parochial system served the people.[86] But after Leipzig, Möhler seems to have been even further disillusioned with the eighteenth-century solutions of Halle and Jena which had clearly proved to be inadequate to the task of Christian renewal in a revolutionary age. He was confused as to which model of Christianity to turn to as a guide for the future.[87]

He found the answer in Berlin. This discovery came amidst another experience of urban alienation:

----

[84]Lösch, Möhler, I, 67-68, 72-73, 80-81.

[85]Ibid., pp. 67-68.

[86]Ibid., pp. 80-82.

[87]Ibid., pp. 72-73, 86-87.

I travelled to Berlin not without a certain anxiety....I found myself to be very anxious there during the first days...harassed by the extremely high cost of food and lodging, by the excessive police-like ambience. When I spoke with anyone I was afraid.... When I went out in the street, especially during the night with no one around, I was afraid that someone would steal my watch or my money which I kept with me all of the time.[88]

Möhler particularly feared the police, to whom he had regularly to report in order to have his papers cleared. He wished that"the streets had been shorter and the days had been longer."[89] But discomfort was dissolved in the theology of Schleiermacher and the history of Neander, to the extent that he wrote his uncle Messner, who had insisted that he stop at the Prussian capital, "My trip would not have had such great worth if I had not visited Berlin according to your plan."[90] He was overwhelmed by the religion of the city:

This place where Schleiermacher, Neander, Marheinecke, Strauss... teach deserves alone a half year visit. The spirituality, the deep earnestness, with which scientific investigation is carried on, the true religiosity which penetrates all the teachers, the unusual recognition of the contributions of other churches...the love of the students and the lively interest in their education as well as for their spiritual advancement distinguishes this theological faculty above all others.[91]

Above all Schleiermacher had given this memorable spirit to the University of Berlin. He was central to and the symbol of a great flowering which had taken place within north German Protestantism in the years preceding Möhler's trip, a revival which was characterized by Lord Acton as equal to the Renaissance:

The prostration of religion on the continent at the close of the last century was shared by the Protestants in an equal measure [with the Roman Catholics]. But it was followed by a revived literary activity among them, to which there is no

---

[88]Ibid., pp. 82-85.

[89]Ibid., p. 83.

[90]Idem.

[91]Ibid., pp. 89-90.

parallel in modern history except the revival of the fifteenth century, to which it bears a real resemblance.[92]

From Weimar to Bonn and Heidelberg and finally in Berlin, Protestant theology was being awakened by the same impulses which had stirred the south. Möhler was not the only example of a Romanist touched by this Protestant theological shift, for, as Acton noted, this new "Protestant theology with its restless spirit of inquiry, has gone along by the side of the Catholic, exciting and awakening, warming and vivifying: and every eminent Catholic divine in Germany will gladly admit that he owes much to the writing of Protestant scholars."[93]

Friedrich Ernest Daniel Schleiermacher was at the height of his power and influence when Möhler entered Berlin. He was, at fifty-seven, something of a national institution, a man who had rallied the German spirit against the French in 1813, had helped unite the Lutheran and Reformed Churches in Prussia, had been one of the founders of the University of Berlin, and had given a new intellectual respectability to adherence to the Christian religion. That in a faculty whose philosophy section included Fichte, Hegel, and Schelling, in which Ranke taught history and the Humboldt and Grimm brothers offered instruction, he could be a dominating intellectual force and attract as many as one hundred and forty students to his classes is testimony to the spell of his ideas and presence, which worked on Möhler as well. There are many parallel themes in Schleiermacher and Drey, for they were both shaped by the same general intellectual influences, and perhaps this accounts for Möhler's immediate understanding of Schleiermacher.

The difference between the two was that Drey had received Romantic notions second hand through theological channels, while Die Romantik were Schleiermacher's own friends. Schleiermacher lived with Novalis

---

[92]J. E. E. D. Acton, Essays on Church and State (London, 1952), p. 66.

[93]J. E. E. D. Acton, The History of Freedom and Other Essays (London, 1922), p. 311.

and in his theology there is the imprint of "Die Christenheit oder Europa," the message that the faith of the fathers and mothers of the past had provided a social unity which could never be supplied by the religion of reason. Schelling was a close friend, and his organic thinking about history and institutions was applied by Schleiermacher to the church. In Halle Schleiermacher lectured that the "Church is a continuing and changing whole," that because of its organic character the church was able to unite men and provide the unity in society which Novalis had suggested it had provided in the past.[94] Schleiermacher's discussion of the unity in the church is based on two points, one a rejection of the religion of reason and the other an affirmation of the social nature of faith.

Despite this epistemological subjectivism, Schleiermacher advocated that the richest consciousness of God is preceded by fellowship with other Christians sharing a similar religious experience: "If there is religion at all, it must be social, for that is the nature of man, and it is quite peculiarly the nature of religion."[95] In Uber die Religion of 1799 he attempted to introduce Protestants to the value of communal religion. A religion of the self, he said, would lead to isolation and alienation. Such is overcome by joining a universal whole to which religion provides the entrée. "To consider each individual as a part of the whole, each limited being as a representative of the infinite: that is religion."[96] To those who argued that founding Christianity upon experience would lead to spiritual anarchy and extreme subjectivism, Schleiermacher answered that this was precisely the importance of a communal understanding of

----

[94]Gustav A. Benrath, "Evangelische und Katholische Kirchenhistorie im Zeichen der Aufklärung und der Romantik," Zeitschrift für Kirchengeschichte, 82 (1971), 211. For a summary of recent Schleiermacher scholarship with bibliographical guide see B.A. Gerrish, "Friedrich Schleiermacher," in Ninian Smart, op. cit., pp. 123-156.

[95]W. B. Selbie, Schleiermacher (London, 1913), p. 58.

[96]Ibid., p. 56; Hervé Savon, Johann Adam Möhler. The Father of Modern Theology (Glen Rock, New Jersey, 1966), p. 13.

faith, for Christianity has been preserved in its objectivity primarily because it has been the religious experience of a community.

From his Moravian background, Schleiermacher had learned that worship could become a common experience of spirit which formed men and women into a true brotherhood of equality and love:

> Would that I could depict to you the rich, the superabundant life in this city of God, when citizens assemble, each full of native force seeking liberty of utterance, and full at the same time of holy desire to apprehend and appropriate what others offer. When one stands out before the others he is neither justified by office nor by compact: nor is it pride or ignorance that inspires him with assurance. It is the free impulse of his spirit, the feeling of heartfelt unanimity and completest equality, the common abolition of all first and last of all earthly order.[97]

This non-hierarchical Christian communion provided a stronger bond than other institutions—nation, family, and university. But Schleiermacher did not deprecate these bodies. In reacting to Kant's ethics, he taught that healthy moral and political life depended upon the extent to which individuals could be integrated into such institutions. Christian regeneration and sanctification were defined as processes by which persons entered into the life of a community. Thus, baptism was seen as the reception into fellowship, the Lord's Supper as a means for renewing union in the Spirit.

The influence of these Protestant ideas upon Möhler is beyond question. When his first book Die Einheit came out in 1825 the German theological booksellers said that the young Tübingen professor had Schleiermacherized Catholicism.[98] In an 1827 review of his friend Adam Gengler's Uber das Verhaltnis der Theologie zur Philosophie in Theologische Quartalschrift, Möhler discussed specifically what he had taken from the Berlin theologian. The idea that "the Church is the social manifestation of the Christian Spirit" which is essential to

---

[97]Selbie, op. cit., p. 58.

[98]Karl Eschweiler, Johann Adam Möhler's Kirchenbegriff (Braunsberg, 1930), p. 35.

Möhler's Die Einheit had been taught him by Schleiermacher. Similarly the concept which Möhler used to question the absolute dominance of the hierarchical principle in Roman Catholicism, that the church is grounded in the experience of the Holy Spirit found in unity with other Christians in the communal church, whose unity itself is the work of the Holy Spirit, is based on pages of Schleiermacher's 1811 work Einleitung in das theologische Studium. Möhler's definition of sin and heresy as assertion of individuality comes from a similar source.[99]

Yet the same article reveals that Möhler was hostile to many characteristics of Schleiermacher. A great difference was evident in definitions of Spirit. In Schleiermacher the Holy Spirit evolves into Gemeingeist, the common feeling of the faithful. Möhler maintained that the divine spirit evident in the members of the church remained the Third Person of the Trinity. There was no osmosis of divinity into humankind. Möhler suspected that Schleiermacher was taking a Socinian view of atonement in his lectures, and he was suspicious of the Protestant's explanation of the divinity of Christ, that the Deity, who is in some measure displayed in every human being, was in larger measure revealed in Christ.

Möhler therefore looked for a more orthodox exposition of the communal church, one which, following the advice of Planck, could be located in the past. He found his answer in the Berlin lectures of August Neander on the history of the church in the patristic era. Neander was one of a group of young disciples who used Schleiermacher's terminology to defend more orthodox theology. August Twesten, Schleiermacher's successor, Ernst Hengstenberg, who taught that the Hebrew Bible was as important to Christianity as the New Testament, August Tholuck, a man concerned with the purely emotional aspects of religion, Sack, Lücke, and Nitzsch were all part of the same circle.

Neander was born a Jew in Hamburg, was converted to Christianity by Schleiermacher's Halle lectures in 1806, and began teaching history

---

[99]Savon, op. cit., p. 61. Möhler's review appeared in ThQ (1827), pp. 513-515.

first in Heidelberg in 1811 and then in Berlin after 1813. He became the historian of the experience of Christian community. Neander set before the German public the liturgical practices of the church of the past centuries. He began his career with studies of the fourth century, Uber den Kaiser Julianus und sein Zeitalter, 1812, and the eleventh century, Der heilige Bernhard und sein Zeitalter, 1813. He then wrote books on the Gnostics, Genetische Entwicklung der Vornehmsten Gnostischen Systeme, 1818, and the eras of Saint Chrysostom, Der heilige Chrysostomus und die Kirche in dessen Zeitalter, 1820, and Tertullian, 1825. Neander also presented histories which counteracted the treatises of Strauss which attached a mythological label to early Christianity. These books were on Christ's life, Das Leben Jesu Christi, and the apostles, Geschichte der Pflanzung und Leitung der christliche Kirche durch die Apostel, 1837.

Of all these works the most massive and memorable is the great history of the early Christian centuries, Allgemeine Geschichte der Christlichen Religion and Kirche. Möhler was in Berlin while Neander was lecturing from the notes of the first volume (it came out in 1825) which covers the first three hundred years. The volumes which deal with the fourth to sixth centuries were published in 1828, the sixth to eighth in 1834, the eighth to eleventh in 1836, and the eleventh to the thirteenth in 1841.

In his lectures Neander presented this historical material in the context of a contemporary dilemma. He wrote to J. E. Ryland in England that he felt that he was living "in a time of great crisis," and that the spirit of God was working in a generation called to set right the imbalances of Christianity.[100] A great disaster had occurred. The Aufklärung had turned the faith into a natural and rational ideology. Equally dangerous had been the Evangelical development of the German pietists who eschewed the material aspects of Christianity. The classical view had been that the church conveyed divine power to

---

[100]Quoted in A. Neander, History of the Planting and Training of the Christian Church (Edinburgh, 1842), p. VI.

humankind through material means. The central theme of the thousands of pages Neander wrote is the incarnation, God joining matter and spirit and the human and the divine through Jesus Christ.

Neander suggested that the church is the mystical organism which joins heaven and earth, eternity and time, essence and becoming. The main purpose of the institution had not been to espouse dogma but to engender a way of life among men and women which would balance the material and spiritual:

> Christianity claimed for its service the faculties of knowledge, no less than those of feeling....Christianity is based upon a supernatural revelation; but this revelation would be appropriated and understood by the organ of a reason which submits to it; since it is not destined to remain a barely outward thing to the human spirit. The supernatural element must be owned in its organic connection with the natural, which in this finds its full measure and complement. The fact of redemption has for its very aim, indeed, to do away with the schism between the supernatural and the natural;--the fact of God's becoming man is in order to effect the humanization of the divine, and the deification of the human.[101]

Neander discovered that the characteristic of social and religious communalism dominated every aspect of early Christianity. "The whole outward form of the Church and of Church life betokened a community propagating itself in opposition to the dominant power."[102] Irenaeus, Justin Martyr, Ambrose, Cyril of Jerusalem are shown to have viewed the eucharist as spiritual participation in Christ's body by means of fellowship with the human components of his body on earth, the people. The Fathers are said to have taught that the eucharist produces "a unity of godly communion among the redeemed...all filled, after this common consecration, by the one same Holy Spirit are ordained a true priesthood--a spiritual people."[103] The sacraments were held to be "symbols of the invisible fellowship between him [Christ], the Head of

----

101Ibid., pp. 186, 507.

102Ibid., p. 283.

103A. Neander, The Life of St. Chrysostom (London, 1845), p. 35.

the spiritiual body, and its members, the believers, and of the union of these members not only with himself, but with one another."[104] Neander stressed that the Fathers regarded Christ as present as much in the assembly of the congregation as in any symbolic or sacramental sign. Clement of Alexandria is representative when he said:

> It is not the place, but it is the congregation of the elect, which I call the Church....Fellowship in prayer and devotion was considered a means of promoting holiness, since it was known that the Lord was present with his Spirit, in the midst of those who were assembled together in his name....[105]

Because "there was no distinction of spiritual and secular" among patristic Christians, the communal element was carried over into secular existence:

> The essence of the Christian community rested on this: that no one individual should be the chosen, preeminent organ of the Holy Spirit for the guidance of the whole; but all were to cooperate, ----each at his particular position, and with the gifts bestowed on him, one supplying what might be wanted by another,----for the advancement of the Christian life and of the common end....There could no longer be a priestly or prophetic office...on which office the religious conscious-ness of the community was to be dependent....Such a priestly caste could find no place within Christianity. In removing out of the way that which separated men from God, in communicating to all the same fellowship with God, Christ also removed the barrier which had hitherto divided men from one another.[106]

At Carthage money and food were provided when any of the believers were sick. Common goods were shared at Alexandria. Prayer produced social unity because in the early church there was "...a view of prayer as an act embracing the whole life."[107] Neander provided descriptions, drawn from Tertullian, of how the ancients united daily for spiritual songs and readings in order to sanctify with prayer all the more important

----

[104]Neander, History of the Planting, p. 304.

[105]Ibid., p. 289.

[106]Ibid., pp. 179, 181.

[107]Ibid., p. 285.

portions and transactions of the day. Greetings, entertainment, and public occasion were sealed by liturgical prayer:

> It was in prayer, that the brotherly fellowship, the mutual sympathy of the members of the one Body was to be specially expressed; each was to pray in the spirit of all, and to present the interests of all the brethren, which he regarded as his own, before the great Head of the Church....Thus Cyprian in his exposition of the Lord's prayer, says, "The teacher of peace and of mutual fellowship was desirous, not that each individual should pray for himself alone, but that each should pray for all. We say not my Father, but our Father....Ours is a common prayer; and when we pray, we pray not for individuals, but the whole church, because, being members of the Church, we are all one."[108]

Christ had provided a sacramental and liturgical means for the unification of society which produced social stability in the early church and could be applied once again to Germany:

> Just as the unity of that higher Spirit must reveal itself in the manifoldness of the charismata, so must all these peculiarities, quickened by the same Spirit, serve as organs, mutually helping each other for one common end,...with the inner fellowship, Christianity produced among its professors from the first a living outward union, whereby the distantly separated were brought near to each other. This union must be realized in a determinant form, which later was conditioned by the existing forms of social life....[109]

These ideas were immediately attractive to Möhler. He reported to his colleagues and his uncle that Neander, because of his use and understanding of sources, his religiosity, his earnestness, his clarity in lectures, his living exposition of Christianity, and the beautiful pictures which he had painted of the church of the Fathers, was the most impressive figure that he had heard on his travels.[110] He was intrigued by the manner in which Neander used science for the benefit of the church rather than to destroy her ancient customs. "This scientific activity is carried on most excellently by Neander, an

---

[108]Ibid., p. 287.

[109]Ibid., pp. 181, 201-202.

[110]Lösch, Möhler, I, 83-84.

unequaled historian, who carries forward earnest and worthwhile projects of Church history."[111] He sent this message to Württemberg from Berlin:

> Here there is an industrious, heartfelt, deep, truly scientific life and effort. Science exists here in its true essence. It embraces both thinking and living. I was amazed by Planck. But what is Planck next to Neander? Planck swims on the surface. Neander comprehends all in the deepest deep!....Neander's lectures will be unforgettable to me....His private life is penetrated by an illuminating religiosity as well. It is as simple in mode as that of a village schoolmaster....He knows no streets in Berlin other than those around the University buildings. He knows no one among his colleagues as thoroughly as he knows Origen, Tertullian, Augustine, Chrysostom, and St. Bernard....I went often to see him, when he was alone as well as when he was in society. I spoke with him about the great historical subjects and works which I have had in view....[112]

To Möhler's friend and successor as dean of the cathedral at Würzburg, Heinrich Kihn, this contact with Neander was the central turning point of Möhler's life, for it was the inspiration to study the Fathers, the inspiration that shaped all his later work:

> He himself gave two different explanations for the solidification of his point of view, his trip to north Germany and his study of the Fathers.[113]

Through the Theologische Quartalschrift Möhler introduced Neander to the Roman Catholic priests of Württemberg. In 1824 he recommended the Protestant's Chrysostom as "true Christian Church history." The reviewer "wishes this book could come into many hands," because of its evidence that once priests and people formed one community in the church, with a single moral code for lay folk and hierarchy, and in which ordination was a gift recognized by the body of Christians.[114]

----

[111]Ibid., p. 89.

[112]Ibid., pp. 83-84.

[113]Kihn, op. cit., p. 23.

[114]J. A. Möhler, "John Chrysostom von Neander," ThQ (1824), 262-280, partic. 263, 280.

131

When Möhler returned to Württemberg the government required him to teach church history for seven hours each week. He conducted a lecture series on the patristic era and discussed Clement of Alexandria an additional two hours weekly. Phrases from the church history lectures are a combination of Neander and Drey: "It is necessary to have an understanding of Christian history in order to grasp the sense and spirit of Christianity."[115] The fundamental law of history is the action of God working in concert with humankind to bring a higher life to human beings:

> Church history is the development among mankind of the new life brought by Christ--the deployment of circles of men brought into a relationship with God through Christ into the entire human family--a gradual regeneration of mankind.[116]

Forty pages of notes are devoted to praise of church historians, most of all of "Neander who has added to and continued most excellently" the tradition of the church by his rediscovery of patristic sources.[117] Two hundred pages of notes are devoted to various early Fathers, and their treatment of the themes of unity and community. The patristics course used the works of Jerome, Augustine, Leo, Gregory the Great, Athanasius, Chrysostom, Gregory of Nazianzus, and Basil the Great to illustrate these topics.[118]

To one friend Möhler wrote that this literature was "the tableau of my being. The serious study of the Fathers has aroused in me a great awakening. In them I have discovered a very living, a very true, and a very full Christianity."[119] He confided to his friend Lipp in 1825:

----

[115]MS notes Kirchengeschichte, II Periode, taken down by J. B. Müller, 1827, 115, MS HSGh 1278 Wilhelmstift, Tübingen, pp. 1-2.

[116]Ibid., p. 8.

[117]MS notes Kirchengeschichte, Winter Semester 1827-1828, MSGh3280 Wilhelmstift, Tübingen, p. 52.

[118]MS notes Patrology, Winter Semester, 1827-1828, Wilhelmstift, Tübingen.

[119]Knöpfler, op. cit., pp. 42-43.

Earlier I had only the word, only the naked concept of
Christianity...The earnest study of the Fathers excited me.
In them I have discovered for the first time
a...Christianity as Christ himself wanted it....[120]

He openly advocated patristic ecclesiology as the contemporary
model in his canon law lectures. A visible community which overcomes
alienation is placed in opposition by Möhler to the Aufklärung model of
church as a collection of morally responsible individuals. By 1824
there is a German Roman Catholic teaching his students that "The Church
is a holy community in its original form...the Church exists in its
highest form as a society."[121] We witness Möhler in these lectures
ordering his pupils to go out and foster communities, free from the
control of the state and not dependent on any primate, bound together
only by love and belief.

----

[120]Lösch, Möhler, I, 251.

[121]Einem Schüler des Herrn von Möhler, Abriss des Katholischen
Kirchenrechts für Geistliche und Studierende (Stuttgart, 1853), pp. 1,
17. This book was a publication of Möhler's 1823-24 canon law lectures
at Tübingen done anonymously, but perhaps by J. B. Leu.

CHAPTER III

From Einheit to Symbolik

Möhler's life after his return from Berlin contrasted sharply with
that of Dom Guéranger. His work in the church lasted only twelve
years, from 1825 to 1838. Unlike the wandering French abbot, he
journeyed no farther than Munich in the east, Baden-Baden in the west,
and the Rhineland in the north. He wrote only two books of any
consequence, Die Einheit in der Kirche and Symbolik, which created a
storm, however, equal to that surrounding the French abbot's liturgical
tracts. He did not seek such controversies, but preferred the simple
life of a professor in the romantic, half-timbered German university
town of Tübingen where his existence was circumscribed by the narrow
streets which led up from his tiny rooms in the Wilhelmstift to the
lecture halls of the university on the heights of the city near the
Protestant parish church. The controversies unleashed by his books
disturbed the tranquility of his life consciously patterned after that
of Neander in Berlin. It was not a happy life. Guéranger always had
the comfort of his fortress home at Solesmes to retire to. Möhler, on
the other hand, like Newman, was hounded from the Protestant university
he loved into the precincts of Roman Catholic institutions where he
never felt at home.

The first stage in Möhler's career was the production of Die
Einheit, a relatively short essay based on his patristic research and
teaching. In 1827 a three-volume work, Athanasius der Grosse, lacking
the freshness and insight of his first work, appeared. The next year
he issued a political tract of some importance on St. Anselm. From
1829 until 1831 a series of articles in the Theologische Quartalschrift
prepared the ground for his great synthesis, the Symbolik of 1832.

133

134

These reviews and treatises reveal the wide range of Möhler's knowledge
and interests, for they cover such areas as the false decretals of
Pseudo-Isidore, Islam, Swedenborgianism, Gnosticism, the condition of
the church in the fifteenth and sixteenth centuries and the French
Saint-Simonians. Another series of lecture courses on the
controversies separating Protestants and Catholics also prepared the
way for the Symbolik. Neue Untersuchungen was his last book, a defense
of the Symbolik, comparable in quality to Athanasius. His life closed
with a series of polemical articles, circulated throughout Germany,
dealing with the political position of Catholics.

Die Einheit and Athanasius made Möhler well known throughout
Germany. He received offers of professorships from several of the
leading universities of central Europe. These were blocked, however,
by the mounting opposition of Protestant and Catholic leaders who would
not countenance the Tübingen theologian's theories about the nature of
the church. Until the publication of Symbolik, Möhler's relations with
the Protestant faculty were amicable. After 1832, however, very great
differences arose which resulted in his departure from the university.

In 1826, a young man was appointed "extra-ordinary professor" at
Tübingen. Ferdinand Christian Baur was Möhler's opposite number in the
Protestant Stift and a near contemporary. Each was the shining light
of his own seminary. Both had been influenced by Schleiermacher and
his followers and by Hegel. Baur adapted a Hegelian methodology to the
style of New Testament exegesis of Schleiermacher, which became the
foundation of the so-called Tübingen Critical School and led on to the
demythologized Christianity of his students Friedrich Strauss and Adolf
von Harnack. In the Symbolik, Möhler attacked this as mere pantheism.
Baur responded with "Der Gegensatz des Katholicismus und
Protestantismus," which argued that the revived superstitions of
Möhler's own brand of Catholicism should not be allowed in modern
Württemberg.[1] In this attack, Baur was joined by the entire Protestant
----
[1]F. C. Baur, "Gegensatz des Katholicismus und Protestantismus, nach
den principien und Hauptdogmen der beiden Lehrbegriffe, mit besondere
Rucksicht auf Hrn. D. Möhlers Symbolik, etc.," Tübinger Zeitschrift für
Theologie, Third Quarter, 1833, pp. 1-43.

135

faculty as well as by his co-religionists in Prussia, Prof. Marheinecke of Berlin and Prof. Nitzsch of Bonn, and even by the government of the Kingdom of Württemberg. Möhler replied with his Neue Untersuchungen. A great pamphlet war thus broke out in Tübingen in 1833. But in the end, as in the case of Tract 90 in England, the violent theological controversies displeased government and university alike, and Möhler's removal became the only solution.

By September 1834 Möhler was so spiritually and emotionally exhausted that he wrote his friend, J. J. I. Döllinger, the church historian in the faculty at Munich, asking that he find him a place in that university, for he was out of sorts with all his colleagues at Tübingen and not of the same spirit as the inhabitants of that place. He reiterated his request in 1835 and wrote that after Württembergian troubles and controversies he was longing to be refreshed by "dearly beloved Catholic Bavarian beer, rather than the oldest Prussian Rhine wine and its neighbor, the Neckar wine."[2] Döllinger reports in his memoirs that when he discovered that his correspondent was being oppressed by the "rationalistic-protestant spirit of Tübingen," he went at once to the King of Bavaria to secure Möhler's appointment to the new faculty at Munich, which the king sought to make into a center of Catholic learning for all of Germany. Ludwig I, Döllinger found, had long wanted this "pearl of Tübingen University" for his establishment, and he agreed to call Möhler immediately as ordinary professor in church history at a salary of 1800 florins.[3] The government of Württemberg now gave tacit assent to Möhler's departure from its university by doing nothing to keep him.

In March 1835 a bitter Möhler wrote his brother as he prepared to shake the dust of Tübingen from his feet:

---

[2]Stephan Lösch, Johann Adam Möhler. Gesammelte Aktenstücke und Briefe, I (Munich, 1928), p. 242.

[3]Ibid., p. 231; J. Friedrich, Johann Adam Möhler der Symboliker. Ein Beitrag zu seinem Leben und seiner Lehre, aus seinem eigenen und anderen ungedrückten Papieren (Munich, 1894), p. 34.

> You can imagine that my apologetic and polemical writings have begotten evil blood, and that, therefore, I have lived here amid great tension. The government has taken notice as well and involved itself in this controversy. Now, this is the outcome of various deliberations: I will take myself out of the range of their shots...to Munich. That which is truly Christian is received much more readily in Bavaria than here in this land, where one destroys what another has built.[4]

The night before he left, a large number of students gathered under his window with torches to demonstrate support for their departing teacher. A young priest, Albert Werfer, remembered Möhler's farewell speech in the torchlight in which he said that it was hard to relinquish his Tübingen post because he was leaving behind a wonderful circle of students. Werfer came away from the gathering convinced that Möhler "was attached deep in his heart to his dear Fatherland and Tübingen."[5] As the expatriate made his way across southern Germany with his few belongings he stopped at an inn near Augsburg. He shared his table with a woman who was returning to her sister's house in Stuttgart, and in the midst of the meal, worn out with work, travel, and controversy, he cried, "Oh if I could only return again with you to Württemberg."[6]

In May 1835 his spirits were lifted as he arrived in Munich to the cheers of students. Young people and professors hurried to meet him. Grand dinners were given in honor of the author of che Symbolik. In the Munich theological faculty Möhler was assigned the duty of lecturing on the history of slavery, the Saint-Simonians, the development of monasticism, and the later periods of ecclesiastical history. This odd allocation of professional talent (the eminent church historian Döllinger was teaching theology and Möhler history) prompted Lord Acton to comment,

> As Möhler, who was essentially a theologian, deserted divinity to compose inferior treatises on the Gnostics and the fake decretals, Döllinger, by choice and vocation a divine, having religion as the purpose of his life, judged

---

[4]Lösch, op. cit., p. 391.

[5]Ibid., pp. 486-487.

[6]Idem.

that the loftier function, the more spiritual service, was historical teaching.[7]

These lectures and a serious conflict between the Prussian government and the Catholic population of the Rhineland over mixed marriages determined the work Möhler was to publish during his last months, a series of controversial essays on relations between Christianity and the state, on the true function of the church in contemporary affairs, and on the role of monasticism.

These articles suggest that Möhler was slipping into a mood of despair as he surveyed the secularization of north German life on the one hand, and, after several months in Munich, he also felt alienated from the hyper-Catholic, clerical, and theocratic atmosphere of the Bavaria of the conservative Round Table movement. He confided to his Benedictine friend Beda Weber in 1837,

> Therefore it has come to this, that I am completely out of harmony with many of the tendencies of our UltraCatholics. ...My spirit hungers after more eternal, more enduring nourishment.[8]

The king learned of this disenchantment and in order to move Möhler closer to his dear Württemberg appointed him dean of the cathedral at Würzburg in March 1838. Möhler's end was thus in his beginning, for that very episcopal city of Würzburg in the neighborhood of Igersheim had inspired him as a boy to an idealized glory of the church.

So much work within such a short span of years dictated an austere existence. A man who spent most days writing about the importance of communities passed his adulthood in almost complete isolation. He once remarked that "the study of sources is my life."[9] Joseph Lipp, who

---

[7]J. E. E. D. Acton, The History of Freedom and Other Essays (London, 1922), p. 379.

[8]Lösch, op cit., p. 520.

[9]Stefan Lösch, Prof. Dr. Adam Gengler 1799-1866. Die Beziehungen des Bamberger Theologen zur J. J. I. Döllinger und J. A. Möhler (Würzburg, 1963), p. 161. He thought that the study of historical sources should be a part of the life of every priest. A large number of the articles which he wrote for the Theologische Quartalschrift centered about the need for Roman priests to become acquainted with historical works in order to understand the spirit of Catholicism as it

138

became the second Bishop of Rottenburg, and Dr. Döllinger were his only close friends. After he went to Tübingen he remained isolated from any centers of the Catholic faithful, for there was no Roman church in the town. In Munich he was equally separated. He wrote to Dr. Döllinger that all he required for accommodation was a study room and a sleeping room, with a guest room attached. Möhler took his meals in his study so that he could work while he ate. He even celebrated the eucharist alone in Munich in the tiny round Trinity Church, far from the university church of St. Ludwig.

These years were interrupted by one other personal crisis. One month of each summer vacation was spent at a spa. In 1832 he went to Bad Boll near Göppingen, a day's journey from Tübingen, in order to take the baths and strengthen his declining health. There he met a young Protestant woman from Stuttgart, Emilie Sigel, and developed a brief, platonic, but nonetheless passionate interest in her. The interest was brief because the baths did not restore Emilie's health and she soon died. A scene which followed is another in Möhler's life which might have been taken from Hölderlin. In a misty night, lighted by a full moon, Möhler threw himself upon the grave of Emilie, tore at the dirt, and cried, within earshot of Protestants who took down the words for posterity, that his life was over.[10]

Möhler was made aware of developments in the Anglican Church on those occasions when he travelled to the far side of the Black Forest

----

existed in earlier eras. ThQ (1826), 324-331, (1827), 91-104, (1828), 719-731, (1831), 77-90.

[10]Emilie appears to have also been a friend of the famous David Friedrich Strauss, who arrived at the age of 32 at Tübingen and was allied to Baur in the anti-Möhlerian struggle. Strauss' tale of Möhler's attachment was published in H. B. Oppenheim, Deutsche Jahrbücher für Politik und Literatur. Bd. 13 (1864), 385-0392; D. F. Strauss, Kleine Schriften, II (Leipzig, 1866), 352-380, and Heinrich Maier, Briefe von D. F. Strauss und Ludwig Georgii (Tübingen, 1912). This tale is alluded to also by some Catholic authors, viz., Alfons Erb, Gelebtes Christentum: Charakterbilder aus dem deutschen Katholichen der 19. Jahrhunderts (Freiburg, 1938), p. 218; Philipp Funk, "Die Geistige Gestalt Johann Adam Möhlers," Hochland, 271 (1929-30), 102; Lösch, Möhler, I, 367.

and dwelt among the affluent English vacationers at the spa of Baden-
Baden. These visits widened his confessional horizons and introduced
him to the beginning of the movement which valued once again the
Catholicity of the Church of England. Six days after John Keble's
Assize Sermon which began the Oxford Movement he discovered the
Anglican community at Baden-Baden. He wrote of this introduction
later:

> My doctor had sent me to Baden-Baden for the cure, where I
> had spent a week. The most remarkable thing that I got to
> know there was the Anglican liturgy. There in Baden many
> Englishmen live in the summer. They reserve the Spital
> church for their use and in fact on Sunday it is completely
> filled up with the devout. One hundred and fifty men and
> women from those islands are generally there in the church.
> I got to know the thinking of the English clergy and one of
> them imparted to me his appreciation of the Liturgy.[11]

Weakened by cholera in 1836, by the grippe in 1837, and by a
journey back to Igersheim and Mergentheim taken too soon after his
recovery, worn out by constant work, Möhler died on Maundy Thursday
1838. His funeral, held on the Easter vigil, was an occasion for the
government of Bavaria to make a demonstration of Catholic solidarity in
the face of the threats of Protestant Prussia. The royal ministers
were there, as was the chapter of the cathedral, the professors of the
university, and a large contingent of students. The propagandists
immediately attempted to turn the dead theologian into the victim of
the Württembergian Protestants, and dwelt only upon the Möhler of the
period of the Symbolik, ignoring the earlier controversies engendered
by the more liberal Die Einheit. The Allgemeine Zeitung made a
prophetic appraisal of the importance of Möhler as theologian, rather
than as political symbol, on the day of his death:

> Thousands of people in Germany, yes, even in Europe, feel the
> loss of such a man to be irreparable. Through his works,
> namely, his treatment of the unity in the Church, his life of
> Saint Athanasius, and his Symbolik, as well as through a
> series of first-rate articles in the Tübingen theology
> quarterly, is grounded his designation as one of the premier

----

[11]Lösch, Adam Gengler, p. 102.

140

Catholic theologians of the new time.[12]

The outer form of Möhler's life suggests two periods, nine radical years of Die Einheit and those of the more conservative traditional exposition of the Symbolik. But the Allgemeine Zeitung suggests rightly that there was a constancy about Möhler's theology throughout his life. His numerous articles and his books from both periods are focused upon the single mission of writing Catholic theology for a new age. The underlying assumption is a belief in the necessity of communal forms of life for the survival of civilization, and his conclusion is that only the Christian church as an institution can fulfill this need. Therefore the territorial concept of the church which had dominated German ecclesiology during the thousand years of the Holy Roman Empire is dismantled in his writings and replaced by the pristine structure of a spiritual community.

All other sentiments in Möhler's works are corollaries of this ecclesiological concept of community which is stated in a different manner in the two periods of his career. In the argument of Die Einheit the ecclesial shape of the community is free, unstructured, based on love and the Romantic religious definitions of Schleiermacher, Schelling, Neander, and Drey. In the period of the Symbolik the argument is made more traditionally Roman Catholic by being couched in the terms of orthodox Roman theology with Hegelianism tinting the discussion. In the Symbolik the phrase "communal church" is appropriated to past institutional realities, the hierarchy, and the eucharist. It is placed in opposition to Protestant, Febronian, and Wessenbergian ecclesiological paradigms. Between 1825 and 1832 the tension between life and form in Möhler was resolved in the Symbolik's conclusion that forms are necessary for the survival of the lived experience of Christianity. The less subversive idiom of his last books and articles made his ecclesiological shift more palatable to German Catholic hierarchies and faculties, while it frightened Protestant princes and ministers.

----

[12]Allgemeine Zeitung, 15 April 1838.

Some said that in recalling the churches to the ideal of community
he "expressed the religious consciousness in the spirit of his time"
which led to "the regeneration of theological science."[13] One
countryman, after closing Die Einheit and Symbolik, exclaimed, "Truly,
here at last we possess a German theology."[14] Möhler, it was concluded,
had done for German idealism and romanticism what Aquinas did for the
neo-Aristotelianism of his day. Because his concept of the church was
the product of the marriage of contemporary philosophical language with
the history of the first three Christian centuries, it was understood
and survived in the universities of central Europe. The force of this
combination was so great that one commentator remarked "...the history
of the spiritual awakening and renewal of Catholic Germany must be
connected with his name and bound to his memory...."[15]

The dissemination of Möhler's ideas to the Württembergians and
then to the Germans was carried out in one manner by his students.
Möhler was an impressive teacher. His holiness and visionary spirit
gathered about him a school of students who then took his message to
the parishes of his native land. Those who became university teachers
transmitted it to their institutions in Germany as well as Austria and
Switzerland. Others yet, took it to abbeys. Möhler was similar to
Pusey and Newman in England in his ability to draw young people to his
camp. Outside of his scholarly work, teaching remained Möhler's most
important and dedicated activity. Even after his appointment as
ordinary professor in Tübingen, he continued to devote seven hours a

---

[13]Heinrich Kihn, Professor Dr. J. A. Möhler ernannter Domdekan von
Würzburg. Ein Lebensbild als Beitrag zur Geschichte der Theologie der
Neuzeit (Würzburg, 1885), p. 19. Karl Bihlmeyer, "J. A. Möhler als
Kirchenhistoriker, seine Leistungen und Methode," ThQ (1919), 134,
also expresses the notion that in mastering the ability to speak of the
church in the language of the day Möhler had something to do with the
regeneration of German Catholicism.

[14]Bernhard Hanssler, "Johann Adam Möhler: Theologie der Kirche,"
Hochland, 35, II (1938), 26.

[15]Balthasar Wörner, Johann Adam Möhler. Ein Lebensbild (Regensburg,
1866), p. 388.

week to church history lectures and three to early Christian literature.

Johann Baptist Hafen, one of the pupils who propagated the Tübingen professor's ideas in the Württemberg parishes summed up the testimony of many individuals to Möhler's great influence at the lecture desk:

> He discovered the good and brought it into the light....He perceived the powerful working of the divine spirit in the Church.[16]

In scholarly circles, the reactions to Möhler's second medium of influence, his major works, were also favorable, even though at first they did not gain the approval of the hierarchy. Both Die Einheit and Symbolik became at once, and continued to be, sources of inspiration for various sectors within the Catholic community. Heinrich Kihn, Möhler's successor as Dean of Würzburg, recognized the fount of Möhler's great influence, despite his short life: "With his great classical works, Möhler became the teacher of an entire generation."[17] In 1879, Dr. Döllinger remembered the effect produced by the first edition of Die Einheit on his circle:

> The ardor and fervour, which emerged from this book, the ingenious, clever and witty picture of the Church, drawn from

---

[16]J. B. Hafen, Möhler und Wessenberg, oder Streng-kirchlichkeit und Liberalismus in der Katholischen Kirche in allem ihren Gegensätzen mit besonderer Rücksicht auf die Katholischen Geistlichen Württembergs (Ulm, 1842), p. 11. Another pupil remembered Möhler's influence on the Tübingen students to be not so much as great teacher but as spiritual father. A Munich student said that he was "drawn to this theology because Möhler's soul (despite the controversies) exuded no animosity and no hatred," Alois Knöpfler, Johann Adam Möhler. Ein Gedenkblatt zu dessem hundertstem Geburtstag (Munich, 1896), pp. 75–76, 80–81, 82. P. B. Gams, who attended his courses in 1834 and 1835 and then became a Benedictine said that it was primarily Möhler's depth and interior quality and his love for the church which caused his lectures to be crowded. W. G. Volk attested that in Munich an atmosphere of priestly purity and high spiritual ideals hung about the former Württembergian which was not common in that city. Lösch, Möhler, I, 483–485, 507.

[17]Fritz Vigener, "Gallikanismus und episkopalistische Strömungen im deutschen Katholizismus zwischen Tridentinum und Vaticanum," Historische Zeitschrfit, III (1913), 563.

143

the spirit of the Fathers of the Church, enchanted all of us
young men.[18]

When, in January 1828, Johann Michael Sailer had put down Möhler's

Athanasius, he wrote about it to the Bavarian Minister of Cults von

Schenk:

> I would like to call your attention to a new, striking
> publication in the field of theological literature, which has
> gladdened my heart in an extraordinary measure....I have not
> read a book like it....(It is filled with) profundity and
> clarity, fervor and peace, freedom of thought and orthodoxy,
> sagacity and classical exposition....[19]

Goyau, the observer of the developments in German ecclesiastical life

in the nineteenth century, remarked that at the end of the century the

Symbolik was regarded as the great classic which had inspired the young

clergy with dogmatic principles. By the time Goyau was writing, it had

gone into fourteen editions and it was still a tradition for Tübingen

students to learn entire chapters of it by heart.[20]

-2-

But there were important differences in Möhler's exposition of his

central themes as expressed in Die Einheit and the Symbolik. Between

1825 and 1835, like so many European theological schools, like Dom

Guéranger and Dr. Pusey, like Wagner, Napoleon III, Hegel, Walter Pater

and Bismarck, Möhler moved steadily to the right, to reliance upon the

authoritarian structures of the past. Möhler realized that his initial

vision of the church required objectivization and protection from

----

[18]J. Friedrich, op. cit., p. 9.

[19]Lösch, Möhler, I, 257.

[20]George Goyau, L'Allemagne religieuse. Le Catholicisme (1800–
1848), II, 2 (Paris, 1905), 41. One observer remembered this effect of
the editions of the Symbolik: "It worked like an electric shock on our
souls and brought forth inside and outside the Catholic Church a fresh
movement of the spirit." Kihn, op cit., p. 12. Three learned Roman
authors of the nineteenth century in Germany, the historian Hurtir, the
Jesuit Hammerstein, and the philologist Bickell were converted from
Protestantism to Catholicism by reading the Symbolik.

absorption into the state. As a result, he concluded that the ancient
organs of the church, whether they be monastery, episcopate, sacrament,
or papacy, could be reformed to become the matrix of the new
Catholicism. In the technical language of ecclesiology, Möhler's
evolution was from communal Presbyterianism to episcopal corporatism
grounded in the papal primacy.

In his conversations with Beda Weber at the Meran resort in 1837,
Möhler remembered Die Einheit as being neither the fullest nor most
mature expression of his thought:

> I would hardly like to be remembered completely for this
> work. It is the product of an enraptured youth, who is
> thinking candidly about God, Church, and world. But many
> things which are stated there I can no longer defend. All is
> not fittingly understood and convincingly developed
> [there].[21]

But it was the foundation and basic expression of all that came later.

Die Einheit is concerned with the Catholicism of the first three
centuries. Möhler's belief in a true "spirit" of the Christian people,
tarnished and repolished through 1900 years, is underscored by the
subtitle of the work, The Principle of Catholicism Exhibited in the
Spirit of the Church Fathers of the First Three Centuries .[22] He saw
that the Catholicism of those centuries grounded every individual into
the immediate community and thence into the universe at large. Thus,
unity (Einheit) is produced, in the church, in society, in the
universe. The ideal of unity, expressed in various forms, is the
central ideal of Catholicism exhibited in the unity of the spirit of
the church, the mystical unity of the church, the intellectual unity of

----

[21]Lösch, Möhler, I, 513. Only two editions of the Einheit have been
published, one in 1825 and one in 1925. All references in this work
are to the Mainz edition of 1925. Thirteen complete German editions of
the Symbolik have come out, five by 1838 and the last in 1924. All
references in this work refer to the translation by James Burton
Robertson published in New York in 1844.

[22]Throughout, Möhler argues that the Fathers' main concern was
unity, and the basic proofs of all his concepts are drawn from the
Fathers Origen, Ignatius of Antioch, Clement of Rome, Justin, Cyprian,
Irenaeus, Tertullian, Augustine, Eusebius, and Clement of Alexandria.

the church, the unity of humankind in the church, the unity of the church expressed in the local bishop, in the metropolitan, in the collective episcopate, and in the primate.

All of these Christian unities are placed in apposition to the current multiplicity produced by forces of disunity: the destruction of the old German church system and the inability of the hierarchy to adapt to new economic and political circumstances, the new state system and the end of old communal unities within society.[23] The exposition of the various unities produced by Christianity is divided into two parts, corresponding to the two sections of Die Einheit. The unities of the first half are gathered under the general heading "unity of the spirit of the Church" and those of the second, "unities of the Body of the Church." This division gives a key to the meaning of the book. The initial chapters discuss how the "spirit" expressed in the mystical, unified life of the people is translated into "bodies," hierarchy, sacraments, concepts and dogmas, which would not be valid if imposed from above. Heretical revolts, although properly coming from below, have been an injection of multiplicity and egoism into the Christian organism.[24] The second part continues with a discussion of the symbolic, hierarchical exteriorization of the spiritual unity in persons who stand at the center of the life of the community—bishops, priests, metropolitans, and popes.

In Möhler's manuscript lectures on canon law, the church still appears simply as a form of human society, created by man. In Die Einheit, the community is completely spiritual and built by the Holy Ghost. In the former, the community is separated from God; in the latter, it unites the world with God. In the lectures, it is in the form of men's society; in Die Einheit, it is the form of God's community. The ecclesiological notion which ties the 1825 work

----

[23]The fourth chapter of Die Einheit discusses various forms of multiplicity without unity.

[24]Einheit, p. 44. Möhler says that the essence of each heresy is placing the importance of the individual above all the rest of creation, Ibid., p. 108.

146

together is that:

> The unity in the Church is [based] on the community, founded
> by Christ through the apostles, surviving because of the love
> of the believers which finds its origin in the Holy Ghost
> ....The communication of the Holy Ghost is the condition of
> Christianity in us. He unites all believers into a spiritual
> community, through which he continues to communicate to
> believers, through love....Only in the community of believers
> do we become acquainted with Christ.[25]

This is already a step beyond Schleiermacher and the Romantics, for in Die Einheit it is the power of God which breaks the bars of material alienation separating individuals and creates a church, whereas in Schleiermacher's books the organic grouping of believers into a community receives its initial impulse from the needs of men and women. But the Christian Romanticism of Schleiermacher and Drey is not entirely dissipated in Die Einheit. Christianity in Die Einheit is still a heightened mode of existence which involves a transcendence of the material realm.[26] The Holy Ghost, it is clear, is the Geist of German idealism masquerading in Catholic garb.[27] The evolutionary organicism of Schelling is recalled when Möhler says that the treasure of this life principle which allows believers to dwell in unity is continually being renewed and made young.

In fact, the communal argument of the Romantics is presented so strongly in Die Einheit that it appears to exclude the old-fashioned Roman Catholic conception of hierarchy, to the point that a free church polity appears to be advocated. In Möher's rage against ecclesiastical classes, in the midst of his excitement in the rediscovery of the laity, in his revolt against the Febronians and Josephists, he lessened the role of the hierarchy and primacy in creating Christian unity. However, his contemporaries could detect a role for the hierarchical

----

[25]Ibid., p. 7. Quoted also in Alois von Schmid, "Der Geistige Entwicklung Johann Adam Möhlers," Historisches Jahrbuch, XVIII (1897), 329.

[26]"The Church is viewed as an immediate godly power, as a life in and through the Holy Ghost." Einheit, pp. 96-97.

[27]"The Holy Ghost is also the spirit of truth." Ibid., p. 18.

structure within the Möhlerian church of the future. It is expressed in the first ecclesiological definition of the second section of Die Einheit: "The Church is the outer visible form of an inner, holy, living power of love the body of which is built from the inside out by the spirit of believers."[28] In outlining the history of the development of the church's unity in the first three centuries Möhler shows that the community of love required an exteriorization of that love. The hierarchy became a visible reflex of the love of the community. At the very moment that Lamennais was uttering similar statements in France, Möhler in Germany was arguing that bishops are "the train bearers of the people's sovereignty." The German makes clear that the distinction between hierarchy and laity is only a difference of distributed gifts. The bishops are the community's unity made visible in one person and locality:

> The middle-point of the diocese is the bishop, the person who is the reflex of the love of the community. There are clerics and lay, named nothing other than that. They are differentiated by various gifts. The failure to observe this godly economy creates a situation which lacks freedom. There is a general priesthood of all Christians.[29]

Likewise, doubt is shed in Die Einheit upon the notion that the pope is the essence of the Catholic Church. The papacy is shown to be merely a historically determined symbol. Möhler was prophetic in foreshadowing the solution by which Vatican II solved the dilemma which had separated Gallicans and Ultramontanes since the early nineteenth century by suggesting that the unity of the church is symbolized by the binding of primacy and episcopacy into a collegial body in which both play a role, a union established as much in "Gesamtheit des Episkopate" as in "Primate."[30]

Priesthood and liturgy were also defined as externalized products of the communal unity of the Christian people, rather than its cause as

----

[28]Ibid., p. 129.

[29]Ibid., p. 129; also similar sentiments on pp. 137, 140, 163.

[30]Ibid., p. 171.

in Guéranger. The priest now receives his mission only from the community of the faithful. Ordination becomes in Die Einheit a recognition of a gift which already exists, rather than an imparting of the grace of the sacrament from the hierarchy:

> Ordination is the outer demonstration of nothing other than the recognition by the entire Church that the Spirit is in a certain believer,...that the love of a certain number of believers is represented.[31]

The Athanasius, Möhler's next book, was brought out in 1827 by Florian Kupferberg, a Catholic publisher of Mainz who issued works with Ultramontane overtones. This was a far cry from Die Einheit, published by the Protestant Heinrich Laupp of Tübingen, and banned from Hapsburg dominions by the Austrian censors.[32] One of Möhler's students, Joseph Martin Mack, mentions that he and his contemporaries learned from Die Einheit to construct the church from inside out, from the inner feelings of the believers to the outer structure, and from the Athanasius, from under to above, from the people to the visible community.[33] The Athanasius represents a transition from Die Einheit to the Symbolik. Here Möhler abandons the inner-outer dialect of Schleiermacher and shifts his emphasis from the visible community founded by the Holy Ghost to the presence of Christ in the church through a continuation of his incarnation. For the first time Möhler suggests that the community of believers is the extension of the incarnation, the body of Christ: "The Savior manifested Himself in that He walked as a man among men, but still a greater revelation of

---

[31]Ibid., p. 168. A long note on pp. 243-256 discusses the participation of all Christians in the calling of spiritual leaders. There is a lengthy proof of this from the Fathers including primarily citations from Origen, Augustine, and Gregory of Nyssa.

[32]Möhler wrote to Gengler 10 December 1832, "Do you want a publisher? One who comes to mind is Knicher but I don't allow myself to be published by Protestants. That is why I have put myself under Kupferberg." Lösch, Adam Gengler, p. 95.

[33]J. R. Geiselmann, "Johann Adam Möhler und die Entwicklung seines Kirchenbegriffs," ThQ (1931), 1-91. J. M. Mack quoted in Lösch, Möhler, I, 540.

Him was to be the history of the Christian Church...."[34] The effect of the emphasis upon the visibility of the community and its foundation upon Christ in the ecclesiology of Athanasius was to place the human "outside and before God," and to correct the Sabellianism which Möhler now feared he had inherited from Schleiermacher and defended in Die Einheit.[35] In the Athanasius Möhler questions the orthodoxy of Schleiermacher's reconstituted trinitarian language and openly wonders if the Romantic ideology is compatible with Christianity. Schleiermacher is identified with Sabellius, who suppressed transcendence:

> According to Sabellius the Holy Spirit is the Spirit of the whole, that is, of all the faithful. The Spirit is only in the totality, for since the Spirit is the divinity itself, each Christian would be Christ if the Spirit were present as such in each individual. Thus Schleiermacher expressed himself when he comments on Sabellius' thought.[36]

Schleiermacher confused the spirit immanent in the whole with God. This is unacceptable not because the human is raised in the evolutionary process, but the divinity is shown to be evolving in the Christian community. Möhler wrote, "I wish to remark before all, that it has been taught of Christ always that He is God and that He did not become God only in hymns and exuberant effusions of Christian feeling."[37] God is not separate from the creation in this Sabellian/

----

[34]Athansius der Grosse und die Kirche seiner Zeit (Mainz, 1827), p. 162. Quoted also in H. R. Nienaltowski, Johann Adam Möhler's Theory of Doctrinal Development: Its Genesis and Formulation (Washington, 1959), p. 23.

[35]In 1832 Adam Gengler wrote a series of articles for the ThQ on the Protestant theologian Johann Carl Friedrich Rosenkranz who taught at Halle and Königsberg and was known for his attacks upon Schleiermacher. At that time, in January 1832, Möhler wrote to Gengler that Rosenkranz, with his anti-Schleiermacher arguments, had shown him the dangers of the Romantic theology. The works of Rosenkranz which had been important for Möhler were Der Zweifel am Glauben (1830) and an article in the Berliner Jahrbücher für Wissenschaftliche Kritik (1831), "Kritik der Schleiermacherschen Glaubenslehre."

[36]Athanasius, III, 285.

[37]Athanasius (Mainz, 1844), p. 275.

Schleiermachian pantheism and that results in the Athanasius
anthropology of the Christian standing "outside and before God." In
the Athanasius Möhler is arguing that Christianity will rapidly become
meaningless if the Gospel is reduced to Romantic religion. The
collective feeling of the church is created by Spirit but is not
Spirit. There is protection in Athanasius against a complete osmosis
of divinity into humanity.[38] That was the theme of the doctrinal
controversies of the ecumenical councils of the fourth century in which
the historic Bishop Athanasius played a prominent role. With these
1827 volumes Möhler's plan becomes clear. He reconstructed various
stages of the growth and progress of the "principle of Catholicism" to
serve as inspiration and defense in the face of the most pressing
contemporary challenges to Christianity. There is, consequently, as
much emphasis upon dogma and history in Athanasius as there had been
upon life and freedom in Die Einheit. The freedom of the community,
which had been valued in 1825, is now in Möhler's second book connected
to theological orthodoxy and hierarchical conformity. The pope is
regarded as "the head with which all members of the Church must be
bound."[39]

The threat of the cultural totalitarianism of the state is the
theme of articles on St. Anselm of Canterbury, which later came out as
a book but appeared in the last Theologische Quartalschrift of 1827 and
the first number of 1828 as "Die Scholastik des Anselmus." Möhler sees
here a similarity between the condition of the church in Württemberg
and that of Christians in England in the 11th century. In 1828, in the
new diocese of Rottenburg which was coextensive with the kingdom of
Württemberg, the choice of Johann Baptist von Keller as first bishop
was dictated by the secular government. The ministers of Württemberg
wanted only an "anointer" and in fact von Keller cleared every
administrative step with the government's Catholic Church Office in

---

[38]Josef Rupert Geiselmann, Die theologische Anthropologie Johann
Adam Möhlers: Ihr Geschichtlicher Wandel (Freiburg, 1955), p. 128.

[39]Athanasius, II, 73-74, quoted in Schmidt, loc. cit., p. 351.

Stuttgart.[40] It was to such a situation that <u>Anselm</u> was addressed:

...When the sovereign, without the concurrence of the Church, elects the Bishops, whose qualifications are here immaterial, ...he thereby claims a power of the Church, as though it were an emanation of sovereignty. This is an error.[41]

In England, the church had recognized that only the freedom of the ecclesiastical community could guarantee the liberties of the individual:

The freedom of individuals presupposes the freedom of the body; for when an individual really forms, as he should, an organic member of the whole, his destiny is deeply and wonderfully implicated in the fate of the entire body.[42]

Monasticism and celibacy had been the means in those days, according to the <u>Anselm</u>, through which the church had preserved her independence. The Wessenbergians had preached against the centuries surrounding St. Anselm's life, for they had been dominated by "medieval

----

[40]Franz Stärk, <u>Die Diözese Rottenburg und ihre Bischöfe</u> (Stuttgart, 1928), pp. 57-58. Stephan Lösch, <u>Die Diözese Rottenburg im Bilde der Offentlichen Meinung, 1828-1840</u> (Rottenburg, 1927) reveals that at every meeting of the chapter of the cathedral of Rottenburg, including that at which the bishop was chosen, a secular commissioner who held the title of counselor was present and allowed to veto any matter. Möhler was so conscious of the ecclesio-political situation that some individuals consider that his incorporation of hierarchical structures was a result of his disenchantment with the weak puppet hierarchy of Rottenberg. He wrote one friend, "Our bishop is something of a rascal, who is not worthy of the name which he carries." Goyau, <u>op. cit.</u>, p. 141. He wrote to Döllinger in April, 1830, "Our official ecclesiastical situation is as bad as it possibly could be. Our episcopate is a deformed thing, which is no longer worthy of the name...." Heinrich Fels, <u>Johann Adam Möhler. Der Weg seines Geistlichen Werdens</u> (Limburg, 1939), p. 132. And he wrote to his correspondent Gengler in April 1833, "As far as the ecclesiastical situation is concerned...we have become prostituted, especially with our unworthy, completely demoralized bishop; as you know, I look forward to nothing good." Lösch, <u>Adam Gengler</u>, p. 97.

[41]<u>Life of St. Anselm, Archbishop of Canterbury: A Contribution to a Knowledge of the Moral, Ecclesiastical, and Literary Life of the Eleventh and Twelfth Centuries</u>, trans. by Henry Rymer (London, 1842), p. 97.

[42]<u>Ibid.</u>, p. X.

darkness and slavery."[43] But Möhler saw that the "principle of Catholicism" had survived during those years, developing resources which could now be drawn upon in Württemberg:

It is much to be regretted that the men of these days are totally ignorant of the writings of the scholastics but constantly revile them,--men who oppose themselves to every authority, and yet, when asked what it is they so violently combat can with difficulty give you an answer.[44]

The Symbolik continues the study of the evolution of the "principle" into the era of the formal dissolution of the unity of the Western church, the sixteenth century. The rift between Protestants and Catholics is reduced to a conflict between an objective version of Christianity and a subjective one. As in Möhler's other works, the subtitle, Exposition of the Doctrinal Differences Between Catholics and Protestants as Evidenced by their Symbolical Writings, elucidates the author's intent. The purpose of the Symbolik was to correct the ignorance of the parish clergy, concerning the essence of both Protestantism and Catholicism. It had long been the custom in Germany for Lutherans and Calvinists to deliver lectures and print books on the customs and creeds of the other German religious bodies for the benefit of their clergy. Now, with the new notion of scientific culture solidly engrafted within the Catholic theology of Tübingen, it was incumbent, Möhler felt, to enter with the utmost precision and depth into the nature of the differences which divide "religious parties," for the Roman Catholic clergy as well as for their flock.

There was an ecumenical motive as well in the Symbolik, for it was to remove the differences between Protestants and Catholics. After citing numerous instances of common sacramental theology of Lutherans and Romans, Möhler exclaims:

This is the point at which Catholics and Protestants will, in great multitudes, one day meet, and stretch a friendly hand one to the other. Both, conscious of guilt, must exclaim, "We all have erred--it is the Church only which cannot err;

---

[43]Hafen, op. cit., p. 31.

[44]Ibid., p. 23.

we all have sinned—the Church only is spotless on earth."[45]
Möhler is careful to extol the orthodoxy of reformers of the caliber of
Luther and Calvin in most of their theology, but he was aware that true
ecumenism would come only when the differences of the religious
communities were expressed in the deepest sense and that the sort of
doctrinal indifferentism of the Aufklärung as exhibited by the
Wessenbergians would only lead to danger for the church. Therefore,
the Symbolik is not without a certain element of polemic in pointing
out those doctrinal points which made Roman Catholics more capable than
Protestants of preventing the secularization and rationalization of
Christianity and the disappearance of its separate communal existence.

The Symbolik juxtaposed Catholic and Protestant treatment of
central theological points: justification and sanctification, the
church, the sacraments, and the four last things, death, judgment,
heaven and hell. Möhler refused to allow to any Tridentine or post-
Tridentine catechism the character of a public confession of the true
principles of Catholicism. Enough of the Möhler of Die Einheit remains
to say, with Dr. Pusey, that the only Catholic writings of symbolic
authority are the credal statements of the councils of the first seven
centuries of Christian history. Next to the Catholic pronouncements on
the four central points of the faith, he places the views of the
Lutheran symbolical books, Luther's own long and short catechisms, the
famous Augsburg confession, and the Formula of Concord, compiled by
Andrew of Tübingen in 1577. The number and extent of the Calvinist and
Reformed symbols summarized and discussed is even more varied than that
of the Roman and Lutheran. The foundation of the Calvinist symbolical
notions included in the figuratively parallel columns of the volume are
all the synodal decrees of church bodies who based their concepts on
Calvin's writings. Included as well among the columns of the Reformed
are the ideas of the Zwinglian Confessio Tetrapolitana, the symbolical
formula of the four Zwinglian cities on the borders of Württemberg,
Strasburg, Constance, Memmingen, and Lindau, the three Helvetic

---

[45]Ibid., p. 349.

Confessions compiled by Henry Bullinger, Leo Judas, and Simon Grynaeus, the more Calvinist version of the Thirty-nine Articles of the Church of England brought out under Edward VI by Cranmer and Ridley in 1553, the Heidelberg Catechism of Frederick III, Count Palatine, of 1562, and the Confession of the Marches, promulgated by the Margrave of Brandenburg, John Sigismund. The more sect-like and more recent variations of classical Protestantism—the Methodists, Baptists, Quakers, and Swedenborgians—are treated with cursory glances after the more established schools have been dealt with.

The encyclopedic character of the Symbolik will fool the casual reader. Möhler had not been deterred from the great plan of his life. The exposition of the evolution of the "principle of Catholicism" is continued here as well, into the period of the Reformation and after. This is the theme which ties the details of the symbolical formulations together. He weaves two ecclesiological strands from the confessional statements. Möhler, as did Dr. Pusey, suggests that the seeds first for rationalism and idealism and then for a purely secular society were sown unwittingly by the orthodox Protestant reformers. Luther's opposition of Law and Gospel, his Gnostic-Manichean dualism, is connected directly to the eighteenth-century Aufklärung. The eucharistic pantheism of Zwingli is shown to lead on to Hegelian idealism.

Also with Dr. Pusey, the heart of the difference between Protestantism and Catholicism is reduced to a varied interpretation of the doctrines of justification and sanctification. The Protestants, according to Möhler, separate the two. The Catholics unite them. Protestants reduce justification to a subjective process and thereby open the way for the development of a secular society by reducing the necessity of ecclesial communities proffering objective grace and denuding the body politic of any but secular institutions.

The issue of justification is a lively one again because of its importance for the solution of the pressing nineteenth century problem of alienation. Möhler understands that the opinions on this question are predicated by two different views of the human in Protestantism and

Roman Catholicism. The Protestants looked to the individual's relationship with God; the Catholics to the individual's communion with fellow humans in the church. These

> conflicting doctrines [justification and sanctification], deal with the origin and the nature of the internal life of those united with Christ, [and]...with their external union and communion with each other. Thus, by carefully investigating them we can be led to enlarge on the theory and essence of this outward community according to the views of the different confessions.[46]

To Möhler it was clear that from the classical Catholic point of view a holy community had once existed between God and humans which had been destroyed by self-love. Through the inner working of the Holy Spirit accompanied by the cooperation of creatures in receiving grace through the objective material sacraments, man and woman could be transformed and led back into that holy communion. Justification, by reception of the sacraments, is inseparable from sanctification for the Catholic:

> The Catholic Church, above all things, insists on a radical internal change (for justification to take place). ...The Catholic can attain the forgiveness of his sins only when he abandons them, and in his view the justified man,—the man acceptable to God,—is identical in every respect with the sanctified.[47]

It is just within the context of differentiating the Catholic

---

[46]Symbolik, p. 114. The idea of writing a Symbolik which points out the basic difference of Protestants and Catholics and of writing a book on justification and sanctification appears to have occurred to Möhler at the same time. J. A. Möhler, "Rezension: G. B. Winer, Vorstellung des Lehrbegriffs des verschiedenen christlichen Kirchen Parteien," ThQ (1826), 111-138 is an article in which he mentions for the first time theories of justification as the fundamental idea which separates the two Christian communities. This article also contains Möhler's first mention of the term "Symbolik" and is the first sign of his interest in discussing the fundamental ideas of the Christian communions. Since the whole point of Winer's book was the comparison of Protestant and Catholic views of justification, it is safe to assume that Möhler took the fundamental idea of the Symbolik from him: "The later Lutherans reproached Luther, because he mixed justification and sanctification, but he did not mix the two."

[47]Ibid., p. 198.

theory of justification from the Protestant that Möhler's definition of faith emerges which, while not abandoning Aufklärung notions on this subject, goes beyond them. The faith which justifies—and here he is very close to the theories of both Lamennais and J. H. Newman—is more than a rational assent. It is a response of the whole man:

> If faith passes from the understanding and the feelings to the will, excited through the understanding; if it pervades, vivifies, and fructifies the will through the new vital principle imparted to the latter engendering in this way the new man created after God;...if love is enkindled out of faith,...then only after faith and love doth regeneration or justification ensue.[48]

Möhler's definitions of faith and justification pointedly mix "religion" and "morality":

> The Catholic Church considers religion and morality as inwardly one and the same—both equally eternal—while the Protestant Church represents the two as essentially distinct, the former having an eternal, the latter a temporal, value.[49]

In Die Einheit love was the mysterious bond engendered by the Holy Ghost which ties individuals into the Christian community. In the Symbolik, it is the medium which overcomes the dichotomies "religion" and "morality." Love joins grace and works, righteousness and sacraments. The elements of love in Christianity insure that it is a religion of moral as well as intellectual activity. In chiding the Protestants for excluding morality, good works and sacraments in their theory of justification by faith alone, Möhler was at one with the Oxford Movement. He criticizes the Reformed from Luther to his contemporary F. C. Baur and joins them to other subjective anti-Catholic tendencies in the history of Christendom, Gnostics, Fraticelli, Lollards, Beghards.

Since the Symbolik is a great attack upon subjective religion, its ecclesiology could not be quite the same as that of Die Einheit. In the 1825 work, the church is created by the experience of the Holy Ghost, but in the volume of 1832 the church is a communal form of

---

[48]Ibid., p. 204.

[49]Ibid., p. 263.

Christ continuing to live upon earth. The institutional visibility of the church is important to Möhler as a further protection of the objectivity of Christianity. The founding of the church upon the continuous presence of Christ on earth reinforces its visibility. The danger of subjectivity is avoided by Möhler's insistence that the Kingdom of God must allow the encounter of man with God in an exterior way.

By the final pages of the ecclesiological section of the Symbolik, Möhler has clearly progressed from his earliest Romantic construction to the notion of a church founded on authority. Now the unity in the church is not analogous to the relation of the Third Person to the other members of the Trinity, but to the hypostatic union made manifest in the incarnation: "The Church is human and divine at the same time; it is the unity of both;...it has therefore a divine and human side in an undifferentiated way...."[50] The unity of the community of believers is here rooted in Christ, and it is maintained solely by solidarity of church and hierarchy: "The union with Christ is the same as union with his community; the inner unification with him the incorporation into his Church."[51] The organs of the church in the Symbolik are not mere mystical principles of unity but are the arches upon which the community of believers is constructed. A visible head is required, and therefore there is strong emphasis upon the primate:

> The entire representation which the Church gives of itself, as a visible form which stands in the place of Christ, would have been lost, or much more, would never have come about without a visible head.[52]

The bishop is no longer the reflex of the love of the community but rather its ground:

> If the episcopate is to form a body which is united in both an interior and exterior manner...then the episcopate itself

---

[50]Ibid., p. 310; Herman Tüchle, Die Eine Kirche zum Gedenken J. A. Möhlers 1838-1938 (Paderborn, 1939), p. 194.

[51]Idem.

[52]Tüchle, op. cit., p. 195.

must command a [spiritual] means, through whose existence everything [in the community] is held together and compacted.[53]

Hierarchy and people possess the authority of Christ. They are his body extended into the earthly realm: "The Church is the continually present Christ....Christ himself remains an authority only insofar as the Church is an authority."[54]

This is the final development of the theory of the church as the body of Christ which was to stand behind the radical notions of the role of the congregation in relation to the sacramental presence of Christ in the liturgical movement and in the new Catholicism generally. But the communal element was not lessened in this incarnational ecclesiology. A community in the corporeal shape of Christ was guaranteed visibility and objectivity because Möhler accepted, as a true man of the time of the Idealists, that only the social form of an idea could last and gather intensity:

> And as in the world nothing can attain to greatness but in society, so Christ established a community,...a living, well-connected, visible association of the faithful sprang up...there is his Church, his institution, wherein he continues to live, his spirit continues to work....Thus, the visible Church, from the point of view here taken, is the Son of God.[55]

The eucharistic and liturgical discussions of the Symbolik flow from the incarnational ecclesiology. The incarnation is continued and made present in the individual in the eucharist. Möhler rediscovered, as did Dr. Pusey, the crucial importance of the incarnational sacramental theology of the early Fathers for nineteenth century conditions. The objective element of the sacraments is insured by the use of ordinary materials to convey the spiritual presence. The sections on the mass in the Symbolik were written in such a way as to stand in concrete opposition to the logos-mysticism of Romantic

---

[53]Ibid., p. 196.
[54]Ibid. p. 199.

[55]Symbolik, p. 333.

pantheism and were a direct attack, as was Dr. Pusey's eucharistic theology, on Protestantism's skepticism that earthly materials could be pervaded by a spiritual element. All the religious energies of humankind, the Symbolik argues, are set in motion by sacraments which guard against "entertaining the opinion that religion consists of mere moral and dialectic results, in human feelings, considerations, and resolves...."[56]

-3-

The ecclesiological evolution from Einheit to Symbolik, from Spirit to incarnation, is reflected in the articles which Möhler wrote for the Theologische Quartalschrift, the journal which also carried his ideas to the clergy of Württemberg and to the Catholic theological faculties of the German universities. The articles provide the specific details of Möhler's system as well as more exact historical information to counter his opponents in theological, political and cultural struggles. The Möhlerian books are the great abstract charters of the ecclesiology of the new Catholicism while the Quartalschrift articles offer more practical liturgical, parochial, and methodological instruction for parish priests and theologians.

The articles of Möhler's first period are attacks on several specific enemies from the past. In his very first published endeavors in 1823, Möhler ridicules the "Kopflage" emotional religious individualism of the pietists, the followers of Jacobi, and those Catholics who had not advanced beyond Sailer. That same year he criticized Ferdinand Walter who in 1822 had published a widely read defense of the hierarchical principle in the German Church, Lehrbuch des Kirchenrechts mit Berücksichtigung der neuesten Verhältnisse, which voiced the opinion that "the Church is in essence canon law." Möhler's review, filled with the anti-papal and pro-episcopal bias which came out months later in Die Einheit, was an adaptation of Drey's theory of

---

[56]Ibid., p. 280.

organic historical development as the chief determinant of ecclesiastical institutions. Here the corporate will of the episcopate is representative of the intentions of the faithful and "the papacy is a product of ignorance and barbarity." Möhler, however, adds as an aside, "but ignorance and barbarity are not the product of the papacy." General councils, whose deliberations are not shaped by juridical or theological laws but by the current configuration of historical forces, are here regarded as the voice of the Christian people. A matter of faith is either believed by the whole Catholic population or it is not. Papal approbation cannot make it what it is not. It is a contradiction in terms to say that a doctrine is Catholic when assented to by only one individual, the pope. In his attacks upon Walter, Möhler is bitterly hostile to what is mechanical rather than organic in Christianity and to any restriction on the freedom of conscience of ordinary lay believers. The church, he is convinced, exists only by the conviction of the faithful who must remain absolutely free: "No one remains in it [the Church] without a constant renewal of this act of freedom."[57]

However, Möhler chided as well those who misunderstood the role of the episcopate. He used the occasion of the appearance of Johann Theodor Katerkamp's Des Ersten Zeitalters der Kirchengeschichte, a defense of the grandeur of the prince-bishops of the Holy Roman Empire, to point out that the higher clergy became more important than the rest of the Christian body in that era only because they were nobles and were rich. In a review of the next year he criticized Charlemagne and his bishops and characterized the majority of medieval bishops as hunters and soldiers, often enemies of monasticism who stood in the path of the developing spirit of Christianity. In these reviews he

----

[57]J. A. Möhler, "Rezension: Walter, F., Lehrbuch des Kirchenrechts mit Berücksichtigung der neuesten Verhältnisse," ThQ (1823), 263-299, especially 287. Anti-hierarchical arguments also appeared in the next year in two other canon law reviews, ThQ (1824), 280-285, attacking the hierarchical principle embodied in Austrian canon law. Prof. Walter had his revenge. It was he who advised Archbishop von Spiegel of Cologne to forbid Möhler's appointment at Bonn.

161

draws upon Cyprian to defend his theme that the church as a community
of love should reform such leaders. In these critical pieces, the
kingdom of God is "the union of men of good will,...the community of
all these men with God and Christ...," rather than being divided into
classes—noble bishops and the rest. All the members of the church
form one body of which Christ alone is head.[58]

This community is related in an intimate way to the liturgy in the
Theologische Quartalschrift. The requirement of liturgical reform is
added to the scheme for the revival of the communal life of the church.
Discussing Tertullian in the course of a review of a book by J. N.
Locherer on the history of the early Christians, Möhler agrees with
Tertullian who discovers the foundation of the Christian community in
its liturgies: "...in the Lord's Prayer we pray to be included in a
living community with Christ;...in the Lord's Supper this is fulfilled
in the highest sense."[59] He interpreted the eucharistic sacrifice, the
highest expression of community, as the chief work of the parishes, the
joint service of both people and priests.[60] He wrote against noncommunal liturgical celebrations, such as solitary masses, for these
activities tended to introduce a magical element into Christianity.[61] He
called for a return of the cup in communion to lay people because that
had been the use of the church of the Fathers and had remained in the
orthodox Eastern churches, and it seemed necessary for the community to
partake of the blood of Christ if it were taken seriously as the body

---

[58]J. A. Möhler, "Rezension: Theodore Katerkamp, Des Ersten
Zeitalters der Kirchengeschichte," ThQ (1823), 484-532; "Karl der
Grosse und seine Bischöfe. Die Synode von Mainze im Jahre 813," ThQ
(1824), 367-427.

[59]J. A. Möhler, "Rezension: J. N. Locherer, Geschichte der
christlichen Religion und Kirche," ThQ (1825), 99-108, 665-692, partic.
690.

[60]J. A. Möhler, "Karl der Grosse," ThQ (1824), 416-426.

[61]Ibid., pp. 416-422; J. A. Möhler, "Einige Gedanken über die zu
unserer Zeit erfolgte Verminderung der Priester und damit in Verbindung
stehende Punkte," ThQ (1826), 438.

of Christ.[62] In the reviews of Walter's volumes on canon law Möhler mocks Walter's argument that the language of the liturgy should be Latin because of its antiquity, and the use of the German language is enjoined as an expression of communality.[63] Priest and people must stand together, united through the use of the people's language at the most important moments of the mass.

The liturgy of baptism, which had fallen into such neglect, is the object of Möhler's solicitude in a review of 1824. The rite of Christian initiation should be performed so as to call attention to two facts: that in baptism all Christians are made priests of Christ and that in this sacrament a religious character is imparted to the whole of society.[64]

Lest Möhler's reforms be confused with those of the Wessenbergians, he made careful distinctions. He spoke for a liturgy based on patristic models, they, on the forms of the first century. The liberals stressed sermons and lessons. He was for the mass. They allowed the state an important role in the determination of church services. Möhler considered this a pollution. In 1825 in several reviews he produced evidence from both Fathers and Schleiermacher to

---

[62]J. A. Möhler, "Rezension: H. J. Schmitt, Harmonie der morgenländischen und abendländischen Kirche. Ein Entwurf zur Vereinigung beider Kirchen," ThQ (1824), 648; "Rezension: L. Schaaf, Die Kirchenagenden-Sache in dem preussischen Staate," ThQ (1825), 287-288.

[63]J. A. Möhler, "Rezension: F. Walter, Lehrbuch des Kirchenrechts mit Berücksichtigung der neuesten Verhältnisse," ThQ (1823), 263-299, especially 294-298; "Renzension: L. Schaaf, Die Kirchenagenden-Sache in dem preussischen Staate," ThQ (1825), 286.

[64]J. M. Möhler, "Rezension: S. Brendel, Handbuch des katholische und protestanten Kirchenrechts,: ThQ (1824), 84-113, esp. 105. Möhler, like Guéranger, regarded the liturgy to be the greatest art form of the church, in fact the greatest form of collective art ever produced by men. The outward beauty of the liturgy, he argued, expresses the inner harmony produced by the perfect unity of the church. At the same time Möhler remarked on the need to return to a simpler style in liturgical aesthetics and in architecture, a call very much like that of the later liturgical movement. Paul-Werner Scheele, Einheit und Glaube (Vienna, 1964), p. 175f.

support this position. While the Wessenbergians were defending the right of the prince to legislate marriage laws and customs, Möhler began to publish material suggesting protection of its sacramental and liturgical character, which revealed the unpleasant fact that the Roman Catholic Church and Protestant governments were of different persuasions in regard to the matter of wedlock.

Whereas in his large books Möhler had refrained from identifying the Wessenbergians as the disreputable Catholic party which was the object of his scorn, he abandoned that restraint with the appearance of his liturgical pieces and became even vehement in a series in defense of priestly celibacy. The Wessenbergians began agitating in the late 1820's for the abolition of celibacy. In 1828 celibacy was officially attacked at the Meersburg Seminar, and the lay professors of the University of Freiburg asked permission of the government of Baden to allow priests to marry. They gained the support of local clergy. Möhler delivered a devastating reply to these clergy not in the Theologische Quartalschrfit but in Der Katholik. This journal had been founded by two priests, Räss and Weiss, who introduced the controversial manner of the Mennaisians and the tone of Veuillot to German readers. It was the sort of paper which was critical of the Symbolik because the author acknowledged his debt to certain Protestants. It was, however, the mouthpiece for Möhler's more authoritarian pronouncements, his articles on Islam and Swedenborg, Gnosticism, and the state of the Church in the fifteenth and sixteenth centuries. Of all of these, Möhler's article on celibacy, "Beleuchtung der Denkschrift für die Aufhebung des den katholischen Geistlichen vorgeschrieben Zölibates," was the most important.[65] Here, shoddy Wessenbergian scholarship is unmasked and the appeal for married clergy associated with the end of the freedom of the Christian community. The argument first introduced into Anselm and later developed extensively

---

[65]Der Katholik, 8 (1828), Bd. 30, 1-33, 257-297. This article also appears in J. A. Möhler, Gesammelte Schriften und Aufsätze, ed. by J. J. I. Döllinger (Regensburg, 1839), 177-267.

164

in Symbolik is made use of here. Celibacy guarantees the freedom of
the community by preventing assimilation into secular society:
"Celibacy...bears an unmistakable witness to the dissimilarity of the
Church and the state...."[66] A free community is necessary for the
survival of civilization.   Möhler labels as the destroyers of
civilization those Catholics who would remove the ancient safeguards
which guarantee the survival of the institutional church.   Duttlinger
and Rodek, priests who had introduced anti-celibacy legislation into
the Landtag and to the Grand Duke of Baden as well as to the
Archibishop of Freiburg, are "dangerous Catholics." The followers of
Wessenberg, all of those who have written for and read the Freimüthigen
Blätter, the circle of Fridolin Hüber and Weinmann, and all who have
participated in the Meersburg Seminar are enemies of the church.
Catholics who stand in too close a relationship with state power are
postulating a "frivolous" reform and are transforming Christ's body
into a "frivolous" institution. So are those in the school of
Werkmeister who "stood until the end of his life completely outside the
belief of the Church...[and] was also one of those who struggled
violently against the discipline of the Church."[67]

Devotion and enthusiasm would return to the parishes of Baden and
Württemberg with dedicated priests who would be "spiritual father[s] to
the community" at every moment--at birth, sickness, death, and times of
joy. Celibate priests would transmit spirituality to the towns, for

----

[66]Möhler, Gesammelte Schriften, I, 256. The connection between
Möhler's hatred of the Catholic liberals and their attempts to force
the church to give up celibacy and his identifying this issue with that
of the church's freedom from the state was made clear in a letter to
Adam Gengler in August 1831 when Möhler accused von Cammerer, the
director of the Catholic Church Office at Stuttgart, of being behind
the whole movement for giving up celibacy which had formed itself into
the anti-celibate society. "...The society has been formed after his
idea," he wrote and he also said that "the association has no talent,
science, or eloquence." Lösch, Adam Gengler, p. 67.

[67]Ibid., pp. 177-267, particularly pp. 183, 256, 257.

their renunciation of marriage would stand as a symbolic revolt against the sensual character of the age.[68]

He turned directly on Protestant governments along with their Catholic apologists in his final series of articles. As early as 1830 Möhler predicted that a great struggle for freedom from the state would break out, beginning among the Catholic population of the Rhineland who lived under the Prussians. Berlin seemed dangerous for it represented the religious and political theories of Hegel, a completely secular philosophy of objective spirit which he interpreted to be in opposition to the Catholic notion of objective religious spirit. Hegel offered an apology for a society totally dominated by the Protestant state.

Möhler's fear seemed realized in 1836 when the Prussians incarcerated the Archbishop of Cologne, Klemens August von Droste-Vischering in a Rhenish castle because he refused to sanction a Prussian cabinet order which decreed that mixed marriages should be blessed by the Roman clergy. Möhler had first raised the importance of this issue in an 1825 piece on the forced union of the Calvinist and Lutheran churches in northern Germany. A Berlin decree of that year had ordered that the children of mixed parentage should be educated in the confession of the father. Möhler interpreted this as a further ecumenical adventure of the Prussians which would now mix Protestant and Catholic churches in a superficial manner.[69] In the last two articles of his life, printed in the Augsburg Allgemeine Zeitung in February 1838, he placed the events in Cologne in the context of a

----
[68]Ibid., pp. 240-243, 245, 250. In his letters to Gengler Möhler praised solid parish priests who devoted their lives to the building up of the religious community. On 20 December 1829, he wrote to Gengler to greet one of these good and careful pastors, "Greet Herr Pfarrer Schnetzer, who is a man of God so worthy of love. I greet him with all my heart. You ought to really get to know him." Lösch, Adam Gengler, p. 61.

[69]J. A. Möhler, "Rezension: Ph. Marheineke Über die wahre Stelle des liturgischen Rechts im evangelischen Kirchen-Regiment," ThQ (1825), 261-277; "Rezension: J. A. Theiner, Variae doctorum Catholicorum opiniones de iure statuendi impedimento matrimonii dirimentia," Ibid., 462-486.

larger question, "If there will be no higher power than the state in Europe, then human freedom has come to an end." In these pages Möhler calls for resistance to the intrusion of the state into the affairs of the religious community in Württemberg and throughout Germany, for he interprets the struggle of the Cologne population as a sign of the rebirth of religion in Europe, that the world of the eighteenth century had indeed ended:

> That pleasant and sensual age, that comfortable time which for many is still unforgettable, had reached its high point when the spokesmen for the various confessions, in a gesture of reconciliation, had given each other their hands over a Christianity which many believed at the gates of the tomb. What was called a mixed marriage at that time was really a union from the same metal. In the spouses it was not two religions that met, but the absence of both.[70]

-4-

The variations of Möhler's thought are set within the continuing themes of his theology and mission:

> My whole pursuit is to lead back to the inner essence of Catholicism,...to reanimate belief again and illuminate it and to advance the truth and devotion in the Church which so many either fail to appreciate or completely misunderstand ....The Catholics [today] are lacking boldness, self-confidence, wholeness, conscious trust in the inner

---

[70]J. A. Möhler, "Uber die neueste Bekämpfung der Katholischen Kirche," Gesammelte Schriften, II, 229. Möhler's initial attacks on shallow 18th-century attempts at ecumenism occurred as a review of the English latitudinarians' gestures in such a direction, contained in a general article on the English situation. "Rezension: J. Milner, Ziel und Ende religiöser Kontroversen," ThQ (1828), 337-347. The growing anti-Josephist element of Möhler's thought in the articles resulted in an increasing valuation of the importance of the papacy in the articles as in the books. The symbolic turning point in the articles is another review of Walter's canon law in ThQ (1829), 565-572, where the papacy is labelled a bulwark against "the unchurchy direction of the Josephists (Wessenbergians)," p. 566, and in the 1829 essay "Fragmenten aus und über Pseudo-Isidor," ThQ (1829), 477-520, in which the pope is called "the most excellent voice of the Roman church."

excellence of [Catholicism]....It is the arousing of these
things which I consider a great and holy assignment.[71]

Möhler believed that he was witnessing two simultaneous processes in
his lifetime. Just as the principle of Catholicism had been shaped by
historical forces before, he felt that a new form of the church was
needed for the current historical era. "Without a doubt we have been
standing and waiting for such a new era," he wrote in regard to the
Mennaisians' struggle against the materialistic society of modern
France.[72] Furthermore, the church was in real danger of disappearing.
"The Mother requires the help of her sons," he wrote to Gengler in
1827.[73] Christians were, for the first time in 1500 years, living in a
continent of unbelief and materialism without spirit. This soulless
situation was most advanced in England where an overemphasis upon
machines and factories was crowding out the world of spirit. Möhler
wrote an article in which he described England as a desolate place
where factories were being built during a time of feverish economic
activity but not churches. He compares the religious poverty of such
cities as Liverpool, Manchester, Glasgow, and Birmingham to a period of
less advanced material success when splendid cathedrals were being
erected throughout the British Isles. No adequate parochial machinery
was providing for the Christian needs of the new English towns,
although the bishops were rich.[74] The challenge to Christianity in
England is shown to have implications for all of Europe, for, with Dr.
Pusey, he understood the crisis in one country to be the crisis of all
Europeans:

> ...the union which exists between all the members of the
> European collective is so close and constant, that what takes

---

[71]Lösch, _Adam Gengler_, pp. 134-135.

[72]J. A. Möhler, "Rezension: Damiron, _Essai sur l'histoire de la
philosophie en France au XIX siècle_," _ThQ_ (1830), 590.

[73]Lösch, _Adam Gengler_, P. 42.

[74]J. A. Möhler, "Rezension: M. Miler, _Briefe an einem Pfründer_;
....M. Rubicon, _De l'Action du Clergé dans les Sociétés Modernes_," _ThQ_
(1830), 118-151.

the lead in one of the members must be necessity insert itself soon into all the others.[75]

To Möhler this nineteenth century situation bore an important resemblance to the era of the Fathers, who also had to survive in a secular culture. The modern church, faced with an increasingly hostile science and philosophy could look to the Christians who had combatted the pagan Roman Empire for three hundred years for useful guidance:

> Each person who stands in awe of a philosophy which presents an un-Christian character is close to historical circumstances strikingly similar to those of the first Christians....Therefore it is not unsuitable to refer to the leading ideas and the activities of the Fathers of the Church, who lived and worked under similar conditions....We find ourselves now approximately in a similar time and situation in which and for which Augustine composed his most famous and unsurpassed writing, Civitate Dei....[76]

The Fathers had baptized classical civilization. Möhler called upon his contemporaries to do so once again, to repeat the work of men who followed Cyprian and Augustine and "...warmed the iron bosoms of the chilly north, and melted them into a heat, whereby all the gold and silver of our modern European civilization were by degrees purified from dross."[77] Therefore a central concern of Möhler's career was to write a theology "of the spirit of the times." His attempts to rack and strain the language of the Romantics and idealists so that the words of philosophy would convey a Catholic message came from his belief that in the present it was necessary that the Christian writer be able to address the non-Christian literary population in the rhetoric of modern science, art and numbers. It was essential then that the theological concepts arising out of an earlier historical

---

[75]J. A. Möhler, "Rezension: J. Milner, Ziel und Ende religiöser Kontroversen," ThQ (1828), 339.

[76]J. A. Möhler, "Ein Wort in der Sache des philosophischen Collegiums zu Löwen," ThQ (1826), 93; "Rezension: A. Gengler, Das Glaubensprinzip der griechischen Kirche," ThQ (1831), 652-659, especially 654.

[77]Symbolik, p. 349.

period not be used to shield the church from meeting the threat of
machines and factories, as was later the case in Pius IX's Syllabus of
Errors of 1864:

> One, who thinks that the form and aspect that the Christian
> spirit of his time gives to him is its unique and absolute
> form, is involved in the accidental and is incapable of
> evaluating a period different from his own....[78]

Cultural isolation is dangerous because it involves infidelity to the
principle of the incarnation: "What the Lord wants to change today
will not be changed by magical means, but by instruments adapted to the
times."[79]

If the church could be thus armed Möhler predicted a revival which
he already detected among those in Germany, France, and England who
were addressing the times. The main obstacle to a revived church and a
reformed society was not materialism but individualism: "Individuality
is in its nature limiting; it is not spiritual;...it is local,
temporary, accidental, grounded in the material and transitory."[80] The
individualist is the modern heretic: "because he is all-sufficient to
himself, is he a savage, and because he is a savage, he suffices for
himself."[81] From Paul we get the notion of the infirmity of the
individual man and woman and the absolute necessity of aiding the human
by attachment to a community. Without the external bonds of communal
association there can be no civilization:

> The more polished and civilized the members of a state, the
> more are they bound together by wise ordinances, holy laws,
> venerable customs and manners, which wisely determine the
> mutual relations of rights and duties; so that, in fact, with
> every higher degree of internal freedom, the outward bonds
> are proportionally straigtened. On the other hand, the
> greater the state of barbarism, the greater is the external

---

[78]J. A. Möhler, "Rezension: E. Ullmann, Gregorius von Nazianz der
Theologe, ThQ (1826), 325.

[79]Hervé Savon, Johann Adam Möhler. The Father of Modern Theology
(Glen Rock, New Jersey, 1966), p. 58.

[80]Einheit, p. 107.

[81]Symbolik, p. 343; Einheit, pp. 44, 108.

170

independence; so that the wildest savage is, in a material point of view, the most free.[82]

Möhler realized that he was not the only anti-individualist. He found, however, certain "so-called reforms" to be pernicious, because they could not actually re-establish the communal basis of European society. He describes Socialism with scorn. The evil of the modern world will not be cured by exterior amelioration, by perfecting machines and modifying the state. Of all the Socialists, he chose to warn the Württembergians against the Saint-Simonians as representatives of contemporaries who sought to overcome industrial alienation but, in fact, were prevented from the realization of their goal. The true community must extend beyond the human. This is something even the Saint-Simonians are unable to do:

> Saint-Simonism is an image of modern France. It is unwilling to do without religion, but it has not enough will to believe truly and regulate by its belief all its feelings, its thought, and its way of life. It makes a God of everything so as in reality to have no god, just as there is no king when all are kings. It changes all men's tasks and actions into a cult so as to dispense with the one true worship.[83]

Socialists are at bottom materialists. What is needed is spirituality.

It is the same with those on the right who look at the state as the transcendental community. In Möhler's pages Hegel stands for all of those who interpreted the state as the ideal social body. In the second and third editions of Hegel's Encyclopädie, religion is a subjective feeling, but when it is embodied in visible forms and becomes a church it must be subject to the laws of the state, the supreme revelation of the absolute mind. Some have traced a large Hegelian influence in Möhler, particularly in his notion that human

---

[82]Ibid., p. 344.

[83]J. M. Möhler, "Rezension: Doctrine de Saint-Simon; Lettres sur la Religion et la Politique; Religion Saint-Simonienne; Doctrine Saint-Simonienne; Résumé général de l'exposition faite en 1829 et 1830; Religion Saint-Simonienne, Enseignement Central, Tableau Synoptique de la doctrine de Saint-Simon," ThQ (1832), 305-332, partic. 327.

freedom must be grounded in an objective community.[84] There were occasions when Möhler slipped into overt Hegelianism. Not the least such event was a sermon before the King on the celebration of the latter's birthday at Tübingen in September 1829. The state and the church are denominated two separate communities which must exist side by side for the mutual freedom of both. The external brace of the state is pictured as a necessity: "...true freedom is possible only in the state...."[85]

In the state, as in the church, there occurs a binding of the individual into a whole. There can, however, be no state without freedom, and this is the crucial point at which Möhler corrects Hegel's system, for it is the ecclesial community which makes the freedom of the secular community possible. Karl Eschweiler has inquired into the coincidence of Möhler's and Marx's adaptation of Hegel:

> Möhler's Catholic Church concept is a certain revision of the Hegelian concept of the state...like another great revision of Hegel, Karl Marx, except that where Hegel says state, he [Möhler] replaces it with Catholic Church....[86]

Möhler reasons against Hegel, who posits the sittlichkeit of the state, that moral influence must originate from without the human, from, in fact, the cross of Christ. The church has continued this moral experience for 1800 years, and without its free existence there will be no goodness in society.[87] General civilization necessitates institutions which transcend borders and national interest. The church

---

[84]Karl Eschweiler, Johann Adam Möhlers Kirchenbegriff (Braunsberg, 1930); and Geiselmann in Die theologische Anthropologie.

[85]Johann Adam Möhler, Anzeige der Feier des Geburts – Festes Seiner Majestät des Königs Wilhelm von Württemberg...Einer historischen Betrachtung des Verhältnisses der Universitäten zum Staate (Tübingen, 1829), p. 18.

[86]Eschweiler, op. cit., pp. 146-147; Geiselmann discusses a similar use Möhler makes of Hegel in J. A. Möhler, Die Einheit der Kirche und die Wiedervereinigung der Konfessionen. Ein Beitrag zum Gespräch zwischen den Konfessionen (Vienna, 1940), p. 158.

[87]Möhler, Gesammelte Schriften, II, 239-240.

alone can forge a viable community of nations: "...the more this communion and mutual dependence is extended,...the more the notion of what is foreign disappears, the more is humanity exalted."[88]

When, however, the year of the composition of the Symbolik was reached, Möhler had reduced the questions of freedom and of the relation of the individual to a community to an entirely religious issue:

> The union of men in social life...[has been] certainly not possible without religion....This indestructible propensity in man to unite and to associate with his fellows, is at bottom eminently religious....The man all evil would have felt no social inclinations....[89]

Religion overcomes the individualistic because alone within its realm is the spiritual joined to the material, a necessary process in which the single person must take part in order to escape the confines of ego.[90] Christianity is uniquely capable of combining people into a community.

The true Catholic knows that Christ is found only in the midst of a real community. "In the community of believers is the son of God grasped by him who lives in the middle of the unity...."[91] Each individual receives the inner Christian life principle, the inner power of belief only from that totality...."[92] Furthermore, a community is necessary for the survival of personal religious commitment:

> ...should the religious man not live in a community, which has the indestructible consciousness of possessing the truth...he would necessarily become prey to the most distracting doubts, and his faith would either take no root, or soon again wither.[93]

---

[88]Symbolik, p. 155.

[89]Idem.

[90]Einheit, p. 107.

[91]Einheit, pp. 13, 14, 16, 17, 110.

[92]Ibid., p. 23.

[93]Symbolik, p. 341.

The communal church engenders civilization by ameliorating the lives of men and women engrafted into its body. Without such activity they would go astray. Individual miracles declined because the power of the cross was embodied in a vigorous social form. The power of this religious society was valued by Möhler because it stamps its image on all who come within its circle.[94]

A community is required because to no single individual has religious truth been transmitted:

> ...all of the gifts of the Holy Ghost are only in all of the Faithful....The single believer as an individual can err.... The Church is the body of the Lord....He dwells in the community; all His promises, all His gifts are bequeathed to the community, but to no individual as such since the time of the apostles....Were the Church to conceive the relation of the individual to the whole in an opposite sense, and consider him as personally infallible, then she would destroy the very notion of community; for communion can only be conceived as necessary when the true faith and pure and solid Christian life cannot be conceived in individualization.[95]

Möhler had written that only a spiritual force could break down the walls of egoism and that spiritual energy breaks into the realm of the material in the midst of the Christian community. The collective life of the faithful is, then, the form through which the life of Christ comes into the world. The church is the present form of Christ. By making an organic collective the medium for the presence of his work on earth, Christ himself protects his own continuing incarnation from becoming individualized and subjective:

> Nay, as in Christ, the divinity and the humanity are to be clearly distinguished, though both are bound in unity; so is he in undivided entireness perpetuated in the church. The Church, his permanent manifestation, is at once divine and human.[96]

The church is then the Christian religion in its objective form—its living exposition:

---

[94]Ibid., p. 342.

[95]Einheit, pp. 24, 25; Symbolik, pp. 336, 351.

[96]Ibid., p. 333.

...the word of Christ...found, together with his spirit, its way into a circle of men, and was received by them, it has taken shape, put on flesh and blood; and this shape is the Church, which accordingly is...the essential form of the Christian religion itself.[97]

Such statements are clear evidence that Möhler was attempting to revive the early church's great faith in the general priesthood of all Christians. He was suggesting that the difference between priests and lay persons is only a variation of the gifts of the Holy Ghost.[98] Therefore, Möhler stressed the great significance of baptism,

the introduction into the Church—the reception into the community of the faithful...the anointing with oil [of] the new priest, for every Christian is, in the spiritual sense of the word, a priest...who hath renewed the most living communion with God in Christ. At Baptism, symbol is crowded on symbol to denote that a permanent change is to occur.[99]

The rite of baptism signifies that "...the Church is above all nothing other than the believers."[100] If the visible church is the product of an inner spiritual power conferred upon all alike, then any office within the church must be also the reflex of the power of the believers, and the unity of the church must not come from the hierarchy or state, but from the life of the people of God.[101] Even the development of Christian theology is conditioned by the development of the Christian life of the believers, lay men and women:

As these doctrines existed prior to [theological] opinions, so they can exist after them, and can therefore be scientifically treated without them, and quite independently of them. This distinction between individual opinion and common doctrine presupposes a very strongly constituted

---

[97]Ibid., p. 334.

[98]Einheit, p. 143.

[99]Symbolik, pp. 290, 335.

[100]Einheit, p. 129.

[101]Ibid., pp. 17, 131.

community, based at once on history, on life, on tradition,
and is only possible in the Catholic Church.[102]

The communal ecclesiology lies behind Möhler's belief in the
church's capability of solving social conflict, for it alone could
effect human reconciliation. When he suggested that Christians say not
"credo ecclesiam societatem inaequalem," but "credo ecclesiam
sanctorum communionem" he meant that the church should turn an unequal
European society into an equal European community. This is one of
the most important points which Möhler attempted to convey to his
contemporaries: that Christianity should transform daily life, that
Christianity is not concepts and dogmas, but essentially a life lived
in common.[103] Faith and all theological knowledge are a mere
categorization, concretization, and exteriorization of that life. Life
comes before all else:

> Christianity does not consist in expressions, forms, and
> terms....It is an interior life, a holy power; therefore all
> doctrines and dogmas have their value insofar as they express
> the internal which always is presupposed....Faith is not here
> considered as a reality exterior to the believer which would
> only be present in him through concepts, but a special life
> communicated to us. Orthodox gnosis, then, is an
> elaboration of the Church's faith, the scientific development
> of what is contained in the heart of the believers.[104]

Even though Christianity is a life of love lived within a
community, tradition, liturgy, and hierarchy-externals-are necessary to
convey the religious experience of past generations which cannot be
concretized completely in intellectual forms:

> The community, the essence of the Catholic Church, is a
> feeling that cannot be expressed by language; concepts here
> are powerless....If Christianity first lived in the heart of
> our Lord and the hearts of his disciples before becoming
> concept, reasoning, and letter, we have to affirm that the
> spirit was prior to the letter, and that he who has the
> quickening spirit will understand the letter that expresses
> it....Tradition is the expression through the centuries--at

---

[102]Symbolik, p. 99.

[103]Enheit, pp. 13, 14.

[104]Ibid., pp. 25, 43. 93.

every moment living, and at the same time taking body--of the Holy Spirit who animates the totality of the faithful.[105]

Tradition is incorporated into symbols which are necessary to Christendom because the feeling of the community cannot be expressed otherwise: "The holy symbol is thus an expression of unexpressable feeling--what a word cannot convey....We cannot speak directly of God, but only in figures, derived from finite objects."[106] Symbols change too, Möhler suggests, as the life of the community changes.[107]

The hierarchy is symbolic as well, and Möhler explains that its development resulted from the need to build the unity of the community about a figure. The unity of the spirit of the church for Möhler is incorporated in priests, bishops, and popes who are middle-points at local, diocesan, and universal levels for the protection of the objectivity of communal feeling when it is translated into Catholic teaching.[108] Since they are the exteriorization of the body of the church, the commission of priests, bishops, and popes comes from the faithful:

> The bishop is the personification of the community's love; he is the center of all....Who could be better fit to teach the faith than he who is the image of love?...Since the bishop should offer a living image of the love of all, all should share in his election; all have to testify that he surpasses them in love for Christ and in power to proclaim him....As for the exterior, ordination consists in nothing else than this: the Church testifies that the Spirit is present in this member of the faithful and makes him capable of representing the love of a certain number of believers, while at the same time binding him to the whole Church. In ordination, then, the Holy Spirit is not conferred so much as recognized, since He has already given himself to the ordinand under the form of a particular gift.[109]

----

[105]Ibid., pp. 20, 34, 121; Savon, op. cit., pp. 42-44.

[106]Einheit, p. 118; Anselm, p. 161.

[107]Einheit, p. 120.

[108]Ibid., p. 134.

[109]Ibid., pp. 137, 138, 139, 168.

But Möhler also said, "Hierarchy is not the perfect expression of living tradition. Living tradition is incarnate in...the cult, in the ascetic and mystical life of the Church."[110] In liturgies, prayers, and hymns public faith is expressed. There, nature and art become infused with spirit by the company of the faithful.[111] Since Christ is present himself only at the gathering of the Christian community, forms of worship must be capable of conveying an atmosphere of communal, objective devotion.[112] Möhler denigrated subjective piety, preaching detached from the liturgy, private masses, and masses without communicants. The liturgy, he informed his followers, should include the participation of the congregation, the sharing of the eucharistic cup, the frequent reception of communion, and the incorporation of traditional folk ways along with the worship of the clergy. These improvements would add fresh vigor to parish life in Württemberg.

Möhler envisioned a new eucharistic theology growing out of communal and incarnational ecclesiology as a means to solve the pastoral search for a proper spirituality which could overcome rampant nineteenth century materialism and individualism. He understood the eucharist to be a bridge which could overcome the contemporary separation of spirit and matter, as did Dom Guéranger.

In the eucharist the spiritualization of the human takes place by material means, the bread and wine of the mass. The human, belonging to the world of the senses, stands in need of a sensible type to attain and preserve consciousness of what passes in the supersensual part of the universe.

It is the sacraments which join the church most readily to the

[110]J. A. Möhler, "Rezension: Th. Katerkamp, Des ersten Zeitalters der Kirchengeschichte erste Abteilung: die Zeit der Verfolgungen," ThQ (1823), 498-499.

[111]Einheit, p. 119. It is this concept of the liturgical symbol in Möhler which served as the inspiration for a similar point in Romano Guardini, Trapp, op. cit., p. 231.

[112]Ibid., p. 119.

world of everyday life and insure that it maintains contact with
secular society:

> ...the sacraments contribute the more to cherish Christian
> piety, as they are well calculated to humble arrogance by the
> reflexion, that, as man had ignominiously delivered himself
> over to the dominion of the lower world, so he needs its
> mediation to enable him to rise above it.[113]

Eucharistic worship becomes more important than any other activity
of the church, for there Christ appropriates the merits of his
sacrifice and the individual loses individuality and is integrated into
the community:

> The assembled congregation declares,...that in itself,
> without Christ, it discovers nothing--absolutely nothing--
> which can be agreeable to God: nay, nothing but what is
> inadequate, earthly, and sinful. Renouncing itself, it gives
> itself up to Christ,...in this act of self-renunciation, and
> of entire self-abandonment to God in Christ, the believer
> has, as it were, thrown off himself, excommunicated himself
> ...in his existence as separated from Christ....Hence he is
> in a state to enter into the most intimate fellowship with
> Christ, to commune with Him, and with his whole being to be
> entirely absorbed in Him.[114]

Möhler's sacramental theology became quite useful to modern
Catholic theologians. The definitions of the eucharist as the meeting
point of objective and subjective elements of religion are central to
such leading modern Catholic works as K. K. Rahner's Personale und
sakramentale Frömmigkeit (1958), L. Scheffczyk's Von der Heilsmacht des
Wortes (1966), E. H. Schillebeeckx's Christus, Sakrament der Gottbege-
gnung (1960), O. Semmelroth's Personalismus und Sakramentalismus
(1957). Möhler's vision that the eucharist is the ground of the
communal solidarity of the Church is defended once again in A.
Winklhofer, Kirche und Sakramente and the Second Vatican Council's
constitution on the church, chapter two, article 11 and chapter 4,
article 33:

> It is through the sacraments and the exercise of the
> virtues that the sacred nature and organic structure of the

---

[113]Ibid., p. 280.

[114]Ibid., p. 316.

priestly community is brought into operation. Incorporated into the Church through baptism, the faithful are consecrated by the baptismal character to the exercise of the cult of the Christian religion....Taking part in the Eucharistic Sacrifice, which is the fount and apex of the whole Christian life, they offer the divine victim to God, and offer themselves along with it. Thus, both by the act of oblation and through Holy Communion, all perform their proper part in this liturgical service, not indeed, all in the same way but each in that way which is appropriate to himself. Strengthened anew at the holy table by the Body of Christ, they manifest in a practical way that unity of God's people which is suitably signified and wondrously brought about by this most awesome sacrament....The laity are gathered together in the People of God and make up the Body of Christ under one Head. Whoever they are, they are called upon, as living members, to expend all their energy for the growth of the Church and its continuous sanctification. For this very energy is a gift of the Creator and a blessing of the Redeemer. The lay apostolate, however, is a participation in the saving mission of the Church itself. Through their baptism and confirmation, all are commissioned to that apostolate by the Lord Himself. Moreover, through the sacraments, especially the Holy Eucharist, there is communicated and nourished that charity toward God and man which is the soul of the entire apostolate.[115]

The Möhlerian fusion of sacramental theology and ecclesiology into one whole based upon the incarnation of Christ, resulting in a new Christo centric liturgical and ecclesiastical life, is also canonized by Vatican II in the seventh article of the first chapter of the constitution on the church:

In the human nature which He united to Himself, the son of God redeemed man and transformed him into a new creation. ...By communicating His Spirit to His brothers, called together from all peoples, Christ made them mystically into His own body. In that body, the life of Christ is poured into the believers, who, through the sacraments, are united in a hidden and real way to Christ....Through baptism we are formed in the likeness of Christ...truly partaking of the body of the Lord in the breaking of the Eucharistic bread, we are taken up into communion with Him and with one another.

---

[115]The Documents of Vatican II, Walter M. Abbott, General Editor (New York, 1966), pp. 27-28, 59.

...In this way all of us are made members of His body but
severally members one of another.[116]
These documents attest the survival of Möhler's most important
contribution, his translation of the Romantic community into an
incarnational ecclesiology made manifest in a social theory of the
eucharist.

This was, after all, what he discovered as he journeyed from Die
Einheit to Symbolik. And here, once again, we run into the Abbé
Gerbet who influenced Dom Guéranger's life at a similar juncture. The
theory of ecclesiology and sacraments of Gerbet provided the connection
in Möhler's 1832 Symbolik between eucharist and society. Möhler's
eucharistic theory provided a place for the hierarchy in his own
communal understanding of the church which was never entirely
abandoned.

Here we observe how the mutual influence of two theological
schools led to an important advance. After Philippe Olympe Gerbet had
founded the Mémorial catholique in France in 1824, as an organ for
the publication of the views of Lamennais, he became enamored of late
German Romanticism and those Catholics who engrafted it into their
theology. In February 1828 Gerbet wrote a long article in the
Mémorial praising Möhler. He reproduced the German's idea that the
basis of heresy is the exaltation of the ego and the destruction of the
harmonious life of the church.[117] In 1829, while Möhler was planning the
Symbolik, Gerbet published Considérations sur le dogme Générateur de
la piété catholique. In it he argued that humankind could be united
by the eucharist, which could integrate the individual into modern
society:

> ...the eucharistic communion is the intermediary of the union
> between God and men....Catholicism is the universal faith in
> the presence not abstract, but real and effective of God

---

[116]Ibid., p. 20.

[117]Mémorial catholique, February 1828, p. 81.

among men. The [eucharistic] cult is the permanent organ of his presence in our soul.[118]

Gerbet explains that hierarchy and the existence of the church itself are "generated" in the eucharist which is essentially a social, not an individual act. This social character applies not only to the Catholic sacramental system but to priesthood and hierarchy as well. All the people united in the church form the mystical body of Christ: "Because all is social in Catholicism, because its origins are in the common tradition, the greatest gifts of divine love are conferred not to the individual, but to the Church as a whole."[119] The eucharist is the ground of society, of religion, and Christianity as well: "the eucharist is in the plan of Catholicism at the center of any associations of piety."[120]

Möhler first heard of Gerbet from Augustine Theiner, professor of canon law and exegesis at Breslau, whom he met during his visit to the north German universities. Theiner traveled all over Europe and kept in touch with his friend at Tübingen. It was from Theiner that Möhler first learned of industrial conditions in England and of French society in Paris during the time of the 1830 Revolution. It was from these reports that Möhler's picture of "the inflexible terrorism of unbelief" was constructed.[121] For eight months during the Revolution of 1830 Theiner was in contact with Lamennais and his school as well as other friends of Guéranger, Eugene Boré, Scorbiac, de Salinis, and Montalembert.

Above all he was impressed with Gerbet. In April 1830 Möhler informed Döllinger that he was reading the Mémorial catholique and he

---

[118]P. O. Gerbet, Considérations sur le dogme Générateur de la piété catholiquie Paris, 1829), pp. 81, 83.

[119]Ibid., p. 116.

[120]Ibid., p. 230.

[121]Lösch, Adam Gengler, p. 199.

lamented that the work of the editor Gerbet was not better known.[122]

During the same period Möhler wrote to his brother, "There are many extremely good writings coming out of France for the betterment of the Church...."[123] Möhler later told Beda Weber at Meran that he was "horrified" at the products of Lamennais himself, at the bitterness which had flowed from his pen, at the contempt which he had aroused in unspoilt minds for the Catholic system and by the way that he had racked and strained the Christian faith in order that it might become a useful servant for his various publications.[124] "But his students Lacordaire, Gerbet, and Montalembert have been a consolation and the plumes of France given to the Church," Möhler said in his church history lectures.[125]

In 1831, Möhler introduced Gerbet "to the reading public of the German Catholic world who so little know him" in an article in the Theologische Quartalschrift.[126] Here Möhler not only encourages the Germans to read Gerbet, but he adopts his theology for himself. He sets down for the first time many of the notions linking eucharist, incarnation, and communal church which became the heart of Symbolik. The most attractive aspect of Gerbet, "which in speech and style make [his] work included among the most beautiful products of the new French theologians," is that he provided a connection of the sacrament to society.[127] Möhler agrees with Gerbet's argument that a purely rational faith could have no meaning for a materialistic world. A spiritual

----

[122]Friedrich, op. cit., p. 22.

[123]Lösch, Möhler, I, 262–264.

[124]Alexander Dru, The Church in the Nineteenth Century: Germany 1800–1918 (London, 1963), p. 73.

[125]Kirchengeschichte von Johann Adam Möhler, reconstructed by Pius Boniface Gams, III (Regensburg, 1868), 473.

[126]J. A. Möhler, "Rezension: Ph. Gerbet, Considérations sur le dogme Générateur de la piété catholique," ThQ (1831), 328–357.

[127]Ibid., p. 333.

element could be conveyed only through a material medium. God must be made present among men and women in a physical act. For the communal life of the church to have any influence upon society as a whole, it must be symbolized in a concrete, ritual, liturgical form.

The German stops to consider how warm, how useful, and how necessary these French sentiments are in the face of cold mechanical forces:[128]

> ...the presence of Christ in the Sacrament [is] the permanent or continuing Incarnation of God....The eucharistic communion is the method through which the permanent Incarnation is individualized, the [means] through which the continuing divine power has an effect on each man.[129]

Here Möhler foreshadows what he would confirm in the Symbolik, "We observe here no criticism, but on the other hand only a complete agreement with the spirit of the Abbé Gerbet."[130]

---

[128]Ibid., p. 349.

[129]Ibid., pp. 343-344.

[130]Ibid., p. 357. In the 1832 ThQ there were two series of articles which discussed Gerbet and the school of Lamennais in general in France. One was Augustin Theiner who wrote "Blicke auf die Kirche Frankreichs," another was Adam Gengler's reviews of Lamennais' Défense de l'Essai sur l'indifférence which contained within it a discussion of Gerbet's Coup d'oeil sur la controverse chrétienne depuis les premiers siècles jusqu' à nos jours. On May 9, 1832, Möhler sent Gengler advice on two Gerbet books, one the Coup d'oeil, and the other his Des doctrines philosophiques sur la certitude. On May 11 he sent Gengler more information on Gerbet's Coup d'oeil, on which occasion he argued that German students in theology school should be introduced to the works of the French, and on June 7 he suggested that Gengler write more articles on Lingard, Lamennais, and Gerbet. Lösch, Adam Gengler, pp. 82-84, 88. For more analysis of the Möhler-Gerbet relationship see R. W. Franklin, "Guéranger: A View on the Centenary of His Death," Worship, 49 (1975), 318-320.

CHAPTER IV

From Württembergian "Ultramontanes" to

German New Catholics

The way from Möhler to Vatican II, with its replacement of
juridical descriptions of the church with communal language was direct
yet hazardous.[1]   Success appeared too soon.   K. J. Hefele, Möhler's
student, successor at Tübingen, and Bishop of Rottenburg, went to Rome
as a peritus to prepare documents for the First Vatican Council,
including the preliminary schema on the nature of the church.   This
"Dogmatic Constitution on the Church Prepared for the Examination of
the Fathers of the Vatican Council" defines the church as a mystical
body which must be free from any control or influence by the state.
The schema was to have been considered in connection with the
definition of papal infallibility.

But older ecclesiologists, led by Archbishop Manning of England,
accustomed to thinking of membership in the church in terms of more
tangible data, were uncomfortable in an atmosphere in which the church
was looked upon as an evolving organism, as a mystery embracing not
three sharply divided groups, clergy, religious, and laity, but as a
single large community, made up of many smaller bodies.   Afraid of the
enhanced role of the laity, they tore the "Dogmatic Constitution on the
Church" from its context in 1870.

In the thirties and forties of the twentieth century the air was
filled again with Möhler's thought on the church as a mystical body.
In 1943 Pius XII protected juridical aspects of Roman ecclesiology,

----

[1]Vatican II's Dogmatic Constitution of the Church, ed. by Peter
Foote, et al. (New York, 1969), p. 6.

184

this time with the compromise encyclical Mystici corporis which did allow that each Christian is a member of Christ's body, but associated that body unequivocally with the Roman primate. Mystici corporis, however, was a parent document of Vatican II, for it stimulated new social and theological thought and advanced the efforts of the lay apostolate. Tübingen, Rottenburg, and Württemberg provided the links which joined Möhler to the Second Vatican Council one hundred and twenty-five years after his death. As his thought suffered a variety of fortunes outside Germany, it continued in the University of Tübingen after being absorbed into the parishes of Württemberg, into the episcopal palace at Rottenburg, and into the neighboring and influential Benedictine abbey of Beuron.

-2-

Möhler's departure from Tübingen was followed by revived efforts of the Aufklärung Catholic Wessenbergians and the Protestant government to vilify him, discredit his thought, and drive his pupils from teaching posts into service in local parishes. This proved to be a mistake. The leader of the diocesan Wessenbergians, B. A. Pflanz, did the most to discredit Möhler by linking him to a "curialistic" plot to destroy the carefully balanced peace which existed between Protestants and Catholics in Württemberg. The organ and outlet for Pflanz's attacks was "that light of Aufklärung" in the diocese of Rottenburg, Die Freimüthiger Blätter.[2] Here Pflanz interpreted Möhler's presentation of Christianity on the one hand as "ultra-Catholicism" and on the other as a product of "naive simplicity" and "overly sweet sentimentality."[3] Möhler's notions forced citizens to form too strong an allegiance to the Roman Church. Pflanz named Möhler's struggle the "Symbolikstreit,"

----

[2]Franz Stärk, Die Diözese Rottenburg und ihre Bischöfe, 1828-1928 (Stuttgart, 1928), p. 74.

[3]B. A. Pfanz, Review of F. C. Baur, Der Gegensatz des Katholicismus etc., Freimüthige Blätter über Theologie und Kirchenthum, VI (1835), 208.

and he urged that any adherents to the Symbolik be removed from positions of authority, particularly in educational institutions, for the spirit of the Symbolik "is formally unscientific."[4] The growing party of the Symbolik, Pflanz feared, wanted to return Germany to medieval darkness and re-establish the absolute power of the priesthood and the papacy. Freedom of thought would thus come to an end and a re-institution of "the religion of shepherd and herd,....lifeless mechanism,...outer rules,...forms,... praying monks occupying chancels, ...fairy tales and legends,...belief among the common people without proof, without Christ, would follow."[5]

Pflanz suggested that the secular state held the right to purge the Tübingen faculty of these new Möhlerian Ultramontanes because "...the Church is not autonomous... [but] is in the state...[and the state] fulfills the duty of her protector...."[6] The government should determine "what the uses and piety of the believers are,...the rites... and church discipline, without fear of Rome or its powers."[7] The education of the parish priest must be of great concern to the secular state, for he is to be a bureaucrat and an educator with strong ties to the government: "the law demands of the parish priest above all things that he diligently and with zeal instruct the young people in Christianity....The priest is the local school inspector...."[8]

When Pflanz actually served as a parish priest, at Moosheim between 1836 and 1843, he demonstrated that his central concern was to

---

[4]Pflanz, Review of Baur, p. 175.

[5]B. A. Pflanz, "Der römische Stuhl und die Kölner Angelegenheit," Freimüthige Blätter IX, 2 (1838), 22.

[6]B. A. Pflanz, Die Ausübung des Schutz und Ober-Aufsichtsrechts protestantischer Fürsten über ihre katholischen Landeskirchen durch eigene, aus Katholiken bestehende Kollegien mit besonderer Rücksicht auf Württemberg (Stuttgart, 1833), p. 2.

[7]Ibid., p. 29.

[8]B. A. Pflanz, Ansicht über die Verhältnisse der Katholiken in Württemberg (Stuttgart, 1843), p. 32; Pflanz, Die Ausübung des Schutz, p. 25.

bring education and Aufklärung to his people. His major project during these years was to found two schools and to hire an educational official with the rank of professor to teach his flock.[9] Outsiders noted that during his pastorate the school was more "diligently" attended to than any other concern in the parish.[10] From the pulpit, Pflanz reviled the participation of any of his parishioners in Rogation processions. He openly advocated the blessing of mixed marriages. He taught his congregations to learn from the so-called Cologne affair, in which the archbishop of that city chose to go to jail rather than follow the directives of the Prussian state on the matter of mixed marriage. Here was more evidence of the subversive Ultramontanes, acting as agents of Rome, disturbing the confessional peace of Germany. The laws of the state should be respected in such matters.[11]

The blessing of mixed marriages was precisely the issue on which the Möhlerians attempted to fight the intrusion of the government into the affairs of the church. It was because of this issue that Möhler's students were driven out of Tübingen into the parishes. The cases of Joseph Martin Mack, Thomas Moser, J. B. Hafen, F. A. Scharpff, K. J. Hefele, illustrate that these very "Möhlerian" parish churches, turned into small models of the communal, unified, liturgical church described in Möhler's books and articles, became the sanctuary of the Möhlerian party in Württemberg and enabled Möhler's descendants to emerge as a dominant force in the Tübingen faculty and the diocese of Rottenburg. From pulpits and lecterns they spread their teacher's theology throughout Germany.

There was no one whom Pflanz, or the government, or the Stuttgart Catholic Church Office despised more than Joseph Martin Mack. Pflanz attacked Mack in a series of articles in the Freimüthiger Blätter in 1840 as a "partisan of the Curia among us," stirring up the local

---

[9]MS Pfarr-Visitationen—Moosheim, 1837, Diocesan Archive, Rottenburg.

[10]Ibid., 1841.

[11]Pflanz, Der römische Stuhl, pp. 72-73.

clergy over the question of mixed marriages just as other priests had been agitated by Roman agents in the Rhineland.[12] Josef Martin Mack was born in 1805 in the village of Neuhaus not farm from Igersheim. In 1827 and 1828 he studied with Möhler at the Wilhelmstift. He was made a "Hilfslehre" in the Catholic faculty, and in 1835 was promoted to the post of ordinary professor of moral theology. From the very first, Möhler showed great interest in this pupil, perhaps because they both came from the Frankish part of Württemberg. After his departure for Munich, Möhler wrote to Mack often, and on his last trip to Igersheim in September 1837, he went out of his way to see him. Mack wrote that he came to a new appreciation of Catholicism from digesting the Symbolik and to a new conception of the church as an institution founded on the people from Die Einheit and Athanasius.[13] To him, Möhler was "the first theologian of Catholic Germany." The Tübingen faculty as a whole had brought a "new impulse of science and life" to Württemberg and "new hope" to the Catholic population.[14]

Möhler's influence is evident in Mack's first books on the scriptures, Über die ursprünglichen Leser des Briefes an die Hebräer and Commentar über die Pastoralbriefe des Apostels Paul (dedicated to Möhler), for he used the commentaries of the Fathers, particularly Eusebius, Jerome, and Theodoret, to illuminate the texts. He hoped, furthermore, that the volumes would not be used merely by learned academics, but that they would find their way into the hands of parish

---

[12]Freimüthige Blätter, XI (1840), 275-371; J. M. Mack, Catholica: Mittheilungen aus der Geschichte der katholischen Kirche in Württemberg (Augsburg, 1841), p. 190.

[13]Stephan Lösch, Johann Adam Möhler, Gesammelte Aktenstücke und Briefe, I (Munich, 1928), 542; Josef Rupert Geiselmann, "Johann Adam Möhler und die Entwicklung seines Kirchenbegriffs," ThQ (1931), 3. For a summary of the position of the Möhlerian Party see R. W. Franklin, "Humanism and Transcendence in the Nineteenth Century Liturgical Movement," Worship, 59 (1985), 342-353.

[14]J. M. Mack, Die Katholische Kirchenfrage in Württemberg mit Rücksicht auf die 35ste Sitzung der Kammer der Abgeordneten (Schaffhausen, 1845), p. 24.

priests.[15] Even as a professor of scripture, Mack defined the church as a community of belief and life, as an institution which binds men and women to God:

> The community of Christians should be called the community of God, because God has called [the members of] the community together, because he holds them together, he directs them and leads them into perfection....The community should also be named the House of God, because it is a family of God; since the members of the community are children of God, he is their father and they are brothers one to another....God is present in the midst of this community through his word....[16]

In the Katholische Zustande of 1838 Mack related the continued existence of the Catholic Church as a free community to the survival of the spiritual power of the pope and the local episcopate. He drew upon patristic literature to prove that Rome is necessary for the unity of the church, and he said, quoting Cyprian, "the community with the Roman bishop is the same as the community of the Catholic Church....There is no Catholic Christian who is not bound in unity with the Roman primate."[17] He suggested that to hold such opinions does not class one as an advocate of the Curia, an Ultramontane. Christ himself left the guardianship of his church to bishops, not to the state, and the freedom of the bishops from control by the state is necessary as a fulcrum of belief and love around which the Christian community can gather.[18] Thus, freedom from observation by the police, freedom of belief and rite, and complete separation of church and state are necessary.

As professor of moral theology, Mack was professionally concerned with the subject of marriage as it affected the people of the diocese. In the 1839 issue of the ThQ he published "Uber die Einsegnung der gemischten Ehen" challenging the Württemberg law of 1806 which forced

---

[15]J. M. Mack, Commentar über die Pastoralbriefe des Apostels Paul (Tübingen, 1836), p. vii.

[16]Ibid., pp. 264, 280.

[17]Mack, Catholica, pp. 7, 9.

[18]Ibid., pp. 27, 30.

parish priests to pronounce a benediction over mixed marriages, for that injunction infringed upon their spiritual office. A refusal to give such nuptial benediction, Mack wrote, would be a rebuff to Stuttgart and to the Wessenbergians, who advocated the state law not because they understood the meaning of a Catholic benediction, but because for them it was of no significance, a kind of magic spell.[19]

The archives of the Ministry of Cults at Stuttgart show that once Möhler had left Tübingen for Munich in the spring of 1835, the Minister of Cults von Schlayer warned his agents to be on the lookout for the appearance in the university of other "pioneers of the curialistic, papalistic, Ultramontane spirit."[20] It was von Schlayer himself who began the campaign for the removal of Mack in 1839, on the charge that he was working against the confessional peace established by the religious edict of 1806. Von Schlayer wrote to the Vicar General at Rottenburg on 27 December 1839:

> Mack has been a countryman and a close friend of Möhler. He should have been a healthy and congenial sort of man. Then came the injuries which his book has delivered to the government....He has been led in this direction by the Möhlerians and the adherents of Rome–Munich....He can naturally no longer remain with us in a teaching capacity; one must find for him the first good parish which comes up. This party must see that the government is watching and takes these affairs seriously....Fresh blood must be brought into the Tübingen faculty.[21]

The Vicar General wrote back his agreement that the appearance of "the spirit of this new theological school can be dated from Möhler."[22]

On February 9, 1840, von Schlayer wrote to the king that Mack must be removed from his teaching position because "the young Catholic

----

[19]J. M. Mack, Uber die Einsegnung der gemischten Ehen. Ein theologisches Votum (Tübingen, 1840), p. 51. This book is a reprint of the ThQ article.

[20]Max Miller, "Die Tübingen katholische-theologische Fakultät und Württemgische Regierung vom Wessenberg und J. A. Möhler (1835) bis zur Pensonierung J. S. Drey," ThQ (1952), p. 26.

[21]Ibid., p. 32.

[22]Idem.

priests of the land are looking to this 'hierarchical' party for their new views and directions, this new party which the very presence of Möhler in the scientific world called into being."[23] On the order of the king, the Chancellor of the University of Tübingen, von Wächter, announced that Mack's article on marriage was an attack on the principle of the Parität Staat, which, of necessity, included the blessing of mixed marriages according to the law of 1806. By a royal edict of February 13, 1840, Mack was sent to the parish of Ziegelbach which produced yearly the comfortable income of 1900 gulden. He was allowed to keep his title of professor.

On April 1, 1840, the exile Mack was invested as "Pfarrer" or rector of the parish of Ziegelbach, and he remained there until his death in 1885. The parish chronicle records that "he took care of the people of his parish with professional distinction and civility. In the church service, he was a pater langsam, teaching in his sermons the [Christian faith] in a way understandable to the people."[24] In 1847, Mack printed the best sermons he had preached at Ziegelbach "for all true Catholics in the diocese of Rottenburg" in Haus-Postille für Pfarrer in Ziegelbach Katholiken. Recalling the spirit of Origen, Clement, and Augustine, he told his audience "that the office of preaching is...in the Church simply for building up the body of Christ."[25] He presented the same picture of the church as in his 1838 work, that of a unified community whose impact should be felt in both the religious and secular lives of the parishioners:

> This ecclesiastical community in which we live stands by us through all things: it receives us in the first hours of our earthly existence....Through our whole life it directs us, in the hour of our death it is not separated from us, after our

---

[23]Ibid., p. 33.

[24]MS Series parochorum Ziegelbachensis. Chronik der Pfarrei Ziegelbach (begun by Pfarrer Biesinger in 1887), article "Joseph Martin Mack," p. 2.

[25]J. M. Mack, Haus-Postille für Pfarrer in Ziegelbach Katholiken (Tübingen, 1847), I, 13.

death it prays for us....[Christ] speaks of it as one body
with one spirit.[26]

The rector's sermon on the feat of St. Sebastian in Ziegelbach parish
stressed again that each Catholic Christian is a living member of the
mystical body of Christ, and that this truth is exhibited by having
"communities of the pious and sinners" formed into brotherhoods like
that of St. Sebastian.[27] In 1870, in fact, Mack refounded the
Confraternity of St. Sebastian, which had died out during the early
part of the nineteenth century, for the performance of common spiritual
exercises and the commemoration of dead members. The strength and
popularity of the society can be gathered from the parish records at
Ziegelbach.[28]

The centrality of the eucharist in the life of the people was also
taught at Ziegelbach. Mack invited his parishioners to constant
reception of the sacraments, for the church is most fully the community
of all holy believers during the eucharistic acts themselves.[29] The
kiss of peace and reception of communion are expressions of brotherly
love.[30] He preached on the importance of regular attendance at the mass
on Sundays and feast days. Empty places are an affront to the Lord.[31]
To encourage participation, he restored the church in 1852-53 from his
own funds. He also urged the revival of the Rogation processions,
which he saw as an extension of the sanctifying power of the
eucharist.[32] Other small changes were introduced to indicate the
communality of the Christian life. On the Sunday of first communion,

---

[26]Ibid., pp. 69-71, 75, 116, 344, 345.

[27]Ibid., pp. 178, 187.

[28]MS Records of the Sebastians-Bruderschaft in Ziegelbach,
1870-1890, Parish Archive, Ziegelbach.

[29]Mack, Haus-Postille, II, 18.

[30]Ibid., p. 59.

[31]Ibid., pp. 205, 298.

[32]Ibid., pp. 497, 498.

Mack invited the entire congregation to renew their baptismal vows with the children. The first communicants said the <u>Confiteor</u> with the priest at the foot of the altar.

Visitors to Ziegelbach soon began to notice a change. In 1833-34, "the condition of the parish [was] inferior. The church services were hardly in order at all....The parish buildings [were] dilapidated."[33] The first visitor to come during Mack's tenure noted that for the past eighteen years, the parish, even though it had a good income, could only have been described as "so schlimm." Now, there were a society of 40 men and 60 women for the purpose of attending mass together, processions, and pilgrimages from the parish twice a year, as well as church services three times each Sunday.[34] In 1841, it was remarked that "...Prof. Dr. Mack has already in a short time demonstrated a great zeal as a parish priest....He has increased the liturgical feeling of the parish,...reformed the Good Friday devotions,...put the 'Bettstunde' in order,...emphasized the altar sacrament...[and he] gives instructions and edifying talks to the members [of the parish]."[35]

In 1844, 1854, 1859, it was recorded that in Ziegelbach ecclesiastical functions were "diligently attended."[36] By 1866, a diocesan investigator wrote back to Rottenburg that the entire population of the village appeared to be present at a 7:30 A.M. celebration of the eucharist, which was done "with extreme liturgical care." At the "communion of the faithful, around thirty persons" went forward, a large number of them young men.[37] This was in a population in which Mack baptized 892 children, an average of nineteen for each of forty-five years. There was an average of four marriages yearly. None

---

[33]MS Pfarr-Visitationen—Ziegelbach, 1833-34, Diocesan Archives, Rottenburg.

[34]Ibid., 1840.

[35]Ibid., 1841.

[36]Ibid., 1841, 1854, 1859.

[37]Ibid., 1864.

of them, needless to say, was mixed, and none was to be until 1920.[38] When a diocesan visitor appeared in 1898, he noticed that the people and priest sang together in Latin the Credo, the Agnus Dei, and a communion anthem, that there were still communions at the Sunday eucharist, and that a new eucharistic confraternity, Corpus Christi, had been formed. The state of the parish at the turn of the century was, in short, "very good."[39]

The Stuttgarter Zeitung had said that Mack, as an Ultramontane, was separated from his people, from the loyal citizens of the fatherland.[40] The Schwabian Mercury similarly attempted to portray Mack as lonely, unhappy, and outcast among the fields of Ziegelbach.[41] But the population of his parish demonstrated their loyalty. At a meeting on March 25, 1886, 5000 Marks were voted as a foundation in honor of "the ministry of Prof. Mack in Ziegelbach." On January 28, 1887, the villagers elected to erect a monument to Dr. Mack in the church yard commemorating his accomplishments at Tübingen as well as in the deanery of Waldsee.[42] More importantly, the district of Ziegelbach voted Mack into the Chamber of Deputies in Stuttgart for every term between 1845 and 1868. There, he made two important speeches. One, on April 21, 1845, protested the censorship of the Roman Catholic Church in Württemberg. On April 29, 1845, he gave free expression to what had never been said publicly in Stuttgart before. Mack deplored the situation of one-third of the population of the kingdom, who were not free in matters of religion. The Catholics, he said, should be able to order their own church services: "the rules for the outer liturgy must

---

[38]MSS Taufregister, Eheregister, 1840–1885, Parish Archive, Ziegelbach.

[39]MS Pfarr-Visitationen—Ziegelbach, 1898, Diocesan Archive, Rottenburg.

[40]Mack, Catholica, pp. vii, viii.

[41]Idem.

[42]MS Protokoll-Kirchenstiftungsrat, Parish Archive, Ziegelbach.

stand...under the direction of the Church itself."[43] He asserted that communication with Rome should be open and free, and he repeated his statement that "there are no Catholic Christians who are not also in a community with the Roman bishop."[44] The head of the diocese, he reminded the legislature, was not the Catholic Church Office, but the bishop: "...he is, according to divine ordinance, the head of the whole diocese, the middle-point of belief and love,...the champion chosen by God for the Church....His office includes the duty to support [the Church] with his knowledge and prayers to the point of martyrdom." In the end, he chided the official spokesmen of the diocese for not fulfilling their role and protecting the interests of their flock. As long as the episcopate refused to fight, priests and people must.[45]

Ziegelbach became a platform from which Mack addressed the kingdom and a model of the parochial structure proposed by the Möhlerians. Other priests, however, were not given the chance to work similar transformations. In 1841, the Catholic Church Office suspended Pfarrer Henle of Pottringen for speaking out against the mixed marriages order. In 1840, Pfarrer Zell suffered the same fate, because his "Ultramontane sermons" disturbed the religious peace of the neighboring countryside. The next year the police questioned Chaplain Sauter of Gmünd and Pfarrer Schmitt of Nagerlsburg because of the "Ultramontane directions" of their ministry. On September 8, 1845, Dr. Wenzeslaus Mattes, student of Möhler and tutor at the Wilhelmstift, preached a sermon in the parish church at Renquishausen on the occasion of the ordination of his nephew, Paul Mattes. The title was, as might be expected on such occasion, "What is a Priest?" "A priest is one who has been ordained. ...Just as the Lord ordained his disciples, so today does the bishop with his hands outstretched and using the same words, 'receive the Holy Ghost,' ordain the priest."[46] The clergy must not be related to the

---

[43]Mack, Die Katholische Kirchenfrage, p. 5.

[44]Ibid., p. 13.

[45]Ibid., p. 16.

[46]Wenzeslaus Mattes, Was ist der Priester? (Tübingen, 1846), p. 37.

outward society of men, the state, but the inner community of love, Christ's church. The connection of the priest to his community is the central note of his calling: "The priest is ordained for the service [of the Church]....He serves the Church alone....He is married to one particular community; to it he dedicates his power,...his activity, his life...."[47] The congregation at Renquishausen stopped up their ears at these words. The rector declared that he would never again allow Mattes to preach in his church.[48] Pfarrer Desaller from Kolbingen told the preacher that if he heard of such a sermon again he would denounce him to one of the ministers of the state for disturbing the confessional peace.[49] On November 10, 1845, the Catholic Church Office sent Mattes a remonstrance for this "Ultramontane demonstration."[50] On January 26, 1846, Stuttgart removed him from the Wilhelmstift.[51]

Other Möhlerians began, therefore, to be a bit more circumspect in their actions and writings. Thomas Moser, whose surviving lecture notes at the Wilhelmstift testify to his faithful attendance of Möhler's classes, was made rector of Dürnau in 1843. From 1858 to 1875 he was "Pfarrer" in Friedberg, whence he went to the village of Sauggart. Moser translated the Möhlerian teaching into an active revival of parish life and institutions in all three towns. When the diocesan visitor came to Dürnau, a village of 372 souls, in 1844, he noted that the church was "well visited," the people participated in the activities of worship itself, and there was a "diligent" reception of communion.[52]

The church calendar for 1867 shows the liturgical changes which

----

[47]Ibid., p. 52.

[48]Ibid., p. 6.

[49]Ibid., pp. 8-9.

[50]Ibid., p. 10.

[51]Ibid., p. 20.

[52]MS Pfarr-Visitationen--Dürnau, 1844, Diocesan Archives, Rottenburg.

were introduced by Moser in Friedberg. There were vespers and special devotions for the confraternities on the evening of every Sunday and feast day. There were processions at Palm Sunday and Rogation ceremonies on Saint Mark's Day and at the feast of the Ascension. The eucharist was celebrated daily with high masses on every saint's day and during the octave of Corpus Christi. If 1867 is typical, Moser continually emphasized the importance of receiving the eucharist, and preached on that subject on the second Sunday in Lent, on the occasion of the first communion of the children of the parish, and on the fourteenth and twenty-first Sundays after Trinity.[53] Participation in the leading confraternity of the village, the Herz-Bruderschaft, increased during Moser's tenure to a yearly average of 9.45 new members. Membership in the confraternity doubled to 18.35 new members per annum in the twenty years after Moser's departure in 1875.[54] Outsiders who came through Friedberg during these years noticed that "the believers exhibit a religious demeanor....The Gregorian chant is well executed...and the communion of the faithful is very numerous and from all classes....In general around 140 [people came to communion at a visitation service out of a population of 336]."[55]

Under Moser's successors in the nineteenth century the liturgical emphasis at Friedberg continued. The patronal festival was solemnized in 1876 with a procession, a high mass celebrated by three sacred ministers, and vespers. On that occasion, one year after Moser had left, 320 people received communion out of a population of 336.[56] When Leo XIII announced a Jubilee in 1881, "the community participated in rather large numbers."[57] In 1891 the parish began to go together once

---

[53]MS Verkündigungbuch, 1857–1867, Parish Archive, Friedberg.

[54]MS Taufregister, Eheregister, Herz-Bruderschaftregister, Friedberg, 1837–1900, Parish Archive, Friedberg.

[55]MS Pfarr-Visitationen—Friedberg, 1865, 1876, 1877, Diocesan Archives, Rottenburg.

[56]MS Pfarrchronik, "1876," Parish Archive, Friedberg.

[57]Ibid., "1881."

198

again on a yearly pilgrimage to Schöneberg. During the last twenty-five years of the nineteenth century, Friedberg parish had the reputation of being a place which was "liturgically correct," which used the Latin mass, and in which the people were very diligent in attending church services and receiving the holy sacrament.[58]

Moser went on to be priest in the village of Sauggart. During his last year there, 1884, the bishop was informed of "the zeal of the priest in that place, [and] his diligent work." The official diocesan visitor noted that 60 people received communion in the church during the visitation service out of a population of 270, and he seemed to be surprised that 25 of those were men. The demeanor of the congregation was noted to be "religious and devotional" and the church was "worthily" decorated.[59]

Johann Baptist Hafen was another student of Möhler. After his ordination in 1834, he wrote Möhler und Wessenberg. Here his teacher is described as the harbinger of the revival of the church, for "he discovered the good and brought it into the light....The unity and freedom of the Church came before everything for him....He called forth in Tübingen,...in Württemberg, and...in Germany...a renewed theological spirit."[60] Through Möhler, Hafen came to love the Middle Ages: "In the Middle Ages one discovers a character different from any other period....There, one observes Christianity influencing the whole of life....Of course, in that time one had no steam presses, no factories, and no railroads, and, of course, the monks wrote bad Latin, and so on....But what a rich peace that time had....It was a time in which culture and science were free and self-determined, not burdened by any

----

[58]MS Pfarr-Visitationen—Friedberg, 1876, 1886, 1896, 1897, Diocesan Archives, Rottenburg.

[59]Pfarr-Visitationen-Sauggart, 1883, Diocesan Archives.

[60]Johann Baptist Hafen, Möhler und Wessenberg oder Strengkirch-lichkeit und Liberalismus in der katholischen Kirche in allen ihren Gegensätzen mit besondere Rücksicht auf die katholischen Geistlichen Württembergs (Ulm, 1842), p. 11.

form of dictatorship."[61] The church could have such an influence on society once again if priests took seriously their ordination "and if the old discipline was re-established, if confraternities were founded for the people once again, if pilgrimages were brought back, and the German ritual and song-book given up."[62] Such peace as had existed in Europe would come once again if the church found its unity not in the nations but as a community under the pope.[63]

In 1851 Hafen was appointed to the parish church at Gattnau, where he remained until 1870, an assignment he took so seriously that he wrote a history of his neighborhood. There, he reveals that the parish was itself beset by disunity, divided into a faction which favored the Wessenbergian-governmental direction of the church and another which deplored it. The gulf was so great that the two groups did not worship together.[64] In such a setting, Hafen preached:

> The Christians who are justified [live] in an ecclesiastical community....We are grounded in a Christian community with all who believe in Christ....This must find expression in the society of a parish church....[65]

He argued such union could be established by the reception of holy communion:[66]

> [The eucharist is]...the inner bond of the loving Jesus with loving hearts....With the reception of the body of Christ you

----

[61]Ibid., p. 33.

[62]Ibid., p. 64.

[63]Ibid., p. 64.

[64]J. B. Hafen, Gattnauer Chronik oder der Pfarrbezirk Gattnau und die nähere Umgebung im Spiegel der Geschichte (Lindau, 1854). MS Pfarr-Visitationen--Gattnau, 1833-1835, 1840-1842, 1847-1848, Diocesan Archives, Rottenburg, also recall the parish division and relate it to the retention of processions and other old forms of devotion by part of the population and a fight over whether a new priest's house should be built and a wall placed around the church.

[65]J. B. Hafen, Predigten auf alle Sonn- und Festtage (Stuttgart and Sigmaringen, 1844), pp. 181-183.

[66]Ibid., p. 87, pp. 616-617.

enter fully into the community....The celebration of the
eucharist is the middle point of all holiness, all worship of
God.[67]

Hafen preached that participation in other liturgical ceremonies also
united the members of the parish.[68] He defended Rogation and
eucharistic processions, and the exercises of the confraternities as
"feasts of love and unity."[69] The liturgical year, Latin, vestments,
the liturgy itself "...create unity,...depth...and impart the godly
into the world of man."[70]

Over the years the liturgical life of Gattnau was transformed.[71]
Hafen began daily services. All feasts, Sundays, and saints' days were
hallowed with the celebration of a high mass, as well as the office of
vespers in the evening. Vigil services were held before feasts, the
devotions of the stations of the cross daily during Lent, and exercises
in honor of the Holy Ghost on the afternoon of feasts of the first
class. Rogation processions sanctified the fields on the feast of
Saint Mark and in the days after Ascension.

In 1866 the Dean of Tettnang wrote the bishop that now at Gattnau,
"the parish is very much at peace."[72] During the visitation service
there were 130 communions in a population which had an average of 50
baptisms each year throughout the twenty years of Hafen's tenure.[73]
Even in 1876, after Hafen had been gone for six years, the demeanor of

----

[67]J. B. Hafen, Predigten Anreden zur Feier der ersten heiligen Kommunion, 2nd ed. (Lindau, 1869), pp. 67, 76, 94, 106.

[68]Hafen, Predigten auf alle Sonn- und Festtage, p. 844ff.

[69]J. B. Hafen, Eintausend Entwürfe zu Predigten auf alle Sonn- und Festtage des katholischen Kirchenjahres, 2nd ed. (Lindau, 1866), pp. 739-747, 753-758, particularly pp. 754, 815.

[70]Hafen, Predigten auf alle Sonn- und Festtage, pp. 844-845.

[71]Hafen, Eintausend Entwürfe, pp. 12, 56-57, 140, 256, 260, 199ff.

[72]MS Pfarr-Visitationen--Gattnau, 1865-1866, Diocesan Archives, Rottenburg.

[73]MS Taufregister, 1850-1870, Parish Archive, Gattnau.

the parish was "very devotional," "liturgically correct," "with numerous communions of the faithful" at the visitation service.[74]

Franz Anton Scharpff studied theology and classical philology with Möhler at Tübingen from 1828 until 1833. Möhler called Scharpff "one of my most promising students."[75] He then lectured at Ellwangen, Rottweil, and in the Catholic Faculty at Giessen, near Mainz. Möhler imparted to Scharpff "...his love of the Church and the striving after the mastery of a deep, living ecclesiastical science."[76] On one occasion, the disciple remarked, "Still more did J. A. Möhler direct me to a living understanding of the spirit and essence of the Church and its history,...[to] the love of the Church as the real continuation of the Incarnation—the eternal word, the vessel full of grace...renewing the lost life of mankind." Scharpff transferred Möhler's interpretation of the church even more into the context of the modern factory system. In opposition to the alienation caused by contemporary economic conditions, he placed the daily use of holy communion and liturgical prayer: "The sacraments are the chief means by which we are related to the reality of holiness....We have certain forms and ceremonies to use as the means of grace."[77] Scharpff saw that the basis of society must be religion, which in the light of new social and political turmoil should assume more communal forms:

> I greet with joy the activities of the living societies [in the parishes], the 'Vincent,' the 'Elizabeth,' the 'Boniface'....They must do even more. They must close ranks with the older confraternities and take part in the eternal consecration of the Church....Above all they [the confraternities] lift the Catholic spirit in a land where for

---

[74]MS Pfarr-Visitationen—Gattnau, 1876, Diocesan Archives, Rottenburg.

[75]Lösch, Adam Gengler, pp. 85-86.

[76]Heinrich Fels, Johann Adam Möhler. Der Weg seines geistigen Werdens (Limburg, 1939), pp. 18-19.

[77]F. A. Scharpff, Vorlesungen über die neueste Kirchengeschichte, I (Freiburg, 1850), 122, 124-125; II (Freiburg, 1852), 3-4; Lösch, J. A. Möhler, I, 536.

202

a hundred years each Catholic was languishing in a situation of bondage.[78]

To foster communal rather than individual prayer in the diocese, Scharpff published a liturgical collection based on the psalms and communion, Katholisches Gebet- und Betrachtungsbuch, with the hope that the individual, using such a book, would learn to pray in the unity of all believers, and "participate in public worship services and in the celebration of the holy mass itself."[79]

In 1852 he became parish priest of the town of Mengen. In 1865, after the completion of Scharpff's tenure, it was noted that the parish celebrated the eucharist worthily and correctly and that "the communion of the faithful was rather numerous--around 90 to 100" each Sunday.[80] In 1876 the town founded a Corpus Christi brotherhood and returned to the use of a Latin mass "celebrated liturgically correctly."[81] The liturgical character of the parish was still strong in 1897. One hundred and forty people came to communion at a visitation service and there were two hundred members in one confraternity and seventy in another.[82]

In 1862 Scharpff was called to Rottenburg to take care of the cathedral parish of St. Martin, where, after 1866, he worked under the new dean, Anton von Ohler "who celebrated the sacred mysteries in a warm and reverent manner."[83] In this parish, which had become the

----

[78]Scharpff, Vorlesungen, I, 136.

[79]F. A. Scharpff, Katholische Gebet- und Betrachtungsbuch (Freiburg, 1876), pp. iii, v. Scharpff, Vorlesungen, I, 269, 282-183, demonstrate Scharpff's awareness that the Puseyites were saying much the same thing.

[80]MS Pfarr-Visitationen--Mengen, 1865, Diocesan Archives, Rottenburg.

[81]Ibid., 1876.

[82]Ibid., 1897.

[83]Carl Joseph Hefele, Gedachtnissrede auf dem 20 Juli 1879 im Herrn entschlafenen hochwürdigen Herrn Dom-dekan Dr. von Ohler gehalten bei dessen Beerdigung am 22 Juli 1879 (Rottenburg, 1879).

cathedral partly because it was a model Aufklärung church, where no
festival services had been allowed on weekdays, and processions and
vespers had been severely restricted, Scharpff preached that if the
corporate, social character of Christianity were recognized once again,
if monasteries were refounded, and if Catholics rediscovered that
"belief is the spiritual bond which binds us together," then "even the
workers of industry will develop a warm, open, devotion to our
belief."[84] Thus, stressing the importance of daily attendance at the
eucharist, he began celebrating an early mass for the workers as well
as a parish mass on weekdays. He solemnized feasts with high masses
and festival vespers, observed the traditional Holy Week rites, held
processions during Ascension-tide, on St. Mark's Day, and in the octave
of Corpus Christi, and conducted eucharistic devotions every day during
Advent.[85] Out of a population of 3,014, he had 694 communions at Easter
in 1864 and 388 people joined the parochial eucharistic confraternity
between 1862 and 1880.[86]

The cathedral of the diocese could be transformed in this manner
because Karl Joseph Hefele became bishop of Rottenburg. Hefele was
born in a village close to Ellwangen from whose rationalistic gymnasium
he graduated. In 1827 he came to the Tübingen Wilhelmstift and was
quite close to Möhler during the years of the writing of the
Symbolik:

> Of all the Tübingen professors of the Catholic faculty,
> Möhler had the greatest influence on him....Through Möhler
> Hefele was led into the spiritual direction in which he
> developed and into the field of scientific activity....The
> form of Möhler lighted Hefele along the way of his entire

[84]Franz Anton Scharpff, Predigt bei der Feier des elfhundertjährigen
Jubiläums des Stiftkirche zu Ellwangen am Feste Maria Geburt (Schwäb.
Gmnd and Rottenburg, 1864), pp. 15, 18, 19.

[85]MS Verkündigungbuch-Gottesdienstordnung, 1837, 1867, Parish
Archive, Rottenburg.

[86]MS Corpus Christi Bruderschaft-Register, 1862-1880, Parish
Archive, Rottenbrug.

existence...[His] lectures were guides for Hefele's whole
life, the holy ideal, which...grasped his soul....[87]

It was probably because Möhler maintained old friendships in
Mergentheim that Hefele was appointed to serve as parish priest there
in 1833 after his ordination. Möhler's friends were a group of laymen
who, under the leadership of the businessman Jakob Röser (1796-1849),
were dedicated to fighting Wessenbergian and governmental influence in
the diocese. The Röser circle had been successful in retaining
"Pfarrers" who would respect the liturgical tradition of Mergentheim.
Of the three who followed Hefele, in fact, one, Anton Greiss (1846-
1866) was described as being "very satisfactory to the community," and
another, George Kautzer (1866-1875), had been a pupil of Möhler at
Tübingen. While Hefele was in the parish, he respected the rites of
Mergentheim. There were solemn vespers and a high mass on every feast
and many of the daily masses continued to be elaborate celebrations
with music. The office of vespers was said every Sunday. The Corpus
Christi confraternity had their own corporate spiritual exercises on
Sunday afternoon. During Holy Week there were services with
processions contrary to governmental orders, and Rogation processions
on St. Mark's Day, and for the several days after Ascension. Pentecost
was kept with a special singing of the Te Deum in the afternoon and the
octave of Corpus Christi was celebrated with benedictions, high masses,
and processions. The office of vespers was said daily by members of
the congregation during Advent.[88] After Hefele's arrival, the diocesan
visitor noted, along with "the religiosity of the public church
services," that the offices of nocturn and lauds were said publicly on
some feasts, and that a "good number" of people attended the mass.[89]

---

[87]August Hagen, Gestalten aus dem Schwäbischen Katholizismus
(Stuttgart, 1950), pp 8, 13; Wilhelm Reiser, Worte gesprochen am Sarge
des am 5 Juni 1893 im Herrn entschlafenen hochwürdigten Herrn Bischof
Dr. Karl Joseph v Hefele (Rottenburg, 1893), p. 6; Stärk, op. cit., p.
113.

[88]MS Verkündigungbuch, 1833-1836, Parish Archive, Mergentheim.

[89]MS Bo-Kap A, Mergentheim Visitationen, 1830-1831, 1837-1838,
Diocesan Archives, Rottenburg.

After his experience in Mergentheim the future bishop emerged in the front rank against Wessenberg and the remnants of Aufklärung Catholicism. He wrote, "We must press against...cold rationalism, and make sure that it has no influence in our time."[90] He fought this struggle from various vantage points, the first of which was as professor of church history at Tübingen.

In 1835 Hefele took the examination given to find a replacement for Möhler at the Wilhelmstift. He doubted his success:

> The Catholic Church Office will never put me in that place and I will have to be content with Rottweil or another gymnasium. [Yet] the faculty in Tübingen and the Senate have given me the greatest majority [in the election to the vacant chair].[91]

But in 1837, he was allowed to fill the position, over the objections of Stuttgart. In the first ten years of academic activity he fought his battles through historical works. In his lectures at Tübingen Hefele brought the Möhlerian ideas back before the young people training to be priests in the diocese. The professor of church history illustrated the new "Kirchlichkeit" of the Möhlerian party by drawing on historical examples. One-third of his lectures were devoted to the patristic era. Although Hefele made a greater distinction between priest and laity in the first Christian centuries than Möhler had, the structure and nature of the church is described still essentially as a community.[92] Parishes, dioceses, and provinces are all parts of one great organism, which reaches its height in the pope.[93] The central act of this community is the eucharist, portrayed

---

[90]Stärk, op. cit., p. 77.

[91]Stefan Lösch, Briefe des jungen Karl Josef Hefele (Rottenburg, 1938), p. 43.

[92]MS K. J. Hefele, Unpublished Lectures on Church History, GH 3281 HSI, GH 3287 HSII, Wilhelmstift, Tübingen.

[93]Alois Knöpfler, Lehrbuch der Kirchengeschichte. Auf Grund der akademischen Vorlesungen von Dr. Karl Joseph von Hefele, 2nd ed. (Freiburg, 1898), p. 77.

as both communion and sacrifice.[94] In his lectures on pastoral theology Hefele also called his students to the development of a new liturgical/sacramental life in the parishes.[95] He put out an explanation and guide to the breviary and missal hymns, Die Hymnen und Sequenzen im Brevier und Missale alphabetisch geordnet in 1860. Collections of essays on the history of ritual forms and ceremonies and on the Christian archeology of the area were distributed to establish historical authenticity in the rites and liturgical art of Württemberg.[96] In 1852 he founded the Rottenburg Diocesan Society for Christian art to pursue these goals.

Hefele was successful in his endeavors at renewal within the Kingdom of Württemberg and the diocese of Rottenburg despite the opposition of the Protestant government and the surviving Aufklärung Catholics of the party of Wessenburg. In 1845 Cultminister von Schlayer attempted to remove him from the Catholic faculty. Chancellor Wächter petitioned the king for the same purpose in 1846. But by that time enough parish priests of the Möhlerian party had been elected to the legislature to force the state to grant concessions to the church, and by 1848 the government was not only publicly allowing the Catholics more freedom, but it was appointing men, like Anton von Ohler, to the cathedral chapter at Rottenburg who clearly belonged in the Möhlerian camp. The Wessenbergian party had lost control of the university.

Hefele participated in these political maneuvers. Even while he was a parish priest, he appealed to the people to work to obtain justice and self-determination for the Catholic Church. Between 1833 and 1842 he circulated fifty-four petitions for this purpose. By 1842 he had secured enough votes to win a seat in the Stuttgart legislature from the northern Mergentheim-Ellwangen district. He was opposed by

---

[94]Ibid., p. 107.

[95]MS K. J. Hefele, Pastoraltheologie, HSGi 2350, Wilhelmstift, Tübingen.

[96]K. J. Hefele, Beiträge zur Kirchengeschichte. Archäologie, und Liturgik (Tübingen, 1864).

the government and was described as an "Ultramontane, a Jacobin, an immature person, an unripe head, an adherent of the modern school."[97] But he was elected by a large majority in January of that year and in February he entered the chamber where he acted as a sort of shadow bishop and leader of the Möhlerian party. In March 1842 Hefele began to issue strong calls for the autonomy of the church in the election of its bishops, and in the determination of its cult and liturgy. Through Hefele's efforts by 1857 a "Konvention" was signed between the papacy and Württemberg which allowed virtual self-determination to the Catholic theological faculty. In January 1862 a new "Law Governing the Relations of the State to the Catholic Church" was passed which granted the diocese a free choice in electing its bishop, appointing priests to parishes, ordering instruction and liturgical services.

Hefele himself was the first bishop to be elected under the new system. On December 29, 1869, he was consecrated in the cathedral at Rottenburg on the Feast of Thomas Becket, martyr for the freedom of the church. He was assisted at this ceremony by Abbot Maurus Wolter of the recently re-opened Benedictine abbey of Beuron, by Anton Scharpff and by Anton von Ohler. Josef Martin Mack preached the consecration sermon.

Hefele set about reforming the diocese of Rottenburg "to bring the ecclesiastical sense and ecclesiastical life to growth and maturity...."[98] He immediately embarked on a parochial visitation during which he visited 24 parishes, confirmed 15,000 Catholics, and consecrated five churches.[99] Until 1893 he spent four or five weeks each year confirming in the parishes. 275,000 people were signed with chrism in the diocese during his episcopate.[100] On these trips he

---

[97]Hugo Roth, Dr. Karl Josef von Hefele Bischof von Rottenburg. Ein Lebensbild (Stuttgart, 1893), p. 7.

[98]Roth, op. cit., p. 12.

[99]Stärk, op cit., p. 150.

[100]Ibid., p. 165.

preached the sacraments, zeal for the festivity of church services, and the need for restoring the beauty of God's house. He favored corporate forms of spiritual life. Thus, he founded several confraternities for laity and priests in his diocese, such as the Lehrlingsverein, Raphaelsverein, Afrikaverein, Gesellenverein, and Kaufmannischenverein and built houses for their meetings. He established an institute in Siesen to aid girls employed in factories and he supported societies of Catholic workers (Kolpings Societies) at Ulm, Gmünd, Mergentheim, Rottenburg and Stuttgart.

-3-

With Hefele as bishop, with the support of Rottenburg parish priests and people, with the new legal situation in Württemberg, Tübingen became once again a center of Möhlerian ecclesiology. The unquestioned leader of the Catholic faculty in the second half of the nineteenth century was J. E. Kuhn (1806-1887). He studied with Möhler from 1825 to 1830 and replaced J. S. Drey in the dogmatic chair when the government, in its last great show of force, forced Drey from his post. Kuhn served in the legislature from 1848 to 1850 and then he took up the mission of using theology, reconciled to idealistic philosophy, as a weapon to combat emerging neo-scholasticism.

In his theology Kuhn chose to expand Möhler's concept of living tradition by repeating that "the individual is what he is only as a living member of a community,..."[101] Against the habitual post-Tridentine Roman Catholic conception that there were two sources of tradition, the Bible and the oral teaching of the church, Kuhn maintained Möhler's understanding that there was only one, the collective life of the body of believers. To Lord Acton, Kuhn's investigation of the evolutionary development of that tradition

---

[101]Karl Adam, "Die katholische Tübinger Schüle zur 450-Jahrfeier der Universität Tübingen," Hochland, 24, II (1927), 587.

resembled that of Newman.[102] In his works, Kuhn traced the growth of each dogma from the apostolic age through later assaults of heresy. Kuhn's theology caught the attention of Napolean III, who remarked to Stuttgart's ambassador to France: "In Württemberg, thanks to the scientific education which the priests receive in your schools, you have found the means to solve the most pressing ecclesiastical difficulties."[103] To the next Tübingen generation, scientific scholarship became the dominant interest. Of the successors of Hefele and Kuhn, Franz Xavier Funk (1840-1907) and Paul Schanz (1841-1905) took the university from its Romantic-organic leanings to a critical, positivistic approach to church history through their textual criticism of the documents of the patristic synods.

In Munich there were two divergent views of Möhler at the end of the nineteenth century corresponding to the division of the Munich Catholic theological faculty into conservative and liberal camps. The two camps had become sharply defined even before Döllinger and the liberals differed with the conservatives over the question of papal infallibility. Alois von Schmid, one of the leaders of the conservative faction, was the first German scholar to investigate the nature of the development in Möhler's ecclesiology from Die Einheit to Symbolik in an article of 1897, which hinted that the evolution pointed toward an acceptance of the Ultramontane/infallible theory of the papacy.[104] Therefore, the communal ecclesiology as presented in Die Einheit and continued in the Symbolik is de-emphasized by Schmid as it was also by Fritz Vigener who reproduced the Ultramontane scheme of Schmid in the 1913 article "Gallikanismus und episkopalistische Strömungen." Lord Acton, too, caught up in the debates of the Munich faculty, came to regard Möhler as a conservative reactionary. He still

---

[102]J. E. E. D. Acton, Essays on Church and State (London, 1952, p. 165.

[103]Goyau, op. cit., p. 286.

[104]Alois von Schmid, "Der geistige Entwicklung Johann Adam Möhlers," Historisches Jahrbuch, XVIII (1897), 323-356, 572-599.

regarded the Symbolik with Döllinger's Reformation to be the strongest book which Catholics had produced in the nineteenth century.[105] But he placed Möhler on his lists of those with whom "Ultramontanism is not error but sin."[106] Acton chided Dr. Döllinger for forcing Möhler on him:

> ...I was so bewildered by what you told me of Möhler. For I do not know how to assign degrees of guilt to the several Ultramontanes. The papacy sanctions murder; the avowed defender and promoter of the papacy is necessarily involved in that sanction....Bossuet seems to you far better than Bellarmin, Möhler better than Bossuet....Conrad of Marburg would now-a-days burn nobody. He would go as near it as the times allow. Until last year I always spoke with reverence of Möhler. Indeed I might reply that I have spoken differently when I have spoken under your influence....I have been tempted to attribute something to your friendship for Möhler....[107]

But a more liberal camp directly under the influence of Döllinger, of Hefele, and of Möhler himself continued to present the fresh, inductive, invigorating writer of Die Einheit to the Catholic public. To Dr. Heinrich Kihn in 1885 Möhler "took a great interest in the [modern] Church, in its suffering and joys. He emphasized repeatedly that in the contemporary world it was impossible, without a varied scientific education [for the Church] to have an effect on the literary world. ...The high ideal of the community and unity of the Church gave him his spiritual impulse and, to his speech, a poetic coloring."[108] Döllinger's protégé Johann Friedrich published a biography of Möhler in 1894 which described the spreading influence of the warm spiritual conception of the church which Möhler had taken from the Fathers and

---

[105]J. E. E. D. Acton, The History of Freedom and Other Essays (London, 1922), p. 408.

[106]Conzemius, op. cit., III, 258.

[107]Ibid., pp. 287, 289, 290.

[108]Heinrich Kihn, Professor Dr. J. A. Möhler ernannter Domdekan von Würzburg. Ein Lebensbild als Beitrag zur Geschichte der Theologie der Neuzeit (Würzburg, 1885), pp. 25, 32.

caused to be propagated all over Germany.[109]

Alois Knöpfler, Möhler's second successor in the church history chair at Munich, who had been a student of K. J. Hefele at Tübingen, presented a Möhler who was champion of science and freedom in the church. Knöpfler stressed that the theology, history, and liturgy of the Fathers were the ground of Möhler's entire corpus.[110] By studying the writings of the Fathers, Knöpfler wrote, Möhler came to a new picture of Christianity—organic, unified, built upon the common bond of priests and people in which Rome served as the middle-point, but not the controlling point of ecclesiastical life.[111]

Karl Adam was educated under the influence of the liberal camp at Munich and he brought the image of the Möhler presented in Knöpfler's biography back to Tübingen in the first half of the twentieth century.[112] Born in the village of Pursruck in the Oberpalz region of Bavaria, not far from Württemberg, Adam grew up in a family of eleven children presided over by a professor father. He attended the University of Munich and was _Privatdozent_ there from 1908 until 1917. Finding the sterile scholasticism of most Roman Catholic institutions distasteful

---

[109]J. Friedrich, Johann Adam Möhler der Symboliker. Ein Beitrag zu seinem Leben und seiner Lehre aus seinem eigenen und andern ungedruckten Papieren (Munich, 1894), p. 9.

[110]Alois Knöpfler, Johann Adam Möhler. Ein Gedenkblatt zu dessen hundertstem Geburtstag (Munich, 1896), pp. 42-53.

[111]Ibid., pp. 54-55, 64, 69, 116.

[112]The anti-neo-scholastic tradition of Matthias Joseph Scheeben was also keeping alive Möhler's theology. Scheeben, born in the Rhineland area around Cologne, became professor of dogmatic and moral theology at the seminary of the archbishopric of Cologne where he taught against an infallibilistic/hierarchistic interpretation of the church. "...In his teaching on tradition and in his ecclesiology the influence of Möhler on Scheeben is established." Leo Scheffczyk, "Der Weg der Deütschen katholischen Theologie in 19 Jahrhundert," ThQ (1965), 300. From Möhler, Scheeben learned to use the vocabulary of mystical theology. From Tübingen, he learned of a pneumatic/communal construction of the church. Scheeben seems to have been the conduit through which Möhler's departure in theology was communicated to the Benedictine liturgists Boniface Wolff, Germain Morin, Ursmer Berlière.

and hating equally the atmosphere of pronounced subjectivism and neo-Kantianism of other German intellectual centers, Adam went to Tübingen, drawn, as he later wrote, by "the vital power of revelation [it presented] in opposition to the dry, sterile school theology...."[113]

Tübingen mingled a warm breadth of Catholic belief with zeal for the reform of the church. In Tübingen, "the belief of the Church is not dead rigid letters, but living, real spirit."[114] There, "the question of the existence of God is not an issue of learned academics, but comes from the depths and secular circumstances of the life of men."[115] Above all, Adam came to Tübingen because its theology had traditionally been enunciated in opposition to subjectivism and individualism. In his inaugural lecture of 1919, he described the spirit of the Tübingen School as having new meaning in the context of the German post-World War I revolt against individualism. He placed Tübingen, the liturgical movement, the Catholic youth movement, Guardini, and his own work in opposition to the modernists, von Hügel, Tyrrell, and the English Jesuits, and within the tradition of the orthodox communal philosophy of Catholicism:

> It was innate in the first Christian consciousness and averred continually in the line Paul, Ignatius, Cyprian, Augustine: the Spirit works in and through the community; the community is the particular organ of the Spirit. Not the "I" but the "we" is the carrier of the Spirit. This is just the point in which the Catholic differs from the Lutheran in the profoundest sense. Only in the theology of Schleier-macher do we find a corresponding thought....Catholic theology is thus found only in the religious consciousness of the community.[116]

In the midst of a crisis of German culture Adam offered Möhler's picture of a spiritual community, the living unity of believers:

---

[113]Fritz Hofmann, "Theologie aus dem Geist der Tübinger Schule," ThQ (1966), 265.

[114]Adam, loc. cit., p. 591.

[115]Ibid., p. 598.

[116]Karl Adam, Glaube und Glaubenwissenschaft im Katholizismus (Rottenburg, 1923), pp. 32-33, 40.

'As the life of sensual man,' so remarked Möhler once, the
founder of the Catholic Tübingen school,...'once came from
the creator's hand'...so now from the same source there can
be imparted the power to begin a higher form of life, a new
godly life....[117]

In a series of lectures in 1923 at Tübingen, Adam expanded on these

thoughts. When published as the Spirit of Catholicism in 1924, Karl

Adam's expositions became one of the most important documents in the

history of the Roman Catholic Church in the period between the two

world wars. Karl Sonnenschein, a Berlin publisher, described the

atmosphere which surrounded Adam's Tübingen public lectures of 1923:

Not since the days of Johann Adam Möhler did a voice in
Tübingen so clearly catch the attention of the outside world.
The largest auditorium at Tübingen was too small to accommodate all the auditors. One saw there a great part of the
faculty of the Protestant Stift and not a few of the secular
professors, which was until then unheard of. Adam's words on
the Church as the developing body of Christ struck many, even
the Catholic theologians, as fire from heaven....[118]

Catholic communalism was offered as a replacement for the dying

European culture of the individual. It was not a movement born in

isolation, but was part of "a gradual revolution of our whole mental

attitude" caused by the "influence of early Christian ideas, of social-

ism and of the Great War...."[119] For its part, religion must become a

matter of a supra-personal unity, not relegated to the narrow concerns

of the faithful soul:

...The organ of the redeeming Spirit...its incarnation and
manifestation, is not the individual personality, but the
community as community....The Church possesses the Spirit of
Christ, not as a "many" of single individuals, nor as a sum
of spiritual personalities, but as a compact unity of the
faithful, as a community that transcends the individual
personalities....[120]

----

[117]Ibid., p. 33.

[118]Alois Dangelmaier, P. Anselm Schott. Der Mensch, Priester und
Liturge (Reimlingen, 1971), p. 108.

[119]Karl Adam, The Spirit of Catholicism (London, 1929), p. 34.

[120]Ibid., pp. 32, 36.

The Catholic faith stresses the continually evolving presence of Christ in the middle of the Christian community:

> This conviction that the church is permeated by Christ, and of necessity organically united with Him, is a fundamental point of Christian teaching. From Origen to Augustine and Pseudo-Dionysius and thence to Thomas Aquinas, and thence on to our own unforgettable Möhler....[121]

Adam's ecclesiological definitions in the Spirit of Catholicism implied, as did Möhler's, that pope, curia, bishops were simply the administrative organs of the church not its essence. In 1931, his lectures were translated into Italian, and Adam was soon informed that the book was about to be placed on the Index. "For the theological ear in Italy it sounded strange if theological truth was not expressed in Roman language."[122] Many in Germany were mobilized to protect him. Romano Guardini, the German bishops, his colleagues on the Tübingen faculty, Reichschancellor Brüning, and others interceded with the Vatican. The Spirit of Catholicism was spared final condemnation, but the Vatican insisted that the work and its foreign translations must be removed from all Italian booksellers. Before his death in 1966, Adam was to see one more controversy ignited by the 'questionable' orthodoxy of his notion of the church as the body of Christ when it was impugned in the 1940 work of Dominicus Koster, Ekklesiologie im Werden.

After the éclat of the lectures, Adam dedicated himself to working out from 1925 to 1950 the liturgical, aesthetic, and theological implications of the communal dimension of Catholicism. He set his theology, as Möhler had, fully within the context of a crisis in European civilization in Christ Our Brother (1930), Christ and the Western Mind (1931), The Son of God (1934), Jesus Christus und der Geist unserer Zeit (1935), and One and Holy (1951). Many of the old Möhlerian themes were now couched in the language of inter-war Europe. Adam understood Western civilization of the 1930's to be not only non-Christian, but actually hostile to Christianity and in a greater state of decadence

---

[121]Ibid., p. 15.

[122]Alfons Auer, "Karl Adam," ThQ, 150 (1970), 131-140, note 8.

215

and crisis than even Möhler had pictured it. Such conditions were related by Adam to the West's abandonment of Christianity. The springs of civilization would flow again when the religious spirit could be infused again into modern culture. Just as the faith of Christ had created the original unity of Western civilization, it still remained the only basis upon which the interlocking parts of that structure could be formed into a unified whole. The Christian West's great achievement had been to assert the kingship of Christ not only over the individual soul, but over economic, cultural, and political life as well, to form a Christian cosmos in which every aspect of natural existence culminated in a supernatural existence. The secularization of science, economics, and politics was responsible for the destruction of cultural unity in the West.

Karl Adam's solution to the dilemma was but a repetition of Möhler's phrases of the 1830's and 1820's. Cosmic, superterrestrial love is the road out of the ego, the temporal, the disunified. Civilization will be renewed if men and women return to the communal religious models of early Christianity:

...It is indeed collectivism which in the rhythm of spiritual movements will replace in the not far distant future the western individualism....There is more need than ever for us to find our way back to this essential fundamentally Christian attitude irrespective of temporary conditions, and to oppose to the approaching materialistic cosmopolitanism of socialists and communists the Body of Christ, that organism which forms the unbreakable supernatural union of "the many in the one bread."[123]

Adam addressed his program to revive Möhler's teaching for the twentieth century not only to radical German Catholic intellectuals, but also, through his lectures, to the future generation of scholars and priests.[124] Two of Adam's students worked along with him in

---

[123]Karl Adam, Christ and the Western Mind. Love and Belief (London, 1931), p. 43.

[124]The following unpublished lectures which Adam gave in Tübingen are preserved in MS form at the Wilhelmstift: Einleitung in die Dogmatik (30pp.); Die katholische Lehre von der Gnade (65pp.); Lehre von der Shöpfung (75pp.); Die Lehre von den Sakramenten; Christologie und Soteriologie (77pp.); Mariologie (40pp.).

spreading Möhler's theology from Tübingen to the rest of the German Catholic world. Stephan Lösch spent his scholarly life editing all of Möhler's letters and researching the intellectual influences which transformed him from the visionary of Die Einheit to the polemicist of the Symbolik. Lösch's lectures at Tübingen in the courses Einleitung in das Neue Testament and Der Romerbrief, focused on the theme of community in the structure, government, and liturgical life of the first Christian churches.[125] J. R. Geiselmann investigated the intellectual environment of Möhler's life which had caused his ecclesiology to evolve from the free communalism of Die Einheit. Geiselmann, more than anyone else before Vatican Council II, was responsible for transmitting to his students the outline of the contents of Möhler's books, the traditions out of which his ideas had developed, and the forms of opposition his theology had met in the past.[126]

The close relationship of Adam, Lösch, and Geiselmann to some twentieth century bishops of Rottenburg insured that Möhler's ideas continued to be implemented in concrete form among Württemberg

----

[125]Stefan Lösch's published works are: Briefe des jungen Karl Joseph Hefele (Rottenburg, 1938); J. A. M. Gesammelte Aktenstucke und Briefe, I (Munich, 1928); "J. A. M. und die Theologie Englands im 19 Jahrhundert," Rottenburger Monatschrift für praktische Theologie, 6 (1922-3), 198-202; 221-227; Prof. Dr. Adam Gengler 1799-1866 (Würzburg, 1963). The following unpublished lectures by Lösch are preserved in MS form at the Wilhelmstift: Einleitung in das Neue Testament; Der Römerbrief.

[126]G. C. Berkouwer, The Second Vatican Council and the New Catholicism (Grand Rapids, 1965). Geiselmann's considerable published works consist of: J. A. M. Die Einheit der Kirche und die Wiedervereinigung der Konfessionen (Vienna, 1940); Geist des Christentums und des Katholizismus (Mainz, 1940); Die katholische Tübingen Schule (Freiburg, Basle, Vienna, 1964); Lebendiger Glaube aus Geheiligter Überlieferung (Mainz, 1942); The Meaning of Tradition (Freiburg, 1966); Die theologische Anthropologie Johann Adam Möhlers. Ihr Geschichtlicher Wandel (Freiburg, 1955). For his numerous ThQ articles, see bibliography. The following unpublished lectures by Geiselmann are preserved in MS form at the Wilhelmstift: Allgemeine Sakramentenlehre; Grundlegung der Dogmatik; Die Lehre von der Kirche; Die Kirche als Form der Offenbarungsreligion.

Catholics. In fact, by the 1940's the bishops had taken the lead from the Tübingen faculty in propagating some aspects of the revival of the communal dimension of the church. This development took place amid a 7 percent rise in the Catholic population of Württemberg and a steady increase in the cultural, political, and intellectual influence of the Roman Catholic Church in that part of Germany.[127]

In the light of the rapid urbanization of the Catholic population, communion statistics, which more than any other reveal the extent to which the adoption of the communal renewal was taking place, are revealing. In the first half of the twentieth century, the number of communions in Württemberg quadrupled:[128]

1909	3,245,634
1910	3,527,774
1920	7,575,414
1925	7,764,927
1930	8,972,627
1935	11,653,308
1940	11,541,681
1943	12,501,880

The bishops, deans, and the officials of the diocese in Rottenburg were contributing to this revival. In 1941 Bishop Sproll issued a new prayer book which replaced all the "I-forms" of prayer with "we-forms." Old moralistic, sentimental devotions were supplanted by patristic collects. In November of that year Sproll announced that the theme of pastoral instructions for 1942 would be "the Church as the Continuing Christ,...the Body of Christ...how this Body grows through baptism, the sacraments...the Church as the people of God...its appearance more than sixty times in the prayers in the missal...as 'populus, plebes, gens, familia.'"[129] In 1948 the Vicar General of the diocese wrote to parish priests that the times called "not for a façade Catholicism but for an

----

[127]Hagen, op. cit., III, 199. Population in Württemberg rose from 2,169,480 in 1900 to 3,533,034 in 1950 and the percentage of Catholics from 30 percent of the population to 37.1 percent. Idem.

[128]Ibid., III, 265.

[129]MS letter of Bishop to pastors, 28/11/1941, Bischof-Ordinariat Rottenburg No. A8490, Diocesan Archives, Rottenburg.

inner Catholicism, not a Sunday Christianity, but a workday Christianity—that will be the solution of the future. Catholicism now must be expressed in regular attendance at the liturgy,...in the participation in common prayer and singing....There is the necessity of a strong lay Christianity...in the receiving of the communion by all the members of families."[130] In June 1948 the bishop warned his priests that "a distinction must be made between objective and subjective piety and, particularly in these times, any "sect-like" spirit must be sacrificed for the existence of the Catholic community....The subjective element in the parishes must be weeded out....The warmth of personal piety must not be allowed to stand in the way of the Church's own piety, the dogma and liturgy of the Church...."[131]

A final glance at the development of a few Württemberg parishes indicates the extent to which the Catholic communal revival had spread in one corner of Germany before the Second Vatican Council. In Mergentheim, whose population remained stable at 6,000, the total yearly communions witnessed a dramatic increase, from 31,690 in 1909 to 274,317 in 1955.[132]

In Igersheim between the wars the five lay religious communities included one hundred and ninety-eight people out of a population of 1,000, and the total number of communions rose at this rate, from 4,500 in 1909 to 44,692 in 1949.[133] The number of communions in the parish of Ergenzingen in the central deanery of Rottenburg increased sixfold in a population of 1,000, from 5,000 in 1910 to 32,000 in 1960.[134] The

----

[130]MS letter of General Vicar Hagen to parish priests, 21/7/1948, MSI 76, Diocesan Archives, Rottenburg.

[131]MS letter of General Vicar Hagen to parish priests, 21/7/1948, MSI 76, Diocesan Archives, Rottenburg.

[132]MS Kommunion-Register, Parish Archive, Mergentheim.

[133]MS Pfarr-Visitationen—Igersheim, 1922, 1932, 1934, 1937, 1939, 1940,1944, and 1951, Diocesan Archives, Rottenburg. The data in the earlier reports reaches back to 1909.

[134]MS Kommunion-Register, 1910-1960, Parish Archives, Ergenzingen.

219

clergy of the cathedral parish of St. Martin, which numbered approximately six thousand souls in the twentieth century placed a great emphasis, from the nineteen thirties to the nineteen fifties, on enrolling all the parish in one kind of religious "gemeinschaft" or another.[135] Communions in the cathedral rose from 40,025 in 1909 to 151,890 in 1949.[136]

The parish church in Riedlingen underwent an architectural reform in 1933-34 which expressed the communal understanding of worship and facilitated the active participation of the congregation. Thus, the altar of the church was made clearly visible and seemingly closer to the people by removing the baldacchino, rood cross, heavy communion rails, and surrounding statues, candelabra and tabernacles. Growing participation in eucharistic worship through the early part of this century is reflected in total communion statistics for this parish church, which served 2500 souls, which rose form 17,890 in 1909 to 87,810 in 1951.[137]

Ziegelbach was more conservative in its acceptance of a changing role for the laity. There was not a dramatic upturn in the reception of communion by laypersons; yearly communions stood at 4,801 in 1926 and had moved only to 6,200 in 1971.[138]

The development of Friedberg, with a population of 250, was similar to Ziegelbach's. Diocesan visitors reported that "the communal consciousness of the parish is good" but that spirit was channelled into lay religious societies rather than in frequent reception of communion.[139]

----

[135]MS Report No. 19522, 27 December 1950, Boz7a; MS Letter of Dean Semle, 30 November 1935, Boz7a, Diocesan Archives, Rottenburg.

[136]MS Parish Statistic Books, 1901-1943, Dom Archiv, Rottenburg; MS Pfarr-Visitationen-Dom, 1935, 1950, Diocesan Archives, Rottenburg.

[137]MS Pfarr-Visitationen--Riedlingen, 1912, 1925, 1936, 1942, 1952.

[138]MS Pfarr-Visitationen--Ziegelbach, 1931, 1946, 1951; MS Kommunion-Register, Parish Archive, Ziegelbach.

[139]MS Pfarr-Visitationen--Friedberg, 1954, Diocesan Archives, Rottenburg.

Moosheim followed the pattern of Riedlingen. There in 1935-36 the church was redecorated in a simple, classical style with all Baroque furnishings removed from the building to allow the congregation to follow and understand the eucharistic action.[140] At Gattnau the pattern of transformation in the frequency of communion also appeared. There were 5,100 total communions in 1912 and 29,050 total communions in 1955.[141]

-4-

The call for a revival of the church founded on a communal ecclesiology spread out into Germany from Württemberg, in the wake of the force and popularity of Karl Adam's essays and the weight of Lösch's and Geiselmann's scholarship. One reformer remembered, "The romantics of the 1920's turned more to that youthful work of Möhler's, to Die Einheit, and were influenced by it in a strong fashion."[142] The first edition of Die Einheit to appear since its initial publication in 1825 came out in 1925. The impact on many minds of the appalling consequences of the Great War, the collapse of states and traditions, the ruins of former political and economic greatness, drew many Germans to the vigorous life, the eternal youth of the old, original church, in Karl Adam's words, to the "complete community, the orbis terrarum, as the medium wherein we grasp this Christ."[143]

The pages of Hochland, which had been communicating the cultural insights of German Catholics to the German public at large since the turn of the twentieth century, were the forum in which the breadth of

---

[140]MS Pfarr-Chronik, Parish Archive, Moosheim.

[141]MS Pfarr-Visitationen--Gattnau, 1937, 1942, Diocesan Archives, Rottenburg. MS Pfarr-Visitationen--Gattnau, 1920, 1929, 1937, 1942, 1951, 1956, Diocesan Archives, Rottenburg.

[142]J. R. Geiselmann, J. A. Möhler, Die Einheit der Kirche und die Wiedervereinigung der Konfessionen (Vienna, 1940), p. 89.

[143]Adam, The Spirit of Catholicism, p. 10.

221

the Catholic heritage of the 1830's was drawn on as a source of rejuvenation for the twenties. Philip Funk was the Hochland writer who constantly advocated a return of the theology of Möhler, particularly Die Einheit:

> The task before us is to continue what was then begun, to take up anew what escaped them, to develop and work out the problems they left behind them. For if the present or the immediate past (the pre-war decade) can be reckoned a turning point, that is only so insofar as it is a wave of the turning point which occurred a hundred years ago, breaking on our shores. However new the problems appear, however newly dressed up they may be, all of them need to be brought back to the basic problems engaging the men of those times, re-examined and simplified in that light....In a time of a new unfolding of Church and Catholic consciousness...Möhler stands as the exponent of a pure, spiritual, form of tradition and Church sense.[144]

In the 1930's a number of books and articles set Möhler within the framework of the evolution of German secular intellectual history.[145] The most important and influential was Karl Eschweiler's Johann Adam Möhlers Kirchenbegriff which revealed the affinities of Möhler and the left Hegelians and Marx. Before his election as supreme pontiff, Pius XII had been influenced by Hochland and Eschweiler during his period of service as papal nuncio to Germany. As primate of the Roman Church, Pius XII applied Möhler's theology of the mystical body not only to his discussions of the church but also to the sacraments, which are described as the means through which the faithful are engrafted into the body of Christ, and to justification which is identified with sanctification. By the sacraments the divine community of the church is incorporated.

144Alexander Dru, The Church in the Nineteenth Century: Germany 1800-1910 (London, 1963), pp. 120-121; Philipp Funk, "Die geistige Gestalt Johann Adam Möhlers," Hochland, 27, I (1929-30), 109.

145Sebastian Merkle, "Möhler," Historisches Jahrbuch der Görres Gesellschaft, 58 (1938), 249-267, 59 (1939), 35-68; Bernhard Hanssler, "Rundschau über Möhler," Hochland, 36 (1939-40), 510; Bernhard Hanssler, "Johann Adam Möhler. Theologie der Kirche," Hochland, 35, II (1938), 17-26; Alfons Erb, Gelebtes Christetum Charakterbilder aus dem deutschen Kath. des 19 Jahrhunderts (Freiburg, 1938).

In his Marian pronouncements of 1950 and 1954 Pius XII made use of other elements which had been part of the Möhlerian tradition, by attesting that the Christian people as a whole are endowed with a religious sense and are witnesses to tradition. At the same time, however, he insisted that the church is a visible and hierarchic community, not just a vague mystical body, a dream fellowship born out of and sustained by love.

At Vatican II those who advocated a restoration of the communal dimension of Roman Catholic ecclesiology were a dominating force. The German bishops of course gave voice to what had become a part of their tradition. Bishop Jaeger of Paderborn stressed that an Ecumenical Council should take cognizance that the entire Christian people carry on the work of Christ and that the oneness of the people of God should be given expression in the eucharist. Bishop Hengabach of East Germany reminded the fathers that on Pentecost the Holy Spirit fell on both apostles and laity, and Cardinal Döpfner remarked that the church is a mystery in which pope, bishops,and people are all coordinate members of one organic community.

The French bishops supported the Germans. Bishop Marty of Reims gave one of the clearest expositions of the church as a social organism. Bishop Rastouil suggested that Catholic teaching admitted only one general priesthood, that of all the baptized and confirmed. Bishop Elchinger of Strasbourg told the Council that its mission was to dispel the prevailing, deep-rooted sense of religious individualism in the West and to make the doctrines of Catholic community a reality and daily experience. Too many Christians approached the sacraments in a purely personal sense, for their own satisfaction, without any awareness of the corporate nature of their membership in the mystical body.

The "Dogmatic Constitution on the Church" which the Council produced was the "principal object of the attention of Vatican II" to Pope Paul VI.[146] The idea permeating the constitution is that the

---

[146]Preface to Ecclesiam Suam in Peter Foote, et al., edts., Vatican II's Dogmatic Constitution on the Church (New York, 1969).

church is the people of God, to whom belong all the rights and the obligations of the mystical body. Here, in language which was now the ultimate statement of Catholicism, the hierarchy is a ministry of service. The great mystery of the church can be expressed in no more fitting terminology than that of "body of Christ":

> By communicating His Spirit to His brothers...Christ made them mystically into His own body. In that body, the life of Christ is poured into the believers who, through the sacraments, are united in a hidden and real way to Christ... partaking of the body of the Lord in the breaking of the Eucharistic bread, we are taken up into communion with Him and with one another....[The Church thus forms]...one interlocked reality which is comprised of a divine and a human element. For this reason by excellent analogy, this reality is compared to the mystery of the Incarnate word. Just as the assumed nature inseparably united to the divine word serves Him as a living instrument of salvation, so, in a similar way, does the communal structure of the Church serve Christ's Spirit....[147]

And humankind too, for in setting the priority of the whole over the individual, the world-wide Roman Catholic Church had become once again, in theory, an institution for the fellowship of men and women, "an instrument for the achievement of union and unity."[148]

----

[147]Ibid., pp. 16, 18.

[148]Ibid., p. 6. For the comments of two twentieth century neo-Möhlerians on the ecclesiological background of Vatican II see Marie-Dominique Chenu, "A Council for All Peoples," and Yves Congar, "Moving Towards A Pilgram Church," in Alberic Stacpoole, Vatican II Revisited (Minneapolis, 1986), pp. 19-23, 129-154.

CHAPTER V

Oxford and Berlin

"What an extraordinary thing that is," said Dr. Döllinger, "that enthusiasm about vestments! Growing fanatical about a chasuble! It is a thing that you would find in no other country [other than England], and about a chasuble of all vestments, which is certainly neither graceful nor convenient. We are used to them, and they don't strike us as particularly bad. But I cannot understand why those who care for such things do not go to the Greek Church for their models."[1] Dr. Döllinger included the ritualists in the Church of England in his review of the state of religion as he presided at a dinner party in his house in Munich at the close of the nineteenth century. He had already discussed the situation in the diocese of Rottenburg in which Hefele had been forced to submit to the Vatican I decree on infallibility. "His submission," replied the doctor to a question, "is the result of great debility of character. He is, I know, at the present moment very unhappy in his mind. He has not the courage to state the plain truth and take the consequences."[2] As for France, the religious revival with pilgrimages in honor of the Sacred Heart reminded him of a Bavarian village church he had seen with a banner "Holy Trinity, pray for us." "All this sentimental dramatizing of religion is thoroughly French."[3]

----

[1]MS Alfred Plummer, Conversations with Dr. Döllinger (1870, 1871, 1872), p. 33. All manuscripts, unless otherwise noted, are found in the Pamphlet Room, Pusey House, Oxford, titled by the names of the authors, but without classification numbers.

[2]Ibid., p. 32.

[3]Ibid., p. 15.

224

The conversation returned to England. "I don't think Dr. Newman can be very satisfied with his position," Döllinger said. "He cannot like the state of things in which he finds himself. He must find it difficult...."[4] And then he spoke of Dr. Pusey and the movement he had led with Newman at Oxford in the thirties and forties. Döllinger had first written to Pusey in 1842, "...an acquaintance with your writings has given me a very high idea of the importance of your vocation in the Church of God, and I am persuaded that you are called upon to do great service not only to your own Church, but also to the Catholic Church in general....Roman Catholics [in Germany] are turned in fear and hope towards Oxford; it becomes more and more probable that your great and memorable movement will have essential influence also on the course of religious development....I have read almost all your works....There is far more in them, with which I can entirely agree, nay—what seemed to be written out of my own soul....Everything, with us in Germany also, points more and more distinctly towards a great religious consummatio, towards a drawing together of kindred elements...."[5] And in 1867 Döllinger wrote to Pusey, "I am convinced by reading your Eirenicon, that inwardly we are united in our religious conviction, although externally we belong to two separated churches. There can be no fundamental difference of opinion between us....About your excellent Eirenicon I should have written to you long ago, if that which I want to say of it were not too much for a letter."[6]

It was the same Döllinger who in 1835 came to the help of Johann Adam Möhler whom "he never ceased to venerate as the finest theological intellect," whose works and vision of Catholicism he introduced to Cardinal Wieseman, Lord Acton, and to his students at Munich until 1891.[7] It was Döllinger who published Möhler's best articles and

---

[4]Ibid., pp. 40-41.

[5]MS letter of Döllinger to Pusey, February 7, 1842.

[6]MS letter of Döllinger to Pusey, May 30, 1866.

[7]J. E. E. D. Acton, The History of Freedom and Other Essays (London, 1922), p. 377.

226

papers as <u>Gesammelte Schriften und Aufsätze</u> in 1838 and 1840 and gave public lectures based on the <u>Symbolik</u>, "the best book of its kind,"[8] from 1841 to 1854. It was not coincidence which led a Catholic who venerated Möhler to value Pusey.

Pusey's pursuits were not confined to the Oxford Movement alone, that activity of dons and younger clergy in the ancient English university between 1833 and 1845 for the protection of traditional privileges and beliefs of the Church of England; nor to Tractarianism, the adherence to the doctrines and practices advocated by the Oxford divines in a series of ninety <u>Tracts for the Times</u>. The system of Christianity which was developed by Pusey and his followers was not merely a revival of an older form of Anglicanism, which the terms "Oxford Movement" and "Tractarianism" popularly connote. To a great extent, it was a new creation, based on ancient patristic sources rather than Anglican ones. Even the term "Anglo-Catholicism" is too restrictive, carrying the suggestion that Tridentine Roman Catholicism and religious nationalism had been the normative influences. Döllinger recognized the same spirit of the new Catholicism in Pusey which he had observed in Möhler. The Puseyites were, in fact, the English counterparts of those continental Europeans whom we have labelled "the new Catholics."

Pusey shared much more with Möhler than a repudiation of the Reformation. He, too, appealed from modern private judgment to the collective voice of antiquity. He and his followers also struggled to reassert the sacramental nature of God's revelation within a hostile university, from the pulpits of an officially disinterested church, in the courtrooms and Parliaments of a government which held the power to define doctrine as well as promulgate liturgical legislation. Pusey in Oxford and England, as Möhler in Tübingen and Württemberg, introduced foreign sources into his native religion: north German scholarship, antique sacramentalism, and patristic ecclesiology. He appeared no

---

[8]Döllinger quoted in Heinrich Fels, <u>Johann Adam Möhler, Der Weg seines geistigen Werdens</u> (Limburg, 1939), p. 134.

less a controversial advocate of change than the German. The evolution of the religious thought of this highly conservative man repeated the pattern observed in Möhler. New theories were advanced after his traditional paradigm of Christianity was challenged by external social, political, and intellectual pressures.

No one would have thought in 1820 or even 1828 that Dr. Pusey would become the exponent of the new and the foreign. He began life as a model of country respectability, of Berkshire Toryism, and Oxford High Churchism. He was born into Pusey House in Berkshire and Grosvenor Square in London in 1800, four years after Möhler, six months before Newman, the younger son of a gentle family of extreme Tories. His father, youngest child of Viscount Folkestone, had an equal horror of Whigs and atheists and when speaking of them together would use "and" rather than "or." His mother, daughter of the Earl of Harborough, was a typical lady of the days of Fox and Pitt. When at home in Grosvenor Square she took a sedan chair to South Audley Street Chapel. When, at the death of her husband, the palladian Pusey House and surrounding park in Berkshire fell to Edward's older brother Philip, Lady Lucy took Fairford Park, the scene of Cromwell's daughter's marriage to Ireton, which was seven miles from Oxford along the London Road, where she could be close to Edward and his children and to which he could escape from the ecclesio-political battles raging along the Isis. Dr. Pusey said in later years that from her he was educated in the teachings of the Book of Common Prayer and that from her explanation of the cathechism which she had learned from older clergy he was brought up in the belief in the doctrine of the real presence of Christ in the eucharist. Clerics in her memories contrasted to the priests and bishops whom Edward knew as a youth, country clergy who played whist and went to dinner parties.

The first stages of the education of Edward Pusey marked no transgression of the established order, for he went, as expected, to Eton and in 1819 to Christ Church at Oxford. In the summer of 1822 he "took," according to Bishop Bagot, "the best First ever known," a distinction he appears to have shared with Keble, Mr. Gladstone, and

Cardinal Manning.[9]   The following Easter he was elected a fellow of Oriel College, a mark of great intellectual distinction in that day. In the Oriel Common Room he met John Henry Newman.

In 1828 Dr. Nicoll, having held the Regius Professorship of Hebrew at Oxford for six years, died, some said of the dust of the Bodleian. He was chiefly remembered for one of the longest sermons ever preached at the University Church of St. Mary's, which proved from Genesis IV:7 the primitive institution of sacrifice. His chair had no great significance, for Hebrew was thought the concern of the Jewish Dispensation and hardly the concern of a Christian. But to the Regius Professorships were attached solidity, permanence, and influence by virtue of their connection to a canonry of Christ Church, the cathedral of Oxford, and to the Senior Common Room of Christ Church, the most aristocratic Oxford college. Pusey had been very close to the Regius Professor of Divinity, Dr. Lloyd, since 1822. When the Duke of Wellington became Prime Minister, he made Lloyd Bishop of Oxford and, when the Hebrew Chair fell vacant, Lloyd recommended Pusey to the Prime Minister. Wellington and Peel, moderate reforming Tories, who were not on principle opposed to the Test and Corporation Acts, which relieved the political disability of Dissenters, and in the end supported Roman Catholic Emancipation, needed a man like Pusey with whom the country clergy could identify but who could at the same time keep up the Oxford reputation for scholarship as evidenced by his recent work on German rationalism, who was conservative but possessed of a reformist vein, and who was neither identified with the strict orthodoxy of the old High Churchmen or the emotionalism of the Evangelicals.

Pusey's intellectual standard appeared a theological counterpart to Peel's reforms in the British Home Office.   The don joined the statesman in his abandonment of the exclusive Toryism of the past, and Pusey voted for Peel in the Oxford bye-election in which Peel was defeated because of his support for Catholic Emancipation. On November 13, 1828, Wellington offered Pusey the Hebrew Professorship at Oxford.

----

[9]MS letter of Bishop Bagot to Rev. F. E. Paget, March 1, 1836.

Bishop Lloyd insisted that he accept, for he valued Pusey as an advisor and wanted him in close proximity. The next day Pusey forwarded the Prime Minister his acceptance.

The death of Dr. Lloyd, the Bishop of Oxford, in 1829 interrupted Pusey's advancement. For the next five years he withdrew from the intrigue and gossip of the clerical republic on the Isis where personal inclinations and antipathies as much as principle helped to form religious parties. He was absorbed with compiling the Bodleian catalogue of Arabian and Near Eastern manuscripts.[10] It was this occupation which caused Pusey in this half decade to be remembered as "little fitted for active intercourse with others...[he] is shy, and expresses himself with hesitation and obscurity....Accordingly, he is bent on the study of Divinity and somewhat censures those who are less laborious in this branch of duty...[and neglect]...these duties for general society for which he has comparatively little taste...."[11]

Chronic illness plagued Pusey throughout his life and often shaped the course of his career, especially in the twenties and thirties. It is unclear what the exact nature of this constant ailment was. He refers to it as "a cough" or "my chest," but it was severe enough to keep him away from Oxford for long periods of time, a situation which on occasion he appears to have used to advantage. His life was despaired of in 1832. He was still far from well in 1833. In 1834 he tried to write a tract on keeping company with notorious sinners, but he wrote Newman that "I...have never found myself fit for it on the days I set apart for it."[12] Later in 1834 his illness was so severe that he was forced to spend the spring on the Isle of Wight.

His constant sickness was not helped by his refusal, when convalescing away from Oxford, to interrupt his scholarly pursuits.

----

[10]E. B. Pusey, _Bibliothecae Bodleianae codicum mss orientalium catalogi, partis secundae volumen primum Arabicos complectens_ (Oxford, 1835).

[11]MS letter of Pusey to Miss Barker, dated "between October 4 and 16, 1827."

[12]MS letter of Pusey to Newman, 1834?.

Pusey was a compulsive worker. The diagnosis of an illness which forced him to stay in Brighton for four months in 1828 was described as "headaches [caused by his] working too hard."[13] He told his son Philip that when a schoolboy of eleven he had kept at his books ten hours a day.[14] His brother Philip had written him from Cordova in 1821, "I conclude that this letter...will find you immersed in books and papers with a dressing gown on at ten o'clock after six hours study and perhaps a stocking performing the office of a night cap on your head."[15] While in Germany, Pusey read from fourteen to sixteen hours a day, and quite often throughout middle age he worked all the night through. When eighty-three, he was still at "incessant labour" for ten to twelve hours a day. Constant exertion coupled with illness gave him the reputation of anti-social grind, even among adherents to the principles of the Oxford Movement. Pusey's emergence into society was a rare and memorable event. At the height of the Oxford Movement at the dedication festival at Littlemore in 1838, W. G. Ward exclaimed with a loud voice in Pusey's hearing, "Bloxam is going to give a ball tonight, and Dr. Pusey has promised to dance at it!"[16] But such dedication to work would become useful in the transmission of the tenets of new Catholicism.

Throughout the early eighteen twenties and the thirties, which were the crucial period of his life, Pusey was completely caught up in his relationship with Maria Barker. She was the youngest daughter of Fairford Park, fifteen miles from Pusey House, owned by a family no less wealthy and cultivated than the Puseys, but whose townhouse was in Cheltenham, not London, whose politics were Whig not Tory, and whose religion was Evangelical bordering on Dissent. Edward sent her a ring in 1819 but her parents did not wish to marry their brilliant and

----

[13]MS letter of Pusey to Miss Barker, March 17, 1828.

[14]MS letter of Pusey to son Philip E., February 19, 1844.

[15]MS letter of Philip Pusey to Pusey, December 30, 1821.

[16]MS Bloxam Collection, June 13, 1888.

well-dowered daughter to a younger son. He must at least have a place. Edward's parents distrusted the character of Fairford Park as well. The lovers waited until one father died in 1827 to announce the official engagement, and until the other passed away in 1828 to solemnize the wedding. Through these years Edward was a constant visitor and correspondent of Cheltenham and Fairford Park. The circumstances of their approaching engagement awoke him from gloom into a sunshine which lasted ten years.

By 1836 when his health began to improve and he had finished the Arabian catalogue, she developed a cough and became so ill as to be forced to spend months in the Channel Isles. At the same time, it had become obvious to him that the established pattern of English religious life which had provided him with a situation and platform in Oxford, research materials and time for writing, had broken down. The ecclesio-political destruction of the traditional English world of religion started later than in France and Germany, on February 26, 1828, when Lord John Russell introduced a motion into the House of Lords to repeal the Test and Corporation Acts in order to relieve Dissenters from the statutory prohibition against their serving in municipal corporations or crown offices without first receiving communion in an Anglican church. The successful passage of this bill spelled the end of the system of governance which had overseen the Church of England since the days of Hooker's Laws of Ecclesiastical Polity. Reform continued in the years following Catholic Emancipation and episodic anti-clerical riots, during which the bishop of Bristol's palace was burned down. In the 1833 Church Temporalities Bill, eight episcopal and two archiepiscopal sees of the Church of Ireland were designated for suppression, their revenues to be taken over by the state. On the basis of a "Plan of Church Reform" advocated by Peel's Evangelical brother-in-law, a standing body of Ecclesiastical Commissioners was formed in 1835 to remove religious abuses. In 1836 two more bills were introduced by Lord John Russell. One proposed to remodel the English bishoprics in respect to size and income. A second sought to abolish Anglican cathedral and collegiate preferments.

Pusey's reaction to these events was less hysterical than that of old-fashioned Oxford High Churchmen such as John Keble. If he did not welcome all the changes, he saw them as leading to needed reform. The Hookerian structure was that "disgraceful and injurious system,"[17] he wrote after the passage of the first of Lord John Russell's measures. "That vote, I hope, will be a new era for us, and that we, as well as our ancestors, shall trust more in the goodness of our cause than in the might of legislation."[18] To his brother Philip, a member of the House, he wrote, "You have an anxious time in the House of Commons....If times of trial for the Church come, they will be times of purifying."[19]

More than Parliament, the Oxford professor feared the impact of the industrial system and the sharp rise in the population of his country. He was not dogmatically hostile to the products of industry for he wrote his brother, "I suppose we have no notion of the effect of railroads yet....Although I do not see it as a matter of principle not to go upon them."[20] At the same time he wrote to Mr. Gladstone, that "I have no objection to a tax on the richer clergy, or any reduction of our incomes....But if the Church Rates were to be abolished here, I had much rather have the maintenance of the material churches left to the Christian feeling of the public....There is an abundant field for every exertion in our manufacturing, or mining districts....I much fear that large resources will be comparatively wasted in augmenting what are called the small livings...while those places which are really heathenizing our land, our great towns, will be in fact neglected...I am, day by day, more convinced that we stand upon a fearful crisis and that each year is preparing for the ultimate decision as to the fate of the English Church. A few more years more, and the day of probation may be

---

[17]MS letter of Pusey to Miss Barker, February 28, 1828.

[18]MS letter of Pusey to Miss Barker, April 7, 1828.

[19]MS letter of Pusey to brother Philip, June, 1839.

[20]MS letter of Pusey to brother Philip, August 19, 1839.

over."[21]

In his early sermons and pamphlets Pusey preached that "our modern towns have their characteristics—the chimneys of our manufactories, and the smoke of our furnaces....Which of these exhibits the picture of a 'wise and understanding people'?....The population of the large towns is left heathen....We have in our crowded cities, or our deserted villages, deprived of their birthright the children of our Christian land; have allowed God's good seed to spring up empty, barren, unfruitful...."[22]

Pusey despaired of the form of Christianity which could survive in Manchester, Leeds, and Birmingham:

> ...As before the distress of the manufacturing districts, the prevailing feeling was not merely being indifferent to but above all religion—and this is one of the phenomena, which makes me fear most for our country: And I fear a crisis is approaching (whether it come in the next tens of years or no) in which Christianity will have to struggle for its existence among us....I have long been anxious to see some effort made to amend the heathen condition of our great towns; and have used what occasions I had to call attention of others to it.[23]

Pusey perceived that the impact of the demographic revolution of the eighteenth century was being felt in the churches as well. The

---

[21]MS letters of Pusey to Gladstone, February 15, 1833; March 6, 1836.

[22]E. B. Pusey, Churches in London with an Appendix Containing Answers to Objections Raised by the "Record" and Others to the Plan of the Metropolis Churches' Fund (Oxford, 1837), p. 5; E. B. Pusey, Remarks on the Prospective and Past Benefits of Cathedral Institutions in the Promotion of Sound Religious Knowledge and Clerical Education. 2nd ed. (London, 1833), pp. 150–151; MS E. B. Pusey, Twelve Sermons, p. 13; E. B. Pusey, A Sermon Preached at the Consecration of Grove Church on Tuesday, August 14, 1832 (London, 1832), p. 21; E. B. Pusey, "The Preaching of the Gospel. A Preparation for our Lord's Coming," Parochial Sermons Preached and Printed on Various Occasions (Oxford and London, 1865).

[23]MS letter of Pusey to Miss Barker, February 12, 1828. For more analysis of Pusey's views on the industrial revolution see R. W. Franklin, "Pusey and Worship in Industrial Society," Worship, 57, (1983), 386–411.

most populous diocese in the country in 1831 was Chester, which included the city of Manchester, with only 616 parishes to serve 1,833,958 people. In London, the churches had room for one-tenth of the population, for during the last years of George III's reign Dr. Porteous, the Bishop of London, had built no more than six edifices in the entire metropolitan district. At that time, 5,000 out of the 11,000 parishes of England were without resident clergy. Even in the thirties, under the more enlightened episcopacy of Blomfield, sixty-four London parishes were without permanent priests. Sections of the city were turning into sinks of iniquity, and this was causing, according to Pusey, spiritual starvation of many hundreds of thousands.

In the 1830's Pusey published Answers to Objections...to the Plan of the Metropolis Churches' Fund to demonstrate, with the use of statistics, the current inadequacy of the church in dealing with the growth of the English population. Dr. Pusey gave the following figures to illustrate his point:

Spiritual Destitution of London

No. parishes	Population	Church Room	Proportion	Clergy	Pro. of Clergy
4	166,000	8,200	not 1/20	11	not 1 for 15,000
21	739,000	66,155	not 1/10	45	not 1 for 16,400
9	232,000	27,327	not 1/8	19	1 for 1,230

Unprovided for in 34 parishes: 3,756,954
Sittings required: 252,318

East and North-East of London

Parishes	Population	Churches	Proportion	Clergy	Proportion
10	353,460	18	1 for 19,000	22	1 for 14,000[24]

Pusey wrote Newman in 1838 that they must "correct the stupidity with which people look on at such skeletons of the true fabric; one clergyman where there ought to be a bishopric."[25] He preached at Salisbury Infirmary in September 1833, that to meet the needs of the

---

[24]Pusey, Churches in London, p. 16.

[25]MS letter Pusey to Newman, August 15, 1838.

country's growing population a church should be built every day of the year.[26]

In addition to the seismic shocks of the industrial and demographic revolutions there arose new intellectual challenges to Pusey which were intensified by the religious difficulties of his future wife, Maria Barker. She worried about contradiction in scripture and had "a great inclination to question where [she] ought to have believed."[27] Throughout 1827 and 1828 she poured out the misery of her unbelief to Dr. Pusey in a long series of letters:

> Religion has certainly never been to me the source of comfort and serenity which it has to others....I could frequently only find peace of mind in banishing the subject from my thoughts....[28]

She lacked a theological context into which to fit and translate the words of the scriptures:

> I took up my pen, because I was too sleepy to read; I have been trying what I could understand of the Epistle to the Galatians. The four first chapters, which are all I have looked at, are full of expressions I do not understand.[29]

Dr. Pusey himself seems to have shared Miss Barker's doubts. He also was searching to fit the words of scripture into a theological pattern:

> I understand entirely every part of your case....After this proof of weakness, the advice of one who was so little able to cure himself will have lost some of its value....My discomfort was raised to the utmost, by, you will scarcely believe, reading parts of Rokebey....From the autumn of '22 till September '27, I never ventured to open a book of poetry or to enter any scenery in which there was any chance of excitement.[30]

----

[26]MS E. B. Pusey, Sermon preached at Salisbury Infirmary, September, 1833.

[27]MS letter of Miss Barker to Pusey, December 3, 1827.

[28]MS letter of Miss Barker to Pusey, October 3, 1827.

[29]MS letter of Miss Barker to Pusey, October 22, 1827.

[30]MSS letters of Pusey to Miss Barker, October 16, 1827 and October 29, 1827.

Amid his doubts and fears as well as in the situation of England now affected by industrial and demographic changes, Pusey perceived that none of the established English religious parties were fit to provide a remedy. Maria Barker's familial Evangelicalism, born in the Methodist conventicles, was by the twenties the fashionable religion of watering places like Cheltenham, Bath, and Tunbridge Wells, where it was preached in both church and chapel. Pusey saw the Evangelical revival as a contradictory, self-denying apostleship of individuality. The new Evangelical desire to participate in a common spiritual life was satisfied not by the historic church, but by extra-ecclesiastical societies. John Wesley himself had become a proponent of a theory of justification similar to that of the Lutherans which Möhler had seriously questioned in the Symbolik. There was a strong analogy between the Lutheran-Wesleyan emphasis on fides informis, in contrast to the fides formata caritate of the Symbolik as the sole justifying principle, and Kant's doctrine of moral goodwill, which wills no particular act, but merely its own universality, as the sole principle of morality in human actions.

Pusey disapproved of the Evangelical and Wesleyan doctrine of "present salvation" for it created a tyranny of religious individualism:

> ...It seems to me a main and very extensive error in the
> school to which he (an Evangelical) belongs, to forget the
> extent of the natural varieties of Conformation of the human
> mind, and to suppose that the object of Christianity is
> rather to produce one uniform result, than to modify,
> chasten, exalt, sanctify the peculiar character of each
> ....Religion is opposed both to superstition and credulity
> ....They have only enslaved themselves to these stern and
> hard masters. There is but one slavery, a slavery to
> self....[31]

Pusey distrusted the Evangelical absorption in subjective feeling to the near exclusion of the sacraments as channels of grace. He mocked, in a letter to John Keble, Evangelical self-righteousness in regarding

----

[31]MS letter of Pusey to Miss Barker, "between October 4 and 16, 1827."

as Popish, and therefore untrue, formalistic deviations from the
religion of subjective emotionalism:

> Some folks' lethargy could not be roused any other way: e.g.
> I heard today that William Palmer of Magdalen College prays
> before a picture of the Blessed Virgin: I think that we must
> begin to circulate, per contra, that the Rev. D. W. has a
> picture of Rowland Hill, or Wesley or Baxter, as his
> Saint....[32]

There were also the English Roman Catholics. In Pusey's boyhood
"the Roman Catholic religion hung about some few ancient English
families like a ghost of the past. They preserved their creed as an
heirloom which tradition, rather than conviction, made sacred to them
....Romanism was in England a dying creed, lingering in retirement in
the halls and chapels of a few half-forgotten families."[33] Occasional
conversions to the Roman Catholic Church were thought the acts of
eccentric dons and demented aristocrats. In 1798, the Rev. H. Digby
Beste, fellow of Magdalen College, went over to Rome. Lord
Cholmondeley (1792-1870) joined the Roman Church as did the
Leicestershire squire Ambrose Phillips de Lisle in 1824 who took the
Hon. and Rev. George Spencer with him in 1830. Kenelm Digby the author
became a Roman Catholic in 1823 as did Augustus Pugin the architect in
1834.

Pusey classed Tridentine Roman Catholicism also as a product of
modern subjectivism and individualism. But he recognized that this was
an outer core of deformed practice which masked the surviving Catholic
truth among the Romans. He wrote to Miss Barker in the twenties that
"the R.C.'s though they have mingled up superstitions with, and
adulterated the Faith, have yet retained the foundations: I do not
mean to deny the practical idolatry into which they have fallen: or
that the 'good works' of self-emaciation, hairshirts, flagellations,
etc., have not had a merit ascribed to them which interfered with the
merits of Christ....The danger was that it might be practically more,

---

[32]MS letter of Pusey to Keble, Autumn, 1838.

[33]G. W. E. Russell, Dr. Pusey (London, 1907), p. 41.

yet so as rather to lead to idolatry, than to an interference with the Atonement."[34] The "gross and carnal" promulgation of the doctrine of transubstantiation in 1215 marred the eucharist to Pusey by associating the real presence of Christ solely with the action of an individual priest. Neither the people nor the corporate church were seen to have the power to call down the presence of Christ. The codification of transubstantiation was followed by concomitant abuses, such as purgatory and indulgences, stemming from a great emphasis on individualistic exercises and a complex of private masses without communicants or congregation.[35]

Pusey came to the conclusion that both Rome and ultra-Protestantism were products of the individualistic spirit of the late Middle Ages. Both rejected the ancient notion of the church as a corporate Communion of Saints interceding as a body before God:

> The Romanist and Ultra-Protestant are alike rigorous in opposite ways....[The Roman] must fain obtain to himself a personal interest in their (the Communion of Saints) intercessions, appropriate them to himself, make them personally his friends, and so he steps beyond Antiquity. ...[He] condemns as "impious" those who deny that they are to be invoked, or assert that the invocation of them to pray for each of us individually is idolatry: he ends by making them his mediators....The Ultra-Protestant, revolted at this abuse, will not hear of their interceding at all, proscribes all thought of it, cuts himself off—not from their communion and fellowship, but from all sense of it and its blessedness ...and either restrains the doctrine of the "Communion of Saints" to the charities of this life, or makes it a mere abstract statement that all the redeemed belong to one body.[36]

Furthermore, both Rome and Protestantism looked to individuals as the

----

[34]MS letter of Pusey to Miss Barker, February 28, 1828; MS letter of Pusey to Miss Barker, April 7, 1828.

[35]E. B. Pusey, Tracts for the Times, Catena Patrum No. IV. Testimony of Writers of the later English Church to the Doctrine of the Eucharistic Sacrifice (London, 1837), p. 10.

[36]E. P. Pusey, A Letter to the Right Rev. Father in God Richard Lord Bishop of Oxford, on the Tendency to Romanism Imputed to Doctrines Held of Old, as Now, in the English Church (Oxford, 1839), pp. 202-203.

seat of religious authority, the one to the pope, the other to the ordinary believer seated in his box-pew. "Rome (like Ultra-Protestantism) follows modern traditions, assumes them to be apostolic, simply because she holds them, and she is infallible."[37]

There was still another party in the Church of England to which Pusey could resort. It was the party of his youth, the old High Church, which had devised its own solutions to the disruptions of the modern world. John Keble, though living in semi-seclusion in the Cotswolds as curate in his father's parish at Hursley village after his defeat in the Oriel College election of 1828, was the recognized leader of the Oxford High Churchmen. In the twenties he had imbued a succession of Romantic undergraduates like Hurrell Froude, Robert Wilberforce, and Isaac Williams with the religion of their fathers. Keble represented slight reform based on unchanging Tory High Church principles.

Keble was perhaps the last English apologist of that shibboleth of the old High Church party, political non-resistance to divinely sanctioned authority. He was the vociferous representative of those country clergy who, since the expulsion of the Non-Juring bishops, had been the repository of belief in the Caroline Anglican tradition, regard for the apostolic succession, and the efficacy of the sacraments. The poetry of his Christian Year, composed between 1819 and 1828, and the prose of a sermon on national apostasy preached in the Oxford University Church in July 1833, expressed sentiments easily imaginable on the lips of the divines of Queen Anne's reign. In the face of Parliamentary Commissioners, Whigs, and radicals, Keble remonstrated by calling the attention of the Church of England to its apostolic succession, which would act as a bulwark against the intrusion of the state:

> The Apostolic Church is now in the eyes of the State only one sect among many....Disrespect to the Successors of the Apostles, as such, is an unquestionable symptom of enmity to Him who gave them their commission....I do not see how any

----

[37]Ibid., p. 39.

person can devote himself too entirely to the cause of the Apostolic Church in these realms....[38]

H. J. Rose, who had once written, "We are an Establishment as well as a Church,"[39] was the leader of the Cambridge University High Churchmen and the editor as well of the British Magazine, the official organ of the party. In November 1832, he urged on A. P. Perceval, a peer's son who had been Keble's pupil and was now royal chaplain, the need for immediate action to protect the Church of England from the threat of modern forces.

Within the next few weeks, Rose had lighted upon a solution. After having considered a "journal to defend the Establishment,"[40] quickly transformed into an "organ of communication,"[41] he came upon the idea of issuing "very useful tracts" to defend the High Church position.[42]

At a meeting to plan High Church action convened by Rose at Hadleigh Rectory, Hurrell Froude was the only member of the Oriel Senior Common Room present. His roots in an agrarian parsonage did not alienate him from the other clergy there, William Palmer, a don who was interested in the liturgy, Perceval, and Rose. Keble's influence was evident in the presence of three of his students and in Palmer's call for a national association of "safe, sound, sensible men" who would resist the state encroachment in terms much the same as those of Keble's assize sermon.[43] Perceval suggested the publication of a stout

----

[38]Brilioth, op. cit., p. 101. For a recent look at Keble and the conservative High Church see Walter H. Conser, Church and Confession (Mercer, 1984), pp. 161-214.

[39]MS letter of H. J. Rose to A. P Perceval, August 28, 1833.

[40]MS letter of H. J. Rose to A. P. Perceval, November 17, 1832.

[41]MS letter of H. J. Rose to A. P. Perceval, December 9, 1832.

[42]MS letters of H. J. Rose to A. P. Perceval, June 26 and July 6, 1833.

[43]Christopher Dawson, The Spirit of the Oxford Movement (New York, 1933), p. 54.

"Churchman's Manual"; Rose's idea was taken up by Froude, "a bold rider, as on horseback, so also in his speculations":

> I don't see why we should disguise from ourselves that our object is to dictate to the clergy of this country and I for one do not want anyone else to get on the box....We must make a row in the world....We must have short tracts...and get people to preach sermons on the Apostolical succession and the like.[44]

From the meeting at Rose's rectory, there followed brief, incisive statements of High Church principle to render the ideas of these Oxford dons familiar to the rest of England. In the first two years the tracts were issued almost entirely from Oxford. John Henry Newman wrote the majority. Froude, Keble, Isaac Williams, John Bowden, William Palmer, and Benjamin Harrison contributed. Young dons on horseback distributed them over the countryside to Church of England rectories. By 1835, 60,000 copies of the Tracts for the Times had been circulated.

At first, the discreet men of the High Church in London, and respectable Tories like Edward Copeland, W. F. Hook, Edward Churton, and Archdeacon Joshua Watson, looked kindly and with genuine regard upon these young movers. There was little to fear from a revival of sound Anglican orthodoxy. The opponents of the Oxford Movement acknowledged at first that nothing was being said that could not have been found as well in Laud, Ken, Wilson, Alexander Knox, Archdeacon Daubeny or Bishop Van Mildert. Thomas Arnold wrote, "They are the very non-Jurors and High Church Clergy of King William's and Anne's and George I's time reproduced with scarcely a shade of difference."[45]

From all of this activity Dr. Pusey had been consciously excluded by Rose who identified Pusey with German scriptural views, and thus with rationalism. Pusey wrote to H. P. Liddon and to Dr. Newman:

> My relations with H. J. Rose prevented my being invited to the Hadleigh Conference....I think that it was on account of my unhappy relations with Rose, that I only heard very

---

[44]Ibid., pp. 77, 80.

[45]Ibid., p. 9.

distantly of the first meeting, nor do I think that I knew
distinctly what you were doing....When the Tracts were
begun, and they took an organized shape, I do recollect
thinking how I should do most good identified with it, or
along side of it....[46]

-2-

Education abroad was indeed under suspicion. It was rare for
anyone in England in the twenties to be interested in German. The mere
knowledge of that language subjected a theologian to the same suspicion
of heterodoxy which was once visited on those who knew Greek. Only two
men in Oxford could read German. One of Pusey's correspondents wrote
him that to send a box of German books to Oxford was so rare an
occurrence that one had to find a special commissioner. Rose had been
in Germany in 1824 and 1825 and had brought back tales of a decayed
Christianity. Knowing, however, of Pusey's and Miss Barker's troubles
in the interpretation of the scriptures, Bishop Lloyd suggested that a
young divine might acquire the tools which would be useful in solving
such questions in the German universities. Pusey remembered, "One day
Dr. Lloyd said to me, 'I wish you would learn something about those
German critics...'.My life turned on that hint of Lloyd's."[47]

Pusey left London for Göttingen on June 5, 1825, to return on
November 6 of that year. The object of this first visit to Germany was

---

[46]MS letter of Pusey to Liddon, July 14, 1882; MS unfinished letter
to Newman, 1864. Newman attributed Pusey's absence to illness and
wrote alongside a letter of Nov. 1833: "N.B. This was before Pusey
had joined the Movement—Indeed, he was too ill to take part in it."
For more analysis of the early development of Pusey see also D. W. F.
Forrester, The Intellectual Development of E. B. Pusey, 1800-50
(unpublished thesis, Oxford 1967); Leighton Frappell, "'Science' in the
Service of Orthodoxy: The Early Intellectual Development of E. B.
Pusey," in Perry Butler, Pusey Rediscovered (London, 1983), pp. 1-29;
John R. Griffin, "Dr. Pusey and the Oxford Movement," Historical
Magazine of the Protestant Episcopal Church, XLIII (1973), 137-154; and
H. C. G. Matthew, "Edward Bouverie Pusey: from Scholar to Tractarian,"
Journal of Theological Studies (1981), 101-124.

[47]Liddon, op. cit., I, 72.

to become "acquainted with German and German theology." It was such a success that Pusey returned in the summer of 1826 to acquire Chaldee, Arabic, and Syriac, and to learn to apply modern forms of criticism to the Old and the New Testaments. This time, he studied under the eminent Orientalist Prof. Kosegarten at Greifswald and with the Old Testament scholar Ewald at Berlin. He then went to Bonn to work with Pof. Freytag, the first Arabist of Europe. Remaining until the summer of 1827, he had mastered enough Syriac, Chaldee, and Rabbinic to read the Jewish and Arabic commentators on the Old Testament.[48] His German teachers were in contact with Pusey through the next decades and informed him of the latest German works on biblical criticism. Freytag especially sent him dictionaries, books, and the most recent news on breakthroughs in hermeneutic studies because he could not "express in words how valuable your friendship is to me." He also forwarded a selection of his own works as testimony to his former pupil's learning. Freytag recalled "with the greatest pleasure the time of his [Pusey's] sojourn in Bonn...."[49]

Thus Dr. Pusey became the official Oxford Germanophile, whose task it was to entertain any Teutonic scholars who should happen to be visiting England and Christ Church, to write articles for German periodicals, and to answer the queries of his English colleagues on the mysteries of German scholarship.

Pusey's contemporaries and students detected the importation of German ideas along with German methodology. Baron Bunsen went to Christ Church to visit the Doctor and wrote in his journal: "Breakfasted with Pusey upon ham and speculative philosophy. There is no Englishman I know who has studied this subject so much: he takes in Schelling as easily as Plato....He is a most unique union of a practical Englishman and an intellectual German."[50] A. P. Stanley

---

[48]MS letter of Pusey to Bishop Lloyd, August 29, 1826; MS letter to Pusey to Liddon, January 12, 1879.

[49]MS letter of Freytag to Pusey, July 29, 1827.

[50]Memoirs of Baron Bunsen (Feb. 24, 1838 and April 23, 1838) quoted in Literary Supplement of Agricultural Gazette, March 3, 1879.

produced an account of Pusey's Oxford classes after his return from Germany:

> The whole atmosphere of the Professor's lectures breathed the spirit of Germany to a degree, which I am convinced could have been found in no other Lectureroom in Oxford....All that related to the interpretation of the part of the Scriptures on which he was lecturing--in this instance it was the book of Psalms--was both in matter and manner almost entirely German. The table was piled with German commentaries....The Professor's mode of lecturing was exactly what I remembered in the very fine lectures of Professor Nitzsch which I once attended in the University of Bonn...to these Lectures I certainly look back as to the most instructive which I attended in Oxford--as to those the notes of which are still most useful to me. And it is certainly not from agreement with the peculiar views which the Professor extracted from the Fathers....[51]

The Germans whom Pusey was publicizing in England were those who most influenced Möhler, the school of Schleiermacher, Neander, and Tholuck. From them, he had learned of the Fathers' sacramental-allegorical interpretation of the Bible, and had abandoned his own literal understanding of the words of the scripture and his former belief that the will of God had inspired every verse of the biblical text. He was led to apply the Fathers' mystical explication of the Old Testament to the New Testament and to the doctrines of Christianity as a whole. The sacramentalism of antiquity thus became the foundation of Pusey's Catholicism, and Schleiermacher, Neander, and Tholuck and the school of Romantic Protestant orthodoxy in Berlin became a principal impetus behind Pusey's theological development.

In a letter to Dr. Lloyd in August 1826, Pusey noted "the orthodox [school in Berlin's characteristic of] going back almost exclusively to the Fathers."[52] During both his visits to Berlin, Pusey became personally acquainted with the patriarch Schleiermacher. In 1825, he heard his elucidation of Acts in its entirety and in 1826 was

----

[51]E. G. W. Bill, University Reform in Nineteenth Century Oxford 1811-1885 (Oxford, 1973), pp. 252-253.

[52]MS Letter of Pusey to Lloyd, August 29, 1826.

present for his lectures on Thessalonians and Galatians. In addition, he learned from his books the use the Evangelists had made of the Old Testament in composing the gospels. To Pusey, "Schleiermacher was that great man, who, whatever be the errors of his system, has done more than any other for the restoration of religious belief in Germany."[53]

Through Schleiermacher, Pusey made the acquaintance of the church historian Augustus Neander whose lecture series, "Introduction to the Fathers," he audited in 1825 and whose course on ecclesiastical history and another on the last epistles of Paul he attended in 1826. The bond between the two in the late twenties and early thirties was particularly close and even in the forties Neander wrote to Pusey, "I hope you have not quite forgotten the relations in which you stood to me here, and the Christian communion between us...."[54] In 1847, a student of Neander's, H. Biesenthal, visited Pusey: "I met with a reception as from an old friend, particularly after having given him the message from Neander. He was a great admirer of Neander. He said,'Germany can never be grateful enough to Neander, for he like no one else has annihilated Rationalism vulgaris.'"[55]

In his library, Pusey had Neander's Genetische Entwicklung der vornehmsten gnostischen Systeme (Berlin, 1818), Denkwürdigkeiten aus der Geschichte des Christenthums und Christlichen Lebens (Berlin, 1825), Kleine Gelegenheitschriften praktisch-Christlichen vornehmlich historischen Inhalts (Berlin, 1824), and Allgemeine Geschichte der Christlichen Religion und Kirche (vol. 1-6). He liked to refer to them often. In 1832, for example, he wrote Newman, "I should be also much obliged to you to send me the three first volumes of Neander's Kirchengeschichte (in my study, division nearest to the passage-door,

---

[53]E. B. Pusey, An Historical Enquiry Into The Probable Causes of the Rationalist Character Lately Predominant in the Theology of Germany, I (London, 1828), 115.

[54]MS letter of Neander to Pusey, Nov. 20, 1841.

[55]MS H. Biesenthal, My Relations to Dr. Pusey.

third or fourth shelf)."[56] At the end of his life, Pusey made a final bow to the learning of Neander and his protégé Augustus Tholuck, "Germany had its impulses, imperfect as it was, in Neander, a convert from Judaism, and Tholuck, from Unbelief."[57]

Tholuck, three years younger than Möhler, had fallen into advanced rationalism until rescued by Neander. He attended Schleiermacher's lectures from 1815 until 1820 and there became interested in the concept of the religious community of love espoused by the first Christians. In his own scholarly work, he attempted to popularize the Fathers' methods of using the Old Testament to explicate the New. Because of his interest in Hebrew studies, he was appointed director of the Jewish Mission in Berlin in the twenties and also of the German Bible Society. At first, the friendship between Pusey and Tholuck was nurtured amid language pedagogy. By the autumn of 1826, they had developed a lasting, mutual affection, which was expressed in a long correspondence and frequent visits. It was Tholuck who consistently and unfailingly provided the guidance which helped Pusey to abandon his earlier High Church principles. He addressed Pusey,

> Many a time I imagine myself to be in the lovely garden of Christ Church, and I long to exchange with you thoughts about that which moves your heart and mine....Tell me also your opinion of Hengstenberg's Christology [Hengstenberg had written a conservative work on the Christological interpretation of the Old Testament]; I cannot believe that in any discipline, and least of all in the Old Testament, we ought to step back to the standpoint of the 17th century.[58]

In his personal library, Pusey had Tholuck's earliest work which proposed an entire sacramental-exegetic system, founded upon the Fathers, Auslegung des Briefes Pauli an die Römer nebst Fortlaufenden Auszuegen aus den exegetischen Schriften der Kirchenvater und Reformation (Berlin, 1824). An acquaintance of Pusey remembered, "A

---

[56]MS letter of Pusey to Newman, July 13, 1832.

[57]MS letter of Pusey to Liddon, July 14, 1882.

[58]MS letter of Tholuck to Pusey, June 3, 1829.

visit [in 1835] from Tholuck, for whom he had a warm regard, strengthened Pusey in his anxiety to spend his life in defense of the Christian faith, and he devoted himself in the next few months to the special study of the Sacraments: the result of this was his celebrated Tract on Baptism."[59] Not only the tract, but Pusey's first published work, An Historical Enquiry into the Probable Causes of the Rationalist Character Lately Predominant in the Theology of Germany (London, 1828), came directly from Tholuck. A second volume of the Historical Enquiry, published in 1830, which undertook a defense of the first volume against the criticism of H. J. Rose and others, was also composed under the direction of Tholuck.

While Pusey was in Germany, in fact, Rose's Discourses on the State of the Protestant Religion in Germany had been published, and it openly accused all Teutonic theologians of having abandoned Christianity. Rose advocated a return to the strictest Protestant orthodoxy as the only means to combat rationalism. Pusey was deeply troubled by Rose's book because he knew that "among them [the Germans] were men whose deep piety, sound faith, and extensive views excited his veneration...."[60] One day in 1826 Tholuck and Pusey met at Prof. Weiss's house in Schönhausen and while walking up and down by the trees which edged the road to Berlin, Tholuck asked Pusey to answer Rose's book, and he gave Pusey his notes from his 1825 lectures as cannon fodder for a reply. Pusey accepted. Tholuck envisioned the task of the proposed volume to be a differentiation of "the views of the German rationalists and to make use of information given by German historians who believe in Revelation."[61] Pusey's object in publishing the book, was not so much to give "my countrymen a full view of the course of theology in Germany, as to shake the despotism which Mr. Rose's

---

[59]A. B. Donaldson, Five Great Oxford Leaders, Keble, Newman, Pusey, Liddon, and Church (London, 1902), p. 165.

[60]Pusey, An Historical Enquiry, I, xi.

[61]MS letter of Tholuck to Pusey, June 3, 1829.

opinions were rapidly gaining in this country, and, as I said in my Preface, to give a chart of the country which I wished others to explore...[to shew] them the dangers of a stiff spurious orthodoxy, and the benefits of the bold but Christian course (or rather bold because purely Christian course) which German theology is now taking."[62]

Pusey, like Möhler, used the historical experience of northern Germany to elucidate the religious dilemma of his native country. The English Church had entered a period of crisis similar to that which had befallen the German Church in the previous half century when rationalism had triumphed, and the weakening of religious institutions and Christianity as a way of life had consequently followed. The rise of rationalism is tied by Pusey on the one hand to the lifeless, almost non-Christian Protestant orthodoxy of the seventeenth century, and, on the other, to the preponderance of weak, pious, sentimental emotionalists like Spener. The situation of England in 1828 was almost exactly the same: "The experience furnished by Evangelical Germany is to us as the biography of an individual to one of similar character....Linked as European nations are, every direction which the human character takes in one country must exert an influence over the rest....Still is the whole one great system, no part of which can be affected without indirectly operating upon the rest...."[63]

The solution lay in a new understanding of Christianity which would be provided by reading scripture as "a living word," not "a dead repository of barren technicalities."[64] Pusey rejected the purely rational biblical criticism of Semler, Michaelis and other eighteenth century rationalists as shallow and worthless.[65] Instead, he adopted what he had heard from Schleiermacher and read in Schelling and Jacobi, to trust religious emotion rather than critical reasoning alone for the

---

[62]MS letter of Pusey to Tholuck, April 28, 1829.

[63]Pusey, An Historical Enquiry, I, 2.

[64]Ibid., I, 31.

[65]Ibid., I, 144.

"immediate certainty of knowledge in regard to the deity....The
original seat of religion is in the feeling, not in the understanding."[66]   The application of the teachings of Tholuck and
Schleiermacher's school would overcome "a mere intellectual conception
of Christianity,...a deadening formularism," would lead to "the
extensive re-animation of a living Christianity,"[67] and even give rise
to a "...new era."[68]

The reliance upon the early church, which had provided the
unifying thread for Pusey's interpretation of the modern German
theological school, was further applied to a proper understanding of
Christianity as a whole, a paradigm which he opposed to the decadent
rationalism of the Noetics and the subjectivity of the Evangelicals.
Pusey addressed his contemporaries:

> An acquaintance...with the works of the primitive Christians
> would tend to diminish the wilfulness of spirit and
> impatience of authority which now often harasses our Church;
> a knowledge of their language would terminate many of the
> differences which now sorely hinder the cordial co-operation
> of her [the Church of England's] two great parties....[69]

The Fathers had not been unknown to the Oxford don before his Berlin
sojourn: "One of the reminiscences of early youth was a wish I
expressed to my father to 'read all the Fathers.' The beginning of my
theological library was Montfaucon's edition of St. Chrysostom which my
father gave me in 1824."[70]   Dr. Routh, the venerable President of
Magdalen College who could remember seeing Dr. Johnson on the Oxford
High Street, had himself often discussed the Fathers with Pusey. But
it was the German use of the Fathers which focused Pusey's discovery.
He returned from Berlin with twelve volumes of Chrysostom, and with the

---

[66]Ibid., I, 51, 170.

[67]Ibid., I, 173, 175.

[68]Ibid., II (London, 1830), 90.

[69]Pusey, Remarks on the Prospective and Past Benefits, p. 40.

[70]MS letter of Pusey to Fr. Hall, June 16, 1879.

works of Clement of Alexandria, Tertullian, Gregory of Nazianzus, Cyril
of Jerusalem, Cyprian, Jerome, Irenaeus, and Augustine.[71] He wrote to
W. J. Copeland in the forties:

> Then as to authorities: when not employed in Hebrew, I used
> to live 'in the Fathers'....They have been these many years
> the same comfort to me as modern Roman writers have been a
> discomfort to you....I read them, learn of them, live among
> them, as a child; adopt their words, say what they say, do
> not say what they do not. I live in them as my home....
> Theirs is my native language....I could preach volumes of St.
> Chrysostom and St. Augustine without rebuke. I do not think
> a Roman Catholic could....The current tone of devotion, which
> is now made the popular mode of influencing minds, is quite
> different from that which the Fathers would foster, and turns
> upon another object....The same great work is going on now,
> and a far deeper work than in more prosperous days, and far
> wider....[72]

The patristic writings became for Pusey a standard of faith to
which he could appeal beyond private judgment. He looked upon their
collective witness as a repository of primitive Catholic truth. From
the Fathers Pusey also absorbed the incarnational interpretation of the
church as the body of Christ and of the real objective presence of
Christ in the eucharist. He referred to the centrality of the incarnation for his life and work: "This teaching I learnt in our own Divines
and in the Fathers long before I read a Roman Catholic writer."[73]

The Library of the Fathers of the Holy Catholic Church, whose
publication was begun in 1838 and continued until 1885 when 48 volumes
had been issued, was Pusey's first attempt to propagate the theology of
the Fathers as an initial step towards the reform of the English
Church, to cause her to "...[leave] the narrowness of the so-called
Evangelical party...adding, to their previous warmth and energy, the
depth and reverence which belong to the old Church's view of the

----

[71]MS letter of Pusey to Newman, Nov. 25, 1826.

[72]MS letter of Pusey to W. J. Copeland, 1840's.

[73]Pusey, A Letter to the Right Hon. and Right Rev. the Lord Bishop
of London in Explanation of Some Statements Contained in a letter by
the Rev. W. Dodsworth (Oxford, 1851), p. 38.

Incarnation, as connected with the Sacraments."[74] A re-awakened sense of the objectivity of the Christian faith would spring from the patristic system in which "the greatness of the gift of God does not depend upon the greatness of the minister: it is the very greatness of the Sacraments that man has nothing to do with them: the Priest is only the instrument, the act is the act of God, the gift, His gift entirely."[75]

The Library of the Fathers was the first breach of the new Catholicism into the bastion of Anglicanism. Yet this issuing of books was typical of the practical methods used by the Church of England. It was an intellectual reaction by Oxford dons, was addressed primarily to the clergy, and did not entail revolutionary action, but the distribution of ancient documents: "...[its] main object was to provide for the children of our Church a great body of Catholic teaching...."[76] Pusey had discussed the idea with London clergy and the Bishop of Oxford, but the plans were drawn up principally with Newman in 1836, to whom he had written: "We need some Greek Fathers who shall incidentally speak of the sacraments,...of new creation,...of infusion of new life."[77] In 1837 the publisher Rivington had been secured, a preliminary list of those Fathers to be published drawn up, and 800 subscribers secured who wished to see "the Fathers of the Catholic Church rather than non-Conformist authors in the hands of the clergy."[78]

Pusey's prefaces to the Library drew increasing attention to the Fathers as model for the contemporary reform of the church. At first the reader was simply encouraged to use the volumes to bring out the

----

[74]MS letter of Pusey to Tholuck, March 6, 1837.

[75]Ibid.

[76]Pusey, A Letter to the Lord Bishop of London, p. 250.

[77]MS letter of Pusey to Newman, September 1836.

[78]MS letter of Pusey to Bishop Bagot, Nov. 2, 1838.

meaning of Holy Scripture.[79] The Fathers were presented as repositories of doctrines and devotion for those weary of modern questioning.[80] Later, their sacramental interpretation of scripture was enjoined along with their theory of the unity of the Church based on God's presence within her.[81]

It was in his lectures on Prophecies and Types that Pusey specifically proceeded from patristic biblical exegesis to an application of the Fathers' theories to an entire system of Christianity. In 1829 after an inquiry into the Fathers' interpretation of scripture, he had adopted their way of giving allegorical-symbolical or typical meaning to the prophecies and historical events of the Old Testament: "It appears to me that we must retire from the orthodox-Protestant opinions...to shew that some of the principal of the Fathers had the same views to which we are now coming," Pusey wrote to Tholuck.[82] He had come to the conclusion that the Fathers interpreted the physical world to be typical of or to bear a sacramental relationship to the world of the spiritual and divine.

Underlying this Christian system of types was the greatest sacrament of all, the incarnation, which made possible the unity of the spiritual and material: "...The Fathers speak of two sacraments only in a stricter sense....There is no doubt that the Fathers spoke of many things as 'Sacraments'....In the highest sense there are only two Sacraments, recognized by the Christian Church, and these we find are those especially united with the Incarnation of our Lord, that by which we are made members of His body and that whereby His Body and Blood are imparted to us....The ancient interpretation was much more typical than

---

[79]The Library of the Fathers. The Confessions of Saint Augustine. Revised from a former Translation (Oxford, 1876), p. xi.

[80]Ibid., p. xx.

[81]The Library of the Fathers. Tertullian. (Oxford, 1854), p. xiv.

[82]Ms letter of Pusey to Tholuck, Aug. 13, 1829. For more on this teaching see David Jasper, "Pusey's Lectures on Types and Prophecies," in Perry Butler, op. cit., pp. 51-70.

the modern....I am persuaded more and more, that everything in the book of God's word, as of His world, is highly typical....I should think typical interpretation, Catholic and true...."[83]

These were the early ideas which in July and August, 1836 Pusey organized into his Lectures on Prophecies and Types of Our Lord, which have never been published. Here, Pusey presented the incarnational-sacramental-typical system of the Fathers to a class of eighty students in Christ Church in Easter Term. The undergraduates were introduced to the world of Clement and Origen in which nature was a parable and scripture an allegory. The Catholic sacramentalism of Augustine's view of grace as divine energy infused by physical means was presented as a remedy as much to the official latitudinarianism of Britain in the thirties as it had been to the court Arianism of the fourth century. The method of the lecturer was to expand the habit he had developed in solving Miss Barker's difficulties with the meaning of particular words of scripture by setting those words within the context of patristic doctrine. In the lectures Pusey struggled to convince his Oxford audience that the nature of God's revelation had always been sacramental. The anti-sacramentalism of the latitudinarians (the rationalists) and the Evangelicals (the "pseudo-spiritualists") is portrayed as an assault on the types and the archetypes of the Old and New Testaments which are the foundation of the sacramental exposition of the church and the cornerstone of the Christian faith.

Pusey shows that it is the common practice in the Old Testament for God to use physical elements, burning bushes, oil, the sun, fire, water, to convey religious truth. The Old Testament language fore-shadows the sacraments of the New Testament. Origen, Irenaeus, and Augustine saw Christ and the ceremonies of the church explained in the full manner by the events of the Old Testament. Thus, for example, the eucharist is interpreted as a sacrifice by Pusey because of the centrality of sacrifice among the Jews. Furthermore, the Fathers were so impressed by the union of grace with sacrifice in the Old Testament

---

[83]MS letter of Pusey to Dr. Hook, April 17, 1837.

254

that they also taught that there was a union of the body and blood of Christ with the symbols which conveyed them. Pusey in the lectures, therefore, stressed that the eucharist is the body and blood of Christ imparted by God by the means of bread and wine. Because the Old Testament sacrifice is related to atonement, Pusey connects the New Testament eucharist to a sacrifice for sin. In the eucharist the bread and wine and the community of Christians present are both offered to become the body of Christ and the channel of God's presence in the church.[84]

The proper interpretation of the Old Testament leads naturally to an understanding of the church as the body of Christ. The relation of the Jewish people to God is typical of the relation of the Christian community to the body of Christ. The church is thus viewed in the lectures as a sacramental organism deriving all of its life and meaning from its being the extension of Christ himself: In language reminiscent of Möhler, Pusey wrote:

> From the mutual connection of the Head and His members, the Jewish people wherein they image forth our Lord, reflect also His Body, the Church, as well as in their more direct resemblance....They picture His dealings with His Church, which He formed into one in Christ out of them and of the Gentiles.[85]

The eucharist and the church are both extensions of the incarnation:

> In this Body, we are of His Body partakers....Passages show that we must be of his body to partake of the body. I have quoted more of this passage than was absolutely necessary, because it will illustrate how in these deeper views, our Lord's Incarnation, His mystical Body in the Eucharist, and the mystical Body the Church which is thereby kept alive and held together are blended as parts of the same mystery, bear the same name; so, aptly might the same type under different modifications represent them all.[86]

---

[84]MS E. B. Pusey, Lectures on Prophecies and Types of Our Lord in the Old Testament, "written mainly in July-August '36," p. 107.

[85]E. B. Pusey, Patience and Confidence the Strength of the Church. (Oxford, 1837), p. 8.

[86]MS Pusey, Lectures on Prophecies and Types, p. 125.

Tholuck had reached parallel conclusions on the patristic acceptance of priesthood, eucharist, sacrifice, and incarnational ecclesiology because of typical analysis of the Old Testament in his Das Alte Testament im Neuen Testament über die Citate des Alten Testament im Neuen Testament und über den Opfer- und Priester- Begriff im Alten and Neuen Testamente (Gotha, 1836). But while he treated these findings as scholarly results to be studied, Pusey saw the possibility of applying them to the contemporary English Church. The lectures on Prophecies and Types, in fact, became the foundation of his teaching on justification, the church, and the two chief sacraments, baptism and the holy eucharist.

As a first step, Pusey was led to reject the Evangelical theory of justification by faith and to propose instead a "Möhlerian" merging of justification and sanctification. He adumbrated this theory in his sermons of the 1830's, in the tracts he wrote in association with the Oxford Movement after 1835, and in his public letters to the Bishop of Oxford and the Archbishop of Canterbury. Like Möhler, Pusey maintained that justification is the crux of the difference between Protestants and Catholics. The Protestant idea of justification is one of a purely subjective religious relation to God which looks away from moral and institutional realizations where faith is assured and grace infused. The patristic Catholic insists, instead, that salvation is worked out through the reception of physical sacraments. Christ's death is indeed regarded as the meritorious cause of justification but man's action is also required before this justification can be appropriated. The reception of the sacraments proffered by the church is the process through which man fulfills his obligations. The language of the Bible supports this view:

> Whenever the justification of individuals is spoken of, it is
> expressed that that justification was bestowed upon them in
> time past....It is spoken of as passive on their part, and as
> complete....So, further, and as connected with this, the
> "receiving" of the Holy Spirit, which sanctifies us is also

spoken of.[87]

Becoming holy and being justified are understood as one process by Pusey. The just by an increase in righteousness become more justified and at the same time grow in holiness and union with Christ.[88]

It is the sacraments which bring about this presence of Christ through the grace which they give. By them faith penetrates and is manifested in works:

> Thus people speak of the Christian life as a sort of edifice to be built upon the foundation of Christ's merits....This last appears to me unscriptural: Justification is always spoken of in Scripture as a past act; not, of course, as one ceasing when completed....We are placed, once for all, in a state of Justification: we are made children of God, members of Christ; and so we are "found in Christ" as being "Christ's" and with His whole Church a portion of His mystical Body....This justification is given in Baptism; and all good works are the fruit of it; and the worship, and adoption and the union with Christ then given: this justification, of course, ceases not, unless a man falls from grace: he has been and continues justified....He filled us, and we ought to remain filled with Him and bringing forth fruits. We ought to remain in the vine....The confusion is that men look to justification as a thing, which they are to obtain, not one which has been given them....[89]

Pusey uncovered for Englishmen that "stupendous mystery, man united with God....The dignity of our nature, not as it is in us, but as it is united with Christ, and consequently in us also as His members, is a frequent theme with the ancient Fathers, and must be

----

[87]E. B. Pusey, _Tracts of the Times. Scriptural Views of Holy Baptism with an Appendix_ (London, 1836), pp. 268, 169.

[88]E. B. Pusey, _A Course of Sermons on Solemn Subjects Chiefly Bearing on Repentance and Amendment of Life, Preached in St. Saviour's Church, Leeds_ (Oxford, 1845), pp. 230, 232.

[89]MS letter of Pusey to Mrs. Pusey, Nov. 11, 1835. Newman's famous Lectures on Justification in 1837 were done at Pusey's suggestion. Pusey wrote to Newman on Aug. 11, 1840 (MS letter), "Indeed, you did write your Lectures on Justification at _my_ suggestion: though you, of course, felt the difficulties too,it was at my request that you let yourself to remove them....It seemed somehow a reason why you should not have all this trouble, when you did not undertake it of your own mind."

again with us, if we would bring men...to consider, in good earnest, what is the hope of their calling. On the present system, we shall never build up Christians."[90] He was thus led to revive the Fathers' use of the term "body of Christ" to describe the Church. He wrote his son, "The Mystical Body of Christ is still imperfect, both in its members and its numbers....Day by day, it receives fresh members by baptism....To be 'a member of Christ' is to be a member of His Mystical Body. God the Word became incarnate...to unite us as closely as possible with Himself."[91]

Pusey's Sermons During the Season from Advent to Whitsuntide provided yet another explication on the theme: "the Church is the Body of Christ, as Scripture saith,..."[92] which reunited people alienated from each other as well as from the church as an institution. The doctrine of the mystical body is presented as a guarantee of Christ's presence among men and women: "the Spirit which dwelt in him without measure, He has imparted to us His members, that It may sanctify us, spiritualize our very bodies here...."[93]

Such Christological ecclesiology provided Pusey with a theory of the unity in the church which avoided the pitfalls of both Erastian and Roman doctrines of the church:

> The seed corn, which is His Flesh, gives life by its death; as bread again, His Body; it nourishes to life eternal; and that Body unites together the various grains to which it gave birth....So again, this one image portrays to us the mysterious connexion between the body of Christ, which is His Flesh, and the Body of Christ, which is the Church....For as the bread, consisting of many grains, is made one, so that

---

[90]MS letter of Pusey to B. Harrison, April 16, 1835. On this point see also A. M. Allchin, "Pusey: The Servant of God," in Perry Butler, op. cit., pp. 366-390; and Andrew Louth, "Manhood into God: The Oxford Movement, the Fathers and the Deification of Man," in Kenneth Leech and Rowan Williams, Essays Catholic and Radical (London, 1983), pp. 70-80.

[91]MS letter of Pusey to his son Philip, undated, but probably after Dec. 15, 1879.

[92]Pusey, Sermons during the Season, p. ix.

[93]Ibid., pp. 246-267.

the grains nowhere appear...so are we conjoined, both with
each other and with Christ; there not being one Body for thee
and another for thy neighbor....[94]

Hence, Pusey was led to employ communal language in his
description of the church. In her there is "an invisible spiritual
bond of the communion of Saints throughout the whole body."[95] As early
as 1829, he had described the church essentially as a community of
worship. Forms of faith, service, and of church government had arisen
out of the communal setting of the early Church: "The Christians of
the first century were a separated people, living in constant
commission of religious exercises. The convert was admitted to this
fellowship by the indispensable rite of baptism....The Christian thus
admitted was expected to join the congregation in constant worship...
the exercise of communion [had] a tendency to produce goodwill by
abolishing for a time the reference to self...."[96] Pusey's regard for
the communal relationship among the members of the church continued to
develop after the twenties when he spoke of the "the communion of the
body," and used St. Chrysostom's language to elucidate the mysterious
corporate fellowship which existed within the church.[97] Pusey presents
it as the very nature of the patristic understanding of the Catholic
church that it is formed by the merging of individuals into one
community.[98] Pusey spoke of the church again as a visible, earthly
community:

> The Church of England recognizes with the ancient Church, the
> actualness of the Communion of Saints: that has knit
> together His elect in one communion and fellowship in the
> mystical body of His Son, Christ our Lord; it rejoices in
> God's assurance that through the due receiving of the holy

---

[94]E. B. Pusey, Letter to the Bishop of London, pp. 198, 199.

[95]Pusey, Catena Patrum, p. 6.

[96]MS E. B. Pusey, "Dr. Pusey's Note-book--Our Lady's Priory's
Library," beginning with a poem dated Rome, March 1829, p. 17.

[97]Pusey, Letter to the Bishop of London, p. 194.

[98]Pusey, Letter to the Bishop of Oxford, p. 235.

mysteries "we are very members incorporate in the mystical body of His Son which is the blessed company of all faithful people," and prays, that we may "continue in that holy fellowship;" [He] is content to feel the blessedness of that mystical union...without intruding into that holy fellowship with selfish and unauthorized prayers....[99]

As in the case of Möhler, this communal ecclesiology led on to Pusey's stress on the twofold role of the sacraments both as the means of engrafting the self into the body of Christ and the guarantee of the objective character of faith. To Pusey, the sacraments impressed upon the mind far more powerfully than any words the mysteries of the Christian faith and provided "a peculiar obstacle to [rational religion's] inroads, for their effects come directly from God, and their mode of operation is as little cognizable to reason as their Author: 'they flow to us from an unseen world....'"[100]

Pusey's treatment of baptism and the holy eucharist marked the stages of the increasing penetration of the concepts of the new Catholicism into the Oxford Movement and the infusion into High Church Anglicanism of newly discovered patristic theology of the church and of the sacraments. Pusey's treatise on baptism changed the nature and direction of the Tracts for the Times. At the end of 1834 Pusey's alliance with the Oxford Movement had been initiated by a tract on fasting which Pusey initialed and thereby caused the permanent application of the word 'Puseyite' to the Tractarians. But Tracts 67, 68, and 69 gave the party a fresh position as well as a new name by making sacramental power the chief issue of the movement, supplanting anti-Erastianism and the apostolic succession. Furthermore, Pusey brought to the movement a prestige as Regius Professor of Hebrew and Canon of Christ Church, which Newman and Froude as mere Fellows of Oriel and Keble as curate in a parish could never have supplied. In addition, Pusey had learning, solidity, a family name, and he had been a nominee of the Tories. He was a most distinguished man to take on publicly,

---

[99]Ibid., pp. 204, 205.

[100]Pusey, Scriptural Views of Holy Baptism, p. ix.

and the rational and Evangelical antagonists of the Tracts demonstrated their sense of Pusey's importance by giving his name to the Catholic party. Before his identification with them, the Tracts were flimsy, litter on tables, "the frogs of Egypt." His contribution helped the volumes to goodly dimensions and qualified them for a place on gentlemen's shelves. It seemed that a greater sense of responsibility now emerged from their pages.

But while on the surface Pusey lent sobriety, gravity, and carefulness, he introduced the radical element of patristic Catholicism which in time became obvious to all readers. Even the titles of his early Tracts suggested their relation to Pusey's emerging Prophecies and Types apologetic which used sacramental-allegorical analysis of the Bible to elucidate theology, for they are collectively named Scriptural Views of Holy Baptism, and, after a revision in 1839 which increased the number of pages to 400, Pusey's baptismal Tracts were republished as The Doctrine of Holy Baptism as Contained in the Scriptures and Thence Enlarged upon by the Fathers.

So great, Pusey impressed upon the readers of his baptismal Tracts, was the gift of baptismal regeneration, that extensive suffering, portrayed in the Tract with vivid horror, was required to be rid of post-baptismal transgression. Young men at Oxford grew anxious over such teachings. To quiet their fears, Pusey preached a famous sermon on the holy eucharist. As Regius Professor it was his right to preach the University Sermon in Christ Church Cathedral rather than in the Church of St. Mary the Virgin. At ten in the morning on the fourth Sunday after Easter in 1843 Pusey moved to the pulpit through the crowds which overflowed the shabby, inconvenient, unrestored cathedral. The bowed, grizzled head, the pale, ascetic, furrowed face, cloudy through the use of a poorly wielded razor, dropped into the pulpit out of sight until the single hymn had been sung. Then the harsh, unmodulated voice was heard dwelling upon high-pitched, mysterious, devotional patristic teaching.

Pusey as a preacher cast a solemn spell. He spoke again of the terror of post-baptismal sin and the comfort which a Christian has in

Christ's presence in the holy eucharist, even though the Catholic Christian cannot with the Evangelical think his sins blotted out at once. J. B. Mozley was in the choir: "I suppose," he remembered, "there must [have been] something harsh in Pusey's statements, as they offend[ed] people so mightily....He hits people hard, and offers no apology or consolation for the blow." The holy communion was presented on this occasion as the second great sacrament which guarantees the objectivity of the Christian faith. The "comfort" derived from the eucharist was, according to the Fathers, the belief in a transcendence of sin by the absorption of the self into the body of Christ:

> Where His Flesh is, there He is and we receiving it, receive Him, and receiving Him are joined on to Him through His Flesh to the Father....We are...perfected into unity with God the Father....For having received into ourselves, bodily and spiritually, Him who is by Nature and truly the Son, who hath an essential Oneness with Him, we becoming partakers of the Nature which is above all, are glorified....This Divine Sacrament has, as its immediate and proper end, union with Him who hath taken our manhood into God, and the infusion into us of His Spirit...making us one with His glorified Humanity, as He is One in the Godhead with the Father....101

He had spoken of the eucharist before. As early as 1828 at Cuddesdon he had encouraged constant communion as a means to increase holiness. At Holton church in 1836 he repeated the call to frequent the "holy mystery,....which dwelleth in us, as God, and we in Him...."102 He published Tract 81 which defended the doctrine of the eucharist as a commemorative sacrifice. He described the eucharist in his published letter to the Bishop of Oxford in 1839 as a communication of the body and blood of Christ. But a storm broke over the 1843 sermon. After church, Dr. Faussett, the Margaret Professor of Divinity, applied to the Vice-Chancellor, Dr. Wynter, to put in force against Dr. Pusey the University statute De concionibus. The Vice-Chancellor summoned six doctors of divinity, Jenkyns, Master of Balliol, Hawkins, Provost of

---

101Pusey, Nine Sermons, pp. 14, 17, 27.

102MS E. B. Pusey, Sermon preached at Cuddesdon in August 1828, in Twelve Sermons; MS E. B. Pusey, Sermon preached at Holton in 1836.

Oriel, Symons, Warden of Wadham, Ogilvie, Regius Professor of Pastoral Theology, and Jelf, Canon of Christ Church, to hear the case. Dr. Pusey was not allowed to be present. Jelf was the only doctor not hostile to Pusey and he remarked that the other five cared nothing about the Fathers.

One Puseyite remembered: "The statute had been disinterred from arbitrary times, but not even in the most arbitrary times--the days of the Star Chamber--has there been denied to an accused person the right of making an appearance and saying what he had to say in his defense."103 On June 2, 1843, the court passed judgment, and Pusey was found guilty of "quaedam doctrinae Ecclesiae Anglicanae dissona et contraria protulisse," and forbidden for two years to preach within the precincts of the University. Mr. Gladstone and Dr. Acland urged Pusey to publish the sermon so that the public could judge its heretical quality, but he refused, preferring to submit to authority, however unjust. Thus for the next years Pusey "wandered about an ecclesiastical Cain with the Vice-Chancellor's mark on his forehead, and an Exeter Hall anathema on his head."104

-4-

The Oxford Movement was coming to an end. The attempt to contain the revived Catholicism within established High Anglicanism was proving to be a failure. Blows began to fall from all sectors of the Establishment. Pusey's reaction to the events of the spring of 1843 was merely that "the storm has at last reached me."105 The heroic strictness and the corporate self-denial of the early church were the objects of general admiration, but men grew fearful when preachers

---

103MS Evan Jarrett, Dr. Pusey and the Tracts for the Times, p. 101. Jarrett lived in Pusey's rooms in Christ's Church in 1845 and 1846.

104Liddon, op. cit., III, 138.

105MS letter of Pusey to Newman, May 18, 1843.

talked too much about copying the Christians of the first four centuries in the nineteenth century. Newman, for example, informed the bishops in his first Tract that "we could not wish them a more blessed termination of their course than the spoiling of their goods and martyrdom." "It may reasonably be supposed," remarked Christopher Dawson, "that such good wishes were not to the taste of all of them."[106]

On January 25, 1841, Newman issued the last of the Tracts, Number XC, which contended that the Thirty-nine Articles of the Church of England were reconcilable with Tridentine Catholicism. Tract XC drove the old High Church clergymen out of their alliance with the Oxford dons and the Tridentine Anglicans into the Roman Communion. Those who remained in the Church of England came under the deepest suspicion. Isaac Williams was defeated in the Oxford Poetry Professorship election of 1842 because he was identified as a Tractarian. A plethora of counter-tracts flooded the countryside, such as "Is Our Minister a Puseyite? A Dialogue for the Unlearned," accusing the Oxford Catholics of religious sedition. Lord John Russell wrote the Queen, "The matter to create national alarm is, as your majesty says, the growth of Roman Catholic doctrine within the bosom of the Church. Dr. Arnold said very truly: I look upon a Roman Catholic as an enemy in his uniform. I look upon a Tractarian as an enemy disguised, as a spy."[107] The pamphlet writers mistook the Oxford Movement for a revived Roman Catholicism, one writer mistakenly tracing the Tracts to "the authority of the darkest ages of Popery, when men had debased Christianity from a spiritual system...to a system of forms, and ceremonial rites, and opera operata influences,..."[108] and so did Pusey's Oxford colleagues, as he reported to Benjamin Harrison: "The walls in Oxford have been placarded for the last week with "Popery of Oxford" and its citizens

----

106Dawson, op. cit., pp. 94-95.

107Chapman, op. cit., p. 98.

108J. H. Newman, Tracts for the Times. Letter to a Magazine on the Subject of Dr. Pusey's Tract on Baptism (London, 1840), p. i.

[have] been edified with the exhibition of Newman's and my name as Papists; all done by Rev. P. Maurice of New College...."[109]

In the midst of these difficulties two great personal tragedies pushed Pusey even further from the world of the typical Oxford don and Anglican clergyman into the realm of Catholic mysteries and austerities, practiced behind the walls of Cardinal Wolsey's rooms in Christ Church. In the fall of 1838 Dr. Pusey was told that his wife Maria had tubercular consumption. Her decline was rapid and she was dead by the next Trinity Sunday. Her death seemed "as though it had changed in a degree the character of my subsequent life."[110] As late as July, he "shrank from seeing any human face."[111] This experience deepened his spirituality. The devotional aids and forms of prayer of the Church of England were inadequate to meet his needs. He discovered many new collects in Roman liturgical books. He also searched through the practical Roman system to find an ascetic discipline to contend with a deep sense of sin: "My dear wife's illness first brought to me what has since been deepened by the review of my past life, how amid special mercies and guardianship of God, I am scarred all over and seamed with sin, so that I am a monster to myself; I loathe myself; I can feel of myself only like one covered with leprosy from head to foot...."[112] He determined to live an extremely austere existence for the rest of his life and to devote his money to the construction of parish churches.

Newman took Maria's place. Pusey turned to the Fellow of Oriel for constant advice, and he wrote to Mr. Gladstone that "my whole self

----

[109]MS letter of Pusey to B. Harrison, March 26, 1837.

[110]MS letter of Pusey to Newman, July 16, 1839.

[111]Idem.

[112]MS letter of Pusey to Keble, Sept. 26, 1844. For another view of this relationship see D. W. F. Forrester, "Dr. Pusey's Marriage," The Ampleforth Journal, 78 (1973), 33-47.

is concentrated about Newman,...."[113] Consequently, he was "half-brokenhearted" as early as 1843 when he received the first indications that Newman was heading for the Roman Communion.[114] When Newman finally did go over to Rome, drawing after him, as Mr. Gladstone later said, a third part of the stars of heaven, Pusey completely broke down. At first, Pusey felt some consolation in the hope that Newman was destined to continue in the Roman Church the restoration which had been begun within the Church of England. But by the next year, after a meeting which was the epitaph of their old friendship, he had lost such hope. Their bond continued, but as between those who inhabited separate worlds.

Newman's conversion led Pusey to change his attitude toward Roman Catholicism. He no longer attacked Romanism publicly and worked to prevent the English Church Unions which were springing up around the country from including anti-Roman statements within their constitutions.[115] Such activities caused Pusey to be ostracized by the High Churchmen and to be placed under a ban against preaching in public except at Christ Church and in Pusey village by the Bishop of Oxford, Samuel Wilberforce. In July 1852, his brother Philip Pusey was defeated in a Berkshire parliamentary election after having been accused in a printed election paper of disloyalty to the Church of England. Events thus joined together after the failure of the Oxford Movement to push Pusey to affirm his vision of a new Catholicism more and more in opposition to established Anglicanism.

The assault of the state upon Pusey's Catholicism came first, for in a series of famous court cases, the subjective understanding of Christianity, that individual assent not sacraments brought grace into the soul, was held not to be incompatible with the faith of the Book of

----

[113]MS letter of Pusey to Gladstone, Feb. 18, 1845.

[114]MS letter of Pusey to brother William, Sept. 25, 1843.

[115]This is the subject of MS Roger Greenfield, The Attitude of the Tractarians to the Roman Catholic Chruch, D. Phil. Thesis 1956, Oxford University, Bodleian Library.

Common Prayer. Against such decisions Pusey was forced to rejoin with his objective sacramental theories. In the reign of William IV the Judicial Committee of the Privy Council had been designated the body of final appeal in religious cases, superseding all ecclesiastical courts of the Church of England. Convocation not having sat since 1712, there being no other legislative organ within the Anglican Communion, the Privy Council became, de facto, the forum which defined dogma. In 1849 an extreme Evangelical named G. C. Gorham, who held Zwinglian views of baptism, was appointed to a benefice in the diocese of Exeter. The bishop, Dr. Henry Phillpotts, refused to institute him, because of the doctrine he held concerning baptism. Gorham moved the Court of Arches to compel the bishop to admit him. The Dean of Arches, Sir Herbert Jenner Fust, upheld Phillpotts, but on appeal to the Privy Council, Gorham was ruled not to have gone beyond or come short of the teaching of the Church of England. The Catholics within the Church of England interpreted this as a judgment against Pusey's teaching on baptismal regeneration, as did Pusey himself. An even greater atmosphere of crisis was created when, in the wake of the Gorham Judgement, the Archbishop of Canterbury and the Bishop of London treated the grace and efficacy of baptism as an open question. Anglican Catholic clergymen William Maskell, William Dodsworth, T. W. Allies, Henry Wilberforce, Henry Manning, and laymen James Hope-Scott and Lord Fielding converted to Rome on this issue.

In the wake of the Gorham Judgement, Church Unions sprang up across Britain protesting the presence of the hand of the state in doctrinal definitions. On July 23, 1850, there were great meetings at St. Martin's Hall and Freemason's Tavern in London at which Pusey was principal speaker. On October 15 Pusey addressed another large London crowd on the efficacy of the sacraments and the usurpation of the state. These sentiments were amplified in The Royal Supremacy not an Arbitrary Authority But Limited by the Laws of the Church of Which Kings Are Members. The state had the duty to guard the church but not to define a faith which had descended to the present in one stream of tradition and under the guidance of the Holy Ghost. In this Gorham case "the center of Christian being and Christian faith, the very essence of Sacraments [that they effect] union with Christ" that the Sacraments engraft us in the incarnation, had been disrupted: "a wrong decision, even in a supreme court, cannot alter the faith of the Church. The meaning of the article of the creed: 'one baptism for the remission of sins,' must be that one meaning in which the whole Catholic Church ever understood it. No wrong interpretation put upon it by a Court, nor any wrong judgement passed in neglect of it, can alter the sense in which the Church received it from the Apostles, and still receives it...."[116]

In other court cases in England and Scotland the objectivity of the eucharist became the issue in contention. Ten years after Pusey was condemned for his 1843 sermon on the real presence of Christ in the eucharist, another sacramental controversy arose. In the autumn of 1853 Archdeacon Denison, the rector of East Brent, preached a series of three sermons in the cathedral of Wells on the objective presence of Christ in the holy eucharist. Rector J. Ditcher of South Brent accused Denison of heresy and cited him before the Archbishop of Canterbury. The case was tried at Bath by the Archbishop's Court, and the decision went against Denison. Once again there were protests and petitions, and the tumult produced two important works from Pusey, a long sermon, "The Real Presence Considered as the Doctrine of the English Church," and a heavy catena of extracts proving the objective grace of the eucharist, all drawn from the Fathers and Anglican divines of the seventeenth century.

One intent of both Pusey's sermon and notes was to warn officials of church and state that if belief in the eucharist as a "reality" were proscribed by law, Pusey and his hosts would withdraw from the Church of England. The second intent was to provide historical material to inform the courts and public opinion, and thereby prevent a wrong final

---

[116]E. B. Pusey, The Royal Supremacy not an Arbitrary Authority But Limited by the Laws of the Church of which Kings are Members (Oxford, 1850), p. 5.

and definitive decision on the holy eucharist. In fact in April 1857, the Dean of Arches reversed the decision of the Bath court. His opinion was confirmed by the Judicial Committee of the Privy Council in February, 1858.

By the end of that year and into the next Pusey was worn out. He informed Theodore Heyse in Rome, "I was writing against time in the unhappy controversies by which we are torn, anxious to do what in me lay, that the truth might not be condemned....Your letter found me in the midst of some of that crushing work, which amid these stormy days we have had so often. A Bishop was attacked for believing and teaching what I too believe, so I had to work to help him in his defense."[117] That bishop was Alexander Penrose Forbes of Brechin who was charged with heresy in 1858 in Edinburgh by the synod of the Anglican bishops of Scotland. Forbes, a Pusey disciple, had learned the doctrine of the eucharist directly from his master. The official questioning of the doctrine of the real presence almost drove Forbes out of the Anglican Church. He wrote to Keble, "...my chief difficulty is the Möhler argument....If you recollect Möhler makes the two systems, the Catholic and the Protestant start from a difference of faith on that point [the objective nature of sacraments]....One cannot but feel that the beautiful school of thought following from 1833 has done its work and exists but as a phase of mind in the church. It can in no sense be said to represent Anglicanism."[118] Pusey's eloquent sacramental defense, prepared for Forbes, saved him from condemnation by the Scots and from going over to the Roman Communion.

Slowly, however, such trials were bringing gradual legal acceptance of the Puseyite point of view on the sacraments. In 1868 a case was brought against W. J. Bennett, Vicar of Frome, for "exaggerated and inaccurate eucharistic language." Bennett's eucharistic language was

---

[117]MS letters of Pusey to Th. Heyse, Aug. 27, 1858 and Dec. 26, 1859. See also Peter G. Cobb, "Leader of the Anglo-Catholics," in Perry Butler, op. cit., pp. 349-365.

[118]MS letter of Bishop A. P. Forbes to Keble, Dec. 1860.

in fact so close to Pusey's own that he asked to be included in the case. "I wish to have the opportunity of defending myself," Pusey wrote. "If [Bennet's] doctrine should be condemned, there is, plainly, nothing for us to do, except to resign whatever offices we hold in the Church of England."[119] Such extreme action was not necessary for in July 1870, the Court of Arches ruled "that it was permissible for the English Church to teach that the Presence of our Lord in the Holy Eucharist was objective, real, actual, and spiritual...."[120]

This victory did not deflect Pusey from continuing to develop a theory of community in the church which traversed a _via media_ between state and hierarchy. His ecclesiology, his theory of community based solely upon the mystical body of Christ and the sacraments, was developing through the fifties in his correspondence:

> There are different degrees of oneness....The deepest union of this sort is not of love or mind, but of reality, that real union whereby we are all in Christ, one body, by being partakers of that One Body and filled with His Spirit. ...There is a real oneness in our common creeds, our sacraments, our Apostolic descent, and the indwelling of the One Spirit, and the prayer for one another, although there be not perfect union....Christ's disciples...were to have an oneness which should be an image of that of the Holy Trinity. This is formed especially by the Indwelling of the Holy Spirit and the Sacraments uniting them into one in our Lord....The fruit of that higher union with our Lord by His Spirit and by His Sacraments, should be love....I do not hold (as Archdeacon Manning estimates) that the unity of the Church is a mere unity of will,--a mere being 'at one'--a mere moral or meta-physical unity, but I hold that it is a unity of nature, a numerical unity, a unity enwrought by God, by the one indwelling Spirit, and by the One Body of Christ, of which all partake, a unity of descent, an organic unity--a mystical sacramental unity. This unity involves duties on the part of man as for instance, agreement, harmony, love between those whom the grace of God has made one....If there is now no communion between Rome and England, this is no more than what in former times has happened between Rome and

---

[119]MS letter of Pusey to A. C. Tait, Nov. 6, 1868, in Tait Papers, Vol. No. 85, Lamberth Palace Library, London; MS letter of Pusey to A. C. Tait, May 3, 1866? or 1868?, _Ibid._, Vol. No. 84.

[120]MS Bloxam Collection, p. 804.

Africa, Rome and Asia, etc...In like manner Israel and Judah,
though not "at one" still remained "one." Christ never
speaks of any Head of the Church except Himself. He gives us
many other of his titles...but never that of Head. The
ancient Church acknowledged no monarchy in the Church....You
ask "Where amid divided Churches is there a foundation of
faith higher than private judgement?" I reply that all the
great points have been already secured by infallible general
councils of the undivided Church. The present Church can
testify to that fact as a matter of history without requiring
infallibility...as to the necessity of outward communion, it
has been broken before without destroying unity.[121]

Pusey's theory of community was stated in a final form against the
Roman hierarchical notion in a last important work, the Eirenicon. This
final affirmation of Pusey's new Catholicism came out in 1865 when the
twelve years of the Oxford Movement were once again the topic of heated
debate following the Charles Kingsley-Newman exchange and the
publication of the latter's Apologia in the atmosphere described by the
Athenaeum: "How briskly we gather round a brace of reverend gentlemen
when the prize for which they contend is which of the two shall be
considered as the father of lies."[122]

The Eirenicon claimed for the Anglican Church a share in organic
Catholic unity—that she was a part of the one Catholic Church. The
modern Roman system as described by Pusey is opposed to "the objective
faith....Not only as the life of individuals, but as held by the
church, the Catholic 'faith' [by becoming subjected to the Roman
hierarchical system] will be very much obscured, and may be found among
few only. We have not seen such a triumph of Satan over the faith
here, as that reign of his in the capital of France."[123] Unity and

----

[121]MS letter of Pusey to brother William, Oct. 10, 1851; MS letter of
Pusey probably to Newman, Aug. 17, 1850's(?), in Newman's Papers at
Birmingham Oratory.

[122]Raymond Chapman, Faith and Revolt: Studies in the Literary
Influence of the Oxford Movement (London, 1970), p. 140. For a recent
look at this period and the Kingsley-Newman controversy see "Newman and
the Oxford Counter-Reformation," in A. Dwight Culler, The Victorian
Mirror of History (New Haven, 1985), pp. 90-121.

[123]E. P. Pusey, The Church of England A Portion of Christ's One Holy
Catholic Church, and a Means of Restoring Visible Unity: An Eirenicon
to the Author of the Christian Year (Oxford, 1865), p. 258.

Catholicism find their origin not in the pope or the hierarchy, but in the spirit of God, the sacraments, and the tradition of faith living in the hearts of believers:

> Unity, in part, is the direct gift of God; in part, it is the fruit of that gift in the mutual love of the members of the Church. In part, it is a spiritual oneness wrought by God the Holy Ghost....In one way, it is organic unity derived from Christ, and binding all to Christ, descending from the Head to the Body, and uniting the Body to the Head; in another it consists in acts of love from the members one to another. Christ our Lord, God and Man, binds us to Him by the indwelling of His Spirit, by the gift of His Sacraments. ...We are bound to one another, in that we are members of Him ...and by common acts of worship and intercommunion....Our highest union with one another is an organic union with one another, through union with Him...an union through his indwelling Spirit....This oneness, then, is an actual mystical oneness, inwrought by Christ our Head, uniting the whole Church together in one with Himself in His body....[124]

---

[124]Ibid., pp. 45, 47.

CHAPTER VI

Parishes and Monasteries

Pusey's Eirenicon was an apology for corporate spirituality. To
describe the church as "mystical union" and "sacramental fellowship"
implied theories of collective worship, which were as contrary to the
contemporary Roman Catholic practical system in England as Pusey's
organic ecclesiology was to Roman Catholic individualistic principles
of infallibility and hierarchical concepts of Christian unity focused
almost entirely on the papacy. The first volume of the Eirenicon
suggested that "practical Romanism," by which Pusey meant both
liturgical practice and church government, was at variance with the
Catholicism of the patristic era.

The Eirenicon dealt more precisely with the specific abuses of
"that vast practical system which lies beyond the letter of the Council
of Trent, things which are taught with a quasi-authority in the Roman
Church, than by what is actually defined."[1] Pusey related most Roman
Catholic liturgical aberrations to the deformed celebration of the
eucharist: "the sale of masses as applicable to the departed," "the
denial of the cup to the laity," "celebrating Divine Service in an
unknown tongue."[2] The Eirenicon related these deviations to the
promulgation of the doctrine of transubstantiation in 1215, a
corruption of the eucharist and a revolt against the patristic teaching

----

[1]E. B. Pusey, The Church of England, A Portion of Christ's One Holy
Catholic Church, and a means of Restoring Visible Unity, An Eirenicon
(Oxford, 1865), p. 98.

[2]MS Copy of Pusey's paper on the position of the English Church,
delivered on the 23rd Sunday after Trinity 1846.

272

on the nature of a sacrament. Transubstantiation, as defined at Lateran IV, destroyed the necessary logical and theological connection between Christ's presence in the Christian people as his body and his presence in the eucharist. The extension of the incarnation to the church as a whole, Pusey taught by contrast, makes the eucharistic presence a reality.

The inadequacies of Evangelical and High Church worship for industrial society loomed even larger in Pusey's world. Both the Evangelical and High Church parties offered the specific and the national in parish work and worship when the organic and communal were wanted amid the new social conditions of England. The Evangelicals did not provide the liturgical means for spiritual growth beyond conversion, and High Church clergy were not dealing effectively with the religious state of the great industrial towns. Both were weakened by a limitation of their devotional expression to the mysteries of Christianity to that which could be conveyed through the conventional media of Anglo-Saxon culture. Pusey's falling away from the liturgical practice of the existing parties in the Church of England was more complex than his revulsion against the liturgy as then celebrated by the Roman Catholic Church in England. He searched for institutions capable of expressing the organic Catholicism he had found in the Fathers and which could provide for religious life in common. At the same time Pusey sought forms of worship and devotion which expressed that objective quality of Christianity which he fought for in the courts, in his baptismal Tracts, and in eucharistic sermons. In both instances, the practical machinery of the new Catholicism grew out of the English Establishment: Oxford colleges, Church of England parishes, and the Book of Common Prayer.

Pusey's initial response to social conditions which perplexed him was simple and direct: the building of churches. In his first published sermon of 1832, "A Sermon Preached at the Consecration of Grove Church," he called for a massive program of ecclesiastical construction, and he did so again in his pamphlets on "London Churches"

and "Cathedral Institutions."[3] Mrs. Pusey sold her jewels to fund
metropolitan churches, and in 1837 their horses and carriages were
auctioned for the same purpose. Pusey sought to establish churches
which would be outposts of new Catholic principles. He told Newman in
1836 that "Churches in London" was issued to counter the Evangelicals'
Simeon Trust, a plan to endow parishes which would adhere solely to
Clapham theology.[4] In the same year he suggested to Keble, "I very
much wish that in the arrangement for the new churches...you...may have
a certain degree of virtual influence...."[5] By 1840 Pusey was speaking
of a network of small congregations with Catholic views in each part of
the country.[6]

But, Pusey wrote, "We need not single clergy only, but bodies of
clergy, if the light of the Gospel is ever to penetrate the dark
corners of our great towns...."[7] Not just new churches, but new kinds
of churches, another kind of foundation than the parsonage with one
Anglican priest and family attached to a parish was needed if the city
were to be saved. "What is wanted everywhere for everything is,--not
funds, but men."[8] In the 1830's Hurrell Froude had passed several
months in France where he had read L'Avenir and observed the activities
of the Mennaisian clergy as they attempted to re-Christianize their
country. When Froude returned to England he set down a "Project for
the Revival of Religion in Great Towns" which suggested colleges of
clergy on the model of Oxford as a means for evangelism. Froude's plan

---

[3]E. B. Pusey, A Sermon Preached at the Consecration of Grove Church
on Tuesday, August 14, 1832 (London, 1832).

[4]MS letter of Pusey to Newman, January 22, 1836.

[5]MS letter of Pusey to Keble, October 4, 1836.

[6]MS letter of Pusey to Newman, January 21, 1840; MS letter of Pusey
to Keble, December 1, 1840.

[7]E. B. Pusey, A Letter to the Right Hon. and Right Rev. the Lord
Bishop of London, in Explanation of Some Statements Contained in a
Letter by the Rev. W. Dodsworth (Oxford, 1851), p. 234.

[8]MS letter of Pusey to her brother Philip, July 21, 1845.

did not become public until included in his famous anti-Reformation Remains published as a memorial to him in 1838. Pusey wrote to Newman in August of that year, "The more I think of Froude's plan, the more it seems to me the only one, if anything is to be done for our large towns."[9] He therefore came to the conclusion that the introduction of a mass of clergy might ameliorate the heathenish state of urban populations. Gradually, the monastic character of a modern Catholic solution for Manchester, Leeds, and Birmingham emerged. The new clergy would be celibate and live in community:

> There are surely duties enough, [the bishop of Oxford was addressed publicly], in the Church, where celibacy may have its proper place, and where there is much room for the exhibition of the sterner grace of self-denial....If the degraded population of many of our great towns are to be recovered from the state of Heathenism in which they are sunk, it must be by such preaching of the cross wherein it shall be forced upon man's dull senses, that they who preach it have forsaken all....Why should marriage alone have its duties...and the single estate be condemned to an unwilling listlessness....[10]

For the city of Leeds Pusey envisioned "bodies of clergy...living in simplicity and self-denial...with an earnest desire for the salvation of souls" which would restore to the poor that service of monasticism which the spoliation of the monasteries had robbed from them.[11] But the advocacy of overt monasticism was disguised under the

----

[9]MS letter of Pusey to Newman, August 9, 1838. Froude wrote to Newman in August 1833, "It has lately come into my head that the present state of things in England makes an opening for reviving the monastic system. I think of putting this view forward under the title of 'Project for Reviving Religion in Great Towns.' Certainly colleges of unmarried priests...would be the cheapest possible way of providing effectively for the spiritual wants of a large population." L. I. Guiney, Hurrell Froude (London, 1904), p. 122.

[10]E. B. Pusey, A Letter to the Right Rev. Father in God, Richard Lord Bishop of Oxford on the Tendency to Romanism imputed to Doctrines Held of Old, as Now, in the English Church, 3rd ed. (Oxford, 1839), pp. 215, 216.

[11]MS letter of Pusey to ? , Quinquagesima 1852; MS letter of Pusey to his brother Philip, June 13, 1846.

pretence that mere colleges were being founded. Pusey described his first scheme for the cities to Benjamin Harrison, a former Hebrew pupil then Archdeacon of Canterbury:

> The principal features of the plan are i) they should be a body of clergy living together (say 12) and acting under the parochial authorities. [The living together] is 1) cheaper; 2) more calculated to produce a. an impression and b. unity of action in such places. ii) They should have Daily Service and observe Feasts and Fasts. iii) They should live single so long as they belonged to the college, as in colleges at Oxford. iv) They should be formed gradually, according as the funds should come in; beginning perhaps with three or four, and going on gradually, until you come to 12.[12]

The new clerical colleges and Catholic parishes called for the liturgy to be celebrated in a manner which had not been provided by popular Anglicanism for generations. Pusey's role in this Anglican liturgical revival was very gradually and carefully to associate a richer eucharistic ritual with those new Catholic doctrines which ceremonial set before the eyes of the people. The nature of the theology which was joined to the rites of the Puseyite churches not only distinguishes them from the products of the ecclesiastical antiquarianism of such groups as the Cambridge Camden Society, but also establishes them as the English counterparts of those nineteenth century Continental parishes which were the pioneers of the liturgical movement.

Just as Bishop Lloyd had secured Pusey a position at Oxford and had sent him to Germany, so he also was responsible for awakening him to the beauties of the liturgy. In a series of classes at Christ Church in 1827, the Bishop of Oxford portrayed the Book of Common Prayer as a guide to holiness and brought before his students, including Pusey, those older liturgical sources on which the collects of the Prayerbook were based, chiefly, the liturgy of 1549 in which the eucharist was the first and most important service. Lloyd had been introduced to the Roman Catholic liturgy by French emigrants to England during the French

---

[12]MS letter of Pusey to Harrison, August 13, 1838.

Revolution.[13] He thus shared with Pusey and his contemporaries Roman breviaries, missals, and sacramentaries as guides to an enhanced understanding of the evolution of the liturgy in England.

After finishing Lloyd's course, Pusey wrote to Miss Barker of his discovery of the importance of public corporate prayer, "[it]...does appear to me to afford proof of the superior value and efficacy of united prayer, whether in a family or larger congregations, as having the immediate promise of blessing from our Saviour...."[14] When he joined the Oxford Movement, Pusey united with Anglicans who still found the Prayerbook to be "the incomparable Liturgy."[15] The period of Pusey's adherence to the revival of "Prayerbook Catholicism" was confined to the thirties. Such a static, nationalistic notion of liturgy did not remain with him through the next decade. The despair of his wife's death brought him into closer contact with Roman Catholic devotional books which Lloyd had first introduced him to, and which had been at hand and in circulation at Oxford since the early thirties, when Roman and Parisian breviaries had been brought from France by Froude. Pusey wrote to his brother in October, 1839, "I was wishing to give one of my nieces the new translation of the Hymns from the Paris Breviary. Do you approve? There is nothing Romanist in them. Also should you like or dislike for them a cross on the binding?"[16] In Tract 81 Pusey suggested joining silent prayers from Roman liturgies to the Prayerbook rite:

> To further these ends, to obviate the embarrassment which may naturally result to individuals, from feeling themselves in possession of a doctrine greater than they have hitherto had...they can readily associate with an action, outwardly so simple as that of placing upon the altar the elements of

---

[13]Ferdinand Baldensperger, Le mouvement des idées dans l'emigration française (New York, 1968).

[14]MS letter of Pusey to Miss Barker, November 28, 1827.

[15]R. C. D. Jasper, Prayer Book Revision 1800-1900 (London, 1954).

[16]MS letter of Pusey to Newman, July 16, 1839; MS letter of Pusey to his brother Philip, Oct. 21, 1839.

278

bread and wine,--as also for the sake of the blessing of the
prayers themselves, we subjoin two forms wherewith the
obligation was of old accompanied. This the priest may
silently pray, (for the Church places no restraint upon
silent prayer.)....Clergymen...can but offer some prayer, or
at least think thoughts which are prayers.[17]

At the same time, his associates were reading the liturgical theories
of Dom Guéranger, and advocating a revival of liturgical ceremonial
within the Church of England.

Frederick Oakeley, Fellow of Balliol, was particularly identified
with the movement for ritual. He had attended Lloyd's lectures on the
liturgy and to him they were the first impulse toward a revival of
Catholic solemnity within the Church of England. Oakeley had done
nothing extreme, however, until 1841, when during a visit to the
Trappist monastery founded by the Roman Catholic Leicestershire squire
Ambrose Phillipps de Lisle in 1837 he beheld the splendors of Roman
ritual and Gregorian chant. De Lisle, a supporter of the liturgical
reforms of Dom Guéranger and a frequent host for monks of Solesmes
traveling in England, shaped his Trappist monastic ritual according to
the French liturgical movement. When Oakeley discussed liturgical
revival in an article in the British Critic, "Rites and Ceremonies,"
he was in effect reviewing the first volume of the Institutions
liturgiques of Dom Guéranger. Guéranger's arguments in favor of the
development of ritual are used to support Oakeley's contention that
Catholic liturgical performance must now be joined to the rites of the
Book of Common Prayer to correspond to the Catholic principles which
were being enunciated within the Church of England. It is the
non-national Catholicity of the Institutions which is most appealing
to the Fellow of Balliol:

We cordially go along with the author whose work we have been
reviewing, in what we may call his unnational spirit.
...National theories...appear to us to involve a subtle

----
[17]E. B. Pusey, Tracts of the Times. Catena Patrum No. IV.
Testimony of Writers of the Later English Church to the Doctrine of the
Eucharistic Sacrifice etc. (London, 1838), pp. 54-55.

Erastianism, besides betokening an inadequate estimate of the fulness and freedom of Gospel privileges.[18] In other articles Oakeley suggested that one of the best means for the Anglican churches to overcome their nationality and reassert the unity of the undivided church was by the adoption of the eucharist as the chief form of Christian worship marked out in its importance by ceremonial accretions which did not appear at Morning and Evening Prayer, and by the singing of Gregorian chant, which, as Guéranger argued, more than any other music exhibits the proper Catholic aesthetic, simplicity and purity.[19]

Pusey considered Oakeley the liturgical pioneer ("Oakeley went to Margaret Street [church in London] and began Ritualism"), but liturgical transformation became the badge of that entire party which accepted Pusey's doctrinal views. In 1842 Montalembert, an ally of Guéranger, wrote to de Lisle, "Thanks to the Tablet and the Catholic I can follow with an anxious eye and heart every step your Puseyite friends are taking; and I do so with the most heartfelt sympathy....It is a thousand times more important not to put the slightest impediment in the way which the Puseyites are so marvelously treading in...."[20]

This Anglican liturgical revival came gradually to engraft more and more Catholic ritual into the English churches. Pusey feared to introduce and defend any foreign rite until it could be demonstrated to congregations and public alike that the ceremonial was the necessary visible expression of new doctrine. His initial liturgical project was a translation of the Sarum Breviary. That venture attracted no financial supporter, and he was forced to compile an office book by hand for his son Philip which contained services for the seven canonical hours. Again in 1844 he attempted to publish an English breviary based on Roman forms but was prevented by Keble, who imagined

---

[18]British Critic, XXX (July, 1841), No. LX, 422-465.

[19]Ibid., No. LVI, 371-90, No. LXVIII, 278-320.

[20]MS letter of Pusey to Liddon, July 14, 1882; E. S. Purcell, The Life and Letters of Ambrose Phillipps de Lisle (London, 1900), p. 236.

that the public would recoil from the invocation of the saints contained therein.[21] Pusey next turned his attention to publishing books of Roman Catholic devotion adapted to the Church of England as guides to public and private worship during the seasons of the liturgical year. These editions of "adapted books" occupied him from 1844 to 1847:

> In editing my little Roman Catholic books, my own object has, perhaps, a little skewed, i.e. I began them with the simple object of building up and guiding our own people....In the present time there is a craving after a higher life; stricter and more abiding penitence; deeper and fuller devotion; mental prayer...more habitual recollection in Him amid the duties of daily life....People feel that they lack instruction; they see dimly what God would have of them,--they see not how to set about it....

These devotional aids were addressed to souls conditioned by Evangelical propaganda, who found themselves alienated from formal liturgies:

> ...These very devotions are strangely suited to win devout souls, who, with imperfect knowledge, yet love with a reverent kindled piety the Person of the Redeemer. While a school among us depreciates these, they will be prized by those who seem, on other points, most opposed to the teaching of the Church.[22]

The "adapted books" presented forms of worship "most powerfully expressive of our incorporation into Christ."[23] The first of these liturgical tracts were translations of commentaries done by the 17th-century French cleric Jean-Baptiste-Elie Avrillon (1652-1729). A Guide for Passing Advent Holily, Translated from the French and Adapted to the Use of the English Church came out in 1844 and The Year of Affections; or, Affections of the Love of God, Drawn from the Canticles for Every Day in the Year in 1845. The preface to the 1844 book described the various liturgical customs of Advent (the use of purple

---

[21]MS letter of Pusey to Keble, January 9, 1844.

[22]MS letter of Pusey to Newman, July 19, 1844?; Pusey, Letter to Bishop of London, p. 97.

[23]Pusey, Letter to Bishop of London, p. 193.

and the disallowance of the Gloria), and invited readers to daily
fasting and holy communion in that season. Pusey then put out
Scupoli's The Spiritual Combat as a companion source for interpreting
Lenten rites. In 1845 and 1847 he edited volumes of J. M. Horst's The
Paradise for the Christian Soul, Enriched with Choicest Delights of
Varied Piety. "One object alone he had before him," wrote the editor,
"to furnish to minds who were yearning after deeper devotions,
practical guidance, a more spiritual and inward life, aids in passing
holy seasons aright...."[24] Pusey's last "adapted book" was F. Surin's
The Foundations of the Spiritual Life, brought out in 1847.

After 1850 Dr. Pusey found himself called upon to defend publicly
liturgical change that had been challenged by Protestant opinion and
brought to wide attention by a series of court cases. These legal
defenses of the ritualists corresponded to his advocacy of the
objectivity of the sacraments in the Gorham, Denison, Forbes, and
Bennett cases. His concern was to annex the sacramental cases to the
ritual cases in the public mind, and at last Pusey came to vindicate
ritual as an expression of sacramental theology. One observer summed
up his thirty years of progress toward a richer ceremonial in
eucharistic worship: "His duty now was to defend what had come to be
called 'Ritualism,' as expressing what he held to be revealed truth
about the Sacrament of the Altar."[25] In November 1865, the Evangelical
spokesmen Wilson, Auriol, Champneys, Dale, and Miller formed a Church
Association for the purpose of prosecuting any English clergymen who
performed liturgical rites which transgressed the letter of the rubrics
of the Book of Common Prayer. A number of important clergy, W. J. E.
Bennett of Frome, A. H. Mackonochie of Saint Alban's, Holborn, Liddell
of St. Paul's, Knightsbridge, Purchas of Brighton, Sidney Faithorne
Green of Miles Platting (who was incarcerated in Lancaster Castle 595
days for using incense) and John Bell-Cox of St. Margaret's, Liverpool

---

[24]J. M. Horst, Paradise of the Christian Soul, ed. by E. B. Pusey
(Oxford, 1845), p. ix.

[25]G. W. E. Russell, Dr. Pusey (Lond, 1907), p. 132.

were brought to public trial. In the autumn of 1866 a campaign against the use of the chasuble and other eucharistic vestments was begun in the columns of the Times. In 1867 English bishops passed a "Resolution on Ritualism" which deprecated the eastward position at the celebration of the eucharist (traditional English usage directed that the celebrant stand at the north end of the "holy table"), lights, incense, genuflection, and the elevation of the host. The document seemed to Pusey to condemn the doctrine of the objective presence of Christ in the sacrament. In the summer of 1866 he spoke to the English Church Union on the charge that these liturgical changes were the work of a cranky fringe: "There is no danger of superficialness now. Thirty years of suffering, thirty years of contempt, thirty years of trial, would prevent anything from being superficial." Ritual, he said, should be valued by the churchman as "symbolized doctrine."[26] Pusey wrote to his brother William in 1866 on the ritualistic parishes: "...I understand that it is a lay rather than a clerical movement, and that the clergy adopt it at the will of the people...insofar as they [the eucharistic vestments] are lawful and they meet a wish of the people and contribute to piety, I cannot but be satisfied with the result."[27] In a University sermon in 1867 he offered himself for prosecution in place of those clergy who were being brought to trial. In that same year he prepared a petition setting forth the opinion that in adopting daily celebration of the Holy Communion, with rich liturgical ceremony marking it out as the chief Christian service, "We act in harmony with the principles and law of the C. of E....having at heart the promotion of the Glory of God in the due and reverent celebration of the Holy Eucharist, as the central act of Divine worship."[28]

In the 1870's the Evangelical anti-ritualist movement reached a

----

[26]H. P. Liddon, Life of Edward Bouverie Pusey, IV (London, 1898), 213.

[27]MS letter of Pusey to brother William B., February 11, 1866.

[28]E. B. Pusey, Declaration on Eucharistic Belief and Worship (Oxford, 1867).

height of frenzy just at the moment when the liturgical war against Guéranger and the Benedictines reached a climax in France and the Kulturkampf was initiated in Germany. The corresponding political attack in England was the passage, in 1874, of the Public Worship Regulation Act. The outlawing of the six points of Puseyite ritual in a proposed bill was produced by Disraeli's desire for an anti-Popish, anti-Irish sop, the Evangelical passions of some members of the House of Commons, and the prejudices of Archbishop Tait who had been one of the four Oxford tutors who condemned Newman's Tract XC in 1841. The P.W.R.A. allowed that any parishioner aggrieved by the introduction of ritual into the services of the parish could bring the local clergy to trial. The passage of the bill provided another occasion for Pusey to defend ritual as a legitimate expression of Catholic doctrine. When he appeared at a monster rally of the E.C.U. at St. James' Hall in London to speak, the audience rose and cheered for a few minutes as if prepared for a fight:

> Surely people must suspect that we have a strong hold on the minds of England that we are to be extirpated thus promptly [by the passage of this law]. People may regard us as a pestilence, but anyhow we are not a pestilence which seizes persons without their will. [Prolonged cheering.] It was attempted in vain last night [in the House] to provide that the complaints [against ritual] should be made by resident parishioners. The "aggrieved parishioners" may still be living in the backwoods of America, w. some petty tenement in the parish [Great sensation].[29]

Pusey advocated the eastward position once again. Standing before the altar at the eucharist implied an acceptance of the real presence and bowing after the consecration was a demonstration of adoration of Christ present in the sacrament. In letters to the Times he replied, to the defenders of the P.W.R.A., that the legislation was a rebuff to

----

[29]E. B. Pusey, P.W.R.A. Speech at English Church Union June 16, 1874 (London, 1876). For recent analysis of the question of ritualism in the parishes see James Bentley, Ritualism and Politics in Victorian Britain (Oxford, 1978); Geoffrey Rowell, The Vision Glorious (Oxford, 1983), pp. 116–140; Judith Pinnington, "Rubric and Spirit," Roger Arguile, "Parishes and People," in Kenneth Leach and Rowan Williams, Essays Catholic and Radical (London, 1983), pp. 95–147.

the demand of the people in the parishes to "set these truths visibly before us."[30]

Prosecution under the P.W.R.A. continued until Pusey's death, and he accelerated his public support of Catholic ritual and defense of those parish priests who made the liturgy the chief means of teaching their people. Controversy grew in the parishes, such as in St. Barnabas behind the Oxford University Press, which flaunted advanced eucharistic ceremonial. Pusey was the representative of such parishes before angry bishops:

> I am sorry to hear of the strife and bitterness in some of the parishes in your Lordship's large diocese, [he wrote the bishop of Oxford]....As far as I have seen the assailants have been the Church Associationists: The Ritualists and their defenders have only wished to do their Master's work in peace....Your Lordship must know that toleration is allowed to every school of clergy except the Ritualists....St. Barnabas is a great power for good in Oxford.[31]

The case of Pelham Dale allowed Pusey to point publicly to a solution which the ritualists had found to the dilemma of theological communication—a physical, corporate language of Christianity for laity who found the intellectual constructs of Anglicanism repellent. Ritual was a means of transmitting the Christian religion to the poor and unlearned and the rich and intelligent. "The strength of Mr. Dale's case," Pusey wrote, "is that he filled his church with communicants...."[32] He praised the vigor of Mr. Dale's congregation when compared to the perishing efforts of the Low Churchmen in the diocese of Manchester: "The ritual movement has, I believe, been eminently a lay movement. The clergy taught the truth; the congregations said, 'Set it before our eyes' and gave the expensive vestments, etc....The strength of the Ritualists lies in their united congregations." And to the London English Church Union Pusey remarked:

----

[30]Liddon, op. cit., p. 271.

[31]MS letter of Pusey to Bishop of Oxford, June 21, 1881.

[32]MS letter of Pusey to Liddon, November 21, 1880.

Mr. Dale is in prison, not as some say, for the use of vestments, but for the great truth which the persecutors too acknowledge it to be their aim to exterminate, which they hope to exterminate though...the outward ritual has taken hold of the hearts of people. The congregations which love it are very devout...nothing [in these liturgical matters] should be done without the good will of the people.

Pusey's final ritualistic fight concerned the imprisonment of S. F. Green in Lancaster for the use of incense. On this occasion he stirred up again a storm of protests, letters and petitions which publicized the suffering of the ritualists in the most tragic terms and provided empirical evidence in the press of the success of their parochial endeavors. Public opinion was turning against the Church Association which became popularly known as "Persecution, Ltd." The Association, in fact, gradually lost support and prosecuted the last ritualist, Bishop King of Lincoln, in the 1890's.

-2-

Because the Puseyites were often excluded from the ladder of preferment in the Church of England, prevented from preaching within established parish churches, and sometimes excluded from college fellowships, Catholic ideals and liturgical practice spread through England by means of a series of new organizations, secret societies, committees and brotherhoods in the universities, through a network of newly founded parishes created especially for the purpose of maintaining Catholic doctrine and discipline, and a complex of men's and women's monastic institutions. Here the ideals of the new Catholicism were kept alive when under attack by the Establishment. In 1864 Pusey labelled such a semi-clandestine system "organic acting within the Church. Without something organic, whose business it shall be to agitate, year by year, [the Catholic revival] would be but an explosion on the surface."[33] The seclusion and uncertain identification of those who constituted these societies and who

---

[33]MS letter of Pusey to Keble, August 29, 1864.

contributed the money to the foundation of Catholic institutions suggest the danger to reputation which such views entailed.

The first secret association for Catholics within the Church of England was the Brotherhood of the Holy Trinity founded in Lincoln College, Oxford, in 1844 by A. P. Forbes and H. P. Liddon. The Brotherhood was established for the study of theology and history under Pusey's guidance and for the observance of a common rule of life "to aim at simplicity in dress, to avoid theatre and opera, to eat meat only once a day, no wine or beer; plainest food."[34] Thirty-one undergraduates enrolled of whom we know Forbes, Liddon, the future architect Butterfield, Robert Payne, Alexander Wilson, E. C. Lowe, and Lionel Boyce. But as early as 1836 Pusey had invited Mr. Gladstone to begin organizing support for Catholic projects among adults in the great world of London:

> ...I am wished to send an account, of what number of acquaintances I could calculate upon, as contributors, upon such a large and safe scheme; and I trust that it will be of much service, as well in promoting the great object of bringing the Gospel home to many, who are now living as Heathens in the center of our Christian land,...I wish at present for numbers not names; at least, I am only asked for numbers; I do not wish to commit anyone; but only so far to strengthen the hands of those in authority, as to obtain, if it may be, a comprehensive association, wherein the whole Church may endeavour unitedly to remove an evil, which is pressing upon all. If you can mention the subject to any of our friends as Lord Ashley, etc....[35]

Gladstone became the spokesman for a circle of well placed figures and politicians who provided the financial support for the Puseyites. There appears to be no complete list of these supporters, but their names can be pieced together form the rolls of those who contributed to various monasteries, parishes, and colleges. Lord John Manners, Lord Lyttleton, Lord Campden, Baron Alderson, A. J. Beresford-Hope, J. O. Watts, F. H. Dickenson, R. M. Milnes, W. Monsell, Lord Beauchamp were

---

[34]MS Brotherhood of the Holy Trinity, 1852.

[35]MS letter of Pusey to Gladstone, February 2, 1836.

benefactors. Mr. Gladstone continued to serve as intermediary between these men and Dr. Pusey from the thirties to the eighties. He did not hide and became the most notable lay Puseyite. Lady Frederick Cavendish wrote,

> It was in the year 1867 that we paid our respects to Pope Pius IX....The Pope spoke to us in French, so the word he used for Puseyite was "Pousséiste." He could not pronounce the French "u." He said to me, "M. Gladstone est Pousséiste, n'est ce pas?" To which I replied, "Qui, Saint Père, et moi aussi"--at which he was much amused.[36]

Mr. Gladstone's parish in London was initially Christ Church, Albany Street, the first place of worship to be built in the city by the adherents of Oxford Catholic views. This area of London had once been served by the single church of St. Pancras. The population of the parish in 1801 was 31,779 and that edifice could seat 150. It had grown to 71,838 when a new St. Pancras was built with 3,000 sittings. When the population rose to 103,548 in 1831 five chapels were opened, and by 1841 nine houses of worship of one sort or another were provided for 129,969 people. Lord John Manners sought to have one of the new churches represent Catholic tenets, and a meeting was held in 1836 in the home of the Rt. Hon. Thomas Erskine to raise money and organize support for an Albany Street Church. William Dodsworth, originally a Cambridge Evangelical, then an Irvingite, finally won to Tractarianism, was the most powerful spiritual influence in this part of London when plans were drafted for Christ Church. Since January 1836 he had been holding a series of weekday lectures, on "Apostolical Ministry," under the patronage of H. J. Rose and with a large following of women who found him "an eloquent-prophetic preacher."

Dodsworth was drafted as spiritual leader of the congregation and Dr. Pusey became general Oxford consultant to the project. Pusey contributed £1000 from the sale of his carriages and his wife's jewels to the building. Some of those stones were placed in a chalice which was presented to the parish. The evolution of the architecture of the

---

[36]Russell, op. cit., p. 38.

building, which was completed in 1837, demonstrates how the interiors of English churches were transformed as liturgical change was engrafted into the parishes with the introduction of Catholic doctrine.

Sir James Pennethorne's original Christ Church was the typical classical style preaching box which had been the model for new church building in England since the seventeenth century. Originally there was no chancel, the organ loft was placed above the altar and fronted with red curtains. The altar itself was not raised above the level of the floor. The church was pewed throughout except for a row of free seats in the center. Choir boys sang in the organ loft over the altar. Round the altar, in the first year, sat charity girls dressed in mob caps, white tippets, and yellow mittens obscuring the holy table from view. During the first months of services a clerk in a black gown sat under the reading desk opposite the pulpit and made the responses to the liturgy rather than the congregation. By 1839 the altar was in full view and the clerk had been dismissed. There were still pew openers "in neat caps" who assisted the owners of benches to their places. A preaching hall rather than a room for eucharistic worship was suggested by the presence of three balconies to hold overflow crowds who came to hear great clerics. At first the question asked of those coming from Christ Church was "Whom did you hear?"

Ritual innovations continued apace. By 1843 an altar recess and sanctuary were added, the organ was moved to the west end and choir stalls added to the east. A stone font was placed at the west door and an eagle lectern replaced the wooden reading desk. Dodsworth began a daily celebration of the eucharist at which he elevated the host and faced eastward at the consecration of the bread and wine. The Edinburgh Review described the Christ Church of the forties:

> Dodsworth was a fine preacher. His church services were impressive. There was a flavour of combined learning and piety, and of literary and artistic refinement, in the representatives of Tractarianism, which enlisted floating sympathies; and hence, besides the thoroughgoing "Puseyites," there existed an eclectic following in and around Albany Street, composed of various elements. In some cases it was the old wine of Evangelicalism settling itself into new High Church bottles; in others, literary affinities fastening on

congenial forms of historic or aesthetic sentiment.[37]

Pusey had hoped that his first college of curates could be placed in this Christ Church parish, but the plan was not realized. However, from 1838 to 1843, Pusey looked to Dodsworth as the clerical leader of his party in London, the responsible spokesman who could be counted on to marshal London forces.[38] The Vicar of Christ Church regarded Pusey as his spiritual father: "He had been amongst the foremost to promote in the Church of England those doctrines and practices which, whether rightly or wrongly, are by the generality of persons identified with the Church of Rome."[39] And in the matter of Pusey's relation to the liturgical renaissance he said, "He was the first Anglican clergyman who spoke to me of its revival in the established Church, and I know of many persons whom he has led into the practice."[40] Pusey advised Dodsworth on how to solve those parish administrative duties which were thrown up by the intrusion of the new Catholic doctrines. In 1836 he suggested two celebrations of the holy communion on all feasts, for the number of communicants on those occasions had risen to 1250 and the church, as it had originally been built, could not hold the numbers. "The source of the difficulty doubtless is the miserably defective supply of churches and clergymen for our people. It was never intended that our churches should be fitted up like theatres for holding and hearing and that one shepherd should have more sheep than he can count."[41] In 1837 Pusey taught the Vicar how to administer the eucharist to the sick, in 1839 the ancient method of baptizing, and in

---

[37]H. W. Burrows, The Half-Century of Christ Church, St. Pancras, Albany Street (London, 1887), p. 63.

[38]MS letter of Dodsworth to Pusey, October 19, 1838; MS letter of Newman to Pusey, April 26, 1840.

[39]Williaim Dodsworth, A Few Comments on D. Pusey's Letter to the Bishop of London (London, 1851), p. 1.

[40]Ibid., p. 5.

[41]MS letter of Dodsworth to Pusey, August 17, 1836, Archives, Christ Church, Albany Street.

1841 how to arrange a service of confirmation.[42]

The Regius Professor of Hebrew preached in the parish on Easter Sunday and the first Sunday after Easter, 1840, on the sixth Sunday after Trinity in 1842, on Easter Day in 1843, on the second, fourth, and sixth Sundays after Trinity in 1845, in the summer and during Advent in 1846, on Circumcision, on Septuagesima, in Lent, and on Palm Sunday in 1847, as well as in Advent, and on one Sunday each in 1848 and 1849.[43] After Pusey delivered the Easter sermon in 1843 Dodsworth told him, "Some strangers in church last Sunday could not believe that you were yourself: they started with astonishment at your name: probably wondering how a wild animal could be so tame."[44] In the next weeks, after the condemnation of the University Sermon on the eucharist, he informed Pusey, "The sentence not being of the Church I trust you will feel no scruple in taking my pulpit....How cordially I go along with you in the whole of it, and how gladly I would share w. you...the reproach...which has fallen upon you. The Sermon seems...so entirely Catholic and scriptural....I do hope that you will come and preach in my Church...this would be to me most gratifying."[45] In his own preaching Dodsworth pressed the non-individualistic aspects of Dr. Pusey's theology. Baptism was for him a mystical union which forms all into one in Christ. He understood Christianity to be a denial of the self: "A Christian is one who is 'in Christ.'"[46] He justified the daily services in his parish with a statement that grace is given by God to the church as a whole community and then transmitted to the

----

[42]MS letters of Dodsworth to Pusey, February 2, 1837, November 12, 1839, Easter 1841.

[43]MS Preacher's Book, 1837-1851, Parish Archives, Christ Church, Albany Street.

[44]MS letter of Dodsworth to Pusey, May 6, 1843.

[45]MS letters of Dodsworth to Pusey, June 3, 1843 and July 4, 1843.

[46]William Dodsworth, Holy Baptism; The Grafting into our Risen Lord, Easter Sermon (London, 1850), p. 3.

individual in the midst of constant worship.[47]

The liturgical revival in Christ Church continued with the formation of English canonical hours. These offices were prepared from the scriptures and the Fathers, for the Book of Common Prayer provides for only two offices, morning and evening prayer. Thus an elaborate, one-hour service of matins was performed daily, and it was perhaps there that Mrs. Pardiggle's unfortunate children did "attend Matins with me (very prettily done) at half-past six o'clock in the morning all the year round, including of course the depth of winter."[48] The rest of the divine office was said in shorter but no less elaborate form. In the late forties Christ Church became the first parish in the Anglican Communion to revive the sacramental office of unction of the sick.[49]

Just as more Catholic ritual was being progressively introduced into Albany Street, Dodsworth joined the Roman Catholic Church in the midst of the Gorham controversy, and was received into that communion on December 31, 1850. The Bishop of London called J. G. Burrows to replace him. Burrows continued to emphasize the ritual and social innovation in the parish. William Butterfield redecorated the interior of the church building with a new font "to express honour and reverence for Holy Baptism," and added a Gothic lectern, Byzantine reredos, altar frontals, alabaster pulpit, and stained glass. At the same time a Young Women's Friendly Society for Domestics, a Commercial School, a Young Men's Society, and outdoor services were begun. In 1884 St. Bede's Working Men's Association began to hold annual outdoor processions with crosses, banners, and lanterns. There was a confraternity for communicants after 1872.

The culmination of Burrows' plans to ameliorate worship and social

----

[47]Ibid., pp. 4, 5.

[48]Charles Dickens, Bleak House, ch. 8, quoted in R. Chapman, Faith and Revolt.

[49]T. J. Williams, "A Lost Treasure Retrieved," The Holy Cross Magazine, LXVII, No. 4 (April 1956), 100-106.

conditions, to change architecture and render Christ Church available to the poor came in 1865 in a campaign to abolish pew rents and open the places in church to all. In this endeavor, as in his social activities and ritual changes, Burrows was supported by the Rossetti family who resided in the parish from 1843. Christina was a district visitor for the church and her pre-Raphaelite brother designed stained glass for the Butterfield refurbishing of the fabric. In The Churchman's Shilling she described with outrage and satire the reaction of the leading parishioners when Burrows, in true Puseyite fashion, announced the abolition of pew-rents:

> We have borne with chants, with a surpliced choir, with daily services, but we will not bear to see all our rights trampled under foot, and all our time-hallowed usages set at nought. The tendency of the day is to level social distinctions and to elevate unduly the lower orders. In this parish at least let us combine to keep up wise barriers between class and class, and to maintain that fundamental principle practically bowed to all over our happy England, that what you can pay for you can purchase.[50]

Burrows took this action because

> pew-renting obscures the great principle that the services of the Church are the natural inherent right of all the baptized in the parish, as such, and equally...the laity, instead of supporting their clergyman "freely" for the good of all the parishioners, stipulate for advantages for themselves in return for their payment....[With pew-rents] the congregation thus consists mainly of opulent persons; while out of church, in every other relation of minister and people, the parish priest has to do with many times more poor than rich.[51]

One observer reported that after the taking down of the pews "there was a marked increase of zeal in the congregation generally."[52] Pew-openers were dismissed and laymen volunteered as ushers. Additional souls, deterred by rents before, could now attend the church.

---

[50]Quoted in Chapman, op. cit., p. 175.

[51]Burrows, op. cit., pp. 43-49.

[52]Ibid., p. 48.

The statistics from Christ Church reveal that from its opening the surrounding population was attracted, and the numbers did not diminish during Burrows' tenure. During Dodsworth's vicarate there were 2,081 baptisms in the church. Parents from all classes brought infants to Albany Street for christening, but between 1838 and 1870 there was more than a doubling of the number of professional people who enrolled their children in the parish. Between 1860 and 1870, the period of the abolition of pews, there was a sharp falling off in baptisms from the merchant class.[53]

Communion statistics show that the most dramatic change in eucharistic reception occurred between 1842 and 1845, that period when Pusey enunciated and was condemned for the doctrine of the real presence. Total communions at Christ Church rose from 3,392 in 1837 to 10,927 in 1845.[54]

In the early nineteenth century the district close to Portland Place and Cavendish Square touched extremes of wealth and poverty in a manner in which Christ Church did not, for as well as the houses of the rich it included the costermongers' barrows. The only parish church for the area was All Souls', Langham Place, a great bastion of the Evangelical revival. Within the parish, at the time of the French Revolution, there had been built a temple of Deism, called Margaret Chapel, on Margaret Street, which was very fashionable and was the essence of a Protestant meeting house with galleries, high pews, and a three-decker pulpit in front of a table which served as an altar. Frederick Oakeley was licensed to minister in the chapel in July 1839. He took down the pulpit and reading desk and moved the communion table to a central position, in view of all, giving it a frontal in crimson, and placing a cross and candlesticks upon it. Oakeley did this before his contact with de Lisle and the French liturgical revival. After 1841, in addition to daily service in the chapel which reproduced the

----
[53]MS Register of Baptism, 1840-1900, Parish Archives, Christ Church, Albany Street.

[54]MS Communion Book, Ibid.

model of Albany Street, the breviary hours began to be said in an oratory and were attended by laymen such as S. F. Wood, brother of the first Lord Halifax, Robert Williams, M. P., Mr. Gladstone, and A. J. Beresford-Hope.

The oddness of the services in Margaret Street caused comment throughout London. Benjamin Webb wrote to John Mason Neale, "They have now got up a complete musical mass [at Margaret Street]: the Commandments, Epistle, Gospel, Preface, etc. all sung to the ancient music."[55] In 1845, Richard Redhead, the organist of Margaret Chapel had issued Laudes Diurnae: The Psalter and Canticles Set and Pointed to the Gregorian Tones, the first book of Gregorian chant adapted for congregational worship in the Church of England.

Pusey's relation to Margaret Chapel under Oakeley was as advisor and preacher. He delivered his only important sermon outside of Leeds there during the period of his suspension, on St. Peter's Day, 1845, "The Blasphemy Against the Holy Ghost," which was printed at the request of and dedicated to the Margaret Street congregation. He directed Oakeley on how to regulate fasting in the parish, on what devotional books to assign his flock, and on the best means for adapting the breviary for use in London. In February, 1845, Oakeley turned to Pusey for protection when he feared that the Bishop of London was moving to dismiss him because of his liturgical advances.[56] When Oakeley was indeed expelled, Pusey defended him publicly in On the Recent Judgements in the Court of Arches. Three Letters to "The English Churchman"--Mr. Oakeley's Case--October 5, 1845. Pusey lamented that the true Christian community, which had been created by Oakeley in Margaret Street, might perish now that the "band between priest and congregation is being broken."[57]

----

[55]Peter F. Anson, The Call of the Cloister (London, 1955), p. 318.

[56]MS letters of Oakeley to Pusey, 1839?, 1843?, and February 24, 1845.

[57]Privately printed in London, 1845.

Oakeley's replacement, W. U. Richards, had served Dodsworth and the Vicar of Margaret Chapel while sub-curator of the British Museum and was to remain thirty-six years as vicar of the parish. He did not place the church any longer in the avant-garde of the ritual and aesthetic movement of the Catholic party but developed the Margaret Street congregation into one of the most united, enthusiastic, and vigorous parishes in the Church of England. Richards' goodness and cheerfulness drew Dr. Pusey to him, and so highly did the professor think of him in this respect that in 1850 he dedicated to him his The Church of England Leaves Her Children Free to Whom to Open Their Griefs. This tract, fittingly, deals with the church as a common spiritual mother to all the population, rich and poor. Both as curate and vicar, Richards turned to Pusey, who was also godfather to his child, for advice and support in managing the growing parish. "...No one knows," he wrote to Oxford, "the comfort I have derived from having seen what I have of you—I look to you, even upon you, and am ready to fulfill your wishes and advice to the best of my ability."[58] Pusey advised him on the ministrations of confession and absolution, the adaptation of the monastic system to the parish, the ordering of the services, and the choice of hymns, sermon topics, and assistants.[59]

Pusey's visits to Margaret Street were particularly valued. "Your presence just now," the Vicar wrote in inviting the Regius Professor, "at Margaret Chapel would do much to give confidence to the congregation....My wish was to build up the drooping spirits of our congregation upon you....You will not I hope lightly give up preaching at Christ Church and Margaret Chapel. You have no idea of the good which results form it. You know not how many date their first impressions of seriousness from hearing you....Therefore it is that I urge you...to preach at Margaret Chapel for I know the blessing which

---

[58]MS letter of Richards to Pusey, Whitsunday 1845.

[59]MS letters of Richards to Pusey, July 6, 1843, 3rd Sunday in Advent 1845, early 46, January 23, 1846, ?1847, ?1849.

it is."[60] When the size of the congregation had outgrown the old
chapel, Pusey laid the foundation stone of the new All Saints' Church
on All Saints' Day in 1850. He said this was "the first stone of
another earthly temple, wherein yet He may be pleased to dwell, wherein
He may be pleased to form a spiritual temple, of those knit together in
His mystical body."[61]

All Saints' Church was the first religious building in England
designed to give architectural expression to the new Catholic doctrines
of the mystical body and the eucharistic life. It was built two
decades before the German Benedictines of Beuron began to experiment
with a new liturgical architecture that could better express the ideal
of one eucharistic community gathered for worship. William Butterfield
planned a church to fulfill the goal of the parish stated in a
published letter of 1847 issued by his friend A. J. Beresford-Hope:
"The great object is to secure, upon a permanent and ecclesiastical
footing, more numerous services, and the frequent administration of the
Holy Communion."[62] Butterfield had written to Pusey in 1848 asking for
a list of books which would be most suited to elucidate the theology
which stood behind the new liturgical practices. All Saints' was new
wine in the old bottle of Pugin, for though the inspiration for the
design was revived Byzantine and Gothic, Butterfield provided a great
space for the congregation to form into one body which could be
organically related to the altar so that the worshippers as a whole
could actively join the eucharistic action. The altar dominated the
room and was unobstructed, for there were no pews, nor galleries, nor
elaborate stalls and reading desks. Butterfield also departed from any
historic style in his use of industrially produced and colored brick to

----

[60]MS letters of Richards to Pusey, 1845?, 1846?.

[61]E. B. Pusey, A Lecture Delivered in the Temporary Chapel,
Titchfield Street, previously to Laying the Foundation Stone of the
Church of All Saints in Margaret Street, Marylebone. On All Saints'
Day, 1850 (London, 1882), p. 10.

[62]MS Historic Scrapbook, 10 February 1847, Parish Archives, All
Saints; MS letter of W. Butterfield to Pusey, 1848?.

decorate the eucharistic room and create an atmosphere of joy.

The English architect thus built a church which foreshadowed continental liturgical architecture and at the same time satisfied Puseyite principles—the focus being on a single altar, visible everywhere and not hidden behind a screen. The hallmark of the church was a simple though rich liturgical dignity. An ornamented buttress immediately opposite the archway into the street carried a statue of the Annunciation, the only sculpture of the human form when the church was built. In 1962 Laurence King added a modern wooden screen to the end of the south aisle which bears the figures of W. U. Richards and Dr. Pusey.

The centrality of the eucharist and the greater participation in worship quite naturally caused a sharp rise in the reception of the holy communion in a parish of which the average population was 3000 between 1850 and 1885. The total number of communions at All Saints' Margaret Street quickly rose from 12,043 in 1857 to 24,363 in 1862.[63] From 1875 to 1885 the number of communions in the parish fluctuated between 24,000 and 27,000 yearly.[64]

"Everywhere one finds on the other hand the most barbarous indifference and selfish egotism," Engels wrote of Leeds in 1844, "on the other the most distressing scenes of misery and poverty. Signs of social conflict are to be found everywhere."[65] It was in Leeds in the West Riding of Yorkshire, where short-stapled wools were used for the manufacture of hand-spun woolen yarn and cloth, where the population had risen from 53,000 in 1801 to 123,000 in 1831, that Dr. Pusey himself built and supervised a church which was an experiment to determine whether a clerical college, Catholic dogma, and ritual could bring Christianity to people living in desolate industrial conditions. In 1826 when W. F. Hook became Vicar of Leeds the one parish church

----

[63]Parish Magazine (All Saints' Margaret Street), 1857–1872.

[64]"The Late Vicar of All Saints," The Guardian, June 25, 1873, p. 6.

[65]Friedrich Engels, The Conditions of the Working Class in England, trans. by Henderson and Choloner (New York, 1958), p. 31.

served 120,000 people. The Vicar attempted to provide for the situation in a typically High Church fashion. He created the first parish church services which were modeled on the liturgical practice of cathedrals, with a surpliced men's and boys' choir singing daily matins and evensong at the hour when most mill hands were at work. An act of Parliament divided Leeds into 30 parochial districts. In that closest to Hook's Holy Trinity Church there was widespread aversion to the Church of England. In an area of 11,000 or 12,000 people not twenty families went to church. One of these districts included the east ward of Leeds, on the northeast side of the Aire, an area populated by 6,000 laborers and mechanics who lived in gloomy dwellings around the Black Dog mill. The population density was 300 workers per acre.

Here Pusey built his church. He first planned a building on the site in 1839. From the outset Pusey desired the foundation to be served by a body of men remaining unmarried and living in community. Pusey wished to return to early Christian austerity and simplicity in every aspect of the design of the building. He wrote the Bishop of Ripon that he wanted "old, sacred representations and symbols, which have been long received and recognized" particularly those of the body and blood of Christ.[66] Pusey sketched a plan and sent it to Hook: "It looks as unlike anything Romanist as can be; for it stands in awful simplicity, a strong contrast to Romanist tawdriness....My friend would have liked the stone cross, and that the chapel should be called Holy Cross Chapel...."[67]

The architect was John MacDuff Derick, a student of Pugin, who built a Pugin-like perpendicular Gothic structure in cruciform with long choir, soaring nave and crossing, transepts all glowing with rich colors from walls and glass. A 280 foot tower was planned which would loom above Leeds, but engineers discovered that the site was above a mine shaft, and Pusey in his stubborn way refused to move. He sank

----

[66]MS letter of Pusey to Bishop Longley of Ripon, ? 1844.

[67]MS letter of Pusey to Hook, December 1839.

money for the tower into foundations. Pugin designed rich frontals for the altar-table ("When truth was not denied tables were altars, as well as altars holy tables").[68] Pugin drew the majority of the windows by April 1844 and William Morris did the rest in 1860, all guided by this dictum of Pusey: "I wished to go back to the austerity and simplicity of the older school of Painting (adapting it, as far as circumstances admit, to glass)....I selected the oldest models I could...."[69] The founder donated chalices and ciboria with pearls, diamonds, and rubies fashioned by William Butterfield in 1844. When complete in 1845

> ...the beautiful church, and its windows...all spoke of the mysteries of our redemption, tended so much to further reverence, and to fix the mind on our Lord...[as] the ritual does, when understood, certainly, (as experience shows) does speak to the soul....[70]

But the soul of many a Leeds clergyman, like Trollope's Obadiah Slope, "tremble[d] in agony at the iniquity of the Puseyites....His gall [rose] at a new church with high pitched roof...."[71]

Crowds turned out to see the opening of the new building. "About this period," an observer in the crowd remembered, "a church was being built in Leeds about which all sorts of rumours were being circulated in Lancashire and Yorkshire. No one knew who supplied the funds for its erection, and I believe that the mystery has ..ever been satisfactorily solved to this day."[72] A course of sermons on very solemn subjects, two each day, was delivered during the octave of the consecration. The liturgical character of Pusey's parish was immediately set in this initial week with daily eucharist, morning prayer, and evensong. The social work of the parish was begun with the

----

[68]MS letter of Pusey to Benjamin Webb, January 1844.

[69]MS letter of Pusey to Benjamin Webb, December 28, 1843.

[70]MS letter of Pusey to ? , Quinquagesima, 1852.

[71]Derek Linstrum, "Equating Goodness and Gothic Style," Yorkshire Post, March 17, 1969.

[72]MS Evan Jarrett, Dr. Pusey and the Tracts for the Times, p. 146.

distribution of blankets, clothing and 400 pounds of meat to the poor. Pusey's sermons at this "Leeds' self-appointed Holy Week" dealt with the communal life in the church as ameliorator of the lives of those who lived amid the industrial conditions of England. Pusey placed the doctrines of the mystical body and the communion of saints in the context of loss of community in the modern industrial city:

> It may be a sore loss, greater than we can imagine, that, although confessing in our creeds, "the communion of Saints," we, for the most part have so little felt the privilege of being "fellow-citizens with the Saints, and of the household of God," of belonging to a body, of which such glorious hosts have been already perfected, of being struggling members of the one Body.[73]

All the defilement, shame, and sin of a town like Leeds are taken away from the individual after "being made a member of Christ." That is what baptism, frequent communion, presence daily in the church at service does for the soul:

> He shall change...this our body of humiliation, change its fashion, and clothe it with another, that it may be conformed to and may be partner in the Form of His glorious Body...in His new creation; Himself the Hidden magnet, who having no Form or Beauty when He died for us, draws mightily to Himself all who have that which can be drawn, and drawing, holds them to Himself, imparting to them the virtue which goeth forth from Him, and thereby transforming them into Himself....He, through whom are all things, Himself, through all—inspirations, Sacraments, hidden drawings, the yearnings and cravings of the soul, prayers, meditations, the mysteries of His Incarnation, Life and Death and Resurrection...—draweth all; Himself as God, the beginning from Whom all things are, the End to Whom all things tend.[74]

The men whom Pusey appointed to Saint Saviour's spoke more bluntly about the alienating conditions of the factory. One was John Hungerford Pollen, Fellow of Merton, curate from 1847 to 1851. He attacked

----

[73]E. B. Pusey, A Course of Sermons on Solemn Subjects Chiefly Bearing on Repentance and Amendment of Life, Preached in St. Saviour's Church, Leeds...1845 (Oxford, 1845), pp. 232-233.

[74]Ibid., pp. 178, 300, 301.

...life which is passed in the continual din of revolving wheels, the glare and blaze of furnaces, the mistiness of smoke and flax-dust, with which the air is for ever full... those who know anything of our manufacturing populations are well aware that they offer a field, which the energies of many labours and extraordinary means will not exhaust....They who own the mills...can neither value nor see the evil....So, however it is, and whatever the cause, it is an appalling evil, and it was the knowledge of this evil which caused the building of St. Saviour's church....St. Saviour's was a humble attempt to carry out this conviction, and to give a practical refutaton to those who doubted whether the Church of England could satisfy the longings of those amongst her children who yearned after the deeper and more unearthly gifts, which the Holy Ghost brought down upon the Apostolic body.[75]

Charles Gutch preached openly against the conditions in the surrounding mills while curate in the 1850's:

Souls are being lost on every side for want of plain speaking, crying aloud and sparing not. It is not the preaching of the Gospel to rebuke the poor and let the rich escape....I have heard, from good authority, that there are masters, who insist on their men working whole or half-time on Good Friday, and yet go themselves to Church on that Day.. What do their prayers profit them?...I tremble for the rich, for the masters and employers of the poor, who do not realise their vast responsibilities....They are rich, or waxing rich, and they overpass the deeds of the wicked....Their eyes are set against the poor....Why are there so few churches and schools compared with the population, and such a difficulty in the erection of what we have? Is it not because the rich will not pay tithes and build them....If you will look upon the poor as Christ's members, your own brethren in Him; and will advise, warn, educate, help, sympathise with,--in one word, really love them as if they were Christ Himself...the curse of the blood shed in your mill, now hanging over your house, may yet be wiped away.[76]

Gutch spoke of dehumanization:

Are they only his [the mill owner's] "hands," or machines? Or, are they...his brethren and sisters in Christ? And are

---

[75]J. H. Pollen, Narrative of Five Years at St. Saviour's Leeds (Oxford, 1851), pp. 2, 4, 13, xi, xii, viii-ix.

[76]Charles Gutch, The Sure Judgement of God upon All Sinners, Especially the Rich....A Sermon on a Recent Mill Accident; preached in Saint Saviour's Leeds etc. (London, 1853), pp. iii, 15, 35, 38-39.

their souls not to receive so much care and attention as his dogs, or his spindles?   If they live in a polluted atmosphere, if they learn evil and corrupt each other, if they are left to be seduced and defiled by overlookers and foremen...is not some one individual responsible to God for the state they die in?[77]

The four clergy living at St. Saviour's attempted to form the population into a small cell of the body of Christ through constant services and the provision of the sacraments.   These were proffered as means to overcome industrial alienation, to open mill-hands' eyes to a world of spirit beyond the factories.   From 1845 to 1847 there was daily morning prayer at 7:30 and evening office at 7:30 in the church. On Sunday there were services at 10:30, 3, and 6:30.   The "Holy Eucharist" was celebrated every Sunday after morning prayer and on Holy Days after the 7:30 morning service.   On Tuesday evening there was a sermon and on Wednesday night a class.   The clergy operated three day schools and spent three hours each day visiting.   "The daily services were not numerously attended, but on Sundays there was a considerable congregation.   About 25, I think, attended Holy Communion."[78]

In late 1846 there were additional ritualistic advances.   "We had delightful Services: early communion at 7.   Full choral service with communion and sermon at 10 1/2...then full choral service with Sermon at 1/2 past 7," wrote Richard Ward after the arrival of Richard McMullen as vicar in 1846.[79]   Public baptism was appended to Sunday evensong.   On all solemn occasions the eucharist was sung.   On Christmas Eve there was evensong at 9, a procession, and the celebration of the eucharist at midnight.   This order of service was repeated on New Year's Eve.   On these occasions St. Saviour's was hung in red and there were many candles and flowers.   The eucharist was celebrated after evensong on Maundy Thursday.   Then the church was stripped and left bare until evensong on Holy Saturday, when there was

---

[77]Ibid., p. 42.

[78]Pollen, op. cit., p. 45.

[79]MS Letter of Richard Ward to Pusey, October 29, 1846.

baptism celebrated with a choir of 30 or 40, chanting in a ring about the font. Easter eve ended with midnight communion and on Easter Day the congregation processed with banners. There were eucharistic vestments of all liturgical colors, a processional cross with diamonds, and an altar cross with pearls. "There was a carefulness and reverence about the whole celebration [of the eucharist] that became a teaching of the Real Presence, more comprehensible when so seen than yearly cycles of many sermons. The poor parishioners saw what it all meant."[80] The seats in the church were all movable benches and free. From the outset there had been no pews and no charges for sittings. By 1850 the clergy had created a congregation of 250 communicants with average yearly confirmation classes of 50.[81]

Henry Collins, one of the clergy, went to de Lisle's monastery to study Gregorian chant and when he returned, an observer noted, "the music used in the services of the church [became] mostly Gregorian ....The Hymnal is compiled for the church and made up of hymns both ancient and modern."[82] That collection was Sacred Hymns and Anthems; With the Music as Used in the Church of St. Saviour, Leeds, and it was put to use in Margaret Street. The book contained Gregorian melodies for funerals, Good Friday, Introits, Kyries, and Office Hymns. One difference between the music at St. Saviour's and at Hook's church was that at Holy Trinity only the choir sang as in a cathedral, whereas at Pusey's church there was a certain congregational enthusiasm even in the singing of Gregorian chant.[83]

In 1848 a Guild of the Holy Cross was formed for corporate daily prayer for unity, conversion of sinners, and perseverance of the

---

[80]Pollen, op. cit., p. 105.

[81]Ibid., p. 89; George Peirce Grantham, A History of Saint Saviour's, Leeds (London, 1872), p. 25.

[82]Grantham, op. cit., p. 48.

[83]Alf Härdelin, The Tractarian Understanding of the Eucharist (Uppsala, 1965), p. 5.

faithful of the parish. From that year money was given daily to the poor at the vicar's door and classes for men were held each weekday evening. There were day schools for boys, girls, and infants—for all who could pay two pence per week. The church endowed a fund to provide workers with compensation when ill and another to provide worthy funerals for members of the parish. There was a savings account established for the purchase of clothing, a night school for adults, and a library of 1,000 volumes for workers. Despite the public denunciation of St. Saviour's by Hook after 1845, by the bishop after 1846, despite episcopal inhibition, secessions to Rome, and public trials of his curates, Pusey wrote of his church,

> ...There is a daily Service and Weekly Communion....A person
> might be very happy there;...It has been a new scene to me.
> Boys, mechanics, and mill-girls, using confession, kneeling
> thankfully for the blessing, and bound to the church by a
> stronger band than that which bound them to their late
> pastors. I have left things in a more comfortable state.
> The poor people love me very much, and wish I could come and
> stay among them...: "When will you come again among us?"
> they say, "Those whom you have comforted will want you again
> very much."[84]

James Davies, a country parson from the village of Abbenhall, visited Saint Saviour's in the fall of 1848 and wrote to his mother of the services and music. He described the "deep Solemn Mystery [which was] the character of the whole place." "I felt in a different atmosphere from any that I had ever been in before." A week of attending all the offices produced this reaction: "For till it is incorporated in the Body—till all Personification is destroyed, till the individual offers up all he has, all he is to the Church his good is evil—his mere personal good qualities only tend to division and confusion and every evil work. It is self—that word of Idols and all the worse for making itself like God and Good. I hardly can suppose a place better formed than St. Saviour's for breaking up this Idol. You hear much of the Services of the Sacrament of the Church, but not a

---

[84]MS letters of Pusey to W. J. Copeland, January 16, 1847 and April 11, 1851.

word of sermons or individual Preachers...."[85]

From 1851 to 1859 J. W. Knott was vicar and after him one of his curates, Richard Collins, directed the activities of the parish for eighteen years, a period during which a sort of Wesleyan revivalism was engrafted upon the ritual. Pusey's original conception of St. Saviour's, however, was restored during the vicarate of John Wylde who came to Leeds in late 1877. The eucharistic life was the center of his understanding of parish affairs. On Sundays there were three celebrations of the eucharist and public baptism in the afternoon. On holy days there were two eucharistic celebrations, and one on weekdays. There were processions of the guilds and confraternities through the neighborhood on Easter Day, Holy Cross Day, Whitsunday, and during the octave of Corpus Christi. The confraternities were Holy Cross with 37 members, St. Aloysius with 16, St. Agnes with 18, St. Nicholas with 11, Confraternity of the Blessed Sacrament with 9.[86] Wylde preached on the Holy Eucharist as the means for the sanctification of daily life: "In these times of unbelief and neglect, it seems more than ever binding on Christians to unite together in praising God for His Goodness in giving us the Holy Communion...." The eucharist was the chief way for "binding all Her [the Church's] members into one." He also taught his people the meaning of the liturgical year: "The different seasons of Holy Church are not merely to keep alive remembrance of the varous events....We ought to live in them, that our whole frame of mind--ways of thinking and feeling are affected by them."[87]

Wylde's restoration of the sacramental cycle after the neglect of his predecessors effected an increase in the total number of communions in the parish, an indication of the appeal of the liturgical character

----

[85]MS letter of James Davies to his mother, November 7, 1848, Parish Archives, Saint Saviour's, Leeds. Davies, a vicar at Abbenhall, came to Saint Saviour's yearly until 1868, when he was 93.

[86]Grantham, op. cit., p. 56.

[87]MS John Wylde, Sermons, pp. 49-50, 131, Archives, Saint Saviour's, Leeds.

of St. Saviour's to the district:

Total Communions SSL

1878	2938	1884	4151
1879	3054	1885	4296
1880	3361	1886	4862
1881	3673	1887	5149
1882	4080	1888	5104
1883	4408	1889	4818[88]

Between 1846 and 1870, 2135 children were baptized at St. Saviour's, an average of 125.88 each year in a population of 6,000. The professions of the fathers of the children baptized in the parish further suggest that, in fact, the local population did come to St. Saviour's for the sacraments:

Unskilled worker	13.90%
Skilled worker	23.45%
Factory worker	21.00%
Miner	9.60%
Professional	0.79%
Shopkeepers	2.30%
Artisans	9.03%
Servants	1.12%

In sample years during the next decades the breakdown of professions was:

Year	Total	Unskilled Workers	Skilled Workers	Factory Workers	Miners	Artisan	Shop-keepers	Servant
1975	267	17.67	18.35	19.47	14.23	1.87	2.24	0
1885	297	27.27	22.09	13.80	12.12	4.49	3.03	.33[89]

and points to the increasing preponderance of parishioners drawn from the lowest classes.

Wantage Parish Church stands on a rise above the Letcombe Brook, fourteen miles from Oxford in the Vale of the White Horse at the foot of the Berkshire Downs. The town, like its church, is not all of one

----

[88]Parish Magazine (Saint Saviour's, Leeds), 1878-1889.

[89]MS Register of Baptisms, 1846-1885, Parish Archives, Leeds. For more analysis of the history of this parish see Stephen Savage and Christopher Tyne, The Labours of Years (Oxford, 1965) and Nigel Yates, The Oxford Movement and Parish Life: St. Saviour's Leeds 1839-1929 (Leeds, 1975).

piece. It is the gradual growth of centuries, and in the nineteenth century radical change marked each decade. South of the church, in that century, small manufacturies were put in for the production of agricultural machinery. West of the church, and either side of the brook, there was an unexpected strip of country in the middle of the town. In the east there were houses from the time of the Reformation, but the town was mainly Georgian in outward appearance. Mellow eighteenth-century bricks gave a deceptively rosy cast to the central square and its weekly corn market to which the country people of the Berkshire Downs came to do their shopping. The eighteenth-century rope-making industry was declining, but an iron foundry had been opened which manufactured two specialties, the Berkshire plough and threshing machines. The concern of Nalder and Nalder opened a mill, and in 1840 the Great Western Railway built a station at Challow at which ten trains each day stopped and from which travelers came to Wantage by steam tram.

The population was growing rapidly. In 1801 there were 489 inhabited houses and in 1824, 520. The number of residents rose to 3,056 in 1851 and remained at that level until the turn of the twentieth century.[90] By 1831 in Wantage 407 families received income from jobs in manufacture and trade. Only 98 were employed in agriculture.[91]

Yet Wantage "lay almost outside the pale of nineteenth-century civilization, and retained many characteristics of an earlier date."[92] Property owners paid "quit-rents" to the Lord of the Manor, a wealthy London merchant Sir Henry Martin, to be quit of their feudal agricultural duties. There were no paved roads and no oil street

---

[90]MS Historical Survey, Parish Archives, Wantage.

[91]MS W. J. Butler, Parochialia, 28/1-12, Berkshire Record Office, Reading. These parish diaries occupy 12 very large notebooks and record very minutely the activities in the parish.

[92]Sir Arthur Quiller-Couch, Memoir of Arthur John Butler (London, 1917), p. 343.

lamps, but pubs flourished on every corner. No official in the town was responsible for order. Therefore miscreants fleeing from London were drawn down the canals by liquor and anarchy. Murder rose with the population and soon King Alfred's birthplace was "Black Wantage." Manure lay in the streets. The ditches were not cleaned, and the Grammar School was discontinued in 1832.

A new Puseyite vicar arrived here in 1847, William John Butler (the famous Bishop Butler of the Analogy had also been from Wantage, but they were not related). "The horrid apathy and irreverence of the whole concern, the crowd of idlers, etc., made me rather down-hearted," he remembered of his arrival.[93] Butler discovered many couples in the parish living in an unmarried state. There were large numbers of unbaptized and illegitimate children. His first congregation numbered thirty-five.[94] The vicar determined to introduce the Puseyite system as the means of religious revival in these conditions, and he wrote to Keble:

> In this matter of Wantage it seems to me strange that you should not understand how very serious a thing it is for one like myself, only twenty-eight years old and very much of the sort of study and preparation which a country town needs, to take upon myself the care of 3000 souls to prepare for eternity....I dread it very much. How to encourage a Catholic community under the disadvantage of Protestant or Puritan ways.[95]

Butler began introducing Catholic theology in small doses and more reverent services. He was taken aback by the lack of comprehension of the people, and by the state in which he found the parish church:

> I took morning service. Really at times owing to the strange differences in singing, the slovenly way of conducting the services, the Communion Service from reading desk, etc., it seemed so very odd to end with the Nicene Creed. [The preacher's] sermon was drier than hay. Not a word of sense

---

[93]A. J. Butler, Life and Letters of William John Butler (London, 1897), p. 46.

[94]Butler, Parochialia, 1847, p. 29.

[95]Quoted in A. J. Butler, op. cit., pp. 39, 40 (July 9 and July 22, 1846).

in it. I only wonder so many people can sit through it.
Were I likely to undergo such things continually, I must join
one of the sects with which Wantage is rife....There am I in
a parish of which, I am sure 9/10's do not understand a
single word of the event in question [a liturgical
celebration]....Yet it is impossible to pass these...great
feasts carelessly over....The people here seem hardly to feel
Christmas Day. I observed that they wore their working-day
clothes, and a very scanty attendance at church in proportion
to that on Sundays....The religion of the English peasant is
all confined to generalities....When I came to examine
others, servants, small shopkeepers, and the like, I found so
dense an ignorance on all religious subjects, words seeming
to have literally no meaning in their mouths....[This
Catholic teaching] goes directly against the idea which the
great majority of people form respecting religion. It is, in
a word, sacerdotalism, the one thing they hate because it
opposes itself to human pride and human sensuality.[96]

For a century Wantage parish church had been idle and neglected
and Dissent had entered the breach. Preaching had been the center of
worship. In 1769, under the vicar Thomas Gerrard, a three-decker
pulpit was installed in the chancel obscuring the altar. Galleries to
accommodate listeners at sermons were affixed to the twelfth-century
walls in the seventeenth and eighteenth centuries. Seats in the
galleries were regarded as heirlooms to be left by will. Charles
Liddard explicitly stated in his will, "To my eldest son Thomas the
house he resides in together with pew number one in the old gallery of
the Wantage Parish Church."[97] By the end of the eighteenth century all
but one pane of medieval glass had been knocked out of the windows and
replaced by clear glass.

The eucharist was celebrated only four times a year and the prayer
services held morning and evening on Sunday, never on weekdays, were so
disorderly that the parish vestry required the sexton "to be at the
south transept door to keep order and seat the people." The choir was
"not to interrupt the parson nor to argue or walk about during the
sermon." The churchwardens were to see that measures "be taken to

---

[96]Ibid., pp. 27-28, 32, 37, 213-215.

[97]Kathleen Philip, Victorian Wantage (Oxford, 1968), p. 66.

render the doorways more easily available in case of any panic arising."[98] In 1763 only 646 persons out of the population of the parish had been confirmed and in 1808, 1108 or one-half of the people had received the sacrament of confirmation.[99] The parish derived a small income from the township by providing space in the Lady Chapel to store the Wantage fire engine.

Butler described himself "as one brought up in the school of men like Mr. Keble and Dr. Pusey." When, in the 1850's, segments of the town turned against the Vicar he related the reaction to "fear of Puseyism." They had "caught fear of Puseyism," "fear of Puseyism growing--people in neighborhood speaking out."[100] Butler himself drew up plans for a monastic organization to be established in one of the great industrial towns. Pusey was consulted on the project and suggested that reform based upon a body of clergy and sacramental services might be attempted in a country town. Butler wrote Keble, "I sent the other papers to Pusey as you kindly permitted me, and he seems, as you may suppose, greatly pleased with them, especially with the notion in one of them about making a country parson's cottage the rudiments of a sort of monastery....I have long felt, though I never thought myself fit, that farmers and shopkeepers should be leavened with the Church."[101]

Wantage thus became the country counterpart of Leeds, a model Catholic parish, with a highly developed parochial machinery. "Wantage was essentially a place of work....So did Butler raise the tone of and the spirit of work learned at Wantage that it was never, I believe, lost by the Wantage curates when they went to parishes of their own. Wantage did for the South of England what Leeds did for the North."

----

[98]Ibid., p. 72.

[99]Butler, Parochialia, 1847, pp. 1, 72.

[100]Butler, Parochialia, p. 260.

[101]Quoted in A. J. Butler, op. cit., pp. 31, 42 (July 28, 1845 and August 1846).

The attraction to Wantage as a town open to Catholic views brought this notation in Butler's diary: "I was contacted by Dr. Pusey seeking a house in a Parish where he might find Daily Service."[102]

Pusey preached his first printed sermon at Grove Church in the parish of Wantage in 1832, and he continued to preach at Wantage into the fifties even when quietly forbidden to do so, for Butler recorded on an August Sunday in 1854: "Dr. Pusey kindly preached morning and afternoon."[103] And when under great suspicion after the Gorham decision, Wantage parish sent Pusey a petition of support. "Butler of Wantage sent me the enclosed saying that they of Wantage would do as I."[104] Pusey consulted Butler on the management of and appointments to St. Saviour's, and in 1867 Pusey named him to Bishop Gray of South Africa as replacement for the heretical Colenso as bishop of Natal.

In 1847 Butler began to celebrate the eucharist once a month at the morning service, and there was an early communion on the other Sundays, at which a dozen communicants assisted. Of this "early communion," he wrote, "I am not sure whether it will answer or do harm. It is a very serious step, more serious than perhaps at first sight appears. It seems like the beginning of a great work."[105] Then the eucharist began to be celebrated on weekdays. By 1849 he decided "it would be much better to administer the Blessed Sacrament twice on Sundays."[106] There were three services of Holy Communion on Easter and Christmas by 1850. In 1851 he added a 4:45 A.M. celebration for workers on Sunday and feasts "perhaps a little earlier than necessary" but "rewarded by large attendance."[107]

----

[102]Ibid., p. 94; Butler, Parochialia, p. 118.

[103]Butler, Parochialia, 1854, p. 112.

[104]MS Pusey to Keble, January 21, 1852.

[105]Butler, Parochialia, 7 May 1848, p. 17.

[106]Ibid., Epiphany 1849, p. 81.

[107]Ibid., Circumcision 1851, p. 252.

"Reverence rather than ritual," was the mark of the liturgy of Wantage.[108] The Vicar bore witness to the real presence of Christ in the eucharist by use of vestments, cross, candles, eastward celebrations, and reverent inclinations to the altar. At the same time, Butler encouraged the active participation of the laity in frequent celebrations of the eucharist. "He once exploded in strong wrath in telling me of a young clergyman who had read the Epistle and Gospel in an inaudible voice, and then defended himself for doing so on the ground that the whole service of Holy Communion was a mystery." "I should, indeed, be grieved if," he told a curate, "'non-communicating attendance were to be substituted for regular and frequent participation of the Bread from heaven."[109]

The eucharist was the center of Butler's preaching and his conversations on visits to parishioners. "I cannot free my mind from that which troubles it, viz. the difficulty of raising my parishioners to a higher standard of religious feeling, individually and as a consequence collectively."[110] One old woman with whom he talked of coming to communion was characteristic of many. "She talkt about the fear of coming to what she called 'your table' (O these wretched personal dissenting views)."[111] He discussed the eucharist with the dying and preached on "the need of the Sacrament of the Lord's Supper to restore the armour of God...." at funerals of those whose lives were witnesses to the power of the Sacrament.[112] The eucharist was "the greatest of all Christian acts of service, in truth, the only service which our Lord Himself ordained...the great Communion."[113]

----

[108]A. J. Butler, op. cit., p. 177.

[109]Ibid., p. 358; Butler, Parochialia.

[110]Butler, Parochialia, October 18, 1848, p. 54.

[111]Ibid., September 20, 1848, p. 47.

[112]Ibid., June 30, 1847, p. 24.

[113]W. J. Butler, Ignorance the Danger of the Church (London, 1890), p. 10.

The whole meaning of the Catholic movement in Wantage, he summed up later, was "that self was to be set aside, the Church made everything; that Christ was to be sought upon His altar, ministered to among His poor, obeyed in His Church; that He lived in His members...."[114] Butler understood the church to be a collective ("the divinely appointed Body to preserve the deposit [of faith] intact") and religious life to be best when corporate. ("How are we to succeed, unless we be bonded together, by love. We need greater collectedness....").[115]

New doctrine led to architectural change in Wantage. Butler's dream was "restoring our church to the beauty of holiness."[116] His first activity in 1847 was to remove the fire engine from the Lady Chapel. The minutes of the Commissioners of Wantage record in December 1847, that "Arrangements have been made with Mr. Kent for renting part of the Market House as an Engine House, and it is agreed with him to remove the Engines from the Church forthwith."[117] Butler himself sketched a design for the chancel, which removed the three-decker pulpit, the small altar-table, and galleries, and pews, and replaced them with a large altar, chairs, stained-glass, and religious symbolism on the walls. By 1857 "the old, degraded, ungodly state of God's house" had been repaired at a cost of £1,050 by the architect G. E. Street, who, for a short time, was a member of Butler's choir.[118] William Butterfield, whose nephew William Starey was one of Butler's curates, designed St. Michael's chapel in 1848 and St. Mary Magdalen chapel in 1860 in the new Catholic style that emphasized the corporate character of the celebration of the eucharist.

----

[114]W. J. Butler, What is Our Present Danger? (London, 1891), p. 12.

[115]A. J. Butler, op. cit., p. 443; Butler, Parochialia, Friday after 9th Trinity Sunday, 1849, p. 141.

[116]A. J. Butler, op. cit., p. 90.

[117]Philip, op. cit., p. 67.

[118]A. J. Butler, op. cit., p. 90.

314

Sacramental life and social renewal were inseparably bound
together in Butler's thought and the rector was moved to undertake a
very successful secular reform of the town. In 1847 Butler became
chairman of the Wantage Commissioners. He contracted with a gas
company to lay down pipes for the gas lighting of the town by 37 lamps.
A drainage system was built which reduced the occurrence of typhoid.
The streets were paved. The rector sponsored other innovations. "My
people perish for lack of knowledge," Butler said and wrote of his work
in establishing national schools, "They are to me the great object on
which we expend all strength."[119] The parish maintained a school of
embroidery overseen by the architects Street and Butterfield who sought
to revive the purest style of the art of English church embroidery.
There was a printing press. By the end of the century the church in
Wantage managed 21 institutions, and at least 750 young people were
trained at Wantage schools alone.[120] "At Wantage," said Bishop
Wilberforce, "there was no rest day or night. Everything was done with
full activity by day and, at night, first there were conversations
lasting into the small hours and then the dove cooed and the clock
chimed."[121]

A curate wrote, "Though desires for colored stoles and other
luxuries were repressed, we knew well enough that the Vicar was taking
pains not to give scandal to the Wantage people."[122] Butler knew "that
tradesmen in the town are fully and thoroughly against religious
observance," and that hostility had taken over entire neighborhoods.[123]
"The state of Grove Street is very sad and difficult to deal with. The
people seem utterly reckless, and sneering at religion and at those who

---

[119]Community of St. Mary the Virgin, Butler of Wantage (Westminster,
1961), p. 23.

[120]Quiller-Couch, op. cit., p. 9.

[121]Community, ibid., p. 26.

[122]A. J. Butler, op. cit., p. 177.

[123]Butler, Parochialia, Ash Wednesday, 1849, p. 88.

attempt to go to church."[124] Hostility rose higher "partly and in a great degree to our attempt to restore God's house to fitting comeliness and order. This last rouses all classes against us, dissenters, a great portion of our Church people, and all the low rabble of the place, too glad of the excitement and of giving unchecked to a rude and democratic spirit."[125]

The conflict burst into the open at a vestry meeting on April 1, 1852. "I knew well the exceeding hostility to me," Butler wrote, "but I was not prepared for the fierce opposition I encountered."[126] William Dixon opposed the restoration and vociferous cheering followed anything said against it. T. H. Fawley spoke up because he wished to have a door to his pew. A resident of Lockinge opposed it because he would lose his pew. A parishioner from Charlton "spoke of the mummeries, flummeries, tomfooleries" by which Butler chose to elaborate the service. After a debate of three hours, the proposal was rejected by a large majority.

When Butler carried forward the architectural changes many parishioners joined the Methodist and Baptist churches. The chief mill owners of Wantage were Baptists. Charles Hart, owner of a foundry, gave the foundrymen time off to attend the parish meeting and vote against Butler's restoration. He sent around Johnnie Barr with no Popery handbills. George Stevenson's family had been in the Church of England for centuries, but after growing wealthy from his gas company and tram line he joined the Baptists and wrote,

> The great doctrines of the Reformation had not been overthrown, and though great efforts were made to establish sacerdotalism in Wantage by erecting schools and forming a sisterhood, those who held Protestant principles became more

---

124Ibid., St. Peter's 1849, p. 132.

125Ibid., beginning 1852, p. 397.

126Ibid., 1852, p. 334.

firmly attached to them and the Baptists had never before attained to such a degree of prosperity.[127]

Thomas, the son of that same Charles Liddiard who willed pew number one in the gallery of the parish church to his son, became a mainstay and trustee of the Baptists in the 1850's. By 1859 there were three Wantage Baptist churches and in 1860 a new Gothic Revival Baptist structure was built which contained the old pulpit of the parish church. The crowds were so large at Baptist services that an extra balcony had to be added to the edifice in 1873.

A Methodist church was opened in 1845 and the Wesleyan preacher, Thomas Bush, took as his constant text the wickedness of Puseyism. Methodist baptisms show the result:

Baptisms, Methodist Church, Wantage

1840-1850 -- 36
1851-1861 -- 80
1862-1871 -- 67
1872-1883 -- 88[128]

However, by the end of the fifties Butler wrote in his diary, "The attendance, though not in throngs, has been fair, shewing a general tendency in the parish to take up with Holy Church ways."[129] Between 1851 and 1860 the total number of baptisms in the parish was 878. Between 860 and 1900 the average number of children christened yearly was 105.25. The professional identification of the parents of these babies suggests a decline in the number of merchants and professionals who came to the parish church and an increase in workers:

Year	Skilled worker	Unskilled worker	Small merchant	Sub-pro-fessional	Servant	Profes-sional	Agricul-tural worker
1860	23.63	44.54	11.70	.9	.9	7.27	2.72
1900	29.12	47.57	4.85	5.82	0	6.79	1.94[130]

---

[127]Philip, op. cit., p. 77.

[128]MS Registers of Baptism, Archives, Methodist Church, Wantage.

[129]Butler, Parochialia, Holy Saturday 1849, p. 100.

[130]MS Registers of Baptisms, Parish Church, Wantage.

The total number of communions at Wantage rose at this rate:

1848	2424	1856	3754
1853	3286	1857	3931
1854	3760	1860	3781
1855	3409	1865	4693[131]

By the late sixties Butler felt that his parochial activity had reaped some success. "The complaining jealous temper which tried us so much through 1867 has, in a great degree, subsided."[132] 1869 was "a brilliant successful year."[133] Wantage, with its elaborate machinery and vigorous and fearless vicar, became a model Puseyite parish and training ground for other well-known parish priests and prelates. The town provided evidence that Catholic principles could be translated into practice. It became symbolic of a certain nineteenth century apostolic zeal. W. G. Sawyer, who carried Puseyism north to Yorkshire, recalled at the end of his life, "I went for one day, and stayed for five and a half years. Whatever little work I may have been able to do in the Church of God has mainly been the result of the training I received at Wantage."[134] Charlotte Yonge put down her impression:

Nothing struck me so much as the zest, life, and spirit which pervaded everything. The early service, the merry breakfast, the schools, the parish visiting, the mid-day dinner with the curates, the classes, the evening visits to parishioners, all concluded by a supper as lively as the former meals had been. There was something brilliant and something quaint about it all. [Another remembered] One felt that there was a very atmosphere of high intellect and refined taste—not very many books—Classics and Fathers.[135]

---

[131]Butler, Parochialia, passim, 1848, 1853-57, 1860, 1865.

[132]Ibid., 1868, p. 213.

[133]Ibid., 1869, p. 287.

[134]A. J. Butler, op. cit., p. 93.

[135]Ibid., pp. 237, 287.

CHAPTER VII

The Advance of the New Catholicism

in the Church of England

Benedictines of Germany and France cast the new Catholicism evolving in Roman Catholic parishes into refined theological schemas and liturgical forschungberichten. Roman Catholic universities were gradually penetrated with the communal ideals of the new Catholicism, prelates won over, and urban and rural districts revitalized. The breach with Tridentine ecclesiology and piety was solidified with the two encyclicals of the nineteen forties, Mediator Dei and Mystici Corporis.

A parallel development can be traced in Britain. The parishes, however, were Anglican. The monks were Cowley Fathers and religious of the Community of the Resurrection and the Society of the Sacred Mission. Rather than encyclicals, the corresponding English statement came from Westminster Abbey and was issued by E. S. Abbott, Gregory Dix, T. S. Eliot, A. G. Hebert, L. S. Thornton, and A. M. Ramsey, also in the nineteen forties.

Puseyite parishes, modeled on the pattern which emerged at Christ Church, Margaret Street, St. Saviour's, and Wantage, blossomed into colorful varieties, united by their belief in corporate liturgical action, objective sacramental theories of baptism and the eucharist, and the church as the body of Christ, inspiring an organic theology and practice conceived as a power to redeem a shattered social order. Some Puseyite parishes attracted the rich. Belgravia, "with mink and money blest," had been a spiritually destitute quarter of London. There in 1843 W. J. E. Bennett inaugurated St. Paul's, Knightsbridge, as a place

318

of worship for fashionable ritualists. Daily choral service was begun and St. Paul's became a center of extravagant Catholic loyalties. Pusey preached here occasionally until 1868.

The chief mission church of St. Paul's was St. Barnabas, Pimlico, which was intended for the poorest classes but was soon filled with the rich and well-to-do. Pusey preached the consecration sermon in 1850 which discussed the sacraments as the means to be united in the body of Christ.[1] After the sermon, an old woman came forward to him and said, "That was a fine sermon. With more preaching like that we would have fewer of these cursed Puseyites in our churches."[2] Not only did the celibate clergy of St. Barnabas live in community but the choristers did too, for they sang multiple offices daily and it was necessary that they reside in proximity to the church. They processed into their stalls, bowed at the altar on entering and retiring, wore liturgical colors, and made the sign of the cross. These activities became a public attraction in the year of the Great Exhibition.

Crowds of the curious jammed the three celebrations of the eucharist on Sunday. Lord Shaftesbury, a leading Evangelical, was one, and he wrote to the Times that he would rather worship "with Lydia by the banks of the river side" than attend St. Barnabas. Bennett found a man wandering in church at the consecration. "Well, sir," he replied to the Vicar's questions, "being in London for the Exhibition, I came to see St. Barnabas'; and if I had taken a seat I wouldn't have seen it a bit, so I just wanted to walk round, through the crowd, and examine it at my ease."[3] The throngs became mobs on the four Sundays of November in 1851. The poor and rich were driven in terror from their seats and the choir was pelted with rotten eggs. Bennett was cast out of Belgravia through the combined effects of these detachments of Mr.

----

[1]E. B. Pusey, God Withdraws in Loving-Kindness Also (London, 1850), pp. 4, 24.

[2]"Tales of a London Parish," in G. Wakeling, The Oxford Church Movement (London, 1895), p. 100f.

[3]Maria Trench, Charles Lowder (London, 1882), p. 35.

Westerton, "Protestant Champion of England," and the Bishop of London.
He was replaced in the work at St. Barnabas by Charles Lowder, the
son of a rich banker of Bath, who, while an undergraduate, heard Pusey
preach. He was inspired by Pusey's great sermon on the eucharist of
1843 and felt called "to go the largest heathen city in the world.
...The spiritual condition of the masses of our population,...the
increasing tendency of the people to mass together, multiplying and
intensifying the evil, and the unsatisfactory character of the attempts
hithereto made to meet it, were enough to make men gladly profit by the
experience of those who had successfully struggled against similar
difficulties."[4]   For five years at St. Barnabas Lowder used Puseyite
methods to restore a parish which had been shattered by mob violence so
that there were 483 communions at Easter 1858, and, by 1881, 761 Easter
receptions of the eucharist were recorded.[5]   The experience in Pimlico
convinced him that the church

> must assume a missionary character, and, by religious
> association and a new adaptation of Catholic practice to the
> altered circumstances of the nineteenth century,...endeavour,
> with fresh life and energy, to stem the prevailing tide of
> sin and indifference.[6]

There were other London varieties of Puseyism, appealing primarily
to the upper classes. Baron Alderson founded St. Mary Magdalen's,
Munster Square, in 1849 where incense was first introduced at midnight
on Christmas Eve in 1854. This Gothic Revival edifice was built to
accommodate a congregation of 600, without pews. When Pusey preached
there, the church was filled. The eucharist was the chief form of
worship in Munster Square. After 1856, the high mass on Sunday was
always sung.[7] Other parishes which reproduced St. Mary Magdalen's in

----

[4]Ibid., pp. 26. 65.

[5]Ibid., p. 55.

[6]Ibid., p. 75.

[7]Before incense was used at Munster Square in 1854, it had appeared
briefly at St. Margaret Pattens in 1573, at St. Botolph's, Bishopsgate,
in 1575, at St. Michael's, Cornhill, in 1589, at St. Margaret's,
Westminster, in 1592, and at St. Augustine's, Farringdon, in 1603.

size, class of the congregation, and ritual practice in London were St. Cyprian's, Marylebone, first directed by Charles Gutch who had been trained in St.Saviour's, Leeds, St. Mary Magdalen's, Paddington, John Mason Neale's St. Andrew's, Wells Street, St. Matthew's, City road, St. Bartholomew's, Moor Lane, St. Augustine's Kilburn, and St. Peter's Vauxhall. Spies hired by the Evangelical manufacturer Kensit regularly attended the Church of the Ascension, Lavender Hill, and St. Cuthbert's, Philbeach Gardens, whose vicar was brought to trial for assault because the Sunday suit of a Kensit operative had been splashed with holy water. They uncovered the curate of Christ Church, New North Road, a Mr. Rose, "a fair man, with hair parted down the middle, who sang the Litany in lavender kid gloves."[8]

New churches sprang up also in fashionable suburbs. Butterfield designed St. John the Evangelist, Hammersmith, where services were sung in Gregorian chant from 1859. Saint John the Baptist, Holland Road, was founded by a circle of Christ Church graduates in 1869 who desired to celebrate the liturgical year with great pomp. In the next decade St. Paul's, Bow Common, and St. Stephen's, Shepherd's Bush, became centers of Catholic collectivity.

The City of London churches, once impregnable bastions of anti-Puseyite prejudice, were slowly penetrated. Daily eucharist was begun at St. Magnus the Martyr in the 1890's. Under the rector H. J. Fynes-Clinton, the box-pews and galleries were cut down and the interior redecorated with the addition of a splendid altarpiece, with its Moses and Aaron and cherubs visible from every corner, for new low curving pews enabled the congregation to observe the service at the altar for the first time, and produced those surroundings "the walls of Magnus Martyr hold, Inexplicable splendour of Ionian white and gold."[9] Most of the internal fittings of Wren's St. Mary Aldermary were discarded in 1876-7, and a new altar and low benches installed. Daily eucharist was offered and the parish initiated retreats for the

----

[8]Wakeling, op. cit., p. 117.

[9]Anon., The Church of St. Magnus the Martyr (London, 1970), p. 9.

promotion of the Catholic devotional life among men of the City. St.
Vedast, Foster Lane, had daily service as early as 1852.

St. Mary Abbots, Kensington, is representative of those wealthy,
ancient London parishes outside the City which were revived. In this
instance, the Puseyite was W. D. Dalrymple, who arrived in 1872 and
introduced full choral services and elaborate decoration of the
sanctuary on all liturgical feasts. Special services were provided for
those who could not come to church at the usual time. Grosvenor
Chapel, which Lady Lucy Pusey had attended in the late eighteenth
century, was one of those non-parochial chapels of ease put up at the
same time as Mayfair Chapel, Trinity Chapel, Berkeley Chapel and others
of that type of "preaching box" deriving an extensive income from pew
rents and fees for burial in the vaults contributed by the affluent
residents of the parish of St. George's, Hanover Square. Followers of
H. P. Liddon, Pusey's student and biographer, took over the chapel in
1907 with the comment: "Still, there are uglier churches." It was to
remedy this that extensive alterations in the chapel were carried out
under the direction of Sir Ninian Comper. The three-decker pulpit was
replaced by a free-standing altar, having room for a small Lady Chapel
behind which the sacrament was constantly reserved, in the old English
manner, in a hanging pyx.

Liddon himself restored the liturgical character of St. Paul's
Cathedral. In 1870 he was named Canon, after a decade of seclusion
under the wing of the Hebrew Professor as the last of the "Students"
under the old Foundation of Christ Church, along with R. M. Benson and
Lewis Carroll (C. L. Dodgson). "I think I am right in saying," wrote
Bishop Talbot, "that Liddon was always thinking of himself as a
henchman, one whose duty it was to carry on a great tradition."[10]
Liddon was a spellbinding preacher, and he used these gifts and
constant and colorful services to make St. Paul's into an instrument
which would have a direct impact on the country. When he preached, the
great space under the dome of the cathedral was filled, often with

----

[10]Darwell Stone et al., Henry Parry Liddon (London, 1929), p. 25.

lines of the rich and the poor in front of Wren's great bronze doors winding down into Fleet Street. Liddon put a new ring of bells in the towers, a stone altar and reredos in the sanctuary, and stained glass in the apse. By 1885 there were two celebrations of the eucharist on Sunday. One was at eight and the other was appended to the choral morning service at 10:30. There were two celebrations daily as well, and a third added, at 7:15 A.M. on feast days.

The only district of metropolitan London to be taken over almost entirely by the Puseyites was the East End, the quarter of most abject poverty. The first successful Puseyite pioneer here was Charles Lowder, who was called in 1856 by Bryan King to come and assist him in the parish of St. George-in-the-East. "There is a field in East London," Lowder wrote, "for as noble and knightly adventure as ever was achieved by England's chivalry....[In the East End] they pursue daily the same dull, never-thinking course of existence...."[11]

Lowder walked from the banks and business houses of the City to the first East End borough of Stepney. Within sight of Aldgate was the white pepper-box tower of the Parish Church of St. George-in-the-East which had been built by Wren's chief pupil Nicholas Hawksmoor in 1712-1713. During the 18th century this had been a fashionable district and one-fourth of the parents of the children baptized at St. George were from the class designated "merchant," "professional," and "gentleman." By 1833 the number of yearly baptisms was double what it had been in the previous century, but almost all babies came from families whose fathers were employed in the most menial occupations.[12]

When Lowder reached the church, he climbed the tower, and where there had once been neat captain's homes and gardens, he saw narrow, dirty streets, unventilated courtyards, houses huddled together in unplanned chaos, most without proper sanitary conditions and many in bad repair. Factories, workshops, and warehouses were scattered

---

[11]Trench, op. cit., pp. x, xiii.

[12]MS Baptismal Registers, St. George-in-the-East, 1730-1860, P59/SGE/2/8, London County Council Record Office.

indiscriminately. The open spaces could be counted on one hand. Looking toward the Thames he saw the shanties where dockworkers lived and to the east there were vistas of tenements, markets, tiny roofs and chimneys fading into the distance.

When Bryan King was appointed rector to the 38,000 residents of the parish of St. George-in-the-East, there were four services per week, congregations consisting of thirty people, and five or six regular communicants. The church, with its high box pews equipped with footwarmers, cushions, and bookshelves, seemed to have been built to keep the poor out, even though by 1842 "...of all the families who were in the habit of attending the parish church," King noted, "I only know of three who are yet remaining as residents....There remain...the smaller class of shopkeepers, artizans, and the various classes of labourers employed in the docks, on the river, or in the multiform occupations of London manufacture." In the four streets next to the parish church there were 733 houses, 27 pubs, 13 beer gardens, and 154 brothels. King thought of attracting his parishioners by making the church services less dull. He introduced choral services, increased their number to 54 per week, and, in 1859, adopted eucharist vestments hich had been presented to him by members of his congregation.[13]

In 1856 King began an experiment. His parish was treated as a missionary district and clergy were assigned quarters in which to attempt new methods of evangelism. Lowder was given the docks, and he chose liturgy as his medium of evangelism. St. George's Mission was to him

> avowedly an experiment in the most neglected and depraved part of London, an attempt to bring the blessings of the Church in their truly Catholic character within the reach of the most ignorant and sinful....It is difficult to describe the amount of prejudice, unbelief, and wicked opposition which must be patiently encountered in laying such a

----

[13]Bryan King, Sacrilege and Encouragement, Being an Account of the S. George's Riots and of their Successes (Lond, 1860), pp. 7-11; Bryan King, The S. George's Mission with the S. George's Riots and their Results (London, 1877), pp. 7-9.

foundation soundly and securely.[14]
In the first service held in an iron church along the St. Katherine's
Docks, a glass pitcher was thrown and crashed against Lowder's head.
Protestant sympathizers disliked his grand eucharistic ceremonial—
incense, candles, vestments, processions. But these forms were to him
the outward expression of truths he held most sacred, and a means of
sharing them with the uneducated. Solemn services could take the
residents of the docks from the evil surroundings. He wrote the Bishop
of London, "Evidently something more elastic and energetic is wanting
than the old parochial system; are we to fall back upon Wesleyanism, or
on the Catholic teaching of our Church?..." and to another, "Our solemn
celebrations of the Holy Communion...have made a great impression on
those who had never thus felt Christ preached to them; and we trace
many conversions from these occasions....Think how hard it is to teach
children and grown-up people the respect and reverence due to
themselves as part of the body of Christ, amidst such surroundings of
their daily life."[15]
Two churches were opened seating a total of two hundred and fifty,
where the "Holy Eucharist" was celebrated from 1857 at eight and eleven
on Sunday, and daily at seven in the morning. There were offices at
10:30 and 3:30 on Sundays, and at 8 A.M., 12:30 P.M., and 8 P.M. on
weekdays. Communicants walked to these two churches along the Ratcliff
Highway which was filled with prostitutes. Lowder came to feel
that those who worshipped constantly "really do feel that they are
'members one of another,' and are bound together in the Body of Christ
by the love of God the Holy Ghost. [These mission flocks were] an
astonishing exception to the usual London congregation in the real
family life which characterizes [them]."[16] The clergy ran an
industrial school, Sunday schools for all ages, and communicant and

---
[14]Charles Lowder, Annual Report, St. George's Mission (London,
1859), p. 7.

[15]Trench, op. cit., pp. 107, 140, 142.

[16]Ibid., p. 165.

confirmation classes in the evening.

"The doctrine of the Incarnation of Christ, and the extension of the Incarnation through the sacraments as a means of union with Christ and as channels of grace, usually formed the basis of [Lowder's] cathechizing, and indeed of his religious teaching generally."[17] To further the work in the East End a Confraternity of the Blessed Sacrament, and a Church of England Working Men's Society for "freedom of worship and the preservation of her rights and liberties on the basis of the Book of Common Prayer and the Usages of the Primitive Church," which had a yearly outdoor procession with banners and cross, were instituted. Nor were women, prostitutes, and children neglected. "It will be seen," confided Lowder in 1863, "that the great bond of these associations is the Holy Eucharist. This we gladly believe is forming more and more the spiritual life of the Mission. The attendance on this Blessed Sacrament, as the great service of the Church is steadily increasing."[18] By 1867 there were approximately 200 communions in the mission every Sunday.[19] The congregations had outgrown temporary structures and status, and that year a new parish was created and a new church built, St. Peter's, London Docks.

The new St. Peter's Church, supported principally by Lord Beauchamp, the Earl of Powis, Lord Lyttelton, and Mr. and Mrs. Gladstone, became a center of Catholic community along the London Docks. The edifice was built to accommodate 700 and by the mid-1870's was filled to overflowing at the eleven o'clock "Solemn Eucharist" on Sunday morning. An extra celebration was added in the new building. Numerous processions became colorful occasions for demonstrations of Catholic evangelism in the streets of the East End. There were processions before each of the dedication week sermons by one of the

----

[17]Ibid., p. 148.

[18]Charles Lowder, Annual Report of St. George's Mission (London, 1863), p. 4. Service paper, No. 8182, Pusey House Pamphlet Collection.

[19]Chalres Lowder, Ten Years in St. George's Mission (London, 1867), p. 26.

guilds or confraternities of the parish. There were rogation
processions of choir, clergy, and congregation at 5 A.M. on each of the
Rogation Days, in the evening preceding major feasts, each day in the
octave of Corpus Christi, on the Harvest Festival, and after the
conclusion of the "Solemn Eucharist" of saints' days. Good Friday was
kept with hymn singing and preaching at ten stations on street corners.
Funeral processions became expressions of Catholic solidarity. By
1880, the number of confraternities had risen to eight and there was a
parish nurse, free kitchen, hostel, infant school, night school,
industrial school for girls and convalescent home at Seaford.

The initial prejudice of the general populace which had grown to
open rioting in St. George during services, when the choir was
assaulted with pea shooters and dogs were unleashed in the galleries,
was stilled by 1872 when this cycle of Catholic marches began. When
the Church Association attempted to prosecute Lowder in 1878, 1,600
East End residents signed a petition attesting that "we can personally
testify to the important change, morally, socially, and religiously,
which has been brought about by your instrumentality in this poor and
once spiritually-neglected district."[20]   When two spies came to take
notes on Lowder's ritual practice, a churchwarden, a lighterman, walked
up behind their pews and whispered, "If you go on with this 'ere,
there's half a dozen men behind you will crack your heads."[21]   The
notebooks were put up at once. Lowder was not tried, but he died two
years later. His funeral, when the dock streets were lined with
thousands as the coffin was carried by Benson, Mackonochie, and Bryan
King, became another testimony of success. "Twenty years ago he
entered some of those very streets among the jeers of such as lived
there. He has now left them amid their sobs. They laughed when he
came, and wept when he left...,"[22] one witness reflected, and Dickens'

---

[20]Charles Lowder, Annual Report, St. George's Mission (London,
1878), p. 3.

[21]Trench, op. cit., p. 244.

[22]Ibid., p. 366.

328

son recorded in his Dictionary of London:

> We may fancy that there is some connection between reverent
> ceremonial and spiritual and moral improvement; or,...when
> the Parish Church is a living, bright, and happy centre.
> Life, light, and true happiness radiate into the surrounding
> streets and houses....You will find in full work an agency
> which, if the people of the neighborhood are to be believed,
> has had, in the marvellous transformation which has taken
> place, a more potent influence even than police or Parliament
> combined.[23]

From 1868 the Cowley Fathers, the first Anglican religious order
since the Reformation, were constantly in the parish. In three years,
of the first three Cowley Fathers, R. M. Benson preached along the
docks on nine occasions, S. W. O'Neill twelve, and Charles Grafton
sixteen times. L. S. Wainright, who was an associate of the Cowley
Fathers, also known as the Society of St. John the Evangelist, was
named Vicar of St. Peter's in 1884 and stayed into the 1930's. He was
an example of the second and third generation Puseyite who engrafted
evangelical fervor into the traditions of the liturgical reform.
Wainright was described as a simple preacher who employed Moody and
Sankey's hymns in conjunction with Gregorian chant. The favorite of
St. Peter's became "Shall we gather at the river?" Yet Wainright was
still inspired by the patriarch, Pusey:

> Dr. Pusey spent some time in London. Here is an interesting
> passage from his commentary on Zechariah, touching what he
> felt as he walked our streets: "And the streets of the city
> shall be full of boys and girls playing in the streets
> thereof." Dr. Pusey, on the text, says: "In the dreary
> back-streets and alleys of London, the irrepressible
> joyousness of children is one of the bright sunbeams of that
> great Babylon, amid the oppressiveness of the anxious, hard,
> luxurious, thoughtless, care-worn, eager, sensual, worldly,
> frivolous, vain, stolid, sottish, cunning faces which
> traverse it. God sanctions, by His Word here...our joy in
> the joyousness of children, that He too taketh pleasure in
> it, He the Father of all."[24]

---

[23]Ibid., p. 326; Charles Lowder, Annual Report, St. George's Mission
(London, 1879), p. 3.

[24]L. S. Wainright, Untitled article, St. Peter's Parish Magazine,
January, 1900, p. 13.

Wainright sought to create joy by using dignified liturgy in which the people could participate. He expended effort to make the ritual forms understandable in the schools and classes of the parish. He strove to connect the joy of the eucharistic rites to the daily affairs of the docks. His mission was:

> to make the ritual simple and dignified, as solemn and devotional as possible, that the people might learn from all the outward associations of this solemn service....Festival seasons duly observed, processions, lights, incense, choral services, pictures and music--these accessories of worship are the rightful claim of the clergy and people of such a Church as St. Peter's and they are appreciated by them. The people love and glory in their church. To many it is their only quiet retreat; all that they have to soothe them in the privations of a hard life. It is their home. It is God's house, but it is also theirs and they feel a pride in its adornment.[25]

At the same time Wainright maintained 32 social service organizations so that all welfare needed by the residents of Wapping could come through the church--education, medicine, food, clothing, music, art, handicrafts, recreation, and excursions. The number of Sunday eucharists was increased to four, choral services were performed during Holy Week when the vicar introduced the ancient patristic liturgies of the Sacred Triduum, Maundy Thursday, Good Friday, and Easter Even, which the Fathers had regarded as the height of the liturgical year.

The parochial statistics reflect the response of the population to the combination of richer liturgy and social renewal along the London Docks. In one decade of Lowder's tenure, 1868-1877, 1,643 children were baptized at St. Peter's. The totals from decades during which all baptisms were recorded in Wainright's vicarate were:

1895-1904	1,875
1905-1914	1,319
1915-1924	1,017
1925-1934	709[26]

---

[25]Lucy Menzies, Father Wainright. A Record (London, 1947), pp. 30-31.

[26]MS Baptismal Registers, 1868-1934, Parish Archives, St. Peter's, London Docks.

When Lowder was at St. Peter's, yearly communions numbered:

1868	5048	1871	4964
1869	5783	1879	5493
1870	4715	1880	6293

During the interim between Lowder and Wainright the figures were:

1881 -- 7144
1882 -- 7587
1883 -- 7525

and under Wainright:

1884--9195	1895--6724	1907--5835	1918--5796
1885--7976	1896--7225	1908--6036	1919--5451
1886--6865	1897--6759	1909--5995	1920--5274
1887--7394	1899--6077	1910--6159	1921--5412
1888--7568	1900--5901	1911--6133	1922--5628
1889--7095	1901--5901	1912--6618	1923--6238
1890--6427	1902--5737	1913--6767	1924--6764
1891--7136	1903--5826	1914--7166	1925--6438[27]
1892--7065	1904--6212	1915--6610	
1893--7023	1905--6127	1916--6424	
1894--6597	1906--5982	1917--6100	

There were, in all, seventeen parishes in the East End similar to St. Peter's. At St. John's Drury Lane, St. Matthew's, Bethnal Green, and St. Michael's, Shoreditch, Stewart Headlam spoke of the social implications of the Puseyite sacramental system in clearly political language. He founded the Guild of St. Matthew, the first socialist society in the Church of England, to study political questions in the light of the incarnation.[28]

A. H. Mackonochie combined Wantage and St. Peter's in another poor district of London, Holborn. Baldwin Gardens was set in the immense

----

[27]Charles Lowder, Annual Report[s], St. George's Mission (London, 1868-71, 1879-80); R. J. Suckling, Annual Report[s], St. George's Mission (London, 1881-83); L. S. Wainright, Annual Report[s], St. George's Mission (London, 1884-1897), St. Peter's Parish Magazine, 1900-1925.

[28]For more analysis of the social, political, and intellectual radicalism of these parishes and further bibliography see Kenneth Leech and Rowan Williams, Essays Catholic and Radical (London, 1983), and Geoffrey Rowell, The Vision Glorious (Oxford, 1983), pp. 116-140.

parish of St. Andrew's, Holborn, in the 1860's much the same sort of parish as St. George-in-the-East had been in the thirties. The residents of Holborn were more like Henry Doolittle than the hard-working poor of the East End. J. G. Hubbard, afterwards Lord Addington, hired Butterfield to build a Church of St. Alban's on the plan of All Saints', Margaret Street. He endowed the parish with £ 5000 to support a collge of clergy and called A. H. Mackonoche to dirct the enterprise. The new vicar came from comfortable circumstances. His father was an official of the East India Company, and he entered Wadham College, Oxford. After a few days in Oxford Mackonochie wrote his mother, "I heard Pusey preach on Sunday. He gave a very good sermon on the Power of the Keys."[29] This was the beginning of a development which carried him to Wantage and through the riots at St. George-in-the-East.

Mackonochie brought Butler's methods to London. The vicar of Wantage sent constant paternal advice for organizing, the parish of St. Alban's. The parish was divided into districts which were the responsibility of each curate, as in Wantage. On Monday morning all met in solemn conclave in the clergy house to receive instruction on dealing with the poor, as in Wantage. The monastic hours were said and "the services of the newly formed district were carried on in a very 'Early Church' manner in a sort of catacomb, which was reminiscent of Wantage.[30]

When worship commenced in the completed Butterfield church in 1863, St. Peter's, London Docks, was the model for St. Alban's. From the outset the clergy wore colorful liturgical vestments designed by William Morris. Incense was used at the Introit, Gospel, Offertory, and before the consecration in the mass. There were four eucharistic celebrations on Sunday and feast days and two daily. The music was Gregorian.

----

[29]Edward Francis Russell, Alexander Heriot Mackonochie (New York, 1890), p. 14.

[30]Ibid., p. 40.

The clergy purposed to make the worship of God as magnificent as possible, as a means to the conversion of society. The Catholic faith they taught sought the redemption of humankind as a whole, not single souls, and ritual symbolized the sanctification of the community through the reception of the sacraments. "The Church, then," wrote Mackonochie, "is a Society. As by origin She is God manifested to man; so by the outward form of Her existence She is man affiliated to God: in fact, a Divine Society, just as Her Head is a Divine Name."[31] Mackonochie's ecclesiological definitions implied that Christ is present in the assembled congregation as well as in the bread and the wine of the eucharist, a further justification of ceremonial. "Well then, what is going on here when we meet for our daily morning and evening prayers? The whole body of Christ is bowing itself down upon its knees before God the Father....And so onward we follow Him through the mysteries of the Christian Service."[32]

Solemn rites molded souls into a united body to which alone grace could be conveyed: "We have not to seek after Heaven as so many single individual souls, but we are brought to Him, joined to Him, bound up in Him, made parts of Him, and as parts of Him partakers of His Holy Spirit, and so by that Holy Spirit, all led on together as Members of one Holy Body...."[33] Incense thus bore witness to the incarnation in the assembled flock, "whereby we ourselves, and our Acts and Prayers and Sacrifices, are united to Him."[34] Mackonochie wrote to Pusey, "If you want to touch people's hearts and rouse them, give them a procession ....It comes home somehow to the poor people with a loud call....This

---

[31]A. H. Mackonochie, First Principles Versus Erastianism, Six Sermons Preached at St. Vedast's, Foster Lane (London, 1876), p. 22.

[32]A. H. Mackonochie, Union with Christ through the Services of the Church (London, 1860), pp. 7-8.

[33]Ibid., pp. 3-4.

[34]A. H. Mackonochie, printed letter to St. Alban's Parish beginning "My dear Parishioners and Friends," January 1867, Service Paper No.7854, Pusey House Pamphlet Collection.

warfare, guerrilla though it be, we shall have to pursue...."[35]

To Mackonochie the doctrine of the church as the mystical body of Christ led on to an enhancement and renewal of the role of the laity. Lay persons should join with the clergy in electing bishops and should have the right to veto the appointment of parish priests and sit in ecclesiastical legislatures. His chief curate, A. H. Stanton, was even more radical in drawing secular and ecclesiastical conclusions from sacramental communalism during his years in the parish from 1863 to 1913. He was "firmly convinced," wrote a friend Richard Rowe, "that the basis of ritualism was a belief that all human flesh was loveable and venerable, because Christ had worn the human form, and therefore the most depraved ought to be looked on and looked after as saintly brethren in obstructed embryo."[36]

Stanton was a firebrand of the new Catholicism, a most fascinating, simply evangelical but sweetly ironical preacher:

Romanism is to me a lie, and Anglicanism hopelessly Erastian. ...Ever since they inhibited me I've only been curate at St. Alban's,...I am most unsatisfactory in so much—politically socialistic, in faith papistical, in Church policy a thorough-going Nonconformist.[37]

Preaching Sunday after Sunday at the St. Alban's "Solemn Eucharist" at eleven o'clock, he heaped scorn upon an Establishment whose injustice and hypocrisy were proof enough that it did not know the church to be the mystical body of Christ. He "rejoiced to see Liberty, Fraternity, Equality, on the walls of Paris," during the Commune and said, "When the Republic is set up these streets must really be re-christened."[38] Mackonochie and Stanton organized a "Council of Laymen Communicants of the Congregation" to assist in governing the parish. The Vicar wrote

---

[35]E. Russell, op. cit., p. 224.

[36]Mackonochie, First Principles, pp. 25, 34, 58; G. W. E. Russell, Arthur Stanton (London, 1917), p. 102.

[37]G. Russell, op. cit., pp. 24, 138.

[38]Ibid., pp. 127, 138.

Dr. Pusey for advice:

> You will be able to tell me the extent, limits, and mode of exercising the powers of the laity in ancient times; and to what extent, within what limits power can be put into their hands now.[39]

It was just this creation of a strong community of laymen through ritual and workingmen's clubs, a postman's league, confraternities for every sex and age group, classes, schools, institutes, leagues, societies, free meals, a nursery, medical aid, and recreational facilities which Pusey valued in St. Alban's and pointed out to detractors when its clergy fell under severe Church Association assault. In July, 1866, Lord Shaftesbury wrote in his diary, "On Sunday to St. Alban's Church in Holborn with Stephens and Haldane. In outward form and ritual it is the worship of Jupiter or Juno. It may be Heaven itself in the inward sense....Do we thus lead souls to Christ or Baal?"[40] Methodists disseminated the information that "the lady portion of the congregation belonged to that class who try to combine worldly pleasures with religious dissipation, and who are said to oscillate at certain seasons between the opera box and the confessional box."[41] From 1867 until 1882, Mackonochie was continually prosecuted in one court case after another because of the St. Alban's ritual, a process which caused him to lose his mind. Stanton was inhibited from preaching in any pulpit in England other than his own.

Amid these difficulties Pusey wrote Mackonochie, "...Your strength is and will be in the hearts of your people. These you have won wonderfully. Courts cannot really move you while you have them....If the younger clergy will but win their people first as you have."[42]

----

[39]MS Letter of A. H. Mackonochie to E. B. Pusey, June 25, 1874, Pusey House.

[40]E. Russell, op. cit., p. 133.

[41]Bourchier Wrey Savile, Dr. Pusey: An Historic Sketch: with Some Account of the Oxford Movement during the Nineteenth Century (London, 1883), p. 96.

[42]MS Letter of E. B. Pusey to A. H. Mackonochie, June 28, 1874, Pusey House.

Pusey told C. L. Wood of "Mackonochie's earnestness and success in conversion..." in urging him to stir up the English Church Union for the clergy of Saint Alban's.[43] He wrote to The Times in 1881, "Mr. Enraght and Mr. Mackonochie have not been struggling for themselves, but for their people. St. Alban's was built by a pious High Church layman in what was one of the worst localities in London. It is now full of a religious population, who join intelligently in the service provided for them and love it."[44]

In 1874, two thousand residents of Holborn signed a petition protesting the harassment of Mackonochie. When he died, a great public meeting was convened in the parish under the chairmanship of Earl Beauchamp and Lord Halifax. Sufficient funds were raised to erect a Mackonochie Chapel next to St. Alban's. In 1906, 3,600 parishioners signed another petition in honor of A. H. Stanton, and when he died, crowds lined the streets for his funeral procession from Holborn Viaduct to Charing Cross station.

The religious communalism of the new Catholicism evolved more slowly at St. Alban's after the death of Stanton, and the movement toward the active role of the laity in the religious community of the parish was stifled. Henry Ross, who was Vicar from the end of World War I until 1931, took as the theme of his teaching "Corporate religion," which, however, was expressed simply by adding processions on the eve and before the mass of every feast day and a great parish march of guilds on St. Alban's day.[45]

There is no doubt that the chief period of advancement and success at St. Alban's was the twenty years of Mackonochie's vicarate,

---

[43]MS Letter of E. B. Pusey to C. L. Wood, January 24, 1879, Pusey House.

[44]Letter of E. B. Pusey to The Times, January 12, 1881.

[45]Michael Reynolds, Martyr of Ritualism (London, 1965); G. W. E. Russell, Saint Alban the Martyr, Holborn. A History of Fifty Years (London, 1913); St. Alban's, Holborn, Monthly Magazine 1918-1940; Printed notices of services, 1918-1940, Parish Archives, St. Alban's, Holborn.

1863–1882, when an average of 309.1 baptisms per year were performed.[46]
The great revolution in reception of holy communion also took place
under Mackonochie:

Total yearly communions,
St. Alban's, Holborn

1864 — 3,293	1871 — 13,446
1865 — 4,765	1872 — 13,373
1866 — 17,392	1873 — 14,204
1867 — 18,271	1874 — 12,500
1868 — 16,251	1877 — 13,423
1869 — 15,842	1878 — 13,399[47]
1870 — 12,592	

After being destroyed in World War II Saint Alban's was built up
again with the same dimensions as before, but in a simpler
architectural style with bare walls, clear glass, and a table altar in
closer proximity to the congregation. But these were the only
evidences in the life of the parish of the evolution of the implications of the doctrine of the church as the mystical body of Christ. This
was not the case at All Saints', Margaret Street. Between the wars the
overt communality of the parish was the more in evidence because of the
presence of Anglican Benedictines, under Dom Bernard Clements, as
parochial clergy. After World War II an Institute of Christian Studies
was formed, a lay religious community living together a rule ordered by
teaching, worship, and the exercise of corporate spirituality in one of
Butterfield's buildings. This "experiential body" was constituted to
replace traditional methods of Christian education. The goal of the
Institute was to make the theory of lay apostolate a reality.

In the twentieth-century Christ Church, Albany Street, moved
toward expressing "that which in the main is the object for which a
parish exists, namely, the building up and edifying the body of Christ
which is His Church" by having fewer services and less, simpler, and
more dignified ritual. The climax of this development was a new 10

---

[46]MS Baptismal Registers, 1863–1942, Parish Archives, St. Alban's,
Holborn.

[47]St. Alban's Defense Committee, The Church in Baldwin's Gardens
(London, no date), p. 11.

o'clock "Parish Eucharist" which was to be the gathering of the entire Albany Street community around the altar at one time. The reduction of services and emphasis on this one Sunday "Parish Eucharist" was understood to give expression to the corporate nature of a parish. The Vicar of Christ Church wrote in 1922:

> As in the days of Aaron, so now the vestments, the lights, and swinging censers are to impress both priest and people with an adequate sense of what they are about....[Yet] the simple and open altars of the Church of England [provide a] sense of the real wonder, the veiled splendour of our communion with the Deity.[48]

Of the four parochial outposts of Anglican Catholicism in Oxford in the twentieth century, St. Barnabas followed the pattern of St. Peter's, St. Paul's that of Christ Church, and St. Philip and St. James' that of Margaret Street. St. Mary Magdalen reproduced St. Alban's. Headington, Henley, Banbury, Clewes, Bayne Hill, Abingdon, Newbury Hill, Ipswich, and Kempsford were small towns whose experiences were similar to Wantage. The countryside thus began to be penetrated with Puseyism as well. Of nineteen rural churches in the Sevenoaks area, for example, in 1905, the eucharistic vestments were worn in 17.[49]

Seaside towns appeared susceptible to Puseyism. The rich were attracted to St. Paul's, Brighton, which was similar to Margaret Street and St. Barnabas, Oxford. The interior was decorated by the Pre-Raphaelite Brotherhood. Parishioners of St. Paul's, principally Sir William and Lady Gomm, endowed other Brighton churches: St. Mary Magdalen in Broad Street, St. Bartholomew in the northern part of town, St. Martin, Lewes Road, and St. Michael's, along the sea. Plymouth's churches were for the poor. G. R. Prynne restored St. Peter's, Plymouth, "to the spirit of the catacombs."[50] Robert Dolling, who had

---

[48]Printed letter of Vicar F. Fielding-Ould to parishioners of Christ Church, Albany Street, July, 1922, Parish Archives, Christ Church, Albany Street.

[49]Anselm Hughes, The Rivers of the Flood (London, 1961), p. 18.

[50]Shane Leslie, The Oxford Movement (London, 1933), p. 74.

338

taken part in religious and social work at St. Alban's as a layman, combined Christian socialism and the high mass to bring religion to the poor Postsmouth district of Landport until driven from the parish by Archbishop Randall Davidson because he said masses for the dead.

Northern towns adopted the methods of St. Saviour's, Leeds. In Newcastle Vibert Jackson of the Mission of the Holy Spirit was forced to celebrate the eucharist in the kitchens of the homes of his parishioners after 1907 because the bishop of the diocese refused him a license. He used vestments and incense. The Vicar of All Saints', Small Heath, close to Birmingham, was imprisoned in Warwick Gaol for two months for similar practices, even though he attracted 500 communicants to the parish "Solemn Eucharist" and a congregation of 800 to Sunday evening "Solemn Evensong."[51] James Bell-Cox of St. Margaret's, Liverpool, was incarcerated in 1887 and left behind him a loyal and enthusiastic parish. J. S. L. Burn brought the Catholic revival to the smoky town of Middlesbrough in 1865. He was accused by the local press of practicing "genuflexions and incest" at St. John's Church.[52] Burn founded All Saints' Church himself and ran it according to Puseyite principles for forty years. Crowds came to low mass at seven and high mass at nine on Sunday to participate in a homely, enthusiastic variety of Catholic worship. At the outbreak of the First World War, the eucharistic vestments were worn in nine out of the eleven Middlesbrough churches.

From 1904 through World War II there was a great movement of missionary zeal at Pusey's St. Saviour's, Leeds. A campaign was begun to increase the participation of the congregation in the liturgical services and to have the people sing all the musical parts of the mass. The corporate witness of processions was increased by the addition of a Whitsun Monday march of all guilds and confraternities through the Black Dog district in 1918. There were additional processions during

----

[51]Wakeling, op. cit., p. 258.

[52]Hughes, op. cit., p. 32.

Corpus Christi octave beginning in 1924. In 1914 processions were added on the eve and before the "Solemn Eucharist" of major feast days. By 1910, St. Saviour's parish was able to found two daughter churches in the same neighborhood of Leeds, All Saints' and St. Hilda's.

-2-

In Germany the experience of the liturgical parishes of Württemberg was fashioned into a coherent theology by the Benedictines of Beuron and of Maria Laach. In England the Cowley Fathers, or the Society of St. John the Evangelist, and the Community of the Resurrection were theologicans of the new Catholicism, and monks of the Society of the Sacred Mission were the liturgists. Members of the revived Anglican religious orders were instruments for transforming the parochial experience of the Puseyite parishes into a universal tradition which could be spread throughout the Anglican Communion.

The shape of the theology of R. M. Benson, the founder of the Society of St. John the Evangelist, came not only from his contact with Pusey but also from his experiences from 1857 in the St. George Mission and St. Peter's, London Docks. The person to whom Benson owed the most intellectually and spiritually was Pusey. From Pusey he gained his devotion to the Fathers and the disciplines of the spiritual life. He carried Pusey's anti-individualistic interpretation of Christianity into the rule and polity of the Cowley Fathers. At the same time, in the hard life of the East End parishes he found monasticism in embryo:

> It is true that, although they were not living under what we know as religious vows,...they were wholly dedicated...to God. They were not living under vows; but we must remember that the vows do not constitute the religious life; the religious life is the life of the Spirit within the heart of those who take the vows.[53]

Benson transmitted his theories of communal religion as the panacea of secular society to Cowley Fathers who went out from Oxford to serve

---

[53]M. V. Woodgate, Father Benson (London, 1953), p. 166.

parishes in the East End, India, America, Canada, South Africa, and Japan.[54]   R. M. Benson was convinced that "If we are to live true to God we must live indeed within the organism of the Body...."[55]

The parish church, the local concretization of the body of Christ, was for Benson the only true community, the locus of human fellowship, because of its intimate association with the incarnation solidified in sacraments and liturgies. Thus, Benson wrote, "We have fellowship one with another not for one another's sake, but as a result of our being taken up into the life of Christ the Head."[56] George Congreve, another Cowley Father, wrote of this eucharistic union as an answer to the alienation of industrial society:

> Here at your altar you find the answer to the terrible enigmas of political economy, to the threats of national rivalries, and of individual selfishness....Here we all, whoever we may be, find ourselves gathered before the throne of the Lamb, healed of the burning rivalries, and of all that is unbearable in the pain of differences, which for a moment divide us unavoidably; before the altar we can let go all that forbids our unity in Christ....[57]

Benson and Liddon were the movers of a scheme to open a house and library at Oxford "to promote theological study and religious life in the university" as a memorial to Dr. Pusey. An endowment of £ 50,000 was raised as "The Dr. Pusey Memorial Fund."[58]   In 1903 another considerable legacy was bequeathed by John W. Cudworth because "it was in great measure through attending services at St. Saviour's Church,

---

[54]R. M. Benson, Redemption: Some of the Aspects of the Work of Christ (London, 1861); G. Congreve, ed., Letters of Richard Meux Benson (London, 1916), pp. 54-55, 78, 197; Richard Meux Benson, The Way of Holiness (London, 1901).

[55]Woodgate, op. cit., p. 157.

[56]Congreve, op. cit., p. 287.

[57]George Congreve, Christian Life. A Response (London, 1901), pp. 19, 179.

[58]"Dr. Pusey Memorial Fund," printed paper of November 13, 1882, Pusey House. The principle lay subscribers were Earl Beauchamp, F. H. Rivington, J. G. Talbot, M. P., Sir J. R. Mowbray.

Leeds,...that I became a Churchman."[59] Pusey House was opened in 1884.
V. S. S. Coles, who had been a curate at Wantage for three years, was
librarian and Charles Gore became first principal. Gore was born at
Wimbledon in 1853 into the family of a high civil servant. At Harrow
G. W. E. Russell, whose brother was a curate at St. Alban's, Holborn,
became a close friend. Gore began to steal away from home with Russell
on adventurous weekend expeditions to St. Alban's, describing his
experiences later in a diary: "such a splendid service" with the
Hallelujah Chorus at the end of mass accompanied by full brass band and
"such a magnificent sermon" from Fr. Stanton. Stanton taught Gore to
love the mass, to fast on Friday, and to appreciate the liturgy.[60]
Gore wrote in 1905: "I love, as I hardly love anything in the world
physically...that type and kind of ceremonial worship, which is called
ritualistic by many people and Catholic by its maintainers. It appears
to me personally to be the one kind of ceremonial worship which really
expresses my feelings...."[61] With Russell, Gore visited the Cowley
Fathes at Oxford and developed a profound respect for Benson who
imparted to him his mystical and corporate conception of the church.

Gore demonstrated his adherence to religious anti-individualism by
founding a new monastic order in 1892, the Community of the
Resurrection, for the application of Christian principles to
contemporary social problems. From Benson and the Tractarians Gore
had learned that the human realizes true being only in relation to
community. Central to his theology and action as the twentieth century
began is the Pusey stress on the church as a visible and Catholic
society, the only ontological community. Christ left behind an
institution now described by Charles Gore as "His body, indwelt by His
Spirit...the visible organ through which He is to act upon the world."[62]

---

[59]F. L. Cross, Darwell Stone (Glasgow, 1943), pp. 98-99.

[60]G. L. Prestige, The Life of Charles Gore (London, 19350, p. 11.

[61]Gordon Crosse, Charles Gore (London, 1932), p. 5.

[62]John Gore, Charles Gore. Father and Son (London, 1932), p. 5.

To Gore, the church is the only form of corporate life which discredits and weakens secular individualism. "We are rejecting a mere individualism in all departments of life as false in philosophy, and perilous in practice."[63] Gore's socialism was based upon the belief that Christian fellowship had evolved from the incarnation. He used Darwinian terminology to convey this Puseyite concept to his contemporaries. The mystical life of the church is the climax of the ascent of man, the crown of human nature. Redemption comes to the earth through the eucharistic and the rites of Christian initiation. The sacraments are thus both social ceremonies and means for the sanctification of society, symbols, in the language of Gore, of Christ's immanence in nature. "...Baptism is our regeneration or our incorporation into the new manhood by the Spirit, and involves that deep break with the past...."[64] The eucharist is the means "to bind into an indissoluble unity our fellowship with God and our fellowship with our brother members in the Church..."[65]

Gore carried the practical implications of the revived corporate nature of the church into his several posts. At Westminster Abbey he instituted the daily celebration of the eucharist. As Bishop of Birmingham he strove for the social justice which was implied in his sacramental theology, and in the see of Oxford he advanced the restoration of liturgical piety in the churches of the diocese. When Gore resigned Oxford in 1919 he moved to London to work in the parish of All Saints', Margaret Street, and preach, until the 1930's, at Grosvenor Chapel. Walter Howard Frere, Gore's successor as Superior of the Community of the Resurrection, carried out similar diocesan reforms as Bishop of Truro until 1935.

The Puseyite tradition was also carried into the twentieth century by the Society of the Sacred Mission, an Anglican counterpart to the

---

[63]Ibid., p. 11.

[64]Ragnar Ekström, The Theology of Charles Gore (Lund, 1944), p. 257.

[65]John Gore, op. cit., p. 12.

German Benedictine abbeys of Beuron and Maria Laach, which fostered an English liturgical movement. The Society of the Sacred Mission was founded in 1894 by Herbert Hamilton Kelly, who had come to Oxford in 1879, shy, deaf, and from the opposite end of the social scale than Gore. He was impressed by a course of R. M. Benson lectures on the religious life in 1888 and by John Ruskin's Unto this Last which he had been reading at the time. Kelly determined to found a religious society which would train ordinands who did not have enough money to attain a university degree. He composed a rule centered about a common life founded in the eucharist. Lower class austerity dictated that "the life of all must be kept in real simplicity and poverty" which implied that the bourgeois comforts of established Anglican clerical life were eschewed.[66] In 1903 S.S.M. clergy and students moved into Kelham Hall, near Newark in Lincolnshire, to which was added a new chapel built to give expression to the sacramental communalism of a Society shorn of the romantic externals of many revived monasteries. Kelham chapel expressed the communalism of the new Catholicism:

> One enters the new buildings from the old. The door is closed on the Gothic Revival. On the other side of it comes the complete antithesis, the new work. On the one side, a revival. On the other, what?...Bare brick walls, of a warm friendly texture and colour, but not smooth; bricks, that are honestly glad to be bricks...no art, no carefully devised texture faking, but a curious naive atmosphere of country architecture...a vast open space....Here is a chapel which is a place of assembly...treated with a broad simplicity of handling, its structure of humble materials yet noble in conception.[67]

This structure reflected Kelly's understanding of Catholicism, a vision of the infinite power of God impregnating the smallest material things. The Christian faith, he taught his monks, has to do primarily with the sanctification of ordinary objects through religious life in common. "Catholicity," he wrote in a book of the same, name, "is a vital and essential principle. We may learn a great deal from

---

[66]Peter F. Anson, The Call of the Cloister (London, 1955), p. 142.

[67]Ibid., p. 144.

Tractarians, Ritualists, Anglo-Catholics, even Ultramontanes, from all who died for it, like Fisher and Campion, Cranmer and Laud or like Pusey, died in it."[68]

A. G. Hebert, one of the most important English writers on the liturgy between the wars, was attracted by this definition. After attending Harrow and New College, Oxford, Herbert worked from 1909 until 1911 in the Catholic parishes of Bethnal Green in the East End. He was ordained in 1912, but felt drawn to the novitiate at Kelham in 1914, because he felt:

> ...an outstanding feature of modern life is the lack of true community--the loneliness and isolation of the individual from his fellows, in the modern town suburb where people do not know their neighbors. With this goes the spiritual famine of an age whose intellectual food is the garbage supplied by the press and the cinema. What is lacking is a common faith or belief about the meaning of man's life....[69]

The patristic religion of the incarnation provided an alternative to A. G. Hebert:

> ...The incarnation is the coming of God in the flesh, for the redemption of our actual bodily life and our social relations. Therefore the Christian religion is always something more than an individual piety, or a pursuit of an individual holiness....The Church is not a mere association of individuals who have had similar experiences and unite to form a community. The Church depends on the Incarnation and has been created by God's action.[70]

Hebert found the Catholic movement in the Church of England to be potentially the strongest force for the ideal of community in Britain:

> I have tried to interpret the aim of this movement as a reassertion of the objective side of Christianity, in conscious opposition to the subjectivism which is the common tendency of modern religion....An Anglican view of the Christian faith is in certain ways markedly different from

---

[68]H. H. Kelly, Catholicity (London, 1932), p. 35.

[69]A. G. Herbert, MS The Liturgical Movement, Archives of the Society of the Sacred Mission, Kelham.

[70]A. G. Hebert, MS Some Notes on the Subject of the Conference, Archives of the Society of the Sacred Mission, Kelham.

that of our Roman Catholic brethren in England. While it is true that we Anglicans have in the last 100 years moved a long way nearer both to the Roman Catholic mind and to the orthodox mind, we believe that there is an Anglican something, which has a true place within the Una Catholica, and which is truly in accord with the Patristic writers of the early centuries, to whom our Anglican Divines have always appealed.[71]

This special contribution was that "the Anglo-Catholic movement was first of all a liturgical revival" that men like Lowder, Mackonochie, and Stanton related the liturgy to the amelioration of society.[72] Hebert copied and kept with him a model sermon delivered by R. M. Benson at All Saints', Margaret Street, in 1884 which was to him a short manifesto of the social critique inherent in the new Catholicism:

> God ordained society, but God did not ordain luxury. God ordained society, but God did not ordain idleness, or that any amount of accumulated wealth should free any from the obligation to work and use all their powers for the benefit of society....If you belong to what is called the Upper Class it is your duty to see that you level upwards—that you hold anything you have beyond your daily bread in fellowship with any member of Christ's Body who is in need: that you share freely any benefit you possess, lifting up your breathren to any higher enjoyment you may possess beyond them....If you do not level up, Satan will soon have his way and level downwards. Think not that Poverty is the great eyesore of this city; if we were all poor together we might have God's blessing on our penury; the great eyesore of London is your accumulated wealth. If a man can have no crime imputed to him save this; that he has accumulated riches in the bank: that alone is sin enough to send him to hell.[73]

In much the same way that Karl Adam and Yves Congar fashioned Möhler for their generation, so Hebert restated the message of the

----

[71]A. G. Hebert, MS Christianity in the Modern World, Archives of the Society of the Sacred Mission, Kelham.

[72]A. G. Herbert, Typescript The Liturgical Movement, Archives of the Society of the Sacred Mission, Kelham; A. G. Hebert, MS Starting the Parish Communion, Archives of the Society of the Sacred Mission, Kelham.

[73]A. G. Hebert, MS R. M. Benson, Notes from a sermon preached at All Saints', Margaret Street, in 1884, Archives of the Society of the Sacred Mission, Kelham.

Tractarians for the twentieth century. In Intercommunion, 1932, Liturgy and Society, 1935, Grace and Nature, 1937, and The Form of the Church, 1948, Hebert spoke of the eucharist as the power to redeem the social order. On the one hand worship provided escape:

> On Sundays, in the worship of the Church, it is possible to get clean away from the atmosphere of the mechanized world...to find the peace which the world cannot give nor take away.[74]

But at the same time the liturgy could show the way to the recovery of corporate life in a Europe which had lost any common cultural bond and consequently faced disintegration.

> ...It is chiefly by what they themselves do in Church that the people are educated in the meaning of redemption: and they must learn to see the meaning of the whole of life in the light of the Church's sacred actions....Here is seen the true meaning of "community": the common life of a spiritual family, based on a common faith and a common food....Here is seen the pattern of community which God had ordained, in the midst of a world where men are strangers to one another....We [thus] lose hold of the essence of Christianity if we interpret it simply as a way of holiness, having for its end the salvation and the perfection of the individual soul.... Christianity is the redemption of the body, and of common life, by the Divine action in the Incarnation.[75]

Hebert observed the institution of one principal parish communion at Christ Church, Albany Street. He later found that a movement toward a single eucharist on Sunday, at which the whole parish gathered about the altar, had appeared in 1890 at St. Faith's Stepney, at the country parish of Staveley near Kendal in 1902, at St. Mary's, Horbury Junction, and at St. Ninian's Perth, in 1912, at Temple Balsall in 1913, and at St. John's, Newcastle, in 1927. This arrangement appeared to accentuate the communality of the eucharist, and so Hebert launched the Parish and People Movement with The Parish Communion in 1937 to encourage the active participation of the laity in a single Sunday celebration around a simple, free-standing altar-table. He perceived

---

[74]A. G. Hebert, The Form of the Church (London, 1948), p. 95.

[75]A. G. Hebert, Grace and Nature (London, 1937), pp. 72, 74; A. G. Hebert, Liturgy and Society (London, 1935), p. 158.

this as a necessary reform for the full realization of the social implications of the new Catholicity:

> ...God is already beginning to lead us back to a Christianity that shall be at once evangelical, Catholic, and modern. The Christianity of the future is to be based on the old Gospel of God; and in it the Catholic conception of the Church and of the Sacraments is to come at last into its own.[76]

In November, 1945, the Archbishop of Canterbury invited Dom Gregory Dix to convene a group of Anglicans of the Catholic school at Westminster Abbey to examine the causes of the constant failure of discussions between Anglican Catholics and Protestants and to consider whether any synthesis between Catholicism and Protestantism was possible. In January, 1946, a group was constituted which included E. S. Abbott, Dean of King's College, London, H. J. Carpenter, Warden of Keble College, Oxford, A. G. Hebert, A. M. Ramsey, Professor Divinity in the University of Durham and Canon of Durham, L. S. Thornton of the Community of the Resurrection, and T. S. Eliot. Canon Ramsey was elected chairman, and Dom Gregory Dix and Fr. Hebert secretaries. During 1946 three sessions of the group were held. At a final meeting in January, 1947, no synthesis emerged, but rather a statement of the Anglican definition of Catholicity which is a parallel to Pius XII's encyclicals of the 1940's which are landmarks in the restoration of the corporate dimension of Catholicism.

The committee took notice of the inadequacy of those who, virtually omitting the doctrine of the church from its place in the Gospel, replaced it by a doctrine of the spiritual vocation of the English secular community, as well as those content to practice an introverted and pietistic ecclesiasticism under the name of "Catholic" churchmanship. They pointed to the shallowness of others who, intent upon the idea of Christian leadership in the march of progress, had twisted the Gospel into a pragmatist panacea for human ills. To be a Christian is, they said, to belong to the one "Body," to share in the one visible series of sacramental rites. The unity of the church is a

---

[76]A. G. Hebert, Intercommunion (London, 1932), p. vii.

part of one great social "wholeness" and cannot be understood apart from it. Social unity, in all its aspects, has sprung directly out of the entrance of God into human history in the eschatological event of Redemption. This event includes no less the church which is Christ's body, and the Spirit, who through this body brings into the world the powers of the realm which transcends matter. Thus the members of the church do not constitute a unified social order themselves. It is Christ in his body the church who justifies men and women, and their justification is their deliverance into the unity of his body, the means of which is the eucharist, "a communion and fellowship meal." The mass is a corporate action of the whole body. It expresses the intimate communion of the soul with Christ and the corporate essence of the whole church, as well as the fellowship of the particular local church as a self-contained society.[77]

Eliot, Abbott, and Ramsey had been closely associated with Hebert and the Society of the Sacred Mission, the latter lured by the corporate spirit of the Kelham Chapel while Rector of Boston in the thirties. Each drew out the practical implications of Catholicity; Eliot in essays on Christianity and society; Abbott as Dean of Westminster Abbey, and Ramsey as Archbishop of Canterbury from 1962. Thus the primate of the Anglican Communion during the Second Vatican Council was a spokesman for the new Catholicism. In 1970 the Archbishop lectured in New York on "The Future of the Christian Church" with a leader of the progressive element at the Council, Leon-Joseph Suenens, Primate of Belgium. Canterbury concluded:

> It is of little importance here to know whether this point of convergence is eschatological or belongs to history....It is a process in which the Catholic Church will continue to reform and purify herself, to develop in herself, and if need be to rediscover any values which are hers but which, in her present state in times, she does not integrally honor.[78]

---

[77]E. S. Abbott et al., Catholicity (Westminster, 1947), pp. 1, 13, 14, 15, 52.

[78]Michael Ramsey and Leon-Joseph Cardinal Suenens, The Future of the Christian Church (New York, 1970), p. 66.

Suenens responded:

> We, all of us, have to show that individualism is not
> Christianity. We must point out how profoundly Christianity
> must be a communion of people together with God. We must
> help the young to see that the social conscience, which they
> possess to such a marked degree, only reflects that communal
> dimension of man that is brought to fulfillment in the Body
> of Christ.[79]

Canterbury reacted spontaneously, "I think it is daft--absolutely
daft--that we should have to belong to separate ecclesiastical
establishments."[80] And a witness wrote, "[These lectures] represent
more than another ecumenical event. They are beyond ecumenism; indeed,
beyond dialogue. They disclose a unity of mind and spirit, a
theological unity which already exists, waiting to be realised."[81]

Just as modern liturgical revision became a principal means
through which the twentieth century successors of Pusey strove to
restore the communal dimension of the Catholic tradition within the
Anglican Communion, so the impact of the modern liturgical movement,
transcending denominational boundaries, is also one reason for the
contemporary "convergence" of Roman Catholicism and Anglicanism pointed
to by Lord Ramsey and Cardinal Suenens. A letter of Jan Cardinal
Willebrands, President of the Vatican Secretariat for Promoting
Christian Unity, of July 1985 to the two co-chairmen of the Anglican-
Roman Catholic International Commission draws attention to the
"remarkable process of liturgical renewal in both communions" which has
allowed Anglicans and Roman Catholics to make an explicit confession of
one faith in the eucharist and the ministry which is recorded in the
ARCIC Final Report of 1982.[82]

----

[79]Ibid., p. 118.

[80]Ibid., p. 3.

[81] Ibid., p. 5.

[82]For analysis of this letter see R. W. Franklin, "Apostolicae Curae
of 1896 Reconsidered: Cardinal Willebrands' Letter to ARCIC-II,"
Ecumenical Trends, XV, no. 5 (May 1986), 80-82. On the Puseyites and
ecumenical convergence see Geoffrey Rowell, "The Catholic Revival and
Ecumenical Endeavour," The Vision Glorious (Oxford, 1983), pp. 188-219;
and Robert Greenfield, "Such a Friend to the Pope," in Perry Butler,

Since the Second World War liturgical renewal has borne abundant fruit in the extensive revision of Anglican prayer books around the world. The extent of this activity can be gauged from the fact that Colin Buchanan's Modern Anglican Liturgies 1958-1968 contains fifteen revised rites, to which twenty-two more were added by the same compiler's Further Anglican Liturgies 1968-1975. The development culminated with the 1979 Book of Common Prayer for U. S. Episcopalians and the Alternative Services Book published for the Church of England in 1980.[83]

In virtually every part of the Anglican Communion these liturgies share a remarkably similar shape and emphasis with the rites promulgated in the Roman Catholic Church after Vatican II by Pope Paul VI. Not only do Anglicans and Roman Catholics intend and say many similar things at worship, but there is widespread understanding of the eucharist as the climactic act of the corporate life of the Christian community, an insight expressed by a marked growth in the participation of the laity in singing the service, in more responsive liturgical material and congregational saying of the prayers, and in the laity joining in all-inclusive offertory, communion, and other processions. This rapprochement is one reason why Cardinal Willebrands has stated that the Vatican may be prepared "to acknowledge the possibility" of the validity of Anglican orders so that there may be formal reconciliation of the ministers and people of the two churches.[84]

----

ed., Pusey Rediscovered (London, 1983), pp. 162-184.

[83]Colin Buchanan, Modern Anglican Liturgies 1958-1968 (London, 1968); Further Anglican Liturgies 1968-75 (Bramcote, 1975); Anglo-Catholic Worship: An Evangelical Appreciation After 150 Years (Bramcote, 1983). The most complete summary of this period appears in the final chapter in the second edition of Geoffrey Cuming, A History of Anglican Liturgy (London, 1982). For an American Anglican version of this recent history see Massey H. Shepperd, The Liturgical Renewal of the Church (New York, 1960); The Reform of Liturgical Worship (New York, 1961).

[84]Jan Cardinal Willebrands, "New Context for Discussing Anglican Orders," Origins, XV, No. 40 (March 1986), 662-664.

351

Revision of worship is one constant activity that links the "consummatio" envisioned by Pusey and Döllinger in the nineteenth century with the "convergence" spoken of in the late twentieth century by Ramsey, Suenens, and Willebrands. The transmission of elements of Möhler's new Catholicism into our own time has been intimately associated with the work of the liturgical movement in Germany. One of the leading modern exponents of Möhler, Karl Adam, endorsed the liturgical reforms of the Benedictine monks of Maria Laach as the best means to convey to German Catholics Möhler's sense that the whole church, clergy and laity, is one corporate body:

> The communion with the flesh and blood of Christ which we celebrate in the liturgy in a real communion....The mass is never an individual act, but always essentially a community act...in the sense that participation in the one bread gives the community its true cohesion and unity....It is precisely this communion and fellowship, the normal condition of the living Christian, that the sacrament is intended to secure. ...[and that] is the profound value of the liturgical movement of our days, that it is revealing once more the rich significance of the liturgical formulas, and that it is teaching us to assimilate our own practice to the spirit of the liturgy.[85]

The Benedictine monks of Beuron and Maria Laach implicitly and explicitly taught the Möhlerian ecclesiology while reforming church services in Germany.[86]

It is significant that perhaps the two most influential figures in the enterprise of post-war Anglican liturgical revision, A. G. Hebert and Gregory Dix, were both nurtured in the Anglican religious orders that grew out of Puseyite circles and parishes, and they were shaped by the Continental European liturgical movement of Benedictine monks.

---

[85]Karl Adam, Christ Our Brother (London, 1931), pp. 74-75, 70.

[86]Konrad Jakobs, pastor of Maria-Geburt in Mülheim in the German industrial Ruhr district is only one example of clergy who combined preaching on Möhlerian themes with worship reforms as a means of parish renewal. For analysis see Maria Hopmann, Pastor Jakobs (Freiburg, 955); and Konrad Jakobs, Das Mysterium als Grundgedanke der Seelsorge (Düsseldorf, 1936); Die Pfarrgemeinde als Heimat (Recklinghausen, 1937).

In the 1950's the ideals of Fr. Hebert, adopted by the parish and people movement, spread out and captured almost the whole of the Church of England to the parish communion, rather than morning prayer, as the norm of worship on Sunday morning. Without doubt there is a direct connection between Pusey's desire for a weekly congregational communion at which all would devoutly and sincerely partake and this transformation of the Church of England into a eucharistically oriented body. But at the same time, Hebert relied heavily upon propagating among the English the most important results of the Continental liturgical movement in order to achieve this goal. Hebert's influential book that went through five printings in nine years, Liturgy and Society, relies heavily on the historical research and the theological exposition of the Benedictine monks of Maria Laach.[87]

The sources of that principal insight of Dom Gregory Dix which "ruled supreme" over the post-war project of re-thinking Anglican worship throughout the world, the insight that worship in the patristic church was "done" by the whole gathered community, not said by the priest and "listened to" or "watched" by the people, may also be traced back to Oxford and to the Benedictine monasteries.[88] On the one hand wrote Dix, who entered the novitiate of the Anglican community at Nashdom in 1936 and was first associated with Hebert's The Parish Communion in 1937, "The Oxford Movement turned to the parishes and taught the parish priests and the laity in great numbers to think of the eucharistic action as the patristic authors had thought of it."[89]

----

[87]Peter J. Jaggar, A History of the Parish and People Movement (Leighton Buzzard, 1978); Judith Pinnington, "Rubric and Spirit: A Diagnostic Reading of Tractarian Worship," in Kenneth Leech and Rowan Williams, eds., Essays Catholic and Radical (London, 1983), pp. 95-130.

[88]Colin Buchanan, Anglo-Catholic Worship, p. 7; Kenneth W. Stevenson, Gregory Dix Twenty-five Years On (Bramcote, 1977).

[89]Gregory Dix, The Shape of the Liturgy (London, 1945), p. 717. A short summary of this immensely influential work appeared first in Hebert's The Parish Communion in 1937, a longer draft was read as a paper before the Cowley Fathers in August 1941, and the manuscript was completed in 1943 on the hundredth anniversary of the preaching of Dr. Pusey's condemned sermon on the holy eucharist. For background, history, and commentary see H. N. Bates and F. C. Eeles, Thoughts on

On the other hand, Dix derived "a great deal of valuable study and guidance" from the Continental Roman Catholic liturgical movement that had sought "to return behind the medieval 'clerical' distortion of the eucharist to the truer and deeper conception of the Church...because it has first recovered a more authentic notion of what is involved in the doctrine that the Church is the mystical Body of Christ."[90]

In the Roman Catholic Church, more than any other, the liturgical revival had strong leadership and the highest official support and direction. Roman Catholics produced the most extensive literature on the subject at all levels, from scholarly treatises to popular tracts. They organized by far the largest number of liturgical conferences and published the great majority of liturgical journals for clergy and laity. But because of its policy of non-cooperation with other Christian bodies, at least officially, the Roman Catholic Church largely excluded from its official activities in the renewal of corporate worship the participation of members of other churches until the 1960's.

However, the Benedictine monasteries were hospitable to visiting non-Roman Catholics who sought to study their aims and ideals at close range. The Protestant Friedrich Heiler wrote in the 1920's that "the Roman Church is exercising today a very strong attraction on the non-Catholic world. The German Benedictine monasteries, especially Beuron and Maria Laach, have become places of pilgrimage for non-Catholics, who find inspiration in the Catholic liturgy there practiced."[91]

----

the Shape of the Liturgy (London, 1946), and the most important reviews by Dugmore, Journal of Theological Studies, 47 (1946), 109-113, Jungmann, Zeitschrift für Kirchengeschichte und Theologie 70 (1948), 224-31, and Brou, Ephemerides Liturgicae, LX (1946), 176-8.

[90]Dix, Shape, pp. xvi, 20. For a summary treatment of the influence of the Continental liturgical movement on the English of this period see Horton Davies, Worship and Theology in England: The Ecumenical Century, 1900-1965 (Princeton, 1965), pp. 13-49.

[91]Heiler in Karl Adam, The Spirit of Catholicism (London, 1929), p. 8.

The liturgical movement could not have played its historic part outside of the Roman Communion and within it if it had not been in large measure the enterprise of Benedictine monasticism. It was the contribution of our third figure, Prosper Guéranger who was the first nineteenth churchman to employ the phrase "liturgical movement," above all to associate the Catholic revival and its renewal of worship with the restoration of Benedictine monasticism.

CHAPTER VIII

Dom Guéranger

Guéranger's earliest articles were published in an atmosphere of revolution and violent anti-clericalism. They preceded and followed the political events of July 1830 and the end of the Restoration settlement in France. Between January 1830, when his name first appeared in the Mennaisian Mémorial Catholique, and the publication of his first book, which opposed the Concordat of 1801, the following year, there was dramatic evidence that religion was declining to the point at which a new clerical emigration might be called for. In the winter of 1831 there were riots at St. Germain-l'Auxerrois, the royal church, which forced the closing of places of worship in the capital. The archepiscopal palace of Mgr. de Quélen near Notre-Dame was destroyed. The cathedral itself was invaded. In Lille, Nîmes, Dijon, and Angoulême seminaries and bishops' houses were sacked.[1] Guéranger was visiting his parents in Le Mans during the summer of the Revolution and there in the great square before the cathedral demonstrators gathered on the Feast of the Assumption to shout "Death to the priests." In September an ancient cross which had stood in the midst of the city for centuries was desecrated by a mob.[2]

----

[1]Details of anti-clerical riots and sacking of that period may be found in G. de Bertier de Sauvigny, "Mgr. de Quélen et les incidents de St. Germain-l'Auxerrois en février 1831," Revue d'histoire de l'église de France, XXXII (1946), 110-120; Louis Blanc, Histoire de dix ans (4th ed., Bruxelles, 1846), II, 283; P. Thureau-Dangin, Histoire de la monarchie de juillet (Paris, 1884-1906), I, 189.

[2]Auguste Sifflet, Les Évêques concordataires du Mans. Mgr. Carron (Le Mans, 1914), pp. 35-37; Dom Paul Delatte, Dom Guéranger, Abbé de Solesmes (Paris, 1909), I, 61.

The relative calm which had existed since 1815 among the three groups of social philosophers in France—the Catholic reactionaries de Maistre, Chateaubriand, de Bonald, and Lamennais; the bourgeois eclectic spiritualists following the lead of Victor Cousin; and the socialistic and scientific reformers Saint-Simon, Proudhon, Fourier, and Comte—was broken as the bonds which held religion and society disintegrated. The hostility of the period is reflected in the scolding given the Catholics in February, 1831, by Le Journal des Débats, the official organ of the regime of King Louis-Philippe: "You are not only to blame for your own madness: you are to blame for the madness of others."[3]

French philosophy was dominated in the 1830's by the question of the nature of the social bond. Philosophers had been preoccupied by the need for a solution to the problem of public disorder since the days of Rousseau and the Revolution. The state guarantees social unification, said Rousseau. The subordination of the individual to law makes society possible. Humanity is the organism, countered Comte and the socialists. Reason is the universal bond, lectured Cousin. The Catholic traditionalists insisted that religion is the requirement for solidity. Arguing within that framework, Guéranger suggested that attention be paid to the liturgy, for it is the medium through which Christian ideas can act on groups of men.

For the first time in centuries there was a definition of prayer as a social act. Guéranger's initial discussion of the liturgy and society appeared as "Considérations sur la liturgie catholique" in the Mémorial Catholique during the first months of 1830.[4] Here he maintains the necessity of some form of public cult for the existence of society. Catholic worship is best for this because the church is

---

[3]Philip Spencer, Politics of Belief in Nineteenth Century France (London, 1954), p. 21.

[4]Prosper Guéranger, "Considérations sur la liturgie catholique," Mémorial Catholique, 28 February 1830, pp. 49-57; 31 March 1830, pp. 79-90; 31 May, 1830, pp. 181-189; 31 July, 1830, pp. 241-256.

the most stable institution, perfectly grounded in the natural order of the universe. Beautiful and inspiring pageants create a sense of unity, and the Catholic mass is the most impressive form of popular ritual. The sacramental system, of which the liturgy forms the outer expression, binds individual to community while joining the human to God.

Contemporary interest in the social value of church services in France was so low that the study of the liturgy had been abandoned in ecclesiastical institutions. But to Guéranger exterior ceremonies and the celebration of the eucharist had been essential to Christianity during its first millennium. The liturgy was Christ praying in his mystical body, the voice of tradition, the outer expression of the faith, the external arm of Catholicism on which all else depended.

It was the decadence of the liturgy and the decaying piety of France which had resulted in the decline of the national church to Guéranger, and, filled with the audacity of a man of twenty-six, he told the French bishops that the liturgical traditions of the seventeenth and eighteeneth centuries, which they continued to maintain, were responsible for the rot of society. Liturgical practices dictated by local taste and the presence of the spirit of rationalism in books for worship created confusion and ruined the faith. Particularity and modernity had lessened the utility of worship. If Europe were to be revived, there must first be a restoration of the Catholic cult. The proper aesthetic model was not to be found in fashionable Paris proprietary chapels or at the royal court but in the golden age of the church, the patristic era. If the worship in France were guided by the ethos espoused by the Fathers then it would no longer be surrounded by an atmosphere of modern paganism. Antiquity rather than modernity would be valued, mystery rather than instruction. The liturgy would be pure, purged of heretical elements. The simple commonality of prayer would be stressed. Above all, the forms of the public cult would be universal, subject to the authority of the representative of the entire Christian community.

Guéranger introduced these points, which were an overt attack on the French post-revolutionary ecclesiastical status quo as contained in the Concordat of 1801 between the Vatican and Napoleon, in two articles which came out in the fall of 1830 in L'Avenir, "De la prière pour le roi," and in De l'élection et de la nomination des évêques, published in May, 1831. Here he broke with the classic treatment of church and state which had dominated French treatises on the subject since the Pragmatic Sanction of 1438.[5]

Public worship in 1830 was neither pure, simple, antique, nor unified. There was no church in France which followed Guéranger's patristic model. When T. W. Allies, a young English Puseyite, visited Paris during these years he was struck by the cultic deadness of the city and the lack of any liturgical comprehension. None of the lay people appeared to understand exactly what was happening at a high mass. The priest was silent. The people did not follow his action. Allies reported that many masses were said simultaneously during the chief hour of worship. The chanting in the churches was so poor that no words could be distinguished. The favorite composers for the Opéra delighted worshippers as well. Charles Gounod' Messe Solennelle St-Cécile, composed in the 1850's, is a reflection of contemporary French liturgical taste which could allow a musician to write for the church without altering his secular theatrical style. Gounod made the striking textural alteration of combining the words of the Agnus Dei with the modern sentimental devotional formula spoken by the individual before receiving communion, "Domine, non sum dignus."[6] Gounod's offertory is wholly instrumental, a "prière intime" indicating passive silent prayer rather than an action of offering by the people. At the

----

[5]Propser Guéranger, "Considérations sur la liturgie catholique," Mémorial Catholique, 28 February 1830, pp. 49-57; 31 March 1830, pp. 79-90; 31 May, 1830, pp. 181-189; 31 July, 1830, pp. 241-256.

[6]Compare the individualism of the "Domine, non sum dignus": "Lord, I am not worthy that you should enter under my roof: say but the word and my soul shall be healed" with the communal form of the Agnus Dei: "O Lamb of God, who takest away the sins of the world, have mercy upon us."

end of his mass, the composer of __Faust__ followed the common practice of inserting, as an equal of the ordinary texts, such as Kyrie, Gloria in excelsis, Credo, Sanctus, Agnus Dei, the Gallican prayer for the sovereign "Domine, salvum fac" which Guéranger had argued should be expunged from services. This was not only sung as a "Prayer of the Church," but with greater flourish as a "Prayer of the Army" and a "Prayer of the Nation."[7]

In the Church of St. Marguerite in Paris Allies noted that compline and vespers were said together, but nowhere else did he find the divine office used in public, for it had been reduced to the mechanical duty of a private devotion for the clergy.[8] At the Church of St. Jacques-du-Haut-Pas in the neighborhood of the Sorbonne, noted for an intelligent, Jansenist, and therefore more participatory tradition, the canonical offices were suppressed for the entire year except on the day of the patronal festival. In this church there were twelve chapels, and on Sunday eleven masses were said, many simultaneously; this practice destroyed the meaning of the eucharist as a gathering of the parish family. The cost of a seat in the nave for services was enough to exclude the poor, and there were no organizations to take care of their needs. The three pious congregations which did exist for lay persons within the parish engaged in no liturgical teaching but were organized around the cults of benediction, the Sacred Heart, and the rosary. To the women who joined these three groups, communion itself was a self-contained exercise which occurred not at the principal mass of the day but after one of the dawn masses. In fact, for many years at St. Jacques it was forbidden for lay people to receive the host at the point designated __communio__ within the mass.[9]

---

[7]"Lord, save our Emperor Napoleon, and mercifully hear us when we call upon thee."

[8]T. W. Allies, __Journal in France__ (London, 1849), pp. 22f., 121f., 248f.

[9]MS reports on the parish church of St. Jacques-du-Haut Pas, Archives of the Archbishop of Paris, Visite No. 24, I P 55. Parish Church S.J.H.-P., Paris, Archives Pastorale—Broadside, "Paroisse Saint-Jacques-du-Haut-Pas Fête Patronale," 6 May 1827; Parish Book,

The liturgical life at St. Jacques is a model of what was to be found in other Parisian churches, in the valley of the Sarthe where Guéranger grew up, in Le Mans where he went to school, and in the eastern dioceses of France. In the Church of Notre Dame du Pré in Le Mans, 1550 F represented the average yearly income from the rent of chairs during worship services in the early decades of the nineteenth century as compared to 6,000 F per annum during the last thirty years of the nineteenth century.[10] In the village of Mesnil-St-Loup in the eastern diocese of Troyes, during the entire century there was only one episcopal visitation, the occasion of the 62 confirmations of the century out of a population of 300. Only five of the 350 parishioners in the early part of the nineteenth century regularly received communion at Easter.[11]

If it had been possible to visit all of those churches on a single Sunday, there would not have been a similar set of readings used in any one place, and the texts for the Sunday would have had no logical unity. Almost all the buildings were in a dilapidated state as a result of the appropriations of the Revolution in 1791. The newer popular Paris churches: St. Geneviève, Saint-Philippe-du-Roule, la Madeleine, were modeled after pagan temples, or built as ornamental

---

Broadside, "Paroisse S.J.H.P. Processions du Saint Sacrament 1828"; Expense Accounts, 1842; Broadside "Tarif des Chaises dans la Paroisse S.J.H.-P. Extrait de l'Arrêté du Conseil de Fabrique en date du 22 July 1847." Low masses cost 5 centimes, solemn vespers and benediction 10 centimes, first class feasts 10 centimes, and second class feasts five centimes. Broadside collection, parish registers of baptisms, marriages, and burials beginning in 1800. On the Jansenist tradition of lay participation see F. Ellen Weaver, "Scripture and Liturgy for the Laity: The Jansenist Case for Translation," Worship, 59, No. 6 (November 1985), 510-521.

[10]Parish Church Notre Dame du Pré, Le Mans, France, Parochial Archives, Book of Expenses and Receipts.

[11]Parish Church Notre Dame, Mesnil-Saint-Loup, France, Parochial Archives, MS Historique de la paroisse 1668-1789, manuscrit de la main du Père Emmanuel; Deliberations, Reports, and Expenses of the Council of the Fabric. Registers of baptisms, marriages, and burials of the parish.

361

baubles to honor army or king as Les Invalides had been. These buildings were sacred theatres, great halls of marble and gold, often including galleries and boxes. They expressed the idea that the liturgy was holy drama to be performed by ecclesiastical actors on a stage raised and separated from the passive audience below.

The conception of the liturgy as edifying spectacle reached a climax of development in the royal chapel at Versailles, a sacred drawing room in its architectural form, complete with carpets for the worshippers, a morning counterpart of the opera next door. A court mass was similar to a soirée, often including a divertissement by Lully, and the congregation sometimes faced the orchestra and not the altar. French piety greeted Christ as a divine king within the monstrance or visited him as the suffering prisoner of the tabernacle. The mass-liturgy was understood as a collection of rubrics, compulsory ceremonial for proper reception of a heavenly monarch. The liturgical text was smothered under the weight of profane polyphony; and fashionable masses, surrounded with lights, jewels, singers, pageantry, were "church concerts with liturgical accompaniment."[12]

After the Revolution of 1789, French governments, like their German neighbors, favored a policy of suppressing the liturgical expressions of the people. In the Napoleonic Organic Articles of 9 April 1802, Article 44 severely restricted the number of public solemn processions that were allowed. The only feasts which could be celebrated by the populace on days other than Sunday were Christmas, Ascension Day, and All Saints. Christians were forbidden to leave work and attend any weekday celebrations. The commemoration of all Apostles was restricted to the Sunday nearest the date of the Feast of Peter and Paul. Martyrs could only be remembered on St. Stephen's Day. The extent of the decline of ancient liturgical traditions and the rationalization of worship is indicated by comparing the rite at

---

[12]Waldemar Trapp, Vorgeschichte und Ursprung der liturgischen Bewegung (Regensburg, 1940), p. 219; Louis Bouyer, Life and Liturgy (London, 1962), p. 2; J. A. Jungmann, The Mass of the Roman Rite (New York, 1951), I, 111-113.

Napoleon's coronation in the cathedral of Paris to the ancien régime service at Reims. Profane hands crowned the emperor's head, and there was no communion of the lay persons present. The newest Paris liturgy was used.

France was in the midst of liturgical anarchy when "Considérations sur la liturgie catholique" appeared. The Concordat of 1801 between France and the Vatican had decreed that there be 42 new sees in France, but the papal bull Paternae caritatis reduced that number to 30 in 1822. By 1830 there were many dioceses which were a combination of parishes with varying traditions and no historical unity or continuity of practice.[13] Geographical manipulation by government and church authorities produced a complete state of confusion in worship. In the diocese of Périgueux the local rites as well as three other liturgical traditions were in use. In Nevers, 183 parishes used the ritual and chant of Paris of the eighteenth century, 45 that of Auxerre, 30 the books of Nevers, 18 those of Autun—all of the seventeenth century, and 6 the Tridentine Roman rite of the sixteenth century. The new see of Avignon was created from the suppressed bishoprics of Orange, Carpentras, Apt, Vaison, Cavaillon. The parishes and cathedral of the episcopal city used the medieval Roman-Gallican liturgy of Apt, Orange, and the eighteen century neo-Gallican Paris liturgy, imported immediately before the Revolution of 1789. In 1801, parishes belonging to the diocese of Langres were transferred to Dijon, Troyes, Besançon, and Sens, while Langres was presented churches formerly belonging to Troyes, Châlons, Toul, and Besançon, so that there were five different liturgical traditions. For many years, the cathedral choir in Langres chanted modern neo-Gallican Paris chapters and responses from the Roman liturgy, and sang the hymns of Paris and the antiphons of Rome.

---

[13]These are dioceses which were made up of parishes from many liturgical and musical traditions: Aire, Albi, Auch, Belly, Beauvais, Blois, Chartres, Châlons-sur-Marne, Fréjus, Gap, Langres, Luçon, Marseille, Montauban, Moulins, Nevers, Nîmes, Pamiers, Périgueux, Perpignan, Le Puy, Rodez, Reims, Saint-Claude, Saint-Dié, Sens, Tarbes, Tulle, Verdun, Viviers. On worship and the secular history of this period see R. W. Franklin, "Guéranger and Pastoral Liturgy: A Nineteenth Century Context," Worship, 50, No. 2 (March 1976), 146-162.

In 1830 there were only twelve dioceses in all of France which still maintained the Roman liturgy of 1570.[14] Thirty-four used neo-Gallican Paris rites.[15] Three had those of Toulouse.[16] Two each worshipped from the neo-Gallican books of Besançon, Clermont, Le Mans, and Poitiers. The dioceses of Sens, Rouen, Bourges, Auch, Amiens, Chartres, Bayeux, Beauvais, Orléans, Limoges, Troyes, Toulouse, Soissons, Nantes, Châlons-sur-Marne, Meaux, Nîmes, Versailles, Valence, and Laon practiced local neo-Gallican forms of worship. In 57 French dioceses there were twenty different liturgies, some medieval, some sixteenth century, some seventeenth century, and some eighteenth century, compared to the rest of the 700 dioceses of the entire Roman Church, of which 760 used the Roman rite,and the 80 dioceses of the Eastern Churches, where only seven different rites were to be found.[17] That there was not a geographical unity of worship is shown by the following chart which indicates that not even the dioceses of one ecclesiastical province shared a common liturgy:

----

[14]These dioceses were Aix, Ajaccio, Avignon, Bordeaux, Cambrai, Saint-Fleur, Marseille, Montpellier, Perpignan, Quimper, Rhodez, Strasbourg. See Instructio Pastoralis et Decretum Versaliensis Episcopi (Versailles, 1864). For background and history which explains this complex situation see F. Ellen Weaver, The Evolution of the Reform of Port-Royal (Paris, 1978); Cuthbert Johnson, Prosper Guéranger: A Liturgical Theologian (Rome, 1984), pp. 147-189; and R. W. Franklin, "Guéranger and Variety in Unity," Worship, 51, No. 5 (September 1977), 378-399.

[15]Agen, Aire, Albi, Angers, Angoulême, Arras, Blois, Coutances, Digne, Dijon, Evreux, Gap, Luçon, Meaux, Mende, Metz, Nevers, Paris, Périgueux, Rennes, La Rochelle, Saint-Brieuc, Siez, Tarbes, Tours, Tulle, Vannes, Verdun. More analysis of neo-Gallican liturgies may be found in John Sullivan, "Reports to Rome About the Paris Breviary of 1736," Manuscripta, 22 (1978), 149-157; Guy Oury, "Contribution à l'étude des liturgies néogallicanes du XVIIIe siècle: les messes de Saint Martin," Études Grégoriennes, 4 (1963), 165-183.

[16]Montauban, Nancy, Toulouse.

[17]Jean-François Bergier, Études liturgiques. Histoire de la controverse et da la réforme liturgique en France aux dix-neuvième siècle (Besançon, 1861), pp. 412-413.

Prov.	No. of Dioc.	No. of Liturgies
Paris	6	4
Aix	7	2
Auch	4	3
Avignon	5	3
Besançon	7	4
Bordeaux	7	3
Bourges	6	5
Cambrai	2	2
Lyon	6	3
Reims	5	6
Rouen	5	3
Sens	4	4
Tours	8	4

All of this meant that French Catholics used a wide variety of texts at worship, some of recent composition, did not follow a uniform liturgical calendar or one prescribed sequence of ceremonies, nor did clergy wear similar vestments throughout the country or hang a uniform scheme of liturgical colors in the churches.

The confusion was complicated because the sees often did not sing music which matched their liturgies. The following bishoprics used the chants of Dijon: Langres, Troyes, Bourges, Evreux, Périgueux, Saint-Fleur, Rodez, Strasbourg, Tarbes, Perpignan, Angoulême, Bordeaux, la Rochelle. At Digne, Arles, Marseilles, Fréjus, Montpellier, Carcassonne, Nîmes, Metz, Gap, Ajaccio, Embrun, Auch, Aire, Avignon, Viviers, Seez, Pamiers, Nice, and Chambéry the predominant music was from Digne. The editions of Rennes were used at Valence, in almost all of the churches of the province of Bordeaux, at Versailles, Autun, Tours, Saint-Brieuc and Rennes, those of Malines at Cahors, Verdun, Le Puy, Châlon-sur-Seine, Meaux, Laval and Moutier. The chant of Reims was used in the churches of that province, at Cambrai, Sens, Alby, Arras, Soissons, Saint-Dié, Saint-Claude, Bourges, Limoges, Moulins, Blois, Beauvais, Le Mans, Bayonne, and Saint-Denis. At Amiens, Rouen, and Toulouse local music was sung.[18]

It was observation of this complex and confusing disarray which awakened in Prosper Guéranger the idea that the liturgy was an essential element of Christianity and that its decadence had led to the disruption of the Christian community in France. To Guéranger it was not only an antiquarian issue when processions were stopped and feasts reduced by the government, when ancient readings were excluded from worship, for the liturgy expressed the essence of the church to the people: it molded the habits of the daily life and the thinking of vast illiterate masses.

The liturgical environment in the diocese of Le Mans coupled with the religious and social confusion in his own home town of Sablé also shaped Guéranger's outlook. The members of the Guéranger family were outsiders in a town dominated by enlightened bourgeois Catholics. Julien Pierre Guéranger moved his family to the small town of Sablé, an ancient commercial center on the Sarthe in western France, 50 kilometers from Le Mans, in 1798 when he was instituted in his functions as a teacher by the Directory. If the manner of his appointment were not enough to make him unpopular with the politically conservative natives, he soon became known for his vocal "hatred of the royalty."[19] Even though a politically radical man, Julien Guéranger was an ardent Roman Catholic. He loved church ceremonies and liturgical functions and all of his life he had the habit of reciting the breviary offices daily to himself. He was destined by his father, a tinmaker in Le Mans, to be a priest, but the Revolution closed all the seminaries in the region in 1791. He moved to the small village of Sainte-Suzanne and was married according to the clandestine Roman Catholic rite. Municipal documents in Sablé show that the Guéranger family were not faithful to the public Constitutional cult but attended secret Roman Catholic liturgies, often

---

[18]Jules Bonhomme, Principes d'un véritable restauration du chant Grégorien et examen de quelques éditions modernes (Paris, 1857), pp. 268-269.

[19]Antoine de Mazis, MS La Vocation de Dom Guéranger, Archives, Abbey of Solesmes, Solesmes, France, p. 3.

those conducted by Yves-Charles François de la Primaudière, the first Concordat curé of the suburban village of Juigné, who had worked as a Roman Catholic priest at night in the area since 1795. Many of the other families who joined in those services of worship, the Vérité, the Gazeau, and the Marçais, would be the earliest benefactors of Solesmes.[20] Because of his strong religious views Julien Guéranger had serious difficulties with the liberal and anti-clerical educational officials of the area after he became principal of the secondary school. This continued tension and unpopularity with all segments of the town led to his acceptance of a post at Le Mans in 1821.[21]

This is a contemporary description of the environment which shaped the young Guéranger:

> The inhabitants of the countryside are active, sober, work hard, and are economical—it is a Christian town where religion functions. Contact with the city has not altered the customs....The people of the town are industrious and work in commerce...they have an independent and gay character. The middle class is religious. The poor class is hardly religious at all. The comfortable and rich class leaves much to be desired on this subject with the exception of some generally pious women. Many of the houses are charitable, but insufficiently so. There is considerable commerce in grain, anthracite, marble.[22]

The middle-class, small manufacturing character of the parishes of the southern Sarthe was established even before the Revolution when 46% of the land had been owned by the bourgeoisie.[23] In the eighteenth century the high society of Sablé had been the notaries, lawyers, and owners of small factories whose rationalistic character is witnessed by

---

[20]De Mazis, loc. cit., p. 4.

[21]P. Delaunay, Galerie des naturalistes sarthois. Edouard Guéranger (Laval, 1937), passim; L. Callendini, "Le Collège de Sablé," Journal de Sablé, (Sablé, France), 5, 12 (April 1931); L. Callendini, "Le vieux collège," Journal de Sablé (Sablé, France) (16 April 1933).

[22]Parish Archives, Church of Notre Dame, Sablé, France, MS Recherche historique sur Sablé.

[23]Thérèse Greffier, Une petite ville du Maine aux XIXe siècle (Sablé, 1960), introduction.

the opening in 1781 of a non-ecclesiastical charitable bureau in the style of other enlightened circles in the valley of the Sarthe and, in 1789, of a lodge of Masons, whose secretary was a Benedictine from Solesmes, Pierre Morel. By the time of the Revolution six secular houses of instruction had been founded for the population. Much of the prosperity of the eighteenth century had been based on the manufacture of gloves, which on average employed as many as 125 workers. In 1813 there were as many as 80 male and 300 female glovemakers.[24] A fledgling textile industry reached a peak in 1813 with 113 workers employed and 4,000 kilograms of woolen cloth finished in a year. But it was the discovery of anthracite and marble between Sablé and the village of Solesmes in 1809 which totally transformed the character of the region. In 1819 the entrepreneur Landeau began to mine the newly-discovered minerals with hydraulic equipment and "The Society for the Exploitation of the Sarthe and Mayenne" was formed. By 1834, 165 men were working regularly in the mines and in 1849 638, about one-fourth for Landeau. The area was rapidly being transformed into a local industrial center and the population which was 2,500 in 1800 was already 2,612 in 1806, 3,450 in 1822, 3,999 in 1833.[25]

The Guérangers were a part of this flood of new people drifting into the old town. And in his Notes autobiographiques, which he wrote in 1860-1864 for his monks, Dom Guéranger noted his abhorrence of the extremely mixed religious situation in Sablé during this period of war and incipient economic expansion. The Constitutional Clergy, the Petite Eglise—the small group of clergy and ten bishops who refused to accept the 1801 Concordat—and the Roman Catholics were all vying for the attention of the faithful. Guéranger recalls a lack of sympathy in himself for even the most conservative parish priests of the town, for they were judged too "Chouan," too fanatically royalist in their spiritual direction. There is certainly evidence of the truth of what

---

[24]L. Callendini, "Fabrication à Sablé," Journal de Sablé (Sablé, France) (12 February 1933).

[25]Greffier, op. cit., pp. 43, 60.

he said. It appears that he interpreted the church in his town to be representative of all of France and in future discussions of the ecclesiastical ancien régime it was pictured as dominated by the Gallican sentiments of church and king, but king more than church.

The religious history of Sablé is complicated even more because, though liberal elements had been dominant before the Revolution, after March 1793 the area was affected by the great counter-revolutionary movement of western France, the Vendée, which though filled with political elements, such as hatred of conscription, was also a revolt against the religious settlement of the Revolution. In November 1789 all church property in the nation had been seized and the Civil Constitution of the clergy in the summer of 1790 had reduced the church to a state agency and priests to civil servants. The legal oath administered to all priests in January 1791 had created two sets of clergy, constitutional and refractory. The latter were Roman Catholic. A law of August 1792 decreed deportation for refractory priests who refused the oath of submission to the Civil Constitution. The refractories began to be hunted down by revolutionary officials. North of the Loire the Vendée assumed the form of Chouannerie; guerilla bands harassed Republicans and protected the hide-outs of Roman Catholic priests. In the area of Sablé the refractionaries hid in the abandoned priory of Solesmes and during the night administered the sacraments.

In Sablé, the Revolution had been outwardly accepted but not its ecclesiastical reforms. General disenchantment was evident in December 1796 when only 31 citizens voted in the municipal elections.[26] Since the eleventh century, Sablé had been divided into two parishes, Notre-Dame which in the revolutionary period served 1,200 communicants and was staffed by four vicars and a curé, and St. Martin which had one vicar, one curé, and 400 souls. The last ancien régime curé of Notre-Dame, Hanuche, was forced to resign in November 1790 and a Constitutional curé appointed. The parish of St. Martin was abolished

----

[26]Françoise Aveline, MS Sablé-sur-Sarthe durant la période revolutionnaire, at Hôtel de Ville, Sablé, France.

in 1793. The commune changed it into the Club of the Friends of Liberty and Equality. Notre-Dame always remained a church but it was converted into a temple of reason, with dances, chants, and allegorical performance. Reports were continually related to the administrators of the district that the inhabitants did not attend the masses of the Constitutional priests. There was an attempted assassination of one of the government curés at Solesmes; and in 1799 Chollières, the Constitutional priest of Sablé, was killed by a Chouan. When Napoleon finally pacified the area, more than 529 guerillas submitted to the governmental authority, but brigandage continued until 1835. Even during the First Empire the sympathies of Sablé continued to be strongly Royalist and Bourbon.

The first priest after the Napoleonic Concordat, vicar from 1803 and curé from 1816 to 1830, gave very strong Chouan overtones to the religious character of Notre-Dame in Sablé. He was Pierre-Ambroise Gougeon de Lucé, born at Solesmes in 1771. When he was forced to leave his seminary at the Revolution, he joined the Republican Army, but on hearing that his father had been guillotined at Chateau-Gonthier in the year II he joined the Chouan dragoons of de Bourmont in the region of Sablé and rose to the rank of lieutenant. In 1803 he reappeared as a priest. But his conception of the liturgy was witnessed at the major feasts when there was a procession in the church. He would mount the steps of the altar at the head of the body of clergy and command: Forward march![27]

De Luce attempted to keep alive the spirit of religious revival which accompanied Chouan clandestine Catholicism and to channel the missionary efforts of the diocese of Le Mans into his own parish. There was an increase in participation in the religious life of the parish church once the Revolution had ended. From 1790 to 1799 baptisms averaged ten per year, funerals nine, and marriages celebrated in church, two. In 1800 baptisms numbered 43 and in 1820 reached a

----

[27]de Mazis, loc. cit., p. 4, note 16; MS Recherche historique sur Sablé.

peak of 80.   There were 20 marriages in 1800, 30 in 1815, and 36 in 1830.[28]

This cycle of religious decline, depression, and then revival was repeated in the villages surrounding Sablé.   At the time of the Revolution of 1789 the Benedictine priory at Solesmes, which had been founded by Geoffrey of Sablé in 1010 and given the newly-built parish church in 1277, contained seven religious.   The monks were dispersed in March 1791 and the prior Dom de Sageon was thrown into prison at Le Mans.   Henri le Noir de Chantelou of Le Mans acquired the priory and its property for 146,000 F and saved the buildings from the destruction which befell the parish church when Solesmes was invaded by Republicans in 1794.   The curé of Solesmes, the abbé Lefeuvre, adhered to the papal decree condemning the Constitutional Church and was expelled.   The parishioners of the town demonstrated their conservative loyalty by hiding their most famous relic, one of the thorns from Christ's crown, and the parish plate during the entire Revolutionary period.   They refused the sacraments of the parish church under Constitutional rule and were shepherded by abbé Champroux, the former vicar of Juigné, abbé Duqué, formerly of St. Martin at Sablé, and abbé Glatier of Precigné, who hid in the abandoned priory and came out at night.   The extent to which the townspeople avoided the Constitutional sacraments is shown by the flood of participation which began when the Roman priests were restored in 1797.   In that year, there were 43 church marriages and 28 baptisms in a population of only 551.   Baptisms fluctuated between 10 and 20 a year until 1833, whereas during the years of the church of the Constitution there had never been more than four a year.[29]

The same pattern was repeated in many of the churches along the valley of the Sarthe.   At Neuvillalais the church was sold to the merchant Jean-Augustin Freulon and between 1794 and 1806 only 26

---

[28]Parish Archives, Sablé, Registers of Baptisms, Marriages, and Funerals.

[29]Archives, Parish Church of Solesmes, France, Registers of Baptisms, Marriages, and Funerals, Parish Chronicle; Antoine de Mazis, Solesmes sans les Moines (Sablé, 1947).

baptisms were recorded in the town.[30] At Precigné the place of worship was relinquished to bourgeois entrepreneurs. In Brains church 108 infants were baptized in the fifteen years after 1790 in a population of approximately 1,000.[31] At Pincé and Souvigné-sur-Sarthe the churches were not put on the market but the populace avoided maintaining them and, in the first years of the century, they were in an almost unusable dilapidated state.[32]

One religious practice did not die out in the region. That was the strong local devotion to the eucharist. As early as 1685 the Corpus Christi procession began to be celebrated as a great event at Sablé. There was a confraternity of the Holy Sacrament at Notre-Dame in Sablé in 1700. In 1701 a special chapel was raised in Juigné to honor the eucharist. Another sacramental confraternity was begun in 1732 at St. Martin's. At the end of the century Precigné followed the example of Sablé and a similar organization was begun.

As well as the native sacramentalism, Guéranger noted the strong impression made on him by the capture of the pope by Napoleon's troops.[33] In 1799 there was not much popular reaction when Pius VI was taken from Rome to Valence by forces of the Revolution. However, the abduction of Pius VII to Savona in 1808 created a wave of hostile reaction all over Europe and was responsible for contributing a new sense of spiritual authority to the Holy See. It was during the years that Guéranger was growing up at Sablé that the picture of the saintly pope resisting the intrigues of Napoleon was most popular in the region.

At the Lycée David at Angers, to which he was sent by his father in 1818, this regard for the Papacy as the one center of religious

---

[30]Parish Archive, Church of Neuvillalais, France, Registers of Baptisms.

[31]Parish Archive, Church of Brains, France, Registers of Baptisms.

[32]L. Callendini, "Les Églises," Journal de Sablé (Sablé, France) (17 September 1933).

[33]Prosper Guéranger, MS Notes autobiographiques, Archives, Abbey of Solesmes, France, p. 6. Long extracts from this work appear in de Mazis, loc. cit., and will hereafter be referred to as N.A.

authority was cultivated along with the development of a habit of
looking to the past for the solution to the religious problems of the
present. At Angers Guéranger's eucharistic piety was an oddity, and he
was called "the monk" because he was the only student in the first
division who received holy communion at the four great feasts of the
church year.[34]

He came under the influence of the chaplain of the lycée, Jacques
Pasquier. This priest opened him to the new world of the patristic
church by giving him Fleury's l'Histoire ecclésiastique. Guéranger
devoured the 36 volumes of the great Gallican church historian. He
remembered later, "The reading of the Fathers had awakened in me,
during my childhood, the desire to get to know the monuments of the
ancient church....I read the apostolic fathers, St. Justin,
Athenagoras, Tatian, St. Theophilus of Antioch, Hermias...."[35] Then to
balance this Gallican introduction to church history Pasquier gave him
Chateaubriand's Martyrs and more importantly his Génie du Christianisme
in 1819. The Génie was the first of the series of books which turned
Guéranger against the French Catholic apologetic of the seventeenth and
eighteenth centuries. In 1797, in his Essai sur les révolutions,
François-Réné, Vicomte de Chateaubriand had argued that the Revolution
and the religious systems of the eighteenth century were hopelessly
inadequate in making men better. In 1802, in the Génie he continued
his argument by saying that the church was the only institution which
could improve society because it alone was aesthetically perfect. He
did not emphasize the literal truth of Christian theology, that it was
accompanied by prophecies and miracles, as eighteenth-century
theologians would have, rather he stressed the power and value of its
artistry, the certitude embodied in its sublime loveliness. The
artistic beauties of Christianity were the best means for representing

---

[34]de Mazis, loc. cit., pp. 5-6; Delatte, op. cit., pp. 15-20; Le
Monde (Paris, France, 15 (February 1875); M. Antier, Le Lycée David
d'Angers (Angers, 1947), pp. 39-48.

[35]N. A., p. 26.

in symbolic fashion the truths of the universe. The mass was the incomparable solace for souls in a confused age.

Guéranger then read de Bonald's Legislation primitive, a traditionalist treatment of society, and the Romantic Méditations of Lamartine the next year. In 1821 Pasquier gave him de Maistre's du Pape and this work made a profound impression. It not only left him a confirmed Ultramontane, one who defends the power of the pope, but it was an introduction to the philosophy of Lamennais. Joseph de Maistre hated the eighteenth century. He was overwhelmed by the Revolution and could not explain it on the basis of rationalistic principles, so he turned to the experience of the human race, not to the individual reason, as the guide to knowledge. The facts of history indicated the necessity of uniting men into organic wholes, into the mystical unity of nations, and above all into the eternal solidarity of the Catholic church. Society is founded on religion. Faith unites where reason divides, and in the papacy is found the supreme concentration of unity and faith. Therefore, for there to be any sovereignty there first must be a spiritual authority which comes from above and limits secular governments. Only the pope is the legitimate agent of sovereignty, and any governmental decrees, the Articles of 1682, for example, which limit his authority in internal ecclesiastical affairs are illogical and lead to the politics of anarchy and revolution. "This work," Guéranger later recalled, "opened to me a picture of the Middle Ages and the role of the papacy of that era, and I began to distrust Fleury, but there were a thousand things which I did not understand and I was too far from sound ideas on the constitution of the Church....I felt myself to be dominated, but the synthesis was lacking."[36]

The synthesis, as Pasquier had hoped, was found in the new Mennaisian apologetic which was sweeping the young clergy of western France. Lamennais united two currents of French thought, distrust of individual reason and reliance upon the traditions of humankind for the foundation of knowledge, and loyalty to the Papacy as the center around

----

[36]N.A., p. 12.

which a religious renaissance of Europe could occur. The pope became the organ of the sens commun, the voice of the tradition of the people. In Lamennais' system there was at once an emphasis on the importance of the common people and the Holy See. Deeply troubled by the violence of the Revolution of 1789, the Breton priest published a series of Réflexions on that event, in which he attacked the ineffectiveness of the intellectual attitudes of the eighteenth century and called for a Catholic revival as the only means for a European regeneration. The Essair sur l'indifférence en matière de religion, which appeared in 1817, 1820, and 1823, pointed to individualism as the source of disorder. In the Essai men and women are pictured not as isolated entities left to discover truths on their own but as social beings who learn through traditions received on authority. Religion is the highest knowledge revealed in this manner, the ground of society and the cohesive social force.

It was the sens commun, an idea capable of overturning the Cartesian egoism of the past, which attracted Guéranger to Lamennais. On the other hand it was the strength of Lamennais' attack on the sort of Christians who had made him uncomfortable as a youth by their identification of religion with one kind of politics also drew him to the Breton priest:

> Gallicanism received the most terrible blows and succumbed after two centuries of power. Lamennais had on his side the most studious faction of the young clergy who struggled at the side of such an athlete. Du Pape of Joseph de Maistre was too much above the clerical level of those days. What was needed was a brave, eloquent, passionate priest to translate the Roman idea [into practice]. And this priest had been found.[37]

When Guéranger went to the major seminary in Le Mans in 1822 he could write, "I declare myself bluntly to be a Mennaisian."[38] This

---

[37]N.A., p. 28. It should be noted here that most of the nineteenth-century commentaries on Guéranger's life and the works of the Benedictines, particularly the biography by Dom Delatte, as well, attempted to conceal the strong influence Lamennais had on Guéranger for reasons which will be obvious from what is related below.

[38]de Mazis, loc. cit., p. 6.

meant that rather than accept the Gallican theology taught out of <u>Les Institutions philosophiques</u> of the seminary superior Mgr. Bouvier or the compendia compiled by the Cartesian seminarists of St. Sulpice, Guéranger spent those years reading the Bible, for the scriptures were taught only as a minor accessory course, and the Fathers in the 27-volume <u>Maxima Bibliotheca Veterum Patrum</u>. This was done in his free time because there was no ecclesiastical history, no liturgical science, no canon law, and no pastoral theology taught in the seminary.[39]

It was the Ultramontane professors of the school Heurtebize and Lottin, implacable enemies of the old-fashioned Gallican-rationalist members of the faculty Bouvier and Hamon, who urged Guéranger to look in the earliest centuries of the church for the solution to the ecclesiastical problems of the present. In observing the conflicts between Gallicans and Ultramontanes in the major seminary at Le Mans, Guéranger learned that historical research could be a powerful weapon in theological struggles. He spent a free year of research in 1825 reading Irenaeus and Clement of Alexandria. "These editions of the Fathers of the Church enraptured me. Never had I been so touched as by them...."[40]

During July 1826, he was made subdeacon. In the days before the Revolution when the church had been rich it was possible to give a man an easy benefice while he prepared for ordination to the priesthood. Guéranger was forced to find a way to support himself, and so he became master of ceremonies in the cathedral of Le Mans and secretary to the bishop of the diocese Claude-Madeleine de la Myre-Mory. Work in these posts had the double effect of exposing him to the dechristianization of France and introducing him to Roman liturgical forms. He was

---

[39]Louis Callendini, "Les études ecclésiastiques au diocèse du Mans," <u>La Province du Maine</u>, XIV (July 1906), 209ff., 259ff., 296ff., 312ff. Bouvier was a thoroughgoing Gallican and expressed this conception of Christianity in other treatises as well, on Christian contracts, justice, and marriage.

[40]N.A., p. 20.

initiated into the world of the Faubourg St. Germain, to a different, aristocratic remnant of the ancien régime lingering in the great salons of the left bank where a priest could be conservative, royalist, but at the same time fashionably Ultramontane.

Myre-Mory (1755-1829) was a nobleman bishop who had ruled over the see of Carcassonne in the days before 1789 when only five bishops in all of France were not of aristocratic birth. (In 1889 only four nobles held the episcopate in the ninety sees of France.) He had been a friend of Talleyrand, member of the Assembly of the Clergy, and during the Revolution was an émigré to Piedmont, Rome, Salzburg, and Moravia. During his political exile he became acquainted with Roman liturgical forms and began to use the Roman breviary for his private devotion. During the Restoration his family became deeply involved with the ultra-royalist secret society the Chevaliers de la Foi. In 1800 he was appointed canon of Paris and then, because of connections with this clandestine circle, he was named Bishop of Troyes and, in December 1819, Bishop of Le Mans by Louis XVIII.

In 1819 the diocese of Le Mans was recovering from the devastation of the Revolution. If the southwestern part of the see had been conservative and loyal to religious tradition during the Revolution, that could not be said of the city of Le Mans and the eastern sector of the region. In August 1792 and September 1793 there had been public clamor for the enforcement of laws against wearing religious costumes in public and the appearance of ecclesiastics on the street.[41] At the Restoration a majority of the clergy petitioned the first Concordat Bishop, Mgr. de Pidoll, for the removal of all feasts of the Virgin to Sunday. They were against the revival of any of the other Christian celebrations suppressed at the Revolution, except Easter Monday and Circumcision. The churches of the area were deserted during most

---

[41]R. Deschamps La Rivière, "Antoine Maguin et le clergé constitutionnel manceau, 1791-1794," La Province du Maine, XVII (June 1909), 205ff.

religious observances.[42] Piodoll attempted to arrest this decline in
interest in worship and unite his divided diocese by starting a
campaign in 1803 for the rebuilding of churches and in 1804 by creating
local committees in each parish to restore the fabric of the church
structures and the religious life of the villages. He attempted a
liturgical revival in August 1814 and urged the celebration in church
with ancient solemnity of the old feasts of the Circumcision, the
Purification, the Annunciation, the Conception and Nativity of the
Virgin, St. Stephen, St. John the Baptist and the solemn procession for
the Assumption. But he was hampered, by his great regard for Gallican
theory, from introducing any forms of worship not sanctioned by the
government. After he was elected bishop he urged the singing of the
"Domine salvam fac" in the mass, in 1806 the Napoleonic usages were
enforced and in 1815 a Feast of St. Louis was begun, with prayers for
the dead king, Te Deums for his brother the living one, and novenas for
the royal family.[43]

Myre-Mory, influenced by his émigré experience, continued the
reform in the direction of Rome. In 1821 he introduced the Roman
breviary and missal into the convent of the Dames du Sacré-Coeur which
had been opened by his fanatically religious niece Mlle. de Cassini.
By 1823 he was restoring the ancient cathedral of St. Julien.
Myre-Mory required that parts of the cathedral service be sung in
Gregorian chant.[44] In November 1827 Guéranger conducted a service for
the community of the Dames du Sacré-Coeur and for the first time used
the Roman liturgy promulgated in 1570. There the ambitious and
unsettled young man of twenty-two seems to have found the perfect

---

[42]J.-B. Bouvier, Lettre circulaire de Mgr. l'Évêque du Mans au
clergé de son diocese touchant la célébration des fêtes supprimées (Le
Mans, 1851), p. 7.

[43]Auguste Sifflet, Les Evêque concordataires du Mans. Mgr. de
Pidoll, 1802-1819 (Le Mans, 1914), passim.

[44]Auguste Sifflet, Les Evêques concordataires du Mans. Mgr. de la
Myre-Mory, 1820-1829 (Le Mans, 1915), passim; Auguste Sifflet, Le
Chapitre du Mans depuis le Concordat (Le Mans, 1912), passim.

expression of the Christianity he had been searching for in the dusty
folios of the library of the seminary and in the works of the
Mennaisians. The Tridentine Roman liturgy avoided the cult of the
individual and the state which was apparent in the nineteenth century
worship Guéranger saw around him in Sablé and the churches of Le Mans.
He felt that he had discovered the pure source of Catholicism. He
wrote of this conversion:

> In order not to detract from the usage [of the Roman liturgy]
> I conformed to the habits of the chaplain. Despite my little
> penchant for the Roman liturgy which before then I hadn't
> studied seriously, I soon felt myself penetrated by the
> grandeur and the majesty of the style used in this missal.
> The use of the scriptures, so majestic, so full of authority,
> the air of antiquity which emanated from this book, all this
> made me understand that I had discovered in this missal the
> ecclesiastical antiquity for which I already had such great
> passion yet here it was, still alive. The tone of the modern
> [neo-Gallican] missals seemed to me after this to be
> deprived of authority and unction, suffering from being the
> work of one century and one country and also of being a
> personal work....The thought of adopting the Roman Breviary,
> ...could not be late in being nourished in my spirit. I
> reached the point where I did not want to celebrate the mass
> in any other place but at Sacré-Coeur because I did not find
> elsewhere this dear missal which spoke like the Fathers,
> while the other [the rite of Le Mans] spoke like any Johnny
> come lately (le premier venu).[45]

On the Feast of St. Julien in 1828 Guéranger asked and received
permission to begin to use the Tridentine Roman breviary and missal,
and he remembered that "the recitation of these prayers through the day
joined to the daily celebration of the mass in the Roman missal made me
penetrate more each day into intimate depths of the Church."[46]

Myre-Mory lived in the style to which a bishop of the ancien
régime had been accustomed. He enjoyed the service of many servants,
the pleasures of a large table, the delights of the salon, and the
habits of the great lord. In the winter of 1828 he began to feel ill
and decided that a long absence from the cares of his provincial

---

[45]Delatte, op. cit., p. 32.

[46]N.A., pp. 50-51.

diocese was the only cure. He took a leisurely trip with Guéranger, and they visited the country houses of rich relatives, the palaces of brother bishops and finally ended up in Paris living in apartments in the Missions Etrangéres on the rue de Bac amid the reactionary mansions of St. Germain. In the best tradition of the Gallican bishops they stayed away from home for a year and a half, until the summer of 1829 when Myre-Mory fell seriously ill and passed away.

Those trips opened a new world to Guéranger. They went into sections of France which had not been Christian since the Revolution. One day they stopped at the village of Marolles-en-Brie on the edge of the diocese of Paris which had been without a priest since 1789. They were so shocked by the degraded state of the population and the open immorality in the streets, that Cardinal Donet recalled over fifty years later the excited conversation of the young Sarthian priest at the end of that day. Guéranger was already calling for new methods to halt the progressive paganization of his country.[47] When he was introduced to the Archbishop of Paris, Mgr. de Quélen, he talked of the non-Christian France which he had witnessed and he carried the message to the Catholic drawing rooms of the capital.

In February 1829 Guéranger and his bishop took up residence at the Missions Éstrangères which was at the time the center of the spiritual life of the royalist and émigré milieux. Myre introduced his secretary to ecclesiastical society. A Jesuit Père Varin allowed Guéranger to work in the library of the Jesuits on the rue de Sèvres where he continued his extensive reading in the patristic collections. Guéranger's plan at the moment was to shape his research in the Fathers into a defense of the rights of the Holy See.

At the same time on trips to country houses the Mennaisian contacts of school days were re-established, and Guéranger was introduced to other, even more respected, followers of Lamennais. In Besançon, a strong traditionalist center, they met Jean-Marie Donet,

---

[47]F.F.A. Donet, "Guéranger," Le Monde (Paris, France) 25 February 1875.

the future Bishop of Montauban and Thomas Gousset, later to be a leading Ultramontane cardinal. Both men knew Lamennais and Gerbet and provided introductions. They met others in the diocese of Meaux and in Franche-Comte. These visits led Guéranger in February 1829 to write to Lamennais and explain his projects for the defense of the rights of the Roman Church in the dioceses of France as a means to end the decline of religion which he had witnessed.

While Lamennais was publishing his essays on indifference between 1817 and 1824 and overturning the traditional Christian apologetic in the name of the people, he still remained a legitimist in the world of secular politics. In the fashion of almost all French ecclesiastical politicans he never questioned the connection and dominance of the church by the state. But at the time he came into contact with Guéranger he had moved away from that position, arguing that a great modern Catholic revival would come only if the church were freed by the state and became a separate community. In De la religion considérée dans ses rapports avec l'ordre politique et civil, which was published in May 1825 and February 1829, he urged priests to isolate themselves from atheistic society and governments which were little better than agnostic. He condemned the Concordat of 1801 and any system which united church and state. A church based on the people would lead to social justice and would be the only possible basis of religion in the new conditions of the century: "The future is entirely in the moral state of the people, a state that is itself only the natural and progressive development of doctrines that derive from the remote past. ...The Church will become increasingly identified with the people." The church in its new form would be able to provide alternatives to capitalist organization of industry: "...unless there is a total change in the industrial system, a general rising of the poor against the rich will be inevitable...this is not the place to explain what Catholicism can and will do to remedy such great evils and prevent such terrible calamities....Yes, Catholicism will be great in the age that is beginning, in the age of liberty. Its ancient faith will fructify science, which will rely on it,...will revive the dignity of man, attenuate the causes of discord, make all people brothers...."[48]

The German scholarship of the twenties had begun to restore for Lamennais a more historically accurate picture of the institutional church of previous ages. Lamennais learned from Neander of the spirituality of the free Christian community of the first centuries which bore no relationship to the state.[49] He was impressed by the German method of using research into the past as a means for the revival of the contemporary church.

Lamennais began a religious collective at La Chesnaie in 1825 to encourage French historical research. He was joined by Gousset and Donet and also by Gerbet and Salinis, the editors of the Mémorial. The days were divided into hours for prayer, time for study, and lessons in writing, for modern apostles were required to be journalists. In 1828 he formed the Congregation of St. Peter, a flexible, mobile community, designed for new social conditions. The communal element was maintained by the required recitation of the offices of the Roman breviary.

It was natural that Guéranger would be drawn to this circle and turn to Lamennais for guidance.[50] Lamennais advised him not to continue his projected history of the Papacy based on patristic

---

[48]Selections from the letters of Lamennais quoted in Peter N. Stearns, Priest and Revolutionary. Lamennais and the Dilemma of French Catholicism (New York, 1967), pp. 157, 169, 175, 177, 178, 179, 180.

[49]Liselotte Ahrens, Lamennais und Deutschland (Münster, 1930), pp. 43-93, particularly pp. 45, 74, 84-85; Jean-René, Derré, Lamennais, ses amis, et le mouvement des idées a l'époque romantique (Paris, 1962), pp. 139, 210-216, 516, 671. A series of articles in the Mémorial on the Einheit, February and November 1828, and on the Athanasius, July and September 1829, were the first discussions of Möhler in France. Lamennais praised Möhler as the greatest German theologian in a letter from Fribourg (Switzerland), 31 July 1834.

[50]Letters of Guéranger to Lamennais, 19 February 1829 and 3 March 1829, in A. Roussel, Lamennais et ses correspondants inconnus (Paris, 1912), pp. 192-194, 196-197; 15 March 1830, and 12 April 1829, in Ernest Sevrin, Dom Guéranger et Lamennais (Paris, 1933), pp. 62-64, 30-31.

documents, because there were already enough disciples engaged in that field. Another aspect of ecclesiastical science should be investigated, and Lamennais advised that the German patristic scholars should be consulted for information.[51]

Lamennais' discouragement of Guéranger's project on the papacy and the abandonment of his original research in the Fathers on this topic came during a period of vocational crisis. Myre-Mory died in August 1829. The relatives of the bishop were unsuccessful in securing Guéranger a place in the Polignac government under Baron de Montbel, the minister of ecclesiastical affairs. Carron, the new ordinary of Le Mans, did not offer him any offices. The young priest was afraid that he would not be able to combine a religious career with scholarly research.[52]

At this moment it was suggested that he write a few articles and read Gerbet's Considérations. The impressions of the last few years: the beauties of the patristic church, the excellence of the Roman liturgy when compared to the neo-Gallican texts of the last two centuries, the picture of the dechristianization of France, the need for unity and community, all combined with the impact of this book to awaken a liturgical vocation. After reading Considérations Guéranger later recalled these feelings:

> I gave myself up with delight to the ecclesiastical science in a limited goal, but this same concentration had the inconvenience to delay my aspirations towards a snythesis. [Then] my eyes had been opened on a great number of points. The mystical sense had been awakened, the narrow tendencies of false criticism had disappeared. My intelligence was waiting a signal....It was the liturgy which gave me this signal....I envisioned the dogma of the Incarnation as the center to which I had to relate everything, and [I envisioned] the dogma of the Church as enclosed in that of

----

[51]Letters of Lamennais to Guéranger 28 April 1829, Roussel, op. cit., p. 210; 31 December 1829, 22 February 1829, 15 March 1829, Sevrin, op. cit., pp. 26-27, 29-30, 61.

[52]Archives, Abbey of Solesmes, France, MS letter to his brother Edouard, 26 November 1829: "I have a great desire to continue this career."

the Incarnation. The sacraments, the sacramentals, the poetry of the prayers and of the acts of the liturgy, all this seemed to be more and more radiant. I felt that the future of my intelligence was in these fields.[53]

Philippe Olympe Gerbet had founded the Mémorial Catholique in 1824 and became its main editor. He followed Lamennais in most of his concepts. He was also strongly influenced by late German Romanticism. In February 1828 he wrote a long article in the Mémorial in praise of Johann Adam Möhler. He later adopted Möhler's ideas that the basis of heresy was the exaltation of the individual ego and the destruction of the community life of the church. Gerbet also agreed with Möhler that it is love rather than reason which unites men and women into the community of the church.[54]

Considérations was the only important book Gerbet ever wrote. It was immensely popular, re-edited eight times, and praised by Balzac, George Sand, Manzoni, and J. A. Möhler as well. It presented Catholicism as a religion whose forms of prayer were a means of social solidity. In this work Lamennais' system was translated into the language of the eucharistic cult, yet the book went one step beyond Lamennais to argue that humankind could be united by the eucharist. The sacrament of the altar was shown to be the best method of integrating the individual into the new conditions of modern society. Here Gerbet argued that the cult of the eucharist and public prayers were the highest expressions of Catholicism: "The eucharistic communion is the intermediary of the union between God and men.... Catholicism is the universal faith in the presence not abstract, but real and effective of God among men. The cult is the permanent organ of his real presence in our soul."[55]

Considérations emphasizes that although the eucharist meets all

---

[53]N.A., pp. 62-63.

[54]Gerbet's review of Möhler appeared in the Mémorial Catholique, February, 1828, p. 81.

[55]Philippe Gerbet, Considérations sur le dogme générateur de la pieté catholique (Paris, 1829), pp. 81 and 83.

the needs of the soul, it is essentially a social not an individual act. There is not only a social character to the public cult but to the priesthood as well, and all the people united in the church form the mystical body of Christ. "Because all is social in Catholicism, because its origins are in the common tradition, the greatest gifts of divine love are conferred not to the individual, but to the Church as a whole."[56] A public rite is the ground of society, of religion, and Christianity as well: "the eucharist is in the plan of Catholicism at the center of any associations of piety."[57]

After reading this book Guéranger decided to write the articles which Lamennais had called for on the liturgy. He was encouraged in this work by the master of La Chesnaie who related that his disciples were already enthusiastic about Guéranger's ideas on liturgical reform.[58] Gerbet wrote to Guéranger, "Your projected articles seem to be extremely good in my opinion."[59] Although his pieces were based on many Mennaisian concepts, Guéranger was the father of the idea of a new liturgical apostolate. In commenting on the shortcomings of Gerbet's treatment of the eucharist and society, and how he went beyond he said, "...I was ravished by it [Considérations]; but I did not feel in this book the echo of tradition: nothing in it reminded me of the Fathers or of the tone of antiquity; all seemed to go back to yesterday only. That was not what I was looking for."[60]

What Guéranger was looking for was perfectly expressed for him in the Roman liturgy. The four articles of 1830 in the Mémorial are important for Guéranger because they symbolize the beginning of the period in which the liturgy stood at the center of his preoccupations

---

[56]Gerbet, op. cit., p. 116.

[57]Ibid., p. 230.

[58]Lamennais to Guéranger, 15 April 1830, Sevrin, op. cit., p. 65.

[59]Gerbet to Guéranger, 2 February 1830, Ahrens, op. cit., pp. 282-283.

[60]N.A., pp. 62-63.

and his incipient separation from the Mennaisians.[61] For France the
four articles meant the beginning of a violent journalistic controversy
between the Gallican and Roman parties using liturgical issues as
pawns, a war which would last forty years. For the Catholic Church as
a whole they meant that worship would begin to be viewed as of
essential importance as a chief means of communicating the Christian
message in industrial society.

The Mennaisian element of Guéranger's first four articles is
symbolized by the title of the group as a whole, another
Considérations, "Considérations sur la liturgie catholique," and they
continue the journalistic tone of the movement, its vehemence and
hostility against the Gallican bishops. The articles follow Lamennais
in stressing the importance of the liturgy because it is an element of
the church which deals directly with the people and because it is the
expression of their traditions. The revivalist spirit of the movement
of the Breton priest is present in the promise of the regeneration of
society which will come with the abandonment of the liturgies of the
Gallican past.

That is the main thrust of the article of 28 February 1830. The
second article of 31 March 1830 follows La Chesnaie in calling for a
new Christian unity whose locus must be Rome. But this article is a
departure in suggesting that liturgical confusion is the basis of
social disintegration in France. The third piece, of 31 May, on the
necessity of one authority, the authority representing the Christian
people, as the determinant of liturgical form, is Mennaisian in its
attack on egoism in religion. But it was Guéranger who originated the
idea that an end to individuality in piety would cut at the root of the
modern religious problem, that unless forms of worship be non-
individualistic they would not meet the social needs of the age: "The
spirit of the individual, so paltry, so fussy, is more troublesome,

----

[61]Actually there was one small, light-hearted article mocking the
Gallicanism of the Sorbonne which came out before the liturgical
articles, by Guéranger, "Une thèse de théologie en Sorbonne," Mémorial
Catholique, 31 January 1830, pp. 17-25.

causes more agitation and disenchantment the freer it is. The union of the individual soul with truth is not very easy: there is no more the tranquillity of order."[62]   The fourth article on liturgical unction contains a re-emphasis on Gerbet's definition of the incarnational aspect of the church, that new sense of the church as the body of Christ indwelt by the Holy Ghost. But there is also Guéranger's novel description of the proper aesthetic necessary to shape modern Catholicism in the chaste liturgical spirit: grave, severe, simple, scriptural, and unified.

During the summer of 1830 the tone of the Mennaisian movement became increasingly radical. From October 1830 until November 1831 Lamennais and his followers published a new paper, L'Avenir. Its program was a revolutionary Catholic liberalism which called for complete religious liberty, the disruption of the union of church and state, the suppression of ecclesiastical budgets, the end of the state nomination of bishops and of concordats between the Papacy and governments. The paper was most extreme in its anti-Gallicanism. It asked the bishops of France to throw off the tyranny of the state so that there could be a Catholic revival leading to a regeneration of society. The meaning of the vehement and urgent language was often misunderstood:

> Bishops of France! our brothers in the same priesthood, our fathers because of your apostolic pre-eminence...allow your children to speak to you....To obey our conscience, we shall protest against those who would have the courage to accept the title of bishop from the hand of our oppressors. We make this protest with the contemporary world in mind; we entrust it to the remembrance of all the French people in whom faith and modesty have not perished....[63]

The bishops quite expectedly did not heed that appeal but quickly turned against the men who put out the newspaper. They forbade their

---

[62]Prosper Guéranger, Mélanges de liturgie, d'histoire, et de théologie. 1830-1837 (Solesmes, 1887), p. 93; a quote from the article in the Mémorial, 31 July 1830.

[63]Lacordaire in L'Avenir, 25 November 1830, in Sevrin, op. cit., pp. 146-147.

clergy to read L'Avenir in 1831 and began to work for its end through ecclesiastical and governmental agents in Rome.

It was this change in the nature of the Mennaisian movement which impelled Guéranger to urge the expulsion of any national elements from the liturgy and French customs from the worship of the church. He emphasized the separateness of the liturgical community in "De la prière pour le roi," written for L'Avenir in 1830.[64] On 2 June 1831, L'Avenir announced in big characters, the publication of Guéranger's De l'élection et de la nomination des évêques. It united the spirit of L'Avenir with Guéranger's patristic studies in much the same way that "Considérations" was a joining of Gerbet and the liturgical ideals of the Fathers. The main point of the work is summed up in one phrase, "The Church alone...has the right to choose its bishops."[65] In an age of dechristianization, governments legally without religion should have no claim at all over ecclesiastical affairs. To Lamennais, Guéranger wrote that his great hope was that this work would "...prepare by some more slow and more sure means the great work of the abolition of the Concordats in France...[and]...instruct the Catholics who know neither the times in which they live, nor the past centuries...."[66]

----

[64]They appeared in L'Avenir, 24 and 28 October 1830.

[65]Prosper Guéranger, De l'élection et de la nomination des évêques (Paris, 1831), p. 8.

[66]Letter from Prosper Guéranger to F. Lamennais, June 11, 1831, quoted by Sevrin, op. cit., pp. 167-168. For additional analysis of this period see Johnson, Guéranger, pp. 49-107; and Louis Soltner, Solesmes et Dom Guéranger (Solesmes, 1974), pp. 11-30.

CHAPTER IX

Solesmes

Guéranger's liturgical vocation was the culmination of a decade of disappointment. The next ten years were taken up with the search for "the slow and sure means" to bring about liturgical change. Guéranger understood the necessity of a new institution which would embody his ideas and insure their survival in the church. Experiences during the years 1830 to 1833 convinced him that neither the parish church nor any existing ecclesiastical establishment, including those of the Mennaisians, could accomplish his program. A new institution, free of the control of the state, centered about communal worship and capable of modifying society, was difficult to create because there was no contemporary model for it. The refounding of Solesmes and Guéranger's turn to Benedictine monasticism is an important stage in the development of the new Catholicism for it was through Benedictine monasticism that Guéranger touched France and the world.

During the period of the July Revolution, after finishing his articles for the Mémorial, Guéranger was priest administrator of the parish which used the chapel of the Missions Etrangères for services. He served a population of approximately 15,000 who were divided into streets which included the great houses of the rich, the shops of small traders, and the tenements of the poor. He attempted to care for this representative mass amid revolutionary conditions. He was forced to disguise himself and hide in alleys and doorways as he took the sacraments to the isolated parishioners, for fear that he might be attacked by the anti-clerical forces in the neighborhood.[1]

----

[1]Leon Robert, L'Abbé Guéranger et la revolution de 1830 (Sablé, 1965); the parish was made up of people who lived in these left bank

388

The curé, Dufriche Desgenettes, who was well known for his legitimist opinions, was driven out of the parish during the Revolution of 1830. He had attempted to meet the social needs of his people, but with rationalistic methods. On Sundays he would give three sermons and there were lecture series during Advent and Lent. In order to increase the level of the religious education of the people he began an association for the propagation of good books. That he failed in the attempt to revive his parish church by these means is demonstrated not only by his expulsion at the Revolution, but by the records which show that less than one-fourth of the population of his parish came to communion even once a year.[2]

Guéranger was repelled by the failure of Desgenettes' polite parochial machinery. He wrote to his brother, "I will not go so far as to say that the passion of ministering is impaired in me. No, but I would leave my functions tomorrow with little regret. I find little attraction for this sort of life."[3] The parish church as it then existed was not the instrument for reform because it was not free of the governmental influence exerted through the Gallican bishops.

Guéranger turned to the Mennaisian organization as a means to implement his liturgical scheme. He attempted to amass as much detail as possible on the manner in which Lamennais' communities were organized. In the letters which he wrote to his friend Leon Boré who was living at La Chesnaie there were continued attempts to elicit information on the life there: In what manner did Lamennais distribute the research projects among the various men? What was the role of a rule in the life of a community? Did the piety reflect the community life of the foundation or the individual needs of the men?[4] From

---

streets; rue de Varenne, blvd. Invalides, rue de Bac, rue de Sainte-Placide, rue de Cherche-Midi.

[2]Folder No. 64, Procès-Verbal de Visite of the parish Missions Etrangères, including MS notes on the history of the parish by the curé Roquette, Archives of the Archbishop of Paris.

[3]De Lanzac de Laborie, "Dom Guéranger et son oeuvre," Le Correspondant, CCXXXVIII (10 March 1910), 941-960.

Lamennais and Gerbet, Guéranger learned of the necessity for scientific training before any group of modern ecclesiastics could hope to make an impact on the contemporary world. Ecclesiastical science meant the study of scripture, the Fathers, church history, languages, Christian customs and traditions, all neglected subjects. Lamennais wrote, "...the work which you plan for the restoration of ecclesiastical science could be very useful and I urge you to execute this project...."[5] Although he encouraged Guéranger to establish a society devoted to research, Lamennais objected to its being modeled after any of the great religious orders of the past. He was strenuously opposed to the use of the choral office by modern monks or the spending of long hours in choir celebrating the liturgy.[6]

But it was precisely to an ancient religious order, the Benedictines, that Guéranger had been drawn as early as 1824 when he had been reading and studying the Fathers in the folio editions of the Benedictines of the Congregation of St. Maur. His teacher, Prof. Heurtebize, often told him stories about the Benedictines of Evron and the learned Dom Barbier, who had been his teacher. "These conversations made the liveliest impression on me, and I understood perfectly that in the secular clergy one did not find the means with which to do research into ecclesiastical science."[7]

After becoming disenchanted with parish work in Paris and with the thought in mind of forming some sort of community, Guéranger returned

----

[4]Letter from Prosper Guéranger to Leon Boré, 1 May 1829, quoted by Paul Delatte, Dom Guéranger, Abbé de Solesmes (Paris, 1909), I, 79; five letters of Boré to Guéranger from 22 February 1829 to 6 November 1832 in the Archives of the Abbey of Solesmes show that Boré was sending Guéranger information on community life.

[5]Letter from F. Lamennais to Prosper Guéranger, 2 September 1831, quoted by Ernest Sevrin, Dom Guéranger et Lamennais (Paris, 1933), pp. 190-191.

[6]Delatte, op. cit., p. 83; Robert, Revolution, p. 38; Prosper Guéranger, MS Notes Autobiographiques, Archives, Abbey of Solesmes, pp. 96-97.

[7]N.A., p. 23.

to his native town of Sablé in the summer of 1831. While he had been the chaplain at Sacré-Coeur in Le Mans he had come to know two sisters Euphrasie and Marie Cosnard, daughters of a retired notary of Anjou who had moved to Sablé. These young women had been enrolled in the educational course of the convent and they invited him to spend part of the summer with their family in Sablé. For the first time since his father had left Guéranger returned to the commercial center of the Sarthe. There he met the vicar who had been serving the town for two years, Augustin Fonteinne, a devoted follower of Lamennais. The Cosnards and the vicar shared Guéranger's enthusiasm for old church ruins. On 23 July 1831 they formed a walking party which proceeded along the banks of the Sarthe the few kilometers to the deserted priory church at Solesmes. They went in and sang a hymn before the ensemble of sculptures depicting the burial of Christ and the entombment of the Virgin which had been erected during the Renaissance and were one of the local attractions. When his friends told him that the old and useless church was soon to be destroyed Guéranger was stunned. He decided that he would attempt to buy the buildings and begin his projected religious community there at once. "The idea came to me that if I were able I would unite some young priests on this spot."[8]

After all religious orders had been suppressed by the French Revolution in 1792 and the little Benedictine community at Solesmes had been dispersed, the property belonging to the priory had been bought by M. de Chanteloup. His heirs, who had assumed control of the property in 1825, determined to demolish the structure. Guéranger was faced with three tasks: to find donors to contribute to a fund for purchasing the land and buildings and thereby prevent the destruction, to recruit other men to participate in community life, and to combine the suggestions of Lamennais and others into a practical plan for a monastic community.[9]

----

[8]Leon Robert, Histoire de l'Abbaye de Solesmes (Sablé, 1937), p. 18.

[9]Prosper Guéranger, Notice sur le Prieuré de Solesmes (Le Mans, 1834); Prosper Guéranger, Essai historique sur l'abbaye de Solesmes, suivi de la description de l'église abbatiale avec l'explication des

Extreme haste was dictated by the perilous state of the French church in general:

> The necessity of the Church seemed to me to be so urgent, the current ideas about Christianity were so false and so full of compromises in the ecclesiastical world and in the sector of the laity that I could not see anything which was more urgent than the foundation of a center for the assembling and reviving of the pure tradition.[10]

Guéranger's first inclination was to turn to the L'Avenir group for financial support. He wrote a series of letters to Lamennais and Gerbet appealing for help. But Lamennais was hesitant about having Guéranger's project linked with his paper. Guéranger decided to go to Paris and discuss his projected monastery with L'Avenir men. He found the office in a state of confusion.

> I left for Paris. One of my first visits was to L'Avenir. I arrived at the moment of the crisis of the journal. I very much wanted to see M. Lamennais and M. Gerbet and to speak to them about my projects. The overly political and liberal tendencies of L'Avenir bothered me more and more, but I had confidence in the Catholicism of these men....Lamennais seemed very worried. Nevertheless he listened to me with good will and agreed that there could be nothing done without the religious orders. I answered him that I planned...the re-establishment of a house of Benedictines. He objected that in this order there was the choir; and I answered that it was precisely that which made me choose it and that my associates had the same attraction....[11]

The end of L'Avenir was at hand. Forces had been working for the downfall of the school of Lamennais. In December 1830, Lambruschini the papal nuncio in Paris reported to Rome that the paper was a dangerous journal and that its editor was surrounded by young men more excessive than himself. During 1831 the ambassador of France, prompted by bishops and government, urged the Holy See not to support the new school. Metternich had conveyed his displeasure with the program of the journal to the papal government. Aware of this pressure, Lamennais

---

monuments qu'elle renferme (Le Mans, 1846); N.A., p. 90.

[10]N.A., pp. 94-95.

[11]Sevrin, op. cit., p. 195.

announced the cessation of publication and went with Lacordaire and Montalembert to the papal court in Rome. The three pilgrims reached Rome in the winter of 1831 but were not received by the pope until March of 1832. The pope spoke to them for fifteen minutes about the weather and Geneva. They returned home by way of Munich in August. There they were given a great dinner by Döllinger, Schelling, and Görres, and in the midst of the revels word was received that the pope, in the encyclical Mirari vos had condemned the aspect of the Mennaisian program which called for the adherence of Catholics to the ideas of civil and political liberty, freedom of worship and the press. There was a specific condemnation of the idea that the church was in any need of revival or restoration in order to preserve society. Mirari vos was a prelude to Singulari nos which declared the Mennaisian philosophy of sens commun to be heretical in June 1834. This act dispersed the remaining vestiges of the school of Lamennais. Lamennais pursued an increasingly political radicalism carried on outside the Roman Church while his students assumed various positions of importance within the church, where they masked their residue of Mennaisian ideas in acceptable terms.

Guéranger heard the news of Mirari vos amid his Mennaisian friends at Angers. His reaction was to become convinced that the Benedictine rather than the Mennaisian conception of community was more clearly best for the church.[12] On 20 September 1832 he wrote his bishop, Mgr. Carron, that he would submit to Mirari vos, and that he would like to begin a religious community of his own at Solesmes.[13] But the first of a series of set-backs stemming from suspicion of Guéranger's motives and ideas, because he had written for Mémorial and L'Avenir, now confronted him. The bishop wrote back in October that he could not begin his society until the unrest created by Mirari vos and the

---

[12]Antoine de Mazis, MS La Vocation de Dom Guéranger, Archives, Abbey of Solesmes, p. 35.

[13]Letter of Prosper Guéranger to Bishop Carron, 20 September 1832, quoted in Delatte, op. cit., p. 97.

394

renewal of Chouan guerrilla activity directed at Frenchmen, including the Mennaisians, who threatened the legitimate order of things, subsided.[14] Guéranger began to gather economic and political support while awaiting permission to open his religious house. The first necessity was to raise enough money to halt the demolition of the buildings at Solesmes which had been planned for late autumn.

The initial gifts to Solesmes came from three sources. One was the Catholic families of Sablé, those who had been loyal to the Roman cult during the Revolution and were friends of Guéranger. The Cosnards gave 6,000 F and Mme. Gazeau of Juigné contributed a large sum.[15] Money also came from former followers of Lamennais. The Count Montalembert, the young liberal contributor who had joined L'Avenir in 1831, persuaded Charles de Coux and the Marquis de Dreux-Brézé each to contribute 500 F.[16] A third group of supporters was made up of anti-Mennaisian Ultramontanes and reactionary noblemen. Chateaubriand wrote 11 December 1832 to say that he would become an honorary Benedictine of Solesmes. Cazales, Bailly, Regnon, longing for a return to the social securities of "Christendom," offered support. Marquis Anatole of Juigné, the unimpeachably legitimate descendant of the last ancien régime Archbishop of Paris who lived across the river from Solesmes, guaranteed continued help.[17] Surrounded by such names, Guéranger appeared less revolutionary and more respectable, and on November 8, the bishop relented and allowed the destruction of the buildings at Solesmes to be suspended. On December 19 Carron approved a temporary monastic constitution, and on 11 July 1833, after spending six months raising more money for the basic necessities of life, Guéranger, two priests, Fonteinne and Daubrée, a deacon, Le Boucher, and three

---

[14]P. Delaunay, "La Chouanerie de 1832," Mémoire de la Société d'agriculture sciences et arts de la Sarthe, LIII (1932), 382-452.

[15]Paul Piolin, "Dom Guéranger," Gazette du dimanche (23 April and 7 May 1882).

[16]de Mazis, loc. cit., note 155.

[17]Delatte, op. cit., p. 103.

postulant laymen, Déloge, Henry, Lafayolle, officially began the community life of Solesmes.[18]

In order to appreciate the revolutionary impact of Solesmes it is necessary to recall the individualistic and non-liturgical conceptions of the restorers of other religious orders during the first decades of the nineteenth century. The abolition of all monasteries and convents by the National Assembly on 18 August 1792 was the natural outcome of a long process. An anti-monastic disposition continued in both the government and the populace after the Revolution. The Concordat of 1801 did not mention religious orders. French Restoration governments were officially hostile to such associations. The Jesuits could not be reconstituted under their proper name. On 28 September 1831, 600 men burned the Trappist abbey at de Melleray to the ground. When Dom Verneuil, the former grand prior of St.-Denis, presented a petition to Louis XVIII begging for help in his revival of the Benedictines he asked that they not be put to work teaching and nursing in hospitals. Louis XVIII, however, was not assured that a religious order could be legally re-established if it did not have some useful purpose. It was not enough to do research and to pray and the Benedictine restoration of 1816, like that attempted by Dom Lombard in 1801, had failed for want of support. One segment of the French episcopate, the party of Mgr. Dupanloup, considered monasteries as relics of the church's past and were hostile to their re-introduction and growth.

But the continued appeal of monastic life was demonstrated in 1818 when there had been twenty-nine attempted restorations, seventeen Trappist, six Benedictine, and six smaller orders. In 1820 there were five Trappist efforts and one Cistercian. Almost all of these trials were made within abandoned pre-Revolutionary monastic buildings. Their concepts were also those of the ancien régime.[19] In the Trappist

---

[18]Sevrin disagrees and includes a Gilbert and a Morin among the first monks of Solesmes.

[19]Claude Savart, MS L'Opinion française et le monachisme au milieu du XIXe siècle, B-1, both papers presented at Colloquium on the History of Contemporary Monasticism at the Abbey of Maredsous, 12, 13, 14 October 1972, copies Archives, Abbey of Solesmes.

foundation, at de Melleray under Augustin Lestrange, individual separate meditation was stressed and research and study were eliminated.[20] The English Benedictines who came back to the Abbey of Saint-Gregory at Douai in 1818 and re-opened the prior of St. Edmund in Paris emphasized teaching, parish work, and missionary activity as the vocation of the Benedictine. It was the tradition of the English to maintain great schools for the training of young people. They played a very important part in the Roman Catholic missionary endeavors in Australia and maintained an entire system of Benedictine-staffed parish churches in Great Britain. Their form of spirituality was suited to the individuality of their work, for it was Ignatian rather than liturgical.[21] Even the other religious orders, refounded by followers of Lamennais, had the individualistic rational character of ancien régime foundations. Lacordaire's Dominicans were a preaching order dedicated to the conversion of the individual soul. Basile Moreau, a school friend and contemporary of Guéanger, followed a similar pattern of hatred of Sarthian Gallicanism and attraction of the sens commun while at the Grand Seminary of Le Mans. He also attempted to begin a religious revival in 1832 by founding religious orders, first Notre-Dame de Charité and then the Congrégation des Frères de Saint-Joseph, a body of fifty-eight priests who served twenty-six parish churches. In 1838 he formed the Congrégation de Sainte-Croix whose members essentially were missionaries in the diocese of Le Mans. None of these groups maintained a strong emphasis on common worship. They did not live together.[22]

The life of the men who joined Guéranger at Solesmes may be reconstructed by reading the first rule of 1833, Regulae Societatis

----

[20]Jérôme du Halgouet, MS Les Débuts de la renaissance cistercienne du XIXe siècle, B-2, at Colloquium.

[21]Maur Lunn, MS The English Congregation, B-10, at Colloquium.

[22]P. Philéas Vanier, La très révérend Père Moreau, d'aprés ses écrits, ses correspondances, et les documents de l'époque (New York, 1945); Gaetan Bernoville, Basile Moreau et la Congregation de Sainte-Croix (Montrouge, 1952).

<u>regularis in diocesi Cenomanensi existentis</u>, the constitution of 1837, and the "Règlement" for novices, <u>Religious and Monastic Life Explained</u>. The justification of choosing Benedict as the model of the contemporary monk is found in Guéranger's large unfinished manuscript, La Vie de St. Benoît.[23]

It was the ability of Benedict's monasteries to revive civilization which attracted Guéranger to this form of monasticism. Benedict lived in conditions much like Guéranger's own. There was social chaos caused by the conflict between a decayed culture and a new barbarism. The church, the Papacy, and the monks were the only stable institutions then which had been able to re-establish order and maintain the unity of Europe:

> The popes and the bishops, whose influence worked this trans-
> formation which had as its result the creation of civilized
> Europe, had at their service an element which was never
> short-coming. With its aid they accomplished all of their
> work: this was the monastic element. Above all, the monks
> and the monasteries were the intermediaries who served the
> Christian Church in the noble enterprise which consisted of
> sanctifying, enlightening, and ordering the human existence
> of millions. One is not able to say at the same time that
> this intermediary was distinct from the hierarchy which
> employed it; because monachism was found above all in the
> Popes and in the bishops, so often the products of the
> cloister....The Popes did not hesitate: the foundation of a
> monastery was the best method to effect the reclaiming of
> these wastes which they hoped to see covered with a harvest
> of grace....All that was life during these long centuries,
> all that was light in the midst of the chaos which tore at a
> society attempting to come to birth, proceeded almost
> unilaterally from the monastery, and with the lessons of
> eternal life, the monks shared with the people the knowledge
> of civil life and the aid for material life....It was, again,
> the work of the men of the cloister [to be] fathers of
> nations.[24]

Benedict was a genius to Guéranger precisely because he organized monastic communities that transformed the secular sphere. "...In this

---

[23]Prosper Guéranger, MS La Vie de Saint Benoît, 172 pages in Guéranger's own hand written in 1864, the expansion of an earlier Life, Archives, Abbey of Solesmes.

[24]Guéranger, Benoît, pp. 1-2.

century one is able to admire this work of action."[25] A Benedictine community is the best means for the evangelization of society. The monk "purged of the world and of sin, mortified in his flesh...united to God" is the instrument for the transformation of humankind:

> This love of his brothers, of the Church, which inspires his prayers, his works, and his penitence in the cloister, overflows into human society, and history renders witness to the degree of life which the Church has had in the centuries in proportion to the estimate which has existed for the religious state...and the action which it has exercised.[26]

In the letters to Maur Wolter on the founding of Beuron and in the rule for novices Guéranger stresses that the rechristianization of Europe is the ultimate goal of the prayer and penitence of monks.[27] That same goal could also be found in the life of the monastic patriarch of Monte Cassino who before all else "united his men before God in common prayer."[28] The liturgy was the best form of common prayer. It was the underlying principle of Solesmes that "public prayer should be a communal work and central to all." On many days the monks spent as many as seven hours in the choir for the divine office and for the celebration of the eucharist. The rites and music were gradually perfected so that the beauty of the services would be a witness to the power of the liturgical life set before visitors who happened to attend a mass at Solesmes. Much of the research which occupied the remainder of the day was a preparation of this lengthy liturgical action. This was the primary means of evangelization and distinguished Guéranger's foundation from any other "école d'érudits" or "académie de savants," from the Jesuits and the contemporary Benedictines of England and Italy.[29] Although he realized that certain

---

[25]Ibid., p. 6.

[26]Ibid., pp. 4, 95; L'esprit, pp. 5-6.

[27]Letter of Propser Guéranger to Maur Wolter, 5 May 1863, Archives, Abbey of Solesmes.

[28]Guéranger, Benoît, p. 48.

[29]Mgr. Freppel, Discours sur l'ordre monastique prononcé dans l'église abbatiale de Solesmes à l'anniversaire des obsèques de Dom

modifications were necessary to accommodate Benedict's rule to the altered circumstances of the Sarthe in the nineteenth century, from the very first plans drawn up for Solesmes, he maintained that the divine office, celebrated in choir, in its entirety, according to the Roman rite with the solemn celebration of the mass at the heart, was essential to any community life.[30] Guéranger was intent on translating his theories of social prayer into Benedictine life.

It was for this reason that unlike most post-Reformation monastic reformers he was against long hours of isolated mental contemplation. He returned to the ancient tradition of the community recitation of psalmody as the chief means of meditation. The Psalms "are the source of the true contemplation....After the Fathers of the Desert, it is in the divine office that contemplation has its place...by this concord of voice and spirit."[31] He counseled his novices that at first this would appear to be an absurd waste of time according to contemporary standards: "Let us shrink with horror from the worldly idea that the time passed in choir would be better employed in study or other exercises of piety; as if any work could be compared with the liturgical prayer in dignity, importance, and efficacy."[32]

Benedict's life was the source of the ascetic and aesthetic model of the monk's existence. The principal trait of Saint Benedict that Guéranger derived from his _Rule_ was holy simplicity.[33] "The character of Benedict in all his life is grandeur in simplicity, and all the monastic history of the West attests to the fact that that is

----

Guéranger (Angers, 1876).

[30]N.A., p. 120; Delatte, _op. cit._, p. 312.

[31]Gabriel Le Maitre, "Théologie de la vie monastique selon Dom Guéranger," _Revue Mabillon_, L (1961), 177; _Constitutiones_ (Rome, 1837), R394 and R400.

[32]Prosper Guéranger, _Religious and Monastic Life Explained_ (St. Louis, 1908), pp. 8 and 10. This is a translation of Guéranger's "Règlement" for novices written in 1859.

[33]Guéranger, Benoît, pp. 86-87.

the stamp which has been placed on his institution."[34]   Austerity is the mark of holiness and of gospel perfection.[35]   Guéranger sought to re-establish this Benedictine ideal at Solesmes in the early years in the way in which the liturgy was celebrated, in the conduct of the monks' life, in the style and decorations of the buildings, and in the art and music produced at the abbey.

The Mennaisians who contributed to Solesmes expected that the communal research which had been the central part of the life of La Chesnaie would continue there.   This external pressure insured that Solesmes would be a center of "ecclesiastical science."   The scholarship of the abbey revealed much forgotten knowledge about the liturgy in the past and contributed to a revival of ecclesiastical music.[36]   If the liturgy and community are the first two characteristics of Solesmes, study is the third.   To Montalembert in Rome, who was concerned at the inferior state of French Catholic learning because all of the great centers of religious education had been devastated by the Revolution, Guéranger wrote in January 1832 that he would see to "the necessity of the regeneration of the study of Catholic traditions." Solesmes was being founded for the double goal "of the sanctification of souls and the development of ecclesiastical sciences."[37]   On the same day he wrote to Pope Gregory XVI that the foundation would concentrate all its forces on ecclesiastical science, letters, and Catholic traditions, while the divine office remained at the center of activities.[38]

----

[34]Ibid., p. 120.

[35]Ibid., p. 9.

[36]L'esprit, p. 9.   Guéranger wrote to Bailly that projected editions, journals, and reviews would be the sop thrown to nineteenth-century critics who demanded some useful work.   This printed matter would be the equivalent of liquor and candy manufactured by other abbeys.

[37]Letter of Prosper Guéranger to Charles de Montalembert, 18 January 1832, quoted in Sevrin, op. cit., p. 203.

[38]Letter of Prosper Guéranger to Pope Gregory XVI, 18 January 1832, quoted in L'esprit, pp. 11-12.

But throughout the thirties there was a movement away from this emphasis on research. Scholarship came to play a secondary role to the liturgy and finally at Solesmes it became an adjunct to the renewal of worship, rather than a goal to be pursued for its own sake. In a letter to L'Ami de la Religion in 1833 research had already become "the secondary goal,"[39] and on 6 September 1834 Guéranger wrote, "Our fundamental goal is our sanctification above all, and in second place we put rendering some small services to the Church by devoting ourselves to ecclesiastical science."[40] In the text of the Constitution of 1837 research was only "useful for the service of the holy Church."[41] One of the earliest books published by "the members of the community of Solesmes," Origines de l'église romaine, contains the warning to the reader lest he confuse the monastery with an academy with permanent residents who write without ceasing: "The Benedictine must be knowledgeable, but he is a monk above all."[42]

One of the early indications of Guéranger's wish to make an impact on society was an extensive press campaign which lasted form 1833-1836 and was the first project undertaken after the founding of Solesmes. This was another adaptation of the method of Lamennais, who was the first to make use of newspapers as a proper tool for Catholicism. One of the striking characteristics of Catholicism in the nineteenth century was its reliance on newspapers and tracts. In many cases arguments about theology and piety were fought entirely in the newspapers. It was not only L'Avenir which was the mouthpiece of a party. L'Univers was the primary organ for the Ultramontane wing of the French church and L'Ami de la Religion for the Gallicans. The

---

[39]Prosper Guéranger, Lettre sur Solesmes," L'Ami de la Religion, LXXVII (8 August 1833), 61.

[40]Letter of Prosper Guéranger, 6 September 1834, quoted in L'esprit, p. 10.

[41]Ibid., p. 11.

[42]Prosper Guéranger, Origines de l'église romaine (Paris, 1836), pp. xxv-xxvi.

faithful did not wait for a pastoral epistle, but for the latest issue of their party paper. There were great national religious journals and there were local ones, like the Union de l'Quest which spoke for the Ultramontanes in the diocese of Le Mans and Angers.

The pattern of the first popular articles Guéranger wrote on monasticism was always the same. First he would call attention to the ruin of society caused by the Revolution and the philosophes.[43] He would then argue that modern monasticism is necessary because individuals alone cannot do the work needed to reform society and the church: "In an epoch when historical science is called upon to redo the world, all languishes in the nullity of individual efforts."[44]

The alliance of science and worship at Solesmes would lead to "regeneration" and an end of the isolation of the clergy from philosophy and literature. The work is "eminently social."[45] To de Cazales in Revue européenne, Solesmes would provide a new intellectual defense for the clergy, and to Baron de Mengin-Fondragon who paid a visit to the abbey for La Semaine du Fidèle du Mans the monastery was combatting the low quality of modern religious art and literature by returning to the models of the past. T. A. Bayle, however, realized that this was not an enterprise in religious escapism built on the banks of the Sarthe. "These Benedictines are men of our time...[and are]...using common life as a radiant center to revive the rest of the Church."[46]

---

[43]Prosper Guéranger, "Resurrection des Bénédictins en France," Tribune catholique, Gazette du clergé (19 May 1833).

[44]Prosper Guéranger, "Resurrection des Bénédictins en France," Tribune catholique, Gazette du clergé (19 May 1833).

[45]Guéranger, "Lettre," L'Ami, loc cit., pp. 61-62, Guéranger, "Souscription," loc. cit., pp. 441-445, and Canon Foissat, "Resurrection de l'ordre des Bénédictins en France," Annales de Philosophie chrétienne, VI (1833), 392-98.

[46]E. de Cazalès, "Voyage à Solesmes," Revue européenne, VI (July 1833), 583-595; Baron de Mengin-Fondragon, "Solesmes en 1835," La Semaine du Fidèle du Mans, not printed until 11 and 25 April 1874; T. A. Bayle, "Solesmes," L'Ami des lois (13 and 15 October 1836).

The initial publications of Solesmes reflected the truth of the observations of T. A. Bayle. In January 1836, the Protestant politician and minister of education Guizot awarded Solesmes a contract for the continuation of the Gallia christiana, a project for the editing and publication of the earliest historical documents of the dioceses of France. This had been one of the chief enterprises of the ancien régime Congregation of St. Maur. These planned editions were important for they were used by Guizot as a defense of the legitimacy of the monastery against the accusations of the minister of cults Barthe that the abbey was illegal. They insured an income of 2,000 F a year. In many circles the Gallia editions represented the continuity of Solesmes with the monastic institutions of the French past and were proof that Dom Guéranger was not creating a center of sedition and revolt against the established order.[47] They insured respectability in the right circles and led to favorable attention at Rome. The final result of this acceptance was that in July 1837 the Vatican approved the constitution of Solesmes and the apostolic letter Innumeras inter established that Guéranger was abbot and superior of the Benedictine congregation of France. This action was a first step in establishing the legal independence of the monastery from the French bishops and from the secular powers.

Although the initial historical research and publications of Solesmes were useful, they did not have the liturgical applications which Guéranger thought would be more beneficial. It was the second group of young people who came to Solesmes in the 1840's, who were not followers of Lamennais, who began to use manuscripts in the service of the liturgical apostolate. The most eminent example of this second school was Dom Pitra. He grew up in a village near Chalôn-sur-Saône during the last years of the activity of the Chouans and the Napoleonic Wars. He learned Latin from the curé and began to spend all of his free time deciphering old Greek and Latin manuscripts. In doing this

---

[47]Paul Denis, Guizot et le différend Mgr. Bouvier-Dom Guéranger (Paris, 1911).

work he came across the scholarship of the Benedictines. In 1840 he felt a vocation to the monastic life, and he wrote to Dom Guéranger on 17 April:

> I sadly breathe an air which suffocates me, my soul is altered, hungry for peace, for solitude, for silence, for work and common prayer. I feel especially a kind of passion for study which I am not able to satisfy either in a small seminary where time is wasted in a thousand materialistic details, or in the ministry where every element of work is missing.[48]

In 1841 Pitra entered Solesmes and soon began to travel across Europe copying important patristic and liturgical manuscripts. On 14 July 1840 Paul Piolin, who came from a clerical and Ultramontane family of Bourgneuf-la-Forêt, entered the abbey. He wanted to work and pray in the context of a completely disciplined life. Piolin was drawn to the use of historical research to recall the contemporary church to the purity of the practices of the past.[49]

It was Dom Pitra in England, at the house of Ambrose Phillips de Lisle, who discovered that the men of the Oxford Movement were adopting the French Benedictine prescriptions for liturgical reform which Guéranger found to be rarely adhered to in France. Pitra later remembered that de Lisle

> showed me a beautiful collection of the publications of the new school [the Oxford Movement], and among other things the curious liturgical books; the imitations more or less complete of the Roman liturgy, of the translations of the Breviary of Saint Pius V, of pieces of Gregorian chant...and also a very beautiful prayer on the return of the monastic spirit.

From Charles Wordsworth, Pitra learned that the Anglo-Catholics followed the struggle of the monks of Solesmes against French Gallicanism closely, and he learned that these Englishmen were caught up in much the same war for the freedom of the Church of England. In

----

[48]Fernand Cabrol, Histoire du Cardinal Pitra (Paris, 1893), p. 43; also Leon Gautier, "Le Cardinal Pitra," Portraits contemporains et questions actuelles (Paris, 1873).

[49]Alexander Celier, Dom Paul Piolin (Laval, no date, publisher Chailland).

response to an English Roman Catholic bishop who wanted Pitra's help in defending the use of popular songs rather than Gregorian chants in British churches, Dom Pitra held up the Anglo-Catholics as a better model:

> If your profane chants convert the Protestants as you say, how many others are scandalized. And while ritualists use all their efforts to re-establish the ancient chant of the Church, must we have less care than they do for these traditions?[50]

Pitra published in 1846 Histoire de St. Léger et de l'Eglise de France au VII siècle which discussed the chants and liturgy of that period. In the 1850's he brought out the works of the Latin Fathers in the series Spicilegium Solesmense and the Greek patristic writers in Canons et collections canoniques de l'Eglise grecque. These books were edited for the parochial clergy in order to provide sources which would help renew the church according to the patristic model. Pitra was so successful in this work that he was offered a cardinal's hat in December 1862 if he would come to Rome and work in the Vatican liturgical manuscripts. He was made librarian of the Holy Roman Church. In 1846 Piolin began his 10-volume Histoire de l'Eglise du Mans, in order to reveal that the pure traditions of the early church in the region of western France had been corrupted in the modern era.[51]

In 1854 a young priest of the diocese of Rennes, Paul Jauisons, came to Solesmes because he had failed in an attempt to live the liturgical life in his own parish. The people of his village had refused to accept Gregorian chants as a part of their worship. He had been attracted by Guéranger's arguments in the Institutions liturgiques which maintained that the proper music of the church was the ancient form of chant. He felt that he would never be able to use such music in the secular world. Jauisons took as his job at Solesmes the restoration of the musical manuscripts. He started the Scriptorium

---

[50]Albert Battandier, Le Cardinal Jean-Baptiste Pitra (Paris, 1893), pp. 146ff., 152, 156, 157.

[51]The first volume came out in Paris in 1851, the sixth in 1863. The work was finished in 1875 when Piolin became prior of Solesmes.

Gregorian of Solesmes for paleographical investigation. In 1859 he began to give conferences on the methods of executing early music. By 1860 the first Directorium Chori, a guide to Gregorian singing, had come out and in 1866 Mélodies Grégoriennes was published with the help of the young Dom Pothier. A system was devised and music published so that the people of local parish churches could join in singing Gregorian chants.

Thus in the 1850's and 1860's Solesmes had entered a third period. This was a time of expanding influence over the parochial life of the dioceses, a reflection of the missionary-lay concerns of the volumes of Guéranger's Liturgical Year and the relative ease with which monasticism was being accepted and supported during the years of the economic boom of the French Second Empire. The rate of growth of the monastic population in France between 1850 and 1880 was higher than at any other period of modern history.   In 1852 the Ultramontane bishop Pie wanted the liturgical piety of Solesmes to be adopted within the diocese of Poitiers, and so in 1853 a daughter house of the abbey was established at Ligugé.   By 1858 twelve monks had been solemnly professed there.   The Ligugé Benedictines served some parish churches and acted as diocesan missionaries.   In 1853 five religious were installed at Sainte-Marie d'Acey and in 1863 a city monastery was opened in Marseilles.   By that year there were more than eighty Benedictines at Solesmes and at Ligugé alone.

From 1833 the public reaction to these ideas and institutions was overwhelmingly negative. L'Ami de la Religion denounced the re-opening of Solesmes as useless. There was no justification for the existence of monastic communities in modern times.   The abbey could easily become a new citadel of anti-legitimacy and heresy, in the manner of Port Royal.   It was a dangerous institution filled with men holding seditious opinions.[52]   From 1833 to 1834 L'Ami dwelt on the theme that all the monks were unrepentant Mennaisians who had not submitted to the decrees of Gregory XVI and were therefore disloyal to the nation

----

[52]L'Ami de la Religion, LXXVI (30 July 1833), 607.

and church. The liberal political journals were opposed to Solesmes because it represented a return of the institutions of the ancien régime. Figaro, the journal of the government, mocked the attempt. L'Europe Littéraire remarked that this would be another in the series of scandals which surrounded any effort to establish antique religious institutions. The Constitutionnel denounced it as a "priestly invasion."[53] Others laughed at the pretension of Guéranger and his followers thinking that they were the continuation of the Congregation of St. Maur. The nineteenth-century Benedictines lacked the Maurist erudition and their charity: "These are not the successors of Mabillon and des Brial: there is neither their spirit, nor their method, nor their doctrines."[54]

Conservative Catholic circles in Paris were suspicious because Solesmes was regarded as an anti-legitimist institution, set against the Concordat and the traditions of the Gallican church. The clergy in general avoided Guéranger because of his Mennaisian background. The businessmen of Sablé smiled when Guéranger announced that he was founding an abbey for the needs of the nineteenth century and then turned to the Benedictines as the model for his projects. An example of the distrust of the neighboring population, which continued until the late 1840's, is demonstrated by the case of the death of Louise-Henriette La Bailleul, a rich orphan friend of the Cosnard sisters of Sablé and Dom Fonteinne. She died mysteriously at Sablé in 1844 and left 150,000 F for the work of religion. Fonteinne publicly fought the Bishop of Le Mans to secure these funds for Solesmes. The public was shocked. The rumor that the Benedictines had killed the girl and the open mutterings to that effect in the street were not even halted after a legal autopsy had been performed and the results made known to the public.[55] There is evidence that the old families of Solesmes mocked

----

[53]Anonymous MS Presse articles sur les débuts de Solesmes, 1833-1836, Archives, Abbey of Solesmes.

[54]B. E. C. Guérard, "La Terre salique," Bibliothèque de l"Ecole des Chartes V (Nov. and Dec. 1841), 188.

[55]Ledru, op. cit., pp. 171, 174.

408

what they understood to be a pretension to power and grandeur on the part of their own Guéranger. In the town there was an old officer of the Empire, Anjubault, and when he saw the former secular priest beginning to officiate with the trappings of abbatial dignity he went up and said: "What are you then, Monsieur Guéranger? A bishop is the general, you must be only a colonel."

The government of the July Monarchy expressed a traditional Gallican hostility to orders. But the state officials would have tolerated Solesmes, would not have seen any essential "indecency" in it, if the community had kept to "the modest and useful conditions for which it had first announced itself." The politicians did not like Solesmes to be allied with the Holy See, and they did not like the community to have an influence on the outside world. They were unhappy when Guéranger began to appear in public performing the functions of an abbot. This was against the law of the state. The French Minister of Cults complained in 1838 to the Bishop of Le Mans that Solesmes was illegal and that the government would be forced to take legal action if the church did not discipline these irregular clergy gathered in religious community:

It is not in the government's intention, Monsignor, to tolerate usurpations contrary to the rights of the episcopate and the laws of the state. The concordat of 1801 recognizes as ecclesiastical establishments in France only dioceses and parishes; the article 33 of the law of 18 Germinal, year X, says: "Every function is forbidden to all ecclesiastics, even French ones, who do not belong to any diocese." The suppression of congregations of men does not even allow the discussion of whether the ancient abbeys can be re-established...Every ecclesiastic who claims himself exempt from episcopal jurisdiction becomes thus extraneous....There would be then ground to take some measures concerning M. Guéranger and his associates if they should neglect to return to the early conditions of their association, that is, to live in retreat, without exterior character, to work on ecclesiastical history and other analogous enterprises.[56]

The Bishop of Le Mans from 1834, J.-B. Bouvier, did not require

---

[56]Letter of Minister of Cults Barthe to Bishop Bouvier, 17 August 1838, quoted in Ledru, op. cit., pp. 82-83.

prompting from the state in order to begin harassing Solesmes. He was the same Gallican Bouvier who as the superior of the Grand Seminary of Le Mans had worked against Guéranger's Mennaisian teachers. He did not believe in the continued validity or usefulness of monastic vows in France. To him monastic profession was merely an antique pious ceremony. For that reason from the first he was opposed to having the monks within his diocese. However, he could tolerate monks as long as they did not attempt to influence the laity in the parishes. Then they would be crushed. As a Gallican, he was against any delimitation of the rights of the local bishop and the invasion of a corporation into the work of the diocese which looked to the Papacy and not the bishop for direction. He did not recognize the decisions of Roman congregations as binding within his diocese, and no papal pronouncement could go into force within the see of Le Mans without his approval. Bouvier had respect for the rights of the civil authority in ecclesiastical affairs. He was a man of order and rules who was interested in reviving the 700 parishes in his diocese with more episcopal visits and building programs, but revival could come only on his terms, not from the monks of Solesmes.

It is not surprising, then, that when the government began to complain about Guéranger, Bouvier resolved to discipline the abbot himself. To the minister of cults he wrote that he had opposed the abbot's appearances outside the abbey:

> I shall tolerate even less that he exercise outside his house ecclesiastical functions other than those which I delegate him....I shall not suffer any usurpation of the rights of the episcopate; I owe it...to public order, and I shall know how to discharge my duty in this respect.[57]

This abbatial charade was a challenge to public order in Bouvier's eyes because it was symbolic of rebellion against the Concordat and the beginning of a new system of free illegal religious communities. In episcopal statutes which he sent to all the French bishops he railed

----

[57]Letter of Bouvier to Barthe, 18 August 1838, quoted in Ledru, op. cit., p. 84.

against "the jesting of a certain man. Prosper Louis Pascal Guéranger," who was making a scandal for the faithful. It was "absolutely necessary for the monks and for the edification of the faithful that the abbot restrain himself and remain entirely behind the walls of the monastery."[58]

Bouvier attempted to control Solesmes in several ways. First he threatened to dissolve the community and withhold permission for any future ordinations or professions. He prevented members of the community from exercising their priestly functions in churches outside the walls of the abbey.[59] The bishop also put obstacles in the way of the recruitment of novices. When accused of this by the Holy See he replied,

> It is not because of me that the prosperity of the new Benedictines is threatened and they have become unpopular, it is their conduct and the exaggerations of their abbot, it is their various imprudences which have caused the true scandal in the country....One hardly speaks of them in Sablé without the cadaver of Mlle. Le Bailleul being held against the Benedictines.[60]

Faced with a list of foes, Guéranger succeeded because of continued strong financial support, alliance with the old Mennaisians and Ultramontanes who held important positions in French society and in the church, and because he cultivated spheres of influence at the papal court. The money came from marginal capitalists, members of the upper bourgeosie or lower nobility, an insecure group longing for the certainties of a vanished Christian past and attempting to recreate those times by contributing to the foundation of antique institutions like monasteries. Although funds came from the old Roman Catholic

----

[58]J.-B. Bouvier, Pastoral Epistle, 25 December 1837, quoted in Auguste Sifflet, Les Evéques concordataires du Mans. Mgr. Bouvier. 1834-1844 (Le Mans, 1924), pp. 199-200.

[59]A letter of Guéranger to Bouvier, 4 October 1844, quoted ibid., pp. 559-563, reveals that the monks had been forbidden to act as priests outside the monastery.

[60]Letter of Bouvier to Cardinal Ostini at Rome, 12 October 1844, quoted in Ledru, op. cit., pp. 175-176.

families of Sablé which had contributed at the outset to Solesmes and were distinguished by a loyalty to the Roman Catholic cult during the Revolution, a major source of support in the 1840's and after were the new entrepreneurs of the Sarthe who did not have a reputation for Catholicity, but were converted to Christianity by Dom Guéranger.

The Cosnards, the family of daughters of the ex-notary of Anjou who had invested in land around Sablé, are an example of the original circle who continued to give money for the cause of Solesmes until Guéranger's death. The abbot provided this family with spiritual advice, and the letters which he sent to Euphrasie Cosnard, who came under his influence in 1827, are important for an indication of what these young women sought from Guéranger and Solesmes. In the earliest letters, he wrote to her that her faith could not be sustained in a secular society if she attempted to lead a pious life in isolation from other Christians. Even tough she was a laywoman, she should be absorbed into the church. How would this be possible in the parochial situation of Sablé? In 1828 he suggested that such a Christian life could be maintained by following the liturgical year. The goal of Christianity is communion with Christ, therefore, Guéranger urged Euphrasie "to approach frequently the Holy Communion" and make it the center of her life. "Go to God through the Holy Communion as often as possible, and do not make this an affair, but a daily bread." He asked her support in the building up of Solesmes in order to make this liturgical union with God possible not only for herself but also for other lay Christians.[61]

Leon Landeau, the wealthiest man in the region, represents the newly rich capitalists of Sablé who were won back to Roman Catholicism by Dom Guéranger. He lived in a Gothic revival château, but he made his money in the mines. Landeau was the nephew of the old army officer Anjubault, and he moved to Solesmes after the Napoleonic Wars, a poor fellow who lived with his family in an old mill just below the abbey

----

[61]Leon Robert, MS Lettres spirituelles de Dom Guéranger à Mademoiselle Euphrasie Cosnard, Mélanges Dom Germain Cozien, MS HM c/5-6/22/1958, pp. 4-40, Library, Abbey of Solesmes.

buildings. In 1819 he developed new technical processes for the mining of the anthracite and marble which had been discovered in the environs of the town. He became mayor of the village of Solesmes, and used his influence there to convince other businessmen of the region to back the abbey. He contributed marble for building projects for the parish church and enlargement of the monastic buildings. He attended the liturgical services of the monks every Sunday and on weekday festivals. His support of Guéranger became a controversial point. In the 1843 mayoral election the curé of Solesmes, Jean Jousse, united the town against the mayor who encouraged the monks in "their new and sumptuous monastery."[62] Landeau lost the election but he continued as one of the principal contributors to Solesmes.

The growth of Solesmes was related to an economic revival which occurred at Sablé between the 1830's and the death of Guéranger. The income of contributors like the Cosnards whose money was invested in land went up because there was a period of agricultural expansion. Farming in the area had been destroyed by the years of war and guerrilla activity. This relative cheapness of land accounted for the influx of new buyers. The discovery of rich calcium deposits at Juigné led to the use of that mineral as a fertilizer on the lands of the innovative bourgeoisie. Between the Restoration and the Second Empire the area of cultivation was doubled for cereals and tripled for potatoes.[63] During the years 1861-1875 an apogee of agricultural output was reached. More land was in useful cultivation than ever before in the history of Sablé.

The expansion of the region was a result of the high concentration of new workers connected with the Landeau mines. Landeau recruited marble miners, polishers, and decorators, and local trade grew as it expanded to serve the larger population. Marble production was further stimulated by the arrival of the railroad in 1861 which facilitated the

----

[62]Ledru, op. cit., p. 149.

[63]Thérèse Greffier, Une petite ville du Maine aux XIXe siècle (Sablé, 1960), p. 34.

shipment of the stone.

At the time of Dom Guéranger's death in 1875, the boom came to an end and from 1875-1895 Sablé was in the midst of an economic crisis, brought on initially by the competition of English coal which was brought in by the railroad in 1861. The market for the more expensively produced local coal was destroyed. The decline in anthracite production and the population and power of Sablé is reflected in the fall of the number of coal workers from 638 in 1849 to 60 in 1892.[64] The closing of most of the coal mines resulted in a lower demand for food and a reduction of the amount of land planted in cereal crops. There was a coincident falling-off in employment at the Landeau mines from 662 miners in 1875 to 284 in 1892.[65] It was during the same period that the monks were forced to leave Solesmes because of the decline in monetary and political support.

Solesmes flourished throughout the period of the Second Empire, a time when economic growth characterized the whole of France. Madame Durand is an example of the class of rich bourgeois women from beyond the Sarthe who gave generously to Solesmes in the 1850's and 1860's. Her husband was Jean-Pierre Durand, one of the principal capitalists of Marseilles. She was lonely and felt isolated in that city, for M. Durand did not share her interests in religion. One summer she met the Landeau family by the sea. In 1853 she bought their old house and began to spend one month a year in Solesmes. Soon Madame Durand had become one of the special spiritual children of Dom Guéranger. He appealed to her for funds, and in the midst of a crisis in 1855 she sent him 40,000 F in one letter, and then she raised 132,000 F in 1863 for the foundation of a daughter house of Benedictines in Marseilles.[66]

----

[64]Ibid., pp. 28, 87.

[65]Ibid., p. 87.

[66]Alphonse Guépin, Dom Guéranger et Madame Durand (Paris, 1911), the most significant letters from Guéranger to Durand are 27 December 1853, p. 17; 10 November 1857, p. 32; 9 December 1855, pp. 39-40.

Montalembert and Lacordaire introduced Guéranger to an even more important lady, Madame Swetchine, who was hostess of the leading Catholic salon of Paris. She was an ungainly widow in her fifties who had grown up in the skeptical atmosphere of the Russian court of Catherine II. After being converted to Roman Catholicism by de Maistre she moved to Paris and in 1825 bought a house on the rue St.-Dominique which became filled with so many passionate Catholics, Ravignan, de Tocqueville, de Falloux, and the Mennaisians, that it was remarked that God was also a habitué. "I plunge into metaphysics like a bath," she recalled.[67] But she knew many important people in Paris and at Rome and secured powerful supporters for Guéranger. She was the devoted friend of Madame de Meuban, the sister-in-law of Guizot, who as Minister of the Interior, prevented the government from closing Solesmes and awarded the monks the Gallia christiana.

Madame Swetchine, Montalembert, and Lacordaire raised very large sums for the Benedictines in Paris in the two decades after 1833, from Count Alain de Kergorlay 170,000 F, from senators, from the auditor of the council of state, from the Viscountess de Bussieres, the Marquis de Vogüe, and Viscount Alfred de Falloux. They insured the continual support of Solesmes by old Mennaisians living in the countryside.[68]

----

[67]Philip Spencer, Politics of Belief in Nineteenth Century France (London, 1954), p. 55.

[68]Anonymous MS Notes sur divers sujets relatifs à Dom Guéranger, L. R., Archives of Solesmes, pp. 6-7. These are some of the old followers of Lamennais who gave money to the Abbey of Solesmes:
Paris--de Bailly, Jourdain, Sainte-Foi, Ozanam, Salinis
Nantes--Marquise de Régnon, Mme. de Vaufleury, Abbé Fournier, Abbé
    Coquereau, Abbé Joly
Angers--Jules Morel, Jacques Pasquier, Abbé Banchereau
Le Mans--Lottin, Heurtebize
Mayenne--Abbé de St. Martin, Abbé Jouanne, Abbé Leriche
Bordeaux--Dulac, Scorbiac
A further example of the way the securities of Christendom were offered as the chief inducement to contribution to Solesmes is the appeal Bishop Pie made to prospective supporters. On one occasion in 1875 he attempted to raise money for Solesmes by picturing it as an alternative to the radicalism of the French Revolution, as a means for the religious revival of France. Solesmes is "necessary for the accomplishment of the evangelical counsels and to maintain social equilibrium." He makes it clear that one could not depend on the

Madame Swetchine's friends played an important part in convincing Rome of the legitimacy of Solesmes. This was the most important victory. It is surprising that the pope, Gregory XVI, was extremely hostile to the erection of a Benedictine community with a liturgical apostolate in France, for as Mauro Cappellari, he had been a Benedictine of the Camaldolese reform. However, even though the Italian monastic houses had survived the Revolution and Napoleon, the liturgy was not regarded as an important endeavor among them.

Eventually French Catholics in Rome convinced the general of the Jesuits, Father Rozaven, and Mgr. Bini, the Abbot of St. Paul's Without the Walls, of the basic soundness of the French Benedictines. Mme Swetchine wrote on Guéranger's behalf to all of the persons of influence whom she knew in the Curia. Guizot convinced the French ambassador Count de la Tour-Maubourg to work for the continued independence of Solesmes. The ambassador conveyed the impression that the French government was not hostile to monastic foundations.

In February 1837 Guéranger went to Rome. The Princess Borghese and Cardinal Sala made it possible for him to bring his plans before every member of the Vatican Congregation of Bishops and Regulars. He wrote to his monks: "All of my time is employed in visiting cardinals, prelates, religious, laymen, women, princesses, because, in this country one only advances with such activity, and without it one

---

hierarchy to sustain such a center, that it must be the duty of the aristocracy. He appeals to the memory and custom of past French monarchs who endowed monastic establishments in their time. Pie stresses the fact that Solesmes had been supported by the aristocracy from the first by the family of Juigné and the Princess Hohenzollern-Sigmaringen, and that in the necrology of Solesmes were noblemen—Montalembert, Count Alain de Kergorlary, Marquis de la Tour-Maubourg. After one such appeal Pie received contributions from the following: the Viscountess des Cars, the Duchess de Chevreuse, the Marquise de Courtebourne, the Marquise de Luart, the Marquise de Nicolai, Countess Adolphe de Rougé, and the Viscountess Leo de Turenne. This from Louis-Edouard Pie, Entretien de Mgr. Pie sur L'Abbaye de Solesmes et la Congrégation Bénédictine de France (Paris, 1875).

doesn't advance at all."[69]   The Congregation gave its approval and in the fall of 1837 the pope announced that Solesmes was indeed an abbey and Guéranger the head of the Benedictine Congregation of France.

The Holy See by the apostolic letter Innumeras inter raised the priory of Solesmes to the status of regular abbey and formally conferred the abbatial dignity on the superior of the monastery, Dom Guéranger. The apostolic letter established a French congregation of the order of St. Benedict, holding the place of the old congregations of Cluny, Saint-Vannes, Saint-Hydulphe and St. Maur.   The abbey of Solesmes would now be the principal house of the order in France and its abbot the general superior of the congregation.

Innumeras inter attested canonically that the work of Solesmes was primarily liturgical, that its mission was to be a community working for the restoration of the worship of the church in France. The Holy See recognized that these new Benedictines had a character unlike that of any other religious order.   By the solemn act of 1 September 1837 the Pontiff confirmed the importance of the task of restoring the pure traditions of the liturgy, Sanas sacrae Liturgiae traditiones labescentas confovere.[70]

----

[69]Leon Robert, Un Voyage de Dom Guéranger (Sablé, 1938), p. 11.

[70]Alphone Guepin, "Préface," to Prosper Guéranger, Institutions liturgiques (2nd ed., Paris,1878), pp. xxxv-xxxvi.   See also Jean Leclercq, "Le renouveau Solesmien et le renouveau religieux du XIXe siècle," Studia Monastica, 18 (1976), 157-195; Louis Soltner, Les débuts d'une renaissance monastique, Solesmes 1831-1833 (Sablé, 1974); "Rercherches sur la Pensée monastique de Dom Guéranger," Collectanea cisterciensia, 37 (1975), 209-226.

CHAPTER X

A Liturgical War

"Our intention is to produce a movement," Abbot Guéranger
announced in 1840 in his introduction to the first volume of a series
of publications which came out of Solesmes in the next three decades.[1]
The goal was the adoption of the liturgical reform which had been
presented in the 1830 articles, sanctioned by the Papacy, and supported
by contributors. Guéranger determined that the role of the monks would
not be personal activity in chancelleries and parishes but the
dissemination of the evidence of the Christian practices of the past
uncovered by historical research. Solesmes would be the arsenal of a
struggle with the forces of the ecclesiastical status quo.

Guéranger's liturgical movement was divided into two campaigns.
The first was addressed to bishops and diocesan officials. The three
parts of the Institutions liturgiques (1840, 1841, 1851) demonstrated
the pre-eminence of Roman liturgical forms throughout the history of
the church and criticised the neo-Gallican liturgies compiled in the
seventeenth and eighteenth centuries. In these volumes historical
materials were presented in a polemical manner in order to gain
attention quickly. Three defenses of the Institutions appeared in
public letters to the Archbishop of Reims (1843), the Archbishop of
Toulouse (1844), and the Bishop of Orléans (1846-1847), all justifying
the reservation of legislation on the liturgy to the church as a whole
rather than to individual bishops. These books were for a limited

----

[1]Prosper Guéranger, Institutions liturgiques (2nd ed., Paris,
1878), I, LXXI.

audience, and during Guéranger's lifetime only 2,500 copies of the Institutions and 1,000 copies of the letters were printed.[2]

The production of books, pamphlets, and guides to introduce parish priests and laity to the liturgy was a second aspect of the movement. The journal L'Auxiliaire Catholique which came out of Solesmes every month in 1845 and 1846 contained articles on "the riches and grandeur enclosed in the mystical calendar (the liturgical year),"[3] and a series "Principes de liturgie" provided information so that the parochial clergy "would have precise and exact notions on the liturgy."[4] Appeals to participate in the liturgy were embedded in almost everything that Guéranger wrote, in Les Exercices de Sainte Gertrude, in Histoire de Sainte Cécile, vierge romaine et martyre and Sainte Cecile et la société romaine aux deux premiers siècles. The monks of Solesmes popularized Guéranger's liturgical Christianity by editing his Conferences sur la vie chrétienne, Explication de prières et des cérémonies de la sainte messe, Les Dons du Saint-Esprit, and The Church or the Society of Divine Praise.[5]

----

[2]MS L.R., "Liturgie," Archives, Abbey of Solesmes. Institutions liturgiques (1st ed., Le Mans, 1840) I, (Le Mans, 1841) II, (Paris, 1851) III; Lettre à Mgr. l'archevêque de Reims sur le droit de la liturgie (Le Mans, 1843); Defense des Institutions liturgiques, lettre à Mgr. l'archevêque de Toulouse (Le Mans, 1844); Nouvelle défense des Institutions liturgiques (Le Mans, 1846, 1847). Further analysis of the Institutions see G. Oury, "Les 'Institutions liturgiques' de Dom Guéranger," Esprit et Vie, 9, 10, 11 (1976), 121-126, 139-143, 157-160.

[3]Prosper Guéranger, "Le Lys de frère Eystein," L'Auxiliaire Catholique, I (1845), 449-468.

[4]Anon., "Principes de liturgie," L'Auxiliaire Catholique, V (1846), 350.

[5]Prosper Guéranger, Les Exercices de Sainte Gertrude (Paris, 1863, 1876, 1879); Histoire de Sainte Cécile (Paris, 1849, 1853); Sainte Cécile et la société romaine (Paris, 1874); Conferences sur la vie chrétienne (Solesmes, 1880, 1884); Explication des prières (Solesmes, 1884, 1885); Les Dons du Saint-Esprit (Tournai, 1950); L'Église ou la société de la louange divine (Angers, 1875), Engl. trans., no date, publ. London by "a secular priest."

The greatest work of propaganda was the Liturgical Year, a unique product for that time, unlike anything ever produced in France before.[6] It is a 10,000-page meditation on Christian worship set within the texts and prayers which are used in the divine office and mass every day of the year. Pieces of history, sermons of the Fathers, poetry and hymns from the Middle Ages, and explanations of ceremonies are included as commentaries which initiate the people into the mysteries of the church during the various seasons of the ecclesiastical year. The arrangement and publication of the volumes followed the same divisions as the Roman missal and breviary.

The first part, devoted to Advent, came out in 1841. The second, published in 1845 and 1847, contains the explanation of services from Christmas to the Purification. The third, which continues to the first Sunday of Lent, appeared in 1854 and is called Septuagesima. The fourth segment, also of 1854, comprises the first four weeks of Lent. The fifth, finished in 1857, consists of Passiontide and a detailed description of the rites of Holy Week. The sixth, divided into three volumes which reached the people in 1859, 1862, and 1866, includes the time of Easter. All of these books were arranged so as to arouse interest in traditions of worship which had lost meaning and created little religious response in the minds of the faithful. In providing materials which would educate the public in the significance of Catholic ritual Guéranger meant to end separation—of worship from daily affairs, of the people from the liturgy, of the priests from their congregations.

Although Saint-Beuve is said to have fallen asleep after the first twenty pages of the Liturgical Year, the demand for copies among

---

[6]Only Guéranger's volumes of the liturgical year are discussed here. After his death Dom Lucien Fromage concluded the series with Le Temps après la Pentecôte. For further analysis of this significant work see Louis Soltner, Solesmes et Dom Guéranger (Solesmes, 1974), pp. 77-87; Cuthbert Johnson, Prosper Guéranger: A Liturgical Theologian (Rome, 1984), pp. 340-418; and F. Brovelli, "Per uno studio de 'l'Année Liturgique' di P. Guéranger," Ephemerides Liturgicae, 95 (1981), 145-219.

ordinary people was so great that by 1887 there had been at least eleven editions of some of the volumes in France and translations into English, German, and Italian. When Guéranger died, most commentators agreed that if Solesmes had reached the people of France at all it had been through that monumental work.[7]

The Liturgical Year was a working out for the parochial situation of an idea which Guéranger had discussed with Lamennais in the spring of 1830, a massive life of the saints for the general population: "This is the way to conquer a crowd of people who would not go any other place to search for the teachings of the cathechism....To develop it sufficiently, one would need a volume for each month... placing under their eyes...the customs of the Church in all the centuries."[8]

The Liturgical Year was a carefully assembled attack on the dissociation of the material and the spiritual in religion, the division of society into a secular sphere and an increasingly unimportant and other-worldly ecclesiastical sphere. "Materialism

---

[7]De Lanzac de Laborie, "Dom Guéranger et son oeuvre," Le Correspondant, CCXXXVIII (10 March 1910), 952-953, argues that the collection initiated four generations of Frenchmen into the mysteries of the liturgy. Anon., "Guéranger," Le Monde (17 February 1875), said that the book was a source of holiness for the entire church. A. Saint-Emilion, "Guéranger," L'Evenément (9 February 1875), suggested that compared to the Liturgical Year, Le Génie du Christianisme of Chateaubriand was an informal essay. Never had a Catholic author inspired so many. Jacques d'Anglejan, "Un Défenseur de la tradition religieuse en France au XIXe siècle," La Revue critique des idées et des livres, XIII (25 May 1911), 468, understands the Liturgical Year to be the first work for the liturgical education of the people. The number of editions of the Liturgical Year in France in the nineteenth century were: Advent, nine by 1887, Christmas I, nine by 1887, Christmas II, eight by 1886, Septuagesima, six by 1883, Lent, nine by 1886, Holy Week, eleven by 1887, Easter I, eight by 1887, Easter II, seven by 1885, Easter III, seven by 1886. Translations into English appeared: Advent, 1867, Christmas I and II, 1868, Septuagesima, 1870, Lent, 1870, Holy Week, 1870, Easter I, II, III, 1871; into German: Advent, 1875, Christmas I and II, 1876, Lent, 1877, Holy Week, 1877, Easter I, II, III, 1879-1880; in Italian: Advent, 1884, Christmas, 1885, Septuagesima, 1886, Lent, 1887, Holy Week, 1884.

[8]Letter of Prosper Guéranger to F. de Lamennais, 15 March 1830, quoted by Ernest Sevrin, Dom Guéranger et Lamennais (Paris, 1933), p. 80.

reigns supreme in every country...revolution after revolution has habituated mankind to respect no power but that of might."[9] The decline of spiritual values is changing the character of European society. "We are fast approaching that awful time, when the want of faith will paralyze men's hearts."[10] Europe is beginning to witness the products of a materialistic civilization. Literature is depraved and sterile. Personal relationships have grown cold. The family is declining. There are open displays of pagan savagery.

The church continues, faith is confessed, but the great change has been that Christianity has lost a role in public life. In the past the liturgy at a coronation, royal baptism, state marriage, or funeral of a military hero expressed the connection between religion and secular affairs. "Now-a-days, the Liturgy has none of her ancient influence on society; Religion has been driven from the world at large....As to political institutions, they are but the expressions of human pride."[11] The intimate liturgical tie of church and household has been broken resulting in the end of a spiritual association with the humblest objects:

> Another sign of the decay of the spirit of faith...is disregard of holy practices recommended by the Church...the holiest feelings of religion may blend with the best joys of family and home....How many Catholic houses are there not, where there is never to be seen a drop of Holy Water or a blessed candle or a palm?...the want of...spirit makes [these practices] be condemned as extravagant, unmeaning, and folly.[12]

The Abbot of Solesmes predicted that society would collapse in an

---

[9]Prosper Guéranger, Liturgical Year: Paschal Time, tr. Laurence Shepherd (3rd ed., London, 1909), III, 337.

[10]Guéranger, Paschal Time (3rd ed., London, 1910), II, 247.

[11]Prosper Guéranger, Liturgical Year: Passiontide and Holy Week, tr. Laurence Shepherd (3rd ed., London, 1901), p. 8.

[12]Guéranger, Paschal Time, II, 250, 251; Prosper Guéranger, Liturgical Year: Christmas, tr. Laurence Shepherd (3rd ed., London, 1904), I, 138.

age of capitalism and individual independence because "every creature
is made an object."[13]   If the human is thought to be an atomized
particle of matter, there can be no transcending of the self, no union
by a common non-materialistic medium to fellow creatures or to the
divine. Modern materialistic egoism is an obstacle to the formation of
a community of humankind: "The spirit of independence and of liberty
which reigns today makes belief in God rare, it is one of the wounds of
our time."[14]

By contrast, Dom Guéranger presented the scheme of Christian
salvation as intimately related to social activity. Secular reformers
were calling for associations to combat the disorder created by modern
revolutionary conditions; however, to Guéranger the church alone
creates community because it offers a spiritual element which tends
toward organic convergence:

> But social perfection...the highest form of association, is
> only possible in the Catholic Church through the means of the
> Communion of Saints, by which we participate in the life of
> the mystical Body of Christ....What the circulation of the
> blood is to the natural organism of the human body, that the
> reality of the Communion of Saints is to the supernatural
> organism of the Body of Christ, the Church of the living God.
> ...The Communion of Saints is the medium by which the life
> that energized in the Heart of Jesus Christ, as its center,
> is diffused throughout His Mystical Body, the Church....[15]

The spirit is the only common bond of brotherhood which effects human
unity:

> Human fraternity is manifest in Jesus Christ....Whence do the
> children of the Catholic Church derive the stability, which
> is not affected by time,nor influenced by the variety of
> national character, nor shaken by those revolutions that have
> changed dynasties and countries? The Holy Spirit,who is the
> soul of the Church, acts upon all the members; and as He
> Himself is one, He produces unity in the body He animates.[16]

----

[13]Guéranger, Paschal Time, III, 337; Guéranger, Conférences I, 153.

[14]Guéranger, Les Dons, p. 9.

[15]Guéranger, The Church, pp. vii, ix.

[16]Guéranger, Paschal Time, III, 384; Guéranger, Le Sens, p. 18.

Yet material objects, bread and wine, convey Christ's presence into the church. Reception of the eucharist is the principal means by which Christ "composes men into the body of the Church."[17] It is the eucharist which creates community, for in receiving Christ the walls of self are broken down and the worshipper is engrafted into a great union which surmounts the natural order, Christ's body, the church. Guéranger translates and comments on the "Suscipe sancte Pater" offertory prayers of the mass so as to indicate the overcoming of individuality in eucharistic communion:

> We beseech thee, receive, together with this oblation, our hearts, which long to live by thee, and to cease to live their own life of self....Communion is the means by which our Lord unites all men into one whole....The Sacraments all contribute to make us one Body....Sacraments testify to the fraternity that exists amongst us; by them, we know each other...and by the same we are know.[18]

Guéranger's books argue that a communal conception of Christianity can practically be effected in parish churches by making the eucharist and communion "the center of all...by encouraging participation in the sacrifice."[19] The abbot advised the clergy to teach the faithful "as to Holy Communion,...never [to] isolate it in their respect and love from the oblation itself...[to] receive it frequently...."[20] Christ should be received by the entire community within the eucharist rather than during a pious exercise engaged in by a handful of individuals during an exercise separated from the mass. Communion is the principal act of the Christian life and overshadows every extra-liturgical cult and rational exercise.

That is because Christianity is not individual faith in a preacher's theology or cultivation of an exemplary private devotional

---

[17]L'Auxiliaire Catholique II (1845), 213.

[18]Prosper Guéranger, Liturgical Year: Advent, tr. Laurence Shepherd (3rd ed., London, 1910), p. 71; Guéranger, Explication, p. 200; Guéranger, Paschal Time, II, 261.

[19]Guéranger, Conférences, I, 236.

[20]Guéranger, The Church, p. 3.

life. It is a transformation of the personality into Christ through the infusion of grace. The sacraments are like principles of energy which establish the work of the divine spirit within men and women. It is a eucharistic life which in the end makes men and women acceptable to God:

> The Holy Spirit creates faith within our souls...faith is not the intellect's assent to a proposition logically demonstrated, but...proceeds from the will vivified by grace. ...His aim [the Holy Spirit's] is to form Christ within us. ...The Human element at last disappears....this amiable Saviour deigns to come into each one of us, and transform us ...into Himself....This is, in reality, the one grand aim of the Christian religion, to make man divine through Jesus Christ: it is the task which God has given to His Church to do....21

-2-

The goal of Guéranger's work was to teach bishops, parish priests, and lay people that the essence of Christianity could be grasped by understanding the liturgical year, that the "richness of the liturgy is the powerful means for our entering into the Church's spirit...."22 The beauty of ritual, as well as the contents of the words, have the power to awaken the sense of the religious, for "the spendour of the functions, and the magnificence of the chants, will open our hearts...."23

The publications of Solesmes propagated the view that "the best way of praying is to use the prayers of the Church" because of "the immense superiority of liturgical prayer over individual prayer."24

21Guéranger, Paschal Time, III, 349, 429-31, Advent, p. 31.

22Prosper Guéranger, Liturgical Year: Lent, tr. Laurence Shepherd (3rd ed., London, 1897), p. 144; Heinrich, the German translator of the work, understands this to be its main point.

23Guéranger, Christmas, I, 120.

24Guéranger, Conférences, p. 67.

The ancient prayers are better because they are collective and were written in an age when prayer was "considered as a social act."[25] The ethos of the liturgy is destroyed if it is prayed silently by the priest or used as a private office. For it is an objectively established rule of spiritual order, not the product of a single artist or age, and therefore it can meet the needs of Christians in every class and sector of society. It can solidify a people torn by economic stratification. The stability of society in the time when Europe was dominated by worship "shows the power of the Liturgy to unite men together...what, after Faith, unites us all into one family, is the Church's liturgy."[26] And its decline leads to the ruin of a nation.

> If...a country...were to seek progress by infringing the law of Christian Ritual, it would, in less than a hundred years, find that public and private morality has lost ground, and its own security would be menaced....Every injury offered to external worship, which is the great social link, is an injury to the interest of mankind.[27]

Two reforms were necessary if the liturgy were to play a social role once again in Europe. There would be no community as long as public prayer was merely a province of the clergy. The active participation of all the Christian people in the rites was necessary if worship were to have an impact once again. A comprehension by the public of what happens in the liturgy is a requirement for participation, for

> ...this liturgical prayer would soon become powerless were the faithful not to take a real share in it, or at least not to associate themselves to it in heart. It can heal and save the world, but only on the condition that it be understood....[28]

Solesmes sought to convince the clergy that it was their chief duty to teach the laity so that "they will take an interest in the Feasts of

----

25Guéranger, Institutions liturgiques, I, 1.

26Guéranger, Paschal Time, II, 445.

27Guéranger, Lent, p. 185.

28Guéranger, Advent, p. 5.

the Church, in the ceremonies she employs, and even the rubrics she observes....The Liturgical Calendar...shall be known to them." Parish priests should encourage their people

> on Sundays and Festivals...[to] attend by preference, High Mass...[to] follow all the rites and ceremonies performed by the priests...[to] follow the ecclesiastical chant...[to] avoid distracting their attention from the holy mysteries by other books of devotion...which at these moments would be harmful, by keeping them apart from the sacred Liturgy...[to] be present at Vespers and Compline...[and] to join with Holy Church in the chanting of her psalms and hymns.[29]

The purpose of the thousands of pages produced at Solesmes explaining the meaning of rites and texts, giving directions for the precise moment in a service when it was necessary to stand, make the sign of the cross, say amen, or sing alleluia was

> in order thus to enable the faithful to follow her [the Church] in her prayer of each mystic season, nay, of each day and hour....We have endeavoured to give, to such of the laity as do not understand Latin, the means of uniting in the closest possible manner with everything that the priest says and does at the altar.[30]

So strong was Guéranger's belief that in joining a community at worship the individual was participating in the mysteries being commemorated that he invariably used the word "uniting" to indicate the act of attending a service where worshippers "imitate the piety of the ages of faith, when Christians loved to honour the very least of our Saviour's actions, and so to speak, make them their own, by thus interweaving the minutest details of His life into their own."[31]

The publications of Solesmes, addressed to the laity and to priests, present the church not so much as an institution but as an organism energized by a liturgy which overcomes the antinomy between thought and life. There was a message here for skeptical men and women in the nineteenth century that they had not heard before: They should not investigate Christianity by determining what theologians say but by

----

[29]Guéranger, The Church, pp. 7-13.

[30]Guéranger, Advent, pp. 12, 13.

[31]Guéranger, Paschal Time, III, 174.

what the church does in her liturgy, for Christianity is not so much a matter of personal belief as it is common action. It is collectivity and mystical solidarity, not a way of holiness having for its end the perfection of a handful of individual souls. Christianity is the redemption of the body of humankind by the divine action in the incarnation. Every form of obtrustion of the individual ego in Christian art and worship is out of place. Heresy is the setting of a personal belief against the tradition of the community.

The sacraments and the liturgy give order and discipline to existence and show the way to the recovery of social life. The liturgy solves one of the great nineteenth-century problems, the proper maintenance of a healthy integration of the individual into society. Many solutions were proposed by Guéranger's secular contemporaries for this dilemma. The state, the party, or the proletariat were seen as the human matrix for a renewal of European society. Guéranger said that the liturgy was the form of life. Against the dissatisfied acquisitive human of capitalist societies, Guéranger set the liturgical man—man celebrating with the products of his labor which are transformed into channels of God's grace, man rejoicing in the worshipping community which is grounded in the body of Christ.

Guéranger's second call for reform was directed to the bishops, for the diligent work of the parish priests in urging liturgical participation would produce no unity in church or society as long as each diocese maintained its own particular tradition of services, texts, and music. The second task of Solesmes was to convince the French diocesan bishops of the importance of a basic unity in forms of worship, "that unity...is the essential element of Christianity."[32] Since the church is one transcendent international organism, its prayer must not be the product of the immediate past or of one national tradition. The church must have a universal discourse which stretches into the distant past and into every culture.

---

[32]Guéranger, Institutions liturgiques, I, 149.

The program for reform which Guéranger proposed to the bishops was "the re-establishment of the Roman liturgy in the dioceses of France as the first step" toward renewal.[33] The French episcopate was asked to sacrifice their use of neo-Gallican breviaries and missals of the seventeenth and eighteenth centuries and replace them with medieval Roman-Gallican or Tridentine-Roman brevaries and missals for the sake of the unity and interior peace of a church beset by turmoil. But this the French bishops refused to do. The battle for the adoption of Guéranger's liturgical reform lasted from 1840 to 1870 and was closely fought because it became entangled with the last struggle of the Gallican party in France to maintain an independent position within the increasingly centralized governmental structures of the Roman Catholic Church.

Solesmes was viewed as an agency of Rome; its abbot, an agent; his plans, sedition. The Gallican complexion of the episcopate insured the opposition of the majority of its members to Guéranger. The bitterness of their campaign resulted from the sense that the last bastions of nationalism in the Roman Church and of religious localism in the centralized state were being defended. The bishops who had been appointed during the Restoration understood their mission to be to advance the cause of a return to the political situation before the Revolution. To them Guéranger represented the Napoleonic spirit which had been embodied in legislation which combatted "customary rights," the aristocratic particularities of the ancien régime, in favor of one unique and precise code. The monk raised the double challenge of Rome and revolution. In accepting the Roman-Gallican or the Tridentine-Roman liturgy within their dioceses and removing their worship books

----

[33]Guéranger, Institutions liturgiques, I, XLIII. For analysis in greater detail of the whole complex issue of Guéranger and the Roman liturgy see R. W. Franklin, "Guéranger and Variety in Unity," Worship, 51, No. 5 (September 1977), 378-399; and Cuthbert Johnson, op. cit., pp. 147-246.

of the seventeenth and eighteenth centuries, the French bishops said that they were symbolically giving in to the tyranny of both Rome and revolution.

The first bishop to attack Guéranger for suggesting that Catholic revival was related to a French return to the basic unity of the Roman liturgy was P.-T. D. d'Astros of Toulouse who had been appointed by the king in 1820 and then established a reputation for vigorous opposition to the theories of Lamennais. D'Astros maintained in a stream of books and pamphlets from 1843 to 1846 that liturgical stability is equal to unity and that in changing forms of worship, piety is destroyed and faith endangered. So great a change as the adoption of the Roman liturgy in his diocese would cause the eclipse of the church.[34] D'Astros was supported by laymen of Toulouse. P.-C. Vitrey, the principal of the secondary school at Bourbonne, found that Guéranger's books were unsettling the ranks of the ordinary religious people, all in the name of a zeal for unity which was not traditional in France and resulted in scholarly nonsense and ridiculous practice. Vitrey mocked the learned abbot for discovering semi-Calvinism in the neo-Gallican antiphon Domine, dabis pacem nobis. This is Isaiah 26:12. Another heretical response according to Guéranger is Sive vigilemus, which is 1 Thessalonians 5:10. The revival of the Gregorian chant advocated by Solesmes, Vitrey noted, has caused "horrible cacophonies" in those parish churches where medieval music has been attempted to be sung.[35]

Sixty bishops publicly adhered to the refutation of Solesmes by d'Astros. The liturgical movement, they said in a series of letters,

---

[34]Paul-Thérèse David d'Astros, L'Église de France injustement flétrie dans un ouvrage ayant pour titre: Institutions liturgiques (1st ed., Toulouse, 1843), pp. 8, 44, 76, 143; (2nd ed., Toulouse, 1843), pp. 1-2; d'Astros, Examen de la Défense de Dom Guéranger et courte réfutation de sa lettre à Mgr. l'archevêque de Reims (Toulouse, 1846), pp. 1-2.

[35]P.-C. Vitrey, Observations sur les Institutions liturgiques de Dom Guéranger ou défense des liturgies gallicanes (Mirecourt, 1851), pp. 3, 7, 28.

is the excuse of a party of youthful enthusiasts whose aim is to weaken the authority of bishops. Those revolutionaries have put the rights of the dioceses of France into question and now they have spread discord even into the ranks of the episcopate, the vast majority of whom had always been against using Roman liturgical books in worship. Morlot of Tours wrote that Guéranger's reform was obviously the cause of the young in his diocese. Fruchaud, the bishop of Angoulême, attacked his irreverence. Guibert of Viviers spoke of his "ridiculous and insolent pretensions."[36]

Mgr. Fayet, the Bishop of Orléans, launched an assault in 1845 which was in many respects the most important, for he was a brilliant liberal humanist with a following in non-Catholic circles. His style was less strident and accusatory than the Archbishop of Toulouse and the other members of the episcopate. Fayet's books were gentle and civilized treatises. The arguments, however, remained the same. He wrote that Solesmes is a revolt against the hierarchy. Guéranger's method is to use pseudo-erudition to trap the reader in an Ultramontane snare. He would rather write a book than read one. Working in the school of Voltaire, he creates history out of no other material than his own dreams. His primary illusion is transforming a matter of discipline into an element of religion. The liturgy has no dogmatic character or value.

> There is no necessary relationship between the liturgy and the virtue of religion....The power of religion is only related to interior acts and has nothing to share with the liturgy....When we have saved religion which is perishing, then it will be time to talk about the liturgy.

Mgr. Fayet, product of an age when Christianity was regarded as right thinking, could not comprehend a model of faith in which practical heresy was more dangerous than speculative.[37]

----

[36]Letters of the bishops against Guéranger are in d'Astros, Examen, pp. 69-84; and letter of Morlot, 3 November 1847, Fruchaud, 12 November 1847, and Viviers, 23 November 1847, in Albert Houtin, Un Dernier Gallican. Henri Bernier (Paris, 1904), pp. 437, 438, 441.

[37]Jean-Jacques Fayet, Des Institutions liturgiques de Dom Guéranger et de sa lettre à Mgr. l'archevêque de Reims (Paris, 1845). This book, modified somewhat, became the next year d' Examen des Institutions

The last general rebuttal against "the liturgist of Solesmes who speaks as sovereign legislator of the Universal Church" was begun in 1850 by the bishops of Saint-Brieuc and Chartres. Old themes were repeated. Mgr. David defended the neo-Gallican liturgies on the basis of their beauty. Too many beautiful hymns and sequences were being sacrificed for an illusive and unimportant liturgical unity. Mgr. Clausel de Montals advised his people to avoid "the violent and furious aggressions" of the Abbot of Solesmes. The church is, after all, a federation of national churches, and in the name of innovation to cast scandal upon the customs of one is to weaken the body as a whole.[38] Sectors of the laity of the diocese of Chartres supported their bishop's argument in a petition against a return to the Roman rite.[39]

Priests went about among the parochial clergy agitating for the position of the bishops in the contest with Solesmes. Henri Bernier, the vicar-general of the neighboring diocese of Angers, was a well-known Gallican anti-liturgical activists, a public advocate of individualism and nationalism in religion. He was a church and king man, the product of the Saumur, that region which had strongly supported the Vendée. He could not quite separate the church and the state in his theology, and he argued against any such division in practice. The government to the abbé Bernier was a more trusted administrator of the church than Roman cardinals.[40] Those few passages of the divine office which he used were prayed alone. One half hour of each day was spent in private mental prayer and another was taken up

---

liturgiques de Dom Guéranger et de sa Lettre à Mgr. l'archevêque de Reims (Paris, 1846), pp. 36, 40, 45, 228, 491.

[38]C. H. Clausel de Montals, Lettre pastorale de Mgr. l'évêque de Chartres, sur la gloire et les lumières qui ont distingué jusqu'à nos jours l'Église de France (Chartres, 1850), pp. 3, 11, 32, 33, 45; Lettre pastorale de Mgr. l'évêque de Chartres au clergé de son diocèse ou sont présentées des observations sur le dernier mandement de Mgr. l'archevêque de Paris (Chartres, 1851), pp. 21-22.

[39]M. Roux, Protestation et appel respectueux en faveur de la liturgie gallican chartraine (Chartres, 1860).

[40]Henri Bernier, L'Etat et les cultes (Angers, 1848).

with the rosary. He would write to his spiritual charges and inquire, "How many rosaries have you said today for the repose of my soul?"[41] He emphasized to the curés of his diocese that their time could best be spent preparing sermons rather than trying to implement "the dangerous novelties" of Solesmes.[42]

There were three aspects to this vicar-general's struggle against Guéranger. He traveled about in 1845 preaching against liturgical reform as the work of "neo-Catholics" who were weakening the nation by spreading intolerance and exaggerating the place of ecclesiastical authority in daily life.[43] He attended provincial councils in 1849-50 to argue against adoption of the Roman liturgy in France. He composed circulars and letters, which were distributed by couriers, denouncing his monastic neighbors at Solesmes and pleading for a retention of the French neo-Gallican rites:

> Those people would put everything in a great pyre for the sake of a few hymns and antiphons, and they would produce books to prove to you that you can hardly recite the breviary of your diocese in conscience....They are passionate about uniformity....Uniformity is their mascot, and they will not die until they see all things done in France as they are in Italy.[44]

Their work is useless, but dangerous. To value the great volumes

> of the connoisseurs in liturgy, I would have to...sacrifice my convictions, my appreciations and almost my conscience.... When I hear praised around me "the beautiful, the excellent work" of our neighbors, I have the misfortune, while applauding their serious application, the merit of their vast erudition, the gravity of their language, to find the result of such great efforts pitiable....In my eyes the editions of the seventeenth and eighteenth century are not lacking in purity or chastity nor are they too modern....The words of Moses, of Solomon of St. Paul are neither too simple, too common, nor too old to provide the matter for antiphons and responses. What will these people say of me, if I eliminate

----

[41]Houtin, op. cit., p. 353.

[42]Ibid., p. 16.

[43]Bernier prepared a 600-page MS, Les néo-catholiques, whose contents are summarized in Houtin, op. cit.

[44]Ibid., p. 171.

some prayers in the taste of those which Le Mans has just adopted, the "medieval" office of St. Maurice? Won't they accuse the influence of the "headstrong Gallican" if I reject certain legends which conceal very piquant anecdotes, such as that of the great serpent, which, our venerable and learned neighbors say crepuit medius when it sees St. Julian?[45]

The bishops of Tours, Orléans, Le Mans, Amiens, and Viviers supported the abbé Bernier in a Humble remontrance to Guéranger which was circulated throughout the nation.[46]

Parish priests were also critical of the Benedictine liturgical movement. Le Coniat, the curé at Mennetou-sur-Cher, feared that he would be reduced to having only low masses in his parish because the people could not adjust to Gregorian chants and the ceremonies of the Roman ritual. "There are so many reforms demanded in the Church other than the abolition of the Paris chant and changing the costumes of the choir." Why are the monks threatening the disaffection of the people by forcing these absurd changes?[47] Other clergy complained that too much of their valuable time would be sacrificed in using the longer Roman offices, that the constant repetition of the psalter in the Roman pattern would bore the congregations.[48]

There were, however, some bishops who immediately understood that Guéranger had provided a solution to the practical problems of the dioceses. The first was Pierre-Louis Parisis. He had been born into the family of an Orléans baker which suffered severe persecution for the Christian faith during the Revolution. This experience impressed him with the great need of ecclesiastical reform if the French church hoped to survive the century. He became a priest in the quarter of

---

[45]Ibid., pp. 348-350.

[46]Henri Bernier, Humble remontrance au R. P. Dom Prosper Guéranger (Paris, 1847), pp. 20, 24, 36-37, 103.

[47]Letter of Le Coniat, 21 August 1850, in Houtin, op. cit., p. 447.

[48]P. Toussaint, ed., Lettres sur le bréviaire Romain addressées à un religieux par un curé de campagne (Pont-A-Mousson, 1864), pp. 15, 17; Réponse diverses aux lettres d'un curé de campagne sur le bréviaire Romain (Pont-A-Mousson, 1865), pp. 40-41, 47, 51, 55.

Gien in Orléans and attempted to revive his parish by building a new church. At the Revolution of 1830 he felt that he had failed in his mission when he was thrown into the river by his parishioners.[49] He was made Bishop of Langres in 1834, a fairly large diocese with 432 parishes and 254,000 people, located in the province of Lyon. There he attempted to regenerate religion by reforming his seminary, repairing the cathedral, founding houses for religious communities, and returning to the practice of holding regular clerical synods.

On episcopal visitations he had discovered that there was no unity in the diocese, that half of the parishes had come from other sees and had no sense of belonging to the larger community over which he presided. Mgr. Parisis had come to know of the liturgical reform of Solesmes through his vicar-general, the abbé Favrel, who corresponded with Guéranger. To Favrel, the abbot "had provided a signal service to the Church of France by providing a method for overcoming the liturgical anarchy which had injected a bad spirit" into the nation.[50] The Institutions liturgiques was "the faithful history" which provided a means for the restoration of order.[51] The bishop wrote to Guéranger after reading his liturgical works that he "supports the holy cause which you have defended with so much zeal," and that he had learned particularly of the importance of the unity of tradition.[52]

The Bishop of Langres formally and canonically declared that the Tridentine-Roman liturgy should be re-established in his diocese. It was necessary for him to defend this action before his fellow bishops and diocesan priests, and rebuttal of other bishops criticisms of Guéranger's books was included in Parisis' apologies. Solesmes had

----

[49]Louis Veuillot, Mgr. Parisis (Paris, 1864).

[50]MS letter of abbé Favrel, vicar-general of Langres, to Dom Guéranger, 11 January 1841, Archives, Abbey of Solesmes.

[51]MS letter of abbé Favrel to Dom Guéranger, 16 August 1842, Archives, Abbey of Solesmes.

[52]MS letter of Mgr. Parisis to Dom Guéranger, 31 July 1843, Archives, Abbey of Solesmes.

435

provided help for his parish churches. After thirty-eight years of anarchy "priests and faithful" demanded a remedy and it had been provided, a unity based on Roman forms. "Seeing how many seeds of division were germinating in the bosom of Catholic France we thought that it was necessary not to miss any occasion to strengthen the unity which is the health of us all." The Roman liturgy is the best for the diocese because it is the most ancient, the most universal, the most immutable of all forms of worship.[53]

Mgr. Parisis also encouraged parish priests to extend "the great joy in re-establishing the holy Roman liturgy" by encouraging the people to follow and understand the words of the mass, to sing Gregorian chant, to participate in the performance of the rites, and thereby overcome the detestable state into which the worship of the churches had fallen. Simple music and rites should be introduced in every place "for in the Church the music is for the words."[54] The abbé Favrel reported to Guéranger that in Langres they had created "one people of one expression."[55]

The Bishop of Bourges introduced the Roman liturgy into his 574 parishes "because the reading of the Institutions liturgiques had made a profound impression on us."[56] Mgr. Pie, later to turn Poitiers into an ultra-conservative citadel, came upon the Liturgical Year while he was a curé at Chartres. He wrote the author "that he had done a great work for the Church, priests and laymen," for he had provided a means for the Church to be unified in the face of the Revolution. Returning to the uniform symbols of the past is the best means to overcome the

----

[53]Mgr. Parisis, De la question liturgique (2nd ed., Paris, 1846), pp. 6-8, 11, 20, 36, 37-38.

[54]Pierre-Louis Parisis, Instruction pastorale et mandement de Mgr. l'Evêque de Langres, sur le chant de l'église (Langres, 1846), pp. 4, 15-17, 23-27, 31, 36-38.

[55]Charles Guillemant, Pierre-Louis Parisis (Paris, 1916), I, 185.

[56]Mgr. Berthaumier, Observations critiques sur le bréviaire de Bourges (Crété, 1849), p. 8.

infallibility of the individual, the chief modern heresy.[57] After he became a bishop, Pie established in 1856 the liturgical reform in his 635 parishes as the chief means of a pastoral offensive against the secularism of society in the villages and towns which surrounded Poitiers.[58]

Ordinaries who had been followers of Lamennais accepted the Roman rite quite readily after reading Guéranger's arguments about the unacceptable Catholic nationalism of the neo-Gallican liturgies. Cardinal Donnet converted Bordeaux in 1850, Mgr. Doney promulgated the Roman liturgy in Montauban in 1847, and Gerbet did the same at Perpignan in that year. All the dioceses of Brittany went over to the Roman liturgy between 1846 and 1848 except for Nantes.[59]

Other bishops adopted the Roman liturgy to end social disorder. In 1848 Mgr. Bonnechose of Carcassonne, seeking to control the confusion of his people, "enforced the forms of prayer of the center of the Christian world."[60] On visitations in 1846 and 1847 the Bishop of Tarbes noticed that his people were using liturgies of Paris, Auch, and Rome. He followed the reasoning of Parisis and in February 1849 established "the ancient, universal, unchangeable Roman rite" as a means to arrest a chaotic situation over which he was losing control.[61] That September the diocesan of Angoulême returned to "the common Christian law," for in the presence of popular disruption Catholic

---

[57]Mgr. Baunard, Histoire du Cardinal Pie, Évêque de Poitiers (2nd ed., Paris, 1886), I, 126-127, 431.

[58]Dom Besse, Le Cardinal Pie, sa vie, son action religieuse et sociale (Paris, 1930), pp. 29, 81.

[59]J. C. Doney, "Lettre," L'Univers (10 February 1846).

[60]F. G. Bonnechose, Lettre pastorale et mandement de Mgr. l'Evêque de Carcassonne au clergé de son diocèse pour le rétablissement de la liturgie Romaine (Carcassonne, 1854), pp. 5, 9.

[61]B.-S. Laurence, Mandement de Mgr. l'Evêque de Tarbes, pour le rétablissement de la liturgie Romaine dans son diocèse (Tarbes, 1849), p. 209.

unity is necessary "to counter the new tempestuous forces."[62] Coutances became Roman in its worship because it was felt that now there was a need "to return to the ancient tradition of the Fathers."[63]

The course of the Roman question at Reims suggests that Mgr. Gousset, like other members of the episcopate, was drawn to the reform of Solesmes but deterred from enforcing it because of the vehemence of the Gallicans. Archbishop Gousset notified the abbot that he had read the Liturgical Year "with interest" and that it was a great work of instruction for priests and faithful, but he found he did not have the power to enact the changes suggested in the volumes.[64] The pope was also informed of his dilemma, and Gregory XVI responded from the Vatican on 6 August 1842 that he deplored the variety of liturgical books in France. That settled the matter for Gousset, and he used the papal advice as the principal support for the re-establishment of the Roman liturgy in 1848 and the Gregorian chant in 1852.[65]

Gregory XVI's letter on liturgical unity of 6 August 1842 made an impact on French diocesan officials. After 1842, cathedral chapters began to urge their bishops to adopt some form of the Roman rite, either Roman-Gallican or Tridentine-Roman. In councils and synods, organized coteries won episcopal concessions. The initiative for the 1844 reform in Quimper came from the priests of the diocese. After a unanimous plea from his clergy the Bishop of Gap agreed to the Roman rites in 1845 "in order to fortify us in the midst of tempests which

---

[62]R.-F. Régnier, Ordonnance de Mgr. l'Evêque d'Angoulême qui prescrit le rétablissement du rit Romain (Angoulême, 1849), p. 2.

[63]L.-J. Tréhonnais, Lettre pastorale de Mgr. l'Evêque de Coutances au clergé de son diocèse (Coutances, 1850).

[64]MS letter of Archbishop Gousset of Reims to Dom Guéranger, 21 December 1841, Archives, Abbey of Solesmes.

[65]T.-M.-J. Gousett, Mandement de Mgr. l'archevêque de Reims, pour le rétablissement de la liturgie Romaine dans son diocèse (Reims, 1848), p. 7.

disjoint us more violently than ever."[66]   In La Rochelle 300 priests
demanded a return to the Roman liturgy, which the bishop agreed to as
an expression of Christian unity before the public.[67]

1853 was a year in which parochial officials forced adherence to
the reforms advocated by Solesmes at Amiens, Limoges, Luçon, and Tulle.
In the diocese of Valence the liturgical movement was led by abbé Jouve
who stirred up the parishes by compiling a popular version of the
Institutions, Du mouvement liturgique en France durant le XIXe siècle
and by distributing a monthly leaflet, La Paroisse, revue liturgique,
canonique, etc. which provided simple explanations of the meaning of
Roman texts, descriptions of Roman ceremonies and symbolism, and guides
for the conduct of street processions. The bishop yielded to pressure
from below in 1858 and abolished all the neo-Gallican liturgies in use
in the diocese.[68]

Cathedral canons, those specialists in worship on a large scale,
took the lead elsewhere. The chapter at Périgueux persuaded their
bishop in 1844 that the multiplicity of missals which were allowed in
the diocese was a scandal and a return to "the ancient Roman books" was
proclaimed.[69] The clergy of the cathedral at Saint-Brieuc agreed
unanimously that it was necessary to have "a true and pure liturgy" in
1846.[70] The chapters of Vannes and Moulins were of one mind on the
subject in 1850 and 1852. In Sens, the chapter demanded the establishment of the liturgical reform in January 1847, but it was not

[66]J.-I. Depéry, Lettre pastorale de Mgr. l'Evêque de Gap, au sujet
du rétablissement de la liturgie Romaine dans son diocèse (Gap, 1845),
p. 3.

[67]J.-F. Bergier, Études liturgiques (Besançon, 1861), p. 179; Mgr.
Villecourt, Lettre pastorale de Mgr. l'Evêque de La Rochelle, etc. (La
Rochelle, 1849).

[68]Bergier, op. cit., pp. 244ff.

[69]J.-B. George, Mandement de Mgr. l'Evêque de Périgueux au sujet,
etc. (Périgueux, 1844).

[70]J. J. P. Le Mée, Circulaire de Mgr. l'Evêque de Saint-Brieuc, à
son clergé (Saint-Brieuc, 1846), p. 2.

promulgated by the bishop until 1852. A coalition of well-placed priests bitterly opposed any adoption of Guéranger's ideas and blocked the action for as long as possible. Their rationale was that deficient parochial budgets could not bear the weight of transition to the Roman liturgy.[71]

Other churches were reformed because the diocesan bishop alone was persuaded that the pope's letter to the Bishop of Reims was an endorsement of the criticism of the Gallican liturgies. The Bishop of Rennes spoke through his canon Meslé and said that the pope has expressed a wish for uniformity which must be obeyed. "There are advantages to the new situation. The constant repetition in the Roman rite will afford participation by the humble poor who cannot read but can easily memorize the services."[72] The diocese of Troyes, which had three liturgies after the Revolution, followed the Solesmes reform in January 1847 after receiving a letter from Pius IX expressing a wish that in order to guarantee the authority of teaching in that region in rebellious times the people should enter into liturgical unity. However, "independently...a majority of the priests of the diocese and enlightened faithful declared in favor of a return to the Roman liturgy."[73]

Once again revolution underlay liturgical change. The increasing intervention of the Papacy in favor of the reforms of Solesmes was accelerated after 1848 when the Italian secular movement toward national unity challenged the power of the Holy See in Italy. The policy of Gregory the Great, who sent missions to England and the north when threatened by barbarians in the seventh century, was repeated.

----

[71]Mellon Jolly, Mandement de Mgr. l'archevêque de Sens, etc. (Sens, 1851); Abbé Cornat, De l'introduction de la liturgie Romaine dans le diocèse de Sens (Auxerre, 1848).

[72]J. Meslé, Examen respectueux, pacifique, et religieux des objections et représentations contre le retour aux brèviaire et missel Romains (Rennes, 1843), pp. 59, 64, 82.

[73]J.-M. M. Debelay, Mandement de Mgr. l'Evêque de Troyes, etc. (Troyes, 1847), p. 7.

Pius IX, expelled from Rome in October 1848 by Mazzini and challenged by the anti-clerical laws of the emerging kingdom of Italy, attempted to create countervailing sectors of papal influence by re-establishing the Roman hierarchy in England in 1850 and Holland in 1853. The destruction of the Gallican party in the church of France was a part of this counter-offensive. Guéranger's liturgical apostolate fit into the northern schema of Pius IX. This explains why the character of papal letters on return to the Roman liturgy in France changed from the mild responses of Gregory XVI in 1842 to the direct intervention of Pius IX after 1848.

Books which had attacked Guéranger, beginning with the abbé Bernier's Humble remontrance, were placed on the Index by Pius IX with anonymous defenses of Gallican customary rights, Mémoire sur le droit coutumier and Du droit et du pouvoir des évêques de régler les offices divins dans les limites de leur diocèses. Mgr. Bouvier and other episcopal authors were threatened with the Index unless they corrected their books to conform to the desires of the Holy See. In 1852 the Congregation of Rites decreed that the neo-Gallican liturgies of Le Mans and Beauvais must be abolished. The next year the pope restated his zeal for liturgical unity and purity in France in the encyclical Inter multiplices.

The adoption of the Roman liturgy became as much a political gesture as it had been an ecclesio-political symbol during the period of the early Gallican polemics. Most diocesans quickly accepted it as a means to shore up support for Roman Catholicism, faced as it was by a variety of challenges to the Holy See. The diocese of Fréjus was the first to change because of loyalty. In 1852 the diocese of Blois returned as a demonstration of attachment to the pope. The Bishop of Blois, Mgr. Pallu du Parc, discerned the Holy Spirit leading all into a new period. "This is the epoch of unity in the liturgy." He had been opposed to the "liturgical movement" because it had appeared to be the project of anti-hierarchical priests and laymen. Now he had been led to the knowledge that the simplicity of the Roman prayer, its own "liturgical beauty," and the repetitions which facilitated understanding made it the suitable form "not of individual prayer" but "the common prayer of all the faithful people."[74]

The Dean of Meaux, abbé Pruneau who had been a particularly vehement enemy of Guéranger, withdrew his local breviaries immediately after Rome had made it clear in 1852 that it now considered the French neo-Gallican liturgies to be illegitimate, and the Bishop of Saint-Claude, who had openly favored the beauty and poetry of the neo-Gallican rites even into the fifties, abolished them as a sign of respect for the Holy See now threatened by modern revolution.[75] His action was followed by Aire, Nevers, and Agen in 1853 and in the next two years by Châlons-sur-Marne, Chalon, Autun, Mâcon, Sainte-Dié, Cahors, Montpellier, and Nîmes.[76] The Archbishop of Albi went over to the Tridentine-Roman liturgy in 1857 "thus to complete and reassert union with the Church of Rome."[77] Those ordinaries who had delayed to effect the change were directed to do so again by Pius IX in 1858 and 1859, and Bayonne, Angers, Viviers, Tours, Metz, Puy, Mende, and Nancy bowed before the papal wish.[78] Toulouse, which had been the seat of Mgr. d'Astros, submitted in 1860. The archbishop sadly announced to his people:

...It is not to conform you to our own taste but to fulfill an imperious and sacred duty that you must favorably receive the liturgical reform....It is not a question of art but of conscience....This restoration has been demanded by the Pope in numerous communications addressed to the bishops of

---

[74]L.-T. Pallu du Parc, Instruction pastorale et mandement de Mgr. l'Evêque de Blois, etc. (Blois, 1852, and Paris, 1853), pp. 2, 14, 15, 16, 21, 63-95.

[75]Anon., Notice nécrologique sur M. l'abbé Pruneau (Meaux, 1863), p. 7; J.-P. Mabile, Lettre pastorale, etc. (Sainte-Claude, 1853), p. 18.

[76]Bergier, op. cit., pp. 244ff.; F.-G.-M.-F. de Marguerye, Lettre pastorale et ordonnance de Mgr. l'Evêque d'Autun, Chalon, Maçon, etc. (Autun, 1854).

[77]Un Prêtre du diocèse d'Albi, Livret de la liturgie Romaine, etc. (Castres, 1857).

[78]Bergier, op. cit., pp. 336ff.

Catholicism....We are declaring to you that because of the pontifical bulls, in the matter of liturgy a bishop has no rights. The sovereign pontiff alone possesses the power.... At this very moment 72 dioceses of France have already adopted the Roman liturgy. The others have promised to accept it very shortly....Receive this liturgy which Rome presents to you as the will of this persecuted pontiff, betrayed by some members of his family. May your respectful submission be a filial expiation. Through the invisible solidarity which binds souls among themselves, your inalterable dedication to the see of Peter will hide the defection of those who separate themselves from it.[79]

By 1865 the Bishop of Versailles, who had sanctioned a liturgical education program to teach children obedience to Rome, was able to write of "the salubrious reform of the Roman liturgy...which has brought unity to the Church in France, except for one diocese, where this is not so." By the time of the Vatican Council in 1870 that see, Orléans, had promulgated Roman books.[80]

-4-

In almost all cases this was a pacific transformation. There were, however, vicious struggles in Le Mans, Paris, Angers, Besançon, and Nevers, where sectors of the parochial clergy waged a difficult battle against recalcitrant Gallican ordinaries, and in Lyon where the old traditionalist de Bonald promulgated the reforms, an action which was resisted by his priests.

In Le Mans the gradual return to Roman practices which had been begun in isolated areas by Myre de la Mory was continued as slowly by Mgr. Carron, who, in 1833, changed his missal to make the Holy Week ceremonies conform to the papal celebrations. He refused to go further, fearing the disapproval of a population which equated religion and politics. There was rumor to the effect that any change in what

----

[79]Mgr. l'archevêque de Toulouse, Mandement, etc. (Toulouse, 1860).

[80]H.-A.-M. Dutilliet, Petite catéchisme liturgique ou courte explication des principales cérémonies de l'Eglise Romaine (Paris, 1860); Instructio Pastoralis et Decretum Versaliensis Episcopi (Versailles, 1864).

had been the pre-Revolutionary form of piety would be greeted with outrage and violence. On the basis of this Mgr. Carron, who regarded his chief mission to be the preservation of order, stood firm for the old ways.[81]

Mgr. Bouvier also was aware that some reform of worship was necessary for his diocese, but his hatred of Solesmes and his extreme respect for the liberties of French bishops determined that he would be vehement in rejecting any program for liturgical alteration except one which he alone had drawn up.[82] He was for new liturgies and many liturgies. The alterations suggested by the Benedictines, he argued, were impractical for parish churches and would reduce the clergy to the task of only saying infrequent low masses, for few in this region would attend the new services. Moreover, the Abbot of Solesmes was creating another scandal before the eyes of the public by discussing openly the inadequacies of their worship. It was for the individual bishop to decide such matters, not for parish priests or monks or the pope.[83]

One group in the diocese supported the opinion of Bouvier. The abbé Albin argued that an absolute exclusion of local traditions, for example, the beautiful sequences sung in country churches, would dismay pious souls. M. de Saint-Germain pointed out that the reform of Solesmes was easy for seminarians and monks but would not be taken up by men of the world. The Bulletin d'Agriculture reported that in rural areas where the Roman rite was introduced the populace thought that the religion had been changed. Melchoir du Lac summed up the warning of opponents: "The innovation would have as a result to absent the population, to make them unacquainted with [Christian] teaching.

----

[81]Auguste Sifflet, Les Evêques concordataires du Mans. Mgr. Carron (Le Mans, 1917), pp. 133-134, 171, 175.

[82]Auguste Sifflet, Les Evêques concordataires du Mans. Mgr. Carron (Le Mans, 1921), I, 135.

[83]Abstracts of Collections des Mendements de Mgr. Bouvier, in Ambroise Ledru, Dom Guéranger, Abbé de Solesmes, et Mgr. Bouvier, Evêque du Mans (Paris, 1911), pp. 230-233.

It would have a deadly effect."[84]

But du Lac, although admitting objections, was the spokesman of a circle of laymen who campaigned for reform because it would give them a role in public prayer. The "liturgical revolution" will cause change, they said, but it will be for the good and not injure the parishes at all. These men were supported by the cathedral chapter of Le Mans, the center of clerical propaganda for the Roman rite. Myre de la Mory had altered its complexion by making the leading Ultramontanes of the region honorary canons. René Lottin was named a regular canon in 1831 and Benjamin Heurtebize in 1840. They were joined by other allies of Solesmes, Fillion, Piolin, Gautray, and Pollon de Saint-Chéreau.

There followed a period of bitter controversy between the diocesan Bishop of Le Mans, Mgr. Bouvier, and his chapter. It was not until 1851 that Bouvier was forced to call a synod of the priests of the diocese to debate the liturgical question. That August the canons "challenged Mgr. Bouvier to renounce a new edition of the ritual of Le Mans, which so little conforms to the rules of the Roman liturgy of which the re-establishment is so desirable."[85]

In 1852 the Vatican Congregation of Rites formally condemned the liturgies of Le Mans. Bouvier submitted to the will of the pontiff and the following October grudgingly began the abolition of the rites of Le Mans:

> Although the liturgy of the diocese was one of the most irreproachable of the last century we have taken the resolution together with our venerable chapter, to substitute the Roman liturgy in its place. In doing this furthermore we follow our feelings of profound veneration and complete submission towards the vicar of Jesus Christ.[86]

---

[84]E. Couillard, Notice sur M. l'abbé L.-B. Albin (Le Mans, 1903), p. 9; Bulletin d'agriculture, sciences et arts de la Sarthe, X, 318; Ledru, op. cit., pp. 235-236; Melchior du Lac, La Liturgie Romaine et les liturgies françaises (Le Mans, 1849), pp. 28-29.

[85]Auguste Sifflet, Le chapitre du Mans depuis le Concordat (Le Mans, 1912), p. 84.

[86]Auguste Sifflet, Bouvier, II, 414-415.

This was only a theoretical gesture, and it was not until the consecration of Bouvier's successor, Jean-Jacques Nanquette who had been predisposed to the change after training in the Roman tradition of Reims, that the Tridentine-Roman liturgy was made mandatory throughout the parishes of the region "as a demonstration of faith for the Holy See."[87]

The chapter continued as a force for liturgical renewal. In 1857 there was an effort to insure that the processions of St. Mark and the Rogation days proceeded through the streets and fields and were made into a local event for the people. Dom Gardereau, a monk of Solesmes, was invited as Lenten preacher in the cathedral. Simplified music was established in the parishes. The violins which had traditionally accompanied the figure of Christ in Palm Sunday processions were suppressed. Canon Gontier was a propagandist for a method of singing Gregorian chants which could be used in even the most rustic villages.[88]

In the diocese of Paris there were skirmishes between different forces. There it was the chapter of Notre-Dame in league with the archbishops, the heart of the old Gallican ecclesiastical establishment, who blocked a mandatory enforcement of the Roman liturgy for almost seventeen years after Archbishop Sibour had indicated that such action was necessary. This attitude followed from the great veneration which had been bestowed on the neo-Gallican Paris liturgy for generations as one of the national treasures. The abbé Dassance and M. Tresvaux du Fraval defended their liturgy a great literary masterpiece. Canon Armand Auger added that the destruction of these books would provide further proof to secular enemies of Catholicism of the medieval barbarism of the church. "The introduction of the Roman liturgy would not be able to produce any real advantage for religion and would only

----

[87]J.-J.Nanquette, Lettre pastorale, etc. (Le Mans, 1856).

[88]Sifflet, Chapitre, passim; M. A. Gontier, Méthode raisonnée de plain-chant (Paris, 1859); Le Plain-Chant, son exécution (Le Mans, 1860).

further expose the clergy to the criticism of men of the world...."[89]

The vicar-general of Paris, the old Gallican lion Jean-Henri Prompsault, made the most well-known and widely distributed attack on Guéranger which came from that city. It was an exuberant and futile charge published at the moment when Rome was considering its definitive statement of 1852. Prompsault laughed the excessive laughter of a defeated man. Can the Abbot of Solesmes, he asked, be serious in thinking that a change of prayers would stop the decline of religion? Unity is for medieval automatons not modern men. Diversity is indispensable for congregations of quality. Important people will be driven from the churches.

> The Church, my reverend sir, was established on the unity of faith, the unity of sacraments, the unity of ministries, and the variety of rites....It is diversity and not liturgical unity which conforms to the spirit of the Church.

Should Rome teach the bishops of France, he inquired, and then answered without waiting for reply:

> Rome, the Rome of which you speak is a collection of private persons all with interests of nationality, taste, and vanity. ...These men are the counsellors of the Holy See....Never will they be the tutors of the bishops of France.

Guéranger, the vicar-general suggested, had helped to destroy that wise system of the past which placed the governance of the church under the secular prince thereby keeping out the meddling Romans. For this he "has the ear of the Pope and has been made a member of the Inquisition."[90]

----

[89]J.-B. A. Auger, La question liturgique réduite à sa plus simple expression (Paris, 1854), p. 136; Abbé Dassance, "Lettres," L'Ami de la Religion, CXVI (2 February 1843), 209-214, (21 February 1843), 340; M. Tresvais, "Lettres," L'Ami de la Religion, CXVI (17 January 1843), 97-101; CXVII (27 May 1843), 393-400. Guéranger replied to this praise of a nation's contribution to religion in L'Ami, CXVI (9 February 1843), 251-264; CXVII (15 June 1843), 521-528, and said that "he will always be careful with God's grace, not to be French in matters of religion. Every Christian must be Catholic, and every Catholic must be Roman. I only know that [citizenship] in the world; there are no nations in the Church."

[90]J.-H. Prompsault, Lettre au R. P. Dom Guéranger en réponse à la préface du 3e volume de ses Institutions liturgiques (Paris, 1852), pp. 9, 26, 31, 32, 37, 38, 240.

The Archbishop of Paris of the forties, Mgr. Affre, instructed his priests not to read the Institutions or the Liturgical Year.[91] However, in the fifties the church of Paris was ruled by Mgr. Sibour, who, while bishop of another diocese, had read the Institutions liturgiques and wrote to Guéranger of noticing "...a deplorable state...this multiplicity of breviaries." In 1856 he announced in Paris that the moment had come to re-establish the Roman liturgy because of the need for bonds of unity. "The movement for the liturgy has become a general movement...and resistance by individuals is no longer possible."[92]

There was immediate protest from the clergy that where this had been done "there was an abandoning of the solemn offices and a considerable confluence at the low masses." The Catholics of the Diocese for the Conservation of the Paris Liturgy presented Cardinal Morlot in 1859 with an address protesting "the liturgical fantasies of M. Guéranger" and refusing to adopt "his liturgical system....founded neither on law nor reason...agitated more by passion than reflection."[93]

The church musicians of Paris were the primary defenders of Solesmes. The organist of Saint Eustache endorsed the participation of the people in the Gregorian chant and the explusion of operatic masses as a symbolic gesture.

> In the midst of questions of industry, of business,and material interests which dominate society and seem to absorb the strength and spirit of all, a higher thought ought to take its place in the preoccupations of the noblest spirits

---

[91]Denis Affre, Mandement...sur Institutions liturgiques (Paris, 1843); Mandement, circulaire...sur Institutions liturgiques (Paris, 1849).

[92]MS letter of Mgr. Sibour, Bishop of Digne to Dom Guéranger, Archives, Abbey of Solesmes; M.-D.-A. Sibour, Mandement de Mgr. l'Archevêque de Paris sur le retour à la liturgie Romaine (Paris, 1856), p. 4.

[93]de Laborie, loc. cit., p. 952; Ledru, op. cit., p. 235; Les Catholiques, Requête adressée à son Eminence le Cardinal Morlot (Paris, 1859), pp. 17, 20.

...the practice of the Catholic faith and zeal for its conservation.[94]

Others argued that "the liturgical variations are a...scandal to the people" and that music should be simple enough in churches to allow all the people to join in.[95] A Congress for the Restoration of Plainchant and the Music of the Church at Paris in 1860 voted unanimously that Gregorian music was the best means to these ends.

> Unanimous! Yes, Gentlemen...Plainchant...has been unanimously proclaimed by the Congress as the true song of the Church...the only one which is popular...one of the most powerful means of action on the people.[96]

The Paris rite and chant, however, were not abolished completely until the period of the First Vatican Council, when the pope directly ordered Cardinal Guibert to force all priests to conform to Rome.

In the diocese of Besançon the struggle was not so much over the value of a liturgical change but the rapidity with which the absolute requirement for transformation should be enforced. The archbishop favored a gradual evolution for the sake of his rural population; a fiery circle of priests published a stream of pamphlets calling for total and immediate uniformity with Rome; and they reported their diocesan to the Holy Office. Cardinal Patrizi responded in 1872 naming Archbishop Mathieu a liturgical rebel and summing up how his irregular behavior was viewed at Rome: "After the Vatican Council there are no more Gallicans, there are only Catholics or heretics."[97]

----

[94]F. Danjou, De l'état et de l'avenir du chant ecclésiastique en France (Paris, no date), pp. 1, 15, 56.

[95]Augustin Bourdin, Les liturgies françaises en général (Paris, 1856), p. 221; Théodore Nisard, Examen critique des moyens les plus propres d'améliorer et de populariser le chant (Paris, 1846).

[96]Congrès pour la restauration du plain-chant et de la musique d'Eglise (Paris, 1862), p. 71.

[97]Letter of Patrizi, quoted in Abbé Thiébaud, L'Eglise métropolitaine de Besançon (Besançon, 1872), p. 26. The position of the archbishop was maintained in J.-M.-A.-C. Mathieu, Traduction de la Circulaire au clergé de Besançon touchant la liturgie (Besançon, 1857). We was attacked by: Abbé Ch. Maire, La Liturgie Romaine et la conscience (Besançon, 1861); Réponse aux observations anonymes (Besançon, 1861); Abbé Jean-François Bergier, Études liturgiques;

Unity was even more harshly maintained in Lyon where the parish clergy unanimously rejected "the liturgical revolution" declared by Cardinal de Bonald in 1862. Five representatives were dispatched to Rome with 1,400 signatures petitioning a reversal of the change. The defense was based on cost, that their parishes would be destroyed financially by the adoption of the new rites.[98]

The papal action was swift. The delegates were lectured on filial obedience by the pope, censured in a letter of Patrizi, and their books were listed in the Index. Pope Pius IX, in a series of pointed letters, commanded every recalcitrant church to abandon its local liturgical books.[99]

-5-

This success, although complete, was only official. Scores of parish priests adopted the Solesmes reform under duress. It is a resonable assumption that in the typical church the letter of the services was new, but the spirit was not, for those parishes in which the liturgical reform was used as a medium for the creation of a

---

Explications intéressantes; Un petit mot à l'adresse des prêtres bisontins; Nouvelles explications (all publ. Besançon, 1861); and Entretien sur la necessité d'adopter le Rit Romain (Paris, 1861). Abbé Thiébaud, Crise nouvelle du Bisontinisme agonisant, Profession de foi liturgique (both Besançon, 1861); Introduction du Rit Romain dans l'Eglise métropolitaine de Besançon (Besançon, 1872).

[98]Laymen of Lyon defended their liturgy; L. Morel de Voleine, Recherches historiques sur la Liturgie Lyonnaise (Lyon, 1856); Joseph Bard, De la questoin liturgique par rapport à la sainte Eglise de Lyon (Lyon, 1860). The priests did as well: Bissardon, curé of St.-Bruno, Défense de la Liturgie de Lyon (Lyon, 1864); Abbé Chabert, curé of St. Vincent, Défense de la Liturgie de Lyon (Lyon, 1859). A propos d'un pamphlet contre les curés de Lyon (Lyon, 1863).

[99]Tableau synoptique et réclamation contre une assertion impossible à tolérer (Lyon, 1862); Abbé Rouse, La liturgie de la sainte Eglise de Lyon d'après les monuments (Lyon, 1864), p. vii; Un catholique lyonnais, Liturgie Lyonnaise résumé analytique des débats (Lyon, 1864). Compte rendu de la députation envoyée à Rome par le clergé du diocèse de Lyon (Lyon, 1864), pp. 5, 9, 15, 17, 27, 32.

community began to stand out conspicuously on the religious terrain of France. That a transformation of rites was valued by Frenchmen in the nineteenth century is suggested by the history of a sample of nineteenth century churches where Guéranger's ideas were put into practice.

During World War I, particularly 1915-1917, the line of the trenches ran constantly through the eastern part of the diocese of Troyes. Priests attached to ambulance corps discovered a remarkable village in the valley of the Vanne, not many kilometers west of Troyes. It had been observed that it was the rule in the churches of the district that men did not attend services and the sacraments were abandoned except by small groups of pious old women during Holy Week and Easter. But at Mesnil-St.-Loup the offices were frequented on Sundays and feast days by the entire population, who sang the Gregorian settings and received communion together as one body. It was rumored that this had been the state of religion for sixty-five years.[100]

A newly ordained priest, André Piot, had come to Mesnil-St.-Loup at Christmas in 1849 from the diocesan seminary at Troyes filled with the new liturgical enthusiasm. His first years in the seminary had been taken up with the study of the Greek Fathers. When he heard of the controversies surrounding the Abbot of Solesmes in 1844, he wrote to his family, "I would like to have some information from you on... Father Guéranger...."[101] André finished reading all the volumes of the Institutions and the Liturgical Year which were available, and then he sought out Dom Guéranger to relate his sense of vocation to the liturgical apostolate. He found the abbot in Paris and told him of his plan to take on a parochial cure and there make the Roman liturgy a reality for the simple faithful, a prayer not only of the priest but of the laymen. "That, in the end, is the ultimate goal of the liturgical renovation: it is not an agitation solely to convince individuals, but

----

[100]Bernard Maréchaux, L'Oeuvre pastorale du Père Emmanuel (Saint-Maximin, 1925).

[101]Bernard Maréchaux, Le Père Emmanuel (2nd ed., Mesnil-St.-Loup, 1918), p. 36.

to reach the mass of the faithful...to make the life of the Church the life of the entire populace."[102]

The village in which the twenty-three-year-old André determined to carry out his experiment had been owned before the Revolution by the order of Malta, but the lands had been managed by townsmen from Troyes and Estissac who assumed ownership in 1792. Small industries had grown up in the neighborhood and employed a proportion of the male and female population. The new priest, however, found there to be no civic or religious organizations. One mass a week was celebrated on Sunday morning. He detected a high rate of illegitimacy and noted that in the five years after 1820 twenty-four out of the twenty-eight children baptized did not have married parents. Only ten residents were known to have previously submitted to confirmation in the century. The eucharist was frequented by five aging grandmothers.

André Piot faced this situation by announcing to the villagers in an appeal that

> I want not only to make some Christians, but to make a parish. A non-Christian parish is not a parish. I want to make a parish, that is to say, a collective organism...a body which functions through the tight union of all its members-- common prayer, and chants in common--also communal games on Sunday; in a word, a life of charity in which strong Christians find their place as well as children and new converts.[103]

The first step toward this goal was the introduction of the Roman rites and the Gregorian chant. He used sermons in the mass to teach the people of Mesnil-St.-Loup that the foundation of Christianity is praying together. He preached his own version of the liturgical theology, insisting that the prayers of the mass were the expression of the faith, that by joining neighbors in the eucharistic exercise the individual souls of the parish could be united into the body of

---

[102]Bernard Maréchaux, "Dom Guéranger et le Père Emmanuel. Etude liturgique et théologique," Rivista Storica Benedettina, Vol. V, Fasc. XIX (July-September 1910), 406-417.

[103]Maréchaux, Père Emmanuel, p. 87.

Christ, a fortress in a pagan land. "Babylon is crumbling, but we are constructing a little corner of Jerusalem."[104]

André Piot began classes for children and adults at which he taught the meaning of the Roman liturgical texts "so that they [the parishioners] could pray better and honor God." He compiled a small Méthode facile pour entendre le latin des offices de l'Eglise for instruction in ecclesiastical Latin. At these sessions as well as providing practice in Gregorian melodies, he explained the meaning of the psalms so that the offices might be chanted with intelligence. He interrogated his pupils not only on the teaching contained in the gospels and epistles for each Sunday of the liturgical year, but on the contents of the introits, graduals, and antiphons of every mass. Small cards were printed with the people's part of the liturgy underlined to facilitate participation.

Sunday was made into a demonstration of the union of the parish, a day devoted to the collective cult. There was a simple mass at 8, and at 10:30 the service was sung in Gregorian chant by the entire congregation who were led by four chanters standing about a harmonium placed in the middle of the nave. There was no distinction between "choir" and "congregation." In the afternoon the offices of vespers and compline were sung in the same manner. At Christmas, Easter, and Pentecost the parish became like monastery. All seven of the offices were chanted. The village people were in church from ten until the dawn singing the matins, lauds, and mass of the Nativity, and six hours daily were spent celebrating each of the three days of the Holy Week Triduum, Maundy Thursday, Good Friday, and Easter Even. Evening services with congregational singing were begun for those whose occupations prevented their assistance at the two masses which were celebrated daily.

At the same time there was an important increase in the reception of the eucharist. As early as December 30, 1854 the curé noted, "Our population is only 350 souls, but of this number about 100 approach the

---

[104]Ibid., p. 159.

sacrament and of this number one third are men."[105] One-third of the
village was still taking communion every Sunday as late as 1925. By
1855 at minor feasts like the Purification approximately 70
parishioners received communion, and in the years after 1900 two-thirds
of the faithful were at the altar on Easter.[106]

The curé advanced the communal religious exercises of the parish
by organizing segments of the population of Mesnil-St.-Loup into a
number of lay confraternities. The confraternity of Notre-Dame de la
Sainte-Espérance was formed in 1854 for the purpose of encouraging men
and women to keep the prayer offices in church daily. In the first
year 101 villagers joined. In 1878 the Société de Jésus Couronné
d'Epines was begun primarily for residents who worked in small
factories. Its goal was the "union of souls," "the protection of women
and girls against the contagion of the world," "the observation of
perfect modesty," and "charitable unity and mutual service." The
Society received communion together once a month. In 1878 there were
80 members and by 1903 94 people were participating in its acts of
worship. Another confraternity for men, the Société de la
Résurrection, was attempted in 1888 along with a small monastic house
organized according to the Rule of St. Benedict.[107]

These expanding ecclesiastical activities soon rendered the
existing church of Mesnil-St.-Loup too small for active participation
by the congregation. André applied to his bishop, Mgr. Coeur, for a
new structure in September, 1859 and was refused. It was rumored that
Coeur's hostility stemmed from disapproval of the extravagant
religiosity of the town. He was an old Gallican who feared that
Mesnil-St.-Loup was becoming a Roman nest. Over the years, however,
enough money was raised to begin a new edifice. To the 6,500 F

----

[105]Maréchaux, Oeuvre, p. 48.

[106]Ibid., p. 69; Maréchaux, Père Emmanuel, p. 100.

[107]Maréchaux, Père Emmanuel, pp. 103, 223, 329; André took the
religious name Emmanuel when he founded the Benedictine monastery; MS
Registre de la paroisse, archives, Parish Church, Mesnil-St.-Loup.

contributed by the people was added 10,000 F from the state and 50,000 F left for the work at Mesnil in the will of a rich Paris widow, Madame de Bretteville.

Coeur's successor, Mgr. Ravinet, would no longer interrupt the construction of the edifice after so much money had been raised, and the building was consecrated in 1878. Visitors from surrounding towns were shocked when they beheld the austere structure. A monk of the parish monastery commented on why a simple, bare plan had been chosen:

> Father had dreamed of a romanesque [rather than baroque] edifice: the romanesque is the style properly monastic, it carries the stamp of austerity and of solidity which expresses the religious temperament of the Benedictine....He was unable to realize his desire: it was impossible to have the romanesque built. Gothic was adopted, but a primitive Gothic, very sober, which gives the impression of the romanesque.[108]

That five men went out from Mesnil and were ordained priests and eleven women were professed nuns indicates the religiosity of the village. But more than that, the character of the population as a whole, which was transformed from irreligion into one of the most famous parishes in France after World War I, was a witness to the applicability of Guéranger's ideas. At André Piot's death a few years before that war, the Bishop of Troyes, Mgr. Ecalle, commented:

> What was this parish, then? Its state was generally like that of all those of the region, like so many others it had suffered much....[But] by his [André's] work, by his zeal, by his firmness of principle and in their application, he made of this village a model parish, a community worthy of the first centuries of Christianity. He formed here a body of elite souls....It was by prayer, above all the prayer, that he was able to effect this regeneration....[109]

---

[108]Maréchaux, Père Emmanuel, p. 126; Délibérations, Rapports, et depenses du Conseil de la Fabrique.

[109]Maréchaux, Père Emmanuel, p. 483.

In 1859 Eugène Hiron, who had entered Solesmes as a postulant in 1835 and had subsequently left the monastery in order to propagate Dom Guéranger's reform in the parishes of France, was appointed curé of the left bank Paris church of St. Jacques-du-Haut-Pas. St. Jacques had been one of the centers of Jansenism in the capital. After the destruction of Port Royal in 1711, St. Jacques became the point of assembly for an annual pilgrimage to the graves of Jansenist heroes. The works of the curé Jean Desmoulins, who served until the 1730's, were published in the Nouvelles ecclésiastiques. By the 1830's, however, the proletariat outnumbered the once Jansenist families of gentle birth in the district.

Louis F. M. de Noirlieu attempted to adapt parochial activities to the proletariat from 1840 to 1848. He was a close friend of Frédéric Ozanam, a follower of Lamennais who devised schemes for attracting workers to Catholicism. In 1845 Noirlieu founded an Oeuvre paroissiale des ouvriers de Saint-Jacques-du-Haut-Pas, of which he said, "The goal of the society is to unite workers of various professions in monthly meetings in the chapel of workers where they will listen to religious instruction and various lectures and discourses of interest." Each Sunday night the gospel was read and an instruction given to those workers who did not have time for the eucharistic celebrations. Noirlieu sent leaflets to workshops and bistros announcing that at these gatherings "your priests will form you into the most perfect union." After surveying attendance at these classes, the curé reported, "Pastor of a parish where the population of workers is so numerous, I have the consolation to be able to affirm that here in this district, the families are numerous who practice religion."[110]

In the sixties and seventies Hiron contributed the liturgical element which had been lacking in these pioneer efforts, for Noirlieu had sought his "union of souls" by means of education and instruction.

---

[110]"Règlement de la Société," of the Workers Society of St. Jacques, leaflet printed 1842, preserved in parish archives, St. Jacques-du-Haut-Pas, p. 1; Bulletin—"Aux paroissiens de St. Jacques d.-H.-P.," printed 1842, archives, St. Jacques, p. 8 and p. 1.

The archiepiscopal visitor to the parish in 1849 recalled that little
liturgical care was taken at St. Jacques. The interior structure and
many altars were uncared for. The sacristy was dirty. Liturgical
vestments were torn and the sacramental vessels were thrown about.
"The canonical offices [were] suppressed." Free seats were provided
for the poor, but they were separated from congregation and altar and
placed at the back of the nave. The high mass on Sunday continued to
be dominated by a long sermon. Individual devotion remained the
practice of the five catechetical classes and the three pious
congregations.[111]

In contrast to Noirlieu, Hiron's method of teaching was the
liturgy, and his initial undertaking was to regulate St. Jacques
according to the Roman liturgical calendar and rites.[112] An archiepiscopal reporter was shocked to find that "they do not follow the ancient
usages of Paris in ceremonial," that the breviary offices were said
daily in the church. He recorded "the remarkable dignity of the
offices in this church, that the [Gregorian] chant is well executed,
the music of the services well chosen, and the character of all
religious." There was tension in the parish because of the change in
ritual. The organist, the members of the choir, the sacristan, and
many employees left because of the transition. The treasurer, M.
Borian, resigned rather than spend money for redecoration of the church
or for new liturgical vestments.[113] But M. Hiron was adamant in his
reform. He printed rules demanding that all colors used in services
strictly conform to Rome, that the sanctuary be cleaned and decorated
with care, and that all ecclesiastical furniture be handled with

---

111MS Visite pastorale, 10 March 1849, I P 55, Folder No. 24,
archives, Archbishop of Paris.

112Eugène Hiron, Notice biographique sur M. l'abbé Véron (Paris,
1867), p. 12.

113MS Procès-verbal de Visite--1864, I P 55, Folder No. 24, archives,
Archbishop of Paris.

reverence.[114]

He made a drastic reduction in the price for seats at the main hours of worship in 1868 in order to encourage the poor to participate in the chief liturgical acts, and he was loudly criticized by wealthy parishioners for intrusion upon traditional rights and for demeaning the character of the historic church. The outcry grew, and the curé was forced to print a public defense of the equal prerogative of the poor to share in the liturgy, which ended with an appeal: "Counting on the traditional good spirit of his parishioners, M. Curé hopes that all will aid to effect this reform to the profit of those among us who are less fortunate."[115]

The record of the instruction given by the clergy to one of the catechism classes of the parish, the Catechism of Perseverance, demonstrates how the teaching was changed under the new curé, and reveals one method which was used to inculcate the liturgical tradition. Beginning with the class of February 25, 1866, until the end of the record in 1872, the series was entitled "Explication liturgique du Saint Sacrifice de la Messe." At these lessons a detailed explanation was given of the activities which take place at a solemn mass. Every prayer in the liturgy was translated and explicated. This was followed by a call to participate in the offices and the eucharist. The children were told "in the masses [to] sing while the priest makes his preparation. The people should sing the introit and the Kyrie eleison...and the sanctus." They were taught to make the priest's prayer their own by saying a loud amen. The catechetical instruction suggested that the mass is an action which can only be completed by an activity of the people, the reception of communion by the whole congregation. The last instructions were labelled "L'Année liturgique" and were a recounting of the story of

---

[114]"Paroisse St. Jacques-du-Haut-Pas--Règlement du Prêtre sacristain" in MS collection Visite archdiaconale--1863, I P 55, Folder No. 24, archives, Archbishop of Paris.

[115]"Avis-Tarif des chaises," 1868, leaflet in archives, St. Jacques.

every saint's day and feast with the general theme that the church's year is the living mystery of Christ in the secular cycle of events, that the true Christian is one who celebrates these acts with the church and with the members of the parish.[116]

At the end of his tenure, abbé Hiron began a campaign, carried on in sermons and brochures, which encouraged all the men and women of that district of Paris to assist at the high mass at St. Jacques on Sunday which, he felt, should be the chief communal gathering of the population of the district for worship. He attempted to dissuade his people from attending any of the low masses in the private chapels of religious orders and wealthy citizens which were situated within the borders of the parish. He wrote that "there are too many public offices in the chapels to the detriment of the parish church." The twenty-five non-parochial oratories were dangerous because of their irregular and extra-liturgical exercises. The Chapel of Reparation had "pretentious and extraordinary" cults. The Chapel of the Sisters of St. Michael used neo-Gallican rites. The Jesuits practiced elaborate and non-authorized forms of benediction, rather than the eucharist, as the chief service, as did the Chapel of the Priests of the Holy Sacrament.[117]

Verbal and numerical witnesses indicate that Hiron was successful in reviving St. Jacques-du-Haut-Pas and establishing it for decades in the liturgical tradition of Solesmes. In 1863 he wrote to the Archbishop of Paris of the rapidity with which the new administration was accepted: "The parish of St. Jacques is doubly happy in these days....The priests are honored, the sacraments are frequented, the offices followed, the poor assisted, the work, purged of naturalism

----

[116]MS Cours d'Instruction, Catéchisme de Persévérance, notes on the instruction given at each class, collected in 12 large red volumes preserved in the archives of the parish church, St. Jacques.

[117]"Notes sur les chapelles situées sur la paroisse de St. Jacques," p. 2 preserved in MS Visite archdiaconale--1863, I P 55, Folder No. 24, archives, Archbishop of Paris.

which had sterilized its effects, is encouraging and prosperous."[118]
The archiepiscopal account of the parish in 1864 noted "that this
parish is in a state of transition....However, the number of the
faithful and the revenues have not diminished."[119]

Out of a parochial population of 11,250, approximately 2,000
people took communion at Easter and 40,000 hosts were distributed
annually while abbé Hiron directed the parish. Between 1900 and World
War I, when 18,000 people lived within the borders of St. Jacques, the
total number of communions in the year was still at 50,000, although
8,000 parishioners completed Easter duties, which indicates that the
nineteenth century residents were at the altar more consistently than
their twentieth century descendants.[120]

Another Paris church which evolved into a liturgical center was
Missions Étrangères, that parish in which Dom Guéranger had ministered,
where Desgenettes had roused support for Solesmes in the 1830's and
1840's. It was that fashionable left bank church which began to serve
a quarter of the Faubourg St. Germain, where the majority of the Paris
friends of Solesmes lived. This constituency flocked to the chapel of
the Missions Étrangères in the 1850's after the introduction of the
Roman rite and the Gregorian chant by the curé Jean Louis Roquette, who
had been a colleague of Eugène Hiron at the Church of St. Roch.[121]

Roquette began the exceptional practice of celebrating two high
masses on Sunday as well as twelve simple eucharists. Daily masses

---

[118]MS Letter of Eugène Hiron to Archbishop of Paris, no date, 1863 in
MS Visite archdiaconale—1863.

[119]MS Procès-verbal de Visite—1864, I P 55, Folder No. 24, archives,
Archbishop of Paris.

[120]Procès-verbal de Visite 1864, 1907, 1912, 1924, I P 55, Folder No.
24, archives, Archbishop of Paris.

[121]The new parish church was set in the most fashionable of those
streets and became known as a center for the rich.

were held every half hour from six o'clock until eleven. The offices were sung in plain-chant and during Holy Week and at All Saints all seven were kept publicly in church, with the Roman rites of the Last Supper and the paschal ceremonies performed as well. Even minor weekday feasts of the liturgical year, like the Purification, were kept with great solemnity and a procession within the church. The office of vespers on all great feasts was chanted with incense and glittering vestments. Parishioners paraded through St. Germain on Corpus Christi with the sacrament, on Rogation days singing litanies, with blessed palms on Palm Sunday, and with banners on St. Geneviève and the feast of St. Francis Xavier. A confraternity of the Holy Sacrament was formed which also held periodic processions in honor of the eucharist. The confraternity of St. Francis prepared adults to receive the sacrament of the altar and was the means to encourage frequent reception. A general communion of the parish was held at Easter, Christmas, and Maundy Thursday during the nine o'clock high mass.

In the 1830's, when Guéranger had been a vicar, the parish included 16,000 souls and there were 4,000 communions at Easter. By 1864, when the liturgical transformation was complete, the population had fallen to 15,700, but there were 12.5% more or 4,500 people who ate the paschal eucharist. The congregations were so large that the priests were forbidden to hold services at the chapel of Missions Étrangères. A new parish of Saint Francis Xavier was established and in 1865 began to worship in a vast modified Romanesque structure built behind the Invalides. It soon was filled with 6-10,000 fashionable worshippers on Sunday who came to witness the sumptuous performance of the Roman cult. In 1883, six years before the departure of the abbé Roquette, a report to the archbishop summarized his success in halting the turmoil which had beset this church after the Revolution of 1848:

> The parish of Saint Francis Xavier is well known for its great piety....This reputation is justified. The attendance at the offices is very large and one is able to say that on Sunday morning the church is not commodious enough. The ceremonies are performed with much dignity and the Gregorian chant, inaugurated several years ago, is executed with a great perfection....The piety which characterizes this

wonderful parish is witnessed to by the different confraternities which are full of prosperity. The budget of the parish has been such that continual modification of the fabric has been able to take place.[122]

The curé Grea increased liturgical activity from 1897 to 1917. Sixteen masses were held on Sunday and twelve each day during the week. Classes were begun on the meaning of the liturgy and on the plain-chant, and the congregation began to provide the music at the nine o'clock high mass on Sunday. There were communicant circles formed to encourage reception of the eucharist, and these endeavors produced, in a population of 30,000, yearly communion totals which were:[123]

> 1907 — 108,000
> 1908 — 150,000
> 1909 — 200,000
> 1910 — 210,000
> 1911 — 215,000

Louis Pierret and Georges Chevrot directed St. Francis between the World Wars and continued the elaborate ecclesiastical functions and Gregorian music. A "eucharistic crusade," which included liturgical lectures, was inaugurated in 1925 to further increase sacramental participation, and in conjunction with this a spiritual union for men and one for women were organized; the former had 250 members and the latter 850. The number of celebrations, however, fell to ten on Sunday and seven daily, and this lessened opportunity for approaching the altar is reflected in a fall of communions in an inter-war population of 34,670:[124]

----

[122]MSS Procès-verbal de Visite 1864, 1883, Missions Étrangères-St. Francis Xavier, I P 55, Folder No. 64, archives, Archbishop of Paris; in the same folder are MS untitled notes on history of parish by Roquette, dated 28 March 1854; also in No. 64 are MS Personnel, 1864; MS letter of Roquette to Prefect of Seine on state of parish of 29 March 1868.

[123]MS Procès-verbal de Visite 1912, lists of activities from Bulletin paroissial, beginning 1907, in I P 55, Folder No. 64, archives, Archbishop of Paris.

[124]MS Procès-verbal de Visite 8 February 1925, 1936, I P 55, Folder No. 64, archives, Archbishop of Paris.

```
1920 -- 175,000
1921 -- 178,000
1922 -- 169,000
1923 -- 159,000
1924 -- 138,000
1933 -- 180,000
1935 -- 180,000
```

Yet the curate still noted in 1925 that "the parish is fully living. Communions are very numerous...the church is not big enough on Sunday," and the archbishop said at the same time that the high masses were followed attentively "by an elite interested in the teaching."[125]

But the decline continued and after World War II the average Sunday attendance fell to 7,000. Even then there were urgent attempts to encourage congregational participation as the means of establishing the collectivity of the cult. To facilitiate this a central altar was placed in the middle of the great space under the dome of the church.[126] Yet the rate of sacramental activity during the first decade of the century was never repeated.

Before the 1789 Revolution Le Mans had not only been famous for the flamboyant Gothic cathedral of St. Julien, but for two great abbey churches, la Couture, which served an important women's monastic community, and du Prè, where Benedictines had worshipped since the eleventh century. There were two noble parish churches, Saint Benedict and Saint Pavin. After 1792 la Couture became a seat of government, Saint Pavin was a hall for popular assemblies, and du Prè and Saint

---

[125]MS Procès-verbal de Visite 1925.

[126]Bulletin paroissial, history of post-war liturgical activity in No. 14, January and February 1958, in I P 55, Folder No. 64, archives, Archbishop of Paris.

Benedict were abandoned. At the Restoration all were designated as parish churches. By 1833 their treasuries were depleted from lack of contributions, and in February 1858 la Couture, where the cathedral chapter had intervened to force the clergy to hold Rogation processions, was threatened with being closed by city officials because of infrequent use, and Saint Pavin was deemed worthy of destruction for the same reason. The revolutionary damage there was not mended until the twentieth century.[127]

In 1833 a vicar from la Couture, Ambroise Guillois who had made a name for himself loudly proclaiming the Ultramontane theories of Dom Guéranger's teacher, Prof. Heurtebize, was named curé of the parish of Notre-Dame du Prè. There, in the 8,000 people who lived in the quarter across the Sarthe from the cathedral, he found a cross-section of the population which inhabited Le Mans and a congregation manifesting little love for its church. The windows had disappeared, and all but one of the altars had been cheaply rebuilt of wood. There was no fund for repairs or for the purchase of liturgical ornaments. M. Duchatel, a layman, had contributed 25 F in 1832 to cover the most visible scars of the Revolution, but no more money was raised. The collection for music netted 350 F annually.

Guillois increased the three Sunday masses to eight and the one daily service to six. An annual fund of 300 F was established for architectural repairs. Guillois raised 800 F a year for choral and organ music.[128]

During these years Guillois was also finishing an explication of the catechism which he had begun as a professor at the college of Laval. The first edition of this Explication historique, dogmatique, morale du catéchisme was published in 1838, and a second edition came

---

[127]Robert Triger, L'Eglise de Saint Pavin au Mans (Le Mans, 1900); Sifflet, Carron, p. 175ff.; Mgr. Jean-Jacques Nanquette (Le Mans, 1925), pp. 67, 91, 93; Mgr. Charles-Jean Fillion (Le Mans, 1927), pp. 360, 396.

[128]Ambroise Ledru, L'Eglise de Notre-Dame du Prè au Mans (Le Mans, 1924); MS Budget de la paroisse du Prè, archives, Notre-Dame du Prè.

out in 1843. In both, the third section was "De la grace, des sacraments et de la prière," but the liturgy was never mentioned. Individual acts, particularly the rosary, were emphasized as the chief pious acts. But in the edition of 1852, 602 pages were devoted to the liturgy and nine to the rosary. There was a stress on the centrality of the liturgical year and the eucharist in the work of the Christian church. These pages were a guide to the meaning and derivation of every vestment, gesture, and prayer of the mass, the canonical hours, and the feasts and fasts of the calendar. In 1852 the Roman rites are taken as the norm of the church, for the liturgy is understood to be the means for uniting the Christians into one body and must not be weakened by a marked disunity in outward form. The source for the ideas which expanded the Explication is not hard to determine. Guillois wrote,

> One is able to say with Dom Guéranger that the liturgy, in general, is the ensemble of symbols, chants, and acts—the means with which the Church expresses and manifests its religion toward God....His Institutions liturgiques, of which the third volume has just appeared, have produced an immense good.

In other Guillois books, Le livre de la première communion, Le Sacrifice de l'autel, and Le Dogme de la confession, Christianity is explained as a religion of sacramental participation.[129]

The catechism was used in schools throughout France. It went into eleven editions, was translated into German, and earned the abbé 500 extra francs a year. The inclusion of the Roman liturgy created a small controversy. The abbé Gaultiel, professor at the Parisian seminary of the Holy Spirit, included Guillois in a list of members in an unpatriotic liturgical conspiracy which, he wrote, had brought on the condemnation of the neo-Gallican liturgies by the Congregation of Rites. However, the future Bishop of Le Mans, Mgr. Fillion, and the Jesuit editor of the powerful Roman organ Civiltá Cattolica praised

---

[129]Ambroise Guillois, Explication historique, dogmatique, morale, (et liturgique) du catéchisme (1st ed., Le Mans, 1838); (6th ed., Le Mans, 1852) IV, 11, 698; (7th ed., Le Mans, 1855) IV, IX; (8th ed., Le Mans, 1864) IV, 2, 13, 16, 25.

Guillois' "courageous" and "revolutionary" additions on worship.[130]

A discovery of Guéranger affected his parish as much as his catechism. The curé of Pré loved to read, and the Le Mans book-seller A. Lanier sent him all the French, Latin, German, Italian, and English books he received which dealt with theology. Guillois allotted 200 F a month for books and 127 F for the nine daily papers he took. In 1846 he received the Institutions liturgiques, for 1 F 79, in one of these shipments, and a new pattern of book buying appeared. Roman missals, manuals of ceremonies, pontificals, for 6 F 10, and a Codex liturgicus began to arrive in the parochial mail. Gradually the masses and other sacramental ceremonies of the church were conformed to the new books. In 1847 and 1850 he spent 1960 F repairing the high altar of his church to improve liturgical celebrations. A new organ of eight ranks was bought, and 150 F were spent on ornaments in 1850. The abbé Guillois began to frequent the shop of M. Froget, the ecclesiastical tailor of Le Mans, in order to have vestments cut and sewn in the Roman style and color scheme. Two black copes were ordered in 1848, a violet chasuble in 1849, a violet dalmatic and red chasuble for 1851, and two chasubles for daily masses, a soutane in the Roman style, and a biretta during 1852. And the next year he bought two more chasubles.[131] It can only be assumed that these physical modifications were joined to an introduction in the pulpit and catechism class of the liturgical theories advocated in Guillois' volumes on the catechism. Material was provided there which would facilitate participation in worship.

When M. Guillois died in 1854 he was replaced by Julien Livet, a priest who expanded the activities which his predecessor had begun.

----

[130]MS letters of abbé Gaultiel to Guillois, 3 March 1852, of Canon Fillion to Julien Livet, 21 January 1854, of Joseph Calvetti, 5 November 1853, archives, Notre-Dame du Pré.

[131]Archives of parish contain divers letters and accounts of Guillois outlining the books and papers he bought from A. Lanier, the amounts spent on repairs in church, and the bills from M. Froget. A list of books and when he bought them is included, MS Librairie ancienne de J. Demichelis, made up 5 July 1854, after his death. Other costs of establishing the Roman rite are found in MS Budget.

Two hundred and fifty more francs were spent on calendars, ordos, rituals, graduals, and antiphonaries, and 389 F were designated for cottas to dress the choir, so that every detail of the services would be conducted in the Roman manner. Two hundred thousand francs were devoted between 1858 and 1869 to the completion of the fabric of du Pré and the restoration, which had been begun by M. Guillois, was completed. This attempt to improve the setting for worship was criticized as "useless" and "an inconvenience" by the bishop, the Mayor of Le Mans, and the Prefect of the Sarthe. By 1863, however, the building had been returned to its original late romanesque style and had windows, new altars, mosaics, and paintings. Fifteen hundred people were added to the parish, and the amount collected for worship remained constant until the end of the century, four times what it had been before Guillois arrived.

There was not another parish priest in Le Mans who strove to carry out the spirit of the reforms of the Benedictines of Solesmes until L. Ernest Dubois came to be curé of Saint Benedict in the 1880's. That was a parish which was so poor that one half of its people were registered at the bureau of charity. Dubois began to have four extra daily and six Sunday masses and to say the evening offices in church. All the hours were kept during Holy Week, at Christmas, and on All Saints' and All Souls'. Public processions marched through the streets on St. Sebastian's Day, St. Mark's, St. Julien's, and in Rogationtide. Every important liturgical occasion was kept with a procession in church. A Confraternity of Christian Mothers was formed. Its chief exercise was a corporate reception of communion once a month. The Conference of St. Vincent de Paul and the lay Confraternity of the Work of the Bread of St. Anthony distributed food while encouraging church attendance. In the propaganda distributed by these groups, the abbé stressed that the parish is one family, that the local church is the center of that family, the common house of all the people. "It offers to you all the means of sanctification: offices and feasts...." Above all, the abbé Dubois taught that communion was the basis of a shared parochial life, and therefore should be a collective act, done within the mass. "It is the spirit of the Church to communicate within the mass, not before or after, as often as possible."[132]

The influence of Solesmes upon the twenty-one nearest churches, those parishes which made up the deanery of Sablé, was not often direct. The reluctance of many neighbors to adopt the liturgical ideals of the abbey may be explained by the legitimist politics of the region or by a dread of monks who were attacked by government and bishop. The slow pace of reform could be attributed to the ignorance and laziness of the average country cleric. Not until 1919 was the church at Brains served by a curé who made an attempt to teach the people to understand the liturgy and execute the Gregorian chant in a melodic manner. He was Leonard Sergent, and he kept up the liturgical apostolate in his parish until 1953, no doubt because his brother, Louis Sergent, was professed a Benedictine at Solesmes in 1896 and maintained ties with the village. M. Galbrun, curé of Pincé, established the Solesmes tradition of purified services, processions, liturgical explication, and frequent communion. He valued the monks' work so much that in 1880, when they were first threatened with expulsion from their abbey by the state, he offered them a château in his parish so that they would come and live among his people. These were exceptions, and though the bishops and canons at Le Mans had worked since 1856 for the intelligent use of Roman rites, the village churches at Asnières, Auvers-le-Hamon, Avoise, Courtillers, Gastines, Louailles, Parcé, Precigné, Souvigne, and Vion still maintained a strong tradition of the superstitious devotions of extra-liturgical Catholicism one hundred years later.[133]

---

[132]Robert Triger, L'Église Saint-Benoît du Mans (Le Mans, 1900); Sifflet, Carron, p. 175; Indicateur paroissial. Paroisse Saint-Benoît (Le Mans, 1898), pp. 3, 21.

[133]"Une paroisse de la campagne mancelle. Brains," La Province du Maine, LXX (1968), 142-157. Louis Calendini, "M. Paillard," Journal de Sablé (18 October 1931), collection of Calendini articles "Choses du

In the three churches closest to the abbey, however, the people fell under the Benedictine influence. Two-thirds of the population of the village of Juigné regularly attended eucharistic celebrations at the abbey, but came to their own church for the other sacraments. Eventually the parochial cure of Juigné fell to a Benedictine. Until the Second World War more than one-third of the village received the sacrament at Easter.[134]

In 1851 the care of the parish of Solesmes was undertaken by a monk of the abbey. The fabric of the Solesmes parish church of Notre-Dame was restored to facilitate the proper execution of the Roman liturgy at a cost of 31,000 F contributed by the council of the parish. A sacristy was built. In 1863 M. Landeau gave the church a marble statue of St. Clement and a marble cross for the choir "in the Roman fashion." A rood cross was hung above the altar "in the Roman fashion." A window painter from Paris was hired to decorate the clear panes of glass in the choir, transepts, and nave. In 1880 Dom Foubert further "modernized" the interior to allow more room for processions and to afford the congregation a better view of the rites of the mass.

There is evidence that these physical and liturgical alterations were well received, even among villagers who had been suspicious of Guéranger; for the residents of Solesmes came to the defense of the abbey when it was attacked at dawn on the morning of November 6, 1880, by 250 men of the 26th artillery regiment from Le Mans, acting on the orders of the state to disperse the monks after the passage of the anti-monastic legislation of 1880. Ten young men of the village stood guard with the porter at his gate. M. Chadaigne, the watchmaker, assisted the curé Dom Foubert on the battlements, and at another spot

----

passe," Library, Abbey of Solesmes; Diocèse du Mans, Recherches et réflexions pastorales (Le Mans, 1969).

[134]Doyen de Sablé, MS Procès-verbal de paroisse de Juigné, no date, archives, Notre-Dame de Sablé; MS Registres de la paroisse, archives, Parish Church, Juigné-sur-Sarthe.

on the wall the painter Philipeau and his son stood with the locksmith Foubert and his brother. The Gregorian expert Dom Mocquereau was joined in the tower by Emile Joumier. The women of Solesmes sat as a rampart in the choir, and the town doctor, Rondelou, and the Marquis of Juigné formed a guard of honor about the abbot.

At twelve o'clock on November 6 the under-prefect of the Sarthe ordered an assault on the abbey church. Nine monks and villagers refused to move from the door and were carried by gendarmes into the square. At two o'clock, the door of the church was forced and twenty artillerymen entered the choir. The monks and women began to sing psalms, Te Deums, and mangificats, for once in improper liturgical order. First the choir was cleared of the chanting lay women. One gendarme was said "to have received from the semi-gloved hand of a lady, an intentional slap."[135]

After this disruption of the monastic life, the sacramental participation in the parish church of Solesmes, which had been strong since the 1840's, began to decline even more rapidly than it had after the economic dislocations in the Sablé region in the 1870's.[136]

Sablé experienced a small industrial revolution in the years surrounding 1833 and this was the setting in which Guéranger's ideas had developed. The mining and finishing of marble and coal transformed the town, but the primary impact of industrialization was to double the population:[137]

---

[135]Léon Robert, Histoire de l'Abbaye de Solesmes (Sablé, 1937), pp. 21, 22.

[136]MS Registres de la paroisse, archives, Notre-Dame de Solesmes.

[137]Thérèse Greffier, Une petite ville du Maine aux XIXe siècle (Sablé, 1960), p. 60.

Population of Sablé
1800 — 2,500
1822 — 3,450
1833 — 3,999
1838 — 4,188
1851 — 4,912

There is no doubt that the mines and their shops drew these new residents for when the population rose by 724 from 1838 to 1851, 788 new hands were hired in the marble and coal works between 1830 and 1850. From 1857 to 1866 the population grew by 515, and 455 new miners were employed by Landeau and the other companies. By 1866 over half of the 5,601 people in Sablé, or 2,725, were listed as workers. In 1872, when the industrial revival had slowed, the ratio of worker to total population was 2,541 : 5,549.[138]

These industrial employees were kept in church. For in the period 1800–1850 when the population doubled, the sacramental participation of the town, the number of baptisms and marriages, as well as participation in confraternities more than doubled and remained at a constantly high level until the end of the nineteenth century. No other sector of the parish could have supplied this increase. The registers of Notre-Dame de Sablé reflect this doubling and tripling of the sacramental rate by 1850 and then a leveling.[139]

The organization in the parish which was created to deal with these workers—to provide physical necessities and urge church attendance—was also the point of direct contact between the Abbey of Solesmes and Notre-Dame de Sablé. After the miners held demonstrations during the revolutionary days of 1848 to demand that grievances be met, M. Cosnard, M. Landeau, M. Huve, and Dr. Rondelou, the chief supporters of Solesmes in the region, along with these businessmen of Sablé: Clavreuill, Francy, Gandais, Godefroy, Heurtebize, Karren, and Laforest created a Société de Saint-Vincent-de-Paul, a confraternity for laymen whose purpose was "mutual sanctification, the service and religious

---

[138]Ibid., pp. 28, 60, 73, 78, 80, 87, 90, 101.

[139]MS Registres de la paroisse, archives, Notre-Dame de Sablé.

edification of the poor...the maintenance of good relations between the parish and the holy and knowledgeable religious of Solesmes." Euphrasie Cosnard outlined to the Society methods for helping workers, and Marie Cosnard made a plea to the men to establish an apostolate among the apprentices of the town. A series of lectures were established at which one of the members, a Benedictine, or a Cosnard sister would speak on the liturgy, the eucharist, the importance of communion, and other topics. An annual collection, to which the abbey contributed, was taken up and distributed to families of the miners. Funds were set aside for eucharistic celebrations for the poor. When Léon Landeau died his son Ernest took over the leadership, and the mission of the Society continued until July 30, 1914. After that date there were no more lectures or meetings.[140]

The Society of St. Vincent de Paul gave the people a liturgical education and brought them to church. There, two priests began to reform the austere Chouan tradition of Guéranger's youth and brought color to the worship of the parish. J. B. Saillard, who sat under Heurtebize at the Le Mans seminary and was a friend and colleague of Fonteinne, Guéranger's first follower, had been appointed curé in 1830 by Mgr. Carron. In 1833 he built a new sanctuary, and he completed an organ and a chapel for daily masses in 1843. Processions were conducted through the town after 1839 on the feasts of the Assumption, St. Martin, St. Cénéré, St. Mendé, St. Savinien, and St. Malo.[141] Saillard was succeeded by abbé F. L. Couret, who administered the parish 1848-1880. He had spent the previous fifteen years working for the abbé Guillois at the parish of du Pré in Le Mans. By 1851 Couret had already introduced Roman rites, Gregorian chant, and had increased the number of Sunday and daily masses to four. A special monthly

----

[140]MS Société de Saint-Vincent-de-Paul, Conférence de Sable-sur-Sarthe, Registre No. 1, Procès-verbaux des séances, 14 December 1851-5 February 1876, Registre No. 2, 12 February 1876--, archives, Notre-Dame de Sablé.

[141]MS Recherche historique sur Sablé, archives, Notre-Dame de Sablé.

eucharist was held each first Sunday of the month to encourage communion. Evening offices were said on Sunday and chanted in Gregorian tones on All Saints' and at Holy Week, when the patristic rites were kept, including blessing of the font and paschal baptism. Every Sunday Couret rehearsed from his pulpit the details of the saints who would be commemorated in the liturgical calendar during the week. On Palm Sunday the procession strung along across Sablé to the cemetery. St. Mark's procession went through the fields, and three Rogation processions wound into different quarters of the city for an outdoor mass. The nights of Lent were kept with instructions and readings.[142]

As early as 1851 M. Couret had written Bouvier that the old church which had survived the Revolution was too crowded. He raised 120,000 F for a new structure and was supported by the congregation and Council of the Fabric in his attempt to build a large, open, spacious edifice for his people. But in 1880 the Republican Prefect of the Sarthe refused to allow the plans for the large church which the curé had drawn up, saying that a building of such size would be useless in modern times. The Minister of the Interior and Cults advised against wasting 100,000 F. Couret died, but his successor Drouet continued the fight. Finally, in 1891, a simple Gothic church with grand proportions rose on an island in the Sarthe and was decorated by the people of Sablé.[143]

The new church was well used by M. Drouet, for he built on, rather than diminished, the liturgical care and dignity of his predecessor. he added another mass on Sunday and at feasts, and he began to say the office daily in church and invite the congregation to do so with him. In his sermons he stressed eucharistic communion and urged reception on

----

[142]MS Recherche historique; Sifflet, Mgr. Bouvier, II, pp. 339-340; MS Listes des annonces, 1850-1880, archives, Notre-Dame de Sablé.

[143]La Reconstruction de l'Eglise Notre-Dame et le Conseil Municipale de Sablé (Sablé, 1882), letters of Prefect, p. 12, Minister of Cults, p. 24.

473

weekdays as well as on Sunday, when he designated 7:30 as the time for the corporate communion of the parish. Another public procession was added, to be held along the banks of the Sarthe on the Sunday after Corpus Christi. In 1907 he began a parish bulletin which explained the liturgical meaning of all the feasts of the church year. He instituted instruction in Gregorian chant for children.[144]

---

[144]MS Listes des annonces, 1881-1893, Bulletin paroissial de Sablé, 1907-1932, archives, Notre-Dame de Sablé. For more analysis of relationship between return to the Roman liturgy, popular participation, and the origins of the liturgical movement see R. W. Franklin, "The Nineteenth Century Liturgical Movement," Worship, 53, No. 1 (January 1979), 12-39.

CHAPTER XI

The Liturgical Movement

The experiences of these parishes illustrate the issues which were to haunt the liturgical movement as it spread from the valley of the Sarthe into Germany, Belgium, Austria, and Italy. In urban and rural locales the liturgy was used as an instrument for the recovery of social life. The parish, once merely a territorial unit of the ecclesiastical hierarchy, became a lay religious community. Yet the attraction of incense, golden vessels, purple robes, medieval music, and spotless churches remained to be explained and justified. It was unclear to observers how the liturgy aided the creation of a community or why there had been a flurry of liturgical activity in France in these churches until immediately before the First World War and then a dormant period. Some said the priests capitalized on a surge of Romanticism which disappeared as popular taste moved to more realistic interests. Others remarked that in the liturgical parishes there was established, by various means, a sense of the holy in a civilization which had become desacralized. They said that there had been an appeal to the constituents on a primitive, non-verbal level in a period when religious language was incapable of connecting secular experience and religious emotion.

There is no doubt that the liturgical advocates had discovered an elemental form of discourse. They communicated with gesture, act, and symbol. Splendid rites fixed belief in the senses. Processions and new churches were physical manifestations of the existence of the divine when literature about God was cumbersome. Incense and candles made prayer easier when it was less conditioned by society. The liturgical life provided order, color, beauty, entertainment, emotional release to populations denied the antique festivities and state rites of the ancien régime. The emphasis on singing added an element of joy to the lives of many.

The liturgists rediscovered the efficacy of the symbol in conveying spiritual values to materialistic populations. One foundation of the liturgical revival was Guéranger's return to the symbolic system of the Fathers. In the French parishes the church became the sacred place and the liturgy the medium through which the materials brought by the people, handiwork, fire, oil, salt, wax, water, bread, and wine were made holy. Processions carried religion into places of work in a century when labor was perceived as alien from value. The liturgical year symbolically hallowed time when employment schedules and technology were creating nightless days and seasonless years. Yet at the same time there was a counter-movement here which sought to purify the art, practice, and music of the church of the influence of the secular world so that a neutral space could be created where the natural and supernatural worlds could be joined.

Guéranger's work may be seen as a movement for simplification and the universalizing of ritual symbols. Solesmes was, above all, a revolt against the national and particular in religion. Its argument was that the more objective symbols are, the more are they capable of expressing the interior religious states of many individuals and providing a center around which a community can form, and the simpler the gesture, the piece of music, or the architectural form, the less subjective it is. Simplicity enhances commonality and objectivity. Symbols, gestures, and rituals which can be shared by all classes reinforce the community.

The restoration of active participation of the laity was not a gimmick to entice poor people to come to church. It was a renewal of the ancient function of the eucharistic assembly which alone explains the traditional structure of the mass. The communal form of the eucharist made the parochial community a reality for an hour or two every Sunday. For a moment a sense of unity could be created as the people were engaged in common work, albeit of a ritual variety. The parish was scattered during the week in factories, fields, shops, and homes, but on Sunday there was a community of intention and thought, a united direction of eyes and emotions to an aim beyond the self and the material. The celebration made the community, or in the old scholastic sense, the effect achieved by the eucharist was the church.

The great stress on the adoption of Gregorian chant in parishes and dioceses is understandable, for its monodic form contributed a unified musical structure to the ritual work of the congregation, whereas polyphony or the theatrical popular styles of the nineteenth century stratified the people into voice part classes or separated them from a trained choir. By urging participation, the liturgical pastors sought to give everyone a stake in religion. They did not pander to segments of the population with special pew boxes equipped with foot warmers. All classes were taught to feel at home in the church, not to come merely for the doling out of sacraments but to exercise their priestly function. Guéranger's Gallican critics were right. This was a movement for the democratization of the church. But radicalism was grounded in the world of the liturgy. The social solidity which grew up in the parochial confraternities, for example, was never separated form the prescribed liturgical activities of those bodies.

"Liturgical movement" has come to mean the adoption of this reform at the local level. The phrase was first used in this sense at the height of the liturgical war in the 1850's to point to the adoption of Guéranger's program by diocesan bishops and parish priests. Those who heeded his call, and particularly the clergy of the parishes surveyed here, began a network of liturgical outposts which eventually spread across Europe.[1] The adoption of the Roman liturgy by the dioceses was another initial Guéranger success which was a foundation of the wider liturgical revival, for it was in selected French sees, those of Mgr. Parisis at Langres and Arras and Mgr. Pie at Poitiers, that the liturgy was for the first time used as a weapon of social regeneration and

----

[1]Abbé Jouve, Du mouvement liturgique en France durant le XIXe siècle (Paris, 1860).

ecclesiastical reform. A renewal of worship was used to create a diocesan community, "one people," out of the Gallican administrative units of the past. The struggle of the bishops with Guéranger further popularized liturgical issues and established the liturgy as the primary element of piety, a cornerstone of the constitution of the church not only in France but at Rome.

Yet there is a sense of unfulfillment about the liturgical movement in France. The radical implications of lay participation in the eucharist and divine office outlined in Guéranger's works were never completely realized in practice. The forty lean years in France are to be explained in part by a development which took place within Dom Guéranger and then was carried to greater extremes by his successors. Solesmes ceased to be a center of liturgical advancement. There was a growing conservatism, a turning inward to mysticism and contemplation. No other institution in France replaced the leadership of the abbey of Solesmes.

The creative years had been the period of the constant Guéranger-Lamennais interchange, when theories of social regeneration founded on Rome and the people had been applied to the liturgy. The rest of the abbot's career was taken up with working out that initial insight, for contact with the Breton priest ceased in 1834 when Lamennais left the Roman Church. Friendship with Lamennais' more liberal and intelligent followers, Montalembert and Lacordaire, ended with the split of the vestiges of the L'Avenir party into the Ultramontane and Liberal Catholic camps after the Falloux education law imbroglio of 1848. Guéranger fell increasingly under the influence of reactionaries, Louis Veuillot and Mgr. Pie.

He was hemmed in by the conservative social position of his financial supporters. Already branded a radical by a sector of the episcopate for his initial program, Guéranger was reticent to attempt more. The bishop's hostility prevented the establishment of an elaborate extramural organization for spreading the liturgical reform and training secular parish priests. There was no fresh exposure to the social effects of industrial change after the 1850's, for the abbot and monks did not make long trips and the tumult of the Sabolien industrial revolution was spent. He took care to match the mood of Rome, and Pius IX, who had been a liberal before the Roman revolution of 1848, became increasingly reactionary after 1848.

Guéranger's life then, like so many other nineteenth-century figures, including Wagner and Napoleon III, is divided into pre-1848 liberalism and post-1848 conservatism. The result was that in France, after 1870, liturgical reform was linked in many minds with suspicious theories of papal sovereignty and narrow views of the relationship of Christianity to modern knowledge.

Guéranger's extreme hostility to the natural, which developed during the fifties, weakened the crucial emphasis on the balance of the material and the spiritual in his early liturgical writings, made many enemies, and sullied his reputation. The campaign against science was carried on in a series of seventeen articles which came out in 1857 and 1858 in Veuillot's L'Univers, the organ of the conservative Mennaisians. These articles, later collected as Essai sur le naturalisme contemporain, portray human history as the stage for the activity of the supernatural. The history of the church and the lives of the saints are instances of the work solely of a divine force. This is a decisive shift from the natural/spiritual explanation of the eucharistic life contained in the liturgical essays. It is the Guéranger of the Essai who drew the fire of Lord Acton, who declared that "Dom Guéranger, the learned Abbot of Solesmes, is the most outspoken of these systematic adversaries of modern knowledge."[2]

The dominance of the spirit over the world, of contemplation over public activity, of individual illumination over communal sanctification appeared in twenty-eight mysterious articles in L'Univers from May 1858 until January 1859 under the title Marie d'Agréda et la cité

----

[2]J. E. E. Acton, "Ultramontanism," in Essays on Church and State (London, 1952), p. 58. The most interesting parts of the essay were issued as Prosper Guéranger, Le Sens Chrétien de l'Histoire (Paris, 1945) and the most important articles on the subject are "Du naturalisme dans l'histoire" and "Du naturalisme dans la philosophie," L'Univers (2, 3, 31 January, 21 February 1858).

mystique de Dieu and in the last Conférences sur la vie chrétienne
which he pronounced in the chapter at Solesmes in 1872, 1873, and 1874.
Guéranger took up Maria d'Agréda, who was the author of an imaginative
life of the Virgin Mary (she is the Mystical City of God) and a woman
given to public displays of religious ecstasy yet with some power over
Philip IV, in order to demonstrate the importance of the particular
intervention of the supernatural in the recent history of Catholicism.
The articles are a defense of private revelation, the superstitious
piety of Spain, the cult of Mary, and even the veracity of the girl's
appearance before natives of South America and her visits to the Virgin
herself.   The book on Mary is denominated "one of the most imposing
monuments of the human genius."[3]

He began to teach his monks that meditation was the remedy for an
undisciplined intelligence which could not admit such a "mystical
theology." It led to the "illuminative life" which could result in the
union of the individual soul with God without first experiencing union
with the liturgical community.   In his last days he said that there
were two paths to sanctification. One is active and liturgical, but
the other is passive and contemplative "and the monastic life is
essentially the contemplative life."[4]

The founding in the 1860's of a women's abbey at Solesmes, Ste.
Cécile, was an institutional demonstration of the contemplative ideal
and another step away from the public liturgical mission of the first
abbey. A hushed, reclusive character was given to the new foundation.
In the adaptation of the Rule of St. Benedict for the nuns Dom
Guéranger omitted any reference to relations with the world. Although
the divine office was still held to be "the principal means of

----

[3]Prosper Guéranger, "Marie d'Agréda et la cité mystique de Dieu,"
L'Univers (23 May, 6, 20 June, 18 July, 1 and 15 Aug., 12 and 26 Sept.,
10 Oct., 21 Nov., 5 and 19 Dec., 1858, 16 and 31 Jan., 13 Feb., 13 and
28 March, 11 April, 15 and 29 May, 13 June, 18 July, 7 and 22 Aug., 18
Sept., 9 and 23 Oct., 7 Nov. 1859). The quote occurs in the article of
12 Sept. 1858.

[4]Prosper Guéranger, Conférences sur la vie chrétienne, Volume I
(Solesmes, 1880), 285, 286, Volume II (Solesmes, 1884), 14, 18, 44.

contemplation," the Rule was amended so as to include one-half hour of private mental prayer every morning and afternoon. Other extra-liturgical devotions "inspired by the Spirit of God" are encouraged.[5]

When Dom Guéranger had been buried under the nave of the abbey church beneath the ensemble of statues whose threatened destruction in 1833 had moved him to the refoundation of the Benedictines, his successors did not recreate the spirit of the first decades of Solesmes. There was increased separation from the world, as the liturgy became the preserve of an escapist elite of aesthetes who valued its beauty rather than its power. The second abbot, Charles Couturier, had come to Solesmes because of the Ultramontanism of the place, and he took the most papist and reactionary member of the episcopate, Mgr. Pie, as his principal advisor. Unlike the first inhabitants, he was devoid of talent and never wrote anything except a few letters to the newspapers. Couturier allowed study only as an aid to mystical advancement and when petitioned by his monks to sanction the publication of a journal so that the results of research might have an impact on public opinion, he called this proposal "an exploitation comparable to the manufacturing of chocolates and liqueurs by certain other monasteries."[6]

Paul Delatte, the abbot from 1890 until 1921, was more learned than his predecessor and is known for his commentary on the Rule and for compiling a biography of Dom Guéranger. Yet he too was drawn to the papal rather than the liturgical tradition of the foundation, and he advanced its development in the direction of mystical piety and away from eucharistic devotion. The most important element in the formation of the monk in his monastic theory is the cultivation of supernatural

---

[5]La Règle du bienheureux Père Saint Benoît avec les déclarations rédigées par Dom Guéranger, Abbé de Solesmes, pour l'Abbaye de Sainte-Cécile de Solesmes (Solesmes, 1890). Leon Robert, Dom Guéranger et la fondaton de Sainte-Cécile de Solesmes (Sablé, 1951).

[6]Couturier quoted in anonymous MS L'Esprit des études dans la Congrégation de Solesmes, Archives, Abbey of Solesmes, p. 14; A. Houtin, Dom Couturier, Abbé de Solesmes (Angers, 1899), pp. 211, 247, 323; Henri Tissot, Dom Charles Couturier (Sablé, 1961).

"intelligence." Research is a means to that end. Delatte, however, specifically warns against "passionate intellectual curiosity" as an enemy of the soul.[7]

The withdrawal, the suspicion, the inversion, and finally even the disappearance of Solesmes were conditioned by activities of the state and by the depletion of the abbey's funds. In 1868 the monks were 80,000 F in debt, and by the death of Guéranger the sum had mounted to 500,000 F. On November 6, 1880, the buildings were closed by the Prefect of the Sarthe Lagrange acting on orders of the Republican government at Paris, following the passage of the anti-monastic legislation of the party of Gambetta in March 1880. At the beginning of 1881 the monastery was quietly reoccupied with the tacit approval of Paris. The anti-clerical journals began an uproar. On March 22, 1882, the Minister of the Interior Goblet expelled the monks again. They found refuge in twenty-two houses provided for them by the villagers. A garrison of gendarmes was placed before the abbey gates to prevent clandestine return. In 1895 there was another gradual re-invasion of the monastery which the government did not halt.

The Dreyfus affair, in which secular allies of Solesmes were prominent, destroyed this truce. In the anti-clerical atmosphere of fin de siècle France the government of Waldeck-Rousseau induced the Chamber of Deputies to decree the dispersion of monastic communities and their property in the spring of 1901. The anti-Dreyfusard sentiment surrounding the abbey was evident as cries of "Vive l'Armée! A bas les juifs!" were heard as the monks was forced from their home for the third time in twenty years. On this occasion they traveled to Appuldurcombe in the Isle of Wight where they remained until 1908. Then the monks lived at Quarr on the same island until 1921.[8]

----

[7]Augustin Savaton, Dom Paul Delatte, Abbé de Solesmes (Paris, 1954); Gabriel Tissot, "La pensée monastique de Dom Delatte," Revue Mabillon, I (1961), 111-122; Ambroise Ledru, Dom Guéranger, Abbé de Solesmes et Mgr. Bouvier, Évêque du Mans (Paris, 1911),pp. 335-339.

[8]Robert, op. cit., p. 17; Houtin, op. cit.; Mgr. Freppel, Deuxième expulsion des Bénédictins de Solesmes (Château-Gontier, 1882).

The communities of the Benedictine Congregation of France carried what was left of their liturgical monasticism to other nations where they found refuge from the anti-clerical persecution of the French state. Monks and nuns from Ligugé, Saint-Wandrille, Sainte-Anne de Kergonan, Sainte Marie de Paris, and Saint-Maur de Glanfeuil went to Belgium. The two abbeys at Wisques retired to Holland, and the Marseilles foundation found a haven at Hautcombe in Savoy. The experience of the First World War tended to dampen anti-religious passions in France, and in the twenties the exiled Benedictine monks and nuns began to return. But the 1901 laws halted the growth and influence of French monasticism. By the end of the twenties only 59% of the monasteries which existed in 1900 had been restored. The number of Benedictines had diminished 52%.[9]

The paradox of Guéranger's career was that within what was universally understood to be a reactionary movement at his death were elements which evolved into the expression of Christianity most suited to industrial conditions. It was in Germany that his ideas were widely adopted as a means for saving proletarian quarters for the church. It was in Germany that the liturgical movement developed such power that it became a determinant force in the history of modern Catholicism. There the French abbot's proposals were grafted into the continuing theological tradition of communal ecclesiology maintained by the followers of Johann Adam Möhler. The liturgical movement could not have transformed Christendom had it not been joined to this school which had been judiciously spreading a conception of the communal church. Guéranger had said that the liturgy creates community, while Möhler maintained that the churches were capable of being turned into communal associations. The German had provided a theological justification for the important role of the laity in his theory of the church as the extension of the body of Christ. His works defended the

---

[9]Roger Gazeau, MS L'Essor du monachisme masculin en France, p. 11, Document B-2, Archives, Abbey of Solesmes; Germain Cozien, L'Oeuvre de Dom Guéranger (Le Mans, 1933); Gabriel Tissot, Solesmes en Angleterre (Sablé, 1959).

notion that salvation is conveyed to the group. Möhler's ideas had been taken up by individuals who dealt with Christians who were living amid conditions of rapid industrialization and technological advance.

The first Germans to advocate Guéranger's plans were professors who had been trained in the Möhlerian tradition of the Universities of Munich and Tübingen. Jakob Fluck, the professor of pastoral theology at the University of Geissen, a tiny short-lived school in the diocese of Mainz which was staffed by Möhler students from Tübingen, was one of the initial advocates of Guéranger. He stressed the Frenchman's theory about the liturgy and used it to revive the local church at Geissen, of which he was the priest, by placing a new emphasis upon the round of feasts contained in the liturgical year. In 1854 Fluck began a German translation of the Institutions liturgiques. Josef Amberger who had studied with Möhler at Munich, where he later became sub-regent of the Georgianum in 1841 and professor of pastoral theology in 1845, in the three volumes of his Pastoraltheologie, which came out between 1850 and 1863, propagated the principle of the centrality of the eucharistic feasts in the scheme of salvation. "The Church year," he said, "is the beginning point, the crucial point of all the pastoral activity of the Church....The conveyance of the means for the gradual incorporation of the life and sacrifice of Christ into the believer through the Church is the essence of the Church year." He taught his students, after reading Guéranger, that the mass was primarily a communal act, an affair of the "spiritual family" not of the single soul, and that the mission of the parochial preacher was to encourage the participation of his flock in worship.[10]

Valentin Thalhofer succeeded Amberger at the Munich Georgianum and at the University of Munich in 1863. His two-volume Liturgik, published from 1883 until 1893, kept alive the combined tradition of Möhler and Guéranger for another generation. He differed from Amberger, however, in representing the liturgy as being notable for its role in solving social disputes:

----

[10]Waldemar Trapp, Vorgeschichte und Ursprung der liturgischen Bewegung (Regensburg, 1940), p. 316.

The burning social question of the present would be easy
to solve...if all believers after instruction were invited to
participate in the public celebration of the holy eucharist.
In the time of the first Christians an authentic Christian
socialism prevailed among the believers, which had its origin
and its sustenance in the communally performed church
service.[11]

These teachers are important for joining Guéranger and Möhler, but
they made no impact outside of Bavaria. Fluck, Thalhofer and Amberger
did not have the institutional means with which to reach a large
population or train many parish priests. Once again the role of
propagating the liturgical reform fell to a Benedictine monastery.
This time it was the German abbey of Beuron. That Beuron performed
this function is significant, for it means that as late as the last
quarter of the nineteenth century the monastery was a medium for the
transmission of ideas across national borders.

The father of the Wolter brothers, the romantic youths who rebuilt
Beuron, was a beer brewer, and their mother was a Protestant. They
were very wealthy, however, and grew up amid the rich intellectual life
of the old Rhineland university town of Bonn during the eighteen
thirties and forties. Their father's money allowed them to spend years
leisurely absorbing theology in the atmosphere of J. M. Scheeben, who
had continued Möhler's tradition of writing about the church as if it
were a mystical community, and the heterodox Günther who sought to
reconcile the pope and Kant. They learned French, English, and Italian
and traveled through the north observing the effects of industrialization. They read Bishop Ketteler of Mainz who was advocating a Catholic
solution to social problems, and after the 1848 revolution the brothers
were determined to work for the creation of a Catholic factory system.
In 1856 they journeyed to Rome, attracted by the Güntherian circle
which had gathered in the monastery of St. Paul Without the Walls.
They became Benedictines.[12]

---

[11]Ibid., p. 347.

[12]Virgil Fiala, MS Die Besondere Ausprägung des Benediktinischen
Mönchtums in der Beuroner Kongregation, Document A-4, Archives, Abbey
of Solesmes; Anselm Schott, Leben und Wirken des hochwürdigsten Herrn
Dr. Maurus Wolter (Stuttgart, 1891); Ursmer Berlière, Oraison funèbre

In Rome the Wolters decided to attempt to found a Benedictine house in their native land, and they sought out contributors. Princess Catherine von Hohenzollern, a member of the Catholic side of the Prussian royal family who maintained the Villa d'Este in the papal city, was introduced to them. She was twice widowed and had turned to religion and the establishment of monastic foundations, which appeared to be the new fashion among German royalty after centuries of neglect of such duties. Ludwig I actively worked for the Bavarian Benedictines after 1830, and her Protestant cousin Frederick William IV began a policy of building Berlin churches in 1840 as an aid to the maintenance of the social and political status quo. She offered to install the Wolters in an Augustinian cloister which had been abandoned at the Napoleonic secularization of 1803 and was located within Hohenzollern, a tiny Prussian kingdom within Württemberg which is so close to Möhler's University of Tübingen that the towers of the ancestral Hohenzollern castle can be seen from Tübingen parish church. The princess not only made the new house financially solvent, but by 1863 she had secured its independence from Italian, German, and Austrian Benedictine congregations.

Guéranger had become a well-known figure in the Rome of the sixties. His fame had spread after the swift liturgical reform of the French dioceses. Princess Catherine had visited the abbey on the Sarthe after hearing it praised by Cardinal Pitra and the pope.[13] Perhaps she told Maur, the elder Wolter, to go there to find his model

---

du R. P. Dom Placide Wolter, Archiabbé de Beuron, Premier Abbé de Maredsous (Bruges, 1908); Beuron 1863-1963. Festschrift zum hundert-jährigen Bestehen der Erzabtei St. Martin (Beuron, 1963). The contro-versial early history of the Wolters is covered in Paul Wenzel, Der Freundeskreis um Anton Günther und die Gründung Beurons (Essen, 1965).

[13]Gérard van Caloen, Dom Maur Wolter et les origines de la Bénédictines de Beuron (Bruges-Lille, 1891), p. 38. On the early contacts of the Wolters with Princess Catherine and Cardinal Pitra, see Maurus and Placidus Wolter, MS Tagebuch seiner Reise ins Heilige Land, GEO 440, Library, Archabbey of Beuron; and Virgil Fiala, "Die besondere Ausprägung des Benediktinischen Mönchtums in der Beuron Kongregation," Revue Bénédictine, 83 (1973), 181-228.

of monasticism, for in October 1862 he wrote Guéranger, "Admiration for your success and your illimitable confidence have inspired me," and Maur Wolter asked that he be allowed to visit Solesmes for several months.[14] At Solesmes Wolter said that he found the world of St. Benedict that he had dreamed of and had so long sought to find. He interpreted Guéranger's war against neo-Gallicanism as an anti-Baroque revolt. To Maur, Baroque art and music had been the deadly product of a decadent German Catholicism, and therefore he was drawn at first to the purity and simplicity of Solesmes. He wrote that Guéranger "had established the monastic life in its primitive beauty and purity."[15]

The liturgical character of the Congregation of France was a second attraction. Wolter told Princess Catherine, "Oh, if you could only spend a day singing in the choir services of this family of God. This reverent work [the liturgy] is governed by such regularity, by such careful performance, by a holy earnestness, and above all by a spirit of devotion which is more powerful than ideas."[16] He remarked to his brother Placid, "The Divine Office is the main thing here, and I do not mind spending almost four hours daily...in the choir."[17] He was deeply impressed that Guéranger and his constitution had molded a monastic army capable of influencing the world. Maur reported to Germany that "above all is Guéranger a complete man, full of wisdom, immense experience as a seasoned campaigner (after twenty years of struggle with bishops, monks, and material setbacks), and discretion,

----

[14]MS letter of Maur Wolter to Dom Guéranger, 9 September 1862, Archives, Abbey of Solesmes; he actually had to write two letters to Guéranger explaining his project for building monasteries in Germany. The one of September 9 was not answered and so he wrote Guéranger the same thing again on October 6.

[15]Laurent Janssens, Oraison funèbre du R. P. Dom Maur Wolter, Archiabbé et fondateur de la Congrégation de Beuron (Bruges, 1890), p. 15.

[16]Letter of Maur Wolter to Catherine von Hohenzollern, 19 October 1862, quoted in Fiala, op cit., p. 37.

[17]Letter of Maur Wolter to Placid Wolter, 27 October 1862, ibid., pp. 38-39.

who in all of this activity is seeking in essence to spread sanctification....His monks are truly a holy, splendid phalanx...."[18] Wolter
wrote the princess that above all he had learned that

> it is impossible that the monastic discipline and studies
> would have any permanence without their being connected to
> pastoral activity in the world....The principal mission of
> the sons of Benedict, so reads Dom Guéranger's instructions,
> stands in their building up of the faithful in the world
> through the splendid performances of the church services,
> which work like a heavenly vision on the emotions, enlighten
> the soul, and warm the heart.[19]

Placid Wolter and his friend Benedikt Sauter followed Maur to
Solesmes, and then they all went home to Germany to build there what
they had found in France. The fraternal relation between the two
abbeys was sealed by the dispatch of Dom Bastide to help during the
first days of community life at Beuron and by a series of letters
pledging mutual love. Maur vowed to Dom Guéranger that "I regard your
Paternity (a just title) as the father and the soul of the new
foundation." The French abbot gave a final commission, "Inspire
the love of the holy liturgy which is the center of all Christianity."[20]

In many ways Beuron was a mirror of Solesmes after it was opened
in May 1863. That this could have happened, that Guéranger's vision
could be grounded in another cultural tradition is a demonstration of
the usefulness of his attempt to create a non-national expression of
Catholicism. So much was Beuron a German copy of Solesmes that the
Wolter brothers were remembered as coupling such phrases as "in
Solesmes was it so" and "in Solesmes do they do it this way" to any
decision. The Beuron constitution, approved in 1884, was almost a

----

18Idem. See Louis Soltner, "Beuron und Dom Guéranger," Erbe und
Auftrag, 51 (1975), 5-10.

19Letters of Maur Wolter to Catherine von Hohenzollern, 13 November
and 24 December 1862, ibid., pp. 44, 48.

20MS letter of Maur Wolter to Dom Guéranger, 4 October 1863,
Archives, Abbey of Solesmes; other letters expressing similar
sentiments were sent February 6, 21 and June 16, 1863; MS letter of
Prosper Guéranger to Maur Wolter, 5 May 1863, Archives, Abbey of
Solesmes.

German translation of that of Solesmes. The method of singing Gregorian chant was brought over from the French house. One of Maur Wolter's books, Psallite sapienter, was a publication of Guéranger's argument that monks and lay people should sing the psalms with intelligence. He translated the French abbot's compilation of the Exercises of St. Gertrude as a means to free his countryman "from the subjective bondage of the devotio moderna."[21]

But the Möhlerian element in the training of the founders of Beuron surfaced in a new emphasis on patristic studies, for Möhler had maintained that reform would come from exhaustive research into the age of the Fathers. Maur Wolter compiled an anthology of the theology of that era, Praecipua ordinis monastici elementa, and the counsels of Psallite sapienter are based on the Fathers. It was fitting, then, that Maur should have been awarded an honorary doctorate by Tübingen at the end of his life. Gradually Beuron advanced beyond Solesmes in knowledge of the early liturgy.

The Möhler school had sought to foster an organic communal life among lay Christians as well, and thus the impulse to parochial activity was double in the heritage of Beuron. From the first, contact with the people in the parishes was a fundamental element of Beuroneae activity. Success was prepared in advance, for many of the local churches first penetrated by the Beuron reform were in the neighboring diocese of Rottenburg and had already been served by Möhlerian priests. Placid Wolter immediately began to experiment with the Beuron parish church, and the number of communions in a population of 150 began to rise:[22]

total number of communions,
Beuron parish church

1863 -- 1200

----

[21]Friedrich Nippold, Moderne Klostergründungen. Das Erste halbe Jahrhundert der Beuroner Kongregation (Neuwied, 1910), pp. 30-31. See also Maurus Pfaff, "Dom Prosper Guéranger, Abt von Solesmes," Erbe und Auftrag, 51 (1975), 90-105, 190-204.

[22]Beuron, op. cit., p. 69.

1864 -- 5300
1865 -- 7200
1866 -- 7300
1867 -- 7500
1868 -- 9300

The monks also took over the church at Kleve, and parishoners from Fridingen, Kolbingen, Mühlheim, Stetten, Nendingen, Mahlstetten, and Inendorf began to come to the abbey for liturgical exercises in 1864. That December the monks conducted their first liturgical mission at Leipferdigen in the Württemberg district of Geisingen. This was a form of evangelization which they would carry to all parts of Germany until World War II.

The Schott Missal, produced at Beuron, was the second method of dissemination. Anselm Schott lived between 1843 and 1867 in Staufeneck which was typical of the Württemberg villages which had begun to industrialize in the second half of the eighteenth century. During his youth the place was still dominated by the Schachenmayer woolen mill which employed a large majority of the population. Anselm was lonely there and felt drawn to the security of the church. In 1862 he went to study at Tübingen, and in 1867 he became vicar in the small industrial town of Biberach. He grew dissatisfied with the parochial priesthood after attending a series of lectures on the liturgical life given at the Georgianum in Munich by Valentin Thalhofer in 1865. Bishop Hefele of Rottenburg allowed Schott to enter the novitiate at Bueron in 1868, and he set to work on a German translation of the mass texts for the liturgical year "so that all the people could participate intelligently in the proceedings of worship...and therefore unite themselves and their prayers to the Church." In 1884 his Messbuch der heiligen Kirche appeared on the market and in the preface to the "Vesperale" section the phrase "liturgical movement" was first used in Germany to describe that revival of the church which would be produced if the common people were taught to use the book. By 1906, 100,000 copies of the Schott had been sold and in 1939 1,650,000 impressions were in use.[23]

----

[23]Alois Dangelmaier, P. Anselm Schott. Der Mensch, Priester und Liturge (Reimlingen, 1971), pp. 18, 52-53; Trapp, op. cit., p. 363. See also J. Uttenweiler, Die Geschichte des Laienmessbuches von P.

Other monks of Beuron combined an education in the tradition of Möhler with work for the propagation of the liturgy. Suitbert Bäumer, who came to the abbey in 1865 after studying at Tübingen, wrote on the history of the breviary in order to prove to German clerics that their habit of reciting the office as a private devotion was a distortion of its ancient, public character. Benedikt Sauter was another leading figure who grew up in and combined both the traditions of Möhler and Guéranger. Sauter came from a family of businessmen at Langenenslingen, a town not far from Hohenzollern castle, and he was a chaplain at Bingen when Princess Catherine induced him to enter the monastery. After a novitiate at Solesmes where he studied Gregorian chant under Dom Pothier, he returned to found a chant school at Beuron. Sauter published his most important work, Choral und Liturgie, in 1865 in order to present a simplified version of the leading ideas of the Liturgical Year to the German people. Contained within that book was a call for the laicization of German ecclesiastical music and the adoption of a simpler Catholic aesthetic before there could be any hope of a restoration of the church in Germany. Sauter's book is an attempt to persuade his countrymen that Gregorian chant is the only music that should be admitted in the churches because it is the form of sacred music which meets the needs of modern conditions. It is art which eliminates all unnecessary elements, "which nourishes the clarity of ideas and still has an unearthly beauty." Plain-chant, he wrote, presents the simplest conception possible of music without any elaborate exterior form and therefore is suited to the common people. It is the ideal Christian art which is perfectly harmonious and without artificiality.[24]

Anselm Schott (Freiburg, 1935); and D. Zähringer, Das Messbuch für den Laien (Freiburg, 1959).

[24]Sterbenchronik des Hochwürdigsten Herrn Abtes Dr. Benedikt Sauter (Prague, 1908), pp. 6, 39; Benedikt Sauter, Le Plain-chant et la liturgie (Paris, 1867), pp. 2, 11, 12, 18, 19, 20, 23, 24, 25, 26, 30, 36, 38, 42, 99, 100.

This was no advance beyond the aesthetic theory of Solesmes. But there was progress in Beuron art when monks attempted to apply that aesthetic to ecclesiastical furniture and buildings. The leading artist in the abbey, Peter Lenz, was brought to Beuron by Princess Catherine in order to construct a votive chapel which she was building in thanksgiving for Dom Guéranger's recovery from smallpox in 1866. Lenz stayed on as a monk and director of the art school of the monastery, and his votive chapel became one of the first revolts in Germany against revived architectural styles. It was severe and geometric and attempted to be "spiritual" and "communal" art in the manner of what was thought to be the fashion of the early Christians. But no completely new architectural language had yet been developed to express the liturgical spirit, and there is a vague "Egyptian revival" quality which always hung about the artistic products of Beuron.

Most importantly this Mauruskapelle, and the vestments, chalices, and statues produced at Beuron caught the attention of secular intellectuals in Germany. The liturgical movement communicated by means of art initially with the non-Catholic world. The Historische Politische Blätter remarked in 1890 that at Beuron a way was found for the first time in the century to combine art and prayer. "They made it possible to impregnate art with a spirit of prayer and devotion." The review went on to say that at last a style had been developed by the Beuron Benedictines which honestly expressed the ideals of religion: "...truth and beauty, worthiness and nobility, earnestness and strength, simplicity and economy—these are the ground principles of the Beuron art school." This Benedictine spiritual symbolism made a strong impression on contemporaries at a time when the German artistic avant-garde, particularly Otto Wagner and his pupils at the Wiener Werkstätte, as well as the French were turning against the heavy stuffiness of bourgeois art in the name of symbols which pointed beyond the material. The split between the materialistic academics and the progressives led to the withdrawal of the "Sezession" from the Vienna

492

Academy. The monk Lenz was invited to exhibit with the Sezession.[25]

Beuron's conception of Christianity was spread in a fourth way—by monastic imperialism. There was a period of intense expansion during the twelve years of the German Kulturkampf when the seventy-two residents of Beuron were scattered to other parts of Europe. Then there were the years when Wilhelm II developed a personal interest in the congregation and encouraged it to spread. Soon communities of German religious began to arrive in many countries. In 1880 Benedikt Sauter entered Prague as Abbot of Emmaus, a Czech outpost of liturgical splendor and the Gregorian chant. Seckau was founded in Austrian Styria in 1883. Monks opened a house at Erdington near Birmingham in 1876 and then another foundation was begun at Fort Augusta in Scotland. Other monasteries were opened in Germany at Lubin, Grüssau, Tholey, Neuburg, Kellenried, St. Ottilien, Wimpfen, Trier, Eibingen, Engelthal, Herstelle, Gerleve, Nütschau, Materborn, Benediktsberg, at Neresheim and Weingarten in the diocese of Rottenburg, and in Belgium at Maradret. Volders and Bertholdstein in Austria, Sion in Jerusalem, Singevergarin in Portugal, and Tonogaoka in Japan were begun as well. By 1913, 859 monks and 206 nuns were under the control of Beuron.[26]

Of all these establishments the most important were Mardesous and Mont-César in Belgium and Maria Laach in the Rhineland. The experience of the Benedictines in Belgium was important, for there the first serious strains appeared between the leaders who advocated the radical

----

[25]On the fiftieth anniversary of the founding of Beuron the Bishop of Rottenburg, Paul Wilhelm von Keppler, stressed that one of the primary instruments for the spread of the Beuron tradition in the area had been "its sense and zeal for beautiful art"; Festpredigt zur Feier des 50 Jährigen Jubiläums der Beuroner Kongregation (Beuron, 1913), p. 3; Historische Politische Blätter quoted in Schott, op. cit., pp. 39–40. For more analysis of Lenz and Beuronese liturgical art see Martha Dreesbach, Pater Desiderius Lenz, O.S.B., von Beuron, Theorie und Werk (Munich, 1957); Harald Siebenmorgen, "Die Beuroner Kunstschule: Peter Lenz (P. Desiderius) und seine Mitarbeiter," Das Münster, 30 (1977), 20-36; Harald Siebenmorgen, Die Anfänge der "Beuroner Kunstschule" (Sigmaringen, 1983); Maurus Pfaff, P. Desiderius Peter Lenz (Beuron, 1978).

[26]MS Annales Beuron: 1905-1924, Archives, Archabbey of Beuron.

elements of the liturgical movement and the conservative lay supporters. Innovation was blocked by the upper classes, so in that country the movement dealt almost entirely with workers and became exclusively pastoral. Maredsous was founded in 1872 with the assistance of a circle of rich Belgian burghers of Bruges, the Hemptinne and Desclée families and Baron Jean Béthune, who dreamed of building a little copy of the Middle Ages in their country, populated by monks from Beuron. The Benedictines, however, brought their new simple style with them. There was a long aesthetic wrangle, and the monks lost out to the capitalists. Béthune erected a neo-Gothic palace instead of the austere houses proposed by Lenz. The German monk was not even allowed to paint the walls in the Beuron fashion. He wrote in March 1882, "There has been an important discussion in order to determine what element will dominate the painting here, the romantic Gothic or the primitive Christian. The architect and the founders are for the former, the inhabitants, true Benedictines, are for the latter."[27]

Aesthetic progress was blocked, but there was vigorous experimentation with various methods to determine the most efficient channels through which to reach the industrial populations. Again Möhler, as well as Guéranger, were in the background of this stress on the importance of communication to the laity. The master of the novices at Maredsous after 1879, and the dominant intellectual of the establishment, was Boniface Wolff who had studied the liturgy under Dom Guéranger in 1869 and was introduced to patristic scholarship by Scheeben, the Möhlerian exponent at Cologne. Wolff taught a generation of Belgian liturgists. One of these, Dom Germain Morin, spread the view that the twentieth-century church ought to be founded on the ecclesiology of the Fathers and that the liturgy should become the chief organ of Catholic education in the pages of the Revue

---

[27]Letter of Desiderius Lenz, 3 March 1882, quoted in Jacques-Grégoire Waterlet, MS Le Renouveau gothique au XIXe siècle et l'Abbaye de Maredsous, p. 47, Document B-22, Archives, Abbey of Solesmes; Gisbert Ghysens, "Fondation et Essor de Maredsous (1872-1923)," Revue Benedictine, 83 (1973), 229-257.

bénédictine, which he edited. Another was Gerard van Caloen. He grew up among the Gothic enthusiasts of Bruges, but he moved away from their influence following visits to Solesmes and Beuron. After attending Guéranger's funeral, he felt a call to continue the abbot's work among the Belgian poor.

While prior at Maredsous van Caloen worked from 1878 until 1882 on a simple translation of the missal which incorporated much of the spirit and many of the words of the Liturgical Year. This Missel des fidèles came out in Belgium in 1882 with the prefaced intention that it would cause a return of the faithful "to the true piety and love of the Church their Mother."[28] His Cardinal blocked the translation at first, but the example of what had happened in France concerning the liturgy was recalled, and the missal was allowed along with a review which explained the meaning of rites, Le Messager des fidèles. Van Caloen's second important contribution to the liturgical movement was a paper presented at the third International Eucharistic Congress at Liège in 1883 which sought widespread support for the communion of the faithful within the mass. The idea was attacked by the bishops present, but it soon became the rule in the Belgian churches. Van Caloen commented on the relation of his efforts to the French revival:

> You go on to say that I have been one of the initiators of the liturgical movement in Belgium with the publication of the Missel des fidèles in 1882 and with my paper on the communion of the faithful during the mass...very well. But how imperfect were those first attempts. They rested above everything else on the memorable work of Dom Guéranger and had no other significance other than as the sound of the trumpet opening the way to the veritable and good pioneers of the liturgy....[29]

Van Caloen opened the way for the work of Lambert Beauduin who devoted his life to advancing the anti-individualist and pastoral side of the liturgical movement. In Beauduin two streams of nineteenth-century church history meet and advance together. Born in 1873 into an

----

[28]André Haquin, Dom Lambert Beauduin et le renouveau liturgique (Gembloux, 1970), pp. 8, 9.

[29]Ibid., pp. 16, 29.

upper middle-class family, he worked for eight years as a priest with working men as one of the "chaplains of workmen" appointed by the diocese of Liège to forward the practical application of Leo XIII's Rerum novarum. In 1906 he entered the abbey of Mont-César, founded by the monks of Maredsous in 1899 in the Catholic university town of Louvain, in order to study the liturgy as a framework for living. He was influenced by Guéranger's notion that worship was the instrument for the revival of the churches, but of the monastic setting of the liturgical life he said, "...the great ideal of Dom Guéranger inherited by the brothers Wolter, an ideal which had attracted so many young men and done so much good had now become a bit artificial." He determined to make the parishes the center of the movement.[30]

The first indication of Beauduin's new direction was given during July in 1909 when liberal European Catholics assembled in Belgium for the Congress of Malines as they had been doing since 1863. Cardinal Mercier, who was leader of the conference, wanted the young Benedictine to speak, but no one wanted to accept the report which he had prepared on the liturgy and the workers. Out of deference for the cardinal a place was found in the Christian art and archaeology section for the young man to speak. Under the aegis of Christian art Beauduin delivered the speech which launched a more radical period of the liturgical movement. In his report Beauduin stressed that a common liturgical life would be the source which would revitalize Christianity, especially among workers. An effort should be made, he said, to have all piety grow more liturgical and less individualistic. But in order to make the liturgy once again a living form, it must be understood by all the people, and the world-wide church should undertake such education. "The parish mass," he urged, "[must become] the great weekly meeting of the Christian people in which men unite in brotherhood and are transformed into the whole of Christ."[31]

----

[30]Olivier Rousseau, "Dom Lambert Beauduin et la vie monastique," Revue Mabillon, I (1961), 177.

[31]Louis Bouyer, La Vie de la liturgie (Paris, 1956), p. 82.

This speech attracted great attention in Belgium, and 150,000 copies were quickly sold. It was expanded into a longer version, La Piété de l'Eglise, which came out on the eve of the First World War and quickly became one of the most popular liturgical documents.[32] If in Van Caloen Belgium had received Guéranger's emphasis on comprehension and communion, Beauduin's Piété continued his vision that the church's services could regenerate society, that ritual could be a counterforce to materialism. But in Beauduin's book these remedies are applied exclusively to the industrial city. It is the most violent attack which had yet appeared against modern forms of piety as reinforcement of the alienation produced by capitalism. Individual prayer is said to deform the Catholic mentality. "Religious individualism," he wrote, "is the conception the most opposed to Catholicism."[33] Yet he repeated the central Guéranger phrase which prescribed the social remedy for the times:

> From the first centuries to our own day, the Church has ever given to all her prayer a spirit which is profoundly and essentially collective....This is the most powerful antidote against individualism. It can therefore be said in all truth that whatever the liturgy loses is gained by individualism.[34]

Beauduin abandoned Guéranger, however, in speaking of the parish rather than the monastery as the most important visible community created by collective prayer. He advanced the democratization of the liturgy. It is "the theology of the people" he said.[35] It creates an organism in which sancitification takes place and fraternal relations are solidified. In active participation in worship the individual is lifted beyond the misery and the choking life of the factories. "By means of living the liturgy wholeheartedly Christians become more and

----

[32]D. A. Robeyns, "Les débuts du mouvement liturgique," Questions liturgiques et paroissiales, 19 (1934), 290.

[33]Lambert Beauduin, "La Piété de L'Eglise," Mélanges liturgiques (Louvain, 1954), p. 18.

[34]Idem.

[35]Ibid., p. 19.

more conscious of their supernatural fraternity, of their union in the mystical body of Christ."[36]   The liturgy therefore is not a detail but the whole life of the church.[37]

Dom Lambert surpassed Solesmes in his efforts to influence the parochial clergy.   He did not bother with the bishops.   Weekly inexpensive liturgical guides, reviews, and pamphlets were issued by Beauduin and his colleagues.   In 1909 Vie liturgique, a weekly paper, began to be distributed in Belgium, and in 1910 it was carried into Holland.   In that year Questions liturgiques et paroissiales, a quarterly, was begun in order to defend the liturgical movement in the theological language of the day.   The faithful received books in the Petite bibliothèque liturgique series after 1912.   Annual Liturgical Weeks for the secular clergy were conducted at Mont-César.   Two hundred and fifty priests came in 1910.[38]

The principal German daughter house of Beuron, the abbey of Maria Laach, on the other hand, is remembered for the creation of a theology which justified placing the entire thrust of the liturgical movement in parochial activity.   Maria Laach is an ancient foundation.   It had been converted into a Jesuit college in 1863 and became a Benedictine priory in 1892 when a colony of the Beuron congregation arrived which included Dom Anselm Schott, a leading figure there until 1896.   The liturgical character was reinforced in 1912 when Cunibert Mohlberg, who had been trained by Beauduin at Louvain, arrived.

A highly intellectual and scholarly atmosphere hung about the liturgical movement which came out of Maria Laach.   In the process of defending the liturgy through scriptural and patristic research an elite was formed which later captured the attention of German academics.   Once again there was a return to Möhler, for it was thought that he had developed the best language with which to convey the

----

[36]Ibid., pp. 17-18.

[37]Ibid., pp. 12, 21, 29.

[38]Robeyns, loc. cit., p. 295. See also S. A. Quitslund, Beauduin: A Prophet Vindicated (New York, 1973).

theology of communal Christianity to the universities. In the process of liturgical and patristic research at Maria Laach so much new information emerged concerning the worship of the early church that a new dictum was established: if the liturgy were to be truly the source of renewal of the life and teaching of the church, if vitality were to be restored, changes would have to be made in its performance, even in the Roman rite itself.

This was even more the case between 1913 and 1946 when the abbot of Maria Laach was Dom Ildefons Herwegen, who as a student at Bonn had been won to the inductive theological method of Möhler. He founded a patristic academy at Laach in order to further the revival of the German churches through scholarship. Herwegen's own books undertook to explain the nature of the social solidity produced by the liturgy. The foundation of his argument was Möhler's notion that the basic unit of Christianity is not the individual but the community which is the local manifestation of the body of Christ. Herwegen made use of the term, "Mysterium," to define the process of salvation and unification which occurs within the liturgy. "Mysterium" is a social salvation which destroys secular alienation.[39] His "Kirche und Mysterium" protests the view that the church is essentially a legal institution of bishops and pope. Herwegen posits that it is the concretized form of organic life. The church is, and he uses Möhler's own phrase, "Christ continuing to live on earth." The most important manifestation of that body is the parish. It is held together by symbols and the "Mysterium" which change the existence of members of the local church.[40] "The Mysterium effects the inner transformation of everyday life."[41] It is so

----

[39]Emmanuel von Severus, "Un maître de vie monastique en Allemagne: Dom Ildefons Herwegen," Revue Mabillon, I (1961), 159–165; Was Haltet Ihr von der Kirche? (Münster, 1976).

[40]Ildefons Herwegen, "Kirche und Mysterium," Mysterium, Gesammelte Arbeiten Laacher Monche (Münster, 1926), p. 3.

[41]Herwegen quoted in E. B. Koenker, The Liturgical Renaissance in the Roman Catholic Church (St. Louis, 1954), p. 111.

important that it is "the soul of the essence of Catholicism":[42]

> So long, therefore, as a man comes to know the Church only as
> a legal institution, as the authority in morals and instruc-
> tion, a person finds himself only in the cathecumenate....Her
> mystery reveals itself to him confidingly when he receives
> the flesh and blood of the Son of Man, when he, beginning
> with baptism, passes through the Mystery-life of the
> Church....[43]

Herwegen provided another definition of the mystery of Christianity:

> The purpose of the Christian religion is to sanctify, to
> spiritualize, to deify mankind....This is accomplished
> through sacrifice and sacrament and prayer, that is through
> the liturgy. The purpose of the liturgy is the transfigura-
> tion of human souls.[44]

Odo Casel, another Benedictine of Laach, authored a theology which
was a variation on the theme of Mysterium. When Dom Odo first came to
Maria Laach from a career in patristics at Rhineland universities he
added a new definition of mystery to the liturgical movement. Mystery
is not confined to the presence of Christ in the host or even to the
eucharistic. The mystery of Christ is realized whenever the people
engage in liturgical activity. The crucial component for the effecting
of the mystery is not only the role of the priest but the conduct of
the assembly. On the basis of patristic analysis a connection is
established in Casel's work between the symbolic activity of a
worshipping community and the presence of Christ.

These theories were first outlined in 1922 in the ninth volume of
Herwegen's Ecclesia Orans series of apologetic texts as Die Liturgie
als Mysterienfeier. An expanded and definitive version of Dom Odo's
theology appeared in 1932, Das Christliche Kultmysterium.[45]

----

[42]Koenker, op. cit., p. 35.

[43]Koenker, op. cit., p. 35.

[44]Ildefons Herwegen, The Art-Principle of the Liturgy, p. 16, quoted
in Koenker, op. cit., p. 110.

[45]Other essential articles of Casel appeared in the Laach publication Jahrbuch für Liturgiewissenschaft: "Mysteriengegenwart"--1929,
"Alteste christliche Kunst und Christusmysterium"--1934, "Neuen
Zeugnisse für das Kultmysterium"--1935, "Glaube, Gnosis, und Mysterium"
--1941.

Here there is a radicalization of the function of the lay community in the church, far beyond Möhler's idea that all to some extent share in the priesthood of Christ. Ordinary men and women have now become co-actors and co-operators with Jesus. It is their cooperation which creates the community, Odo Casel said. Mystery produces community, but only if the people are actively participating in worship.

Casel maintained throughout his life that one of the goals of the liturgical movement was to improve the conditions of working Germans. A revived sacramental life would elevate gray and smokey industrial existence. The Mysterium, realized in the equal cooperation of priest and laity at worship, could show the way to the dispersal of the atmosphere of class hatred which was poisoning post-war Germany. Dom Odo pictures the Christian life no longer as an escape from the real world, less an individual adventure under the guidance of personal imagination and sentiment. The liturgy, he said, gives to all who come to it a destiny which is real only insofar as it is an integration into the life of others. Casel demanded that the church not hide from the contemporary world but meet it, live in it, accept it while saving it:

> The world of the sacraments, the world into which the liturgy introduces us, is not a world in its own right, standing aloof from the world of ordinary living. It is rather the meeting-point of the world of the resurrection with this very world of ours in which we must live, suffer, and die....A liturgical life, therefore, is a life of true humanism in the deepest sense of the word, for it is a life concerned with fostering the true interests of human beings as they actually exist in the real order.[46]

The initial medium through which Maria Laach sought to disseminate these ideas was no different from that of Solesmes or Beuron. In 1918 Herwegen began to send out books in the Ecclesia Orans collection, and in 1921 Casel undertook the editorship of the learned journal Jahrbuch für Liturgiewissenschaft which provided reports on the research which was going on behind the walls of the abbey. But a movement which could attract intellectuals, academics and political leaders from Kaiser

---

[46]Odo Casel in Bouyer, op. cit., pp. 327-329.

Wilhelm to Konrad Adenauer found new means to reach a larger audience than the Catholic ghetto. The connection with the universities was built on the cultivation of Herwegen's close association with a group of Catholic lay teachers at Düsseldorf who became interested in introducing the new understanding of the liturgy into the parishes of central Germany. F. X. Münch who had gone to school at Bonn with the abbot and was a member of the Düsseldorf circle was elected secretary of the German Akademikerverbandes, which after 1914 held an annual training session at Maria Laach in the liturgical apostolate for professors. Two leading liturgists of the next generation emerged from these meetings: F. X. Arnold, the theology professor at Tübingen who wrote on the new role of the laity in the church, and Johannes Pinsk, chaplain to Catholic students at the University of Berlin.

A second new conduit was the German youth movement. The Wandervogel groups and the German Benedictines were not only coincident, both springing up at the end of the nineteenth century, but they were each reacting to the bourgeois culture and dominant subjectivism of late nineteenth-century German intellectual life, as well as urban alienation. Herwegen bridged the two movements by teaching young people that the liturgy was the most effective revolt against the subjective. In 1913 the Düsseldorf academics founded the Jungmännerverbandes, a Wandervogel outlet for Catholics, and from the first stamped it with the new liturgical character. The greatest liturgical group, however, was Quickborn, founded in 1920, with its own castle, Burg Rothenfels, magazine, Schildgenossen (contemporary), and communal form for the celebration of mass, Gemeinschaftliche Andacht zur Feier der Messe. There were other similar but smaller organizations: Neuland, Neudeutschland, Neulandbund, Christlich-Deutschen Studentenbund, and in 1936 the Jungmännerverbandes alone numbered 190,000. (There were 20,000 members of the Hitler Jugend in 1931.) It is understandable that the young Catholics increased the simplicity and communality of German eucharistic celebrations. It was hard to pack all the traditional accessories for high mass or benediction in a back pack.

The pivotal figure in this aggregation of Catholicism and the German youth movement, a man who combined Tübingen, Beuron, Maria Laach, the academics, radical politicians and artists, and who talked about the liturgy in a language which became immensely popular all over Europe, was Romano Guardini. Guardini is the symbolic early twentieth-century intellectual who was drawn to the liturgy as much by secular as by ecclesiastical influences. He was, like so many others in the history of the new Catholicism and as his name suggests, a mixture of the European north and south, of Latin form and German thought.[47]

Guardini was born at Verona in 1885, but in 1886 his family moved to Mainz where his father was Italian consul. He began his studies in 1904 at Munich, Freiburg, and Tübingen, the three principal Catholic universities of the south where the memory of the Möhlerian tradition lingered in the interstices of theology. As a youth his time was taken up with Romantic poets, particularly Hölderlin, and natural science, and he came to feel while a student at Tübingen that the church could be the institution to combine life and truth if it shed its guise as "a bourgeois... [and] ...before all a legalistic institution." The ejection of Thomism and Idealism and the adoption of the catholicized phenomenology of Scheler, Peter Wust, and Reinhold Schneider would lead to reform.[48] He read the French Symbolists and then Stefan Georg. From Rilke he learned of symbolic religious experiences which transcended knowledge. He discovered the liturgy as the Catholic expression of a religion which is super-individualistic during a series of short trips from Tübingen to Beuron in 1906, 1907, and 1908. These visits, he later reported, changed his life, for at Beuron he came upon the model of worship and the medium with which the masses could be reached for Catholicism.[49]

----

[47]Robert d'Harcourt, "Romano Guardini et l'éducation liturgique," Ecclesia, CXXXII (1960), pp. 107-11.

[48]Helmut Kuhn, Romano Guardini. Der Mensch und das Werk (Munich, 1961), p. 20.

[49]Romano Guardini, Liturgie und liturgische Bildung (Würzburg, 1966), p. 20.

Guardini participated in the work of Maria Laach from 1917 until 1922 while serving as a parish priest at Mainz. At the same time, he founded the Quickborn Rothenfels castle on a rock above the Main, where the liturgical apostolate flourished among the neo-Romantic youth until the SS arrived in 1939. There he experimented with forms which facilitated the creation of community, such as mass facing the people and the ancient versions of vigil services. Ideas were tried out as well: that Catholicism is the only form of objective truth, that the I can only be emancipated in the we. The pastoral heritage of the youth movement reinforced and expanded in Guardini the old liturgical movement notion that natural and simple materials were the purest sacraments of the divine. By 1923 he was preaching that solidarity based on a youthful Christianity would redeem humankind from an eternal slavery to soulless technology.[50]

A member of the Prussian government heard Guardini speak in this manner, and in 1923 C. H. Becker, the Prussian Minister of Cults, appointed him to a new university chair at Berlin for "Religionsphilo-sophie und katholische Weltanschauung." Guardini was given a truly international platform on the Unter den Linden to espouse the thinking of the liturgical movement. part of his task was to address the students of that non-Catholic university in a language which they could understand, and that produced a rare German phenomenon: theology in a simple style. He went to the extreme in placing Christian ideas within a secular context. At the same time he addressed a larger public in a series of books on Socrates, Augustine, Bonaventura, Dante, Kierkegaard, Pascal, Hölderlin, Rilke, and Nietzsche which were allegorical introductions to the new Catholic point of view.

Guardini was not a systematic thinker. His books were emotional stands against the bourgeois world, calls for the emancipation of

---

[50]Romano Guardini, Neue Jugend und katholischer Geist (Wiesbaden, 1924). Forty-eight letters (1917-1934) of Romano Guardini to Abbot Ildefons Herwegen which document how crucial the Herwegen-Guardini interchange was to shaping the course of the liturgical movement in this period are preserved in the archives of Maria Laach.

European culture from machines, dictators, and atheists. There is a basic assumption that the West is in a state of deep anarchy, that the old culture is dead because its symbols no longer speak to contemporary needs. "Das Erwachen der Kirche in der Seele," his influential manifesto of 1922 diagnoses the crisis of the twenties to be the death-rattle of subjectivism, the heritage of the Enlightenment. The church is depicted as the institution which will erect a new objective order upon the graves of neo-Kantians and neo-Idealists, the running dogs of the captains of industry whose factory system has destroyed the old organic forms of life and separated human from human.

A new resistance to the "I" which for seventy years had dominated German politics, economics, and philosophy is detected by Guardini in the secular sphere, in the name of "Volks-consciousness." It is this which Guardini determines has caused the cultural ferment of the Weimar Republic in Germany. "This vitality grows out of a new consciousness of community. The torrent of community feeling is the creative ground of this new product, its logic and form." The spirit of the times has been playing with a new emphasis on communal bonds, the family and the state. There is a growing awareness among the Germans that "religious life comes no more from the I, but it grows out of the objective form of the community."[51]

Guardini told his Berlin audience that, as opposed to politicians who were offering notions of Volk and Einheit to Weimar Germans, the church's "unity is no chaotic experience, no simple momentary feeling. It creates through dogma, law, and rite a permanent community. Not simply community, but real communion, not religious movement, but life, not spiritual romanticism, but an existence."[52] The church surpasses left and right wing parties because, unlike them, it is founded in freedom, free-will, friendship, and a concern for the salvation of others. "Our community means that each individual feels answerable

----

[51]Romano Guardini, "Das Erwachen der Kirche in der Seele," Hochland, 19 II (1922), pp. 262, 264.

[52]Ibid., pp. 257, 259, 263.

before God for his neighbor."[53]

What insured this communal understanding in a Catholic Church which had lived under the tyranny of subjective religion since the eighteenth century and had been dominated even longer by a hierarchical ideology? "The liturgical movement!," Guardini replied to his own question. It is essential to the survival of the church and the West that the liturgical ideology be widely adopted. He said this in his greatest and shortest work, The Spirit of the Liturgy, which came out in the Maria Laach Ecclesia Orans series in 1918. There is here once again a recapitulation of the theme that a new Western humanism will only come from anti-individualism. The collectivity which is wanting can be achieved in the communally performed liturgy, for in such activity there is a subordination of the self. The individual yields place to the universal. Liturgical acts are a "manifestation of restrained and elevated social solidarity."[54]

Romano Guardini was simply saying to his audience of the twenties that men and women could escape the cleavage of modern life through worship. This conception of how to achieve community stood between two polar groups of German intellectuals. The intellectuals of despair, Lagarde, Langbehn, and Moller van den Bruck, taught that the good life of the past had been destroyed by modernization. The only solution for meaningful existence lay in a rejection of the present and no accommodation with industrial or urban society. Communal life would return to Germany through escape into art, or the mystery of a national religion, or abandonment of the values of the West. The Weimar/Bauhaus intellectuals countered with the argument that art would only restore order out of the chaos of industrialism by embracing the materials and form of the technical world.

Balancing the other groups, Guardini, and Casel and Herwegen as well, urged that the community must not reject existence in the

---

[53]Romano Guardini, Gottes Werkleute (Burg Rothenfels, 1925), p. 46.

[54]Romano Guardini, The Spirit of the Liturgy (London, 1930), pp. 37, 48, 49; Romano Guardini, Auf dem Wege (Wiesbaden, 1923), p. 95.

contemporary world. But the choking life of materialism would be transcended only if men and women adopted a system of values whose end was not man himself but reached beyond man and mere concern with the standard of living. The community is formed by that act of reaching beyond. That act is the mass-liturgy. The liturgy expresses the authenticity, austerity, simplicity, dignity, "other-ness," which overcomes the stuffy bourgeois world.

Because of the combined influence of Romano Guardini, Maria Laach, and Beuron the liturgical movement became so strong in the German parishes that it flourished even during the last years of the National Socialist time when all extra-parochial Catholic organizations were disbanded. During this era of curtailment of old activities the movement became almost entirely parochial. Just before the advent of Hitler a number of powerful local centers had been founded which continued as witnesses throughout the thirties. Heinrich Georg Hörle opened the parish of Heilige Geist in a proletariat section of Frankfurt "in order to make the masses of the industrial city once again a Volk, a living community."[55] Hörle preceded each mass with a call for participation and with a commentary on the significance of the occasion in the cycle of the liturgical year. The congregation prayed aloud with the priest and sang the chants. Hörle reported that "the liturgy grew with the community, and the community grew with the liturgy.... [This parish] is a growth, an organic springing up."[56] He soon had 950 weekly and 2500 paschal communions.

Josef Schrallhamer turned St. Paul's in Munich into "a community in Christ Jesus." The people were taught to sing and pray the mass in a number of new parish organizations, "The Liturgical Assistance Community," "The Children's Liturgical Community," and "The Liturgical Community of Parish Youths." Konrad Jakobs, a friend of Abbot Herwegen, understood his function as a priest to be the transmission of the communality of a Benedictine monastery to industrial districts. At

----

[55]Theodor Maas-Ewerd, Liturgie und Pfarrei (Paderborn, 1969), p. 67.

[56]Ibid., p. 71.

parishes in Essen and Mühlheim in the Ruhr he preached, "The liturgy is
the best means of building up the Christian personality and the
Christian community....Our parish must become a communion parish! ...We
must develop so that Sunday communion becomes the corner-stone of our
Christian life." In his Essen church the number of annual communions
climbed from 7,000 to 70,000 in the years 1925 to 1930.[57]

The German Oratorians Gunkel, Guelden, Becker, and Tellmann used
Betsingmesse and Gemeinschaftsmesse in the parish of the Leipzig
Oratory to keep Christianity alive after post-1933 decrees disbanded
all of their organizations. Johannes Pinsk sought to teach Berliners
through his 1934-1939 "Liturgical Life Movement" that the altar could
be an island of holiness in a Nazi world, that organizing one's life
about the liturgical year would be a subtle internal protest to the
regimentation of the corporatist state.[58] Experiences of liturgical
community in the midst of totalitarianism were recorded in churches at
Cologne, Breslau, and Stuttgart. A priest who was set to work building
German rockets in a forced labor situation described one such occasion:

> That Christmas of 1944, in that rocket tunnel, with the
> German guards around us, we felt boundlessly free. He [the
> liturgical president] spoke, "Please come up, close, all of
> you, and let us all celebrate Mass, that we may not lose what
> we deportees, prisoners, requis found again: the Church of
> the bold, the martyrs, the saints.[59]

By 1940 the movement had grown into such a force that it was formally
sanctioned by all the bishops of the German territories and put under
direct episcopal supervision at the Fulda Conference of that year.

The new theories were carried once again across Europe, this time
by the German army as well as by the Benedictines. In Austria the

---

[57]Ferdinand Kolbe, Die Liturgische Bewegung (Aschaffenburg, 1964),
p. 54.

[58]Johannes Pinsk, "Quelques fruits du mouvement liturgique," Les
Questions liturgiques et paroissiales (1934), pp. 243-248; Alfons
Kirchgässner, "Das Oratorium in Deutschland," Oratorium, 2, No. 2
(1971), 95-115.

[59]Koenker, op. cit., p. 133.

principal leader was Pius Parsch, but J. A. Jungmann also made the
Jesuit University of Innsbruck a center of liturgical scholarship.
Dutch liturgical weeks began in the early forties. Spanish and Italian
centers were Benedictine abbeys, San Domingo de los Silos in the former
and the monastery of Finalpia near Savona in the latter. A parallel
series of liturgical parishes influenced by the Germans grew up in
France in the forties along with those which had evolved directly from
Solesmes. P. Remilleux, who transformed Notre Dame-Saint Alban in
Lyon, was guided by Maria Laach. The monks of Hay-les-Roses undertook
missionary activity in the dechristianized suburbs of Paris by holding
masses in the vernacular in factory work-rooms. The abbé Michonneau
introduced this concept of the local church to the suburban proletariat
at Sacré Coeur de Colombes:

> Let each parish strive to make its liturgy splendid and full
> of meaning. Let each parish make of itself a real community
> ...united within itself....Let every parish priest avoid the
> pitfalls of money, of 'clerical culture,' of remoteness from
> the thoughts and needs of the people.[60]

Odo Casel made a great impact on a group of French Catholics,
Henri de Lubac, Jean Daniélou, Pie Duployé, and P. Doncour. The Centre
de Pastorale Liturgique, a sort of latter day Dominican Solesmes with a
strong parochial orientation, was established by this group in 1943.
Its magazine La Maison-Dieu carried the liturgical mission to the
French-speaking world after World War II and won the approval of the
bishops of sixty-five French dioceses.[61]

The conquest of the Roman Catholic Church by the liturgical
movement was not without controversy, although in the twentieth century
the hostility never reached the level of the anti-Guéranger campaign in
nineteenth century France. The enemies in central Europe were bishops.
Mgr. Gfoellner of Linz condemned the practice of saying mass facing the

---

[60]Abbé Michonneau, Revolution in a City Parish (Oxford, 1950),
p. 189.

[61]P. Duployé, Les Origines du Centre du Pastorale Liturgique (Paris,
1968).

people, and in 1937 he published a defense of reciting the rosary during the eucharistic celebration. Mgr. Conrad Groebner, the Archbishop of Freiburg, called for Rome to destroy the movement before the war. In 1943 the Archbishop of Breslau sought to have the Pope pronounce on the orthodoxy of the Benedictine liturgists. The antagonist in Belgium was the journal Le Patriote, and in France the hostile party in the twentieth century was not made up of bishops but of Jesuits. They launched an assault in the 1913 issues of their journal Etudes. Léonce de Grandmaison, one of the participants in the 1913 campaign, reasoned that the liturgical movement was ending the role of the individual in Catholicism and thereby destroying the church. Devotion, he argued, is the work of the individual and the foundation of the church and cannot be replaced by a purely social Christianity.[62]

Jean-Joseph Navatel, another Jesuit, portrayed the Benedictines as dreamers seeking after a "retrospective mirage." The Catholic mission, he wrote, is conversion. Preaching and teaching are more useful than the liturgy, which is merely "the sensible, ceremonial, and decorative part of the Catholic cult." Corporate worship plays a very secondary and occasional role in the operations of the church. Why should devotion to Joseph, to Mary, to the Sacred Heart be seen as less crucial than the liturgy? Why should the rosary and the stations of the cross be forgotten? The liturgy is powerful only in proportion to the individual belief and devotion which already exist. A good catechetical instruction is better than a thousand voices singing the credo together at Notre-Dame.[63]

As in France, so in the Roman Catholic Church as a whole, the liturgical movement surmounted criticism because of favorable attention at the Vatican. Pius IX, as we have seen, recognized the new

----

[62]Léonce de Grandmaison, "La Religion personnelle," Etudes, CXXXIV (1913), 289-309, 601-626; CXXXV (1913), 33-56, 309-335.

[63]Jean-Joseph Navatel, "L'Apostolat liturgique et la piété personnelle," Etudes, CXXXVII (1913), 451, 453, 456.

importance of the liturgy in his decisive letter to the Archbishop of Lyon in 1864. Leo XIII in warning that social questions would not be solved merely with the application of ethics, pointed to the eucharist as one of the many aspects of the church which would save society:

> Very beautiful and joyful, too, is the spectacle of Christian brotherhood and social equality which is afforded when men of all conditions...gather round the holy altar....[64]

Pius X taught that the liturgy was the source of the true Christian spirit. Yet, in order for that spirit to flourish again it was necessary that liturgical practice be reformed, dignified, and simplified. Three months after his election on November 11, 1903, Pius X issued a Motu proprio which urged the active participation of the faithful in the eucharist. In this announcement the mass is discussed not as something to see or hear, but to take part in:

> It being our most eager wish that the true Christian spirit may flower again in every way and be upheld by all the faithful, before anything else it is necessary to see to the holiness and dignity of the temple, where the faithful gather to gain that spirit from its first and indispensable source: the active participation in the sacred mysteries and the public and solemn prayer of the Church.[65]

Pius X dedicated his pontificate to accomplishing in the entire church that which Guéranger had sought for France, a revival of Christianity by first restoring the dignity and decorum of God's house: by throwing profane and theatrical music out of the churches, by restoring active singing, and by allowing only art inspired by the liturgy to be admitted to places of worship. That Solesmes was the inspiration of these reforms is not only attested in a papal brief to Dom Delatte of 22 May 1904 in praise of Solesmes, but the Motu proprio itself exalts Gregorian chant to the position of the official music of the church and says that "Gregorian chant must be restored to the people so that they may again take a more active part in the liturgy,

---

[64]The Benedictine Monks of Solesmes, Papal Teachings. The Liturgy (Boston, 1962), p. 166.

[65]C. J. McNaspy, The Motu Proprio of Church Music of Pope Pius X (Toledo, 1950), p. 61.

as was the case in ancient times."[66] In 1905 Pius issued a decree, Sacra Tridentina, in support of frequent communion within the mass. The apostolic constitution Divino afflatu of 1911 restored the Sunday and saint's day offices to all churches and the Motu proprio Abhinc duos annos of 1913 reformed the breviary to conform more precisely with the liturgical year.

Pius XI was the first pope to recognize the liturgical movement, the name as well as the thing, to wish it progress, and to quote Guardini in audiences, but it was in the pontificate of Pius XII, specifically in the encyclical Mediator Dei of November 20, 1947, that complete triumph was sensed.[67] The title of the letter itself refers to the underlying concept of Guéranger's system, that the chief work of Christ is mediator between the natural and spiritual world and integrator of humankind into a great supernatural whole. Pius states that it is the church which continues that process through the liturgy: "...the Church prolongs the priestly mission of Jesus Christ mainly by means of the sacred liturgy."[68] There is a definition of the church as a community and an elevation of the liturgy to the first rank of the Catholic constitution. "The Sacred Liturgy is consequently the public worship which our Redeemer as Head of the Church renders to the Father as well as the worship which the community of the faithful renders to its Founder....It is, in short, the worship rendered by the Mystical Body of Christ in the entirety of its Head and members."[69]

There is little doubt that the pope was influenced in his statement by the liturgical movement, for he specifically praises the Benedictines for their renewal of worship, for their work in making ceremonies understood, and for their doctrine of the church. "Bolder

---

[66]Benedictine Monks, op. cit., p. 181.

[67]D. B. Capelle, "Le Saint Siège et le mouvement liturgique," Les Questions liturgiques et paroissiales XXI (1936), 125-147.

[68]Benedictine Monks, op. cit., p. 314.

[69]Ibid., p. 321.

512

relief was given likewise to the fact that all the faithful make up a
single and very compact body with Christ for its Head, and that the
Christian community is in duty bound to participate in the liturgical
rites according to their station."[70] The pope recognizes the idea that
exterior worship is that which makes the unity of Christians possible,
and he goes on to say:

> ...they are to be praised who with the idea of getting the
> Christian people to take part more easily and more faithfully
> in the mass strive to make them familiar with the "Roman
> Missal" so that the faithful, united with the priest, may
> pray together....They are also to be commended who strive to
> make the liturgy even in an external way a sacred act in
> which all who are present may share.[71]

Mediator Dei was the great victory of the new Catholicism in the
Roman Church. All that came later was an expansion of its
implications. In the fifties the Easter Vigil and the vernacular were
gradually restored. Pius accepted the new view of the parish as
community rather than territory in a letter to Cardinal Léger: "...the
parish is the first community of Christian life....It is a community
cut to human dimensions...the symbol of unity and the center of
community life...a really true and active cell of the Body of Christ."[72]

Vatican II was important as a symbolic assent of the entire Roman
Catholic Church to the liturgical movement. Its practices and notions
could no longer be passed off as the illusions of a cranky fringe.
They were now the view of the church. The council stated for a last
time central themes which had first emerged in Dom Guéranger and were
now the official language of the church. The liturgy was defined as
the activity during which men and women are saved:

> Christ, indeed, always associates the Church with Himself in
> this great work wherein God is perfectly glorified and men
> are sanctified....Rightly, then, the liturgy is considered as
> an exercise of the priestly office of Jesus Christ in which

---

[70]Ibid., p. 315.

[71]Ibid., p. 363.

[72]Ibid., pp. 440-441.

---

the sanctification of man is signified by signs perceptible to the senses....[73]

So great is the stress on the liturgy at Vatican II that Guéranger's definition of the church as "the society of the divine praise" is now adopted:

...every liturgical celebration...is a sacred action surpassing all others...the pre-eminent manifestation of the Church consists in the full active participation of all God's holy people in these liturgical celebrations,...[74]

It is the social character of the liturgy which gives it this great role:

Liturgical services are not private functions but are celebrations of the Church....It is to be stressed that whenever rites...make provision for communal celebration involving the presence and active participation of the faithful, this way of celebrating them is to be preferred... this full and active participation by all the people is the aim to be considered before all else; for it is the primary and indispensable source from which the faithful are to derive the true Christian spirit....[75]

But the extent to which these revolutionary ideas had already penetrated the Roman Catholic Church was made manifest when the Constitution on the Sacred Liturgy was first presented to the Fathers of the Council in 1962. It was accepted by a vote of 2,147 to 4.[76]

---

[73]Louis Bouyer, The Liturgy Revived (Notre Dame, 1964), pp. 34, 43.

[74]Ibid., pp. 43, 53.

[75]Ibid., pp. 60, 91.

[76]Saint-Severin, op. cit., p. 131. For a review of this development twenty years after Vatican II see R. W. Franklin, "Humanism and Transcendence in the Nineteenth Century Liturgical Movement," Worship, 59, No. 4 (July 1985), 342-353.

Bibliography

I

France, the German Benedictines, and the German Liturgical Movement

Primary Sources

Parish Materials

Parish Archives

St. Jacques du Haut-Pas, Paris
Missions Étrangères-St. François Xavier, Paris
Juigné-sur-Sarthe
Notre Dame du Pré, Le Mans
Notre Dame, Mesnil-St.-Loup
Notre Dame, Sablé
Notre Dame, Solesmes

Archbishop's Archives, Paris

On St. Jacques du Haut-Pas, I P 55, Folder No. 24.
On Missions-Étrangères-St. François Xavier, I P 55, Folder No. 64.

Other Manuscripts

Annales Beuron: 1905-1924. Archives, Archabbey of Beuron.
Aveline, Françoise, Sablé-sur-Sarthe durant la période révolutionnaire. Diplôme principal presénté devant la Faculté des Lettres de Rennes. 1961-62. Hôtel de ville, Sablé.
Combe, Pierre, Un centenaire, la restauration grégorienne à Solesmes, Mélanges Dom Germain Cozien. Library, Abbey of Solesmes.
Desportes, Charles, La Vocation monastique: Dom Delatte et Huysmans, Mélanges Dom Germain Cozien. Library, Abbey of Solesmes.
du Halgouet, Jérôme, Les Debuts de la renaissance cistercienne du XIXe siècle. Document B-2. Archives, Abbey of Solesmes.

Fiala, Virgil, Die Besondere Ausprägung des Benediktinischen Mönchtums in der Beuroner Kongregation. Document A-4, Archives, Abbey of Solesmes.

Gazeau, Roger, L'Essor du monachisme masculin en France. Document B-1, Archives, Abbey of Solesmes.

Guéranger, Prosper, Correspondence on Institutions liturgiques and other liturgical issues. 1841-1845. Archives, Abbey of Solesmes.

_____, Correspondence with Charles Brandes, 1840-1862. Archives, Abbey of Solesmes.

_____, Correspondence with Maur Wolter, 1862-1863. Archives, Abbey of Solesmes.

_____, Journal 1852-1872. Archives, Abbey of Solesmes.

_____, La vie de Saint Benoît, 172 pages in Guéranger's own hand written in 1864, the expansion of an erlier Life. Archives, Abbey of Solesmes.

_____, Letter to Charles de Montalembert, 18 January 1832. Archives, Abbey of Solesmes.

_____, Notes autobiographiques. Archives, Abbey of Solesmes.

Anon., L'esprit des études dans la congregation de Solesmes. Archives, Abbey of Solesmes.

Misonne, Daniel, La restauration monastique du XIXe siècle et les restaurations anterieures: Interet d'une histoire comparée. Document A-6, Archives, Abbey of Solesmes.

Lunn, Maur, The English Congregation. Document B-10, Archives, Abbey of Solesmes.

Mazis, Antoine de, La Vocation de Dom Guéranger. Archives, Abbey of Solesmes.

_____, L'Esprit des études dans la Congrégation de Solesmes. Archives, Abbey of Solesmes.

Anon., Presse articles sur les débuts de Solesmes, 1833-1836. Archives, Abbey of Solesmes.

Robert, Leon, Lettres spirituelles de Dom Guéranger à Mademoiselle Euphrasie Cosnard, Mélanges Dom Germain Cozien. Library, Abbey of Solesmes.

Savart, Claude, L'Opinion française et le monachisme au milieu du XIXe siècle. Archives, Abbey of Solesmes.

Watelet, Jacques-Grégoire, Le Renouveau gothique au XIXe siècle et l'Abbaye de Maredsous. Document B-22, Archives, Abbey of Solesmes.

Wolter, Maurus and Placidus, Tagebuch seiner Reise ins Heilige Land. Library, Archabbey of Beuron.

Secondary Works

By Prosper Louis Pascal Guéranger:

Conférences sur la vie chrétienne. v. I: Solesmes, 1880; v. II: Solesmes, 1884.

"Considérations sur la liturgie catholique," Mémorial Catholique, 28 February 1830, pp. 49-57; 31 March 1830, pp. 79-90; 31 May, 1830, pp. 181-189; 31 July, 1830, pp. 241-256.

De la monarchie pontificale; à propos de livre de Mgr. l'Evêque de Sura. 2nd ed. Paris, 1870.

De l'élection et de la nomination des évêques. Paris, 1831.

"De la prière pour le roi," L'Avenir, 24 and 28 October 1831.

Défense de L'Eglise Romaine contre les accusations du R. P. Gratry. 2nd ed. Paris, 1870.

Défense des Institutions liturgiques, lettre à Mgr. l'archevêque de Toulouse. Le Mans, 1844.

Défense des Considerations. Paris, 1830.

Deuxiéme défense de l'Eglise Romaine contre les accusations du R. P. Gratry. Paris, 1870.

"Du chant d'Église," L'Auxiliaire Catholique, IV (1846), 220-237.

Enchiridion benedictinum. Angers, 1825.

Essai historique sur l'abbaye de Solesmes, suivi de la description de l'église abbatiale avec l'explicatoin des monuments qu'elle renferme. Le Mans, 1846.

Essais sur le naturalisme contemporain. Paris, 1858.

Explication des prières et des cérémonies de la Messe d'après des notes recueillies aux conférences de dom Prosper Guéranger. 2nd ed. Solesmes, 1885.

Explications sur les corps des saints martyrs. Extrait des Catacombes de Rome et sur le culte qu'on leur rend. Angers, 1839.

Histoire de Sainte Cécile. Vierge Romaine et martyre. 2nd ed. Paris, 1853.

Institutions liturgiques 4 v. 2nd ed. Paris, 1878-85.

Le Jansénisme et la Compagnie de Jésus. Extrait de la Revue d'Anjou et du Maine. 1857.

L'année liturgique. 15 v. Paris, 1841-1901.

La Règle du Bienheureux Père Saint Benoît avec les déclarations rédigées par Dom Guéranger, Abbé de Solesmes, pour l'Abbaye de Sainte-Cécile de Solesmes. Solesmes, 1890.

L'Eglise ou la Société de la louange divine. Angers, 1875.

Les Dons du Saint-Esprit. Tournai, 1950.

trans., Les exercices de Sainte Gertrude vierge de l'ordre de Saint-Benoît. 3rd ed. Paris, 1879.

Lettres à Msgr. l' Archevêque de Reims sur le droit liturgique. Paris, 1840.

Lettre à Mgr. l'archevêque de Reims sur le droit de la liturgie. Le Mans, 1843.

Lettre à M. Hauréau sur sa brochure intitulée: Manuel du Clergé etc. Le Mans, 1843. [written under the pseudonym B. Ulysses Pic]

"Lettre au Courier de la Sarthe," Unvers, 11 March 1835.

"Lettre sur Solesmes," L'Ami de la Religion, LXXVII (8 August, 1833), 61.

"Lettres," L'Ami de la religion, CXVI, 9 February 1843, 257-264; CXVII, 15 June 1843, 521-528; CXVIII, 22 August 1843, 457; CXXVII, 25 December 1845, 725-726.

"Lettre," Le Monde, 29 November 1860.

Liturgical Year. Laurence Shepherd, tr. 9 v. 3rd ed. London, 1901.

"Le Lys de frère Eystein," L'Auxiliaire Catholique, I (1845), 449-468.

"Marie d'Agréda et la cité mystique de Dieu," L'Univers, 23 May, 6 and 20 June, 18 July, 1 and 15 Aug., 12 and 26 Sept., 10 Oct., 21 Nov., 5 and 19 Dec., 1858, 16 and 31 Jan., 13 Feb., 13 and 28 March, 11 April, 15 and 29 May, 13 June, 18 July, 7 and 22 Aug., 18 Sept., 9 and 23 Oct., 7 Nov. 1859.

The Medal or Cross of St. Benedict: Its Origin, Meaning, and Privileges. London, 1880.

Mélanges de liturgie, d'histoire, et de théologie. 1830-1837. Solesmes, 1887.

Mémoire sur la question de l'Immaculée Conception de la Très Sainte Vierge. Paris, 1850.

Notice sur le Prieuré de Solesmes. Le Mans, 1834.

Nouvelle défense des Institutions liturgiques. Le Mans, 1846, 1847.

Nouvelles observations sur les doctrines dites Gallicanes et sur les doctrines dites Ultra montaines. Paris, 1852.

Origines de l'église romaine. Paris, 1836.

Religious and Monastic Life Explained. St. Louis, 1908.

"Resurrection des Bénédictins en France," Tribune catholique, Gazette du clergé (19 May 1833).

Sainte Cécile et la société romaine aux deux premiers siècles. 2nd ed. Paris, 1874.

Le Sens chrétien de l'histoire. Paris, 1945.

"Souscription pour l'oeuvre des Bénédictins de Solesmes," Tribune catholique (23 May 1833); Revue européenne, VI (1833), 440-445.

"Une thèse de théologie en Sorbonne," Mémorial Catholique, 31 January 1830, pp. 17-25.

By other authors:

A propos d'un pamphlet contre MM. les curés de Lyon. Lyon, 1863.

Affre, Denis, Mandement...sur Institutions liturgiques. Paris, 1843.
_____, Mandement, circulaire...sur Institutions liturgiques. Paris, 1849.

Ahrens, Liselotte, Lamennais und Deutschland. Münster, 1930.

Allies, T. W., Journal in France. London, 1849.

L'ami de la religion et du Roi. Paris, 1833, 1837, 1840, 1843, 1849.

d'Anglejan, Jacques, "Un Defénseur de la Tradition Religieuse en France au XIXe Siècle," La Revue critique des Idées et des Livres, XIII, No. 75 (25 May 1911), 456-480.

Annales flèchoises. Le Mans, 1905.

Antier, M., Le Lycée David d'Angers. Angers, 1947.

d'Astros, Paul-Thérèse David, L'Église de France injustement flétrie dans un ouvrage ayant pour titre: Institutions liturgiques. Toulouse, 1843.

_____, Examen de la Défense de Dom Guéranger et courte réfutation de sa lettre à Mgr. l'archevêque de Reims. Toulouse, 1846.

Aubineau, Léon, "Dom Prosper Guéranger, 5 February, 1875," Au Soir (Paris, 1886), pp. 122-136.

Auger, J.-B. A., La question liturgique réduite à sa plus simple expression. Paris, 1854.

Auxiliare catholique, 1845-1846 (only years published).

Balthasar, Hans Urs von, Romano Guardini. Reform aus dem Ursprung. Munich, 1970.

Basil, T. R. P., Antoine Moreau et les origines de la Congrégation de Sainte-Croix. 2 vol. Paris, 1950-51.

Beauduin, Lambert, Mélanges liturgiques. Louvain, 1954.

Bellot, Paul, Propos d'un bâtisseur du bon Dieu. Montreal, 1948.

Bard, Joseph, De la question liturgique par rapport à la sainte Eglise de Lyon. Lyon, 1860.

Battandier, Albert, Le Cardinal Jean-Baptiste Pitra. Paris, 1893.

Baunard, Mgr., Histoire du Cardinal Pie, Évêque de Poitiers. 2nd ed. Paris, 1886.

Bayle, T. A., "Solesmes," L'Ami des lois, 13 and 15 October 1836.

The Benedictine Monks of Solesmes, Papal Teachings. The Liturgy. Boston, 1962.

Benoit, J.-D., Liturgical Renewal. London, 1958.

Bergier, Jean-François, Études liturgiques. Histoire de la controverse et de la Réforme liturgique en France aux dix-neuviéme siècle. Besançon, 1861.

_____, Explications intéressantes. Besançon, 1861.

_____, Un petit mot à l'adresse des prêtres bisontins. Besançon, 1861.

_____, Nouvelles explications. Besançon, 1861.

_____, Entretien sur la necessité d'adopter le Rit Romain. Paris, 1861.

Berlière, Ursmer, Oraison funebre du R. P. Dom Placide Wolter, Archiabbé de Beuron, Premier Abbé de Maredsous. Bruges, 1908.

Bernier, Henri, L'État et les cultes. Angers, 1848.

_____, Humble remontrance au R. P. Dom Prosper Guéranger. Paris, 1847.

Bernoville, Gaetan, Basile Moreau et la Congregation de Sainte-Croix. Montrouge, 1952.

Berthaumier, Mgr., Observations critiques sur le bréviaire de Bourges. Crété, 1849.

Berthelon, Amand, Agonie de la Liturgie Troyenne par un Prêtre qui lui fait ses adieux. Troyes, 1847.

Bertier de Sauvigny, G. de, "Mgr. de Quélen et les incidents de St. Germain-l'Auxerrois en février 1831," Revue d'histoire de l'église de France, XXXII (1946), 110-120.

Besse, Dom, Le Cardinal Pie, sa vie, son action religieuse et sociale. Paris, 1903.

Beuron, Monks of, Beuron, 1863-1963. Festschrift zum hundertjährigen Bestehen der Erzabtei St. Martin. Beuron, 1963.

Bishop, Edmond, Liturgica Historica. Oxford, 1918.

Bissardon, curé of St.-Bruno, Défense de la Liturgie de Lyon. Lyon, 1864.

Blanc, Louis, Histoire de dix ans. 4th ed. Bruxelles, 1846.

Bogler, P. T., Liturgische Erneurung in aller Welt. Maria Laach, 1950.

Bonhomme, Jules, Principes d'une véritable restauration du chant Grégorien et examen de quelques éditions modernes. Paris, 1857.

Bonnechose, F. G., Lettre pastorale et mandement de Mgr. l'Evêque de Carcassonne au clergé de son diocèse pour le réstablissement de la liturgie romaine. Carcassonne, 1854.

Bourdin, Augustin, De Liturgies françaises en général et de la liturgie normande en particulier. Paris, 1856.

Bouvier, J.-B., Lettre circulaire de Mgr. l'Evêque du Mans au clergé de son diocèse touchant la célébration des fêtes supprimées. Le Mans, 1851.

Bouyer, Louis, La Vie de la liturgie. Paris, 1956.

_____, The Liturgy Revived. Notre Dame, 1964.

Brandes, Charles, Uber das Grundprinzip der Weltgeschichte. Maria-Einsiedeln, 1848.

_____, Leben des heiligen Vaters Benedikt. Maria-Einsiedeln, 1858.

Breuning, Klaus, Die Vision des Reiches. Deutscher Katholizismus zwischen Demokratie und Diktatur (1929-1934). Munich, 1969.

Brovelli, F., "Per uno studio de 'l'Année Liturgique' di P. Guéranger," Ephemerides Liturgicae, 95 (1981), 145-219.

Bulletin paroissial de St. François Xavier, March 1904-1958.

Bulletin paroissial de St. Jacques du Haut-Pas, October 1911-.

Bulletin paroissial de Sablé paraissant tous les mois, 1907-1932.

Cabrol, Fernand, ed., Bibliographie des Bénédictines de la Congrégation de France. Solesmes, 1889.

_____, Dictionnaire d'archéologie chrétienne et de liturgie. Paris, 1925.

_____, Histoire du Cardinal Pitra. Paris, 1893.

Callendini, L., "Le Collège de Sablé," Journal de Sablé, April 1931.

_____, "Fabrication à Sablé," Journal de Sablé, 12 February 1933.

_____, "Les Églises," Journal de Sablé, 17 September 1933.

_____, "Les études ecclésiastiques au diocèse du Mans," La Province du Maine, XIV (July 1906).

Callendini, Louis, "M. Paillard," Journal de Sablé, 18 October 1931.

_____, "Le vieux collège," Journal de Sablé, 16 April 1933.

Caloen, Gérard van, Dom Maur Wolter et les origines de la Bénédictines de Beuron. Bruges-Lille, 1891.

Capelle, D. B., "Dom Guéranger et l'esprit liturgique," Les questions liturgiques et paroissiales, XXII (1937), 131-146.

_____, "Le mouvement liturgique," Les questions liturgiques et paroissiales, XIX (1934), 222-224.

_____, "Le Saint Siège et le mouvement liturgique," Les questions liturgiques et paroissiales, XXI (1936), 125-147.

Cappuyn, D. M., "Liturgie et Théologie," Les questions liturgiques et paroissiales, XIX (1934), 249-275.

Casel, Odo, Das christliche Kult Mysterium. Regensburg, 1960.

Un catholique lyonnais, Liturgie Lyonnaise-résumé analytique des débats. Lyon, 1864.

Les Catholiques, Requête adressée à son Eminence le Cardinal Morlot. Paris, 1859.

Catta, Etienne, Dom Guéranger et le Premier Concile du Vatican. Sablé, 1962.

Cattaneo, Enrico, Il Culto Cristiano in Occidente. Rome, 1978.

Cazalès, E. de, "Voyage à Solesmes," Revue européenne, VI (July 1833), 583-595.

Celier, Alexander, Dom Paul Piolin. Laval, no date, publisher Chailland.

Chabert, Abbé, A propos d'un pamphlet contre les curés de Lyon. Lyon, 1863.

_____, Défense de la Liturgie de Lyon. Lyon, 1859.

Chamard, François, Dom Guéranger et M. l'abbé Bernier. Angers, 1901.

Chevalier, F., Instruction sur l'Eglise, adressée spécialement aux fidèles du diocèse du Mans, sous l'autorisation et l'approbation de M. l'Evêque du Mans qui l'a jugée propre à opposer aux efforts d'une nouvelle secte. Le Mans, 1804.

Clausel de Montals, C. H., Lettre Pastorale de Mgr. l'évèque de Chartres au clergé de son diocèse ou sont présentées des observations sur le dernier mandement de Mgr. l'archevêque de Paris. Chartres, 1851.

Clausel de Montals, C. H., Lettre pastorale de Mgr. l'évèque de Chartres, sur la gloire et les lumieres qui ont distingué jusqu'a nos jours l'Église de France. Chartres, 1850.

Cloet, N., De la restauration du chant liturgique. Plancy, 1825.

Compte rendu de la députation envoyée à Rome par le clergé du diocèse de Lyon. Lyon, 1864.

Congrès eucharistique--Sablé. Sablé, 1932.

Congrès pour la restauration du plain-chant et de la musique d'Eglise. Paris, 1862.

Cornat, Abbé, De l'introduction de la liturgie romaine dans le diocèse de Sens. Auxerre, 1848.

_____, De la situation de la question liturgique en France en 1851. Paris, 1851.

Couillard, E., Notice sur M. l'abbé L.-B. Albin. Le Mans, 1903.

Cozien, Germain, L'Oeuvre de Dom Guéranger. Le Mans, 1933.

Dangelmaier, Alois, P. Anselm Schott. Der Mensch. Priester und Liturge. Reimlinger, 1971.

Daniel-Rops, H., "Dom Guéranger restaure la liturgie," Ecclesia, No. 132 (March 1960), 93-97.

Danjou, F., De l'état et de l'avenir du chant ecclésiastique en France. Paris, no date.

Danzer, P. Beda, "Solesmes im Jubelkranz," Benediktinische Monatschrift, XV (1933), 253-260.

Dassance, Abbé, "Lettres," L'Ami de la Religion, CXVI (2 February 1843), 209-214, (21 February 1843), 340.

De la propriété des églises...Exposé des faits pour le Département de la Sarthe. Le Mans, 1905.

Debelay, J.-M. M., Mandement de Mgr. l'Evêque de Troyes, etc. Troyes, 1847.

Delatte, Dom Paul, Dom Guéranger, Abbé de Solesmes. 2v. Paris, 1909.

Delaunay, P., Galerie des naturalistes sarthois. Edouard Guéranger. Laval, 1937.

_____, "La Chouanerie de 1832," Mémoire de la Société d'agriculture, sciences et arts de la Sarthe LIII (1932), 382-452.

Denis, Paul, Guizot et le differénd Mgr. Bouvier-Dom Guéranger. Paris, 1911.

Depéry, J.-I., Lettre pastorale de Mgr. l'Evêque de Gap, au sujet du rétablissement de la liturgie Romaine dans son diocèse. Gap, 1845.

Anon., Dernière réponse aux difficultés présentés par M. Aloys Kung dans ses Nouvelles Notes etc. Toulouse, 1867.

Derré, Jean-René, Lamennais, ses amis, et le mouvement des idées à l'époque romantique. Paris, 1962.

Deschamps La Rivière, R., "Antoine Maguin et le clergé constitutionnel manceau, 1791-1794," La Province du Maine, XVII (June 1909).

Anon., Difficultés presentés par M. Aloys Kung dans son Nouvel Essai etc. Toulouse, 1867.

Dimier, Louis, Choisir les meilleurs textes de Dom Guéranger. Paris, 1937.

Donet, F. F. A., "Guéranger," Le Monde (Paris, France), 25 February 1875.

Doney, J. C., "Lettre," L'Univers (Paris), 10 February 1846.

Dreesbach, Martha, Pater Desiderius Lenz, O.S.B., von Beuron, Theorie und Werk. Munich, 1957.

Dreux Brezé, P.-S.-L.-M. de, Mandement de Mgr. l'Evêque de Moulins pour l'établissement de la liturgie romaine dans son diocèse. Moulins, 1852.

du Lac, Melchior, La Liturgie Romaine et les liturgies françaises. Le Mans, 1849.

Duployé, P., Les Origines du Centre du Pastorale Liturgique. Paris, 1968.

Dürig, Walter, Die Zukunft der Liturgischen Erneuerung. Mainz, 1962.

Dutilliet, H.-A.-M., Petit catéchisme liturgique ou courte explication des principales cérémonies de l'Eglise Romaine. Paris, 1860.

_____, Instructio Pastoralis et Decretum Versaliensis Episcopi. Versailles, 1864.

Duval, Edmnd, Mémoire sur la nouvelle édition du Graduel et de l'Antiphonaire Romaine. Paris, 1825.

la Fage, Adrien de, De la reproduction des livres de plain-chant romain. Paris, 1853.

Falloux, Count de, Madame Swetchine. Sa vie et ses oeuvres. 3rd ed. Paris, 1860.

Fayet, Jean-Jacques, Des Institutions liturgiques de Dom Guéranger et de sa lettre à Mgr. l'archevêque de Reims. Paris, 1845.

_____, D'Examen des Institutions liturgiques de Dom Guéranger et de sa Lettre à Mgr. l'archevêque de Reims. Paris, 1846.

Festpredigt zur Feier des 50 Jährigen Jubiläums der Beuroner Kongregation. Beuron, 1913.

Foissat, Canon, "Resurrection de l'ordre des Bénédictins en France," Annales de philosophie chrétienne, VI (1833), 392-98.

Franklin, R. W., "Guéranger: A View on the Centenary of His Death," Worship, 49 (1975), 318-328.

_____, "Guéranger and Pastoral Liturgy: A Nineteenth Century Context," Worship, 50 (1976), 146-162.

_____, "Guéranger and Variety in Unity," Worship, 51 (1977), 378-399.

_____, "The Nineteenth Century Liturgical Movement," Worship, 53 (1979), 12-39.

_____, "Humanism and Transcendence in the Nineteenth Century Liturgical Movement," Worship, 59 (1985), 342-353.

Frénaud, Georges, "Dom Guéranger et le projet de Bulle 'Quemadmodum Ecclesia' pour la definition de l'Immaculée Conception," Virgo Immaculata--Acta Congressus Mariologici. Rome, 1956, II, 337-386.

Freppel, Mgr., Deuxième expulsion des Bénédictins de Solesmes. Château-Gontier, 1882.

_____, Discours sur l'ordre monastique prononcé dans l'église abbatiale de Solesmes à l'anniversaire des obsèques de Dom Guéranger. Angers, 1876.

Gautier, Leon, "Le Cardinal Pitra," Portraits contemporains et questions actuelles. Paris, 1873.

_____, Vingt nouveaux portraits. No place of publication, no date.

Genestout, F. A., "Dom Guéranger et la restauration de Solesmes," Le Correspondant, CV, no. 1701 (10 August 1933), 391-405.

George, J.-B., Mandement de Mgr. l'Evêque de Périgueux au sujet, etc. Périgueux, 1844.

Gerbet, Philippe, Considèrations sur le dogme générateur de la pieté catholique. Paris, 1829.

Ghysens, Gisbert, "Fondation et Essor de Maredsous (1872-1923)," Revue Bénédictine, 83 (1973), 229-257.

Girard, P., Mission du Mans. Le Mans, 1827.

Giraud, Victor, "La Résurrection de Solesmes," Revue des deux mondes (15 July 1933), 448-454.

Glogger, Placidus, "Monastischer Lenz, Monastischer Sommer," Benediktinische Monatschrift, XVI (1934), 53-59.

Gontier, M. A., Le Plain-Chant, son exécution. Le Mans, 1860.

_____, Méthode raisonnée de plain-chant. Paris, 1859.

Gousset, T.-M.-J., Mandement de Mgr. l'archevêque de Reims, pour le rétablissement de la liturgie romaine dans son diocèse. Reims, 1848.

Gozier, André, Dom Casel. Paris, 1968.

Grandmaison, Geoffrey de, "Solesmes et Dom Guéranger," Le Mois littéraire et pittoresque (February, 1899), p. 269.

Greffier, Thérèse, Une petite ville du Maine aux XIXᵉ siècle. Sablé, 1960.

Grente, Mgr., Statuts synodaux diocesains du Mans. Le Mans, 1847.

Grorichard, Paul, "De Rome à Villersexel," Académie de Besançon (1930).

Guardini, Romano, <u>Auf dem Wege</u>. Wiesbaden, 1923.

_____, "Das Erwachender Kirche in der Seele," <u>Hochland</u>, 19 II
(1922).

_____, <u>Gottes Werkleute</u>. Burg Rothenfels, 1925.

_____, <u>Luturgie und liturgische Bildung</u>. Würzburg, 1966.

_____, <u>Neue Jugend und katholischer Geist</u>. Wiesbaden, 1924.

_____, <u>The Spirit of the Liturgy</u>. London, 1930.

Guépin, Alphonse, <u>Dom Guéranger et Madame Durand</u>. Paris, 1911.

Anon., "Guéranger," <u>Le Monde</u>, 17 February 1875.

Guérard, B.E.C., "La Terre salique," <u>Bibliothèque de l'Ecole des
Chartes</u> V (Nov. and Dec. 1841), 188.

Guibert, Cardinal, <u>Instruction provisoire pour faciliter aux prêtres du
Diocèse de Paris le passage...à la liturgie romaine</u>. Paris,
1874.

Guillemant, Charles, <u>Pierre-Louis Parisis</u>. 3v. Paris, 1924.

Guillois, Ambroise, <u>Explication historique, dogmatique, morale, (et
liturgique) du catéchisme</u>. Le Mans, 1838.

Hales, E. E. Y., <u>Pio Nono</u>. London, 1954.

Haquin, André, <u>Dom Lambert Beauduin et le renouveau liturgique</u>.
Gembloux, 1970.

d'Harcourt, Robert, "Romano Guardini et l'éducation liturgique,"
<u>Ecclesia</u>, CXXXII (1960), 107-111.

Harispe, Pierre, <u>Lamennais et Gerbet</u>. Paris, 1909.

Herwegen, Ildefons, "Kirche und Mysterium," <u>Mysterium, Gesammelte
Arbeiten Laacher Monche</u>. Münster, 1926.

_____, <u>Kirche und Seele</u>. Münster, 1926.

_____, <u>Lumen Christi</u>. Munich, 1924.

_____, "The Nature of Religous Art," <u>Liturgical Arts</u> I (1931), 1-6.

Hiron, Eugène, <u>Notice biographique sur M. l'abbé Véron</u>. Paris, 1867.

_____, <u>Theses</u>. Louvain, 1838.

Hourlier, Jacques, <u>L'église de Solesmes et ses amis</u>. Sablé, 1952.

Houtin, A., <u>Dom Couturier, Abbé de Solesmes</u>. Angers, 1899.

_____, <u>Un Dernier Gallican, Henri Bernier</u>. Paris, 1904.

<u>Indicateur paroissial</u>. Paroisse Saint-Benoît. Le Mans, 1898.

<u>Instructio Pastoralis et Decretum Versaliensis Episcopi</u>. Versailles,
1864.

J. B., "A propos d'un centenaire," <u>Les cahiers du Cercle de la Femme</u>
(October 1933), 197-203.

Janssens, Laurent, <u>Oraison funèbre du R. P. Dom Maur Wolter, Archiabbé
et fondateur de la Congrégation de Beuron</u>. Bruges, 1890.

Johnson, Cuthbert, <u>Prosper Guéranger (1805-1875): A Liturgical
Theologian</u>. Rome, 1984.

Jolly, Mellon, <u>Mandement de Mgr. l'archevêque de Sens</u>, etc. Sens,
1851.

Jouve, Abbé, <u>Du mouvement liturgique en France durant le XIXe siècle</u>.
Paris, 1860.

Kirchgässner, Alfons, "Das Oratorium in Deutschland," <u>Oratorium</u>, 2
(1971), 95-115.

Koenker, E. B., <u>The Liturgical Renaissance in the Roman Catholic
Church</u>. St. Louis, 1954.

Kolbe, Ferdinand, <u>Die Liturgische Bewegung</u>. Aschaffenburg, 1964.

Kuhn, Helmut, Romano Guardini. Der Mensch und das Werk. Munich, 1961.

Kung, Aloys, Nouvelles notes sur la tradition du chant Gregorien. Toulouse, 1867.

Laborie, De Lanzac de, "Dom Guéranger et son oeuvre," Le Correspondant, CCXXXVIII (10 March 1910), 941-960.

La paroisse. Revue liturgique, canonique, littéraire et archéologique. 15 January - 15 June 1861.

Laurence, B.-S., Mandement de Mgr. l'Evêque de Tarbes, pour le rétablissement de la liturgie romaine dans son diocèse. Tarbes, 1849.

Le Mée, J. J. P., Circulaire de Mgr. l'Evêque de Saint-Brieuc, à son clergé. Saint-Brieuc, 1846.

Lecanuet, E., "Montalembert et Dom Guéranger: Lettres inédites," Annales de philosophie chrétienne XI, 113-129.

Leclercq, Jean, "Le renouveau Solesmien et le renouveau religieux du XIXe siècle," Studia Monastica, 18 (1976), 157-195.

Ledru, Ambrose, "Dom Guéranger, abbé de Solesmes," La province du Maine, XVIII (January 1910), 16.

_____, Dom Guéranger, Abbé de Solesmes et Mgr. Bouvier, Evêque du Mans. Paris, 1911.

_____, L'Eglise de Notre-Dame du Pré au Mans. Le Mans, 1924.

Lemenant des Chesnais, L., Oraison funèbre du R. P. D. P. Louis Pascal Guéranger, restaurateur de l'ordre Bénédictin en France. Marseille, 1875.

Les Fêtes du centenaire à l'Abbaye de Solesmes. Solesmes, 1934.

Les Fêtes Jubilaires de l'Abbaye de Saint-Pierre de Solesmes, 9, 10, et 11 Juillet, 1887. Solesmes, 1887.

Anon., Lettera sinodale de Padri del Concilio Provinciale di Parigi, voltata dal Francese etc. Bari, 1856.

Lettre à M. l'abbé Rony, ou observations raisonnées sur les inconvenients et les erreurs d'un nuveau Bréviaire de Lyon. Lyon, 1843.

Lettres sur le Bréviaire Romain addressées à un religieux par un curé de campagne. Pont-a-Mousson, 1864.

Lutz, Heinrich, Demokratie in Zwielicht. Der Weg der deutschen Katholiken aus dem Kaiserreich in die Republik. Munich, 1963.

Maas-Ewerd, Theodor, Liturgie und Pfarrei. Paderborn, 1969.

Mabile, J.-P., Lettre pastorale, etc. Sainte-Claude, 1853.

Maire, Abbé Ch., La Liturgie Romaine et la conscience. Besançon, 1861.

_____, Réponse aux observations anonymes sur l'opuscule intitulé La Liturgie Romaine etc. Besançon, 1861.

Le Maitre, Gabriel, Constitutiones. Rome, 1837.

_____, "Théologie de la vie monastique selon Dom Guéranger," Revue Mabillon, L (1961).

Maréchaux, Bernard, "Dom Guéranger et le Père Emmanuel. Etude liturgique et théologique," Rivista Storica Benedettina, Vol. V., Fasc. XIX (July-September 1910), 406-417.

_____, Le Père Emmanuel. 2nd ed. Mesnil-St.-Loup, 1918.

_____, L'Oeuvre pastorale du Père Emmanuel. Saint-Maximin, 1925.

525

Maret, H.-L.-C., Lettre de M. l'abbé Maret. Paris, 1858.
Marguerye, F.-G.-M.-F. de, Lettre pastorale et ordonnance de Mgr.
l'Evêque d'Autun, Chalon, Maçon, etc. Autun, 1854.
Mathieu, J.-M.-A.-C., Traduction de la Circulaire au clergé de Besançon
touchant la liturgie. Besançon, 1857.
_____, Réponse aux observations anonymes. Besançon, 1861.
Mayer, A. L., "Die Geistesgeschichtliche Situation der liturgischen
Erneuerung in der Gegenwort," Archiv für Liturgiewissenschaft, IV
(1955), 1-51.
_____, "Die Stellung der Liturgie von der Zeit der Romantik bis zur
Jahrhundertwende," Archiv für Liturgiewissenschaft, III (1953),
1-77.
Mazis, Antoine de, Dom Guéranger et l'heritage de Cluny. Sablé, 1949.
_____, Solesmes sans les moines. 1791-1832. Sablé, 1947.
Anon., Mémoire sur le droit coutumier. Paris, 1852.
Mengin-Fondragon, Baron de, "Solesmes en 1835," La Semaine du Fidèle du
Mans, not printed until 11 and 23 April 1874.
Mercati, Angelo, "Una professione di Romanità di Prospero Guéranger,"
Benedictina Anno III, Fasc. iii-iv (1949).
Meslé, J., Examen respectueux, pacifique, et religieux des objections
et representations contre le retour aux brèviaire et missel
romains. Rennes, 1843.
Michonneau, Abbé, Revolution in a City Parish. Oxford, 1950.
Moral, Tomas, "Cien anos despues de la muerte de dom Guéranger," Yermo,
14 (1976), 103-132.
Morel de Voleine, L., Recherches historiques sur la Liturgie Lyonnaise.
Lyon, 1856.
Nanquette, J.-J., Lettre pastorale, etc. Le Mans, 1856.
Navatel, Jean-Joseph, "L'Apostolat liturgique et la piété
personnelle," Etudes, CXXXVII (1913).
Nippold, Friedrich, Moderne Klostergründungen. Das Erste halbe
Jahrhundert der Beuroner Kongregation. Neuwied, 1910.
Nisard, Theodore, Examen critique des moyens les plus propres
d'améliorer et de populariser le chant. Paris, 1846.
Notaires du Synode, Histoire du Synode diocésain du Mans. Le Mans,
1852.
Oury, Guy, "Contribution à l'étude des liturgies neogallicanes du
XVIIIe siècle: les messes de Saint Martin," Etudes Grégoriennes,
4 (1963), 165-183.
_____, "Les 'Institutions liturgiques' de Dom Guéranger," Esprit et
Vie, 9, 10, 11 (1976), 121-126, 139-143, 157-160.
Pallu du Parc, L.-T., A propos de son Instruction Pastorale sur la
Liturgie Romaine. Paris, 1853.
_____, Instruction pastorale et mandement de Mgr. l'Evêque de Blois,
etc. Blois, 1852, and Paris, 1853.
Parisis, P.-L., De la question liturgique. 2nd ed. Paris, 1846.
_____, Instruction pastorale de Mgr. Parisis, Evêque d'Arras. 2nd
ed. Paris, 1854.
_____, Instruction pastorale et mandement de Mgr. l'Evêque de
Langres, sur le chant de l'église. Langres, 1846.

Anon., "Une paroisse de la campagne mancelle. Brains," La Province du Maine, LXX (1968), 142-157.

Pfaff, Maurus, "Dom Prosper Guéranger, Abt Von Solesmes," Erbe und Auftrag, 51 (1975), 90-105, 190-204.

_____, P. Desiderius Peter Lenz. Beuron, 1978.

Phillipps, C. S., The Church in France 1789-1848. New York, 1929.

Pichon, Abbé Frédéric, Étude sur la vie et les ouvrages du T.-R. P. Dom G. A. S. Le Mans. 1876.

Picot, M., "Sur l'usage des liturgies diocésaines en France," L'Ami de la Religion, 2-9 June 1830.

_____, "Sur un réponse de l'auteur des Considérations, etc.," L'Ami de la Religion, 3 July, 9 and 30 August 1830.

Pie, Louis-Edouard, Entretien de Msg. Pie sur L'Abbaye de Solesmes et la Congrégation Bénédictine de France. Paris, 1875.

_____, Funeral Oration of the Right Reverend Father Dom Prosper Guéranger. Dublin, 1975.

Pinsk, Johannes, "Quelques fruits du mouvement liturgique," Les Questions liturgiques et paroissiales (1934), pp. 243-248.

Piolin, Paul, "Dom Guéranger," Gazette du dimanche, 23 April and 7 May 1882.

Un prêtre du diocèse d'Albi, Livret de la liturgie romaine. Castres, 1857.

Prompsault, J.-H., Lettre au R. P. Dom Guéranger en réponse à la préface du 3e volume de ses Institutions liturgiques. Paris, 1852.

Quitslund, S. A., Beauduin: A Prophet Vindicated. New York. 1973.

Régnier, R.-F., Ordonnance de Mgr. l'Evêque d'Angoulême qui prescrit le rétablissement du rit romain. Angoulême, 1849.

Ricard, Mgr., Les grands évêques de l'Église de France au XIX siécle. Lille, no date.

Robert, Léon, L'Abbé Guéranger et la revolution de 1830. Sablé, 1965.

_____, L'Année 1870 à Solesmes. Sablé, 1956.

_____, Dom Guéranger chez Pie IX, 1851-1852. Sablé, 1960.

_____, Dom Guéranger et la fondation de Sainte-Cécile de Solesmes. Sablé, 1951.

_____, Histoire de l'Abbaye de Solesmes. Sablé, 1937.

_____, Les Notes de Dom Guéranger. Sablé, 1953.

_____, Louis Veuillot à Solesmes. Sablé, 1963.

_____, Un Voyage de Dom Guéranger. Sablé, 1938.

Robeyns, D. A., "Les débuts du mouvement liturgique," Les questions liturgiques et paroissiales, XIX (1934), 276-298.

Roe, W. G., Lamennais and England. London, 1966.

Roetinger, Gregory, "Un Centenario di Solesmes," L'Osservatore Romano, 24 February 1934.

Rouse, Abbé, La liturgie de la sainte Église de Lyon d'après les monuments. Lyon, 1864.

Rousseau, Norbert, L'École grégorienne de Solesmes, 1833-1910. Rome, 1910.

Rousseau, Olivier, "Dom Lambert Beauduin et la vie monastique," Revue Mabillon, LI (1961), 265-278.

Roussel, A., Lamennais et ses correspondants inconnus. Paris, 1912.

Roux, M., Protestation et appel respectueux en faveur de la liturgie gallicane chartraine. Chartres, 1860.

The Sacerdotal Communities of Saint-Severin of Paris, Le Renouveau liturgique. Paris, 1960.

Saint-Emilion, A., "Guéranger," L'Evenément, 9 February 1875.

Sauter, Benedikt, Le Plain-chant et la liturgie. Paris, 1867.

Savaton, Augustin, Dom Paul Delatte, Abbé de Solesmes. Paris, 1954.

Schott, Anselm, Leben und Wirken des hochwürdigsten Herrn Dr. Maurus Wolter. Stuttgart, 1891.

Sebaux, A.-L., Vie de Msgr. Jean-Baptiste Bouvier. 2nd ed. Paris, 1889.

Secretary to the Commission Ecclesiastique, Le chant romain de Digne. Digne, 1858.

Severus, Emmanuel de, "Un maitre de vie monastique en Allemagne: Dom Ildefons Herwegen," Revue Mabillon, LI (1961), 249-255.

_____, Was Haltet Ihr Von der Kirche? Münster, 1926.

Sevrin, Ernest, Dom Guéranger et Lamennais. Paris, 1933.

Sheppard, Lancelot C., Lacordaire. London, 1964.

Sibour, M.-D.-A., Mandement de Mgr. l'Archevêque de Paris sur le retour à la liturgie romaine. Paris, 1856.

Siebenmorgen, Harald, Die Anfänge der "Beuroner Kunstschule." Sigmaringen, 1983.

_____, "Die Beuroner Kunstschule: Peter Lenz (P. Desiderius) und seine Mitarbeiter," Das Münster, 30 (1977), 20-36.

Sifflet, Auguste, Le chapitre du Mans depuis le Concordat. Le Mans, 1912.

_____, Les Évêques concordataires du Mans. Mgr. Bouvier. 2 v. Le Mans, 1921 and 1927.

_____, Les Évêques concordataires du Mans. Mgr. Carron. Le Mans, 1917.

_____, Les Évêques concordataires du Mans. Mgr. C.-J. Fillion. Le Mans, 1927.

_____, Les Évêques concordataires du Mans. Mgr. J.-J. Nanquette. Le Mans, 1925.

_____, Les Évêques concordataires du Mans. Mgr. de la Myre-Mory, 1820-1829. Le Mans, 1915.

_____, Les Évêques concordataires du Mans. Mgr. de Pidoll, 1802-1819. Le Mans, 1914.

"Solesmes," Metzer Katholisches Volksblatt, 30 July 1933.

Soltner, Louis, Les débuts d'une renaissance monastique, Solesmes 1831-1833. Sablé, 1974.

_____, Rercherches sur la Pensée monastique de Dom Guéranger," Collectanea cisterciensia, 37 (1975), 209-226.

_____, Solesmes et Dom Guéranger (1805-1875). Solesmes, 1974.

Spencer, Philip, Politics of Belief in Nineteenth Century France. London, 1954.

Stearns, Peter N., Priest and Revolutionary. Lemannais and the Dilemma of French Catholicism. New York, 1967.

Sterbenchronik des Hochwürdigsten Herrn Abtes Dr. Benedikt Sauter. Prague, 1908.

Sullivan, John, "Reports to Rome About the Paris Breviary of 1736," Manuscripta, 22 (1978), 149-157.

Switzer, Richard, Chateaubriand. N. Y., 1971.

Thiébaud, Abbé, Crise nouvelle du Bisontinisme agonisant. Besançon, 1861.

_____, Introduction du Rit Romain dans l'Eglise métropolitaine de Besançon. Besançon, 1872.

Thiébaud, Abbé, Profession de foi liturgique. Besançon, 1861.

Tissot, Gabriel, Au temps ou la Vierge Immaculée conduisait à Sées Dom Guéranger. Sablé, 1958.

_____, Dom Charles Couturier. Sablé, 1961.

_____, "La pensée monastique de Dom Delatte," Revue Mabillon, LI (1961), 201-212.

_____, Solesmes en Angleterre. Sablé, 1959.

Toulouse, Mgr. l'archevêque de, Mandement, etc. Toulouse, 1860.

Toussaint, P., ed., Lettres sur le bréviaire Romain adressées à un religieux par un curé de campagne. Pont-A-Mousson, 1864.

_____, Réponses diverses aux lettres d'un curé de campagne sur le bréviaire Romain. Pont-A-Mousson, 1865.

Trapp, Waldemar, Vorgeschichte und Ursprung der liturgischen Bewegung. Regensburg, 1940.

Tréhonnais, L.-J., Lettre pastorale de Mgr. l'Evêque de Coutances au clergé de son diocèse. Coutances, 1850.

Uttenweiler, J., Die Geschichte des Laienmessbuches von P. Anselm Schott. Frieburg, 1935.

Veuillot, Louis, Mgr. Parisis. Paris, 1964.

Vidler, A. C., Prophecy and Papacy. A Study of Lamennais, the Chruch, and Revolution. London, 1954.

Vigourée, M. A., "Un Essai de synthèse liturgique," Revue du Clergé, 15 May 1906, pp. 1-15.

Villaines, A. L. de, Sablé de Janvier 1874 à Juin 1875. Sablé, 1875.

Villecourt, Mgr., Lettre pastorale de Mgr. l'Evêque de La Rochelle. La Rochelle, 1849.

Vitrey, P.-C., Observations sur les Institutions liturgiques de Dom Guéranger ou défense des liturgies gallicanes. Mirecourt, 1851.

Weaver, F. Ellen, The Evolution of the Reform of Port-Royal. Paris, 1978.

_____, "Scripture and Liturgy for the Laity: The Jansenist Case for Translation," Worship, 59 (1985), 510-521.

Wegman, Herman, Geschiedenis van de Christelijke Eredienst in het Westen en het Oosten. Hilversum, 1976.

Wenzel, Paul, Der Freundeskreis um Anton Günther und die Gründung Beurons. Essen, 1965.

Zähringer, D., Das Messbuch für den Laien. Freiburg, 1959.

II

Germany, Möhler, and Tübingen
in the Twentieth Century

Unpublished Sources

Parish Materials

Parish Archives

Domarchiv, Rottenburg
Ergenzingen
Friedberg
Gattnau
Mergentheim
Moosheim
Riedlingen
Ziegelbach

Rottenburg Diocesan Archives

Dekanatsvisitationen
    Dekanat Mergentheim
    Dekanat Waldsee
Dompfarrvisitationen - Rottenburg
Pfarrvisitationen
    Dekanat Mergentheim
        Igersheim
    Dekanat Riedlingen
        Durnau
        Riedlingen
        Sauggart
    Dekanat Saulgau
        Friedberg
        Mengen
        Moosheim
    Dekanat Waldsee
        Ziegelbach

Other Manuscripts (in the library of the Wilhelmstift, Tübingen, except
                   where noted)

Adam, Karl, Christologie und Soteriologie. Lectures.
_____, Einleitung in die Dogmatik. Lectures.
_____, Die Katholische Lehre von der Gnade. Lectures.
_____, Die Lehre von den Sakramenten. Lectures, (1930).
_____, Lehre von der Schöpfung. Lectures.
Drey, J. S. von, Mein Tagebuch. Articles, essays, reviews,
    (1812-1815).

Geiselmann, Josef Rupert, Allgemeine Sakramentenlehre. Lecture.
_____, Grundlegung der Dogmatik. Lecture.
_____, Die Kirche als Form der Offenbarungsreligon. Lectures.
_____, Die Lehre von der Kirche. Lectures.
Gritz, Martin, Die Stellungnahme der Katholischen Kirchenhistoriker
    Deutschlands im neunzehnten Jahrhundert zu Renaissance und
    Humanismus. Inaugural Dissertation at Tübingen University.
Grütering, Michael, Johann Adam Möhler und die Liturgie seiner Zeit.
    Library. University of Bonn.
Hefele, Karl Joseph, Kirchengeschichte. Lectures.
_____, Pastoraltheologie. Lectures.
Lösch, Stefan, Einleitung in das neue Testament. Lectures.
_____, Der Römerbriefe. Lectures.
Möhler, Johann Adam, notes on Church History Lectures, Winter Semester
    1827-28. Wilhelmstift.
_____, Patrologie. Lectures, 1827-1828.
Müller, Johann Baptist, notes taken on Möhler's Church History
    Lectures, 1827. Wilhelmstift.
Rubinstein, Jonathan B., Society and Politics in Southwest Germany.
    Unpublished Ph.D. dissertation, Harvard University 1968. Widener
    Library, Harvard University.

                        Secondary Works

Works of Johann Adam Möhler

    "Anselm, Erzbischof von Canterbury. Ein Beitrag zur Kenntnis des
        religiösittlichen, öffentlich-kirchlichen und wissenschaft-
        lichen Lebens im 11. und 12. Jahrhundert," ThQ 9 (1827),
        435-497; 585-644; 10 (1828), 62-130.
    Anzeige der Feier des Geburts-Festes Seiner Majestät des Königs
        Wilhelm...auf den 27 September 1829. Tübingen, 1829.
    Athanasius der Grosse und die Kirche seiner Zeit. Mainz, 1827.
    "Beleuchtung der Denkschrift für die Aufhebung des den
        katholischen Geistlichen vorgeschriebenen Zölibates," Der
        Katholik, 8 (1828) Bd. 30, 1-33; 257-297.
    "Betrachtungen über den Zustand der Kirche im 15. und zu Anfang
        des 16. Jahrhunderts, in bezug auf die behauptete Notwendig-
        keit einer, die bestehenden Grundlagen der Kirche
        verletzenden Reformation," ThQ 13 (1831), 589-633.
    "Bruchstücke aus der Geschichte der Aufhebung der Sklaverei durch
        das Christentum in den ersten XV Jahrhunderten," ThQ 16
        (1834), 61-136; 567-613.
    Die Einheit in der Kirche oder das Prinzip des Katholizismus,
        dargestellt im Geiste der Kirchenväter der drei ersten
        Jahrhunderte. 2nd ed. Mainz, 1925.
    "Ein Wort in der Sache des philosophischen Collegiums zu Löwen,"
        ThQ 8 (1826), 77-110.

"Einige Gedanken über die zu unserer Zeit erfolgte Verminderung
der Priester und damit in Verbindung stehende Punkte," ThQ 8
(1826), 414-451.
"Fragmente aus und über Pseudo-Isidor," ThQ 11 (1829), 477-520; 14
(1832), 3-52.
"Gedanken nach der Lektüre des Jesusbuches von Strauss," Hist.
politische Blätter für das katholische Deutschland, 1 (1838),
139-149.
Gesammelte Schriften und Aufsätze. 2 vol. J. J. Döllinger, ed.
Regensburg, 1839-40.
"Hieronymus und Augustinus im Streit über Gal 2, 14," ThQ 6
(1824), 195-219.
"Karl der Grosse und seine Bischöfe. Die Synode von Mainz im
Jahre 813," ThQ 6 (1824), 367-427.
Kirchengeschichte. 3 v. P. B. Gams, ed. Regensburg, 1867-70.
Kommentar über der Römerbrief. F. X. Reithmayr, ed. Regensburg,
1845.
Life of St. Anselm, Archbishop of Canterbury: a Contribution to a
Knowledge of the Moral, Ecclesiastical, and Literary Life of
the Eleventh and Twelfth Centuries. Henry Rymer, trans.
London, 1842.
Neue Untersuchungen der Lehrgegensätze zwischen den Katholiken und
Protestanten. Eine Verteidigung meiner Symbolik gegen die
Kritik des Herrn Professors Dr. Baur in Tübingen. Mainz,
1834-5.
"Sendschreiben an Herrn Bautain, Professor der philosophischen
Fakultät zu Strassburg," ThQ 17 (1835), 421-453.
Symbolik oder Darstellung der dogmatischen Gegensätze der
Katholiker und Protestanten nach ihren öffentlichen
Bekenntnisschriften. Cologne, 1960-61.
Symbolik: or, Exposition of the Doctrinal Differences between
Catholics and Protestants as evidenced by their Symbolical
Writings. James Burton Robertson, trans. New York, 1844.
"Uber das Verhältnis, in welchem nach dem Koran Jesus Christus zu
Mohammed und das Evangelium zum Islam steht," ThQ 12 (1830),
3-81.
"Uber den Brief an Diognetos. Die Zeit seiner Herausgabe.
Darstellung seines Inhalts," ThQ 7 (1825), 444-461.
"Uber die Lehre Swedenborgs," ThQ 12 (1830), 648-697.
"Uber die neueste Bekämpfung der katholischen Kirche," Münchener
Politische Zeitung, 1838.
"Uber Justin Apologie I. c. 6. gegen die Auslegung dieser Stelle
von Neander," ThQ 15 (1833), 49-60.

Reviews by Johann Adam Möhler

In the Theologische Quartalschrift:

1823 Walter, F., Lehrbuch des Kirchenrechts mit Berücksichtigung
der neuesten Verhältnisse, 263-299.

Katerkamp, Th., Des ersten Zeitalters der Kirchengeschichte
erste Abteilung: die Zeit der Verfolgungen, 484-532.

1824 Brendel, S., Handbuch des kath. und protest. Kirchenrechts,
84-113.

Neander, A., Der hl. Johannes Chrysostomus und die Kirche
besonders des Orients, in dessen Zeitalter, 262-280.

Droste-Hülshoff, Cl. A., De iuris Austriaci et communis
canonici circa matrimonii impedimenta discrimine atque
hodierna in impedimentorum causis praxi Austriaca,
dissertatio, 280-283.

Daniel, Vergleichung des gemeinen Kirchenrechts mit dem
preuss. Allgem. Landrech, in Ansehung der Ehehindernisse,
283-285.

Theremin, F., Die Lehre vom göttlichen Reiche, 622-642.

Schmitt, H. J., Harmonie der morgenländischen und
abendländischen Kirche. Ein Entwurf zur Vereinigung
beider Kirchen, 642-656.

1825 Locherer, J. N., Geschichte der christlichen Religion und
Kirche, 99-108; 665-692.

Sincerus, P., Uber das liturgische Recht evangelischer
Landesfürsten, 244-261.

Marheineke, Ph., Uber die wahre Stelle des liturgischen
Rechts im evangelischen Kirchen-Regiment, 261-277.

Anonym, Ideen zur Beurteilung der Einführung der
preussischen Hofkirchenagende aus dem sittlichen
Standpunkte, 278-285.

Schaaf, L., Die Kirchenagenden-Sache in dem preussischen
Staate, 285-292.

Nitzsch, C. J., Theologisches Votum für die neue
Hofkirchenagende und deren weitere Einführung, 292-298.

von Ammon, C. F., Einführung der Berliner Hofkirchenagende,
298-302.

Theiner, J. A., Variae doctorum Catholicorum opiniones de
iure statuendi impedimenta matrimonii dirimentia,
462-486.

Katerkamp, Th., Des ersten Zeitalters der Kirchengeschichte
zweite Abteilung: Streitfragen über Dreieinigkeit und
über die Heilsanstalt in der Kirche, 486-500.

Neander, A., Antignostikus, 646-664.

1826 Winer, G. B., Comparative Darstellung des Lehrbegriffs der
verschiendenen christlichen Kirchen-Parteien, 111-138.

Ullmann, C., Gregorius von Nazianz, der Theologe, 324-331.

Locherer, J. N., Geschichte der christlichen Religion und
Kirche, 726-727.

1827 Krug, Das Kirchenrecht nach Grundsätzen der Vernunft und im
Lichte des Christentums, 73-91.

Hortig, J. N., Handbuch der christlichen Kirchengeschichte,
91-104.

533

Smets, W. (Hrg.), Katholische Monatsschrift zur Belehrung, Erbauung und Unterhaltung, 318-325.
Dannenmayer, M., Leitfaden in der Kirchengeschichte, 325-330.
Sprenke, G. M., Franz Ludwig aus dem freiherrlichen Geschlechte von und zu Erthal, 330-338.
Gengler, A., Über das Verhältnis der Theologie zur Philosophie, 498-522.
Herber, C. J., Statistik des Bistums Breslau, 522-524.

1828 Windischmann, C. J. H., Die Philosophie im Fortgang der Weltgeschichte, 131-134.
Locherer, J. N., Geschichte der christlichen Religion und Kirche, 328-337.
Millner, J., Ziel und Ende religioser Kontroversen, 337-347.
Goldwitzer, F. W., Bibliographie der Kirchenväter und Kirchenlehrer vom 1. bis zum 13. Jhd., 719-731.
Hortig, J. N./Döllinger, J. J. I., Handbuch der christlichen Kirchengeschichte, 97-118.
Räss/Weiss, Religiös-kirchliches Leben in Frankreich während des 17. and 18. Jhds., 146-152.
Katerkamp, Th., Denkwürdigkeiten aus dem Leben der Fürstin Amalia von Gallitzin, 308-324.
Strahl, Ph., Beiträge zur russischen Kirchengeschichte, 324-328.
Walter, F., Lehrbuch des Kirchenrechts aller christlichen Confessionen, 565-572.

1830 Henne, A., Ansichten eines Obskuranten über Kaltholizismus und Protestantismus, 118-151.
Brenner, Fr., Lichtblicke von Protestanten, 602.

1831 Ritter, J. I., Handbuch der Kirchengeschichte, 77-90.
Rudhart, G. Th., Thomas Morus, 91-103.
von Reichlin-Meldegg, Geschichte des Christentums, von seinem Ursprunge bis auf die neueste Zeit, 103-137.
Gerbet, Ph., Considerations sur le dogme generateur de la pieté catholique, 328-357.
Katerkamp, Th., Der Kirchengeschichte vierte Abteilung: Ubergang aus der ältesten Zeit in das Mittelalter, 519-539.
Krabbe, C. F., Leben Bernard Overbergs, 539-551.
Gengler, A., Das Glaubensprinzip der griechischen Kirche, im Vergleich mit dem der römisch-katholischen Kirche und andern religiösen Denkweisen unserer Zeit, 652-569.

1832 Div. Schriften uber den Saint-Simonismus, 305-332.
Pacca, B., Historische Denkwürdigkeiten über Pius VIII, 395-404.

534

1833 Tafel, Th. L. Fr. (Hrg.), Eustathii Metropolitae
      Thessalonicensis opuscula, 147–173.

1834 Bautain, L. E. M., De l'Enseignement de la Philosophie en
      France, au 19. siècle, 137–152.
      Staudenmaier, F. A., Johannes Scotus Erigena und die
      Wissenschaft seiner Zeit, 470–485.
      Tauler, J., Nachfolgung des armen Lebens Christi, 551–557.

      In: Jahrbücher für Theologie und Philosophie, Frankfurt
      a. M.

1834 G. J. Erhard, Geschichte des Wiederaufblühens wissenschaft-
      licher Bildung, vornehmlich in Deutschland, bis zum
      Anfang der Reformation, 173–187.

Other Authors

Acton, J. E. E., Essays on Church and State. D. Woodruff, ed. London,
      1952.
_____, Historical Essays and Studies. J. Figgis, ed. London, 1907.
Adam, Karl, Christ and the Western Mind, Love and Belief. London,
      1931.
_____, The Christ of Faith, The Christology of the Church. New York,
      1957.
_____, Christ our Brother. J. McCann, trans. London, 1931.
_____, "Ekklesiologie im Werden? Kritische Bemerkungen zu M. D.
      Kosters Kritik an den ekklesiologischen Versuchen der Gegenwart,"
      ThQ 122 (1941), 145–166.
_____, Glaube und Glaubenwissenschaft im Katholizismus. Rottenburg,
      1923.
_____, Glaube und Liebe. Regensburg, 1927.
_____, Jesus Christus und der Geist unserer Zeit, Ein Vortrag.
      Augsburg, 1935.
_____, One and Holy. C. Hastings, trans. New York, 1951.
_____, "Das Problem des Geschichtlichen im Leben der Kirche," ThQ 128
      (1948), 257–300.
_____, "Rezenzion: Wilhelm Dilthey, Leben Schleiermachers," ThQ 104
      (1923), 281–2.
_____, The Son of God. P. Hereford, trans. London, 1934.
_____, The Spirit of Catholicism. J. McCann, trans. London, 1929.
Artz, J., "Entstehung und Auswirkung von Newmans Theorie der
      Dogmenentwicklung," ThQ 148 (1968), 63–104.
Aubert, Roger, "Das schwierige Erwachen der Katholischen Theologie im
      Zeitalter der Restauration," ThQ 148 (1968), 9–62.
_____, La théologie catholique au milieu du XXe siècle. Paris,
      1954.
Beil, Alfons, Einheit in der Liebe von der betenden Kirche zur gelebten
      Gemeinschaft. Freiburg, 1955.

Benrath, G. A. "Evangelische und Katholische Kirchenhistorie im zeichen der Aufklärung und der Romantik," Zeitschrift für Kirchengeschichte, LXXXII (1972), 203-217.

Berkowver, G. C., The Second Vatican Council and the New Catholicism. Grand Rapids, 1965.

Bilmeyer, K., "J. A. Möhler als Kirchenhistoriker, seine Leistungen und seine Methode," ThQ 100 (1919), 134-198.

Birnbaum, Walter, Das Kultusproblem und die liturgischen Bewegungen des 20. Jahrhunderts. Tübingen, 1966.

Bolshakoff, Serge, The Doctrine of the Unity of the Church in the Works of Khomyakov and Moehler. London, 1946.

Brunner, Heinz, Der organologische Kirchenbegriff in seiner Bedeutung für das ekklesiologische Denken des 19. Jahrhunderts. Frankfurt, 1979.

Chadwick, Owen, From Bossuet to Newman: the Idea of Doctrinal Development. Cambridge, 1957.

Chaillot, Pierre, "Hommage à J.-A. Moehler pour le centenaire de sa mort," Revue des sciences philosophiques et théologiques, XXVII, No. 2 (April 1938), 161-184.

Congar, M.-J., "Sur l'évolution et l'interpretation de la pensée de Moehler," Revue des sciences philosophiques et théologiques, XXVII, 2 (April 1938), 204-212.

Conser, Walter H., Church and Confession: Conservative Theologians in Germany, England, and America 1815-1866. Mercer, 1984.

Conzeminius, Victor, Ignaz von Döllinger-Lord Acton. Briefwechsel. 1850-1890. 3 v. Munich, 1963-1971.

Daniélou, J., and Vorgrimler, H., ed., Sentire Ecclesiam. Das Bewusstsein von der Kirche als gestaltende Kraft der Frömigkeit Herder. Freiburg, 1961.

Drey, J. S. von, "Die rücklaufige Bewegung im Protestantismus und ihre Bedeutung," ThQ 26 (1844), 4-56.

_____, "Das Wesen der Puseyitischen Doctrin," ThQ 26 (1844), 417-457.

Dru, Alexander, The Church in the 19th Century: Germany 1800-1918. London, 1963.

Erb, Alfons, Gelebtes Christentum Charakterbilder aus dem deutschen Katholizismus des 19. Jahrhunderts. Freiburg, 1938.

Eschweiler, Karl, Die zwei Wege der neueren Theologie Georg Hermes - Matth. Jos. Scheeben. Augsburg, 1926.

_____, Johann Adam Möhler's Kirchenbegriff. Braunsberg, 1930.

Fehr, Wayne L., The Birth of the Catholic Tübingen School. Chico, 1981.

Fitzer, Joseph, Moehler and Baur in Controversy, 1832-38. Tallahassee, 1974.

Foote, Peter, et al., ed., Vatican II's Dogmatic Constitution on the Church. N. Y., 1969.

Friedrich, J., Johann Adam Möhler der Symboliker. Munich, 1894.

Funk, Philipp, "Die geistige Gestalt Johann Adam Möhlers," Hochland XXVII, 1 (1929-1930), 97-110.

Geiselmann, J. R., Geist des Christentums und des Katholizismus. Ausgewählte Schriften Katholischer Theologie in Zeitalter des deutschen Idealismus und der Romantik. Mainz, 1940.

_____, "Der gefallenen Mensch. Die Wandlungendes Erbsündebegriffs in der Symbolik Joh. Adam Möhlers," ThQ 124 (1943), 73-98.

_____, J. A. Möhler, Die Einheit der Kirche und die Wiedervereinigung der Konfessionen. Vienna, 1940.

_____, "Joh. Adam Möhler und die Entwicklung seines Kirchenbegriffs," ThQ 112 (1931), 1-91.

_____, Die Katholische Tübinger Schule. Freiburg, 1964.

_____, Lebendiger Glaube aus Geheiligter Uberlieferung. Mainz, 1942.

_____, The Meaning of Tradition. Freiburg, 1966.

_____, Die theologische Anthropologie Johann Adam Möhlers. Freiburg, 1955.

Geisser, Hans, Glaubenseinheit und Lehrentwicklung bei Johann Adam Möhler. Göttingen, 1971.

Goyau, Georges, L'Allemagne religieuse. Vol. II, Le Catholicisme. (1800-1848). Paris, 1905.

Günthor, Anselm, "Johann Adam Möhler und das Mönchtum," ThQ 121 (1960), 168-183.

Hafen, Johann Baptist, Behandlung der Ehesachen im Bistum Rottenburg in pfarramtlicher und seelsorgerlicher Hinsicht. Rottenburg, 1853.

_____, Eintausend Entwürfe zu Predigten auf alle Sonn- und Festtage des Katholischen Kirchenjahres. Lindau, 1866.

Hafen, J. B., Gattnauer Chronik oder der Pfarrbezirk Gattnau und die nähere umgebung im Spiegel der Geschichte. Lindau, 1854.

_____, Möhler und Wessenberg, oder Strengkirchlichkeit und Liberalismus in der katholischen Kirche. Ulm, 1842.

_____, Predigten auf alle Sonn- und Festtage. Stuttgart, 1844.

_____, Predigten zur Feier der ersten heiligen Kommunion. 2nd ed. Lindau, 1869.

Hagen, August, Geschichte der Diözese Rottenburg. 3 v. Stuttgart, 1956.

_____, Gestalten aus dem Schwäbischen Katholizismus. Stuttgart, 1950.

_____, Der Mischehenstreit in Württemberg (1837-1855). Paderborn, 1931.

_____, "Die Unterwerfung des Bischofs Hefele unter das Vatikanum," ThQ 124 (1943), 1-40.

Hanssler, Bernhard, "Johann Adam Möhler - Theologie der Kirche," Hochland, XXXV, 2 (1938), 17-26.

_____, Die Kirche in der Gesellschaft. Der Deutsche Katholizismus und seine Organisationen im 19. und 20. Jahrhundert. Paderborn, 1961.

_____, "Rundschau über Möhler," Hochland XXXVI (1939-40), 510.

Hefele, Karl Josef von, Beitrage zur Kirchengeschichte, Archäologie und Liturgik. Tübingen, 1864.

_____, Chrysostomus-Postille. 3rd ed. Tübingen, 1857.

_____, A History of the Christian Councils, from the original Documents, to the close of the Council of Nicea, A.D. 325. W. R. Clark, trans. and ed. Edinburgh, 1871.

_____, Die Hymnen und Sequenzen im Brevier und Missale alphabetisch geordnet. Tübingen, 1860.

_____, Kirchengeschichte. 3 v. in 1. No title page.

Hefele, Karl Josef, The Life of Cardinal Ximenes. J. Dalton, trans. London, 1860.

Heiler, F., "Zum Tod von Karl Adam. Ein Brief," ThQ 146 (1966), 257-261.

Anon., Johann Adam Möhler, Der ungeteilte Dienst. Salzburg, 1938.

Kantzenbach, F. W., "Vilmars Theologie der Tatsachen und die Symbolik," Zeitschrift für Kirchengeschichte, LXX (1959), 251-277.

Keller, Erwin, "Die Kostanzer Liturgiereform unter Ignaz Henrich von Wessenberg," Freiburger Diözesan Archiv 85 (1965).

Keppler, F. W., Festpredigt zur Feier des 50 jährigen Jubiläums der Beuroner Kongregation. Beuron, 1913.

Kihn, Heinrich, Professor Dr. J. A. Möhler ernannter Domdekan von Würzburg. Würzburg, 1885.

Knöpfler, Alois, Johann Adam Möhler. Ein Gedenkblatt zu dessen hundertstem Geburtstag. Munich, 1896.

_____, Lehrbuch der Kirchengeschichte, Auf Grund der akademischen Vorlesungen von Dr. Karl Joseph von Hefele. 2nd ed. Freiburg, 1898.

Kolbe, Ferdinand, Die Liturgische Bewegung. Anschaffenburg, 1964.

König, Hermann, "Die Einheit der Kirche nach Joseph de Maistre und Johann Adam Möhler," ThQ 115 (1934), 83-140.

Koster, Dominicus, Ekklesiologie im Werden. Paderborn, 1940.

Kuhn, Helmut, Interpretation der Welt, Festschrift für Romano Guardini. Würzburg, 1964.

Kuhn, J. E. "Nekrolog Möhler," ThQ (1838), 576-594.

Lane, Barbara Miller, Architecture and Politics in Germany. Cambridge, 1968.

Leu, J. B., Beitrag zur Würdigung des Jesuiten-Ordens. Lucerne, 1840.

Leu, J. B., Warnung vor Neuerungen und Uebertreibungen in der katholischen Kirche Deutschlands. Lucerne, 1853.

Linsemann, F. X., Lehrbuch der Moraltheologie. Freiburg, 1878.

Lösch, Stefan, Briefe des jungen Karl Joseph Hefele. Rottenburg, 1938.

_____, Die Diözese Rottenburg im Bilde der öffentlichen Meinung. 1828-1840. Rottenburg, 1927.

_____, Döllinger und Frankreich. Eine geistige Allianz. 1823-1871. Munich, 1955.

_____, ed., Johann Adam Möhler Gesammelte Aktenstücke und Briefe. Munich, 1928.

_____, "J. A. Möhler und die Theologie Englands im 19. Jahrhundert," Rottenburger Monatschrift für praktische Theologie, VI (1922-23), 198-202; 221-227.

_____, Die katholisch-theologischen Fakultäten zu Tübingen und Giessen. (1830-1850). Tübingen, 1927.

_____, Prof. Dr. Adam Gengler 1799-1866. Die Beziehungen des Bamberger Theologen zu J. J. I. Döllinger und J. A. Möhler. Würzburg, 1963.

McGrath, William J., Dionysian Art and Populist Politics in Austria. New Haven, 1974.

Mack, Martin Joseph, Catholica. Augsburg, 1841.

_____, Commentar über die Pastoralbriefe des Apostels Paul. Tübingen, 1836.

_____, Haus-Postille für Pfarrer in Ziegelbach Katholiken. Tübingen, 1847.

_____, Die katholische Kirchenfrage in Württemberg. Schaffhausen, 1845.

_____, Uber die Einsegnung der gemischten Ehen. Ein theologischen Votum. Tübingen, 1840.

_____, Über die Ursprünglichen Leser des Briefes an die Hebräer. Tübingen, 1836.

_____, Zur Abwehr und zur Verständigung. Schaffhausen, 1842.

Maier, Charles S., Recasting Bourgeois Europe. Princeton, 1975.

Mattes, W., Was is der Priester? Predigt. Tübingen, 1846.

Mayer, Anton L., "Liturgie, Aufklärung, und Klassizismus," Jahrbuch für Liturgiewissenschaft, IX (1929), 67-127.

Merkle, Sebastian, "Möhler," Historisches Jahrbuch des Görres-Gesellschaft, LVIII (1938), 249-467.

Michels, Thomas, "Die Liturgie im Lichte der Kirchlichen Gemeinschafts-idee," Jahrbuch I (1921), 109-116.

Miller, Max, "Die Tübingen kath-theologische Fakultät und Württembergische Regierung vom Weg J. A. Möhlers (1835) bis zur Pensionierung J. S. Drey (1846)," ThQ 132 (1952), 22-45, 213-233.

Anon., Möhlers Grab und der Dombau zu Köln (Poem). Schaffhausen, 1843.

Mosse, George L., The Nationalization of the Masses. New York, 1975.

Neander, Augustus, History of the Planting and Training of the Christian Church. J. E. Ryland, trans. Edinburgh, 1842.

_____, The Life of St. Chrysostom. J. C. Stapleton, trans. London, 1845.

Neher, S. J., Statisticher Personal-Katalog des Bistums Rottenburg. Schw. Gmünd, 1878.

Nichols, Peter, The Pope's Divisions. London, 1981.

Niebuhr, R. R., Schleiermacher on Christ and Religion. New York, 1964.

Nienaltowski, H. R., Johann Adam Möhler's Theory of Doctrinal Development: Its Genesis and Formulation. Washington, 1959.

O'Meara, Thomas F., Romantic Idealism and Roman Catholicism. Notre Dame, 1982.

_____, "The Origins of the Liturgical Movement and German Romanticism," Worship, 59 (1985), 326-342.

Pflanz, B. A., Ansicht über die Verhaltnisse der Katholiken in Württemberg. Stuttgart, 1843.

_____, Auchlinige Gedanken über den bekannten Symbolikstreit. Stuttgart, 1836.

_____, Die Ausübung des Schutz und ober-Aufsichtsrechts protestantischer Fürsten über ihre katholischen Landeskirchen. Stuttgart, 1833.

_____, Der Römische Stuhl und die Kölner Angelegenheit. Stuttgart, 1838.

Pflanz, B. A., "Rezenzion: F. C. Bauer, Der Gegensatz des Katholicismus und Protestantismus," Freimüthige Blätter über Theologie und Kirchenthum, VI (1835), 175-281.

Ratzinger, J. and Newmann, J., ed., Theologie im Wandel, Festschrift zum 150 jährigen Bestehen der katholisch-theologischen Fakultät an der Universität Tübingen. Munich, 1967.

Reinhardt, Rudolf, "Dionysius Petavius (1583-1652) in der "Tübingen Schüle," ThQ 151 (1971), 160-162.

_____, "Ergänzungen und Bemerkungen zu Johann Adam Möhler Gesammelte Aktenstücke und Briefe," Zeitschrift für Kirchengeschichte, LXXX (1969), 382-394.

_____, "Im zeichen der Tübingen Schüle," Attempto 25, 26 (1968), 40-58.

_____, "Johann A. Möhler und die Konversion der Malerin Emilie Linder," ThQ 151 (1971), 264-268.

_____, "Korrespondenz aus dem nachlass Johann Sebastian von Dreys," ThQ 149 (1969), 389-391.

_____, "Der Nachlass des Kirchenhistorikers und Bischofs Karl Josef v. Hefele," Zeitschrift für Kirchengeschichte, LXXXII (1971), 361-372.

_____, "Quellen zur Geschichte der kath.-theologischen Fakultät Tübingen. Ein unerwarteter Fund im Nachlass von Prof. DDr. Stefan Lösch," ThQ, 149 (1969), 369-388.

_____, "Unbekannte Quellen zu Hefeles Leben und Werk," ThQ 152 (1972), 54-77.

_____, "Zum Verbleib der Nachlass-Papiere Hefeles," ThQ 152 (1972), 26-29, 40-53.

Reiser, Wilhelm, Worte gesprochen am Sarge des...Dr. Karl Joseph von Hefele. Rottenburg, 1893.

Roth, Hugo, Dr. Karl Joseph von Hefele Bischof von Rottenburg. Ein Lebensbild. Stuttgart, 1893.

Rousseau, Olivier, Histoire du mouvement liturgique. Paris, 1945.

Sägmüller, J. B., "Der Kirchenrechliche Anstoss zu Johann Adam Möhlers theologischer Entwicklung," ThQ 122 (1941), 1-13.

Savon, Hervé, Johann Adam Möhler. The Father of Modern Theology. C. McGrath, trans. Glen Rock, New Jersey, 1966.

Schaff, Philipp, August Neander. Gotha, 1886.

Scharpff, F. A., Katholisches Gebet- und Betrachtungsbuch. Freiburg, 1876.

_____, Predigt auf den 17. Sonntag nach Pfingsten, nach der Besiegung der papstlichen Armee. Freiburg, 1860.

_____, Predigt bei der Feier des elfhundertjährigen Jubiläums des Stiftskirche zu Ellwangen. Schwäb. Gmünd, 1864.

_____, Vorlesungen über die neueste Kirchengeschichte. Freiburg, 1850.

Scheffczyk, Leo, "Die Lehranschauungen Matthias Joseph Scheebens über das Okumenischer Konzil," ThQ 141 (1961), 129-173.

Schmid, Alois von, "Der geistige Entwicklung Johann Adam Möhlers," Historisches Jahrbuch, XVIII (1897), 323-356, 572-599.

540

Selbie, W. B., Schleiermacher. London, 1913.
Einem Schüler des + Herrn v. Möhler, Abriss des Katholischen Kirchenrechts für Geistliche und Studierende. Stuttgart, 1853.
Shaw, J. M., Franklin, R. W., Kaasa, H., Readings in Christian Humanism. Minneapolis, 1982.
Smart, Ninian, Nineteenth Century Religious Thought in the West, Vol. I. Cambridge, 1985.
Stacpoole, Alberic, Vatican II Revisited By Those Who Were There. Minneapolis, 1986.
Stärk, Franz, Die Diözese Rottenburg und ihre Bischöfe. 1828-1928. Stuttgart, 1928.
Stern, Fritz, The Politics of Cultural Despair. Garden City, 1965.
Swidler, Leonard, Aufklärung Catholicism: 1780-1850. Missoula, 1978.
ThQ 150 (1970). Issue completely devoted to the Tübingen School.
Tholuck, August, Leben und Selbstzeugnisse. Gotha, 1930.
Tristram, H., "J. A. Moehler et J. H. Newman," Revue des sciences philosophiques et théologiques, 27, No. 2 (April 1938), 184-204.
Tüchle, Herman, Die Eine Kirche zum Gedenken J. A. Möhlers. 1838-1938. Paderborn, 1939.
_____, "Karl Josef von Hefele," ThQ 152 (1972), 1-22.
Tucker, Robert, Philosophy and Myth in Karl Marx. Cambridge, 1967.
Vermeil, Edmond, Jean-Adam Möhler et l'école catholique de Tubingue (1815-1840). Paris, 1913.
Viering, Fritz, Christus und die Kirche in römisch-katholischen Licht. Ekklesiologische Probleme zwischen dem ersten und zweiten vatikanischen Konzil. Göttingen, 1962.
_____, Ketteler. Ein Deutsches Bischofsleben des 19. Jahrhunderts. Munich and Berlin, 1924.
Werfer, Albert, Karl Joseph v. Hefele, Bischof von Rottenburg. Wurzburg, 1882.
Willburger, August, and Tüchle, Hermann, Geschichte der katholischen Kirche in Württemberg. Rottenburg, 1954.
Wörmer, Balthasar, Johann Adam Möhler. Ein Lebensbild. P. B. Gams, ed. Regensburg, 1866.
Zahn, A., Die ultramontane Presse in Schwaben. Leipzig, 1885.

III

England, Pusey, the Oxford Movement,
and Anglican Liturgical Movement

Unpublished Sources

Parish Materials

Parish Archives

All Saints, Margaret Street, London
Christ Church, Albany Street, London
St. Alban the Martyr, Holborn, London
St. Peter, London Docks, London
St. Saviour, Leeds
Wantage
    1. Baptist Church Archives.
    2. Methodist Church Archives.
    3. Parish Church Archives.

Berkshire County Records Office, Reading. Records of Wantage
Parish Church (D/P143/28/1-12; 1/5-6; 5/2; 7/1-4).

London County Council

    Parish Registers of All Saints, Margaret Street (P89/ALL 2/8
    and 2/1), 1850-1900.

Other Manuscripts

In Pusey House, Oxford

    1. Letters (listed according to the arrangement of H. P.
    Liddon, who collected them into folders):

    Sir T. D. Acland to E. B. Pusey, 1838-1847.
    E. B. Pusey and Bishop Bagot, I:1834-1841; II:1841-1844.
    E. B. Pusey to Miss Barker, 1827-1828; to Mrs. Pusey,
       1828-1838.
    E. B. Pusey to A. J. Beresford-Hope, 1848-1874.
    E. B. Pusey to Mother Bertha, I:1876-1877; II:1878-1882.
    Bishop Blomfield of London to E. B. Pusey, 1830-1855.
    E. B. Pusey to W. J. Copeland, 1839-1882.
    W. Dodsworth to E. B. Pusey, 1836-1850.
    E. B. Pusey and Jane Ellacombe, 1843-1855.
    E. B. Pusey and Bishop Forbes of Brechin, 1856-1873.

Bishop Forbes (of Brechin), Victor De Buck, and E. B.
Pusey, May–December, 1869.
German Correspondents of E. B. Pusey.
E. B. Pusey and W. E. Gladstone, I:1833–1856;
II:1857–1881.
E. B. Pusey to Archbishop Harrison (of Maidstone),
I:1831–1837; II:1839–1880.
E. B. Pusey to Dr. Hook, 1827–1848.
Dr. Hook to E. B. Pusey, 1822–1847.
E. B. Pusey to J. Keble, I:1823–1845; II:1846–1848;
III:1849–1850; IV:1851–1856; V:1857–1860;
VI:1861–1863.
J. Keble to E. B. Pusey, I:1823–1845; II:1846–1850;
III:1851–1856; IV:1857–1866.
E. B. Pusey to H. P. Liddon, I:1848–1870; II:1871–1879;
III:1879–1880; IV:1880–1882.
H. P. Liddon to Pusey, I:1854–1875; II:1875–1882.
E. B. Pusey to Bishop Lloyd, 1826–1828.
Bishop Longley to E. B. Pusey. No dates.
E. B. Pusey to Max Müller, 1862–1880.
E. B. Pusey to J. H. Newman, I:1823–1836; II:1837–1840;
III:1841–1843; IV:1844–1846; V:1861–1867;
VI:1868–1880.
J. H. Newman to E. B. Pusey, I:1823–1840; II:1841–1846;
III:1853–1867; IV:1868–1882.
Frederick Oakeley to E. B. Pusey, 1838–1875.
E. B. Pusey to Sister Clara (Clarissa Powell),
I:1843–1846; II:1847–1881; III:miscellaneous.
E. B. Pusey and Philip Pusey, 1821–1854.
E. B. Pusey to Philip E. Pusey, I:1839–1843; II:1844–
1845; III:1846–1870; IV:1871–1879; V:dates uncertain;
VI:miscellaneous.
E. B. Pusey to William B. Pusey, I:1827–1860;
II:1860–1882.
E. B. Pusey to Miss Maria Trench, 1867–1882.
W. Upton Richards to E. B. Pusey, 1840–1857.
R. Ward to E. B. Pusey, 1844–1847.
Bishop Wilberforce to E. B. Pusey, 1836–1865.
R. I. Wilberforce to E. B. Pusey, 1833–1854.
Isaac Williams to E. B. Pusey, 1838–1855.
E. B. Pusey to C. L. Wood; I:1866–1874; II:1875–1882.
Miscellaneous collection of letters to and from E. B.
Pusey, or about him.
H. J. Rose to the Hon. and Rev. A. P. Perceval,
1832–1836.

2.   Other Manuscripts:

Benson, R. M., The Principles of Brotherhood. An Address Read
Before the Annual Chapter of the Brotherhood of the Holy
Trinity, June 14, 1865.

The Bloxam Collection (includes, besides manuscripts about Pusey of various kinds, also news clippings).

Copeland, W. J., History of the Oxford Movement.

_____, Papers, Vol. II.

Greenfield, R., The Attitude of the Tractarians to the Roman Catholic Church. D. Phil. Dissertation, Oxford University. Copy.

Jarrett, Evan, Dr. Pusey and the Tracts for the Times.

Marshall, E., Notes on Types and Prophecies, Michaelmas 1836, Lent 1837.

Oakaley, Frederick, A Second Letter to the Lord Bishop of London, Containing an Earnest and Respectful Appeal on the Subject of Margaret Chapel. Printed, but not published.

Plummer, Alfred, Conversations with Dr. Döllinger. I:1870, 1871, 1872; II:1872, 1873, 1874, and part of 1875; III:1876; IV:1886.

Powell, Clarissa (Sister Clara), Reminiscences, as taken down by the Rev. T. J. Williams.

Pusey, E. B., and Carter, T. T., Declaration of Confession, 1873.

_____, Lectures on Prophecies and Types of the Old Testament, written mainly in July-August, 1836 (often called "Types and Prophecies").

_____, Paper on the position of the English Church, 1846.

Pusey, E. B., On Inspiration and the Fathers (written before 1839).

_____, Notebook (Begins Dec. 10, 1829), 2 vol.

_____, Notes on his tour of July-August, 1822.

_____, A manuscript on Pelagianism written in 1839.

_____, University Sermon, October 14, 1832.

_____, Sermon preached at Salisbury Infirmary, September 1833.

_____, Sermons preached at Holton, ?1836; 9th Sunday after Trinity, 1836; 12th Sunday after Trinity, 1836.

_____, Sermon preached at Christ Church, 23rd Sunday after Trinity, 1837.

_____, Sermon preached on the Sunday before Advent, 1837.

_____, Sermon preached at Abbeymere, Plymouth, to some inmates prepared for Baptism, April, 1864.

_____, Sermon preached at All Saints, Margaret Street, Ash Wednesday, 1867.

_____, Sermon transcribed by Mrs. Pusey, no date (before 1839).

_____, Twelve Sermons (bound).

_____, Sketch of Devonport Sisterhood in '48.

_____, University Notebooks.

Pusey, Maria, Diaries.

St. Peter's, London Docks, Collection of printed broadsides, announcing special parish services from 1880's and 1890's.

In the Archives of the Society of the Sacred Mission, Kelham

Herbert, A. G., Ad Romanos.

Herbert, A. G., History of a Tour in Italy.

_____, Introduction to the Italian edition of <u>Liturgy and Society</u>. July, 1938.

_____, Letters, 1912–June 27, 1963.

_____, The Liturgical Movement.

_____, Notes on a sermon preached at All Saints, Margaret Street in 1884 by R. M. Benson.

_____, The Objective and the Subjective Sides of Christianity.

_____, Reunion, Anglican and Roman Catholic.

Jones, A. W., H. H. Kelly, S. S. M. 1860–1950: A Study in Failure. D. Phil Thesis, University of Nottingham. Copy.

In the Newman Archives, Birmingham Oratory, Birmingham

Hurrell Froude to J. H. Newman, September 27, 1829; July 30, 1833; September 2, 1833; September 8, 1833; January 25, 1834; July 12, 1834; March 4? 1835?.

J. H. Newman to Charles Gore, May 16, 1885.

William Palmer to J. H. Newman, 21 February, 1870; Easter, 1873.

J. H. Newman to E. B. Pusey, May 20, 1870; September 4, 1870; February 26, 1871; September 20, 1871.

E. B. Pusey to J. H. Newman, August 15, 1851?; August 17, 1850's?; July 2, 1858?; Shrove Tuesday, 1860; March 13, 1845; July 23, 1845; 23 February 1846; ?, 1860's; April 20, 1860; November 27, 1864; January 30, 1865; ?, 1872; 12 March, 1874; April 15, 1874; April 24, 1874; August 7, 1876; May 5, 1880.

In Lambeth Palace Library

E. B. Pusey and A. C. Tait Correspondence, in Tait Papers, Volumes No. 77, 79, 80, 84, 85, 97, 100.

In Bodleian Library, Oxford University

Forrester, D. W. F., The Intellectual Development of E. B. Pusey, 1800–1850, Oxford D. Phil. thesis, 1967.

Secondary Works

By E. B. Pusey

<u>Address at a Meeting of the London Union on Church Matters, Held in St. Martin's Hall, October 15, 1850.</u> London, 1850.

<u>Advice for Those Who Exercise the Ministry of Reconciliation through Confession and Absolution. Being the Abbé Gaume's Manual for Confessors....</u> 2nd ed. Oxford, 1878.

Appendices to the Sermon Preached...on the Fifth of November,
    1837. Oxford, 1838.
"Appendix to the Article on the Psalter," British Critic, XXVII
    (1840), 210-241.
The Articles Treated of in Tract 90 Reconsidered and Their
    Interpretation Vindicated in a Letter to the Rev. R. W. Jelf.
    Oxford, 1841.
Case as to the Legal Force of the Judgement of the Privy Council
    in re Fendall v. Wilson. Oxford, 1864.
The Church of England. A Portion of Christ's One Holy Catholic
    Church, and a Means of Restoring Visible Unity. An
    Eirenicon, in a Letter to the Author of the Christian Year.
    Oxford, 1865.
The Church of England Leaves Her Children Free to Whom to Open
    Their Griefs. A Letter to the Rev. W. V. Richards, Minister
    of All Saints, St. Mary-Le-Bone. Oxford, 1850.
Churches in London with an Appendix Containing Answers to
    Objections Raised by the "Record" and Others to the Plan of
    the Metropolis Churches' Fund. Oxford, 1837.
A Course of Sermons on Solemn Subjects Chiefly Bearing on
    Repentance and Amendment of Life, Preached in St. Saviour's
    Church, Leeds, During the Week after its Consecration on the
    Feast of S. Simon and S. Jude. Oxford, 1845.
The Doctrine of the Real Presence, as Contained in the Fathers
    ...Vindicated, in Notes on a Sermon, "The Presence of Christ
    in the Holy Eucharist." Preached A. D. 1853, Before the
    Univ. of Oxford. 2nd ed. London, 1883.
An Earnest Remonstrance to the Author of the "Pope's Pastoral
    Letter to Certain Members of the University of Oxford."
    London, 1836.
First Letter to the Very Rev. J. H. Newman, D. D., in Explanation
    Chiefly in Regard to the Reverential Love Due to the Ever
    Blessed Theotokos, and the Doctrine of Her Immaculate
    Conception. Oxford, 1869.
An Historical Enquiry into the Causes of the Rationalist Character
    Lately Predominant in the Theology of Germany. Part II.
    London, 1830.
An Historical Enquiry into the Probable Causes of the Rationalist
    Character Lately Predominant in the Theology of Germany.
    London, 1828.
Is Healthful Reunion Impossible? A Second Letter to the Very Rev.
    J. H. Newman, D.D. Oxford, 1870.
A Lecture. Delivered in the Temporary Chapel, Titchfield Street,
    Previously to Laying the Foundation Stone of the Church of
    All Saints...On All Saints' Day, 1850. London, 1851.
Letter to Sir John Conroy. Read at Meeting of Church of England
    Working Men's Society, October 19, 1881. Privately Printed.
Letter to Members of the Church of England Working Men's Society
    Read at Their Meeting in London, on August 6, 1881.
    Privately Printed.
Letter to Church Review, April, 1858, pp. 1-41.

Letter to the E.C.U., Oxford Branch. November 17, 1880; June 9, 1881. Privately Printed.

Letter to The Guardian, October 10, 1869.

Letter to Dr. King. Read at the Meeting of the Oxford Branch of the E.C.U. June 13, 1879. Privately Printed.

Letter to Literary Supplement of Agricultural Gazette, March 3, 1879.

Letter to Morning Post, November 22, 1865.

Letter to Mr. Packman, delivered at a meeting of the S. W. Yorkshire District Union of the English Church Union, October 11, 1881. Privately Printed.

A Letter to His Grace the Archbishop of Canterbury, on Some Circumstances Connected with the Present Crisis in the English Church. Oxford, 1842.

A Letter to the Right Rev. Father in God, Richard Lord Bishop of Oxford, on the Tendency to Romanism Imputed to Doctrines Held of Old, as Now, in the English Church. Oxford, 1839.

A Letter to the Right Hon. and Right Rev. the Lord Bishop of London, in Explanation of Some Statements Contained in a Letter by the Rev. W. Dodsworth. Oxford, 1851.

Letter to The Times, November 23, 1880.

Letter to G. Williams, The Guardian, January 29, 1863.

"Letter to the Hon. C. L. Wood," Supplement to the Church Union Gazette, December 11, 1880.

Nine Sermons, Preached Before the University of Oxford and Printed Chiefly Between A.D. 1843-1855. Now Collected in One Volume. London, 1859.

On the Recent Judgements in the Court of Arches. Three Letters to the English Churchman. Privately Printed, 1845.

Parochial and Cathedral Sermons. Oxford, 1882.

"The Introductory Essay," Essays on Reunion. London, 1867.

On the Clause "And the Son," in Regard to the Eastern Church and the Bonn Conference. Oxford, 1876.

Parochial Sermons. Vol. II. Oxford, 1853.

Patience and Confidence the Strength of the Church. Sermon at St. Mary, 5 Nov. 1837. Oxford, 1837.

Preface, J. H. Newman, Tracts for the Times. No. 90. On Certain Passages in the XXXIX Articles. London, 1865.

Prefaces for the Library of the Fathers: The Confessions of S. Augustine. Rev. ed. Oxford, 1876; The Epistles of S. Cyprian. 2nd ed. Oxford, 1868; Commentary on the Gospel according to S. John by S. Cyril. Oxford, 1874; Tertullian. 2nd ed. Oxford, 1854; Sermons on Selected Lessons of the New Testament by S. Augustine. 2nd ed. Oxford, 1854.

Prophecy of Jesus the Certain Prediction of the [to Man] Impossible. Oxford, 1879.

Public - Worship - Regulation - Bill. Speech at meeting of E.C.U., June 16, 1874. Privately Printed.

The Real Presence of the Body and Blood of Our Lord Jesus Christ the Doctrine of the English Church. London, 1885 (first printed 1857).

547

Remarks on the Prospective and Past Benefits of Cathedral
    Institutions in the Promotion of Sound Religious Knowledge
    and of Clerical Education. 2nd ed. London, 1833.
Renewed Explanation in Consequence of Rev. W. Dodsworth's Comments
    on Dr. Pusey's Letter to the Bishop of London. Oxford,
    1851.
The Responsibility of Intellect in Matters of Faith. A Sermon.
    Preached before the University of Oxford. Advent Sunday
    1872. 3rd ed. Oxford, 1876.
The Royal Supremacy Not an Arbitrary Authority But Limited by the
    Laws of the Church, of Which the Kings are Members. Oxford,
    1850.
A Sermon Preached at the Consecration of Grove Church on Tuesday
    Aug. 14, 1832. London, 1832.
Sermons During the Season from Advent to Whitsuntide. Oxford,
    1848.
Sermons Preached and Printed on Various Occasions. Oxford, 1865.
Sermons Preached Before the University of Oxford Between 1859 and
    1872. London, 1884 (first printed in 1872).
The Spirit Comforting. Sermon at St. Mary the Virgin, Oxford.
    March 18, 1863. Oxford, 1863.
This is My Body. A Sermon Preached Before the University at St.
    Mary's on the Fifth Sunday after Easter, 1871. Oxford,
    1871.
To the Members and Associates of the English Church Union.
    London, 1877; 1879.
Tracts for the Times. No. 18. Thoughts on the Benefits of the
    System of Fasting, Enjoined by Our Church. 3rd ed. London,
    1838.
Tracts for the Times. No. 66. On the Benefits of the System of
    Fasting Prescribed by Our Church. Supplement to Tract XVIII.
    4th ed. London, 1840.
Tracts for the Times. Nos. 67, 68, 69. Scriptural Views of Holy
    Baptism with an Appendix. London, 1836.
Tracts for the Times. No. 81. Catena Patrum. No. IV. Testimony
    of Writers of the Later English Church to the Doctrine of the
    Eucharistic Sacrifice. London, 1837.
Unlaw in Judgements of the Judicial Committee and Its Remedies. A
    Letter to the Rev. H. P. Liddon, D.D. 2nd ed. London,
    1881.
Voices from Within or Disestablishment as Viewed by Churchmen.
    London, 1871.

By other authors

    Abbott, E. S., et al., Catholicity: A Study in the Conflict of
        Christian Traditions in the West. Report to the Archbishop
        of Canterbury. Westminster, 1947.
    Abeken, H., A Letter to the Rev. E. B. Pusey in Reference to
        Certain Charges Against the German Church. London, 1842.

All Saints Paper (All Saints, Margaret Street), Nov. 21,
    1886-1899.
Allchin, A. M., The Silent Rebellion. Anglican Religious
    Communities 1845-1900. London, 1958.
Angell, Charles, A Ritual Controversy in the Victorian Church of
    England. Rome, 1983.
"Anglicanism and Romanism," The British Quarterly Review, April 2,
    1866, pp. 281-338.
Anglican/Roman Catholic Commission in the U.S.A., "Agreed
    Statement on the Purpose of the Church," Ecumenical Bulletin,
    38 (1979), 24-32.
Anglican/Roman Catholic International Commission, The Final
    Report. London, 1982.
A Layman, Anglo-Romanism Unveiled: or, Canon Oakeley and Dr.
    Newman at Issue with the Catholic and Roman Church, and with
    One Another. London, 1866.
Anson, P. F., The Call of the Cloister. London, 1955.
Avrillon, A Guide for Passing Advent Holily. E. B. Pusey, ed. and
    trans. London, 1847.
_____, The Year of Affections. E. B. Pusey, ed. and trans.
    London, 1845.
Bates, H. N., and Eeles, F. C., Thoughts on the Shape of the
    Liturgy. London, 1946.
Benson, R. M., Redemption: Some of the Aspects of the Work of
    Christ Considered in a Course of Sermons. London, 1861.
_____, So-called "Puseyite" Churches, What They Are, and What
    They Teach? London, no date.
_____, The War-Songs of the Prince of Peace. London, 1901.
Bentley, James, Ritualism and Politics in Victorian Britain.
    Oxford, 1978.
Bill, E. G. W., University Reform in Nineteenth Century Oxford.
    1811-1885. Oxford, 1973.
Bonwetch, G. N., Aus A. Tholucks Anfängen. Briefe an und von
    Tholuck. Gütersloh, 1922.
Brilioth, Yngve, Eucharistic Faith and Practice. Evangelical and
    Catholic. A. G. Hebert, trans. London, 1930.
_____, The Anglican Revival. London, 1933.
Briscoe, J. F., ed. V. S. S. Coles. London, 1930.
Buchanan, Colin, Anglo-Catholic Worship: An Evangelical
    Appreciation After 150 Years. Bramcote, 1983.
_____, Further Anglican Liturgies 1968-75. Bramcote, 1975.
_____, Modern Agnlican Liturgies 1958-1968. London, 1968.
Burrows, H. W., The Half-Century of Christ Church, St. Pancras,
    Albany Street. London, 1887.
Butler, A. J., Life and Letters of William John Butler. London,
    1897.
Butler, Perry, ed., Pusey Rediscovered. London, 1983.
Butler, W. J., H. P. Liddon, or the Life of Zeal. A Sermon
    Preached in Lincoln Cathedral on St. Matthew's Day, 1890.
    London, 1890.

_____, What Is Our Present Danger? A Sermon Preached...on Nov. 11, 1891 to Members of the E.C.U. London, 1891.

Carpenter, James, Gore. A Study in Liberal Catholic Thought. London, 1960.

Chadwick, Owen, The Mind of the Oxford Movement. Stanford, 1960.

Chapman, Raymnd, Faith and Revolt: Studies in the Literary Influence of the Oxford Movement. London, 1970.

Christ Church, Parish Magazine, 1920-1939.

Church, R. W., The Oxford Movement. Twelve Years, 1833-1845. Chicago, 1970.

Church Quarterly Review, XVII (October 1879), 199-241 (Reviews of E. B. Pusey, The Doctrine of the Real Presence).

Clarke, C. P. S., The Oxford Movement and After. London, 1932.

Congreve, G., and Longridge, W. H., ed. Letters of Richard Meux Benson. London, 1916.

Coulson, J., Newman and the Common Tradition. London, 1970.

_____, and Allchin, A. M., ed., The Rediscovery of Newman: An Oxford Symposium. London, 1967.

Coulson, John; Allchin, A. M.; and Trevor, Meriol, Newman: A Portrait Restored. London, 1965.

Cross, F. L., Darwell Stone. Glasgow, 1943.

Crosse, Gordon, Charles Gore. A Biographical Sketch. London, 1932.

Culler, A. Dwight, The Victorian Mirror of History. New Haven, 1985.

Cuming, Geoffrey, A History of Anglican Liturgy. London, 1982.

Davies, H., Worship and Theology in England. vol. II. Princeton, 1962.

_____, Worship and Theology in England. Vol. V. Princeton, 1965.

Dawson, Christopher, The Spirit of the Oxford Movement. New York, 1933.

Dix, Gregory, The Shape of the Liturgy. London, 1945.

Dodsworth, W., The Daily Worship of God in His Sanctuary. London, 1842.

_____, A Few Comments on Dr. Pusey's Letter to the Bishop of London. London, 1851.

_____, The Gorham Case Briefly Considered. London, 1850.

_____, Holy Baptism; the Grafting into our Risen Lord. Easter Sermon. London, 1850.

_____, A House Divided Against Itself. London, 1850.

_____, A Letter to the Rev. E. B. Pusey, D.D., on the Position Which He Has Taken in the Present Crisis. London, 1850.

_____, On Baptism. London, 1840.

_____, The Things of Caesar and the Things of God. London, 1850.

_____, What is a Christian? London, 1844.

_____, Why Have You Become a Romanist? London, 1842.

Donaldson, A. B., Five Great Oxford Leaders. 3rd ed. London, 1902.

Ekström, R., The Theology of Charles Gore. Lund, 1944.

Fairbairn, A. M., Catholicism: Roman and Anglican. New York,
   1899.
Faith and Order Commission of World Council of Churches, Baptism,
   Eucharist, and Ministry. Geneva, 1982.
Fifoot, Thomas, To the Church of England the Church of the Working
   Man. An Address to the Working Men of England. London,
   1875.
Forrester, D. W. F., "Dr. Pusey's Marriage," The Ampleforth
   Journal, 78 (1973), 33-47.
Franklin, R. W., "Apostolicae Curae of 1896 Reconsidered:
   Cardinal Willebrands' Letter to ARCIC-II," Ecumenical Trends,
   15 (1986), 80-82.
_____, "Pusey and Worship in Industrial Society," Worship, 57
   (1983), 386-411.
Fries, H., "Newman und Döllinger," Newman-Studien I. Nürnberg,
   1948.
Froude, R. Hurrell, Remains of the Late Rev. R. H. Froude.
   London, 1838-39.
Gibbons, A., and Davey, E. C., Wantage Past and Present. London,
   1901.
Gore, Charles, The Anglo-Catholic Movement To-day. London, 1925.
_____, The Church and the Ministry. London, 1882.
_____, Essays in Aid of the Reform of the Church. London, 1898.
Grantham, George Peirce, A History of Saint Saviour's, Leeds.
   London, 1872.
Griffin, John R., "Dr. Pusey and the Oxford Movement," Historical
   Magazine of the Protestant Episcopal Church, XLIII (1973),
   137-154.
_____, The Oxford Movement: 1833-1983. Edinburgh, 1984.
Guide to the Divine Service in Those Churches wherein the Holy
   Eucharist is Celebrated. 37th ed. London, 1869.
Guiney, L. I., Hurrell Froude. London, 1904.
Gutch, Charles, The Sure Judgement of God Upon All Sinners,
   Especially the Rich, For Their Neglect of the Poor. A Sermon
   on a Recent Mill Accident. London, 1853.
Härdelin, Alf, The Tractarian Understanding of the Eucharist.
   Uppsala, 1965.
Harper, F. W., A Few Observations on the Teaching of Dr. Pusey and
   Mr. Newman, Concerning Justification. Cambridge, 1842.
Harris, Charles, Northern Catholicism. Centenary Studies in the
   Oxford and Parallel Movements. London, 1933.
Hebert, A. G., The Authority of the Old Testament. London, 1947.
_____, The Form of the Church. London, 1944.
_____, Fundamentalism and the Church of God. London, 1957.
_____, Grace and Nature. London, 1937.
_____, Intercommunion. London, 1932.
_____, Liturgy and Society. The Function of the Church in the
   Modern World. London, 1935.
_____, The Parish Communion. London, 1937.
Heurtley, C. A., Remarks on a Declaration of Belief Addressed by
   the Rev. W. Butler...and Several Other Clergymen to the
   Archbishop of Canterbury. London, 1867.

A Layman of the Diocese of London, Dr. Heurtley and the Real
    Objective Presence of Our Lord in the Holy Eucharist.
    London, 1868.
Hills, George, To the Parishioners of St. Saviour's, Leeds, More
    Particularly the Poor...in Their Present Distress of
    Unfaithful Pastors. London, 1851.
Horst, J. M., Paradise of the Christian Soul, Enriched with
    Choicest Delights of Varied Piety. E. B. Pusey, ed. and
    trans. 2 v. London, 1847.
Hubbard, J. G., Letter to The Times, July 18, 1868.
_____, Three Essays. London, 1882.
_____, To the Inhabitants of the District of St. Alban's,
    Holborn. London, 1863.
Hughes, Anselm, The Rivers of Flood. Personal Account of the
    Catholic Revival in England in the Twentieth Century.
    London, 1961.
Jagger, Peter J., A History of the Parish and People Movement.
    Leighton Buzzard, 1978.
Jasper, R. C. D., Prayer Book Revision in England, 1800-1900.
    London, 1954.
Jay, Elisabeth, The Evangelical and Oxford Movements. Cambridge,
    1983.
Johnston, J. O., Life and Letters of H. P. Liddon. London, 1904.
_____, and Newbolt, W. C. E., Spiritual Letters of E. B. Pusey.
    London, 1898.
Kelly, H. H., Catholicity. London, 1932.
_____, An Idea in the Working. London, 1921. (Preface dated
    1908).
King, Bryan, Sacrilege and Encouragement. Being an Account of the
    S. George's Riots. London, 1860.
_____, The S. George's Mission with the S. George's Riots and
    their REsults. London, 1877.
_____, Some Thoughts on Church and State. London, 1877.
_____, A Warning Against the Sin of Sacrilege. London, 1859.
Knott, J. W., A Letter to the Parishioners of Saviour's, Leeds.
    London, 1851.
Knott, W., The Mackonochie Chapel. London, 1891.
Knox, E. A., The Tractarian Movement. 1833-1845. London, 1933.
Knox, W. L., and Vidler, A. R., The Development of Modern
    Catholicism. London, 1933.
Läpple, Alfred, Der Einzelne in der Kirche. Munich, 1952.
"The Late Vicar of All Saints', Margaret Street," The Guardian,
    June 25, 1873.
Leech, Kenneth, and Williams, Rowan, eds., Essays Catholic and
    Radical. London, 1983.
Liddon, H. P., The Aim and Principles of Church Missions. A
    Sermon Preached...on the Anniversary of St. George's Mission.
    London, 1860.
_____, Life of Edward Bouverie Pusey. 4v. 2nd ed. London,
    1893-1898.
_____, Letter to Pall Mall Gazette, January 3, 1869.

Liddon, H. P., The Purchase Judgement. A Letter...to the Right Hon. Sir J. T. Coleridge. Together with a Letter to the Writer by E. B. Pusey. 2nd ed. London, 1871.

Henry Parry Liddon. Centenary Memoir. London, 1929.

Lindstrum, D., "Equating Goodness and Gothic Style," Yorkshire Post, March 17, 1969.

Little, W. J. Knox, A. H. Mackonochie. A Sermon Preached Before the E. C. U. in S. Barnabas' Church, Oxford. London, 1888.

Lockhart, J. G., Charles Lindley Viscount Halifax. London, 1935.

Longley, C. T., The Danger of Neglecting Religious Privileges. A Sermon...Preached Also at the Consecration of St. Saviour's, Leeds. London, 1845.

Lough, A. G., Dr. Pusey: Restorer of the Church. Devon, 1981.

Lowder, C. F., Sacramental Confession Examined by Pastoral Experience. A Letter to...the Bishop of London. London, 1874.

_____, Ten Years in St. George's Mission. London, 1867.

_____, To the Parishioners of St. Peter's, London Docks. London, 1876; 1879; 1880.

Mackonochie, A. H., An Address to His Parishioners. London, 1869.

_____, Blessed is He that Cometh in the Name of the Lord. A Sermon Preached before the University of Oxford at St. Mary the Virgin. Oxford, 1867.

_____, First Principles Versus Erastianism. Six Sermons Preached at S. Vedast's, Foster Lane, on the Wednesdays in Lent, 1876. London, 1876.

_____, Letter to Times, March 31, 1868.

_____, A Letter Addressed to the Record Newspaper, Corrected and Amended. London, 1870.

_____, Missionary Priest. A Sermon. London, 1860.

_____, Parish Church of St. Alban's the Martyr. Letter and Report. London, 1865; 1867; 1868; 1871; 1872; 1874; 1876; 1877; 1879.

_____, Remonstrance: A Letter to the Bishop of London. London, 1875.

Macleod, Robert, Style and Society, 1835-1914. London, 1971.

Manning, H. E., The Workings of the Holy Spirit in the Church of England: A Letter to the Rev. E. B. Pusey, D.D. London, 1864.

Martin v. Mackonochie. Judgement of the Lord Chief Justice of England. London, 1878.

Maskell, William, A Letter to the Rev. Dr. Pusey, on His Practice of Receiving Persons in Auricular Confession. London, 1850.

Matthew, H. C. G., "Edward Bouverie Pusey: from Scholar to Tractarian," Journal of Theological Studies (1981), 101-124.

Meier, Paul, William Morris. Harvester Press, 1978.

Menzies, Lucy, Father Wainright. A Record. London, 1947.

Mozley, Anne, Letters and Correspondence of J. H. Newman. London, 1891.

N.E., "The Late Secessions in Leeds," British Magazine, February 1847, pp. 1-9.

Newman, J. H., Apologia pro Vita Sua. 2nd ed. London, 1913.
_____, An Essay on the Development of Christian Doctrine. 2nd
ed. London, 1878.
_____, Essays Critical and Historical. 2nd ed. London, 1872.
_____, A Letter to the Rev. E. B. Pusey, D.D., on His Recent
Eirenicon. London, 1866.
_____, Tracts for the Times. No. 82: Letter to a Magazine on
the Subject of Dr. Pusey's Tract on Baptism. 3rd ed.
London, 1840.
Anon., "Dr. Newman and Devotion to the Blessed Virgin," The Union
Review, July, 1866, pp. 381-403.
Oakeley, Frederick, "Bishop Jewel," BC, XXX (July 1841), 1-46.
_____, "The Church Service," BC, LIV (April 1840), 249-276.
_____, The Leading Topics of Dr. Pusey's Recent Work Reviewed in
a Letter Addressed to the Most Rev. H. E. Manning. London,
1866.
_____, Personal Reminiscences of the "Oxford Movement." London,
1855.
_____, "Rites and Ceremonies," BC, LX (October 1841), 422-465.
_____, The Subject of Tract XC Examined in Connection with the
History of the 39 Articles. London, 1841.
_____, Things Dispensable and Things Indispensable. Two Sermons
Preached at Margaret Chapel, St. Marylebone. London, 1844.
Ollard, S. L., A Short History of the Oxford Movement. New ed.
London, 1963.
Oxenham, H. N., Dr. Pusey's Eirenicon Considered in Relation to
Catholic Unity. London, 1866.
Pace, G. G., "Act 3:Christian Gothic. Scene 3:Pusey and Leeds,"
Architecture Review, December, 1945.
Palmer, William, A Narrative of Events Connected with the
Publication of the Tracts for the Times. Oxford, 1843.
Perry, William, Alexander Penrose Forbes, Bishop of Brechin. The
Scottish Pusey. London, 1839.
_____, The Oxford Movemet in Scotland. Cambridge, 1933.
Pevsner, Nikolaus, Pioneers of Modern Design. London, 1966.
Philip, Kathleen, Reflected in Wantage. Wantage, 1970.
_____, Victorian Wantage. Wantage, 1968.
Pollen, J. H., Letter to the Parishioners of St. Saviour's.
Oxford, 1851.
_____, Narrative of Five Years at St. Saviour's, Leeds. Oxford,
1851.
Powell, C., Seven Reasons of Working Men of the Parish and
Congregation of St. Alban's Why the Bishops Should Refuse to
Allow the Late Decision of the Judicial Committee of the
Privy Council to be Used Against their Clergy. London, no
date.
_____, Why Working Men Mean to Stand by the Ritualistic Clergy.
London, 1875.
Prestige, G. L., The Life of Charles Gore. London, 1935.
_____, Pusey. London, 1933; Oxford, 1982.
Purcell, E. S., Life and Letters of Ambrose Phillipps de Lisle.
London, 1900.

Anon., "Dr. Pusey's Eirenicon," Christian Remembrancer, January, 1866, pp. 156-189.

"Puseyism and the Church of England," The London Quarterly Review, January, 1895.

Quiller-Couch, Sir Arthur, Memoir of Arthur John Butler. London, 1917.

Ramsey, A. M., From Gore to Temple. London, 1960.

_____, The Gospel and the Catholic Church. London, 1936.

_____, and Suenens, L.-J., The Future of the Christian Church. London, 1971.

Reardon, B. M. G., From Coleridge to Gore. London, 1971.

A Record. The Church of St. Mary Magdalene, Munster Square, 1852-1952. Gloucester, 1952.

Anon., "The Results of Dr. Pusey's Eirenicon," Christian Remembrancer, July, 1866, pp. 155-183.

Reynolds, Michael, Martyr of Ritualism. London, 1965.

Ricard, Antoine, Etude sur monseigneur Gaume. Paris, 1845.

Richards, W. V., "The Dangers of Riches," Sermons Preached at S. Barnabas, Pimlico, in the Octave of the Consecration. London, 1850.

Rigg, J. H., Dr. Pusey: His Character and Life Work. London, 1883.

Bishop of Ripon (Longley), A Letter to the Parishioners of St. Saviour's, Leeds. London, 1851.

Rivington, W., Church Extension in St. Pancras. A Comparative Statement of the Increase of Houses, Population, and Church Accommodation in the Parish of St. Pancras, Middlesex, from 1801 to 1851. London, 1862.

Rowell, Geoffrey, and Cobb, Peter, Revolution by Tradition. Oxford, 1983.

Rowell, Geoffrey, The Vision Glorious. Oxford, 1983.

Russell, E. F., Alexander H. Mackonochie. 2nd ed. New York, 1890.

_____, Father Stanton's Last Sermons in S. Alban's. London, 1916.

_____, Father Stanton's Sermon Outlines. From His Own Manuscript. London, 1918.

Russell, G. W. E., Arthur Stanton. London, 1917.

_____, Dr. Pusey. London, 1907.

_____, The Household of Faith. London, 1902.

_____, Portrait of the Seventies. New York, 1916.

_____, Saint Alban the Martyr, Holborn. A History of Fifty Years. London, 1913.

_____, W. E. Gladstone. New York, 1891.

Sacred Hymns and Anthems; with the Music as Used in the Church of St. Saviour's, Leeds. Leeds, 1852.

St. Alban's Defence Committee, The Church in Baldwin's Gardens: Being a History of the First Thirteen Years of the Church of St. Alban's the Martyr. London, no date.

St. Alban's, Holborn, Monthly Magazine. 1868-1940; 1950-1957.

St.-George-in-the-East, The Church Carries On. London, no date.

_____, The Story of St. George-in-the-East. London, no date.
St. George's Mission, Annual Report. London, 1858; 1859; 1860;
    1861; 1862; 1863; 1864; 1865; 1866; 1867; 1868; 1869; 1871;
    1873; 1877; 1878; 1879; 1880; 1881; 1882; 1886; 1887; 1888;
    1889; 1891; 1892; 1895; 1896; 1897.
St. Gilda's Mission, Annual Report. London, 1857; 1870; 1871;
    1872; 1873; 1874; 1875; 1877; 1887; 1890; 1893; 1895.
The Community of S. Mary the Virgin, Butler of Wantage.
    Westminister, 1961.
St. Peter's, London Docks, Parish Magazine, 1875-1930; 1939-1947;
    1973.
St. Saviour's Monthly Paper, October 1877-1923.
St. Saviour's, Leeds, Parish Magazine, 1904-1928.
Clergy of St. Saviour's, Leeds, The Statement in Reference to the
    Recent Proceedings Against Them. Leeds, 1851.
Savage, Stephen, and Tyne, Christopher, The Labours of Years.
    Oxford, 1965.
Savile, B. W., Dr. Pusey: An Historic Sketch. London, 1883.
Schiffers, N., Die Einheit der Kirche nach J. H. Newman.
    Düsseldorf, 1956.
Shepperd, Massey H., The Liturgical Renewal of the Church. New
    York, 1960.
_____, The Reform of Liturgical Worship. New York, 1961.
Simpson, W. J. Sparrow, The History of the Anglo-Catholic Revival
    from 1845. London, 1932.
Stevenson, Kenneth W., Gregory Dix Twenty-five Years on.
    Bramcote, 1977.
Stewart, H. L., A Century of Anglo-Catholicism. London, 1929.
Stone, Darwell, A History of the Doctrine of the Holy Eucharist. 2
    vol. London, 1909.
Suckling, R. A. J., St. Alban's the Martyr, Holborn. Annual
    Address. London, 1884; 1887; 1889.
Thompson, P., William Butterfield. London, 1971.
Thureau-Dangin, P., The English Revival in the Nineteenth Century.
    New York, 1919.
Trench, Maria, Charles Lowder. London, 1882.
_____, The Story of Dr. Pusey's Life. London, 1900.
Wakeling, G., The Oxford Church Movement. London, 1895.
Ward, Richard, The League of Tractarianism in the Parish of St.
    Saviour's, Leeds. Leeds, 1851.
_____, The Testimony of Bishop Jeremy Taylor to the Seven
    Propositions Selected by the Rev. M. Jackson as Contrary to
    the Doctrine of the Church of England. London, 1836.
Watkin, David, Morality and Architecture. Oxford, 1977.
Webb, C. C. J., Religious Thought in the Oxford Movement. London,
    1928.
Weil, Louis, Sacraments and Liturgy: The Outward Signs. Oxford,
    1983.
White, J. F., The Cambridge Movement. Cambridge, 1962.
Willebrands, Jan Cardinal, "New Context for Discussing Anglican
    Orders," Origins, 15 (1986), 662-664.

Williams, Isaac, _Autobiography_. 2nd ed. London, 1892.

Williams, N. P., and Harris, C., _Northern Catholicism. Centenary Studies in the Oxford and Parallel Movements_. London, 1933.

Williams, T. J., "A Lost Treasure Retrieved," _The Holy Cross Magazine_, April 1956, pp. 100-104.

_____, _Priscilla Lydia Sellon_. London, 1965.

_____, and Campbell, A. W., _The Park Village Sisterhood_. London, 1965.

Willoughby, L. A., "On Some German Affinities with the Oxford Movement," _The Modern Language Review_, XXIX (Jan. 1834), 52-66.

Wilson, R. F., _A Sanctifying Purpose the Secret of Success_. London, 1883.

Woodgate, M. V., _Father Benson_. London, 1953.

_____, _Father Congreve of Cowley_. London, 1956.

Wright, J. Robert, ed., _Lift High the Cross_. Cincinnati, 1984.

Yates, Nigel, _The Anglican Revival in Victorian Portsmouth_. Portsmouth, 1983.

_____, _The Oxford Movement and Anglican Ritualism_. London, 1983.

_____, _The Oxford Movement and Parish Life: St. Saviour's Leeds 1839-1929_. Leeds, 1975.

_____, _Ritual Conflict at Farlington and Wymering_. Portsmouth, 1978.